CW01261430

LAROUSSE
ON PASTRY

This book is printed on acid-free paper.
Copyright © 2009 by Editions Larousse. All rights reserved.
Copyright © 2012 by Editions Larousse for the English edition.
Translation: Martyn Back and Bronia Fuchs-Willig
Text control: Kathleen Micham and Thomas Crane
Editorial production for this edition: Belle Page
Cover design: Suzanne Sunwoo

Published by John Wiley & Sons, Inc., Hoboken, New Jersey.
Published simultaneously in Canada.

No part of this publication may be reproduced, stored in a retrieval system, or transmitted in any form or by any means, electronic, mechanical, photocopying, recording, scanning, or otherwise, except as permitted under Section 107 or 108 of the 1976 United States Copyright Act, without either the prior written permission of the Publisher, or authorization through payment of the appropriate per-copy fee to the Copyright Clearance Center, Inc., 222 Rosewood Drive, Danvers, MA 01923, 978–750–8400, fax 978–646–8600, or on the web at www.copyright.com. Requests to the Publisher for permission should be addressed to the Permissions Department, John Wiley & Sons, Inc., 111 River Street, Hoboken, NJ 07030, 201–748–6011, fax 201–748–6008, or online at http://www.wiley.com/go/permissions.

Limit of Liability/Disclaimer of Warranty: While the publisher and author have used their best efforts in preparing this book, they make no representations or warranties with respect to the accuracy or completeness of the contents of this book and specifically disclaim any implied warranties of merchantability or fitness for a particular purpose. No warranty may be created or extended by sales representatives or written sales materials. The advice and strategies contained herein may not be suitable for your situation. You should consult with a professional where appropriate. Neither the publisher nor author shall be liable for any loss of profit or any other commercial damages, including but not limited to special, incidental, consequential, or other damages.

For general information on our other products and services, or technical support, please contact our Customer Care Department within the United States at 800–762–2974, outside the United States at 317–572–3993 or fax 317–572–4002.

Wiley publishes in a variety of print and electronic formats and by print-on-demand. Some material included with standard print versions of this book may not be included in e-books or in print-on-demand. If this book refers to media such as a CD or DVD that is not included in the version you purchased, you may download this material at http://booksupport.wiley.com. For more information about Wiley products, visit www.wiley.com.

Library of Congress Cataloging-in-Publication Data :

Larousse. On pastry.
p. cm.
Originally published in France by Editions Larousse, Paris.
Includes index.
ISBN 978-1-118-20882-3 (cloth)
1. Pastry. 2. Desserts. 3. Cookbooks. I. Larousse (Firm) II. Title: On pastry.
TX773.L3126 2012
641.86'5--dc23
                                        2011046744

Printed in Spain by Graficas Estella, Estella
10   9   8   7   6   5   4   3   2   1

Grand Marnier ® is a registered trademark of Produits Marnier-Lapostolle Company and Carambar ® is a registered trademark of Cadbury Company, used by Larousse with the owner's approval.

LAROUSSE ON PASTRY

WILEY

JOHN WILEY & SONS, INC.

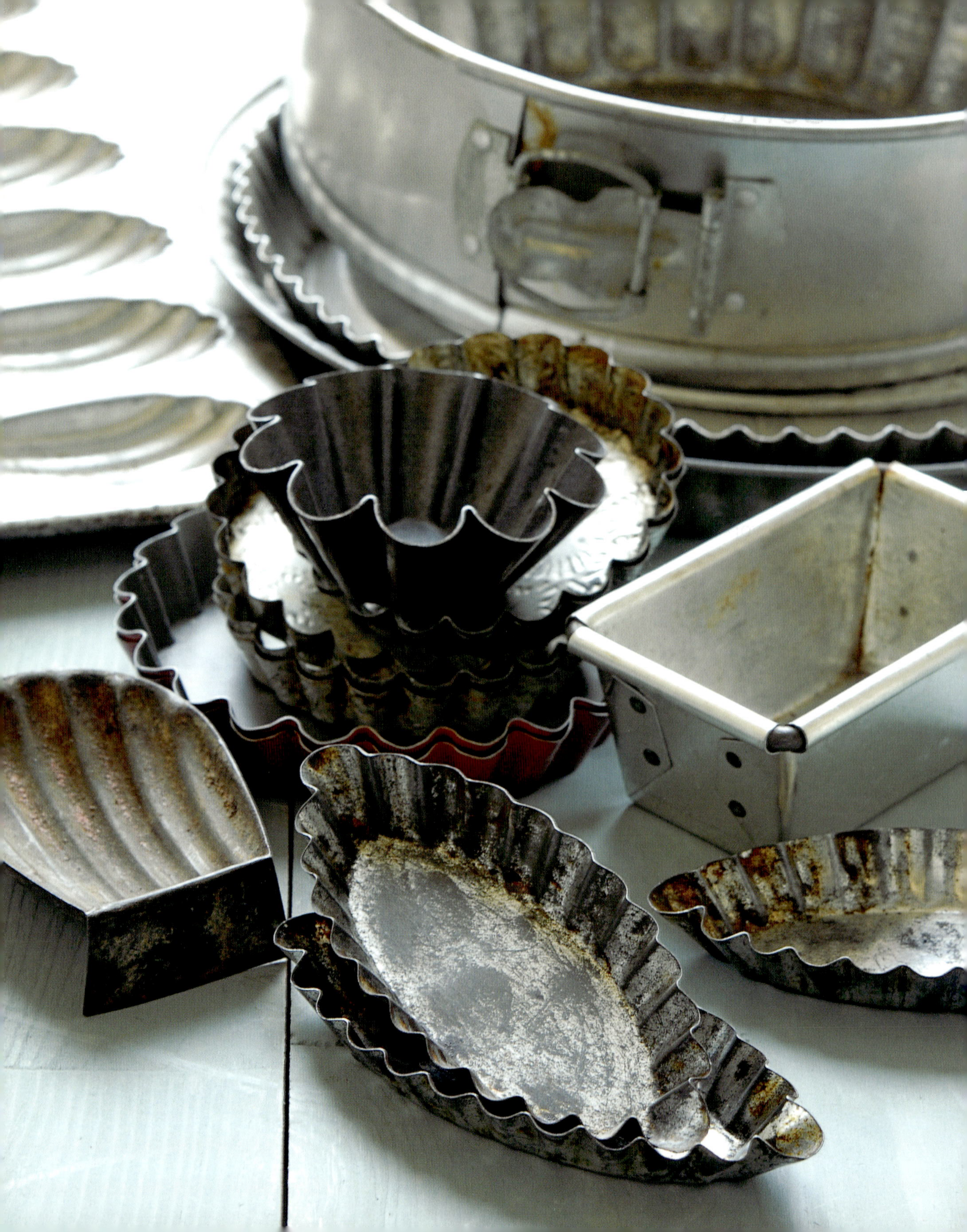

Contents

All-time favorites 7

Oh chocolate! 75

Fancy fruit 141

It's party time! 195

Munchy, crunchy cookies 249

Summer sweets 299

Small snacks 341

Pastry workshop (see details below) 397
Utensils for desserts, pastry and jams 426
Pastry glossary 433
Index of recipes by ingredient & category 438
Index of recipes from A to Z 446

Pastry workshop

Lining tartlet molds 398	Pastillage 414
Blind baking 398	Chantilly whipped cream 415
Shortcrust pastry 399	French meringue 416
Pâte sablée 400	Italian meringue 417
Sweet pastry 401	Chocolate sauce 418
Puff pastry 402	Chocolate frosting 419
Leavened dough 404	Tempering chocolate 420
Choux pastry 405	Chocolate curls and shavings ... 421
Crêpe batter 406	Caramel 422
Fritter batter 407	Simple caramel decorations ... 423
Génoise sponge cake 408	Raspberry coulis 423
Almond dacquoise meringue ... 409	Jams, jellies and marmalades:
Pastry cream 410	one-stage cooking 424
Crème anglaise 411	two-stage cooking 424
Butter cream 412	Jam: cooking method 425
Crème Chiboust 413	Sealing jam jars 425

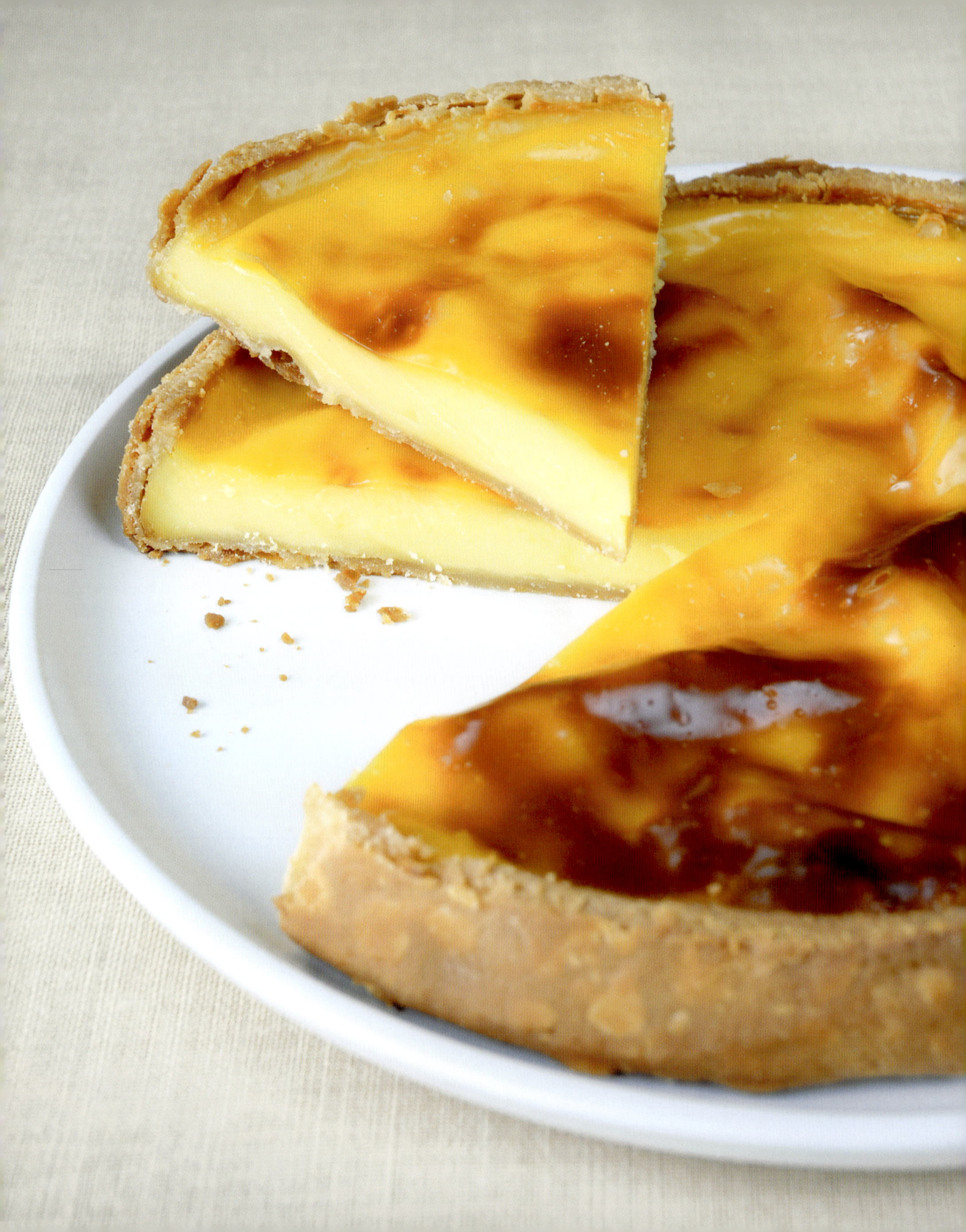

All-time favorites

French-style pound cake	8
Yogurt cake	10
Hazelnut cake	12
Gâteau basque	14
Marble cake	16
Carrot cake	18
Real French sponge cake	20
Montpensier	22
Gâteau nantais	24
Kugelhopf	26
Kouign-amann	28
Caramelized apple cake	30
Normandy apple cake	30
Lemon cake	32
Pear charlotte	34
Prune diplomate	36
Parisian flan	38
Far breton	38
Tropézienne	40
Fiadone	42
Mascarpone pie	44
No-bake cheesecake	46
Apple crumble	48
Cherry clafoutis	50
Baked apples	52
Rice pudding with caramel	54
Rice pudding with citrus peel	56
Traditional rice pudding	58
Semolina pudding with sultanas	60
Crème brûlée	62
Egg custard	64
Little pots of cream	64
Crème caramel	66
Sabayon	68
Floating island	70
Blancmange	72

French-style pound cake

SERVES 6 TO 8
PREP TIME: 15 mins.
COOKING TIME: 40 mins.

- 2 cups flour
  + some for the pan
- 1 cup butter
  + some for the pan
- 5 eggs
- 2 cups sugar
- 2 pinches salt
- 3 tbsp. rum or cognac

Sift the flour. Melt the butter. Break the eggs and separate the yolks from the whites. Whisk the egg whites with a pinch of salt until they form very stiff peaks.

Preheat the oven to 400° F.

Beat the egg yolks, sugar and a pinch of salt until the mixture turns pale. Gradually add the melted butter, then the flour and finally the rum or cognac.

Carefully fold in the beaten egg whites with a wooden spoon.

Butter and flour a 9-inch cake pan. Pour in the mixture and bake at 400° F for 15 minutes; lower the temperature to 350° F and continue baking for 25 minutes.

Allow to cool slightly before turning out.

never fails

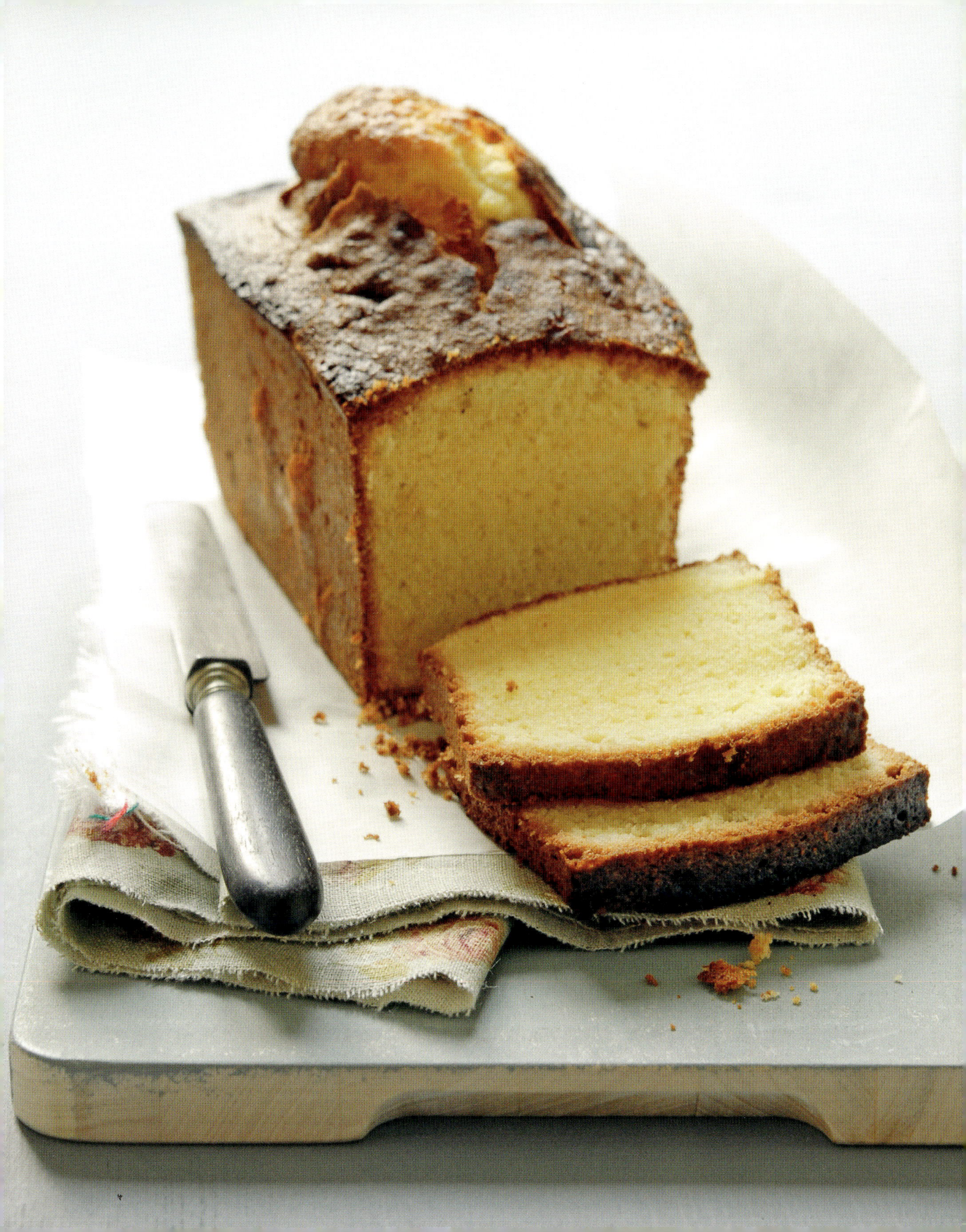

Yogurt cake

SERVES 4 TO 6
PREP TIME: 30 mins.
COOKING TIME: 40 mins.

- 3 eggs
- 1-1/2 cups sugar
- 1 organic orange or lemon
- 1/2 cup oil
- 1/2 cup plain yogurt
- 2 cups flour
- 2-1/2 teaspoons baking powder
- A pinch of salt
- Butter for the pan
- The juice of one orange or lemon

Preheat the oven to 350° F.

Break the eggs and separate the yolks from the whites. Mix the egg yolks with 1 cup sugar in a bowl and beat until pale and frothy.

Grate the orange or lemon zest. Add to the mixture along with the oil and yogurt and mix well. Sift the flour and baking powder into a bowl. Add to the mixture and mix until smooth.

Beat the egg whites with the salt until they form stiff peaks. Gently fold them into the mixture.

Butter a 10-inch round baking pan, pour in the mixture and bake for 25 minutes.

Put 1 cup water in a saucepan and add the lemon or orange juice along with the rest of the sugar. Boil for about 15 minutes. Allow to cool and brush the cake with this syrup.

child's play

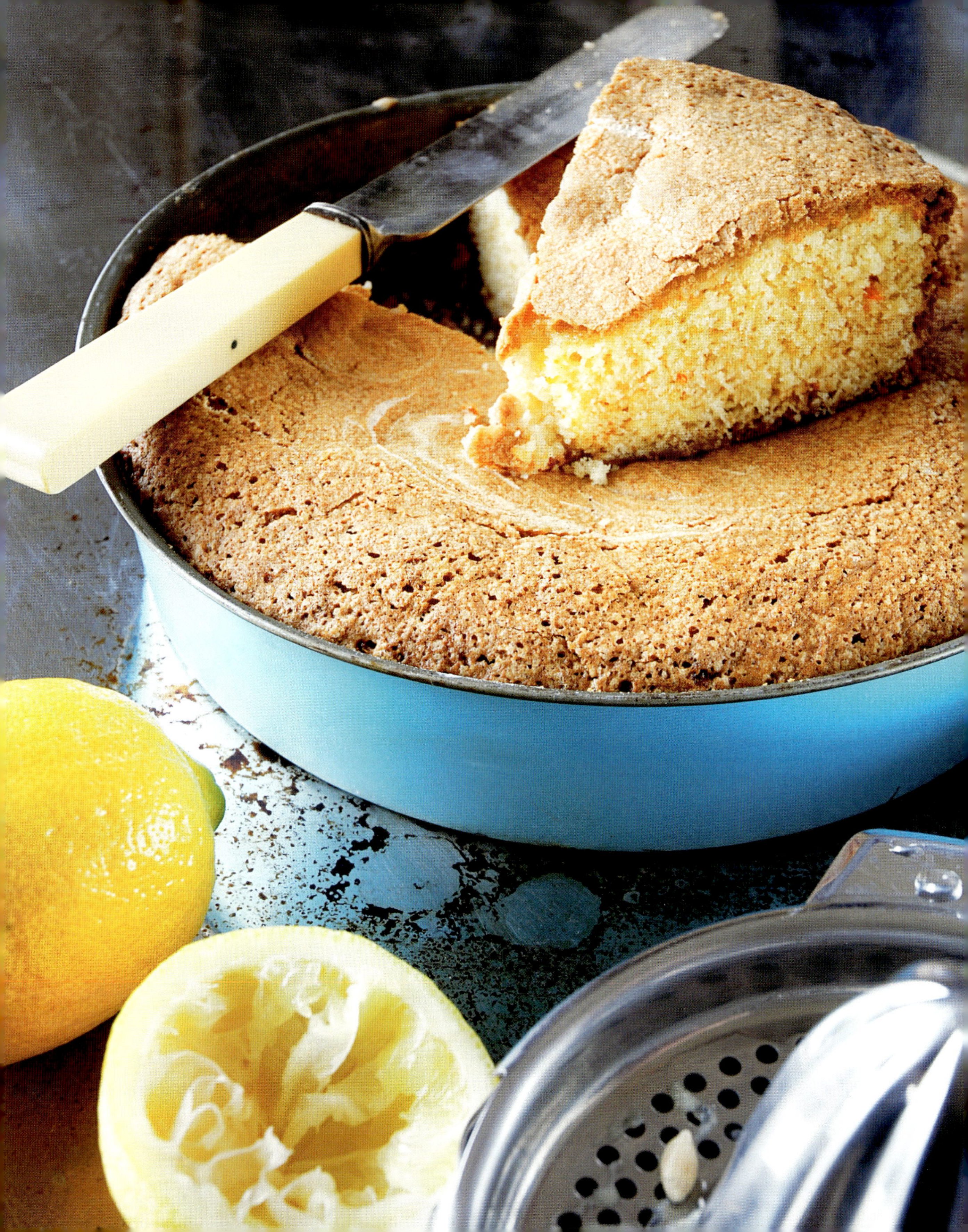

Hazelnut cake

SERVES 6
PREP TIME: 20 mins.
COOKING TIME: About 35 mins.

- 3/4 cup hazelnuts
- 8 egg whites
- 3/4 cup sugar
- 1/3 cup flour
- 7 tbsp. butter
  + some for the pan
- Powdered sugar

Preheat the oven to 475° F.

Crush the hazelnuts with a rolling pin. Place on a baking sheet and place in a hot oven for 3 or 4 minutes to toast them.

Mix the egg whites and the sugar in a bowl. Add the hazelnuts, then the sifted flour, and mix again.

Melt the butter, add to the mixture and mix until smooth.

Reduce the oven temperature to 400° F. Butter a 6-inch round cake pan, pour in the mixture and bake for 30 minutes.

Remove the cake from the oven, allow to cool, turn out and dust with powdered sugar.

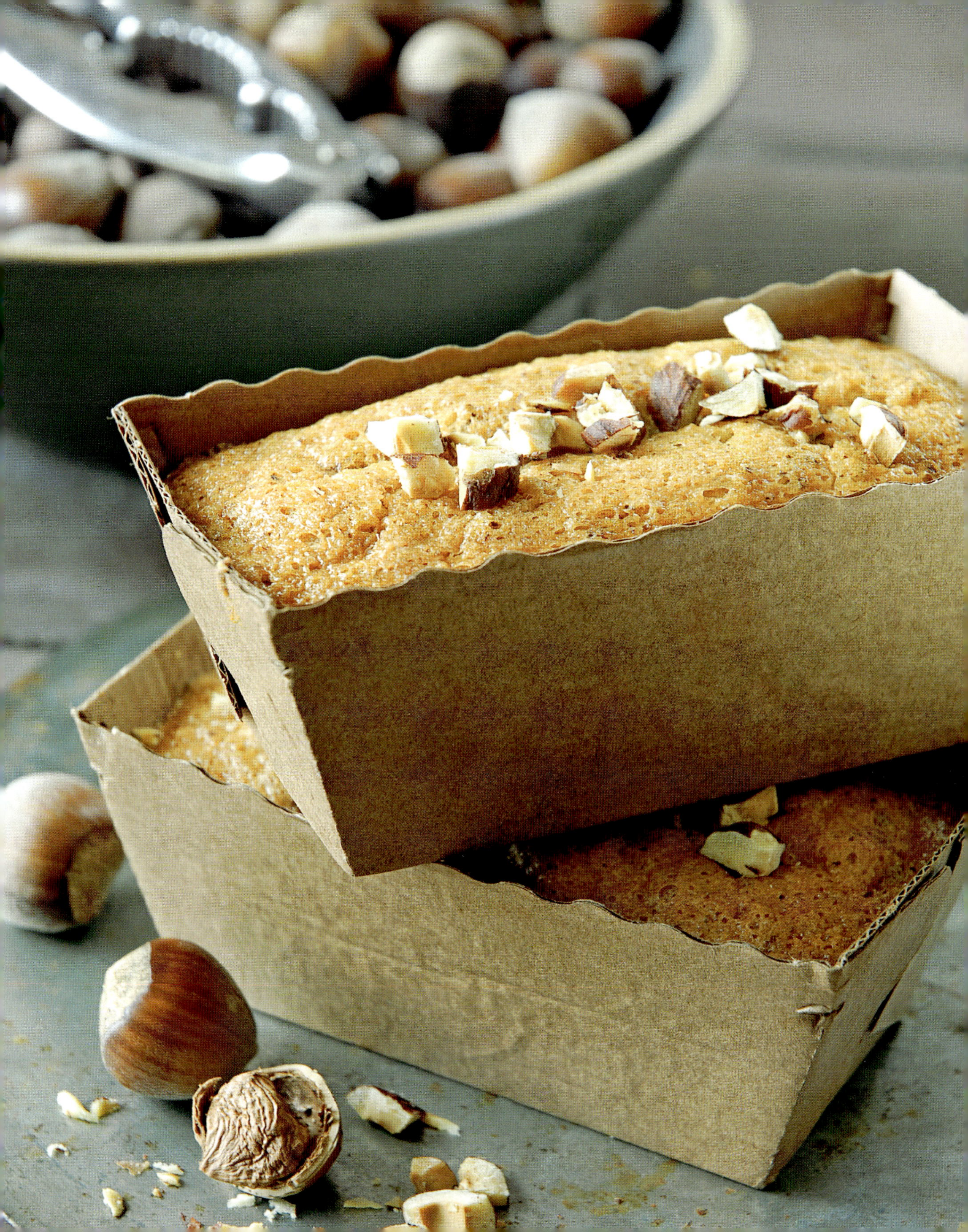

Gâteau basque

SERVES 6 TO 8
PREP TIME: 30 mins.
RESTING TIME: 1 hr
COOKING TIME: 45 mins.

FOR THE PASTRY CREAM
- 1 cup milk
- 1/2 vanilla bean
- 1 whole egg
 + 2 egg yolks
- 4 tbsp. sugar
- 1/3 cup flour
- 2 tbsp. dark rum

FOR THE CAKE MIXTURE
- 2-1/2 cups flour
- 1-1/3 cups sugar
- A pinch of salt
- 1 teaspoon baking powder
- 1 whole egg + 2 egg yolks
- 2/3 cup butter
 + some for the pan
- 1 or 2 tbsp. rum

FOR GLAZING
- 1 egg yolk
- 1 tbsp. milk

Prepare the pastry cream: boil the milk with the half vanilla bean. Beat the whole egg and the extra egg yolks with the sugar until creamy. Beat in the flour, then gradually add the boiling milk. Place in a saucepan and cook over medium heat, whisking constantly until it starts to boil. Remove from the heat, Add the rum and and allow to rest.

Prepare the cake: mix the flour, sugar, salt and baking powder in a bowl. Make a well in the center, add the whole egg and 2 egg yolks, the softened butter cut into small pieces, and the rum. Begin by mixing the ingredients in the center with a wooden spoon, then mix with your hands until you have a smooth dough. Form into a ball and allow to rest in a cool place for 1 hour.

Preheat the oven to 400° F.

Divide the dough into two unequal parts (two thirds + one third). Butter an 8-inch round cake pan. Spread the larger piece of dough in the bottom of the pan, pushing it up the sides.

Pour the pastry cream over the dough. Roll out the other piece of dough to form a lid. Place it on top of the pastry cream in the pan. Dip your fingers in water and seal the edges. Glaze the surface with an egg yolk beaten with a spoonful of milk.

Bake for 20 minutes, then lower the temperature to 350° F and bake for another 20 minutes. Remove from the oven and allow to cool before turning out. Serve warm or cold.

> To make a change
This traditional cake from the mountainous Basque region of southwestern France can be made with cherry jam instead of pastry cream.

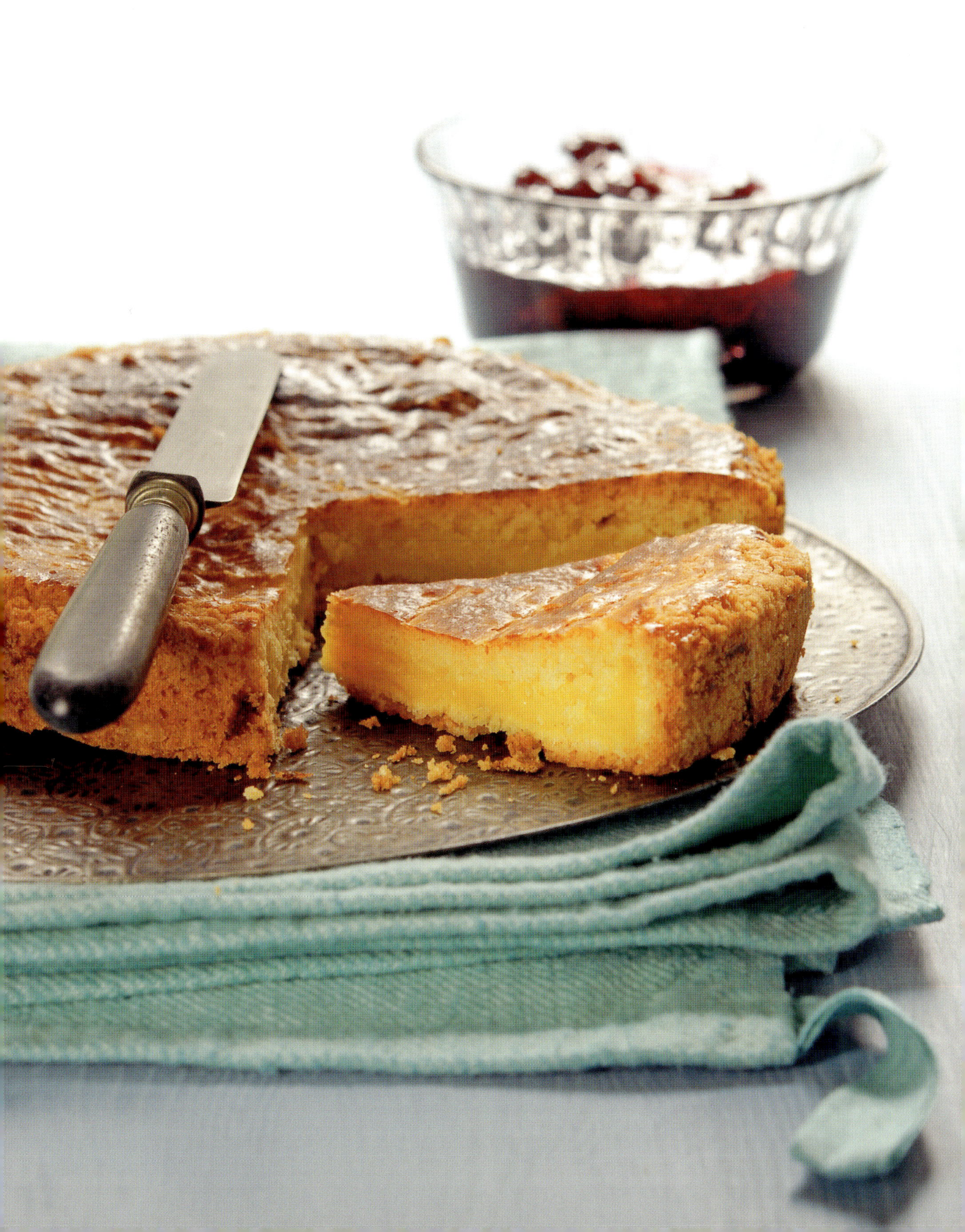

Marble cake

SERVES 6 TO 8
PREP TIME: 15 mins.
COOKING TIME: 50 mins.

- 3 eggs
- 3/4 cup butter
  + some for the pan
- A pinch of salt
- 1-1/3 cups flour
- 1 teaspoon baking powder
- 1 cup sugar
- 1/2 cup cocoa powder

Break the eggs and separate the yolks from the whites. Melt the butter. Beat the egg whites with the salt until they form stiff peaks. Sift the flour with the baking powder.

Whisk together the melted butter with the sugar, then add the egg yolks. Mix well, then add the sifted flour and baking powder and mix again. Fold in the beaten egg whites.

Preheat the oven to 400° F.

Divide the mixture into two halves and mix the cocoa powder into one of them.

Butter a 9-inch round cake pan. Pour in a layer of chocolate-flavor mixture, then a layer of plain mixture. Continue until the pan is full.

Bake for 50 minutes. Check with the end of a knife, which should come out clean.

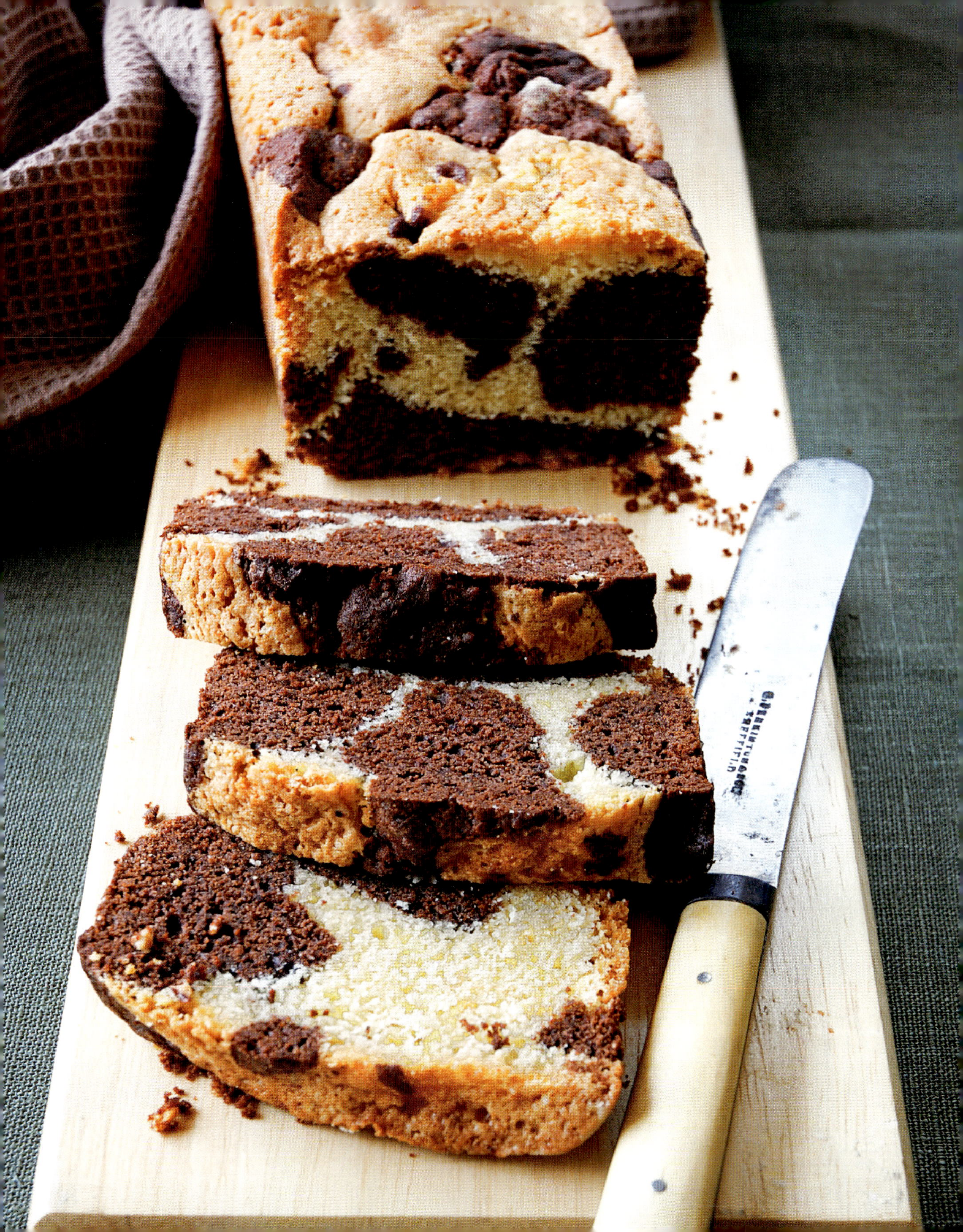

Carrot cake

SERVES 4 TO 6
PREP TIME: 10 mins.
COOKING TIME: 40 mins.

- 1/2 lb. carrots
- 2 eggs
- 1/2 cup sugar
- 1/2 cup flour
- 2-1/2 teaspoons baking powder
- 3/4 cups ground hazelnuts
- 3/4 cup ground almonds
- 2 tbsp. oil
- A pinch of salt
- Butter for the pan

Peel, rinse and grate the carrots.

Preheat the oven to 350° F.

Break the eggs into a bowl and beat them with the sugar.

Sift together the flour, baking powder, hazelnuts and almonds, then gradually add the beaten eggs, stirring constantly with a wooden spoon. Add the oil, the salt and the carrots and stir until the mixture is smooth.

Butter a 7-inch round cake pan and pour in the mixture. Bake for 40 minutes. Allow to cool in the pan before turning out.

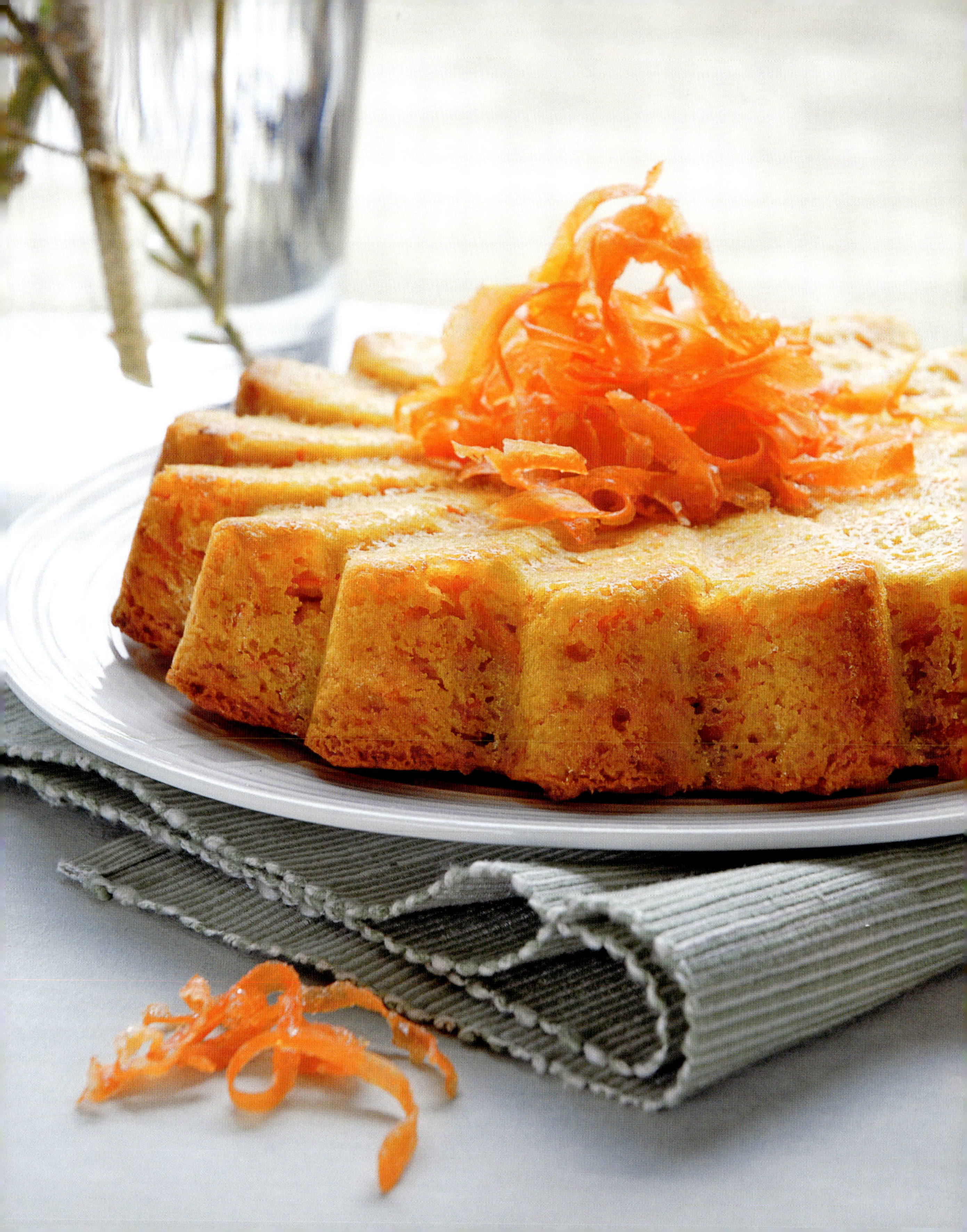

Real French sponge cake

SERVES 8
PREP TIME: 15 mins.
COOKING TIME: 45 mins.

- 14 eggs
- 2-1/2 cups sugar
- 1 teaspoon vanilla extract
- A pinch of salt
- 1-1/2 cups sifted flour
- 1 cup cornstarch
  + some for the pan
- Butter for the baking pan

Break the eggs and separate the yolks from the whites.

Preheat the oven to 350° F.

Put the sugar, the vanilla extract and the egg yolks into a large bowl. Beat until the mixture turns pale yellow.

Whisk the egg whites with a pinch of salt until they form very stiff peaks. Gently fold these into the previous mixture along with the flour and cornstarch.

Butter an 11-inch round cake pan, then dust with cornstarch.
Pour in the mixture: the pan should be only two-thirds full.

Bake for 45 minutes.

Turn out the sponge cake while it is still hot. Serve cold.

> Helpful tip
Check that the cake is cooked with the end of a knife: if the blade comes out clean, the cake is ready.

> Find out more
Why so many eggs? This sponge cake is feather-light because it contains so many egg whites.

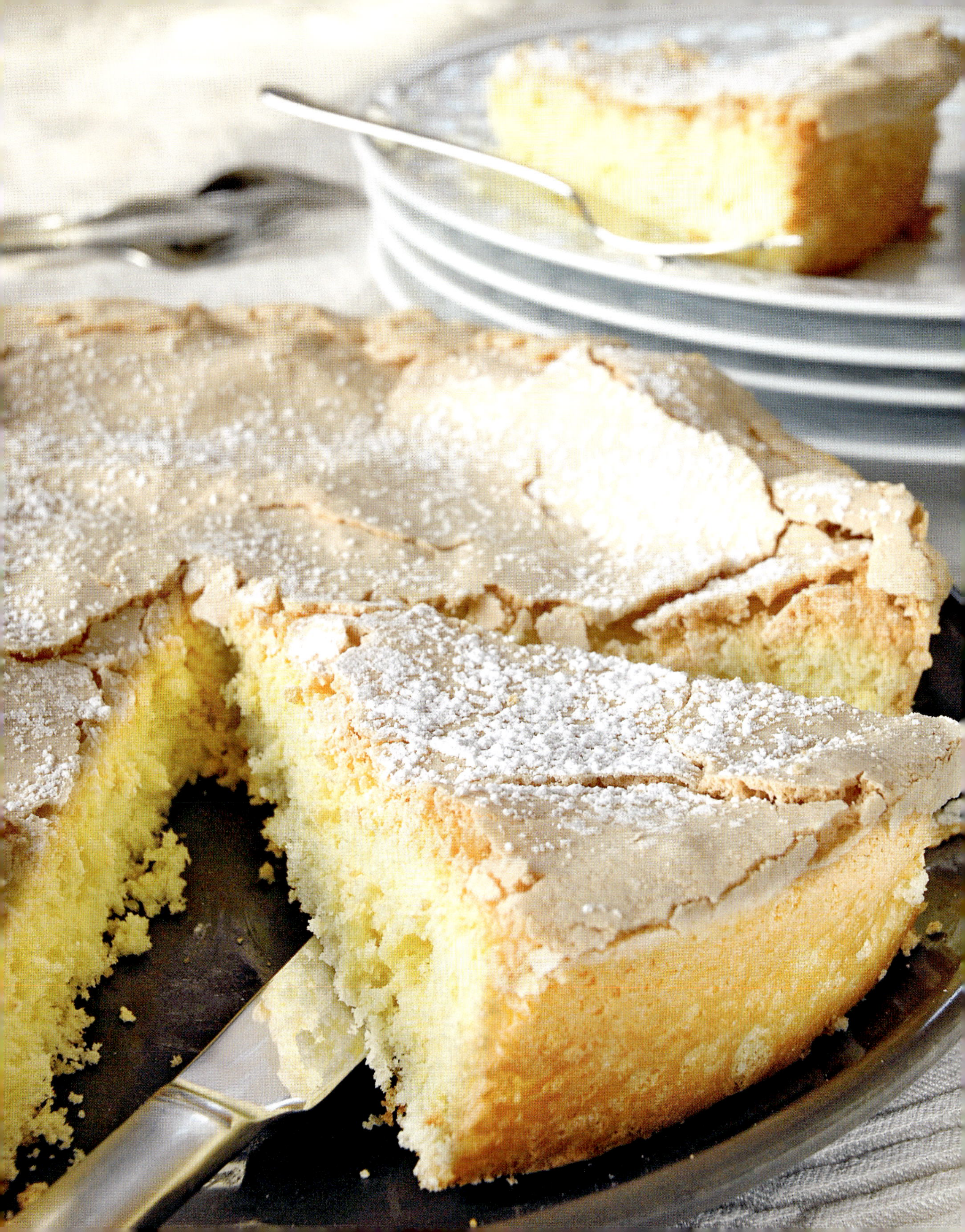

Montpensier

SERVES 4 TO 6
PREP TIME: 20 mins.
COOKING TIME: 30 mins.

- 4 tbsp. candied fruit
- 1/3 cup raisins
- 7 tbsp. rum
- 6 tbsp. butter + some for the pan
- 7 egg yolks
- 2/3 cup sugar
- 1 cup ground almonds
- 1 cup flour
- 3 egg whites
- A pinch of salt
- 1/2 cup slivered almonds
- 5 oz. apricot jam

Soak the candied fruit and the raisins in the rum.

Preheat the oven to 400° F.

Soften the butter. Mix the egg yolks with the sugar and beat them until they turn pale yellow, then add the ground almonds, the softened butter, and finally the flour. Stir well until smooth.

Beat the egg whites with a pinch of salt until they form stiff peaks, and gently fold them into the mixture with a wooden spoon.

Strain the candied fruit and raisins and add them to the mixture.

Butter a 9-inch round cake pan and sprinkle with slivered almonds. Pour in the mixture and bake for 30 minutes.

Turn the cake onto a wire rack to cool. Warm a little apricot jam and brush the surface of the cake with it.

> Helpful tip
This cake is best eaten the day it is made.

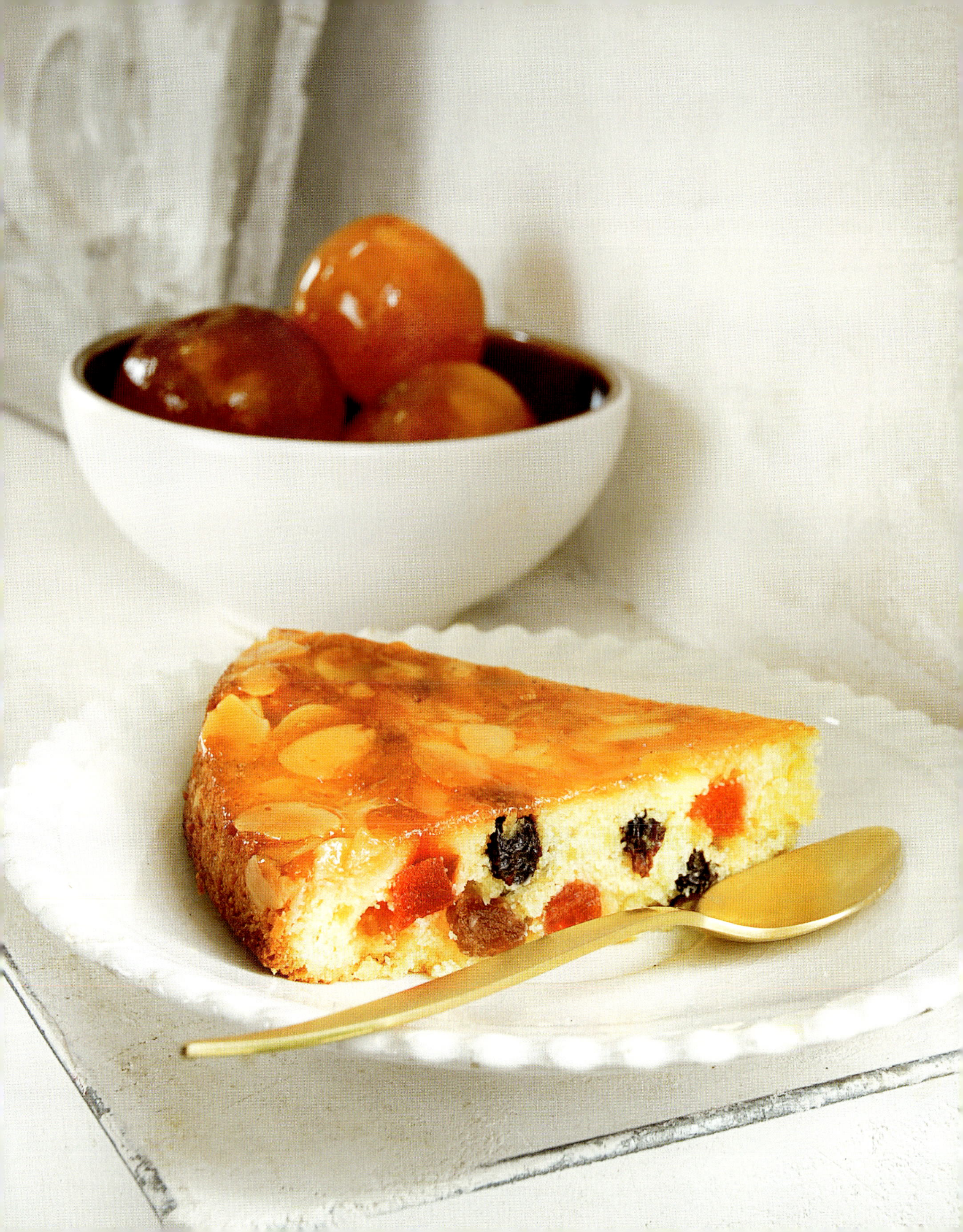

Gâteau nantais (Apricot and almond cake)

SERVES 6
PREP TIME: 10 mins.
COOKING TIME: 40 to 50 mins.

- 1 cup salted butter + some for the pan
- 1-1/2 cups sugar
- 2-1/3 cups ground almonds
- 6 eggs
- 2/3 cup flour
- 2 tbsp. apricot jam
- 6 tbsp. rum

FOR THE FROSTING
- 3 tbsp. rum
- Powdered sugar

Allow the butter to soften at room temperature and put into a bowl with the sugar and ground almonds. Work the mixture well with a spatula until smooth and creamy.

Beat the eggs and stir into the mixture. Add the flour, the jam and 3 tbsp. rum. Beat the mixture until it becomes light and frothy.

Preheat the oven to 350° F.

Butter a 9-inch round cake pan. Pour in the mixture to a depth of 1-1/2 inches and bake for 40 to 50 minutes; if the surface starts to color too much, cover with aluminum foil. Check that the cake is cooked by putting the tip of a knife into the center: it should come out clean. Remove from the oven and pour 3 tbsp. rum over the top. Allow to cool.

Prepare the frosting: mix 3 tbsp. rum with enough powdered sugar to make a thick paste. Spread on top of the cake.

> Helpful tip
This cake is a specialty of Nantes in western France. Its flavors will intensify if you prepare it two or three days in advance.

> Serving advice
You can make delicious apricot jam at home! (see p.384).

> To make a change
Use a cupcake pan to make mini versions of the gâteau nantais.

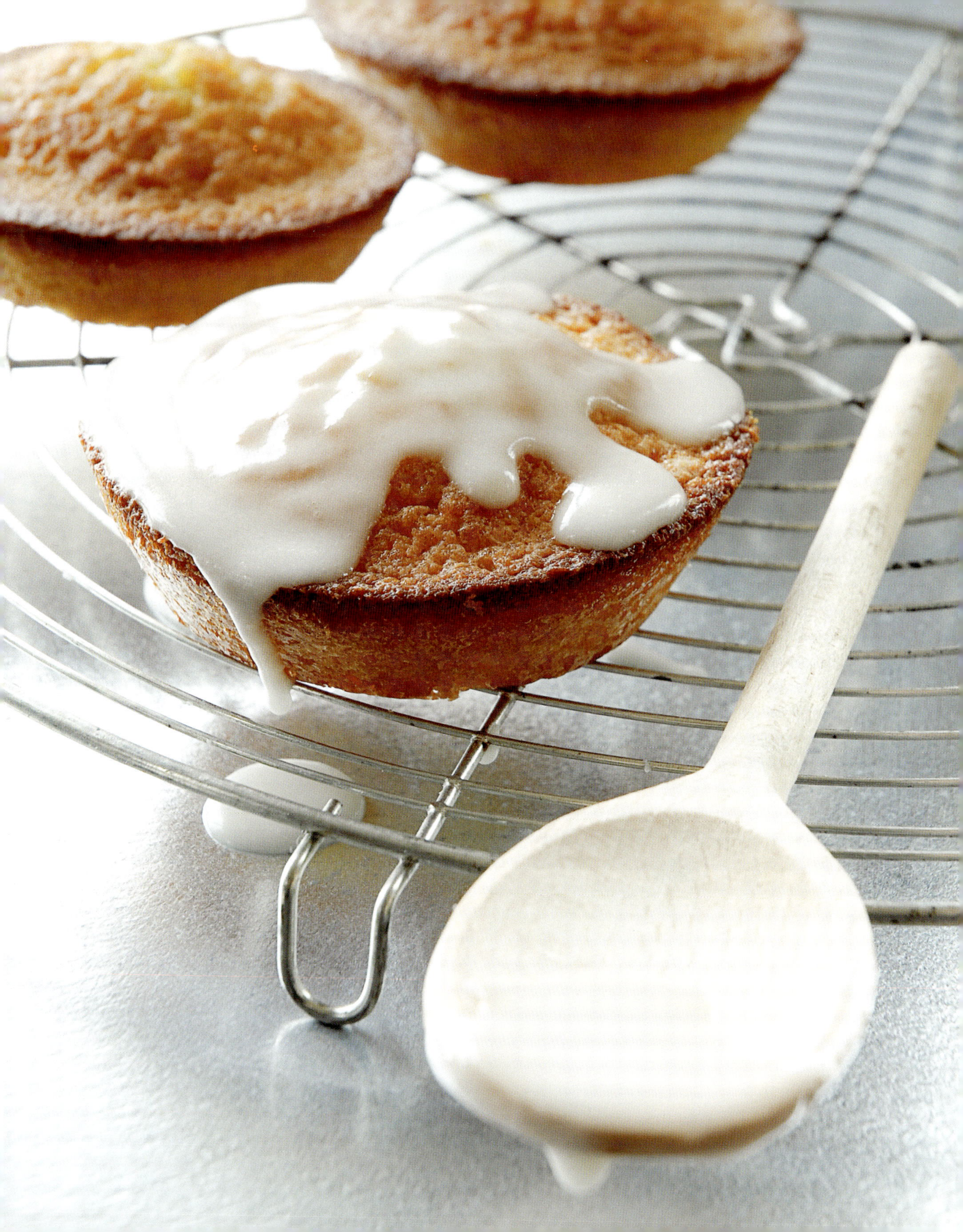

Kugelhopf

MAKES 2 KUGELHOPFS
PREP TIME: 40 mins. (over 2 days)
REFRIGERATION TIME: 4 to 5 hrs
RESTING TIME: 3-1/2 hrs
COOKING TIME: 35 to 40 mins.

- 1/2 cup whole blanched almonds
- 1-1/2 tbsp. butter
- Powdered sugar

FOR THE YEAST MIXTURE
- 1 scant cup flour
- 1/4 tbsp. dry yeast
- 1/3 cup milk

FOR THE DOUGH
- 1 cup raisins
- 3 tbsp. rum
- 1 tbsp. dry yeast
- 1/3 cup milk
- 2 cups flour
- 3 pinches of salt
- 6 tbsp. sugar
- 2 egg yolks
- 6 tbsp. butter
  + some for the pans

The day before, put the raisins and rum in a bowl to soak.

The following day, prepare the yeast mixture: mix the flour, yeast and milk in a bowl and mix well. Cover the bowl with a damp cloth and put into the refrigerator for 4 to 5 hours, until small bubbles start to appear on the surface.

Then prepare the dough: stir the yeast into the milk. Put the prepared yeast mixture, the flour, the salt, the sugar, the egg yolks and the second milk and yeast mixture into a large bowl. Mix well until the dough stops sticking to the sides of the bowl. Add the butter and continue to work the mixture until it stops sticking to the bowl again.

Strain the raisins and add to the mixture. Mix well, then cover the bowl with a cloth and allow the dough to rise for 2 hours at room temperature. It should double in volume.

Butter two Bundt pans and place a whole almond in each hollow ridge.

Place the dough on a floured work surface and divide into two equal parts. Flatten each piece with the heel of your hand, then make two balls by bringing the edges into the center. Roll each ball around on the work surface by pressing lightly with the palm of your hand and making a circular motion.

Flour your fingers and take a ball of dough in your hand, plunge your thumb into the center, stretch the dough a little and place in the pan. Allow to rise at room temperature for 1-1/2 hours; if the atmosphere is very dry, cover with a damp cloth.

Preheat the oven to 400° F.

Bake for 35 to 40 minutes. Turn out onto a wire rack and brush with melted butter to stop them drying too quickly. Allow to cool, sprinkle with powdered sugar and serve.

> **Helpful tip**
If you want to keep these loaves for a while, wrap them in plastic wrap.

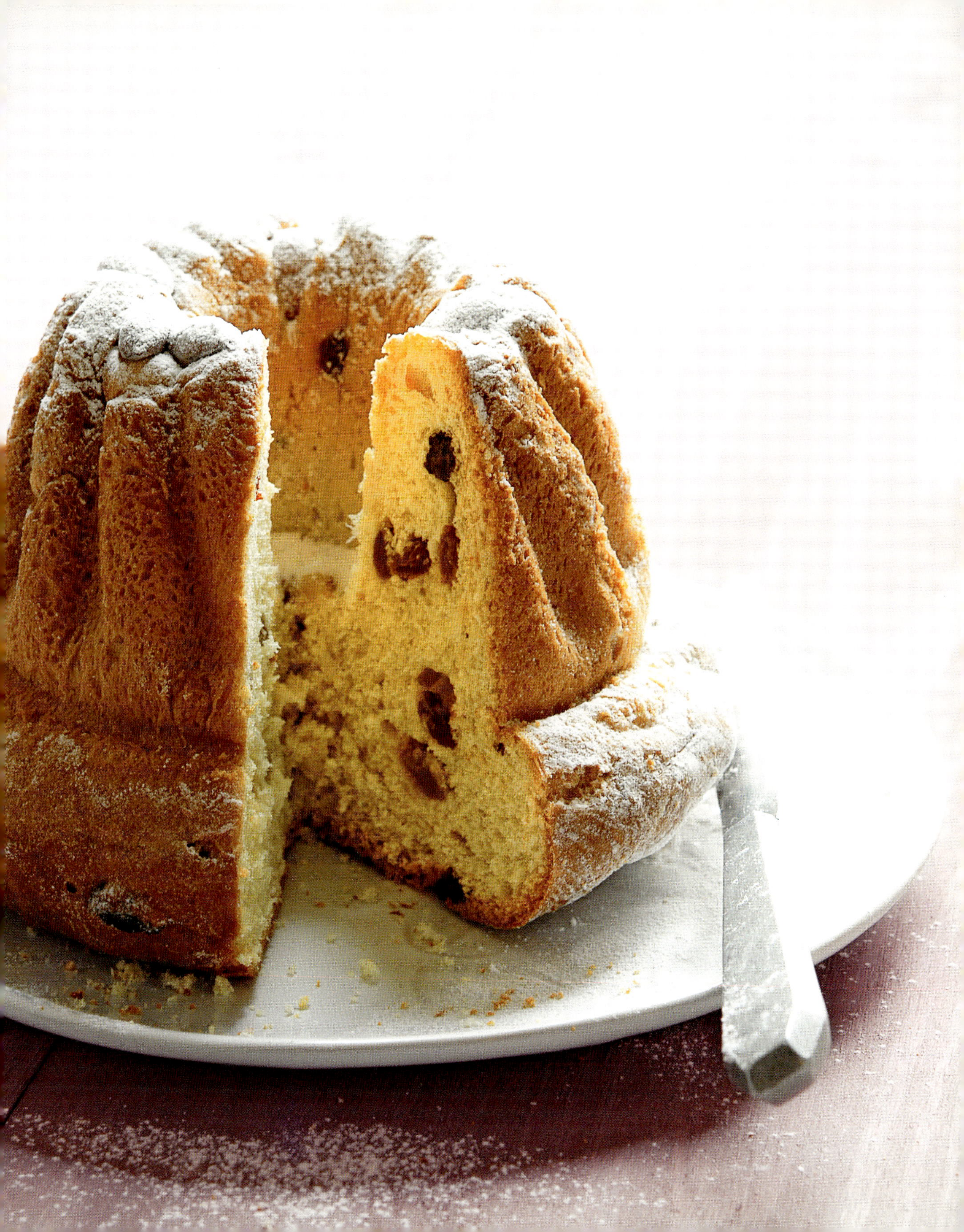

Kouign-amann

SERVES 6
PREP TIME: 40 mins.
RESTING TIME: About 30 mins.
COOKING TIME: 30 mins.

- 1 tbsp. dry yeast
- 16 tbsp. salted butter + some for the baking sheet
- 4 cups flour
- 1 tbsp. melted butter
- 1-1/2 cups sugar

FOR GLAZING
- 1 beaten egg

Mix the yeast with half a cup of warm water. Allow the butter to soften at room temperature.

Sift the flour onto the work surface and make a well in the center. Put the yeast and melted butter in the center, mix into a dough and knead for ten minutes until smooth and supple. Cover with a damp cloth and allow to rise in a warm place (it should double in volume).

Roll out the dough to the thickness of a large pancake. Spread the softened butter on it, leaving a one inch margin around the edge, and pour the sugar over the butter. Fold the pancake into a triangle.

Preheat the oven to 400° F.

Allow the dough to rest for a few minutes, then roll it out again. Fold into four and repeat the operation. Now flatten the dough with your hand to form a circle about 10 inches in diameter. Lay the dough on a buttered baking sheet, make a pattern on the surface with the point of a knife and brush with beaten egg.

Bake for 30 minutes; cover with a sheet of aluminum foil if the cake browns too quickly. Allow to cool on the baking sheet.

> Find out more
This rich, buttery cake is a specialty of Brittany in northwest France.

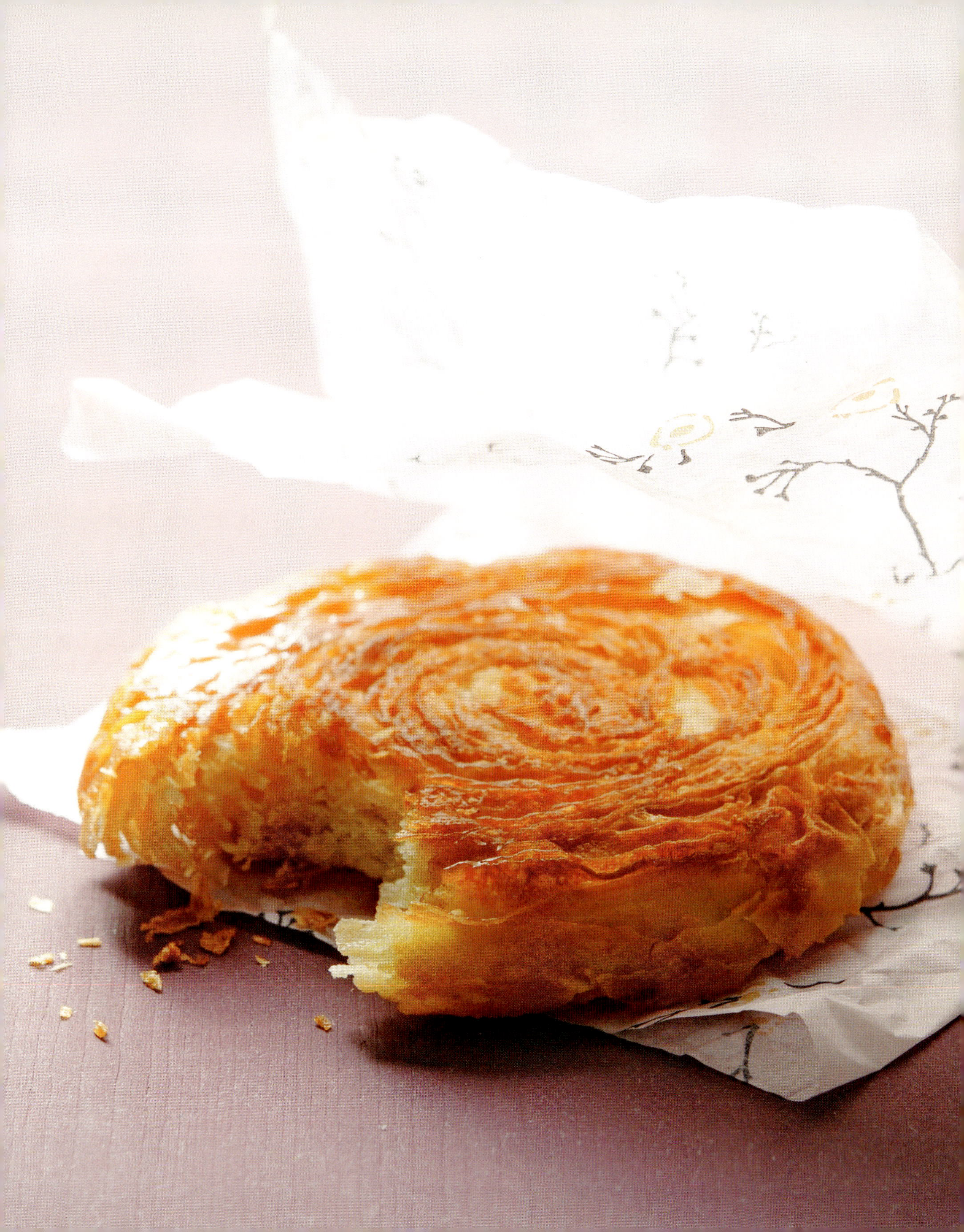

Caramelized apple cake

SERVES 8
PREP TIME: 30 mins.
COOKING TIME: 40 mins.

FOR THE CAKE MIXTURE
- 9 tbsp. butter + some for the pan
- 2/3 cup sugar
- 2 whole eggs + 2 extra egg whites
- 1/2 lemon
- 1-2/3 cups flour + some for the pan
- 1 teaspoon baking powder

FOR THE FILLING
- 1 lb. apples
- 5 tbsp. sugar

Preheat the oven to 350° F.

Prepare the cake mixture: beat together the butter and sugar until frothy. Break the eggs and separate the yolks from the whites. Add the egg yolks to the butter-sugar mixture. Squeeze half a lemon, add the juice to the mixture and mix well. Sprinkle in the flour and baking powder. Mix until smooth. Beat the 4 egg whites until they form stiff peaks and fold them into the mixture.

Butter and flour a 10-inch round cake pan. Pour in the mixture.

Prepare the filling: rinse and dry the apples, cut them in two and remove the cores. Cut the apple halves into thin slices, but don't cut them all the way through so that they stay in one piece. Dip the sliced apple halves into the sugar, then push them into the cake mix with the sugar facing upward.

Bake for about 40 minutes.

Normandy apple cake

never fails

SERVES 6
PREP TIME: 20 mins.
COOKING TIME: 50 to 60 mins.

- 1/3 cup raisins
- 1/4 cup Calvados brandy
- 2-1/4 lbs apples
- 4 eggs
- A pinch of salt
- 4 tbsp. sugar
- 1 cup flour
- Butter for the pan

Put the raisins and Calvados in a bowl and leave to soak.

Peel and core the apples. Cut into small cubes.

Break the eggs and separate the whites from the yolks. Whisk the egg whites with a pinch of salt until they form stiff peaks.

Beat the egg yolks and sugar until they turn pale yellow. Gradually add the flour, then the raisins and brandy. Finally, fold in the egg whites and apples.

Preheat the oven to 350° F.

Butter a 9-inch round cake pan. Pour in the mixture and bake for 50 to 60 minutes, until the blade of a knife comes out clean.

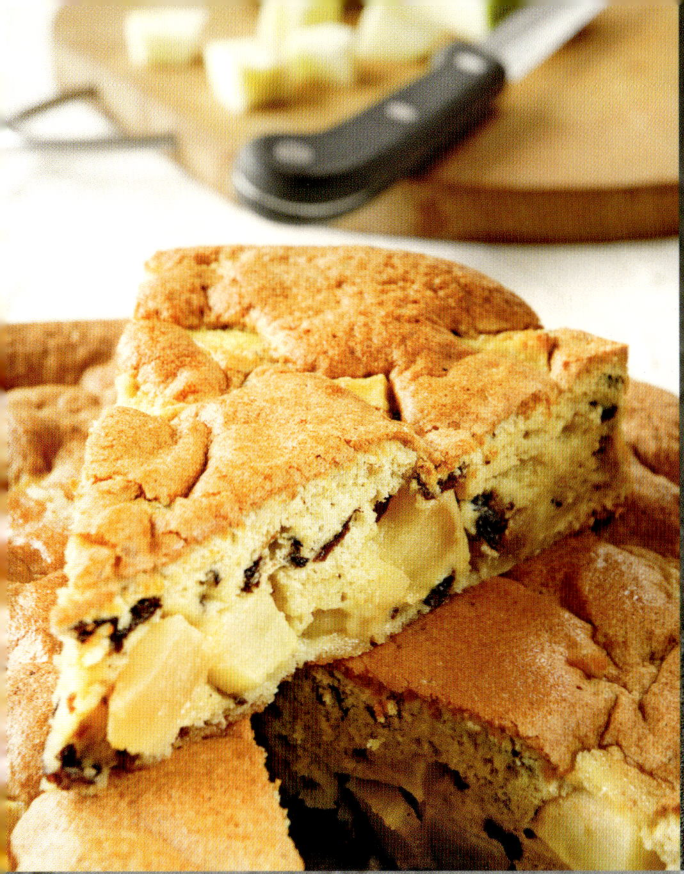
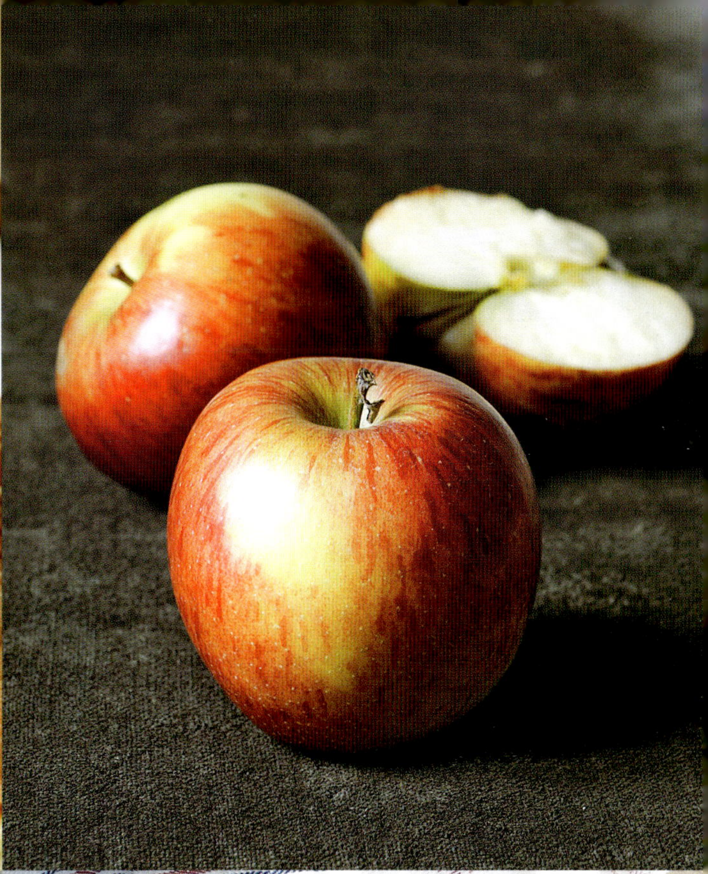
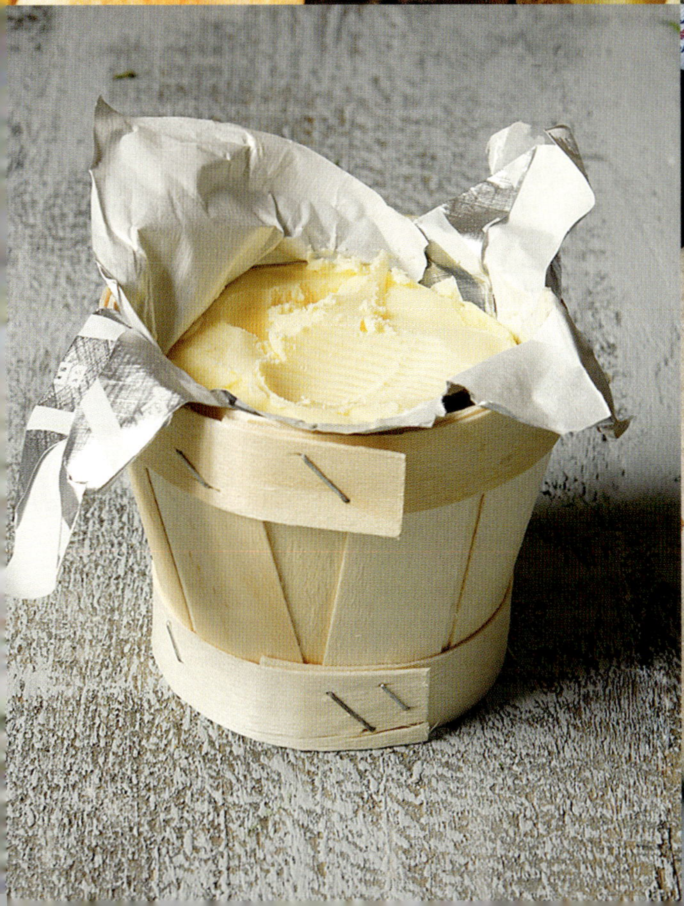
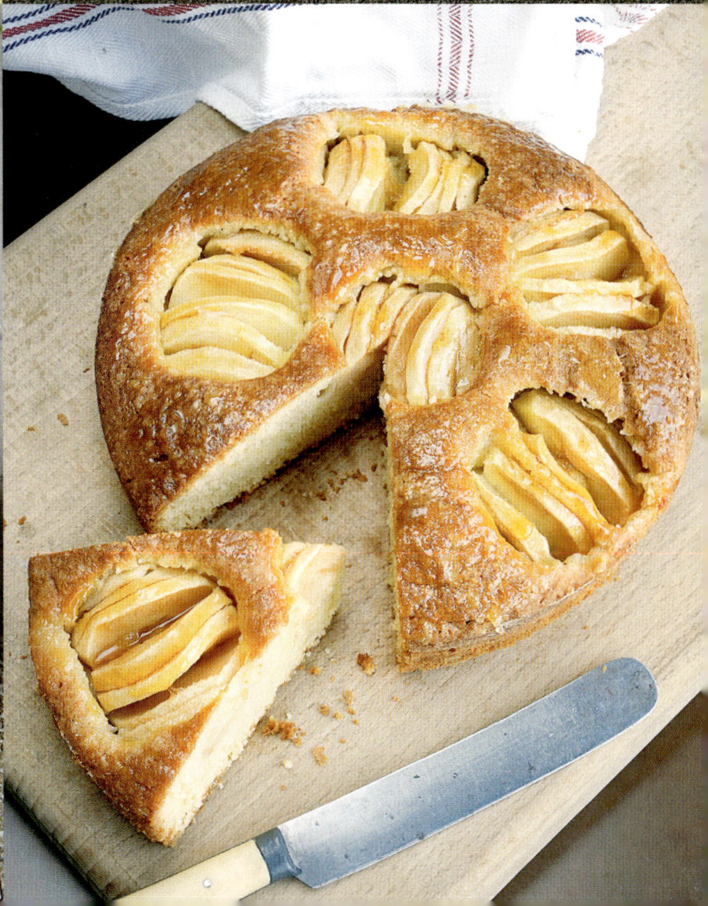

Lemon cake

SERVES 6 TO 8
PREP TIME: 30 mins.
COOKING TIME: 40 to 45 mins.

FOR THE CAKE BATTER
- 1 lemon
- 1/4 cup candied citron or lemon peel
- Just over 3/4 cup flour
- 5 tbsp. butter
- 4 eggs
- 3/4 cup sugar
- 1/2 teaspoon vanilla extract
- 1 tbsp. rum (optional)
- 1/2 teaspoon salt

FOR THE FROSTING
- 1-3/4 cups powdered sugar
- 1 egg white
- The juice of 1/2 lemon

TO DECORATE
- 2 tbsp. candied citron

Remove the lemon zest with a sharp knife and place in boiling water for 2 minutes. Strain, rinse in cold water and cut into thin strips. Dice the candied citron or lemon peel.

Prepare the cake batter: sift the flour; melt the butter in a small saucepan and allow to cool slightly. Break the eggs, separate the yolks from the whites. Beat the yolks with the sugar and the vanilla extract until pale and frothy. Sprinkle in the flour and add the melted butter, the candied citron or lemon, the lemon zest and the rum (if using). Beat until smooth. Beat the egg whites with the salt until they form stiff peaks, then fold them into the mixture.

Preheat the oven to 400° F.

Pour the batter into a 9-inch cake pan and bake for 15 minutes at 400° F. Reduce the temperature to 350° F and bake for 25 to 30 minutes. Check that the cake is done with the point of a knife, which should come out clean. Allow to cool slightly before turning out.

Prepare the lemon frosting: put the powdered sugar, the egg white and the juice of half a lemon into a bowl. Whisk until perfectly smooth.

When the cake is cold, frost it with a frosting knife. Decorate with pieces of candied citron.

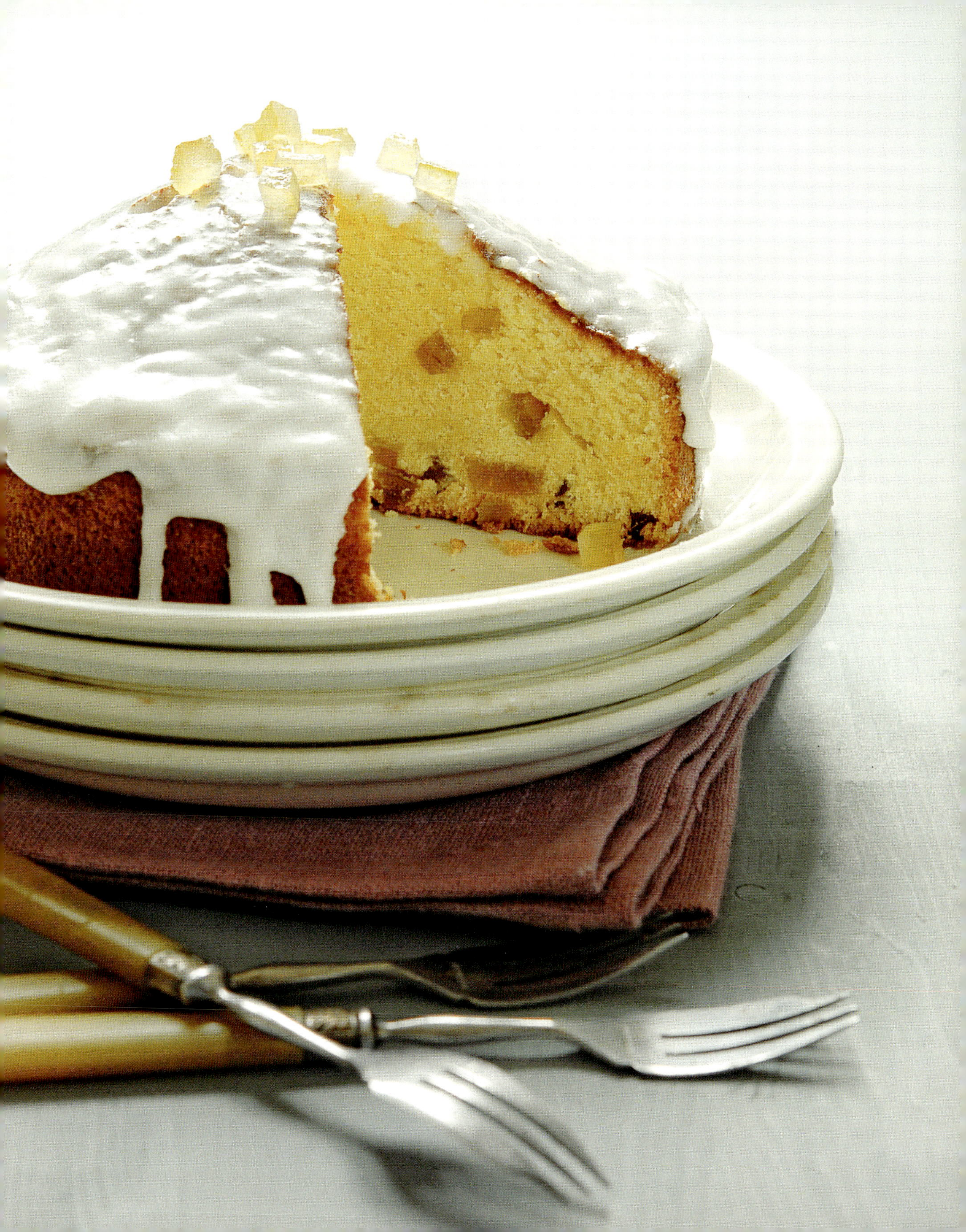

Pear charlotte

child's play

SERVES 6 TO 8
PREP TIME: 1 hr
COOKING TIME: 30 mins.
REFRIGERATION TIME: 6 to 8 hrs

- 2 packets gelatin
- 2 oz. pear brandy
- 1 cup whipped cream
- 24 lady fingers

FOR THE PEARS
- 2-1/2 cups sugar
- 4 cups water
- 3 lbs. pears

FOR THE CRÈME ANGLAISE
- 1/2 vanilla bean
- 2 cups milk
- 6 egg yolks
- 5 tbsp. sugar

First prepare a syrup for the pears by heating the sugar and 4 cups of water together to dissolve the sugar. Peel the pears and poach them whole in the syrup. Check that they are tender with the end of a sharp knife. Make a purée with two of the poached pears: remove the pits and put the fruit in a blender or run it through a food mill; you should end up with about a cup of purée.

Prepare the crème anglaise: split the vanilla bean and put it in a saucepan with the milk, bring to a boil; turn off the heat and allow to infuse for 15 to 20 minutes. Beat the egg yolks and the sugar in a bowl until they turn pale yellow. Remove the vanilla and scrape the seeds from the bean. Put the milk and vanilla seeds back on the heat and bring to a boil. Gradually pour the boiling milk onto the egg and sugar mixture, stirring constantly. Put the mixture on a very low heat, stirring until it thickens. Remove from the heat.

Dissolve the gelatin in a little cold water and add to the hot crème anglaise. Allow to cool, add the pear brandy and pear purée, then the whipped cream. Stir well.

Cut the other poached pears into medium slices and remove the pits. Keep a few slices for decoration.

Line an 8-inch charlotte mold with lady fingers. Pour in a layer of pear custard, add a layer of pear slices, then another layer of custard. Continue until the mold is full. Cover with lady fingers. Cover the mold with plastic wrap and chill for 6 to 8 hours.

Hold the mold under the hot faucet to turn the charlotte onto a serving dish. Decorate with pear slices.

> Helpful tip
Poaching fruit means simmering it gently in sugar syrup.

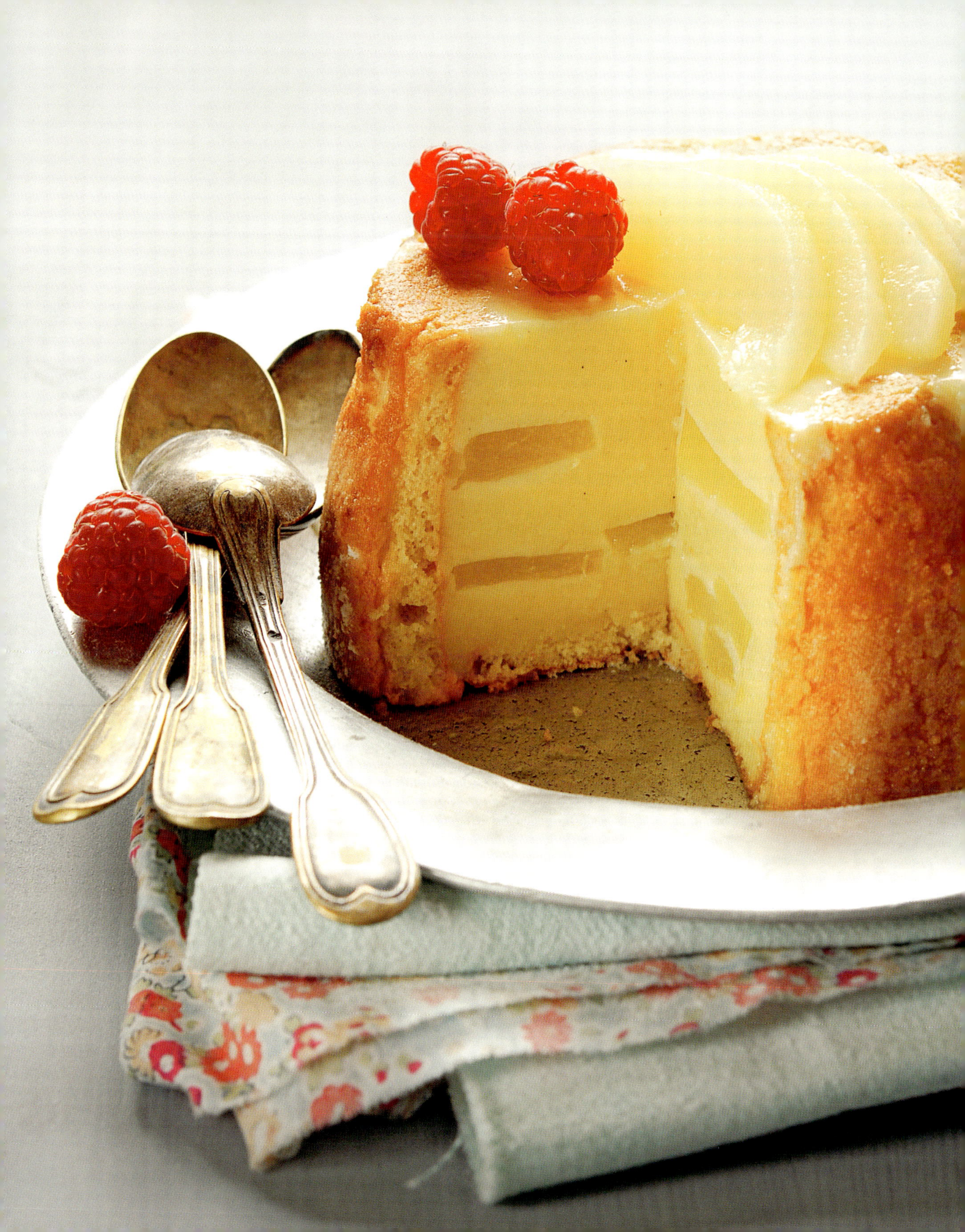

Prune diplomate

SERVES 6 TO 8
PREP TIME: 40 mins. (over 2 days)
SOAKING TIME: 12 hrs
REFRIGERATION TIME: 6 hrs

- 2 cups weak tea
- 1/2 lb. large prunes
- 4 tbsp. sugar
- 2 tbsp. rum or kirsch
- 28 lady fingers

FOR THE PASTRY CREAM
- 4 egg yolks
- 1/3 cup sugar
- 1/4 cup flour
- 1-1/2 cups milk

The day before, make the tea, put it in a bowl and add the prunes. Leave to soak overnight.

The following day, prepare the pastry cream: put the egg yolks and the sugar into a bowl and beat until the mixture turns pale yellow. Sprinkle on the flour and stir it in quickly. In the meantime, boil the milk in a saucepan. Slowly pour the boiling milk onto the mixture, stirring constantly with a wooden spoon to obtain a smooth creamy consistency. Pour into a heavy saucepan. Heat over a very low heat until it thickens, stirring constantly. Remove from the heat as soon as it starts to boil and pour into a bowl.

Put the prunes and tea into a large saucepan. Add the sugar and cook together over a low heat for 15 minutes. Allow to cool, then strain and pit the prunes. Add the rum or kirsch to the cooking liquid. Dip the lady fingers in the liquids and use them to line a 7-inch charlotte mold. Keep the remaining lady fingers to one side.

Pour a small quantity of pastry cream into the mold, follow with a layer of prunes and a layer of the lady fingers you kept to one side, dipped in the prune juice; continue in this way until the mold is full, finishing with a layer of lady fingers. Cover the diplomate with plastic wrap and put in the refrigerator for 6 hours.

Turn the diplomate onto a serving plate and serve.

> Helpful tip
Serve your prune diplomate with crème anglaise flavored with rum or kirsch (see p.411).

> To make a change
You can also use small molds to make individual mini-diplomates.

36 • ALL-TIME FAVORITES

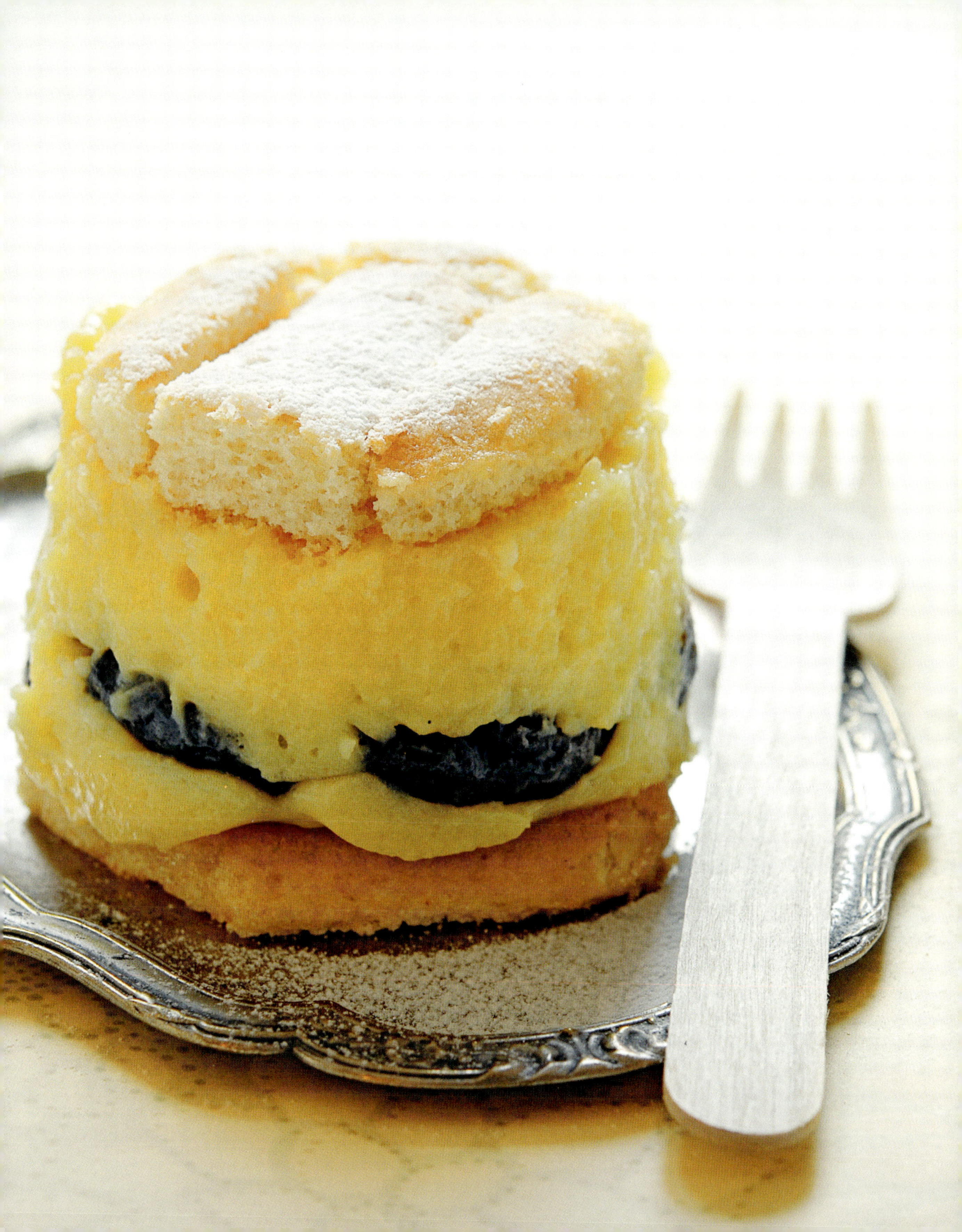

Parisian flan

SERVES 6 TO 8
PREP TIME: 30 mins.
RESTING TIME: 1 hr 30 mins.
COOKING TIME: 1 hr

FOR THE PIE CRUST
- 7 tbsp. butter
  + some for the pan
- 1-1/4 cups flour
- A pinch of salt
- 2 tbsp. sugar (optional)
- 5 tbsp. cold water

FOR THE CUSTARD FILLING
- 3 cups whole milk
- 4 eggs
- 3/4 cup sugar
- 1/2 cup cornstarch
- 1/2 vanilla bean

Prepare the pie crust: cut the butter into small pieces. Sift the flour into a mixing bowl and add the salt, the sugar (if using) and the butter. Rub the ingredients in with your fingertips and add enough water to make a stiff dough. Work the dough with your hands until it is smooth and supple but not sticky (do not overknead). Shape into a ball and allow to rest for at least 30 minutes.

Roll out the dough to a thickness of 1/8 inch. Cut out a 14-inch disk and place on a baking sheet. Put in the refrigerator for 30 minutes. Butter a deep 9-inch pie dish and use the disk of dough to line it. Put back in the refrigerator for 30 minutes.

Preheat the oven to 375° F.

Prepare the custard: split the vanilla bean and scrape out the seeds from one half. Heat the milk in a saucepan. Place the half vanilla bean and the seeds in the milk to infuse. After twenty minutes, filter the milk in a sieve and bring to a boil.

Whisk together the egg yolks, sugar and cornstarch in another saucepan. Pour into the boiling milk in a thin stream, beating with a whisk. Remove from the heat when the mixture reaches boiling point again.

Pour the mixture onto the pie base and bake for one hour.

Far breton

child's play

SERVES 6 TO 8
PREP TIME: 15 mins.
COOKING TIME: 1 hr

- 2 cups weak warm tea
- 1 cup raisins
- 3/4 lb. prunes
- 4 eggs
- 2 cups flour
- A pinch of salt
- 1-1/2 tbsp. sugar
- 2 cups milk
- Powdered sugar

Prepare the tea, add the raisins and prunes and leave for about 1 hour. Strain. Pit the prunes.

Preheat the oven to 400° F.

Beat the eggs. Put the flour in a large bowl, add the salt and the sugar and stir. Stir in the eggs, then the milk. Add the raisins and prunes and stir well.

Butter a 9-inch round cake pan and pour in the mixture. Bake for 1 hour: the top should be dark brown. Dust with powdered sugar and serve cold.

> **Helpful tip**
Far breton is a specialty of Brittany, in northwest France.

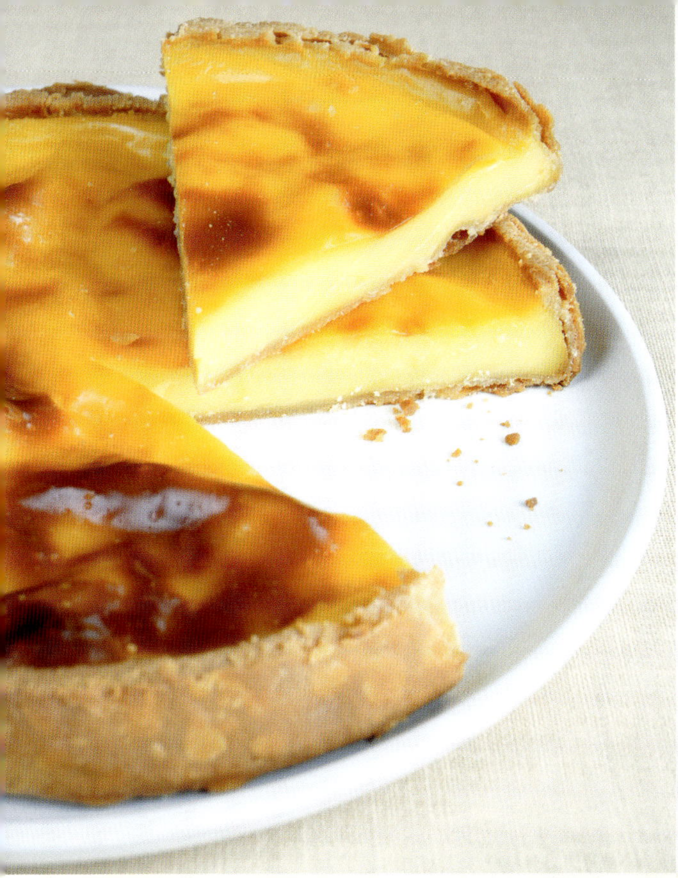
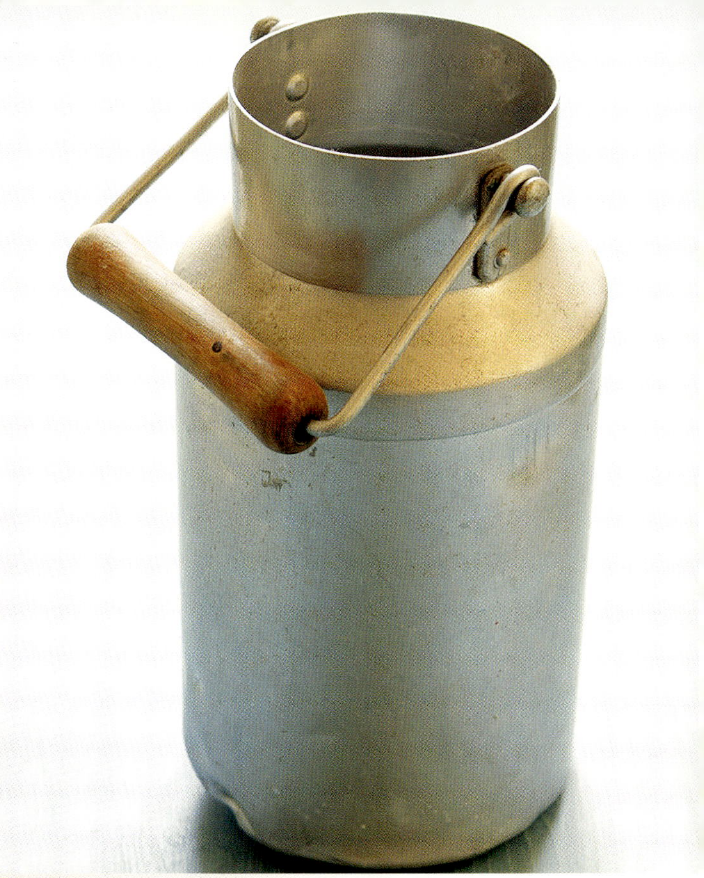
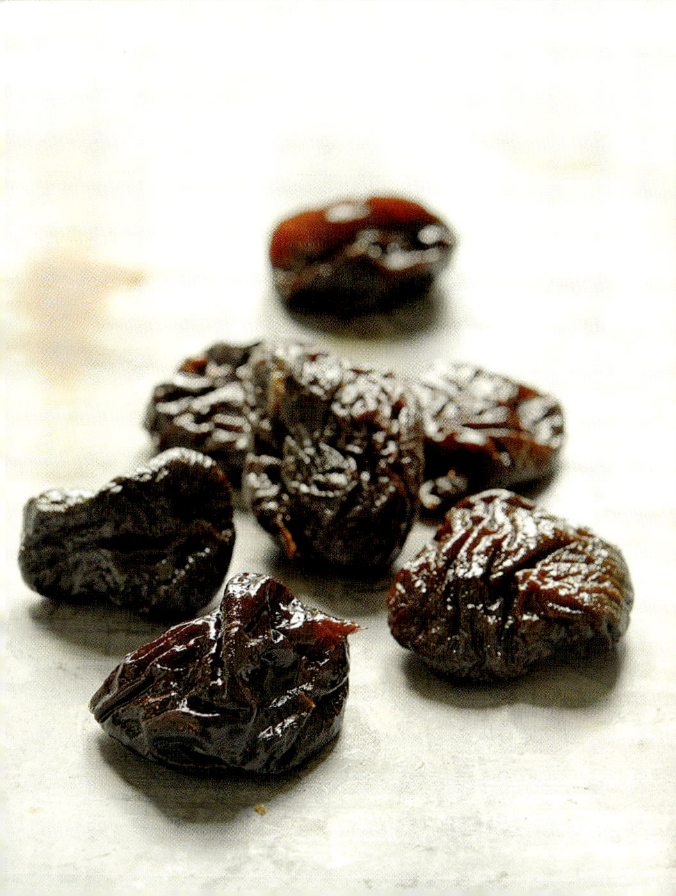
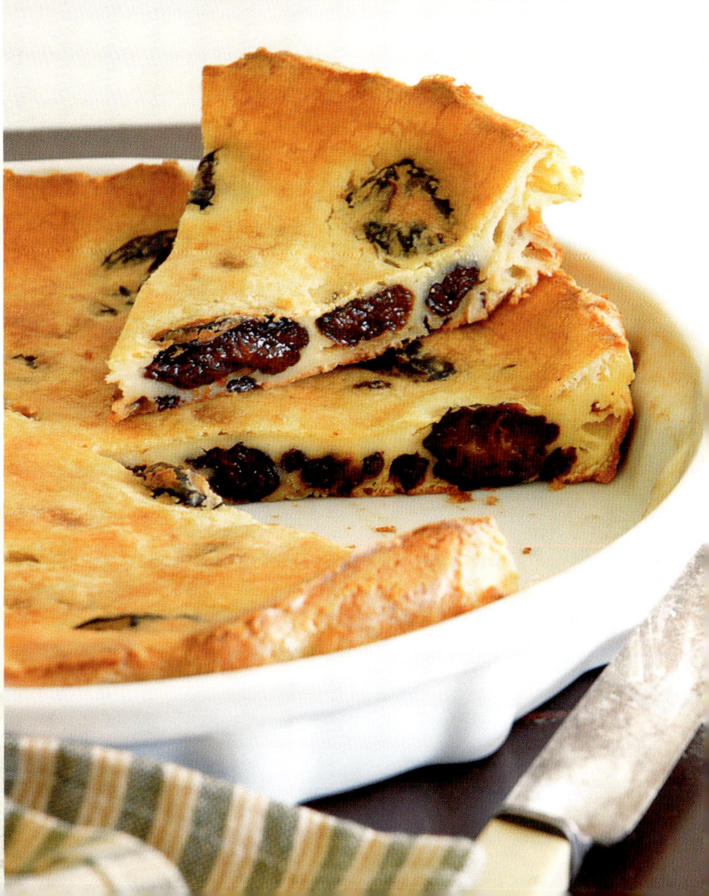

Tropézienne
(custard-filled brioche)

SERVES 6
PREP TIME: 45 mins.
RESTING TIME: 3 hrs
COOKING TIME: 40 mins.

FOR THE BRIOCHE
- 1 scant tbsp. dried yeast
- 2 tbsp. milk
- 1-2/3 cups flour
- 3 eggs
- 2 tbsp. sugar
- 5 tbsp. softened butter + some for the pan
- A pinch of salt
- 2-1/2 tbsp. sugar

FOR THE PASTRY CREAM
- 2 cups milk
- 1 vanilla bean
- 3 egg yolks
- 6 tbsp. sugar
- 1/2 cup flour

FOR THE BUTTER CREAM
- 1 egg yolk
- 2 tbsp. sugar
- 1 teaspoon water
- 9 tbsp. very soft butter

Prepare the brioche: mix the yeast with the warm milk and add 1/2 cup flour. Allow this yeast mixture to rest for 1 hour in a warm place. Sift the rest of the flour, make a well in the center and add two beaten eggs, the sugar, the butter cut into small pieces and the salt. Work this mixture well with your hands, then add the yeast mixture. Knead for 10 to 15 minutes, make into a ball and allow to rest in a warm place for at least 2 hours.

Preheat the oven to 350° F.

Roll out the dough and use it to line a 10-inch pie dish. Beat the remaining egg and brush the dough with it. Sprinkle with sugar and bake for about 30 minutes.

Prepare the pastry cream: split the vanilla bean and scrape out the seeds. Place the milk in a saucepan and add the vanilla pod and seeds. Bring to a boil and remove from the heat. Allow to cool slightly. Beat the egg yolks with the sugar in a bowl for 2 minutes. Add the flour and beat until smooth. Remove the vanilla bean from the milk and pour into the bowl, stirring well. If the mixture is lumpy, blend in a food processor. Put the mixture back in the saucepan over a medium heat and allow to thicken for about 5 minutes, stirring all the time. Remove from the heat and allow to cool.

Prepare the butter cream: beat the egg yolk. Put the sugar and the water in a small saucepan and bring to a boil. Whisk this syrup into the egg yolk, then gradually incorporate the butter cut into pieces. Mix for a few minutes.

Gradually beat the pastry cream into the butter cream.

Turn out the brioche and cut it in two as you would a sponge cake. Sandwich with the cream. Serve cold.

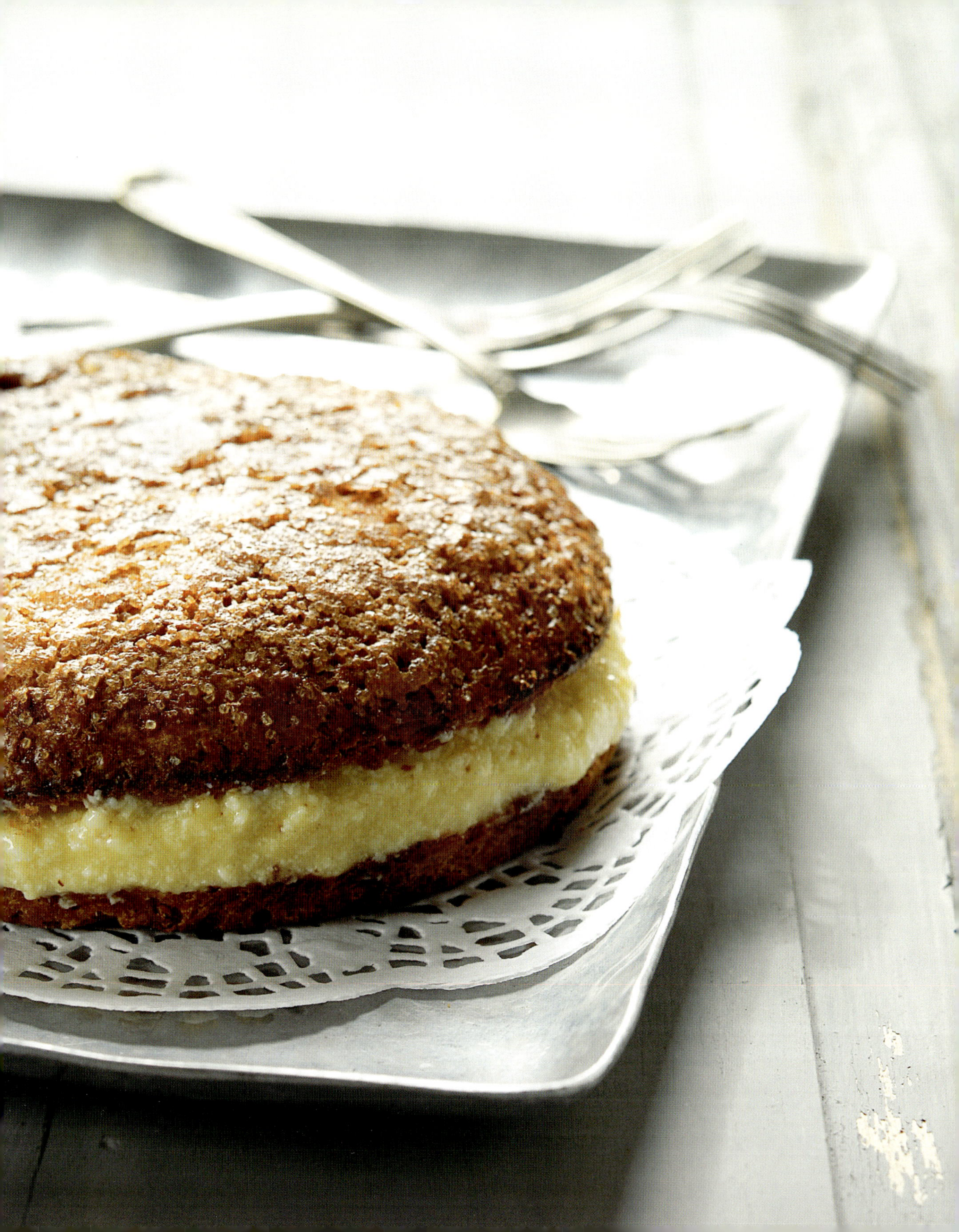

Fiadone

SERVES 8
PREP TIME: 15 mins.
RESTING TIME: 30 mins.
COOKING TIME: About 1 hr

FOR THE SHORTCRUST PASTRY
- 7 tbsp. butter + some for the pan
- 1-1/4 cups flour
- 1 pinch of table salt
- 2 tbsp. sugar (optional)
- 5 tbsp. cold water

FOR THE FILLING
- 2 lemons, preferably organic
- 2 brocciu frais 1 lb each. (Corsican cheese made from sheep and goat's milk)
- 8 eggs
- 1-1/4 cups sugar

Make the pie crust: cut the butter into pieces; place the flour into a large bowl; add salt, sugar (if desired) and butter. Combine these by rubbing together with the fingertips, adding a little water to blend the ingredients. Knead the dough until it is supple (neither too sticky nor too soft). Roll into a ball and let it rest for at least 30 minutes.

Butter a 10-inch cake pan and line with the pastry, making sure it partly covers the sides of the pan.

Preheat the oven to 350° F.

Prepare the filling: rinse the lemons and remove the zest. Place the zest with the cheese, whole eggs and sugar in the blender and mix slowly.

When you have obtained a smooth mixture, pour it onto the pastry and place in the oven for 50 to 60 minutes. After 15 minutes, lower the temperature to 325° F. You can lower the temperature even more if the top of the cake browns too quickly. Serve warm or cold.

> Variation

Prepare a pastry base of crushed dry biscuits mixed with butter, as for a cheesecake. The fiadone can also be made with a rich, crumbly dessert pastry (see p.400).

> Helpful tip

If brocciu cheese is not available, you can use 2 lb. sheep's or goat's milk cheese, or 1 lb. of each, or substitute any other kind of cream cheese.

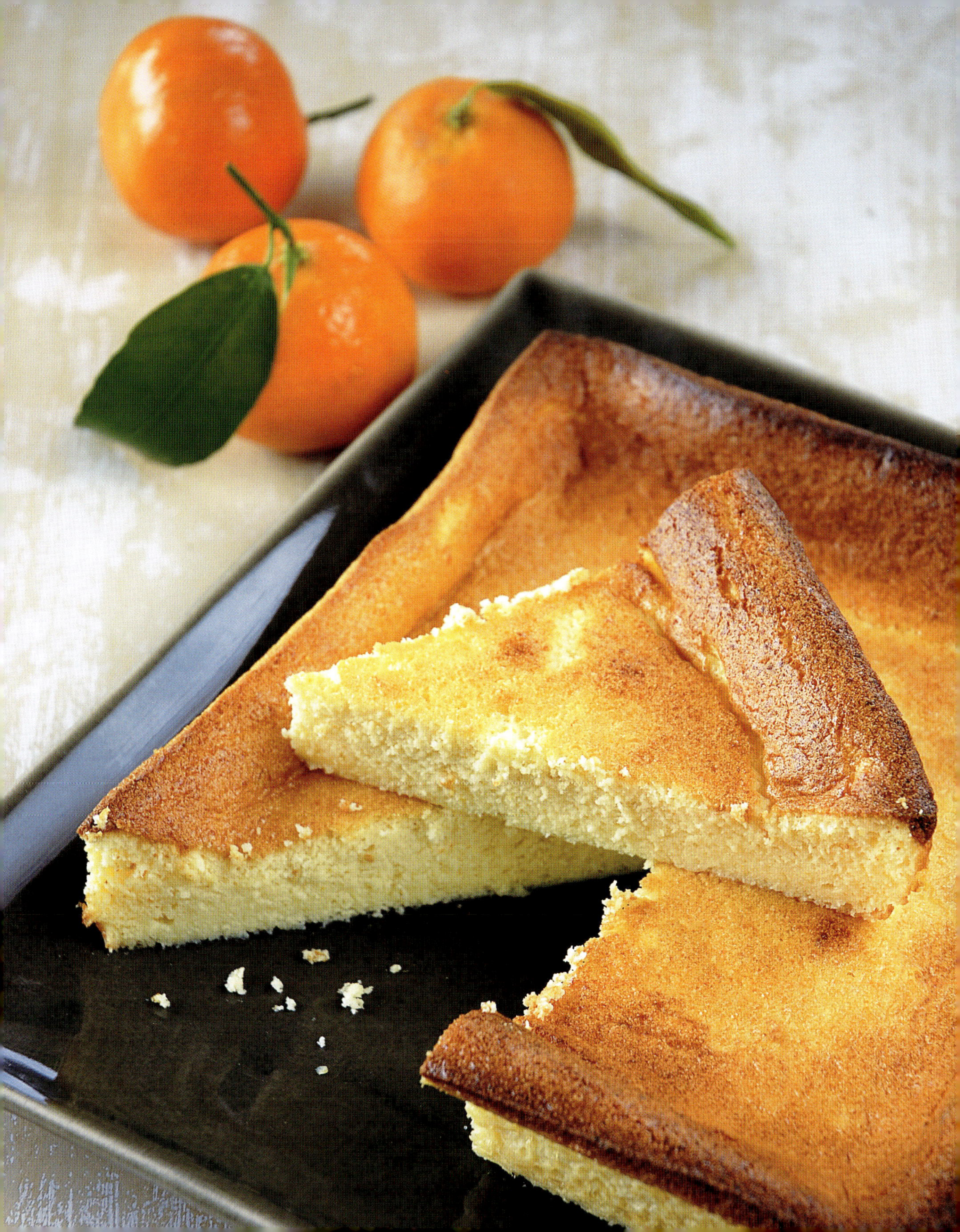

Mascarpone pie

SERVES 6
PREP TIME: 20 mins.
RESTING TIME: 30 mins.
COOKING TIME: 40 mins.

FOR THE PIE CRUST
- 7 tbsp. butter
- 1-1/4 cups flour
- A pinch of salt
- 2 tbsp. sugar (optional)
- 5 tbsp. cold water

FOR THE CREAM
- 1/2 a lemon
- 4 eggs
- 1 cup mascarpone
- 1-1/3 cups sugar
- 2 teaspoons vanilla extract
- 1/2 cup ground almonds

Prepare the pie crust: cut the butter into small pieces; put the flour, salt, sugar (if using) and the butter into a bowl. Rub the ingredients in with your fingertips, then add a little water to form a dough. Knead until supple (it should be neither too soft, nor too sticky). Shape into a ball and allow to rest for at least 30 minutes.

Preheat the oven to 350° F.

Roll out the dough and place in a 10-inch pie dish lined with parchment paper.

Prepare the cream: finely chop the zest of half a lemon. Beat the eggs in a bowl and add the mascarpone, the sugar and the vanilla extract, the lemon zest and the ground almonds. Mix well.

Fill the pie with cream and bake for about 40 minutes. Serve warm or cold.

never fails

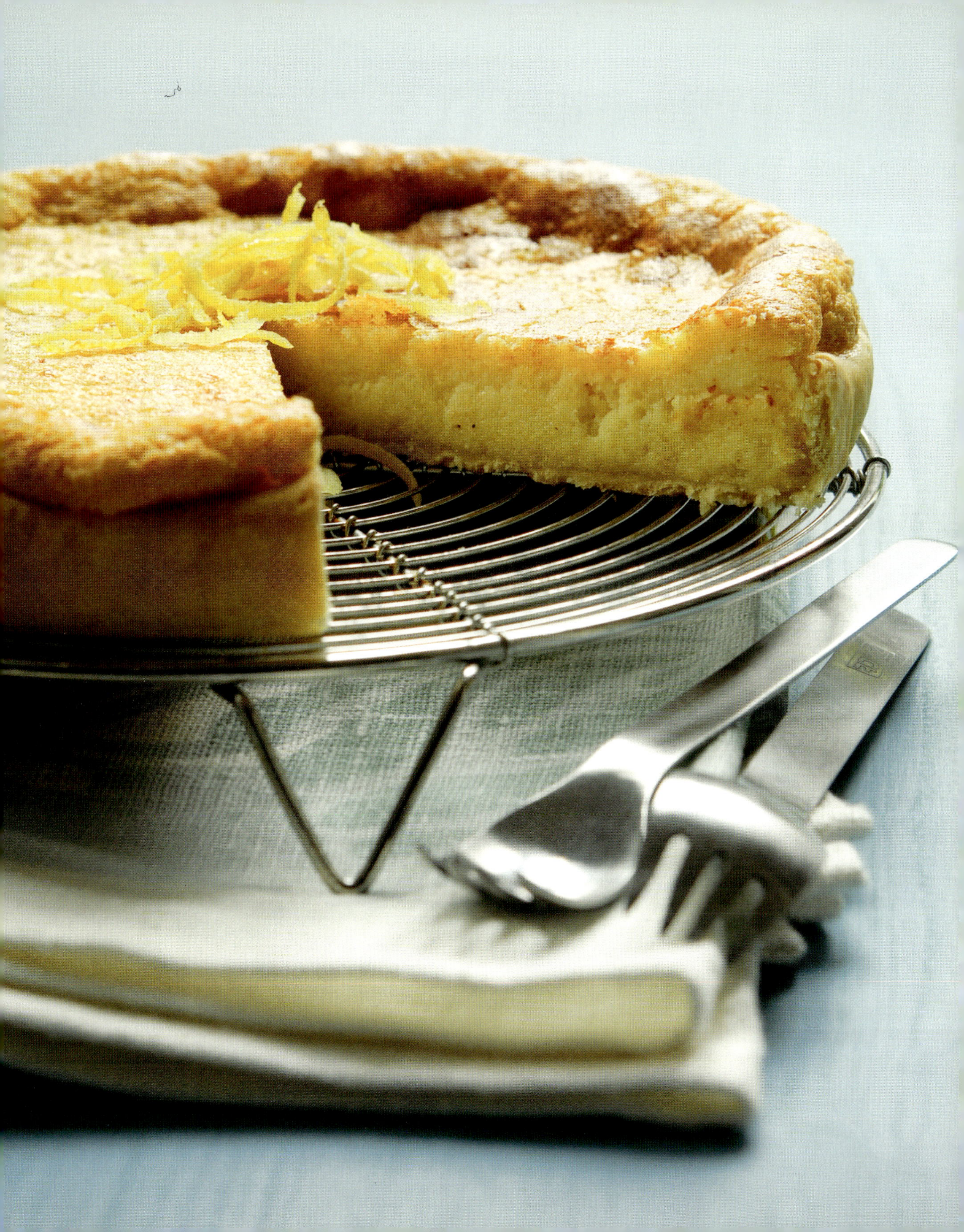

No-bake cheesecake

SERVES 6
PREP TIME: 30 mins.
COOKING TIME: About 5 mins.
REFRIGERATION TIME: At least 4 hrs

FOR THE BASE
- 1/2 lb. shortbread or Graham crackers
- 1/2 cup butter

FOR THE FILLING
- 3/4 packet gelatin
- 1 orange
- 2 eggs
- 6 tbsp. sugar
- 450 g cream cheese
- 13 tbsp. crème fraîche or heavy cream

never fails

Prepare the base: Melt the butter over a gentle heat. Place the shortbread in a food processor with the butter and mix.

Use the shortbread mixture to line the bottom of a 9-inch springform cake pan. Pack the mixture down with the back of a spoon. Place in the refrigerator.

Prepare the filling: dissolve the gelatin in warm water. Finely grate the orange zest and squeeze the juice. Heat the orange juice in a small saucepan. Add the gelatin and stir well.

Break the eggs and separate the yolks from the whites. Mix the yolks with the sugar and the orange zest. Add the cream cheese, the heavy cream and the orange juice. Beat well until the mixture is smooth and creamy.

Beat the egg whites until they form stiff peaks and fold them into the previous mixture.

Pour the filling onto the base and chill for at least 4 hours before serving.

> Helpful tip
This cheesecake is delicious served with fruit coulis.

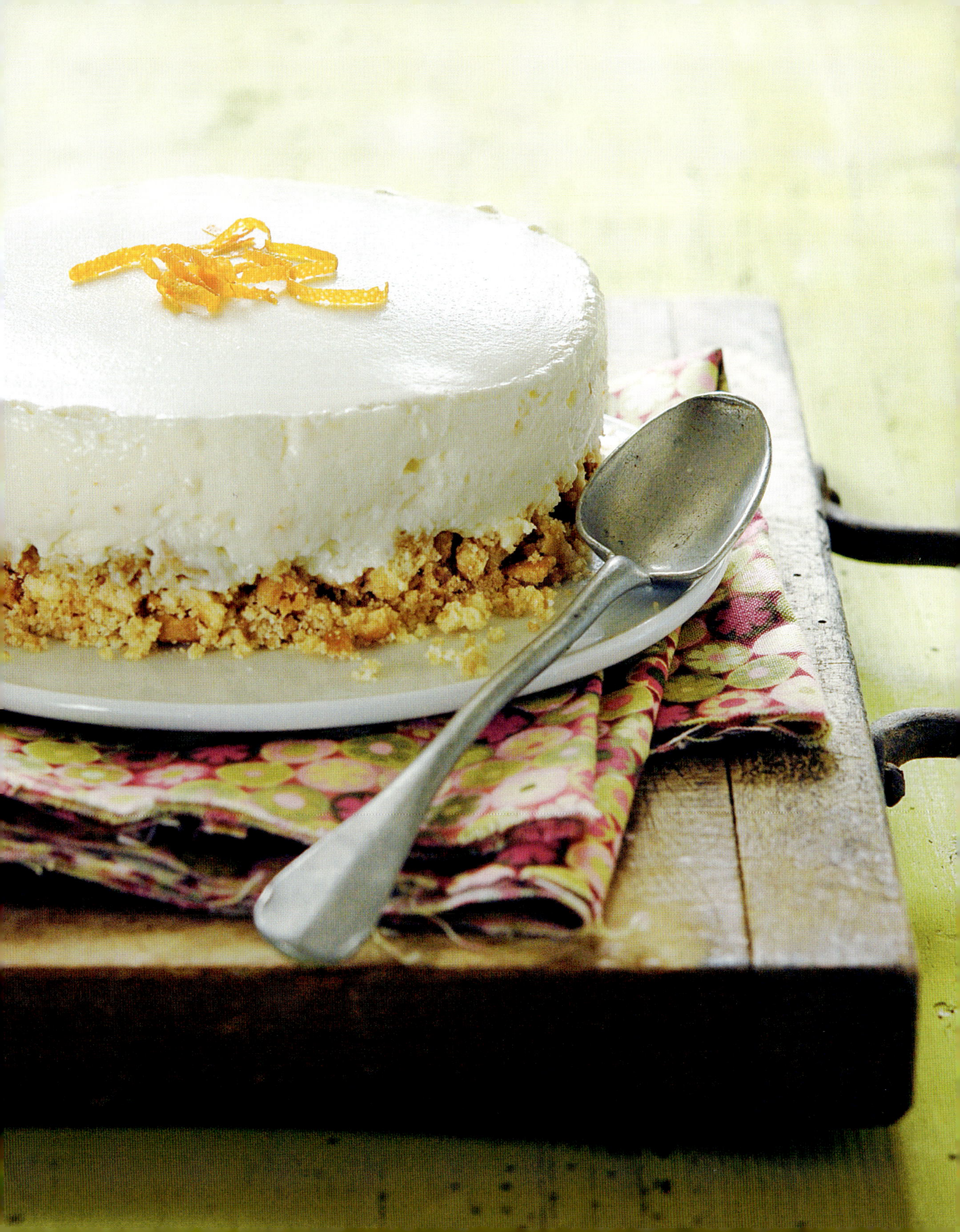

Apple crumble

SERVES 6
PREP TIME: 20 mins.
SOAKING TIME: 30 mins.
COOKING TIME: About 45 mins.

- 2 tbsp. sultanas
- 2 tbsp. rum
- 3 pounds apples
- 1/2 teaspoon cinnamon

FOR THE CRUMBLE TOPPING
- 6 tbsp. butter
  + some for the dish
- 1 cup flour
- 6 tbsp. sugar
- A pinch of salt

Mix the sultanas and rum in a bowl and leave to soak for at least 30 minutes.

Prepare the crumble topping: Mix the flour and the brown sugar. Cut the butter into small pieces and add to the flour and sugar. Rub in with your fingertips until the mixture is the consistency of fine breadcrumbs.

Preheat the oven to 300° F. Generously butter a gratin dish.

Peel and core the apples, cut each into eight wedges and arrange in the dish. Sprinkle over the strained raisins and the cinnamon. Cover with crumble topping.

Bake for 45 minutes, until golden. Serve hot from the dish with whipped cream or ice cream.

never fails

48 • ALL-TIME FAVORITES

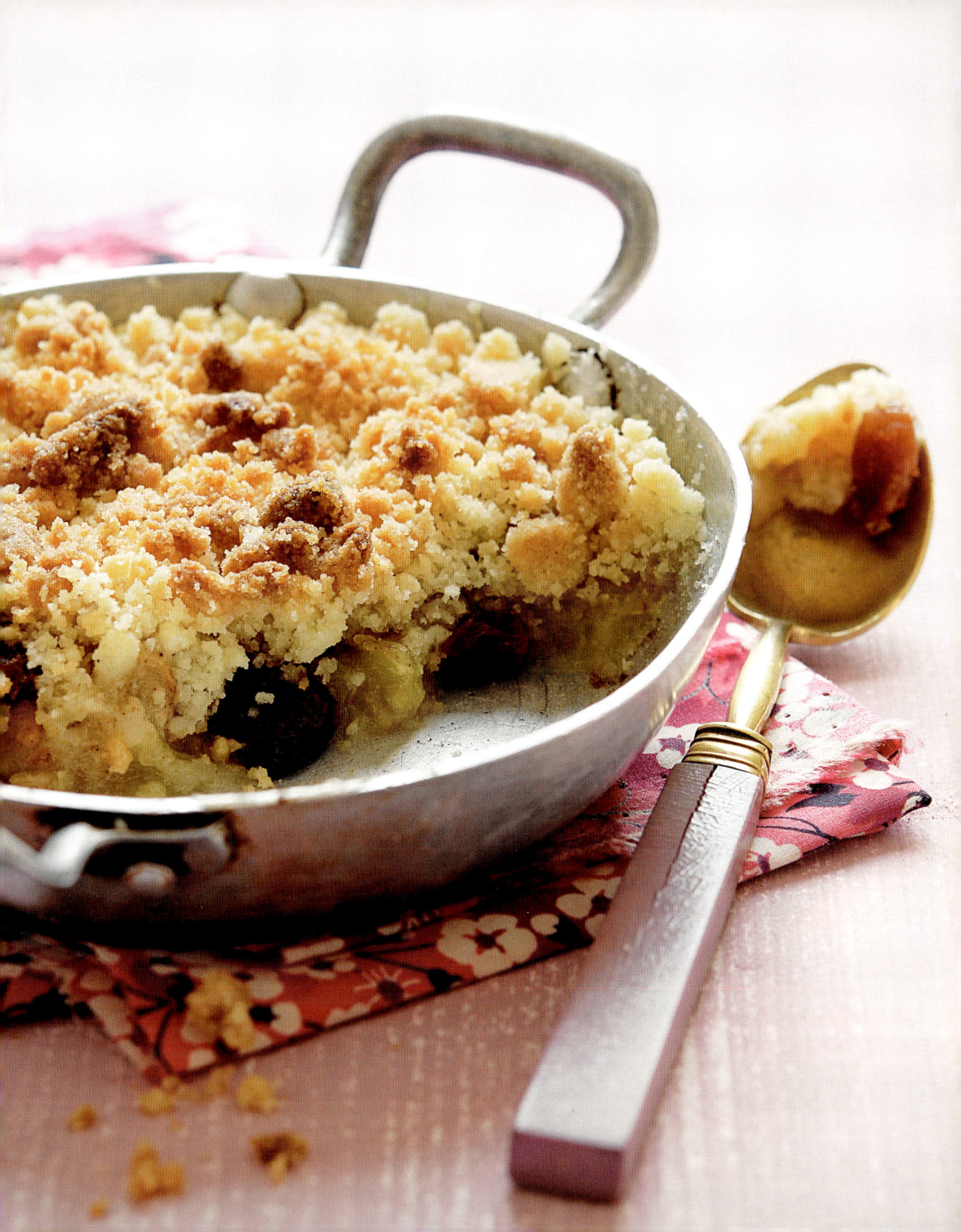

Cherry clafoutis

SERVES 6 TO 8
PREP TIME: 15 mins.
SOAKING TIME: 30 mins.
COOKING TIME: 35 to 40 mins.

- 1 lb. black cherries
- 1/2 cup sugar
- Butter for the mold
- 1 cup flour
- A pinch of salt
- 3 eggs
- 1-1/4 cup milk
- Powdered sugar

Wash the cherries and remove the stems, but don't pit them. Put them in a bowl, sprinkle with half the sugar; stir to distribute the sugar evenly and allow to soak for at least 30 minutes.

Preheat the oven to 350° F. Butter a 10-1/2-inch baking dish.

Sift the flour into a bowl, add a pinch of salt and the rest of the sugar. Beat the eggs and add them to the mixture. Mix well. Add the milk and mix again.

Lay the cherries in the baking dish, then pour the batter over them. Bake for 35 to 40 minutes.

Take the clafoutis out of the oven. Allow to cool slightly and sprinkle with powdered sugar. Serve cold from the dish it was cooked in.

> To make a change
This recipe also works well with mirabelle plums.

never fails

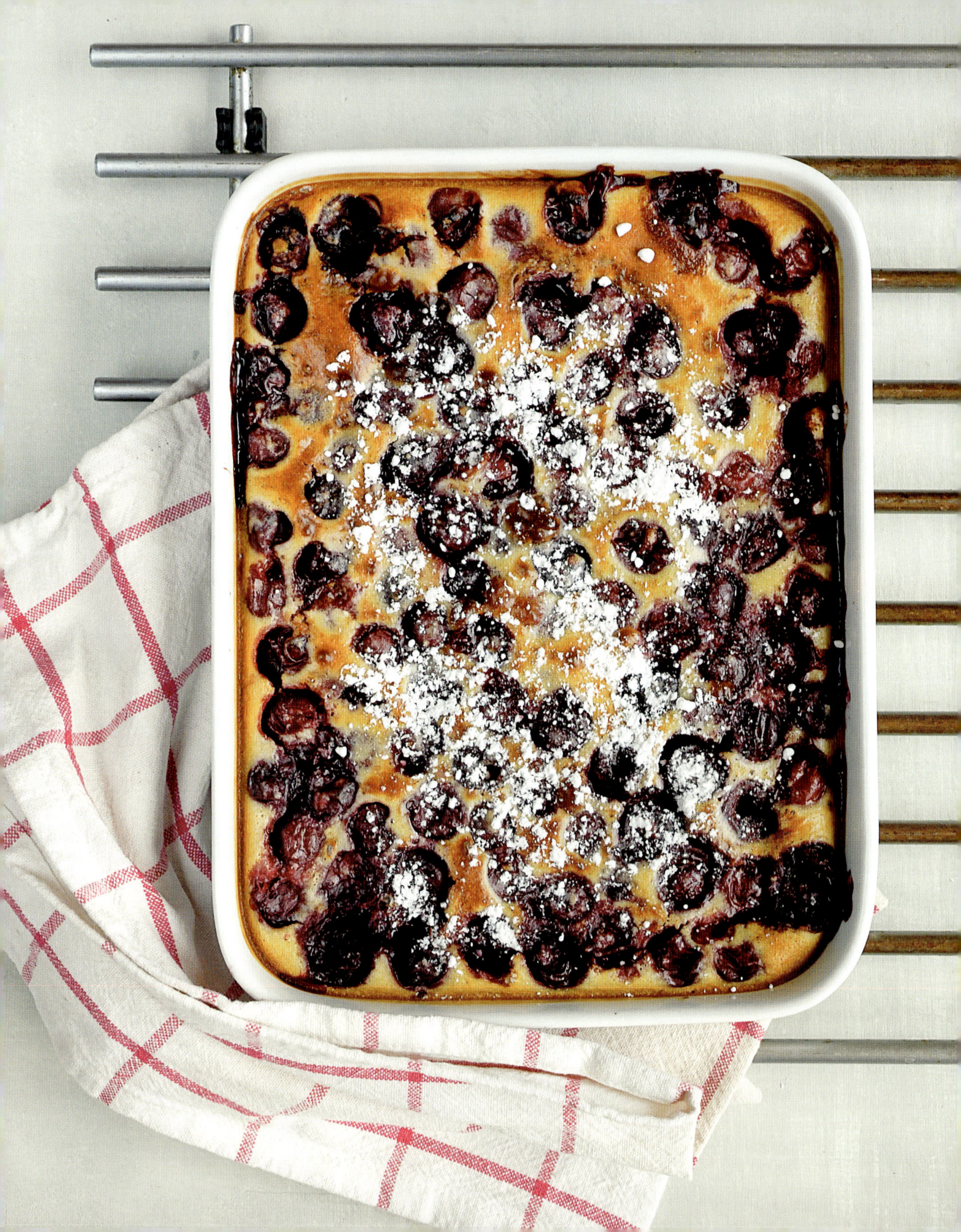

Baked apples

SERVES 6
PREP TIME: 20 mins.
COOKING TIME: 40 mins.

- 6 apples
- 4 tbsp. butter
  + some for the pan
- 5 tbsp. sugar
- 6 tbsp. red currant jelly
- 1/2 cup slivered almonds

Preheat the oven to 400° F and liberally butter a gratin dish. Let the butter soften at room temperature.

Cut a thin slice off the base of the apples so that they don't fall over. Cut the top off the apples to form lids. Dig out the core of the apples to remove the pits.

Blend the butter with the sugar and fill the apples with the mixture.

Arrange the apples in the dish, put the lids back on and pour 2 tbsp. of water into the dish. Bake for about 40 minutes.

Remove from the oven. Spoon a tbsp. of red currant jelly over each apple and sprinkle with slivered almonds. Serve very hot from the same dish.

> Helpful tip
You can serve this dish with caramel sauce, it's really delicious.

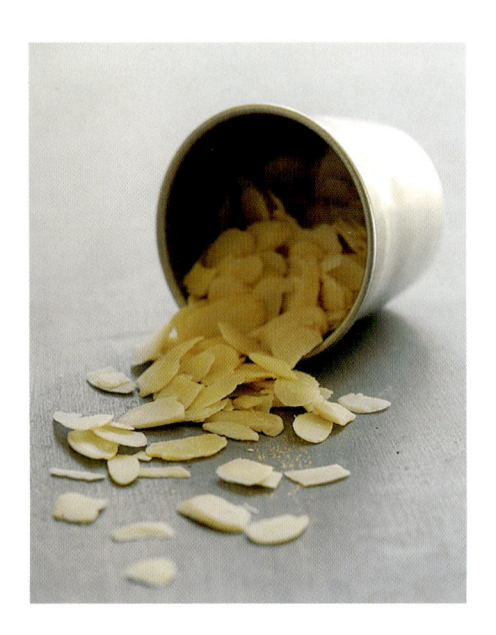

never fails

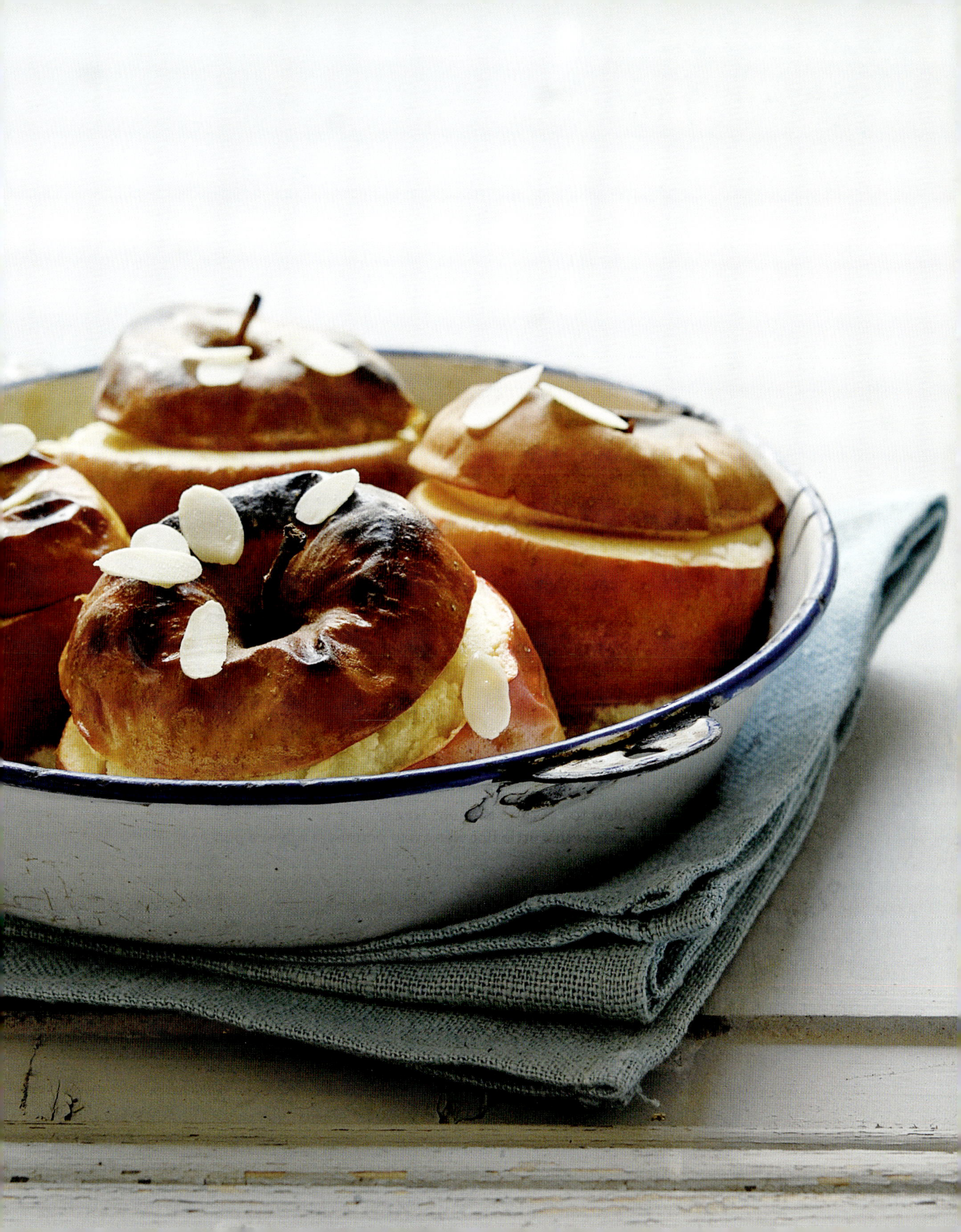

Rice pudding with caramel

PREP TIME: 30 mins.
COOKING TIME: About 1 hr 20 mins.

- 3 whole eggs
- 1/2 cup sugar
- A pinch of salt

FOR THE RICE PUDDING
- 4 cups milk
- 1/3 cup sugar
- 1 vanilla bean
- 1 cup short grain white rice
- 3-1/2 tbsp. butter

FOR THE CARAMEL
- 1/2 cup sugar
- The juice of half a lemon

Prepare the rice pudding: put the milk in a large saucepan with the sugar and the vanilla bean. Boil 2 pints water and pour the rice into it. Wait 2 minutes, strain the rice and place in the boiling milk. Cover, reduce the heat and cook gently for 30 to 40 minutes. When the rice is cooked, stir in the butter, stir well and keep warm.

Break the eggs and separate the yolks from the whites. Remove the vanilla bean from the rice and add the sugar and beaten egg yolks. Beat the egg whites with the salt until they form stiff peaks, then fold them into the rice.

Preheat the oven to 400° F.

Prepare the caramel: mix the sugar, the lemon juice and a tbsp. of water in a large saucepan. Heat together until the mixture caramelizes, pour half of the caramel into an 8-inch charlotte mold, swirling it around to get a layer of caramel on the sides of the mold. Keep the other half to one side.

Pour the rice into the mold. Press it down well and place in a bain-marie. Bring to a boil on the stove, then place in the oven for 45 minutes.

Allow to cool and turn out on a serving dish. Dilute the caramel you set aside with a little hot water and pour over the rice pudding.

child's play

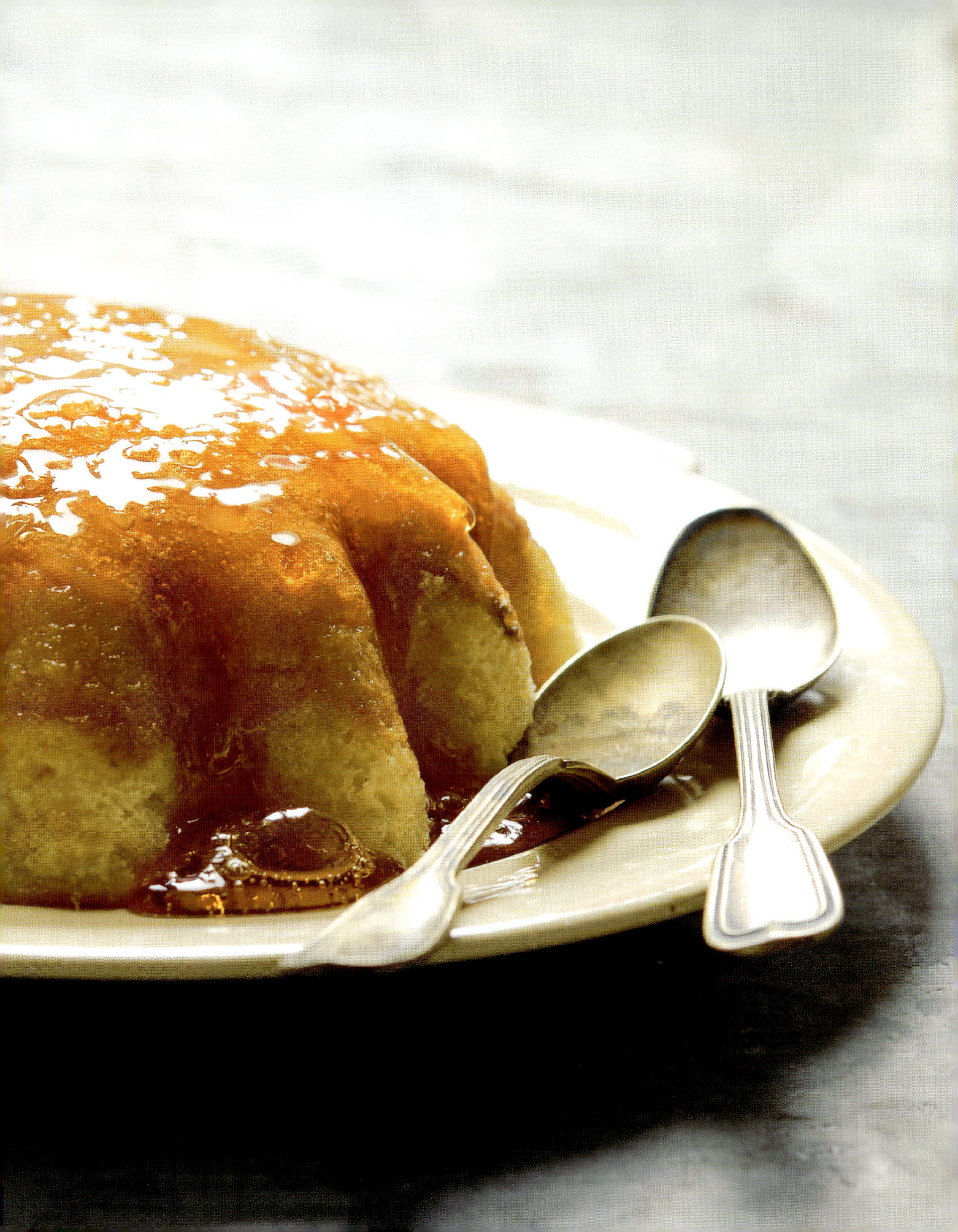

Rice pudding with citrus peel

SERVES 4
PREP TIME: 30 mins.
COOKING TIME: 40 mins.

FOR THE PEEL
- 2 oranges
- 1 grapefruit
- 1/2 cup demerara sugar

FOR THE RICE PUDDING
- 1 cup short grain white rice
- 4-1/4 cups whole milk
- A pinch of salt
- 1 teaspoon vanilla extract
- 1/2 cup sugar
- 2 egg yolks

FOR THE CHANTILLY WHIPPED CREAM
- 2/3 cup crème fraîche or heavy cream

Prepare the peel: remove the peel from the oranges and and the grapefruit without cutting into the pith. Cut into matchstick-sized pieces. Place these in a saucepan of boiling water for 2 minutes, then drain them. Change the water, bring to a boil and repeat the operation. Drain the peel again.

Put the demerara sugar and 1 cup water in a saucepan and bring slowly to the boil, stirring until the sugar has dissolved. Put the peel in this syrup, simmer gently for 10 minutes, then remove with a slotted spoon and allow to cool. Cut the strips into small pieces.

Prepare the rice: bring a large saucepan of water to a boil, add the rice and cook for 3 minutes. Boil the milk in another saucepan with the salt and the vanilla extract. Strain the rice, add it to the boiling milk and bring back to a boil. Turn down the heat and simmer gently for about 40 minutes, until the rice is tender.

Remove the saucepan from the heat, wait a few moments, then beat in the sugar. Beat in the egg yolks and allow to cool completely.

Prepare the Chantilly whipped cream: beat the very cold heavy cream until it thickens. Gently stir in the candied peel and the rice, then pour into a large serving bowl. Place in the refrigerator until needed. Serve well chilled.

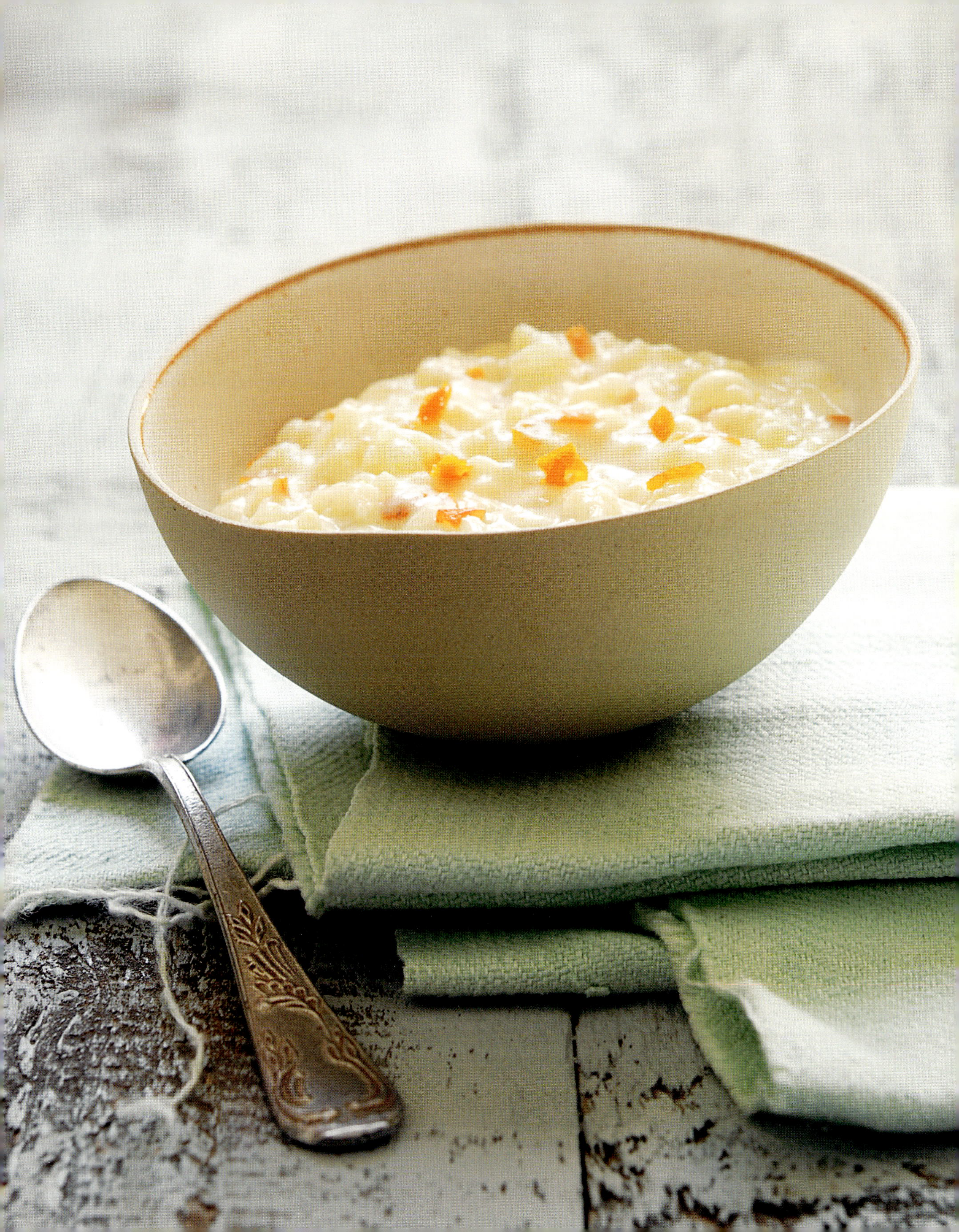

Traditional rice pudding

SERVES 6 TO 8
PREP TIME: 30 mins.
COOKING TIME: 45 mins. to 1 hr 5 mins.

- 1-1/4 cups short grain white rice
- 4-1/4 cups whole milk
- 1-1/3 cups sugar
- 1/2 vanilla bean
- A pinch of salt
- 3-1/2 tbsp. butter + some for the pan
- 8 eggs
- Fine breadcrumbs

Preheat the oven to 220° F.

Wash the rice and place in boiling salted water for 3 minutes to blanch.

Heat the milk and add the sugar, the vanilla and a pinch of salt.

Strain the rice and place in an ovenproof pan, then add the hot milk and the butter. Stir and bring gently to the boil. Cover and put the pan in the oven to bake for 25 to 30 minutes.

Break the eggs and separate the yolks from the whites . Beat the whites until they form very stiff peaks.

Remove the pan of rice from the oven and stir in the egg yolks one by one, then fold in the egg whites.

Adjust the oven temperature to 350° F. Butter a ten-inch round oven dish, sprinkle with breadcrumbs and pour in the rice. Place in a bain-marie and bake for 30 to 35 minutes.

> Helpful tip

This pudding can be served with crème anglaise (see p.411) or a fruit coulis (see p.423).

> To make a change

You can make chocolate flavor rice pudding by adding 3 to 4 oz grated dark chocolate to the rice when you take it out of the oven for the first time and stirring until it has melted.

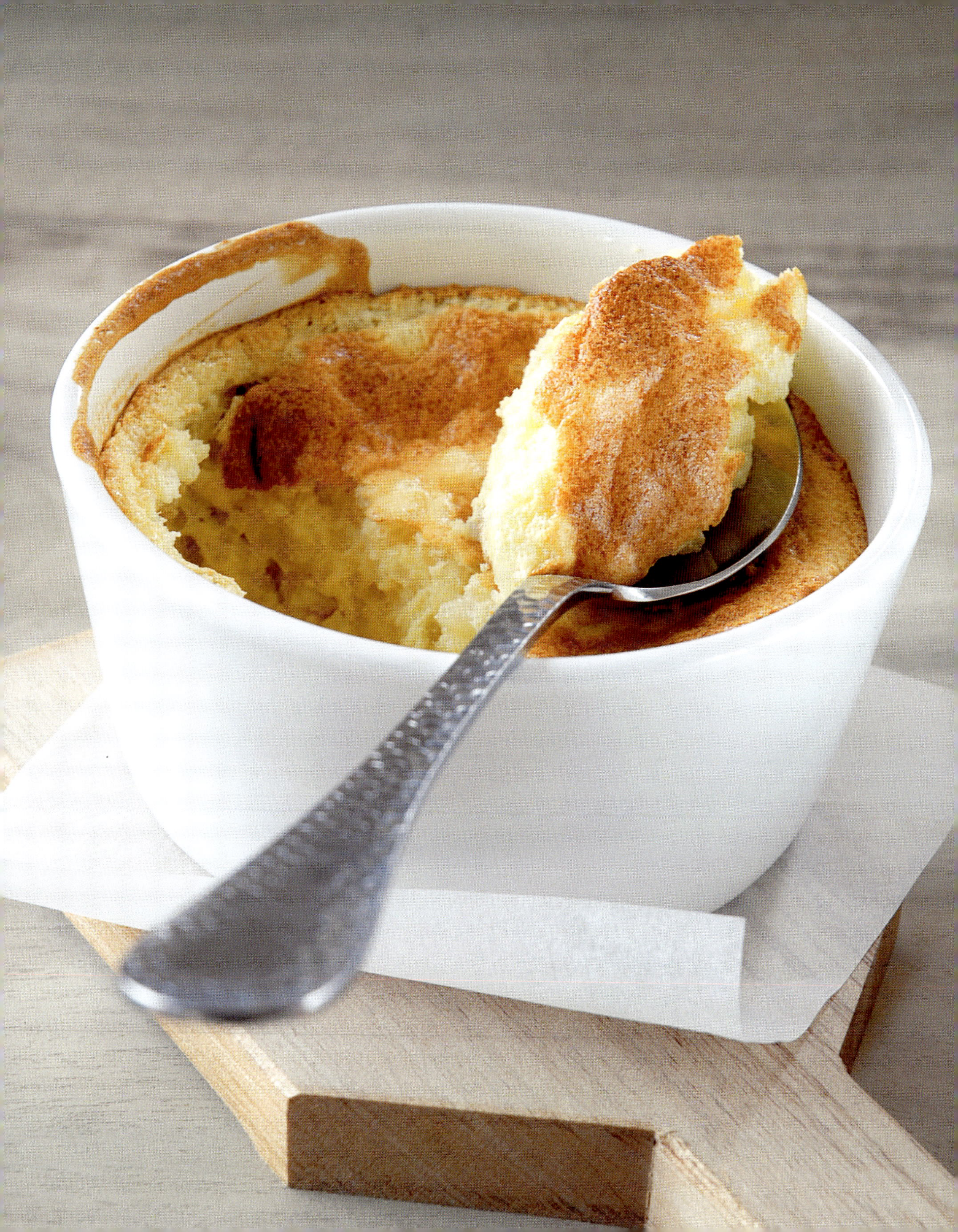

Semolina pudding with sultanas

SERVES 8
PREP TIME: 10 mins.
COOKING TIME: 1 hr 10 mins.

- 1-1/2 cups sultanas
- 1 tbsp. dark rum
- 5 tbsp. water
- 2 cups milk
- 1/2 cup semolina
- 2 tbsp honey
- 4 eggs
- 1 teaspoon peanut oil for the pan

Roughly chop the sultanas and put them in a saucepan with the rum and water. Bring to a boil, cover, and simmer for 3 minutes.

Heat the milk in a saucepan, pour in the semolina and stir with a wooden spoon. Simmer for 3 or 4 minutes. Pour the semolina into a bowl, add the honey, the sultanas and their cooking liquor, and whisk together adding the eggs one by one.

Preheat the oven to 350° F.

Lightly oil a loaf pan with a paper towel dipped in oil and pour in the semolina. Place the pan in a gratin dish and half fill with water. Cover the pan with a large sheet of aluminum foil and bake in this bain-marie for 1 hour.

Allow to cool, turn out and cut into thick slices.

> Serving advice
Serve this pudding with strawberry coulis or raspberry coulis (see p.423).

> Helpful tip
You can also cook this pudding in a steamer for 30 minutes.

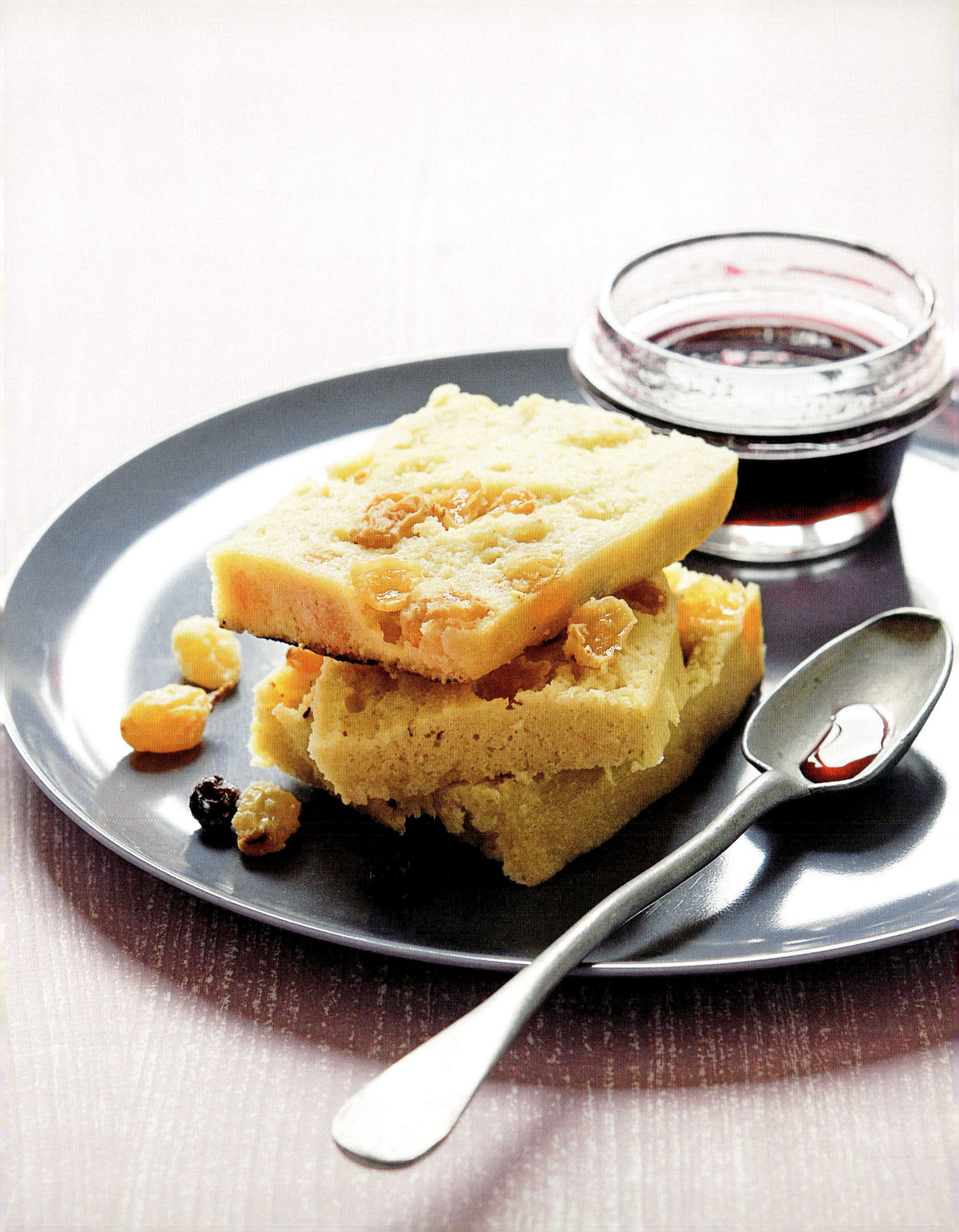

Crème brûlée

SERVES 4
PREP TIME: 20 mins.
COOKING TIME: 30 mins.
REFRIGERATION TIME: 30 mins.

- 1 vanilla bean
- 4 egg yolks
- 2/3 cup sugar
- 1 cup milk
- 1 cup crème fraîche or heavy cream
- 1 tbsp. orange liqueur

Split the vanilla bean and scrape out the seeds.

Preheat the oven to 300° F.

Beat the egg yolks with 1/2 cup sugar in a bowl. Add the vanilla seeds and milk. Beat in the crème fraîche or heavy cream and the liqueur.

Pour into heatproof ramekins. Bake for 30 minutes.

Allow to cool completely (at least 30 minutes).

Turn on your broiler.

Sprinkle the custards with the rest of the sugar and put them under the broiler to caramelize. Serve warm or cold.

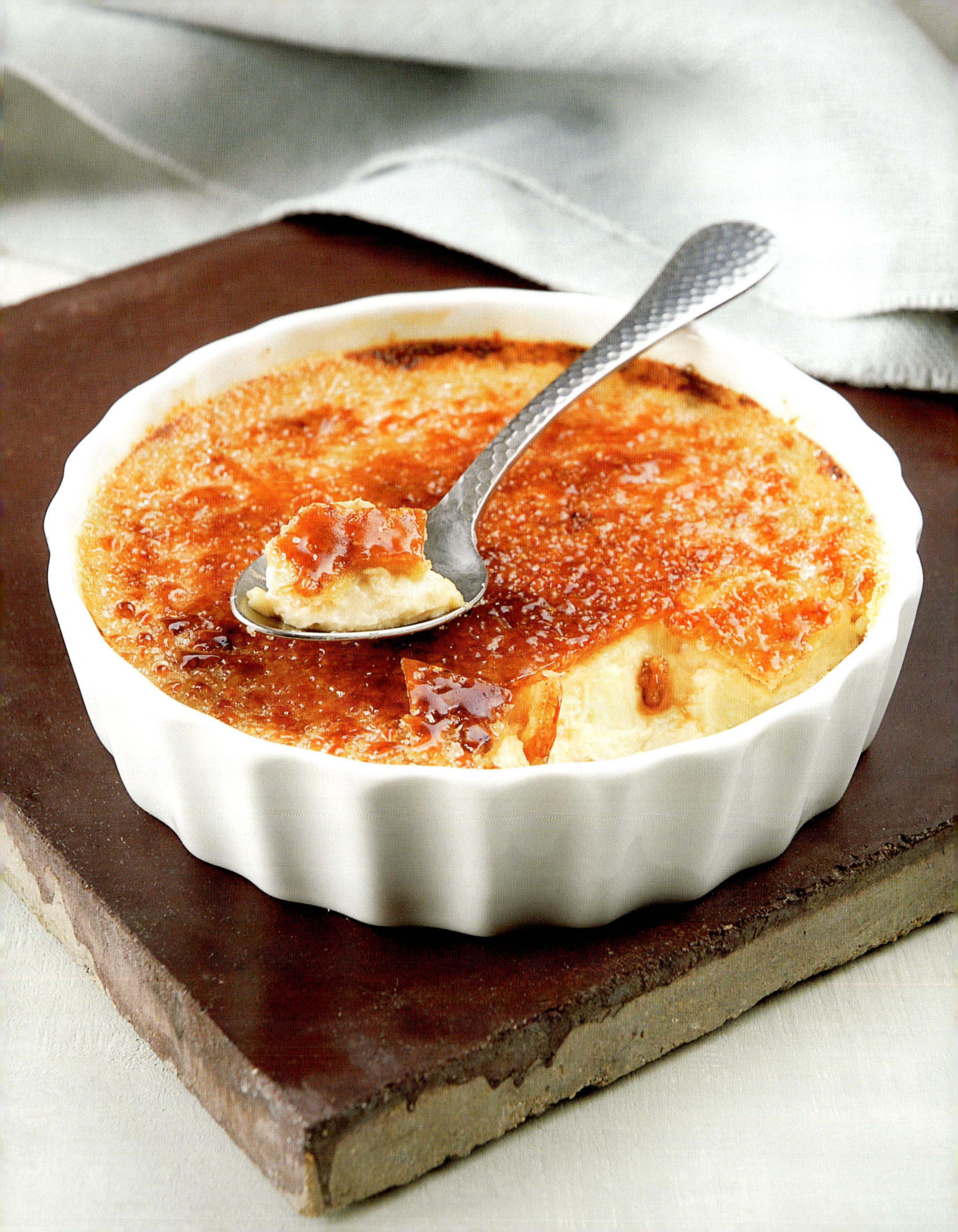

Egg custard

SERVES 4 TO 6
PREP TIME: 20 mins.
COOKING TIME: 40 mins.

- 4-1/4 cups milk
- 2/3 cup sugar
- 1 vanilla bean
- 4 eggs

Split the vanilla bean and scrape out the seeds. Boil the milk with the sugar, vanilla bean and seeds.

Preheat the oven to 400° F.

Beat the eggs in a bowl.

Remove the vanilla bean from the milk. Pour the boiling milk into the bowl, stirring constantly.

Pour into a deep ovenproof dish or into ramekins. Place in a bain-marie and bake in the oven for 40 minutes. Check that the custard is cooked with the point of a knife: it should come out clean.

Allow to cool and place in the refrigerator.

child's play

Little pots of cream

SERVES 6
PREP TIME: 10 mins.
COOKING TIME: 25 mins.
REFRIGERATION TIME: 3 hrs

- 2 cups milk
- 1 vanilla bean
- 2 whole eggs + 6 egg yolks
- 1 cup sugar
- 2 cups crème fraîche or heavy cream

Pour the milk into a saucepan. Split the vanilla bean and place in the milk. Bring to a boil, remove from the heat and allow to infuse for a few minutes.

Meanwhile, beat the eggs and the sugar until the sugar has dissolved. Stir in the crème fraîche or heavy cream. Gradually add the mixture to the saucepan of milk after removing the vanilla bean.

Place the saucepan over a gentle heat and stir until the mixture thickens. When it covers the back of a spoon, pour into 6 individual pots and chill for at least 3 hours before serving.

> **To make a change**
You can flavor this cream with coffee or chocolate. Mix some cocoa powder with some milk (1 tbsp. per pot), or dissolve coffee granules in water (1 teaspoon per pot). Stir in the flavoring just before you fill the pots.

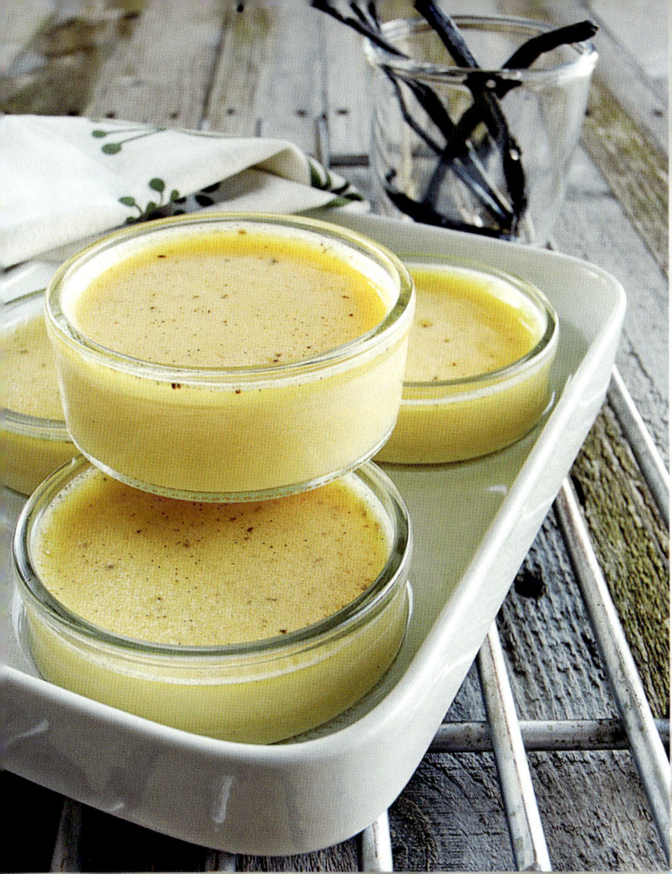

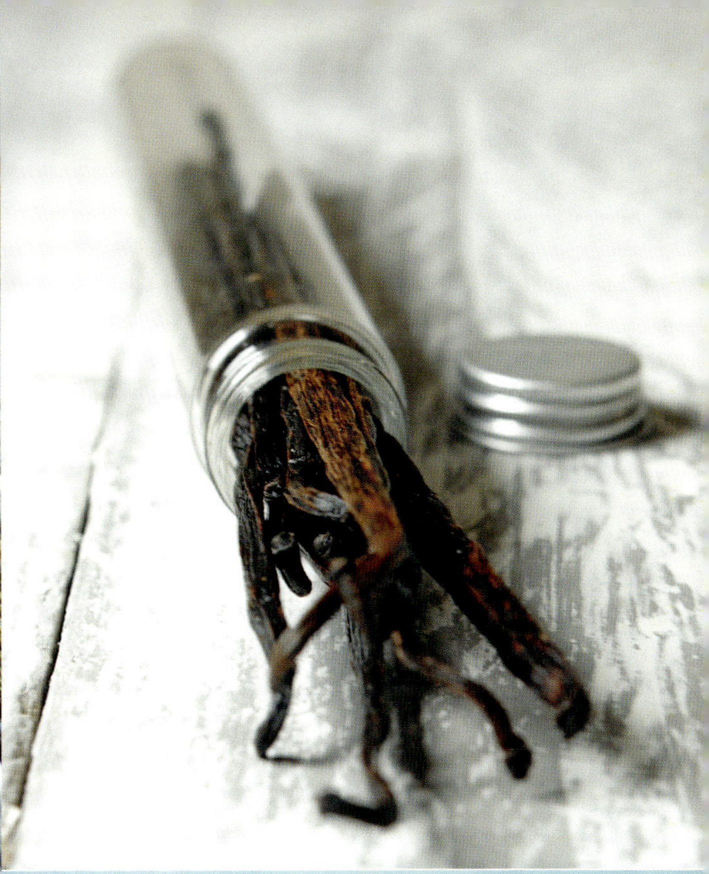

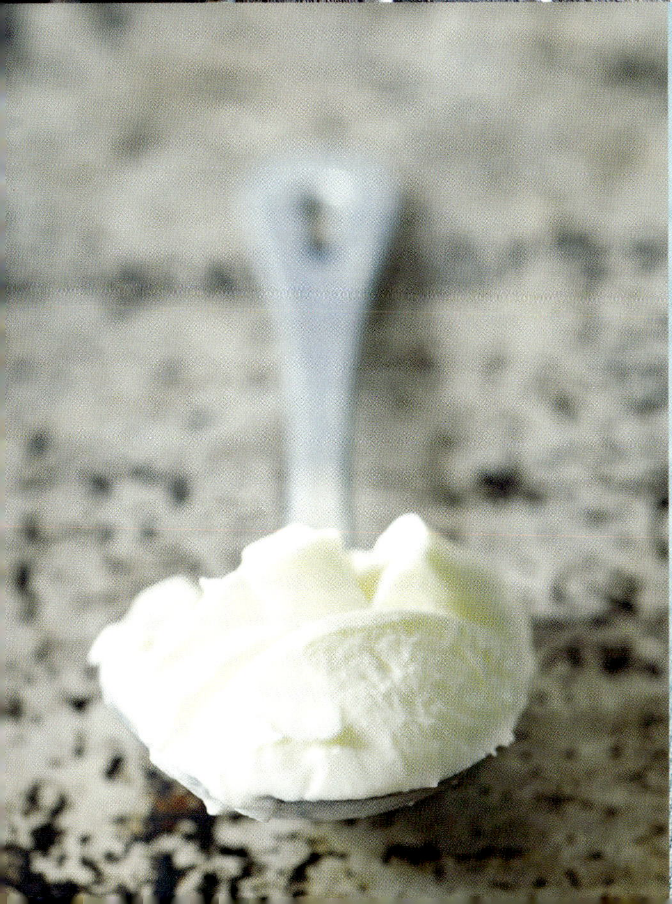

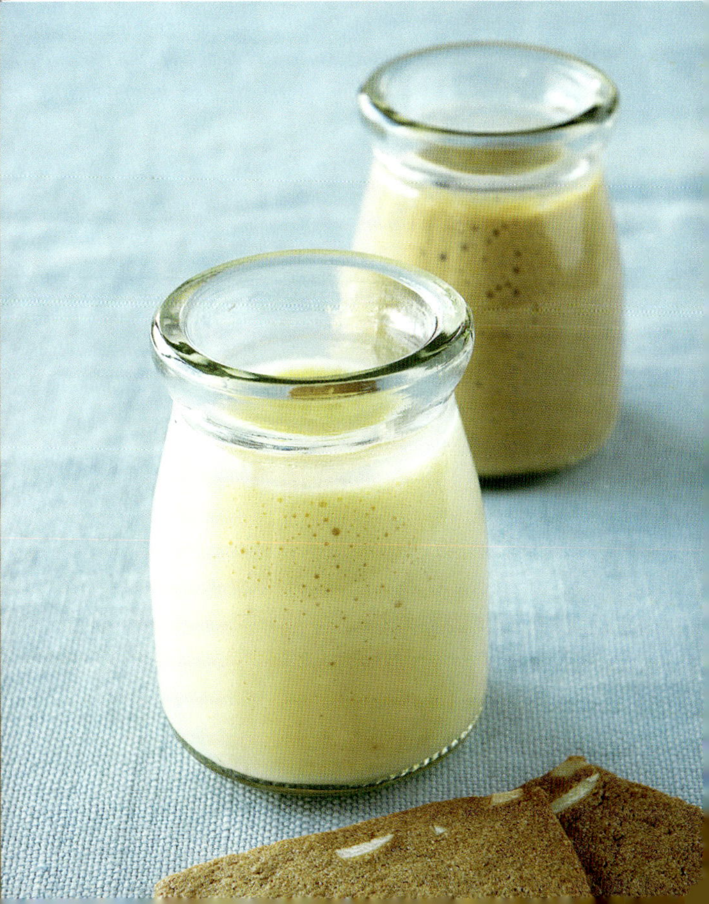

Crème caramel

SERVES 4 TO 6
PREP TIME: 25 mins.
(over 2 days)
COOKING TIME: 2 hrs
INFUSION TIME: 12 hrs
REFRIGERATION TIME: 12 hrs

- 4-1/4 cups whole milk
- 3 vanilla beans
- 4 whole eggs
- 3 egg yolks
- 1-3/4 cups sugar
- 1/4 cup water

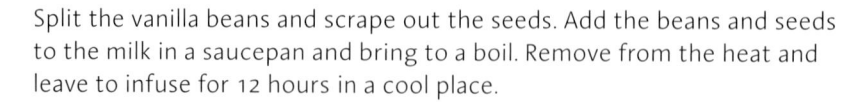

Split the vanilla beans and scrape out the seeds. Add the beans and seeds to the milk in a saucepan and bring to a boil. Remove from the heat and leave to infuse for 12 hours in a cool place.

Remove the vanilla beans and bring the milk to a boil again. In a large bowl, beat the whole eggs with 1 cup sugar for 30 seconds and add the boiling milk, stirring constantly. Strain through a sieve and leave to rest for 15 minutes.

Preheat the oven to 300° F.

Heat the remaining sugar and the water together until they form a deep golden brown caramel. Stop the cooking process by dipping the saucepan into a bowl of ice water.

Quickly pour a thin layer of liquid caramel into 4 to 6 ramekins. Pour in the vanilla mixture. Place in the oven in a bain-marie for 2 hours.

Allow to cool at room temperature, then cover and put in the refrigerator for 12 hours. Run a knife around the side of each ramekin. Invert and give the bottom a gentle tap to avoid splitting the fragile caramel. Turn the creams onto a serving dish. Serve chilled.

child's play

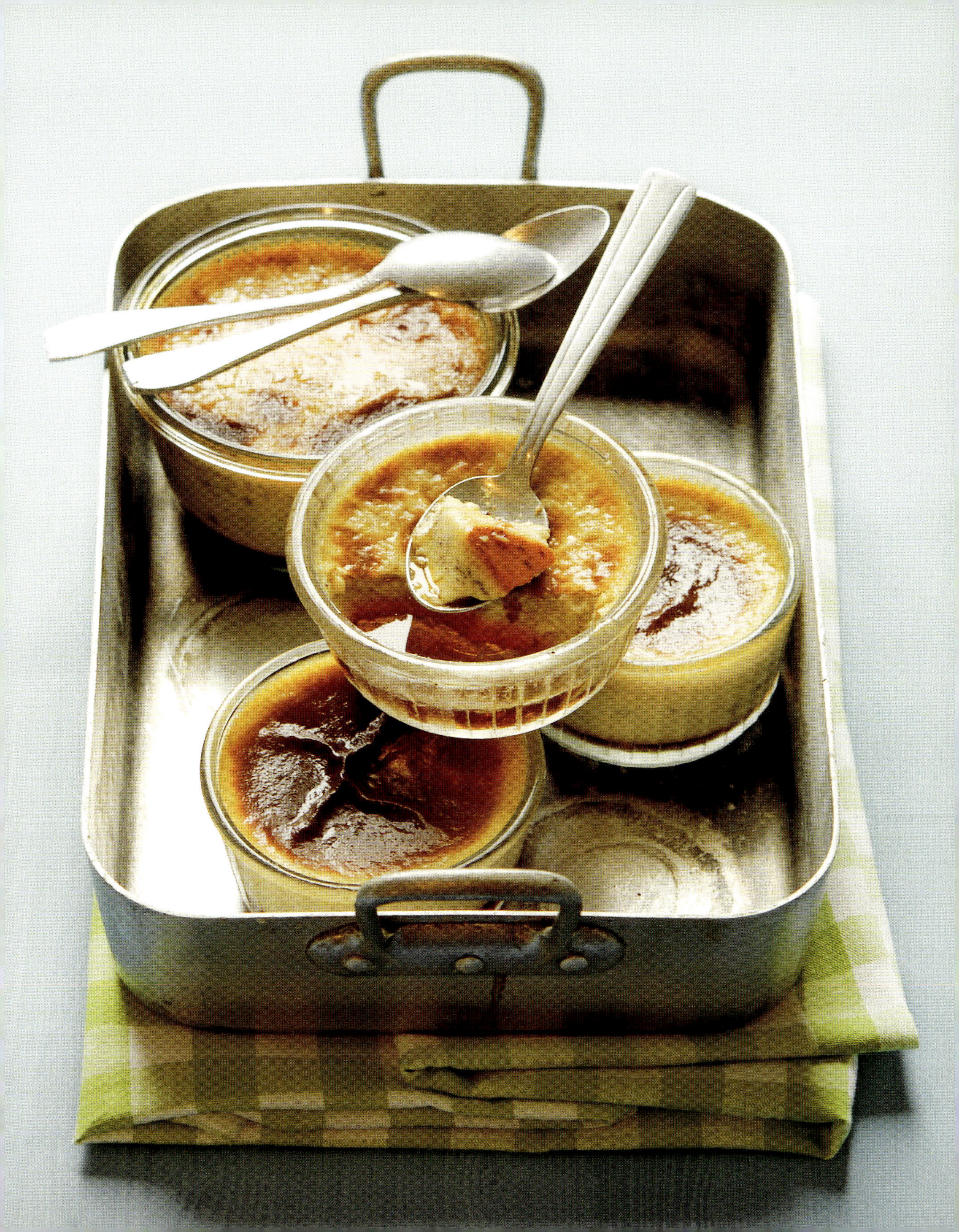

Sabayon

SERVES 4 TO 6
PREP TIME: 15 mins.
COOKING TIME: 2 to 3 mins.

- 6 egg yolks
- 3/4 cup sugar
- 1 cup dry white wine or champagne
- Zest of one lemon (preferably organic), peeled off in large pieces

Heat a saucepan of water.

Put the egg yolks, sugar, wine and lemon zest in another smaller saucepan. Place this inside the pan of simmering water and beat the mixture until it froths up and doubles in volume.

Beat for 30 seconds, remove the lemon zest and serve in individual glasses with cookies or fresh fruit.

> Helpful tip
This dessert can also be used as a sauce for puddings, poached fruit or ice cream.

> To make a change
You can also prepare it with sweet white wine, marsala, port, or with a mixture of white wine and cognac or rum.

quick & easy

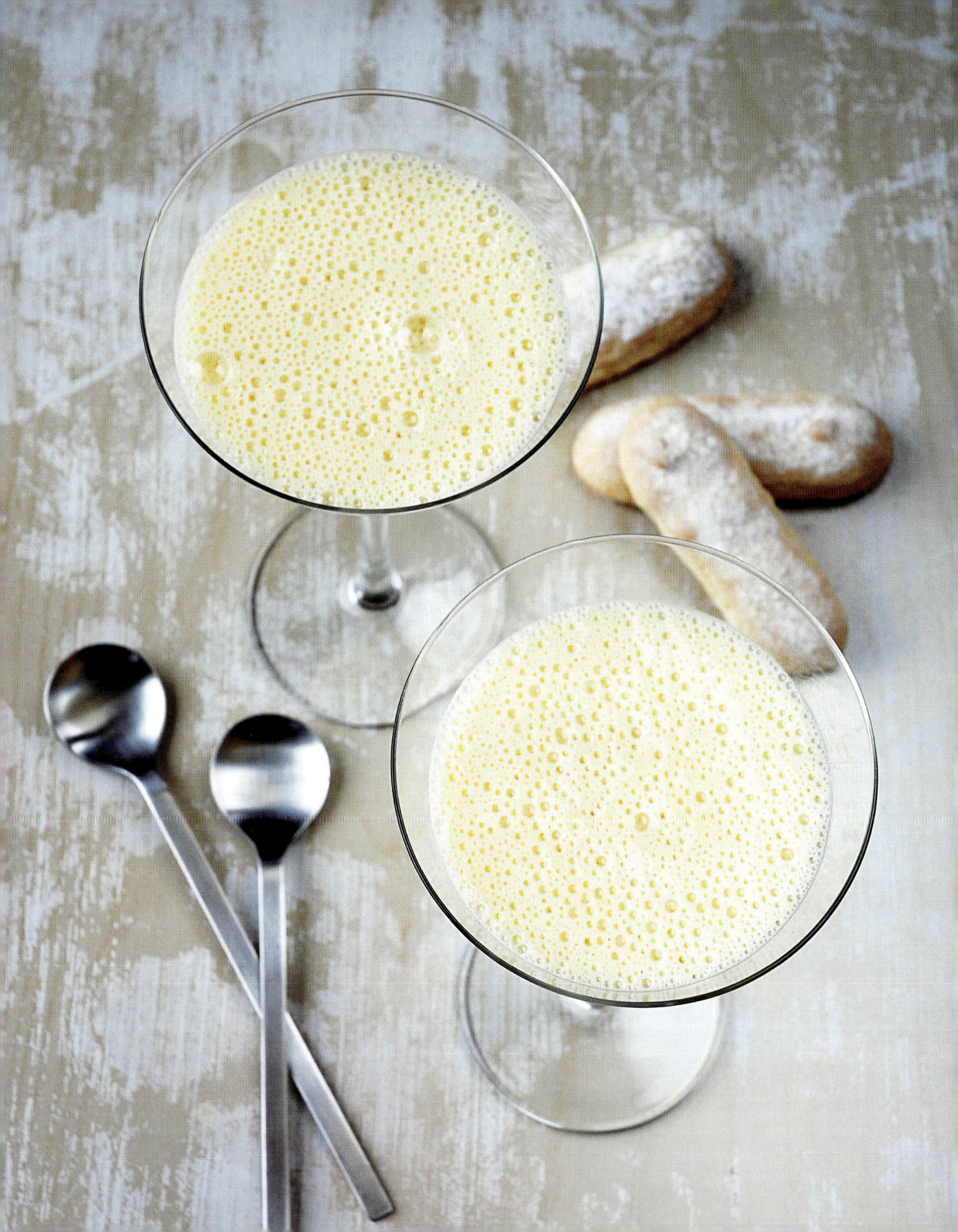

Floating island

SERVES 6 TO 8
PREP TIME: 25 mins.
COOKING TIME: 30 mins.
REFRIGERATION TIME:
At least 1 hr

- 3-1/3 cups milk
- 1 vanilla bean
- 8 eggs
- A pinch of salt
- 1-1/2 cups sugar

FOR THE CARAMEL
- 1/2 cup sugar
- 2 tbsp. water
- Lemon juice

Split the vanilla bean and scrape out the seeds. Boil the milk with the vanilla bean and seeds. Break the eggs and separate the yolks from the whites.

Preheat the oven to 350° F.

Beat the egg whites with a pinch of salt until they form stiff peaks, then gradually add 3 tbsp. sugar.

Pour this mixture into a 9-inch savarin mold. Place the dish in a bain-marie and bake for 30 minutes, until the top begins to turn a pale golden color. Allow to cool.

Meanwhile, prepare the crème anglaise: put the 8 egg yolks and the remaining 1-1/2 cups sugar into a bowl. Beat until the mixture turns pale yellow. Heat the vanilla flavored milk to boiling, then remove the vanilla bean and pour the milk slowly into the egg mixture, stirring constantly. Put back on a very low heat and stir until it thickens. Pour this custard into a bowl that is larger than the savarin mold, and put it in the refrigerator to cool.

Turn out the circle of egg whites from the savarin mold and lay it on top of the crème anglaise.

Prepare the caramel: dissolve the the sugar in the water in a heavy saucepan over a low heat. Increase the heat and watch carefully. When the syrup starts to boil, stop stirring and tilt the saucepan to get an even color and spread the heat evenly. When the caramel is golden brown, pour it onto the egg whites. Place your floating island in the refrigerator until you are ready to serve.

> **Helpful tip**
To stop the caramel from cooking when it is the desired color, dip the saucepan in a bowl of ice water.

> **Serving advice**
Decorate your floating island with toasted slivered almonds or threads of lemon zest.

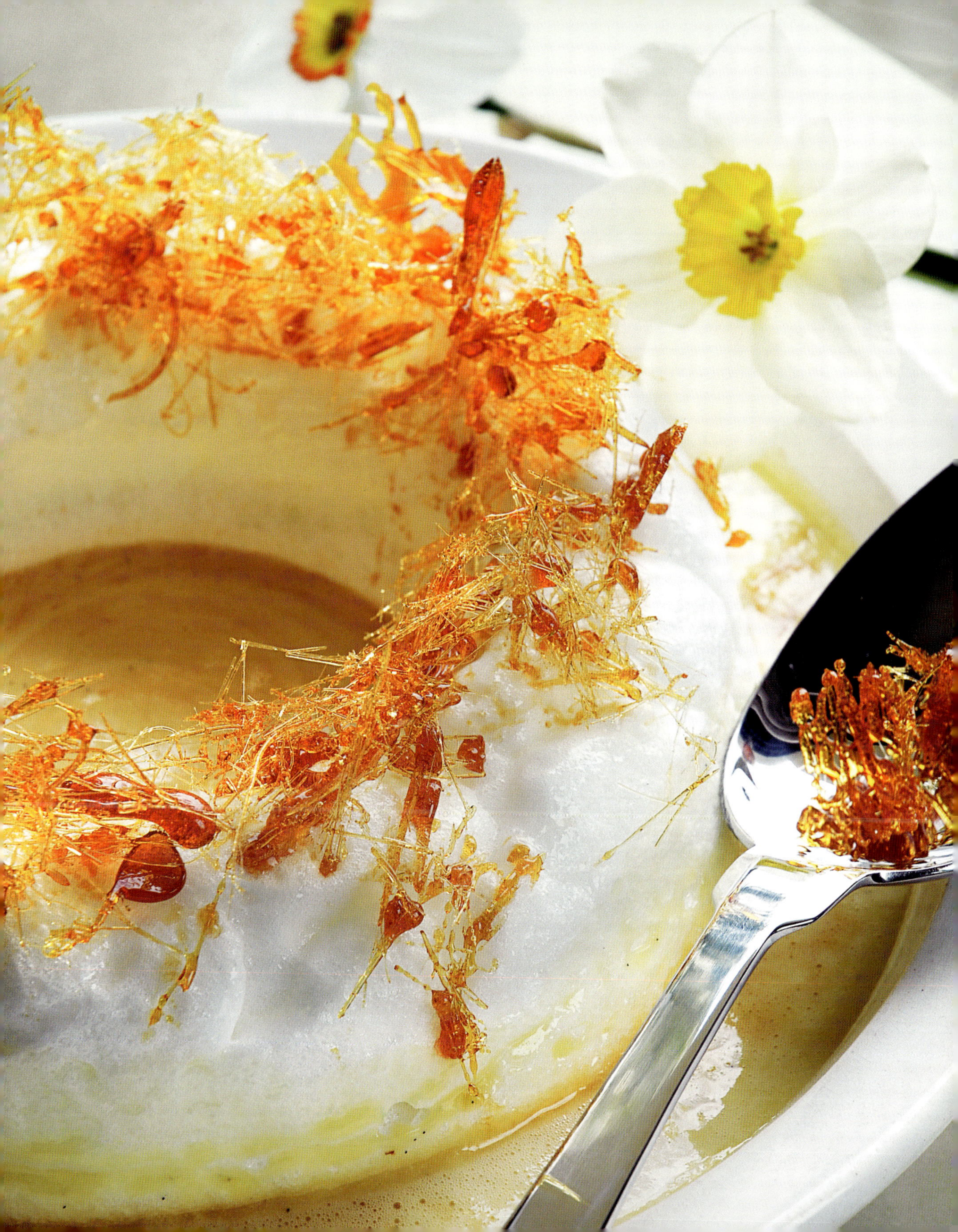

Blancmange

SERVES 4 TO 6
PREP TIME: 40 mins. (over two days)
RESTING TIME: 12 hrs
REFRIGERATION TIME: 4 to 5 hrs

- 2 packets gelatin
- 3/4 cup sugar
- 2-1/2 cups crème fraîche or heavy cream

FOR THE ALMOND MILK
- 7 oz. water
- 6 tbsp. sugar
- 1-2/3 cups ground almonds
- 1 tbsp. kirsch
- 1 drop bitter almond essence

Prepare the almond milk the day before: bring the water and sugar to boil in a saucepan. Add the ground almonds and kirsch and mix well. Blend the mixture in a blender while still hot, then filter using a sieve set over a bowl. Allow to rest in the refrigerator for 12 hours.

The following day, add a drop of bitter almond essence.

Dissolve the gelatin in a little cold water.

Heat one quarter of the almond milk in a small saucepan. Add the gelatin and stir well. Now pour the contents of the saucepan into the rest of the almond milk and mix well. Add the sugar and stir to dissolve.

Whip the crème fraîche or heavy cream. When it thickens, carefully stir it into the almond mixture using a wooden spoon.

Pour the mixture into a 7-inch charlotte mold and place in the refrigerator for 4 to 5 hours.

Quickly dip the mold in hot water and turn out the blancmange onto a serving dish. Decorate with berries.

> Serving advice
Serve blancmange with raspberry coulis (see p.423).

> Helpful tip
Be very sparing with the bitter almond essence because too much gives food an unpleasant taste.

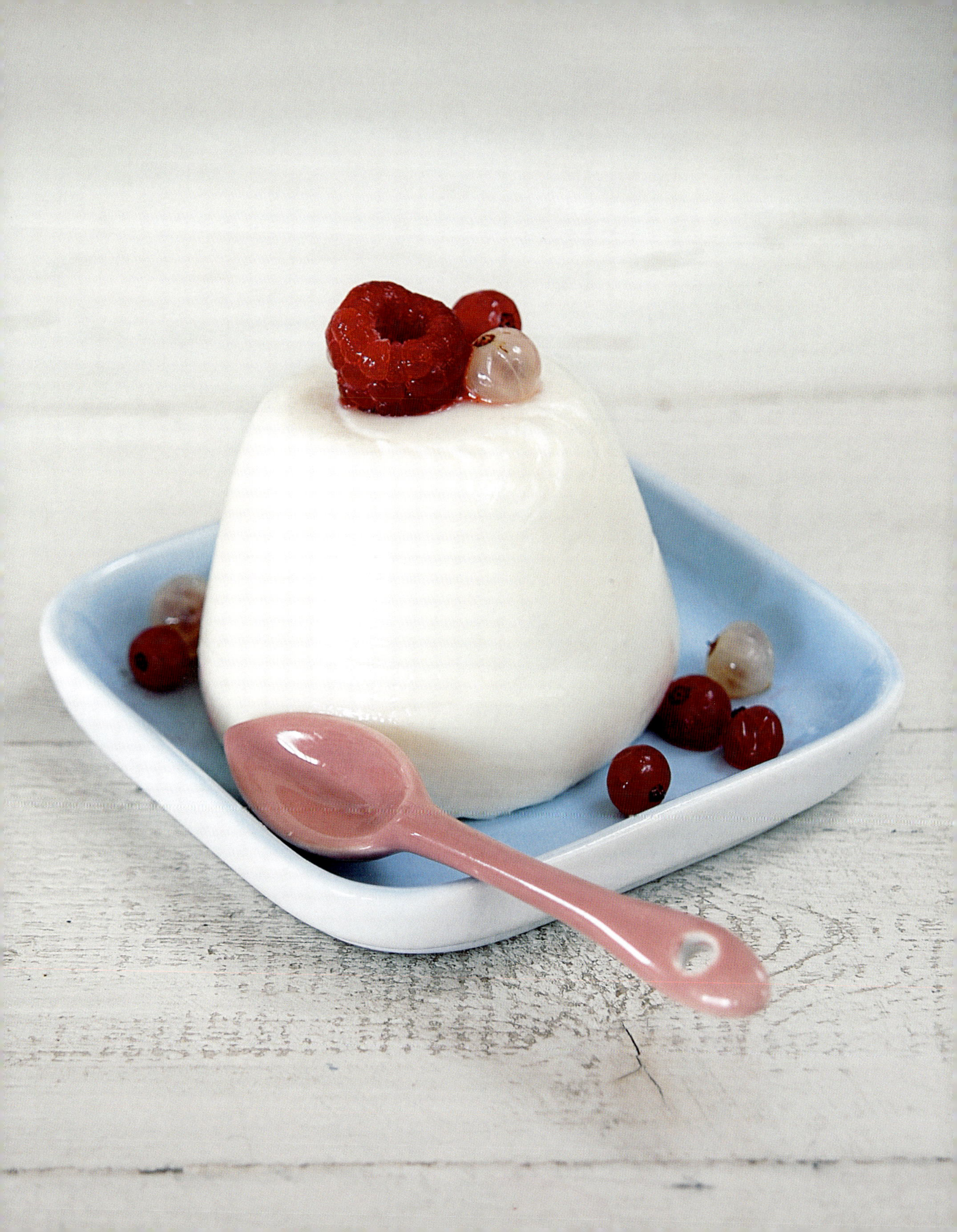

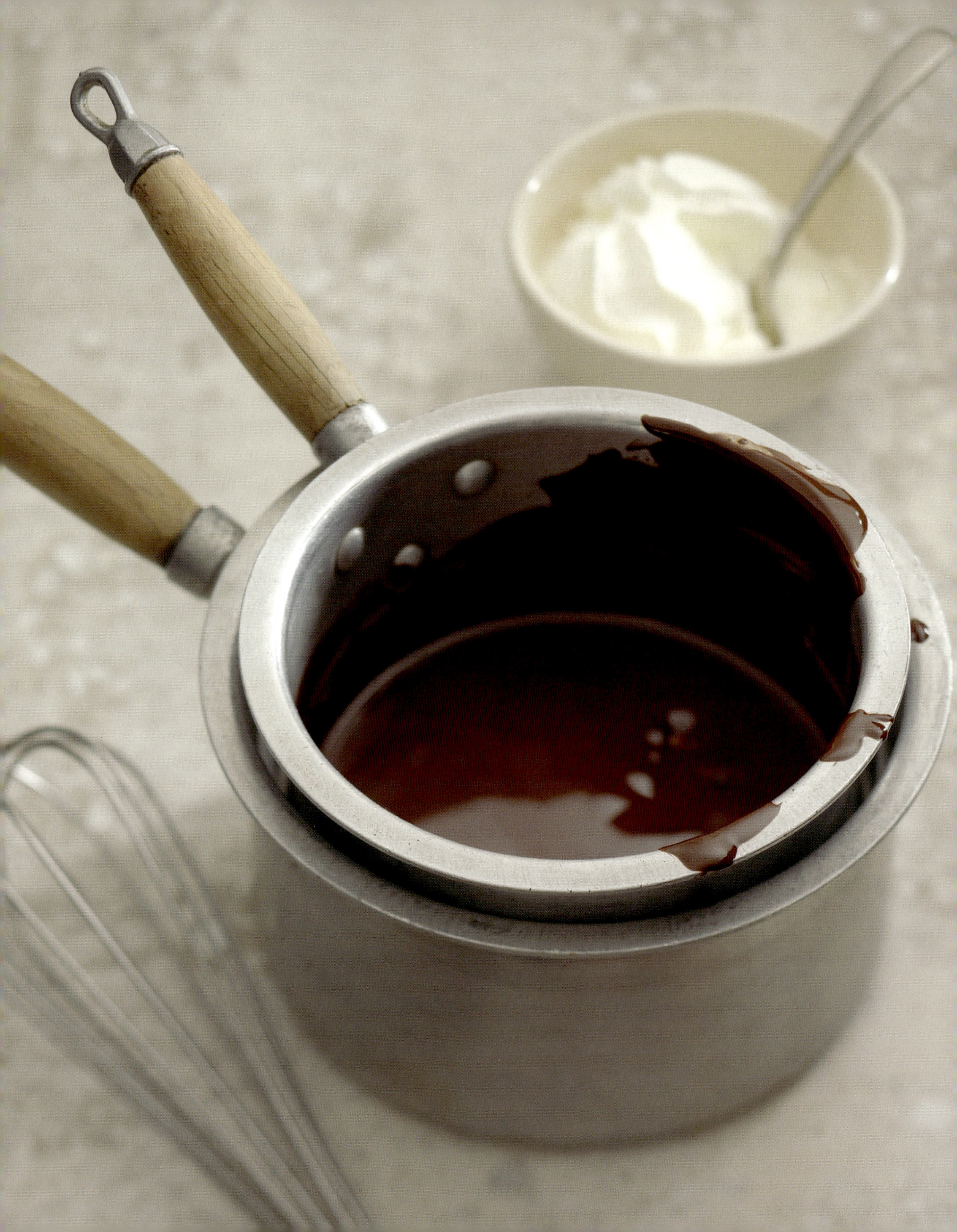

Oh chocolate!

Chocolate charlotte	76
Chocolate fondant cake	78
Chocolate cake from Nancy	80
Chocolate "délice"	82
Pecan brownies	84
Queen of Sheba	86
Chocolate and pear "mi-cuits"	88
Rich chocolate cake	90
Double-choc muffins	92
Spiced chocolate slab cake	94
Chocolate soufflé	96
Chocolate and vanilla Bavarian cream	98
Chocolate pie	100
White chocolate tartlets	102
Banana chocolate pie	104
Chocolate-caramel pizza	106
Chocolate éclairs	108
Chocolate mousse	110
White chocolate mousse	112
Two-chocolate mousse	112
Chocolate marquise	114
Dark chocolate crème brûlée	116
Old-fashioned chocolate creams	118
Chestnut and chocolate verrines	120
Chocolat liégeois	122
Profiteroles with ice cream and chocolate	124
Chocolate-orange cookies	126
Old-fashioned hot chocolate	128
Florentines	130
Chocolate cherries	132
Chocolate caramels	134
Chocolate truffles	136
Chocolate fondue	138

Chocolate charlotte

chef style

SERVES 8
PREP TIME: 30 mins.
(the day before)
REFRIGERATION TIME: 12 hrs

- 24 lady fingers

FOR THE SYRUP
- 7 oz. water
- 4 tbsp. sugar

FOR THE CREAM
- 2/3 cup butter
- 10 oz. dark chocolate (70 % cocoa solids)
- 4 egg yolks
- 7 egg whites
- A pinch of salt
- 5 tbsp. sugar

Prepare the syrup: pour the water into a small saucepan, add 4 tbsp. sugar. Bring to a boil and simmer for 1 minute, until the sugar dissolves. Allow to cool.

Pour this syrup into a small bowl. Dip the lady fingers into it and use them to line a 7-inch charlotte mold. Place in the refrigerator.

Prepare the filling: cut the softened butter into small pieces. Break the chocolate into pieces and put it into a saucepan. Melt it in a double boiler with 1 tbsp. of water, stirring to obtain a smooth creamy consistency. Remove the saucepan from the heat and gradually stir in the butter with a wooden spoon. Add the egg yolks one by one, stirring all the time.

Beat the egg whites to stiff peaks with the salt, then add the sugar.

Mix 2 tbsp. of egg whites with the chocolate cream, then very carefully fold in the rest of the whites.

Pour the mixture into the mold and put in the refrigerator until the following day.

Turn the charlotte out onto a serving dish.

> Helpful tip
Serve your charlotte with berries and whipped cream.
For decoration, make your own chocolate shavings (see p.421) and sprinkle them on the top.

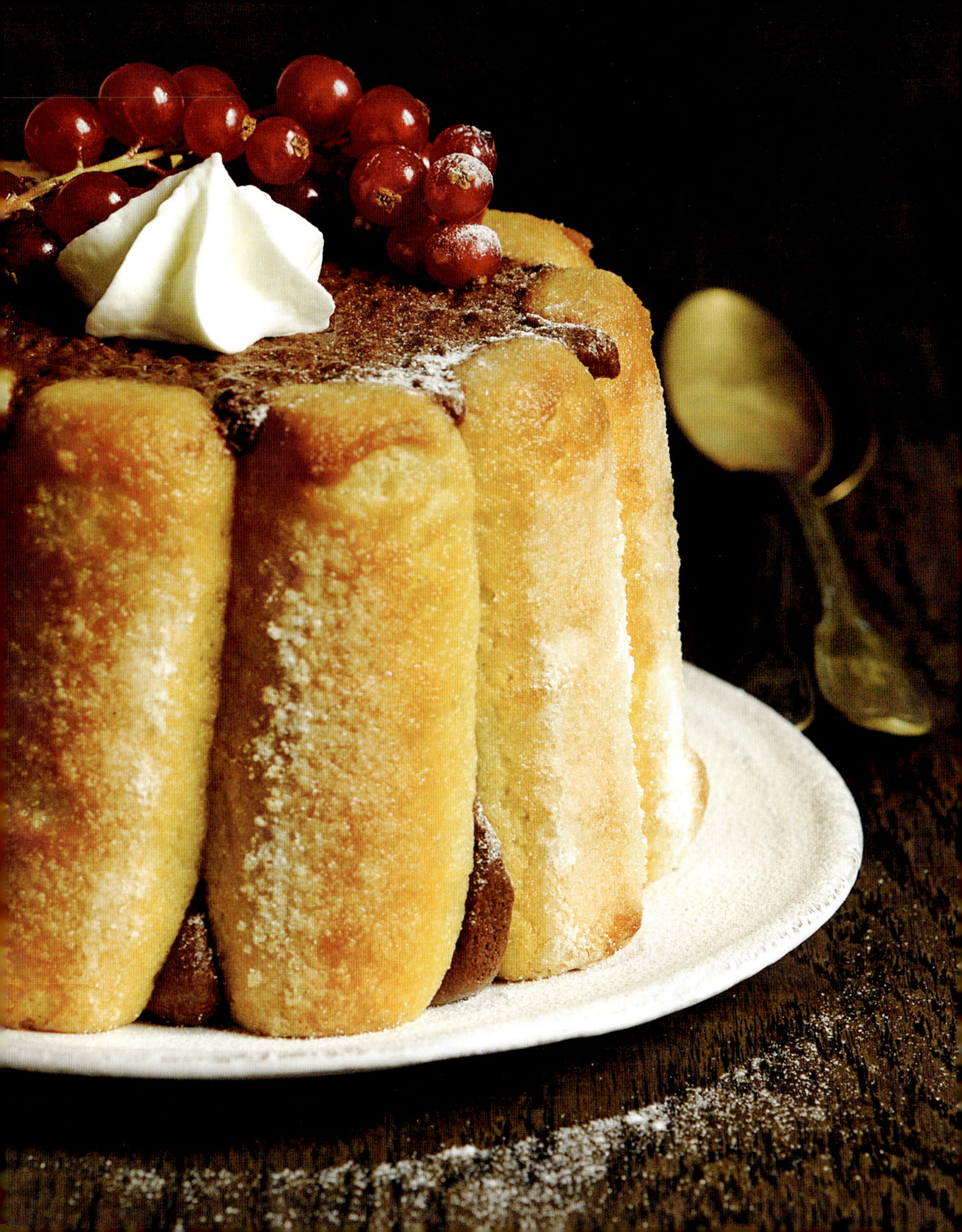

Chocolate fondant cake

SERVES 8
PREP TIME: 20 mins. (previous day)
COOKING TIME: 1 hr

- 1 cup butter
  + 2 tbsp. for the mold
- 1/4 lb. dark chocolate
- 3 eggs
- 1 cup sugar
- 1/2 cup cornstarch
- Powdered sugar

Soften the butter at room temperature. Take the roasting tray out of your oven and preheat the oven to 350° F. Butter a 10-inch round cake pan. Line with a circle of parchment paper, then butter the paper. Stand the cake pan in the roasting tray.

Break the chocolate into small pieces, put them in a bowl and melt in a bain-marie. Remove from the heat and add the butter very gradually, stirring constantly until you obtain a perfectly smooth mixture.

Beat the eggs with the sugar in a bowl until they turn pale yellow. Stir in the cornstarch, then the chocolate mixture. Mix well.

Pour the mixture into the cake pan. Place the roasting tray in the center of the oven and pour in the hot water so that it reaches halfway up the cake pan. Bake for 1 hour.

Allow to cool, turn out the cake and dust with powdered sugar. Serve the cake the following day to allow the flavors to develop.

child's play

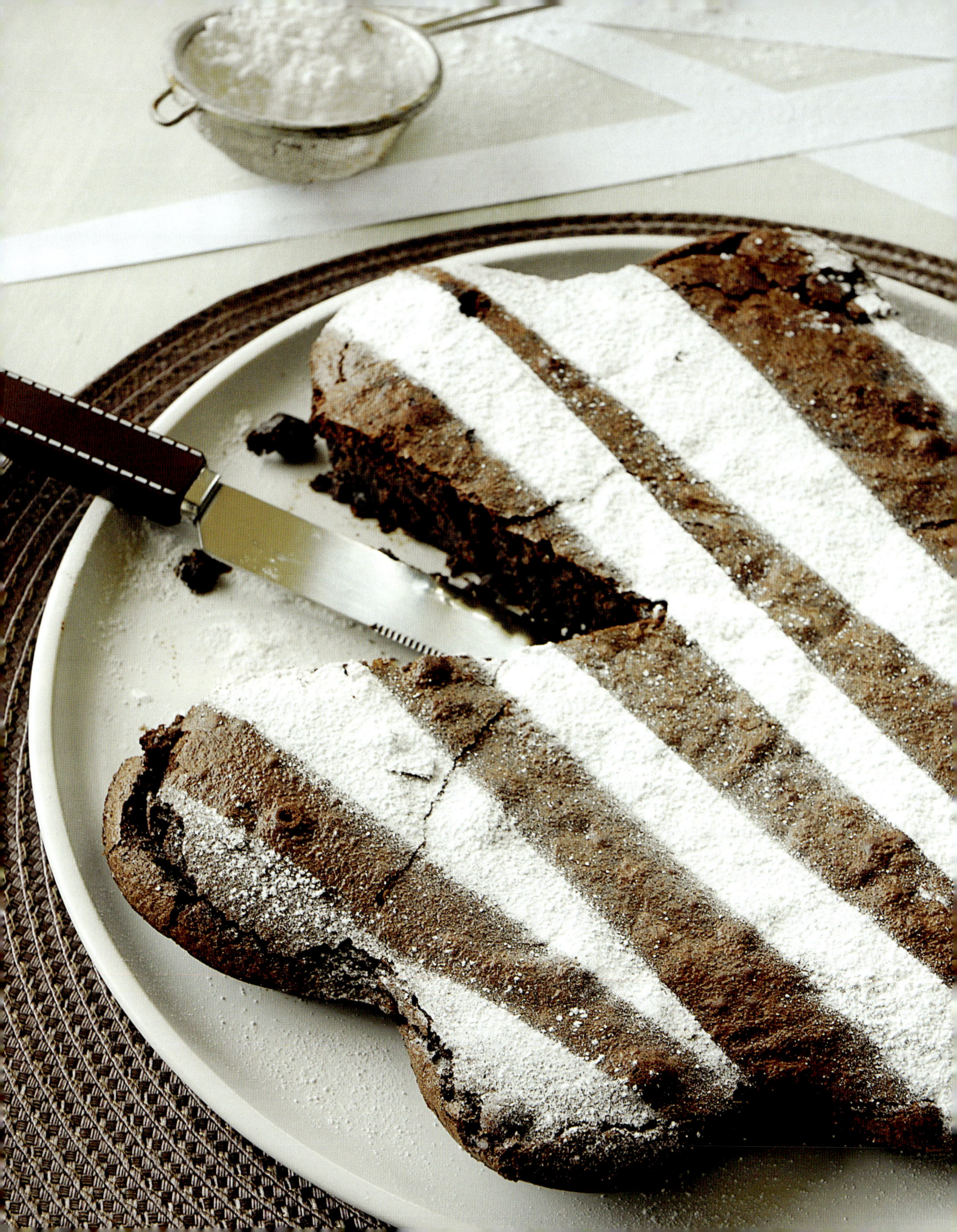

Chocolate cake from Nancy

SERVES 8
PREP TIME: 15 mins.
COOKING TIME: 35 mins.

- 14 tbsp. butter + some for the pan
- 7 oz. dark chocolate
- 6 eggs
- 1/2 cup sugar
- 3/4 cup ground almonds
- 4 tbsp. flour
- Some slivered almonds
- Powdered sugar

Cut the butter and chocolate into pieces and melt in a saucepan placed in a warm double boiler, stirring until smooth and creamy.

Break the eggs and separate the whites from the yolks.

Remove the saucepan from the bain-marie and beat in the egg yolks. Add the sugar, ground almonds and flour and mix well.

Preheat the oven to 300° F. Generously butter an 8-inch round cake pan. Scatter some slivered almonds in the bottom.

Beat the egg whites until they form stiff peaks. Take 2 tbsp. of beaten egg white and stir into the chocolate mixture to lighten it. Now carefully fold in the rest of the egg whites. Bake for about 35 minutes. Remove the cake from the oven and allow to cool slightly. Turn out onto a wire rack and leave until quite cold. Dust with powdered sugar.

> Find out more
The "Nancy" in the name isn't a person but the city in eastern France where this cake originates.

> To make a change
You can also make individual cupcakes with this mixture!

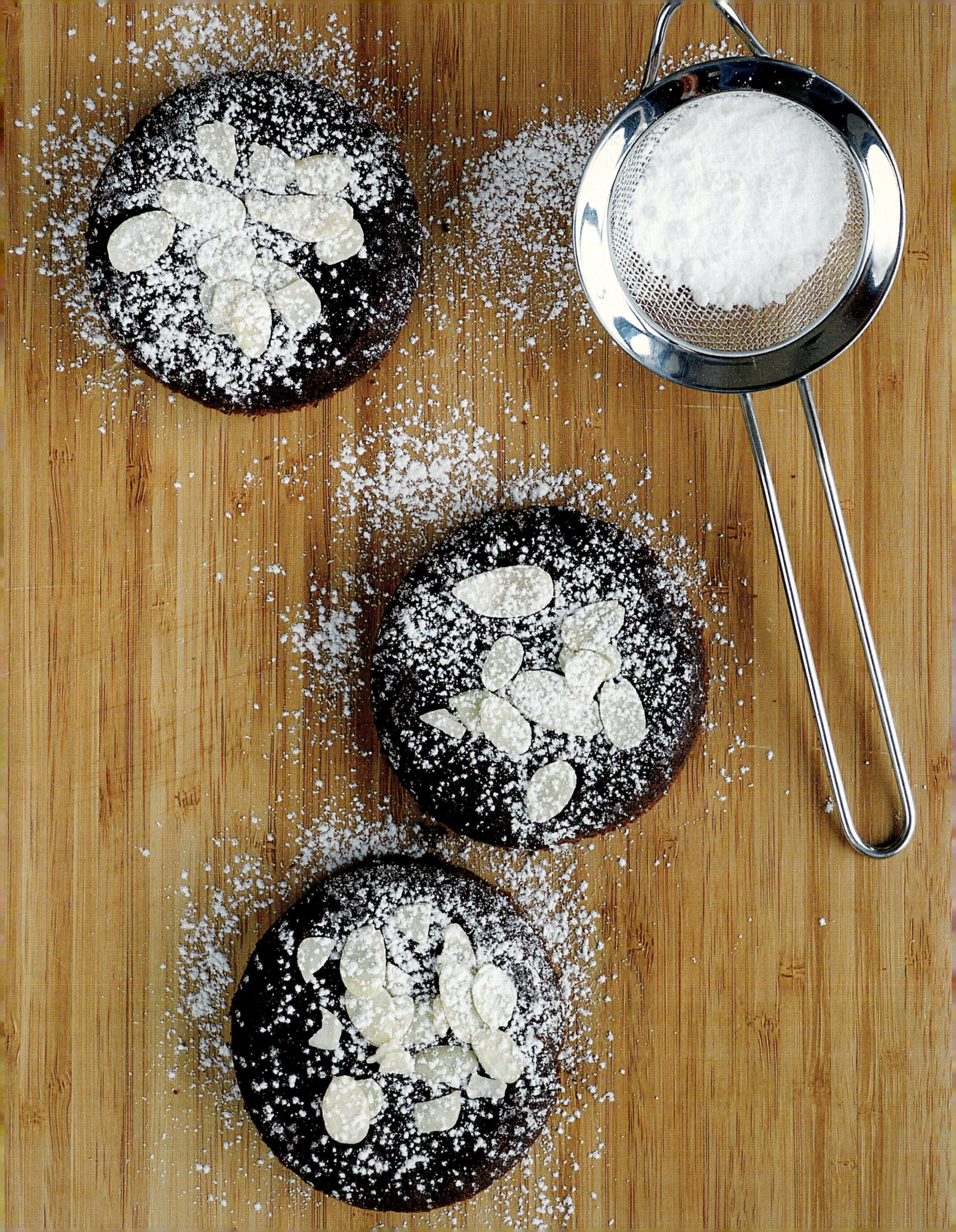

Chocolate "délice"

SERVES 4 TO 6
PREP TIME: 20 mins.
COOKING TIME: 20 mins.

- 2/3 cup butter
  + some for the pan
- 4 eggs
- 1-1/3 cups sugar
- 7 oz. bitter chocolate
- 2 tbsp. flour
- 1 cup ground almonds

Allow the butter to soften at room temperature. Preheat the oven to 425° F.

Break the eggs and separate the whites from the yolks. Beat the yolks with the sugar in a bowl until the mixture is pale and frothy.

Break the chocolate into small pieces and melt in a double boiler. Mix the melted chocolate into the egg mixture. Stir in the flour, almonds and butter.

Beat the egg whites until they form stiff peaks and fold them carefully into the mixture.

Butter an 8-inch round cake pan and pour in the mixture. Bake for 20 minutes. Test with the point of a knife, which should come out slightly damp.

Allow to cool and turn out the cake.

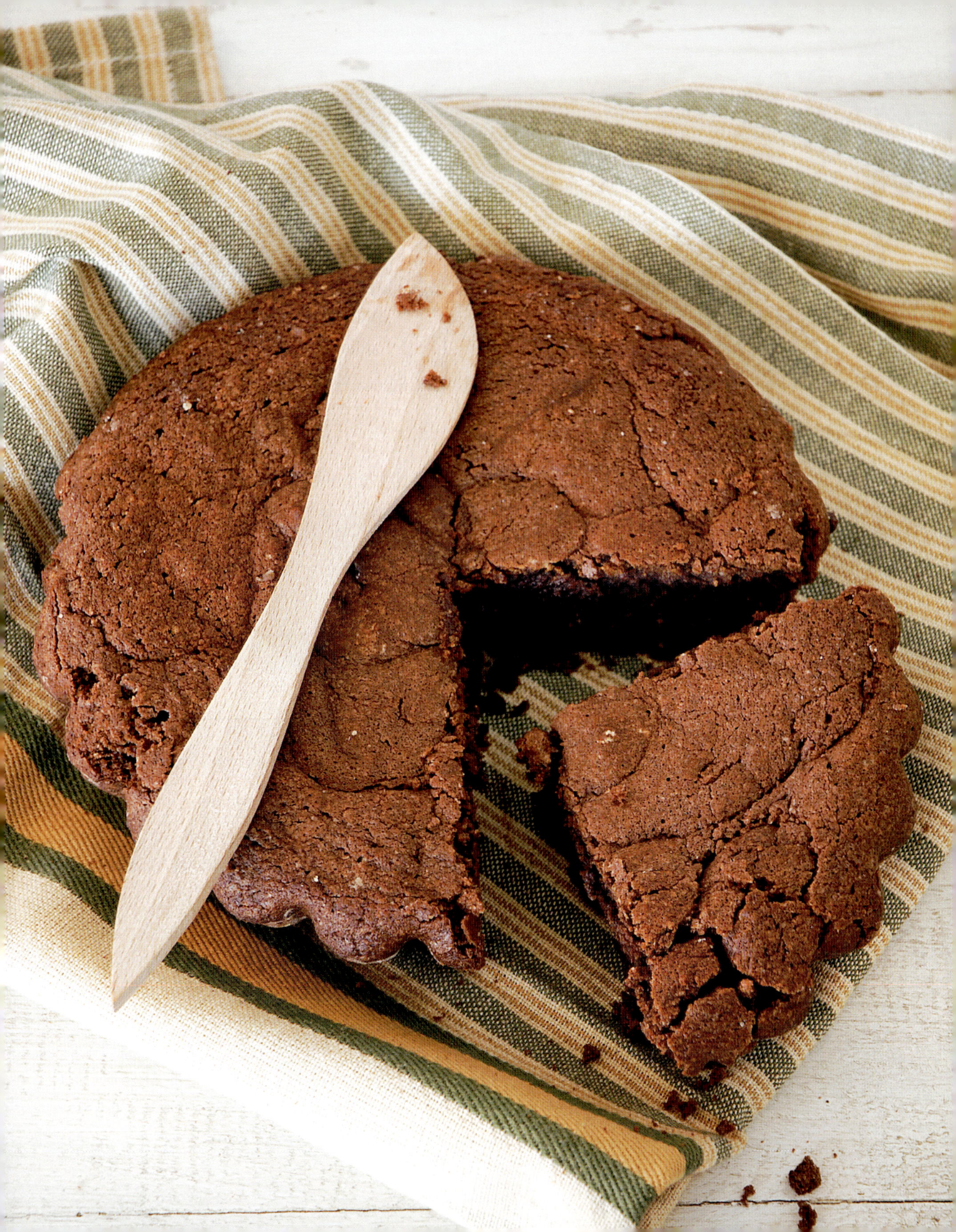

Pecan brownies

30 BROWNIES
PREP TIME: 30 mins.
COOKING TIME: 15 to 20 mins.

- 4 oz. dark bitter chocolate
- 3/4 cup butter
  + some to butter the baking sheet
- 3 eggs
- 1 heaping cup sugar
- 3/4 cup sifted flour
- 6 oz. pecans

Break the chocolate into pieces and melt it in a double boiler (100° F), then allow it to cool slightly.

Cut the butter into pieces and melt that also and allow to cool a little.

Mix the eggs with the sugar. Add the melted butter and chocolate.

Mix the flour and chopped pecans and add to the mixture, stirring with a wooden spatula.

Preheat the oven to 350° F.

Butter a 12-inch square brownie pan and pour in the mixture. Make the surface smooth with a spatula and bake 15 to 20 minutes. The brownies must remain soft: check with the point of a knife, which should come out with some mixture sticking to it.

Allow to cool slightly, then turn the baking sheet upside down over a plate to remove the cake. Cut into brownies and serve.

> Helpful tip

These brownies keep for several days in an airtight container.

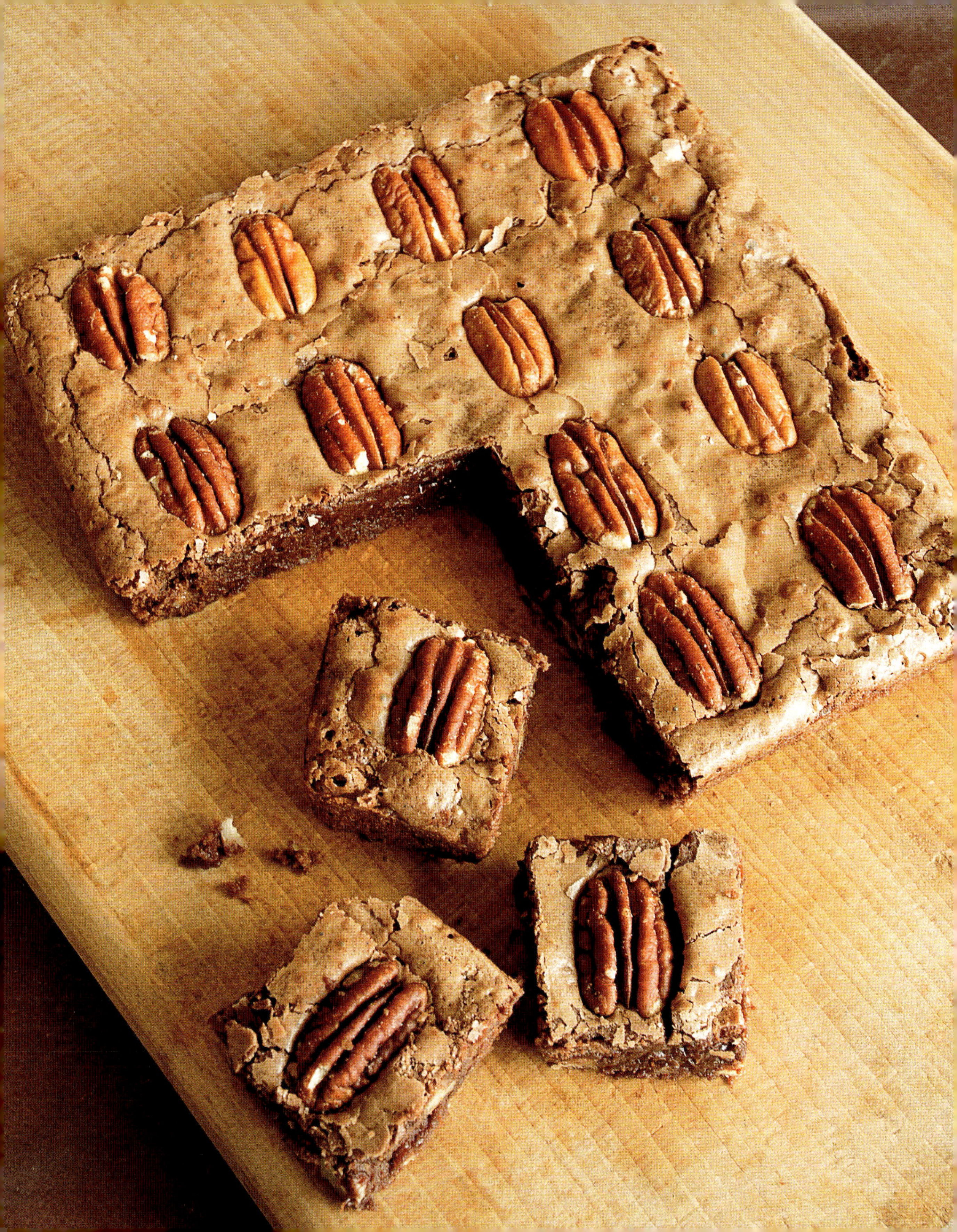

Queen of Sheba

SERVES 6
PREP TIME: 25 mins.
COOKING TIME: 35 mins.

- 5 tbsp. butter
  + some for the pan
- Flour for the pan
- 1/3 cup slivered almonds
- 1/4 lb. dark chocolate
  (60 % cocoa solids)
- 3 eggs
- 1/2 cup sugar
- 1/4 cup cornstarch
- 3/4 cup ground almonds
- 3 tbsp. cocoa powder
- A pinch of salt

Cut the butter into small pieces and allow to soften at room temperature. Liberally butter a round 9-inch cake pan (or a 7-inch charlotte mold) and sprinkle with flour.

Lightly brown the almonds in a dry nonstick pan. Allow them to cool and sprinkle them in the bottom of the cake pan. Place in the refrigerator while you prepare the cake mixture.

Preheat the oven to 350° F.

Cut the chocolate into small pieces and place in a small saucepan with the butter. Melt over a gentle heat or in a double boiler, stirring until you get a smooth cream.

Break the eggs and separate the yolks from the whites. Beat the yolks with the sugar until the mixture turns pale yellow and frothy. Add the cornstarch, the ground almonds, the cocoa, then the chocolate cream, stirring constantly.

Beat the egg whites with a pinch of salt until they form stiff peaks. Quickly mix two tbsp. of the beaten egg whites with the chocolate cream to lighten it, then fold in the rest.

Pour the mixture into the pan and bake for 35 minutes.

Remove from the oven, turn out onto a rack and allow to cool.

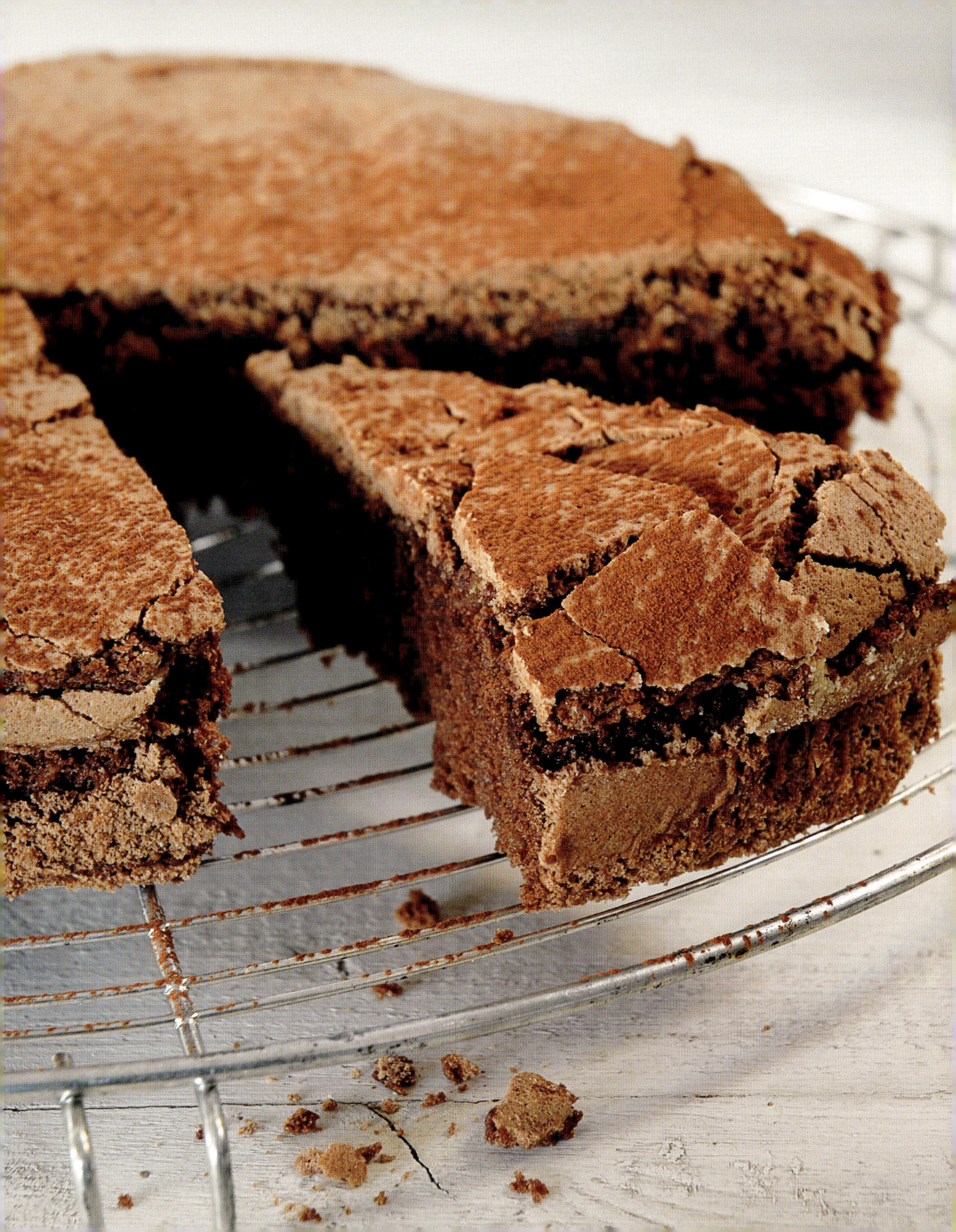

Chocolate and pear "mi-cuits"

SERVES 4
PREP TIME: 25 mins.
COOKING TIME: 10 mins.

- 3 eggs
- 1 pear (not too ripe)
- 1/2 vanilla bean
- 1/4 lb. dark chocolate
- 1/3 cup butter
  + some for the ramekins
- A pinch of salt
- 3 tbsp. sugar
- 2 tbsp. cornstarch
- Flour for the ramekins

Preheat the oven to 350° F. Butter and flour four ramekins.

Break the eggs and separate the yolks from the whites. Peel, core and dice the pear. Split the vanilla bean and scrape out the seeds.

Break the chocolate into pieces and melt in a double boiler. Remove from the heat and beat in the butter in small pieces. Beat with a wooden or rubber spatula until smooth. Add the vanilla, the salt, the sugar and the egg yolks, then the cornstarch and diced pear.

Beat the egg whites until they form stiff peaks. Fold them carefully into the mixture.

Divide the mixture between your ramekins and bake in the bottom of the oven for 8 to 10 minutes. Allow to rest for 2 minutes (no more) and turn out onto plates. Eat without delay.

> Find out more
"Mi-cuit" means half-cooked: these delicious cakes have soft, creamy centers.

chef style

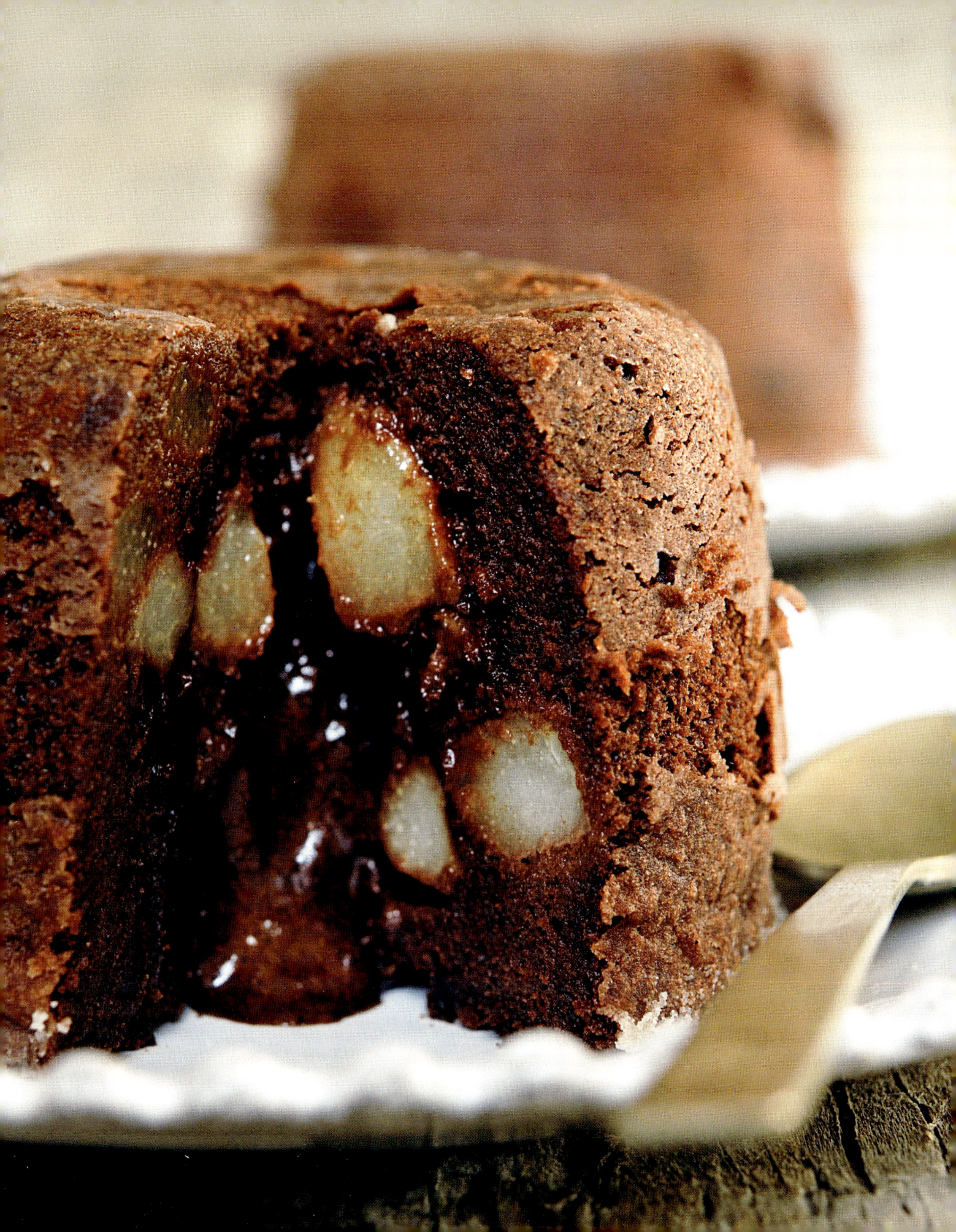

Rich chocolate cake

SERVES 6 TO 8
PREP TIME: 20 mins.
COOKING TIME: 25 mins.

- 1/2 lb. dark chocolate
- 9 tbsp. butter
  + some for the pan
- 8 eggs
- A pinch of salt
- 1 cup sugar
- 1/2 cup flour
- Powdered sugar

Cut the chocolate and the butter into small pieces. Put them into a saucepan and melt together in a double boiler, stirring frequently with a wooden spoon.

Break the eggs and separate the yolks from the whites. Add a pinch of salt to the egg whites and beat them with an electric mixer until they form stiff peaks.

Mix the sugar with the egg yolks in a bowl and beat until they turn pale yellow and frothy (you can use an electric mixer or food processor). Beat into the egg whites, still using a mixer.

Pour the melted chocolate and butter into the bowl, beating all the time.

Stir in the flour and beat again; the mixture should lose some of its volume.

Butter a round 9-inch cake pan. Pour in the mixture and bake for 5 minutes at 475° F, then reduce the temperature to 300° F and bake for 20 minutes longer. Check with the point of a knife: it should come out covered in chocolate.

Take the cake out of the oven and turn out onto a wire rack. Dust with powdered sugar and serve warm.

> Helpful tip
Serve this wonderful cake with chilled crème anglaise.

child's play

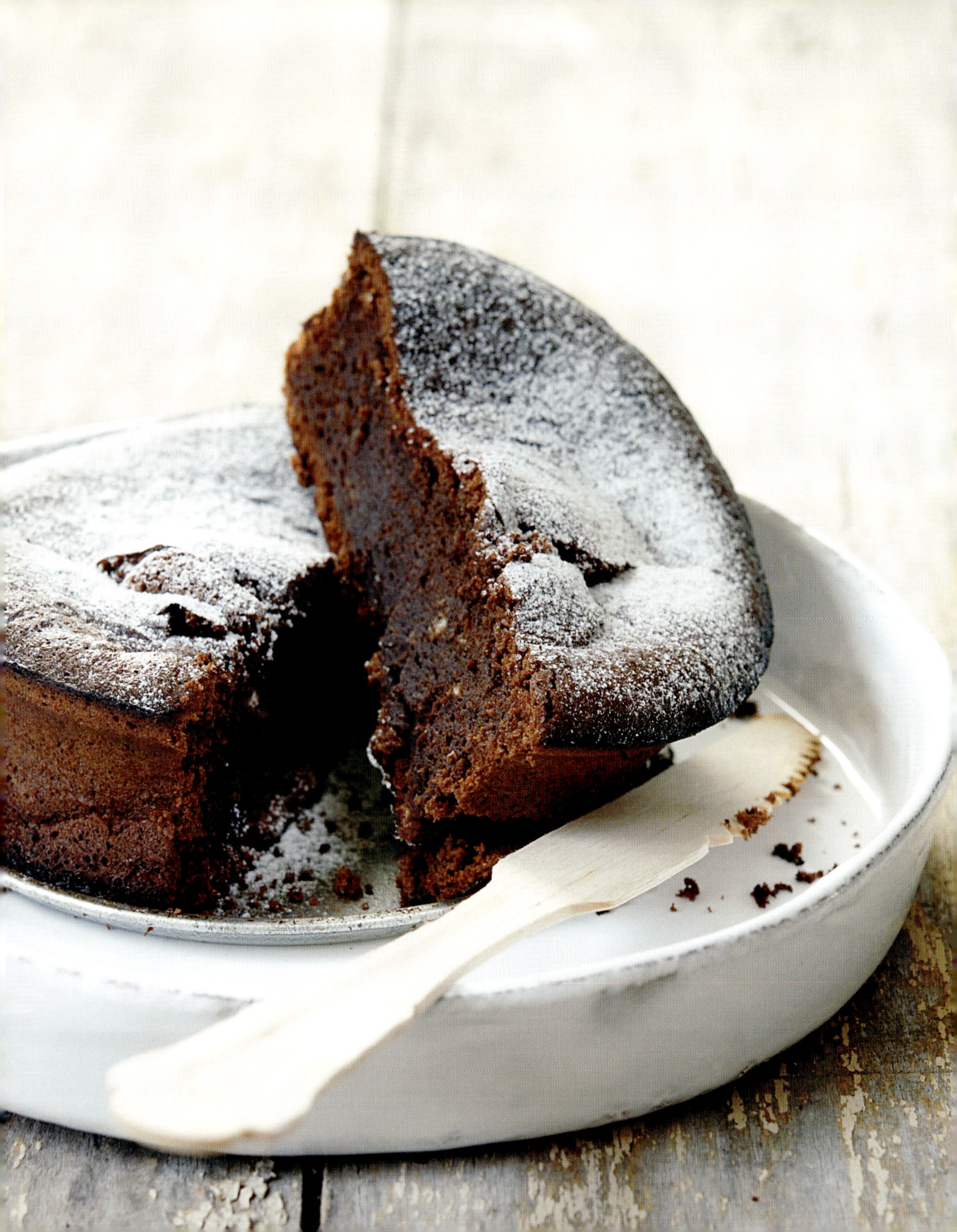

Double-choc muffins

10 TO 12 MUFFINS
PREP TIME: 20 mins.
COOKING TIME: 10 to 15 mins.

- 3-1/2 tbsp. butter
- 2 oz. dark chocolate
- 1/2 cup sugar
- 2 eggs
- 7 tbsp. milk
- 1-2/3 cups flour
- A pinch of salt
- 2 level teaspoons baking powder
- 1/4 cup chocolate chips

Allow the butter to soften at room temperature. Melt the dark chocolate in a double boiler.

Beat the butter and sugar in a bowl until the mixture turns pale. Gradually add the eggs, the warmed milk and the melted chocolate.

Preheat the oven to 350° F.

Mix the flour with the salt and the baking powder. Gradually add to the chocolate mixture. Add the chocolate chips.

Pour into a muffin pan and bake for 10 to 15 minutes.

Serve warm.

> Serving advice
Serve these muffins with a scoop of vanilla ice cream or a fruit salad.

never fails

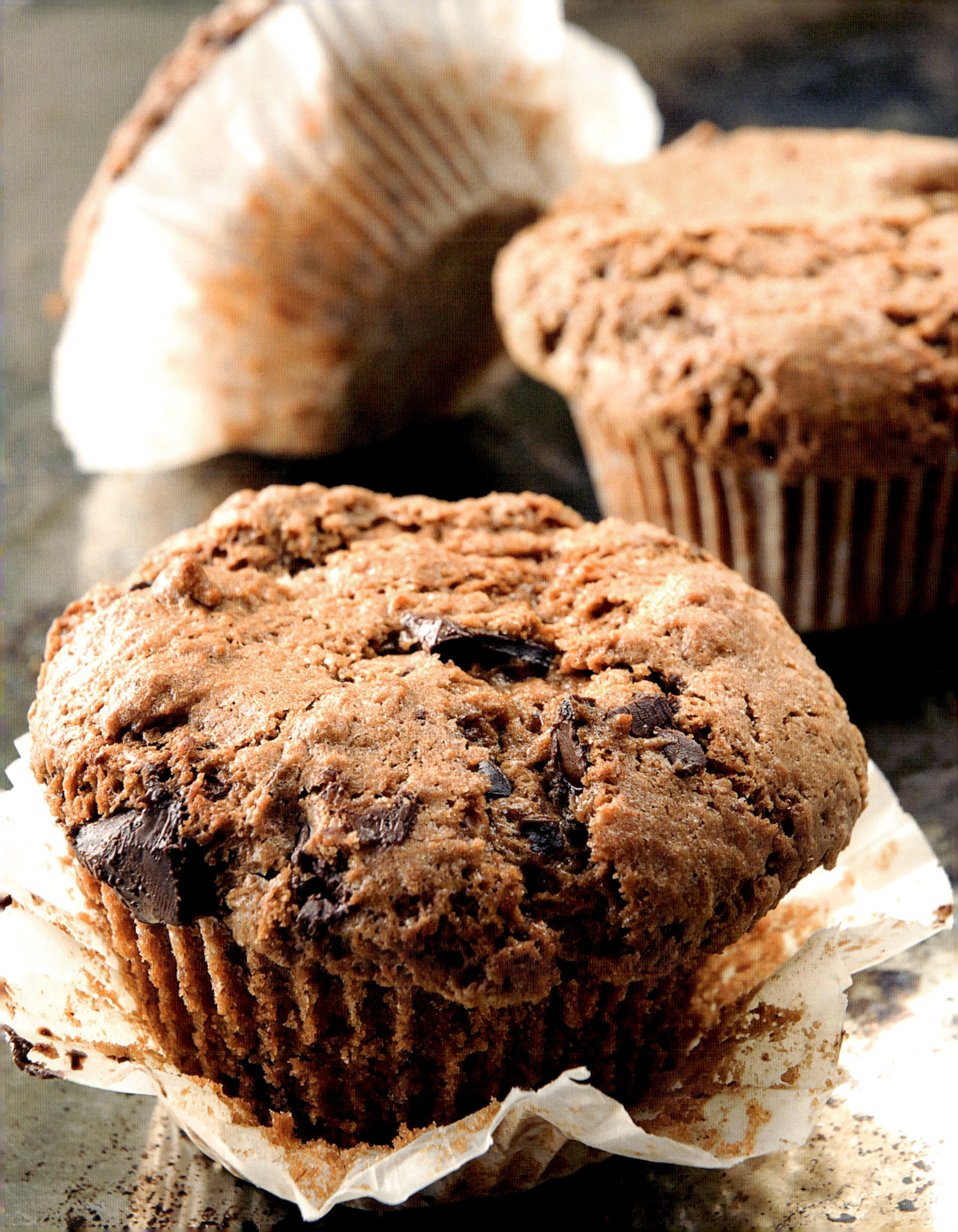

Spiced chocolate slab cake

SERVES 8 TO 10
PREP TIME: 20 mins.
COOKING TIME: 1 hr

- 1/2 lb. dark chocolate
- 1 cup butter + some for the pan
- 2-1/4 cups sugar
- 2/3 cup flour
- 3 eggs
- 1 teaspoon vanilla powder
- A little ground cinnamon
- 2 pinches of each of the following ground spices, mixed together: cinnamon, green aniseed, and cardamom.
- 2 tbsp. dark rum
- Powdered sugar

Break the chocolate into small pieces. Cut the butter into pieces. Pour 1/4 cup of water into a saucepan. Add the sugar and mix. Heat together, stirring with a wooden or rubber spatula. When the sugar syrup reaches the boiling point, add the chocolate, then the butter. Lower the heat and mix well. Remove from the heat.

Preheat the oven to 350° F. Sift the flour into a bowl, add the eggs one by one, mixing well each time. Add the vanilla, the spices and the rum. Beat into the chocolate mixture.

Line an 8-inch square baking pan with buttered parchment paper. Pour in the mixture.

Place the pan in a bain-marie and bake for 1 hour. Allow to cool, then turn out and sprinkle with powdered sugar mixed with a little cinnamon.

> Helpful tip
This cake is even better the following day.

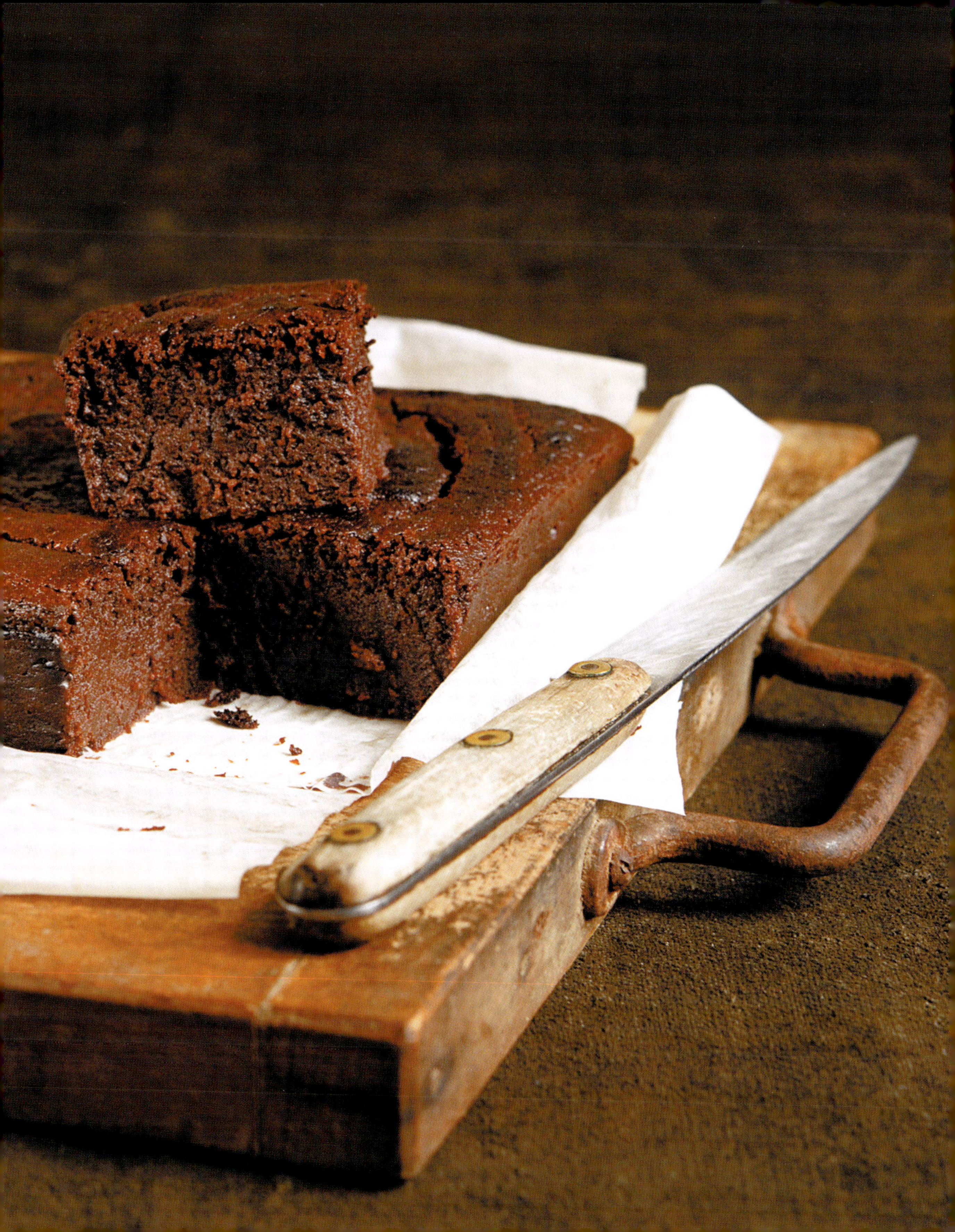

Chocolate soufflé

SERVES 6
PREP TIME: 20 mins.
COOKING TIME: 30 mins.

- 5 oz. bitter chocolate (70 % cocoa solids)
- 6 eggs
- 1/4 cup cornstarch
- 4 tbsp. sugar
- 1 tbsp. butter for the dish
- A pinch of salt
- 1 tbsp. cocoa powder

Cut the chocolate into small pieces.

Break the eggs and separate the yolks from the whites.

Put the chocolate in a saucepan, place in a double boiler and gently melt the chocolate, stirring from time to time.

Remove the saucepan from the double boiler and incorporate the egg yolks one by one, making sure each is mixed in before adding the next one. Sprinkle in the cornstarch and sugar and mix quickly.

Preheat the oven to 400° F. Butter a soufflé dish.

Beat the egg whites with a pinch of salt until they form very stiff peaks. Take 2 tbsp. of egg white and mix with the chocolate cream to lighten it, then very carefully fold in the rest.

Pour the mixture into the soufflé dish and bake for about 25 minutes.

Check that it's cooked by plunging a knife into the soufflé: it should come out slightly damp, showing that the center is still creamy.

Dust the surface with cocoa powder and serve without delay.

> To make a change
Make mini-soufflés using ramekin dishes.

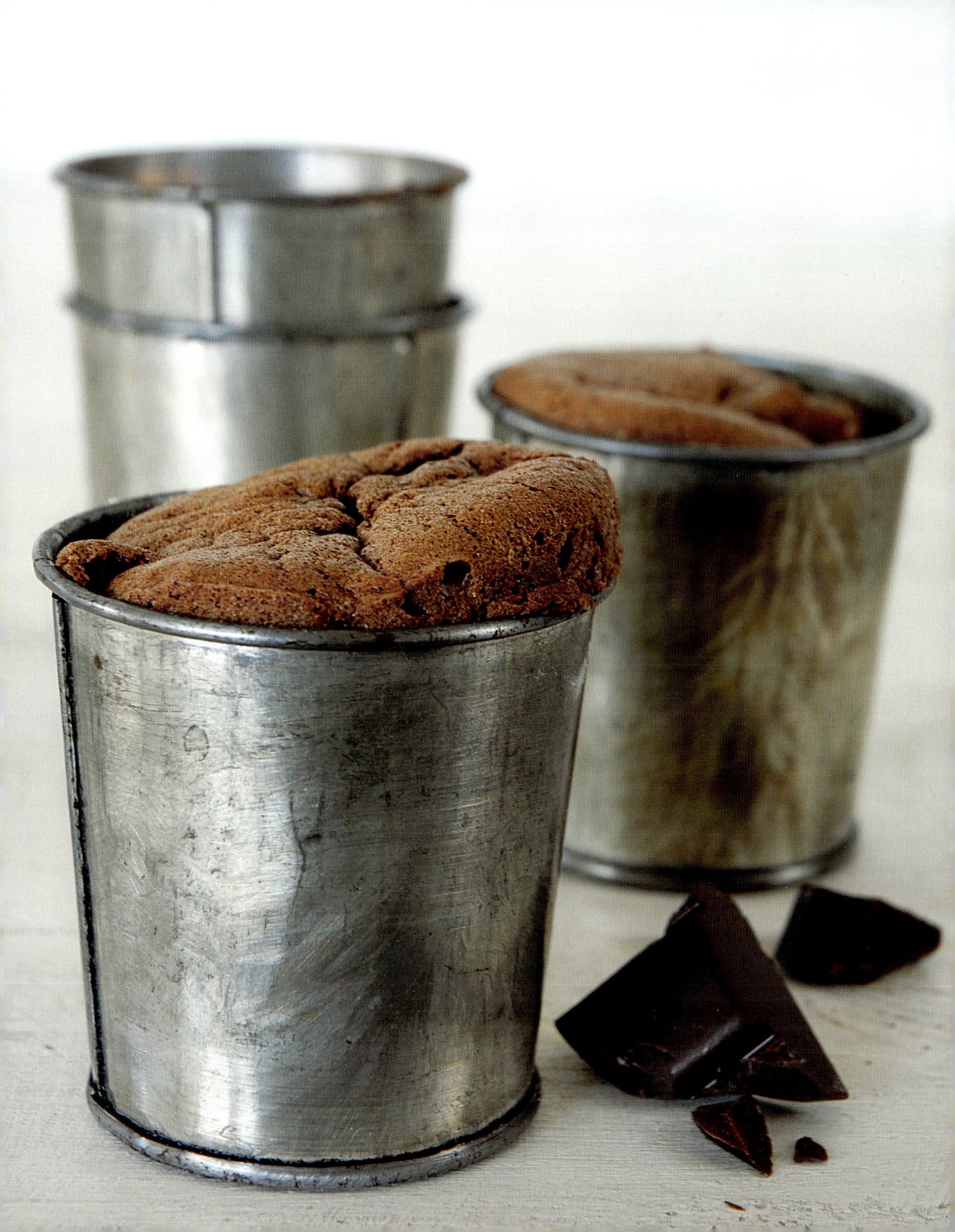

Chocolate and vanilla Bavarian cream

SERVES 4 TO 6
PREP TIME: 1 hr
COOKING TIME: 10 to 15 mins.
REFRIGERATION TIME: 6 hrs

- Sunflower oil to grease the mold

FOR THE CRÈME ANGLAISE
- 1/2 vanilla bean
- 1-1/4 cup milk
- 3 egg yolks
- 2-1/2 tbsp. sugar

FOR THE BAVARIAN CREAM
- 3/4 packet gelatin
- 2 cups crème anglaise (see above)
- 1-1/4 cups crème fraîche or heavy cream
- 1/3 cup whole milk
- 3 oz. chocolate (at least 55 % cocoa solids)
- 2 teaspoons vanilla extract

FOR DECORATION
- Chocolate

Prepare the crème anglaise: split the vanilla bean and put it in a saucepan with the milk; bring to a boil; remove from the heat and allow to infuse for 15 to 20 minutes. Put the egg yolks and sugar into a bowl. Beat together until the mixture turns pale yellow. Remove the vanilla bean from the milk and scrape the seeds from the inside of the bean with a spoon. Mix the seeds into the milk and bring to a boil. Gently pour the hot milk onto the egg and sugar mixture, stirring constantly. Place on a very low heat and stir until the mixture thickens. When it reaches the correct consistency put the saucepan into a bowl of iced water for a few seconds to halt the cooking process.

Prepare the bavarois: dissolve the gelatin in a little water. Add to the hot crème anglaise and stir. Return the saucepan containing the crème anglaise to the bowl of iced water and stir until it begins to thicken. Whip the crème fraîche with the milk (you can use an electric mixer at medium speed) until it thickens. Stir the whipped cream into the crème anglaise with a spatula. Divide between two bowls.

Melt the chocolate in the microwave. Add the melted chocolate to one half of the bavarois and mix well.

Add the vanilla extract to the other half.

Brush a 9-inch round cake pan with oil. Pour in the chocolate bavarois and put in the refrigerator to set.

Remove from the refrigerator and pour in the vanilla flavored half. Leave in the refrigerator for 4 or 5 hours.

Dip the mold briefly in hot water and turn out the bavarois onto a serving dish.

Decorate with chocolate shavings (see p.421).

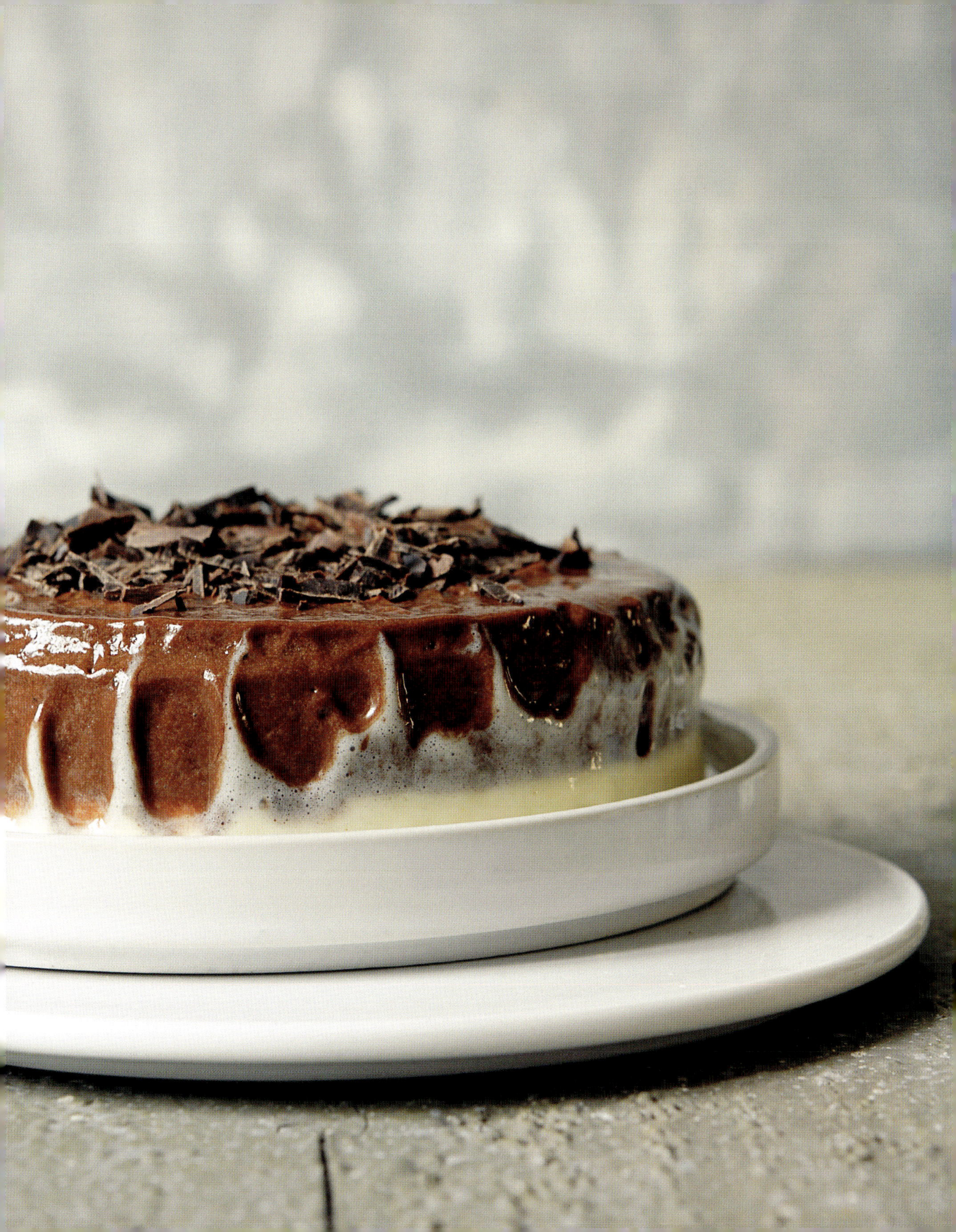

Chocolate pie

SERVES 4 TO 6
PREP TIME: 15 mins.
RESTING TIME: At least 30 mins.
COOKING TIME: About 25 mins.

FOR THE SWEET PASTRY
- 1/4 cup butter
- 1 egg
- 1/3 cup powdered sugar
- 2 tbsp. ground almonds
- A pinch of salt
- 1 scant cup sifted flour

FOR THE GANACHE
- 2/3 cup crème fraîche or heavy cream
- 1/4 lb. dark chocolate

Prepare the sweet pastry: cut the butter into very small pieces; beat the egg in a bowl, add the sugar, the ground almonds and the salt. Beat the mixture with a wooden spatula until it turns pale yellow and frothy. Add the flour all at once and mix quickly with the spatula. Take small quantities of dough and rub them between your fingertips until the mixture has the consistency of fine breadcumbs. Lightly flour a work surface and place the dough on it. Scatter the pieces of butter over the dough and knead to incorporate. Make the dough into a ball, wrap in plastic wrap and allow to rest for at least 30 minutes in the refrigerator.

Preheat the oven to 350° F.

Roll out the dough to a thickness of 1/8 inch. Use it to line a 9-inch round pie dish. Prick the dough all over with a fork, then line with parchment paper and cover with baking beans. Bake blind for 12 minutes. Remove the paper and beans and bake for another 8 to 10 minutes.
Remove from the oven and allow to cool.

Prepare the ganache: heat the cream in a heavy saucepan. Break the chocolate into small pieces and melt in a double boiler (or in the microwave). Gradually add the hot cream to the chocolate, mixing well with a wooden or rubber spatula. Put the ganache in a pastry bag and pipe it onto the pie base. Smooth the surface with a metal spatula.

Chill in the refrigerator until needed.

> Helpful tip

You can use ganache to fill or frost cakes. Don't over-beat ganache, as incorporating too much air makes it keep less well.

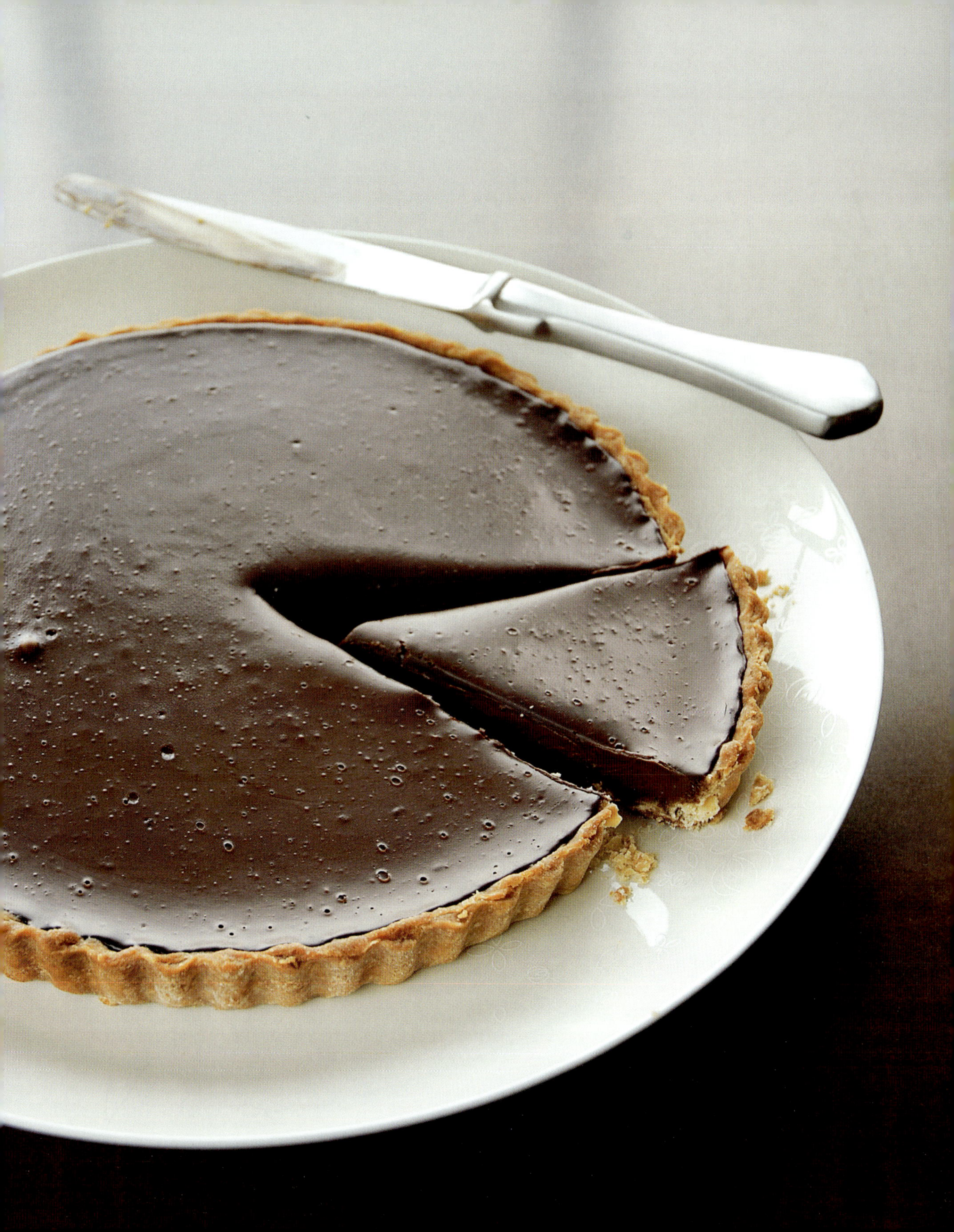

White chocolate tartlets

SERVES 6
PREP TIME: 15 mins.
COOKING TIME: 50 mins.
REFRIGERATION TIME: At least 3 hrs

FOR THE PIE CRUST
- 1 vanilla bean
- 5 tbsp. sugar
- 1 cup flour
- 1/4 cup softened butter
- 1 egg

FOR THE FILLING
- 11 oz. white chocolate
- 1-1/2 cups heavy cream
- 4 egg yolks

Prepare the pie crust: split the vanilla bean and scrape out the seeds. Mix the seeds with the sugar. Sift the flour onto a work surface, then cut the butter into small pieces and rub into the flour until the mixture has the consistency of fine breadcrumbs. Make a well in the center. Break the egg into it and add the sugar flavored with vanilla. Combine the ingredients with your fingertips, but do not knead. Flatten the dough with the heel of your hand, then roll it into a ball and wrap in plastic wrap; allow to rest for at least 30 minutes.

Preheat the oven to 350° F.

Roll out the dough and use it to line six buttered tartlet molds lined with parchment paper. Prick the dough with a fork and bake for 15 minutes.

Prepare the filling: break the chocolate into pieces. Put them into a saucepan with the cream and heat gently until the chocolate has melted. Remove from the heat and incorporate the egg yolks.

Reduce the oven temperature to 275° F.

Fill the tartlets with the chocolate mixture and bake for 25 minutes. Allow to cool at room temperature, then chill in the refrigerator for at least 3 hours.

> Serving advice
Sprinkle these tartlets with a little cocoa powder and serve chilled with some fresh berries.

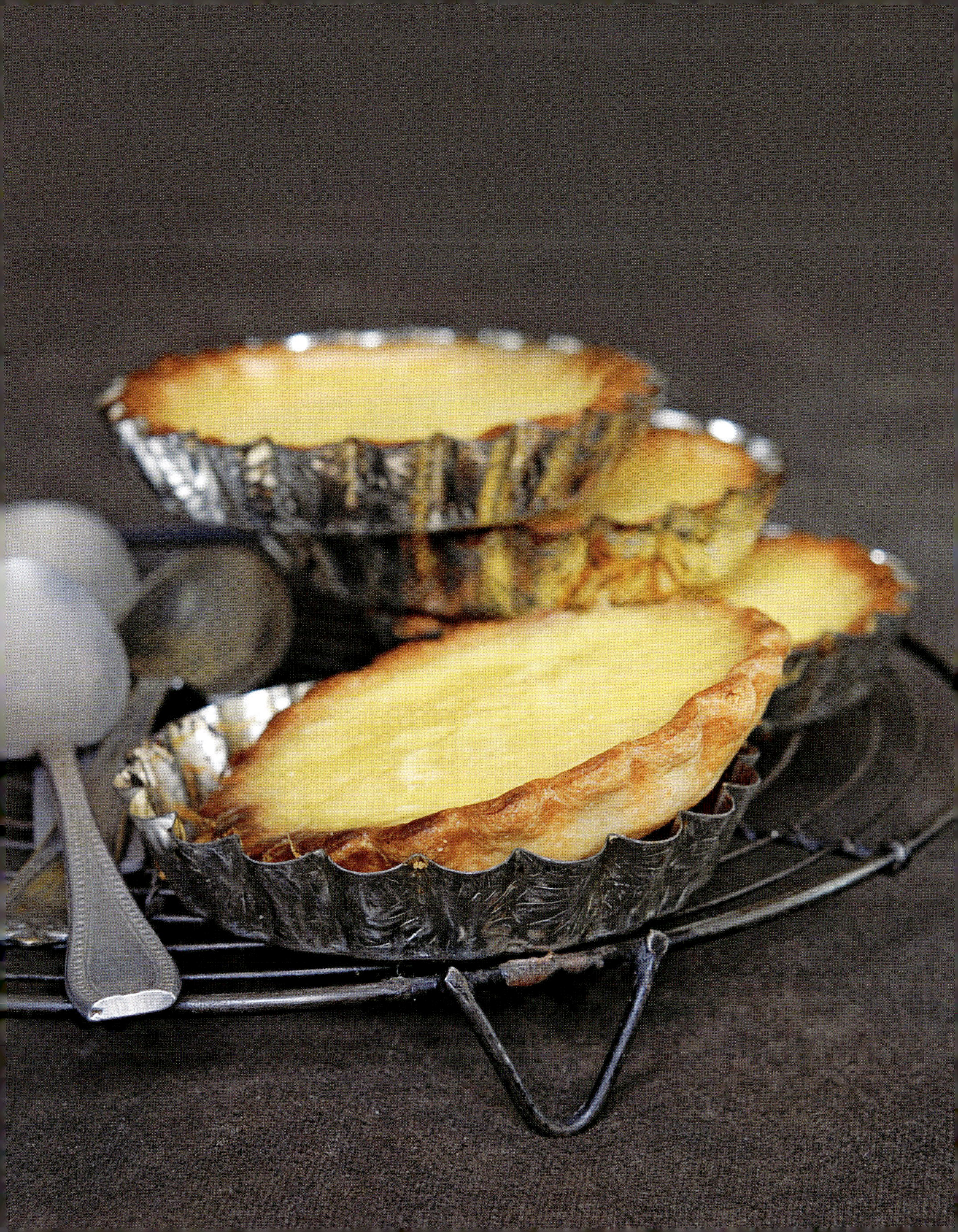

Banana chocolate pie

SERVES 4 TO 6
PREP TIME: 10 mins.
COOKING TIME: 35 mins.
REFRIGERATION TIME: 2 hrs

- 1/2 lb. pre-rolled puff pastry
- 6 oz. dark chocolate
- 1-1/4 cup crème fraîche or heavy cream
- A few slivered almonds
- 3 bananas

Preheat the oven to 350° F.

Lay the puff pastry in an 11-inch pie dish lined with parchment paper. Bake blind for 20 minutes.

While the pastry is baking, break the chocolate into pieces and gently melt in a double boiler. Add the cream and mix well.

Lightly toast the almonds in a hot skillet.

Slice the bananas and arrange two thirds on the pastry. Pour over the chocolate cream.

Decorate with the rest of the banana slices and the almonds. Chill for 2 hours in the refrigerator before serving.

> To make a change
You can also use a rectangular dish for this pie, or even six individual dishes to make tartlets.

> Helpful tip
For blind baking, prick the pastry with a fork, cover with parchment paper and add a layer of baking beans. Bake for a few minutes.

> Home made
To make your own puff pastry, see p.402.

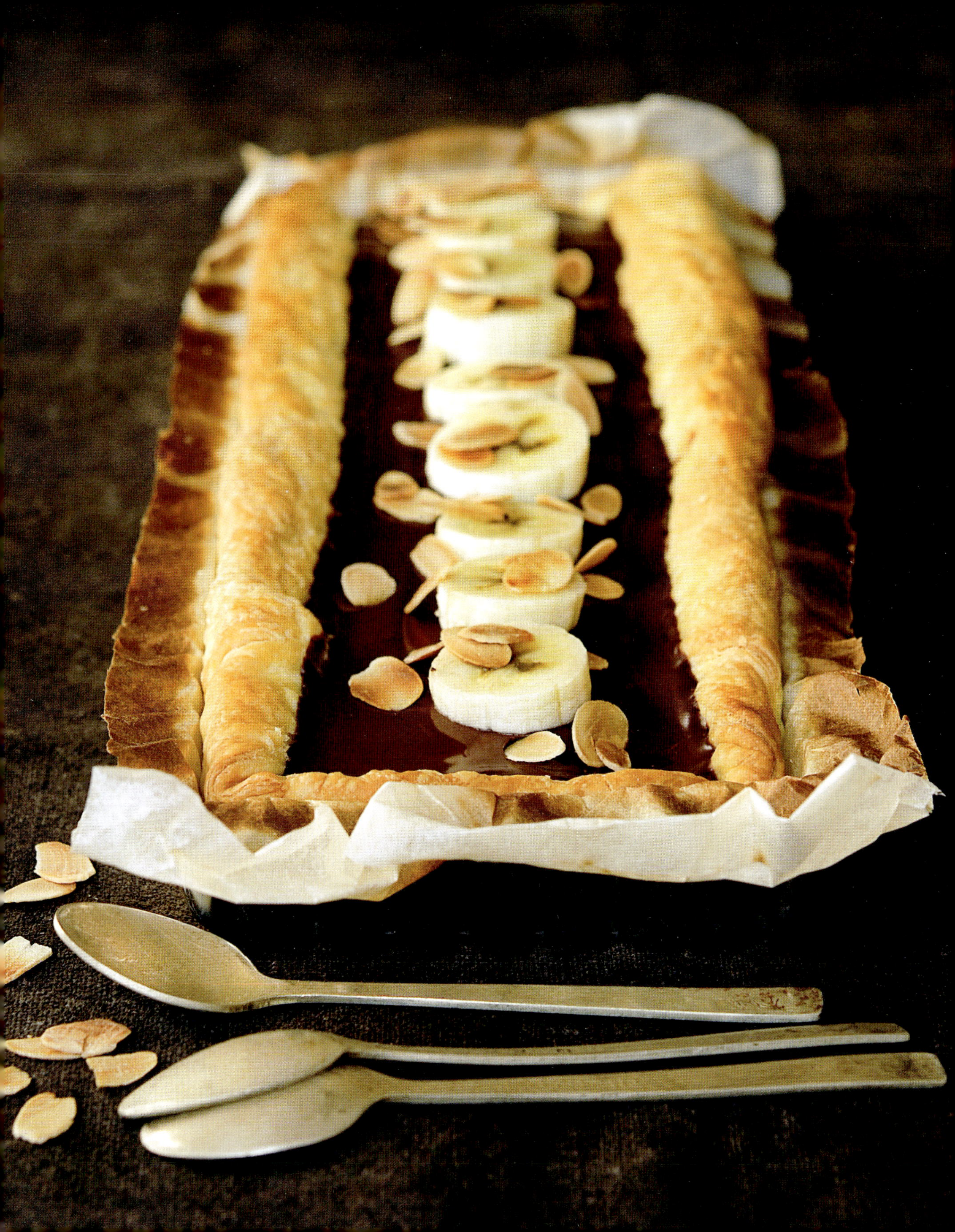

Chocolate-caramel pizza

SERVES 6
PREP TIME: 15 mins.
COOKING TIME: 11 mins.

- 250 g store bought pizza dough
- 11 oz. dark chocolate (at least 70 % cocoa solids)

FOR THE CARAMEL
- 2 tbsp. very cold salted butter
- 1/2 lemon
- 3/4 cup sugar
- 7 tbsp. crème fraîche or heavy cream

Preheat the oven to 470° F.

Roll out the pizza dough and place on a baking sheet lined with parchment paper. Bake for about 5 minutes.

Reduce the oven temperature to 400° F.

Prepare the caramel: cut the butter into small pieces, squeeze the juice of the half lemon and sieve the juice into a heavy saucepan. Add the sugar and heat over a gentle heat until the sugar has dissolved. Do not add any water and do not stir. Brush the inside of the saucepan with water from time to time to clean off any splashes. Meanwhile, gently heat the cream in a small heavy pan. When the caramel is a light golden color, turn off the heat and pour in the hot cream, stirring constantly. When the cream is incorporated, add the pieces of butter and mix with a wooden spatula until the mixture is smooth.

Roughly chop the chocolate. Use a spatula to spread the caramel on the pizza to a thickness of about 1/8 inch, stopping an inch away from the edge. Sprinkle with chopped chocolate and bake for 6 minutes. Serve hot.

child's play

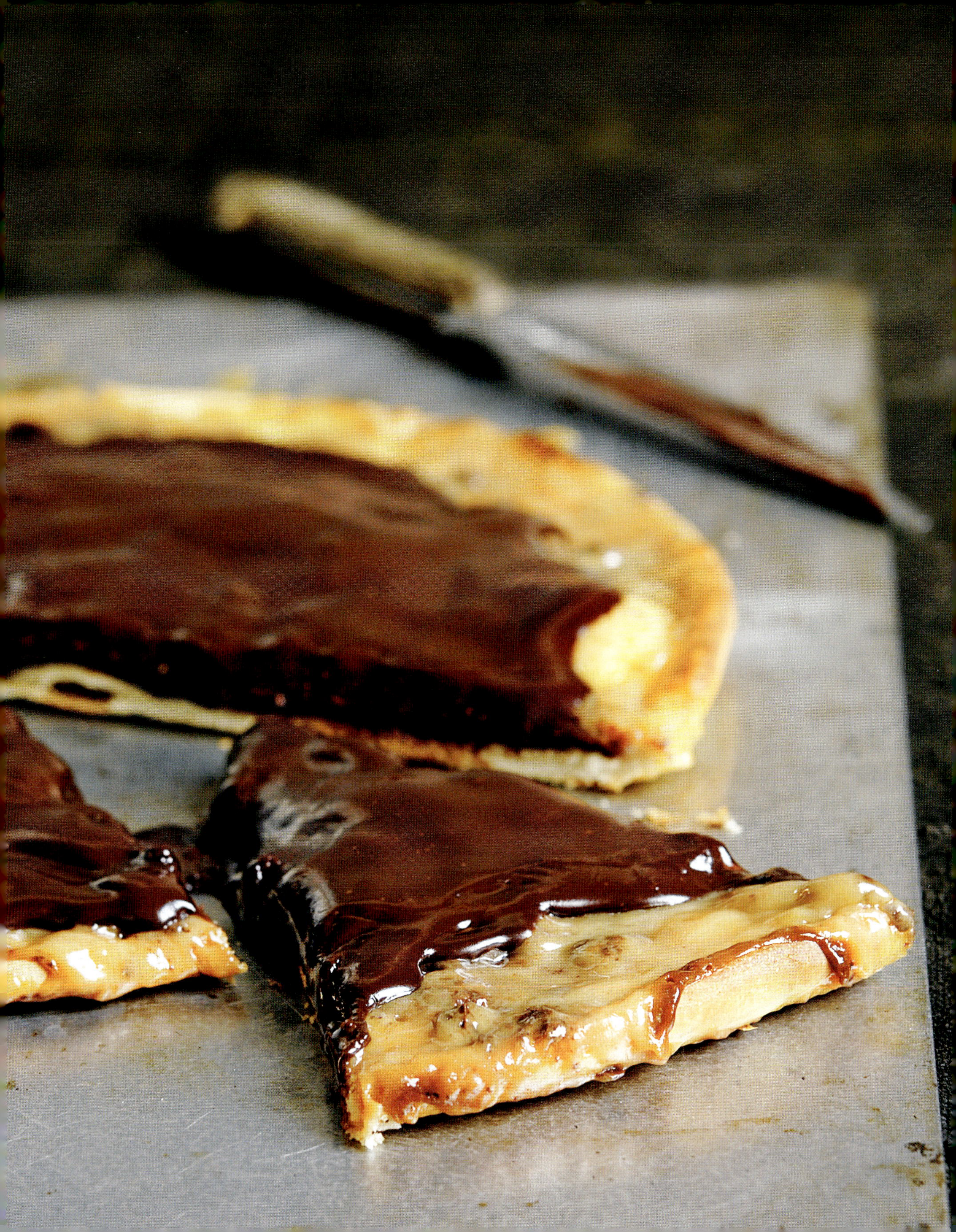

Chocolate éclairs

12 ÉCLAIRS
PREP TIME: 45 mins.
COOKING TIME: 20 mins.

FOR THE CHOCOLATE PASTRY CREAM
- 2 cups milk
- 6 egg yolks
- 1/2 cup sugar
- 1/3 cup flour
- 10 oz. dark chocolate

FOR THE CHOUX PASTRY
- 4 tbsp. water
- 1/3 cup whole milk
- 1 scant teaspoon salt
- 1 scant teaspoon sugar
- 4 tbsp. butter
- 2/3 cup flour
- 2 whole eggs

FOR THE FONDANT
- 1/2 lb. sugar cubes
- 2-1/2 tsp. glucose
- 3 tbsp. cocoa powder

FOR THE FROSTING
- 4 tbsp. sugar
- 1/2 lb. fondant (see above)

Prepare the pastry cream: put the egg yolks and the sugar into a bowl and beat until the mixture turns pale yellow. Sprinkle on the flour and stir it in quickly. In the meantime, boil the milk in a saucepan. Slowly pour the boiling milk onto the mixture, stirring constantly with a wooden spoon to obtain a smooth creamy consistency. Pour into a heavy saucepan. Heat over a very low heat until it thickens, stirring constantly. Remove from the heat as soon as it starts to boil and pour into a bowl. Grate the chocolate and gradually stir into the hot custard.

Prepare the choux pastry: pour the water and milk into a saucepan. Add the salt, the sugar and the butter. Bring to a boil, stirring constantly. Add the flour all at once. Stir with a wooden or rubber spatula until the dough is smooth. When it stops sticking to the sides of the pan, continue to work for 2 or 3 minutes, to dry it out a little. Place in a bowl. Break in the eggs one by one, stirring constantly. Lift your spatula from time to time: when the mixture forms a smooth ribbon, it's ready.

Preheat the oven to 375° F.

Spoon the choux pastry into a pastry bag with a large fluted tip. Take a baking sheet and cover with parchment paper. Pipe 12 six-inch cylinders of pastry. Bake for 20 minutes, leaving the oven door half open after 7 minutes. Put the éclairs on a wire rack and allow to cool.

Prepare the fondant: in a heavy saucepan heat 1 tbsp. water with the sugar cubes and glucose. Heat to soft ball stage (240° F) and remove from the heat. Pour onto a cold marble slab and allow to cool. Work with a spatula, repeatedly spreading out and bringing together the mixture until it is quite smooth and white. Heat in a saucepan placed in a double boiler.

Meanwhile, prepare the frosting: put 4 tbsp. water in a saucepan with the sugar and bring to a boil to make a syrup. As soon as the fondant has softened, add the cocoa powder and pour in the syrup in a thin stream, stirring very slowly with a wooden spoon and being careful not to make any bubbles. As soon as the frosting has reached a thick, smooth consistency, stop adding the syrup.

Put the pastry cream in a pastry bag with a smooth tip. Push the tip into one end of each éclair and fill with custard. Put the frosting in a pastry bag with a flat tip and frost the top of the éclairs. In 5 to 10 minutes the frosting will set and the éclairs will be ready to eat; otherwise, keep in a cool place until needed.

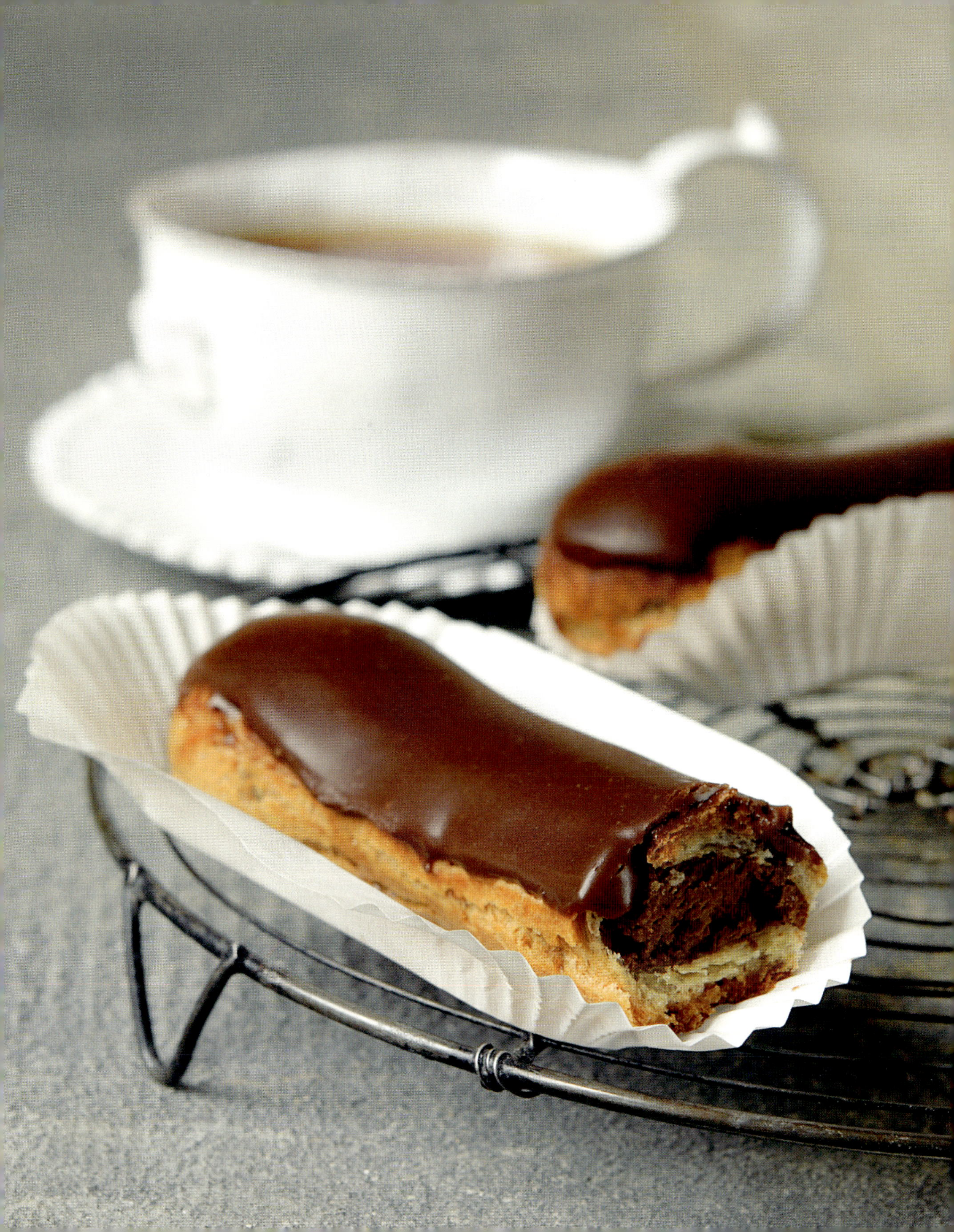

Chocolate mousse

SERVES 4 TO 6
PREP TIME: 15 mins.
REFRIGERATION TIME: 4 hrs

- 2 tbsp. butter
- 7 oz. dark chocolate
- 1 generous tbsp. whole milk
- 7 tbsp. heavy cream or crème fraîche
- 3 whole eggs
- 1 tbsp. sugar

Allow the butter to soften at room temperature.

Chop the chocolate with a knife and place in a large bowl. Put the heavy cream and milk in a saucepan and bring to a boil. Pour over the chocolate and whisk for 1 or 2 minutes until the mixture reaches a temperature of 104° F.

Cut the butter into small pieces and whisk into the mixture.

Break the eggs and separate the yolks from the whites. Put the egg whites in a bowl with the sugar and beat them until they form soft peaks, then add the egg yolks and continue beating for a few seconds.

Take a little egg mixture and mix with the ganache (chocolate cream), then carefully fold all of the ganache into the beaten eggs.

Put the mousse into a large bowl and leave in the refrigerator for 4 hours to set.

> Serving advice
Serve this mousse with cookies or cigarettes russes.

> To make a change
You can flavor chocolate mousse with orange: add the zest of one orange to the melted chocolate.

child's play

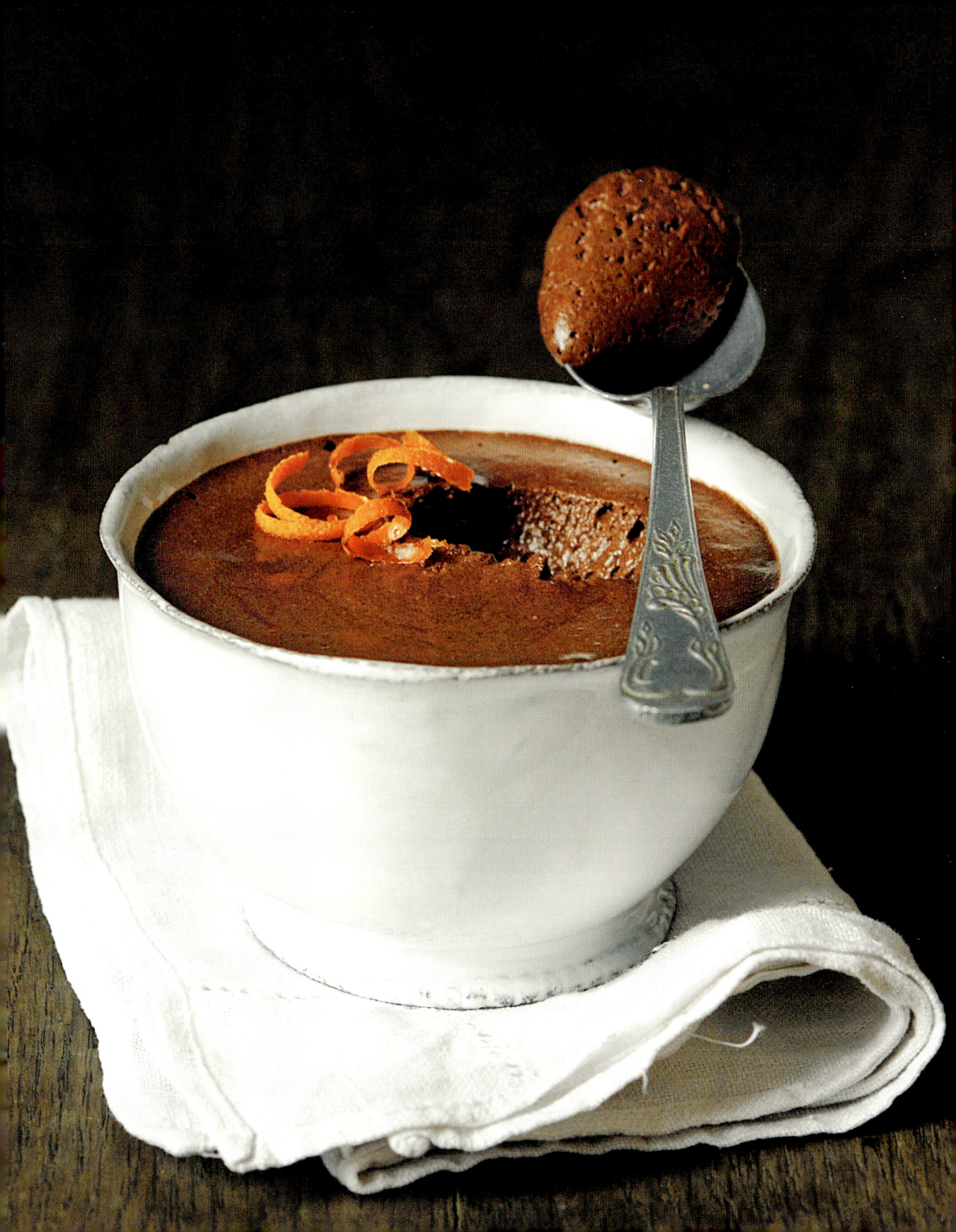

White chocolate mousse

SERVES 4 TO 6
PREP TIME: 20 mins.
COOKING TIME: 10 mins.
REFRIGERATION TIME: 3 hrs

- 1-1/2 cups chilled heavy cream
- 1/4 lb. white chocolate

Keep 3 tbsp. cream to one side and whip the rest in a bowl. Chop the chocolate and melt gently in a small saucepan placed in a double boiler (95° F).

Bring the cream you set aside to a boil and pour it onto the melted chocolate; gently fold in one quarter of the whipped cream, then the rest.

Put the mousse in a serving dish or individual dishes. Leave to set in the refrigerator for 3 hours.

> Serving advice
Serve this mousse with a red fruit coulis.

Two-chocolate mousse

SERVES 4 TO 6
PREP TIME: 15 mins.
COOKING TIME: About 5 mins.
REFRIGERATION TIME: 4 hrs

- 2 oz. dark chocolate (at least 60 % cocoa solids)
- 4 oz. milk chocolate
- 1/3 cup butter
- 4 eggs
- 4 tbsp. sugar
- 7 tbsp. crème fraîche or heavy cream

Break the dark chocolate and milk chocolate into pieces and put them in a small saucepan with the butter, also cut into small pieces. Place the saucepan in a double boiler over a gentle heat. Melt the chocolate and butter, stirring constantly until the mixture is smooth. Remove the saucepan from the double boiler and allow to cool: the mixture should be thick and creamy.

Break the eggs and separate the yolks from the whites. Add 1 tbsp. of sugar to the egg whites and beat them until they form stiff peaks. Add the egg yolks, the cream and the rest of the sugar to the melted chocolate and mix well.

Take two 2 tbsp. of beaten egg whites and quickly stir them into the chocolate mixture to lighten it. Now gently fold in the rest of the egg whites.

Pour into a large bowl, cover and allow to set in the refrigerator for at least 4 hours.

Serve well chilled with crème anglaise (see p.411).

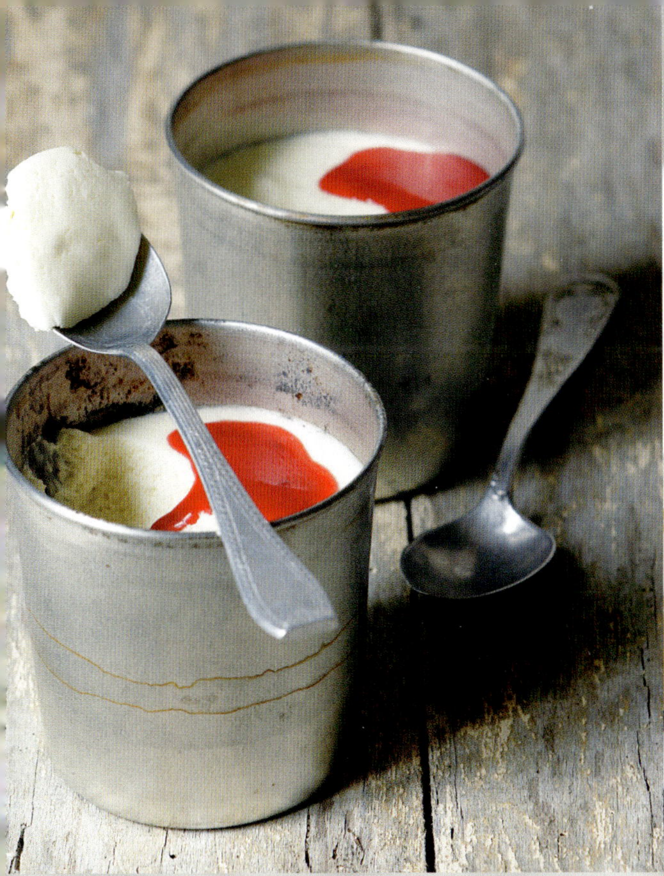

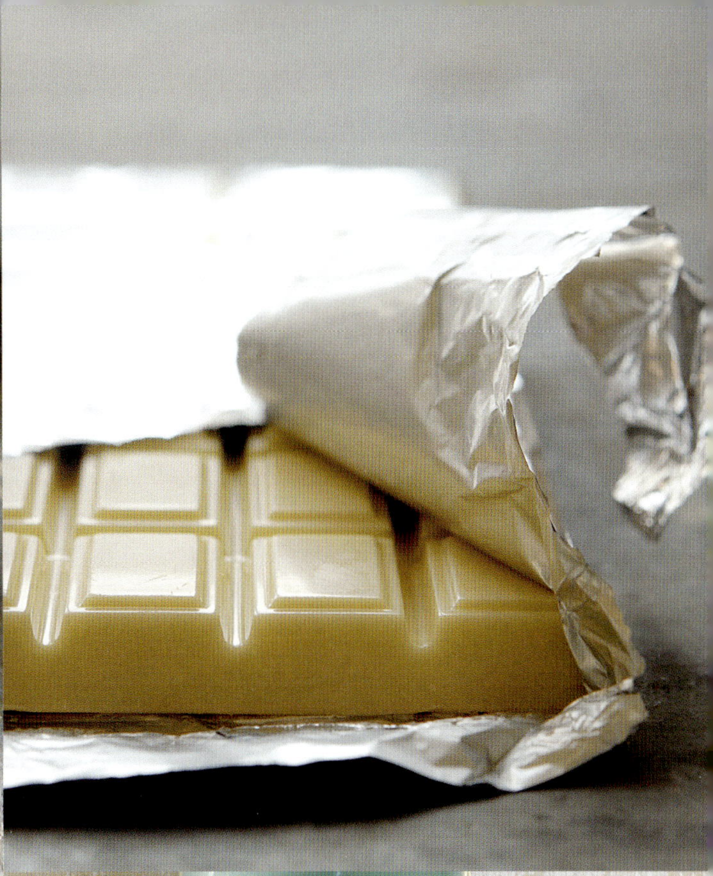

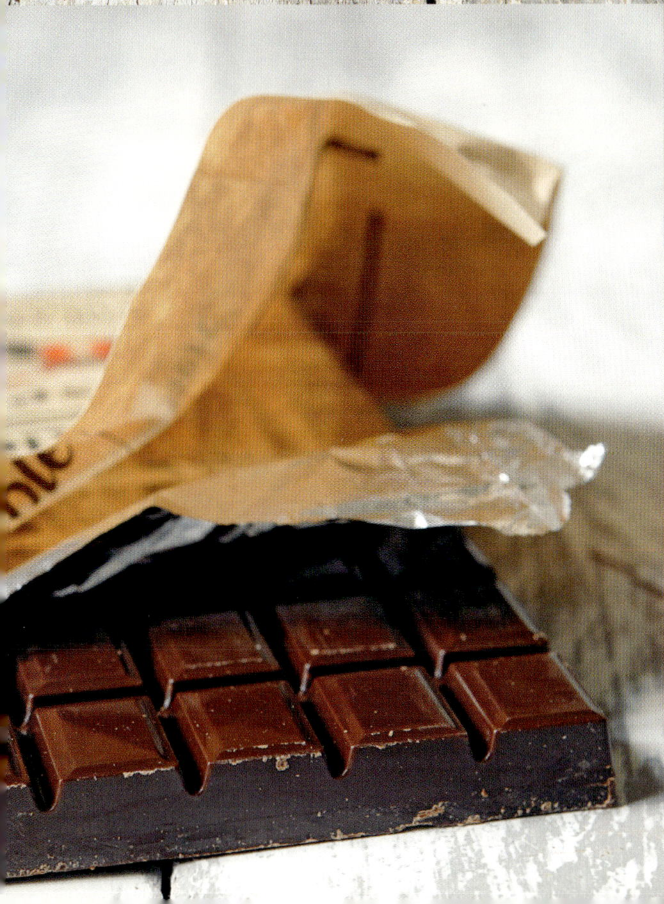

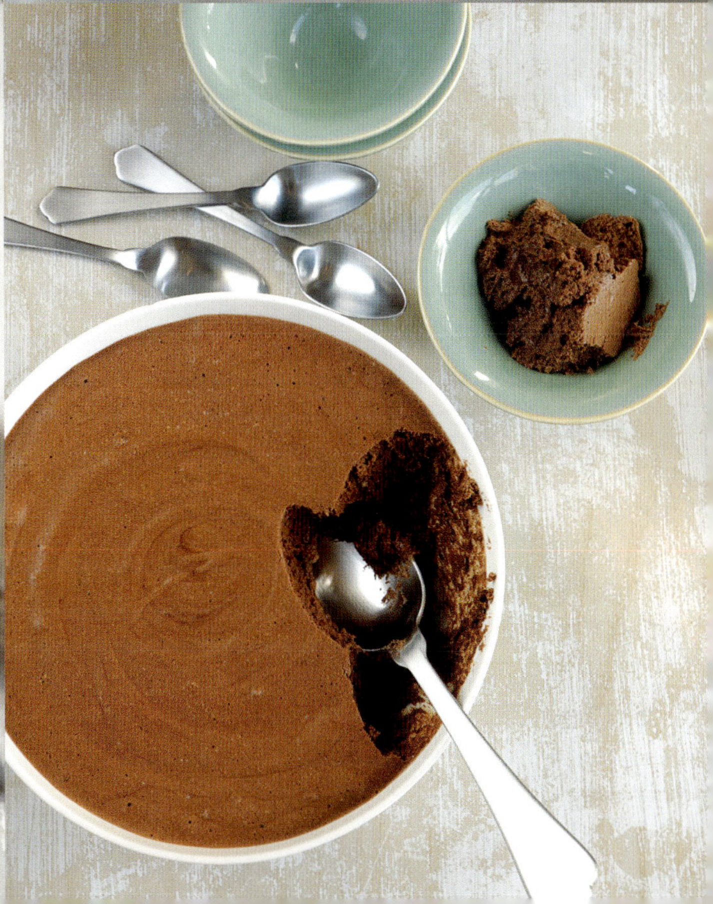

Chocolate marquise

SERVES 4 TO 6
PREP TIME: 20 mins.
COOKING TIME: 3 to 4 mins.
REFRIGERATION TIME: 12 hrs

- 9 tbsp. butter
- 3 eggs
- 7 oz. dark chocolate
- 2/3 cup powdered sugar
- A pinch of salt

Soften the butter at room temperature.

Break the eggs and separate the yolks from the whites.

Break the chocolate into small pieces. Melt in a double boiler or in the microwave.

Add the butter to the melted chocolate and stir, then beat in the egg yolks and the powdered sugar.

Beat the egg whites with a pinch of salt until they form very stiff peaks, and carefully fold them into the chocolate mixture.

Pour into ramekins (or into a round cake pan). Refrigerate for 12 hours before serving.

> Helpful tip

Using a bain-marie means you can melt the chocolate without burning it. Place the bowl containing the chocolate in a pan of boiling water.

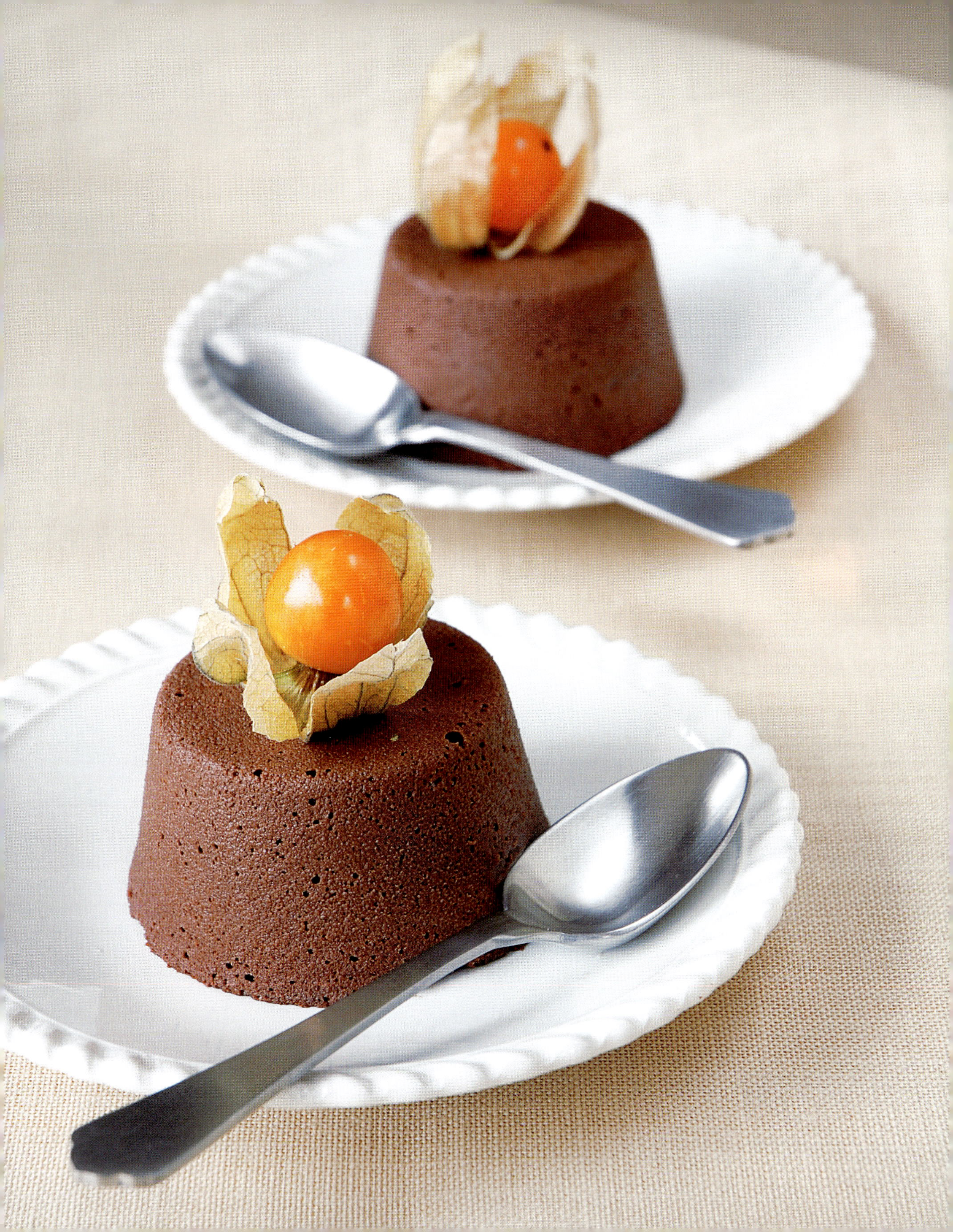

Dark chocolate crème brûlée

SERVES 8
PREP TIME: 15 mins. (over 2 days)
COOKING TIME: About 45 mins.
REFRIGERATION TIME: 12 hrs

FOR THE CRÈME BRÛLÉE
- 7 oz. dark chocolate (at least 70 % cocoa solids)
- 8 egg yolks
- 3/4 cup sugar
- 2 cups whole milk
- 2 cups crème fraîche or heavy cream

TO FINISH
- Brown sugar

The day before, prepare the crème brûlée: chop the chocolate; mix the egg yolks with the sugar. Put the milk and the crème fraîche or heavy cream into a pan and bring to a boil. Add the chopped chocolate and stir. When the mixture is an even color, pour onto the egg yolk mixture and stir well.

Preheat the oven to 225° F.

Divide the chocolate cream between eight ramekins. Bake for 45 minutes. Allow to cool, then place in the refrigerator until the following day.

The following day, take the ramekins out of the refrigerator. Turn on the broiler. Sprinkle the creams with brown sugar and caramelize for 1 or 2 minutes under the broiler. Serve without delay.

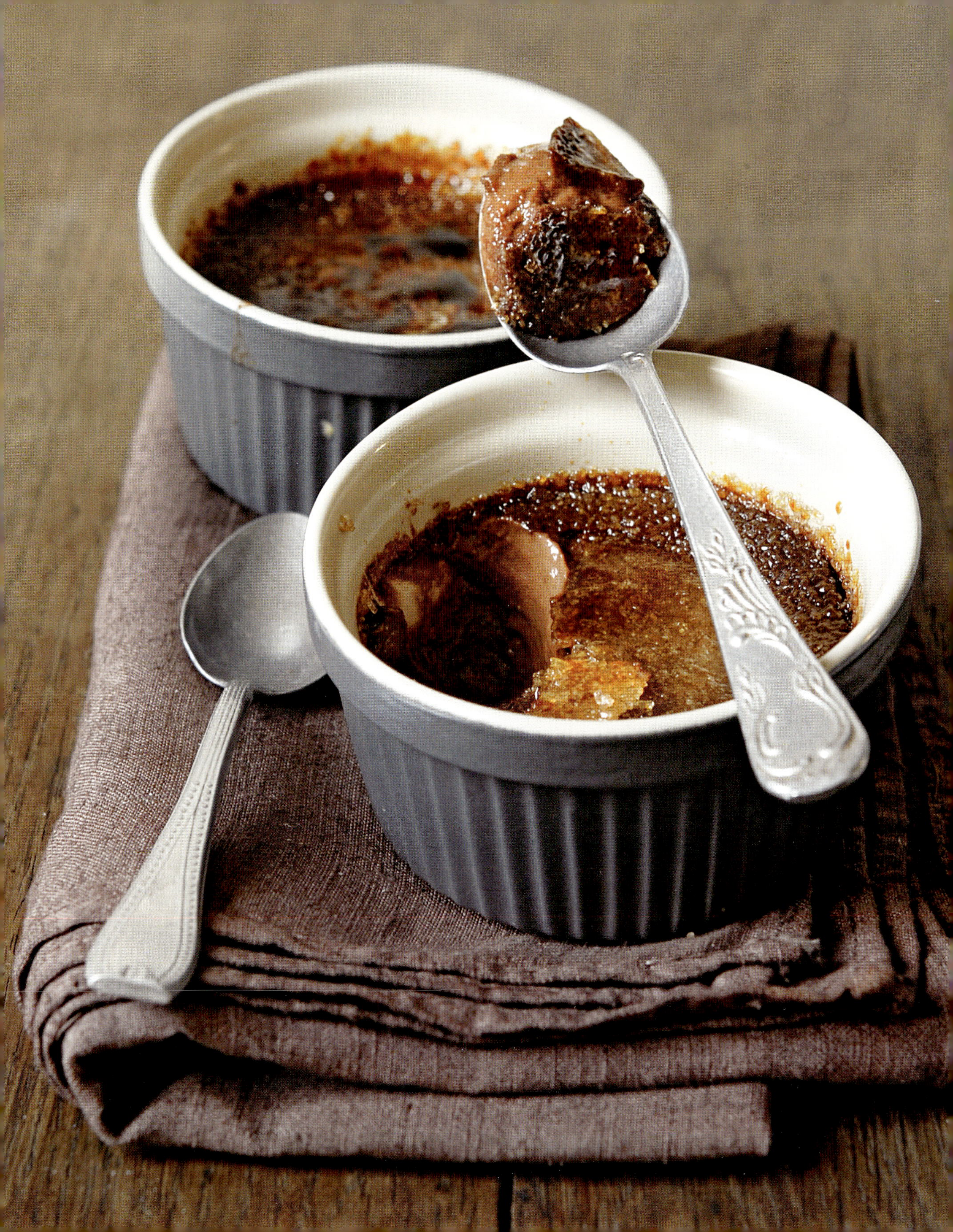

Old-fashioned chocolate creams

SERVES 6
PREP TIME: 10 mins.
COOKING TIME: 25 mins.
RESTING TIME: At least 2 hrs

- 1/4 lb. dark chocolate
- 2 cups milk
- 1-1/2 cups crème fraîche or heavy cream
- 6 egg yolks
- 1-1/3 cups sugar
- 1 level tbsp. cornstarch
- 1 teaspoon vanilla extract

Grate the chocolate into a saucepan, stir in the milk and crème fraiche. Heat together.

In the meantime, beat the egg yolks and sugar until pale yellow and frothy. Stir in the cornstarch and add the milk and cream mixture.

Pour the mixture into a clean saucepan. Heat gently, stirring constantly, until it thickens (do not boil).

Remove from the heat, add the chocolate and the vanilla extract. Stir well. Pour into pretty cups. Allow to cool, cover and chill for at least 2 hours.

> Serving advice

Sprinkle these creams with lightly toasted and chopped unsalted pistachios.

child's play

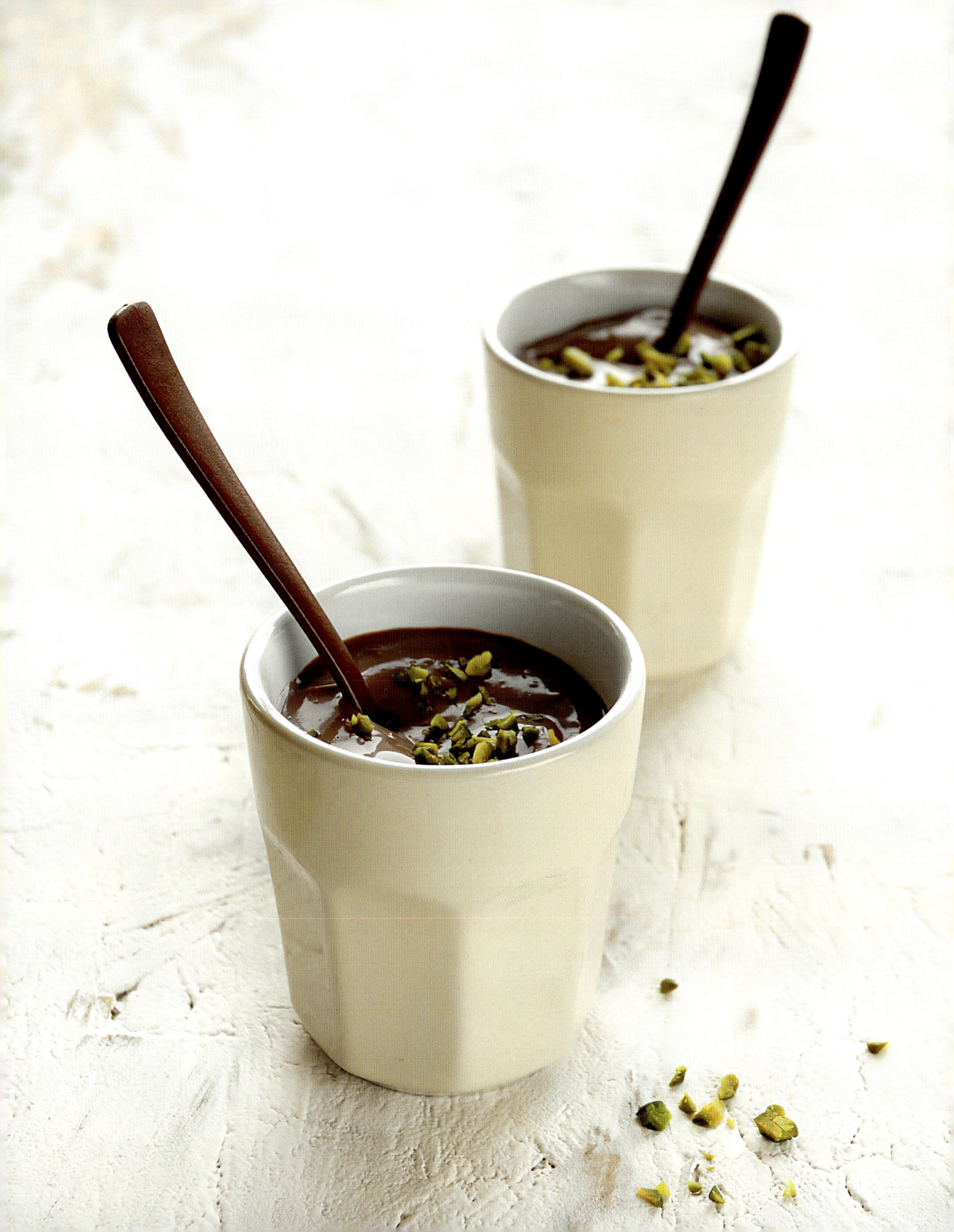

Chestnut and chocolate verrines

MAKES 4 TO 6 VERRINES, FROM 4 TO 5 OZ. EACH
PREP TIME: 15 mins.
COOKING TIME: About 3 mins.

- 4 small meringues (bought ready-made)

FOR THE CHOCOLATE SAUCE
- 4 oz. dark chocolate (70% cocoa content)
- 1/2 cup heavy cream

FOR THE CHESTNUT CREAM
- 1 cup chestnut cream
- 1/2 cup very cold heavy cream

Prepare the chocolate sauce: grate or chop the chocolate into small pieces, put them into a bowl and melt gradually in a double boiler.

Bring the heavy cream to the boil and pour immediately over the chocolate, stirring to obtain a very smooth sauce. Let it cool.

Prepare the chestnut cream: stir vigorously with a spatula until it is supple. Whip the heavy cream until it is firm. Then delicately fold into the chestnut cream, without mixing too much, to obtain a marble effect.

Break the meringues into small pieces and spread over the bottom of the verrines. Pour in one half of the chocolate sauce and then fill up with the chestnut cream. Finish up by pouring the rest of the chocolate sauce over the chestnut cream.

> Serving tip
Spoon the chestnut cream into a pastry bag and pipe into the verrines.

quick & easy

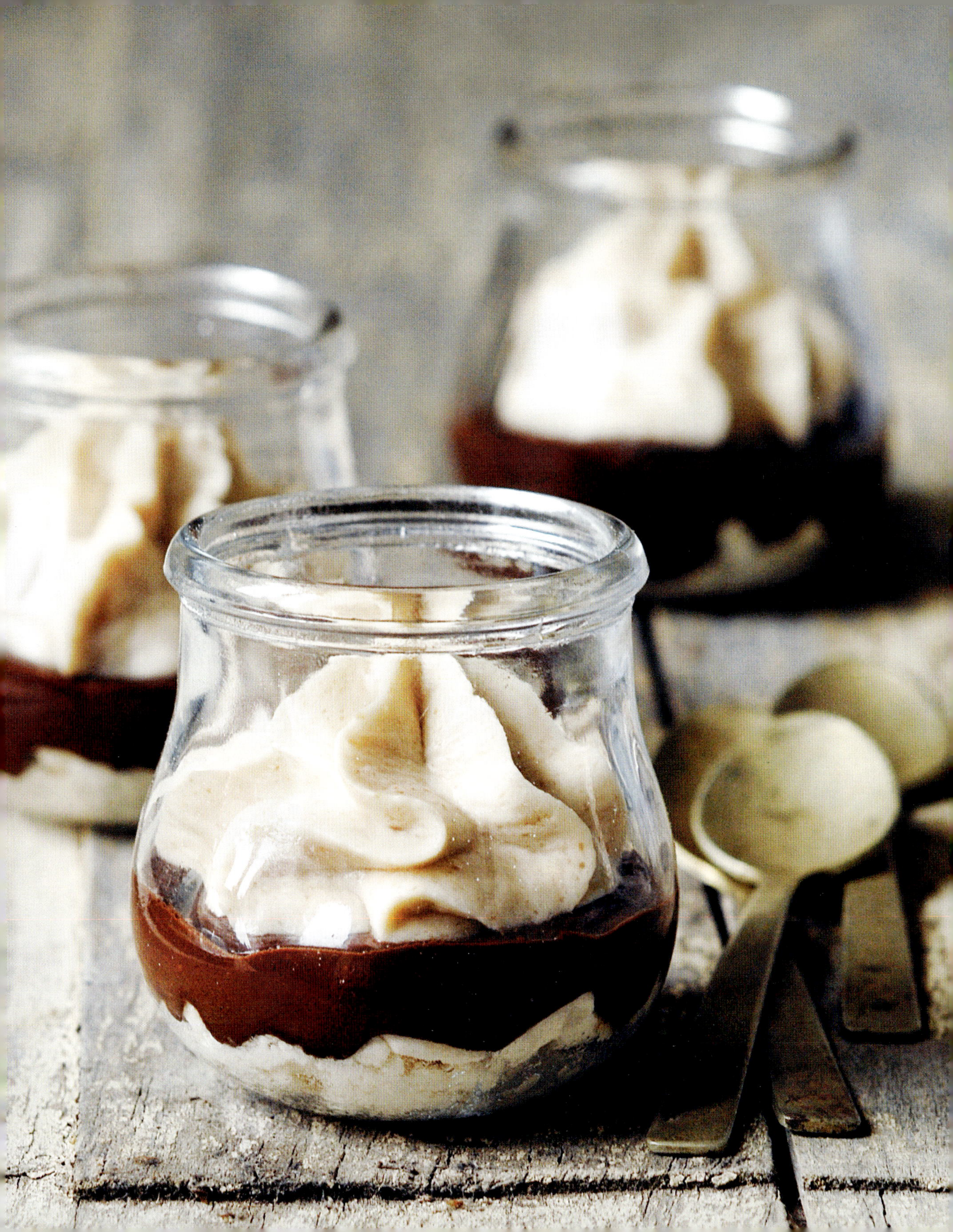

Chocolat liégeois

SERVES 6
PREP TIME: 15 mins.

- 2 pints water
- 1/2 cup sugar
- 9 oz. dark chocolate (at least 67 % cocoa solids)
- 1/2 cup cocoa powder
- 13 tbsp. crème fraîche or heavy cream
- 3 cups chocolate ice cream
- Dark chocolate shavings for decoration

Prepare the chocolate drink: bring the water to boil with the sugar. Chop up the chocolate with a large knife. Add the chopped chocolate and cocoa powder to the boiling water and whisk vigorously with a balloon whisk. Bring to a boil once more, then remove from the heat.

Put the mixture in a blender for 3 minutes, then pour into a large bowl. Allow to cool and place in the refrigerator.

Chill a bowl by placing it in the freezer for 15 minutes. Put the cream in the bowl and whisk until it thickens. Spoon into a pastry bag with a fluted tip.

To serve, take 6 tall glasses and place 2 scoops of chocolate ice cream in each. Pour in the chocolate drink. Finish with a rosette of Chantilly whipped cream. Sprinkle with chocolate shavings. Serve with straws and long ice cream spoons.

> Helpful tip

To make perfect Chantilly whipped cream, the crème fraîche or heavy cream must have been in the refrigerator for at least 2 hours before using. Stop beating the cream when it reaches the required thickness, otherwise it may turn into butter.

quick & easy

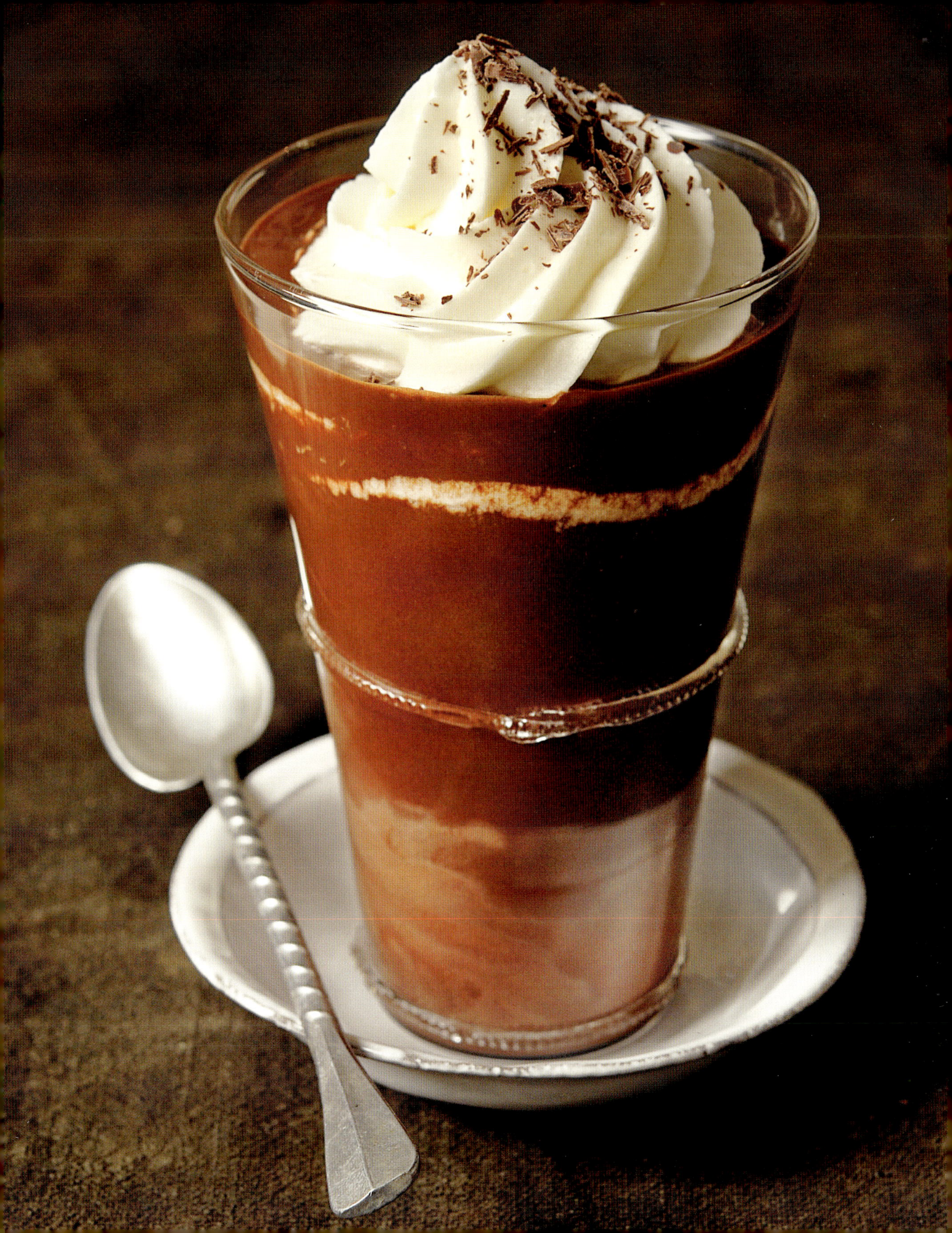

Profiteroles with ice cream and chocolate

MAKES 30 PROFITEROLES
PREP TIME: 40 mins.
COOKING TIME: 15 mins.

FOR THE CHOUX PASTRY
- 1/4 cup water
- 1/4 cup whole milk
- 1 small teaspoon salt
- 1 small teaspoon sugar
- 3-1/2 tbsp. butter
- 1/2 cup flour
- 2 whole eggs
  + 1 egg for the glaze

FOR THE CHOCOLATE SAUCE
- 1/4 lb. chocolate
- 7 tbsp. crème fraîche or heavy cream

FOR THE FILLING
- Vanilla ice cream

Prepare the choux pastry: pour the water and milk into a saucepan, add the salt, the sugar and the butter. Bring to a boil, stirring constantly. Add the flour all at once. Stir with a wooden or rubber spatula until the dough is smooth. When it stops sticking to the sides of the pan, continue to work for 2 or 3 minutes, to dry it out a little. Place in a bowl. Break in the eggs one by one, stirring constantly. Lift your spatula from time to time: when the mixture forms a smooth ribbon, it's ready.

Preheat the oven to 400° F.

Put the choux pastry into a pastry bag with a smooth tip and pipe 30 spheres of pastry the size of a walnut onto a baking sheet lined with parchment paper.

Brush the pastry balls with beaten egg. Bake for 15 minutes, opening the oven door slightly after 5 minutes.

Prepare the chocolate sauce: Finely chop the chocolate. Bring the cream to a boil in a saucepan. Pour onto the chocolate and mix well.

Cut off the top of the choux. Fill with vanilla ice cream and replace the lids. Arrange on a serving dish or in individual dishes. Pour over the warm chocolate sauce and serve immediately.

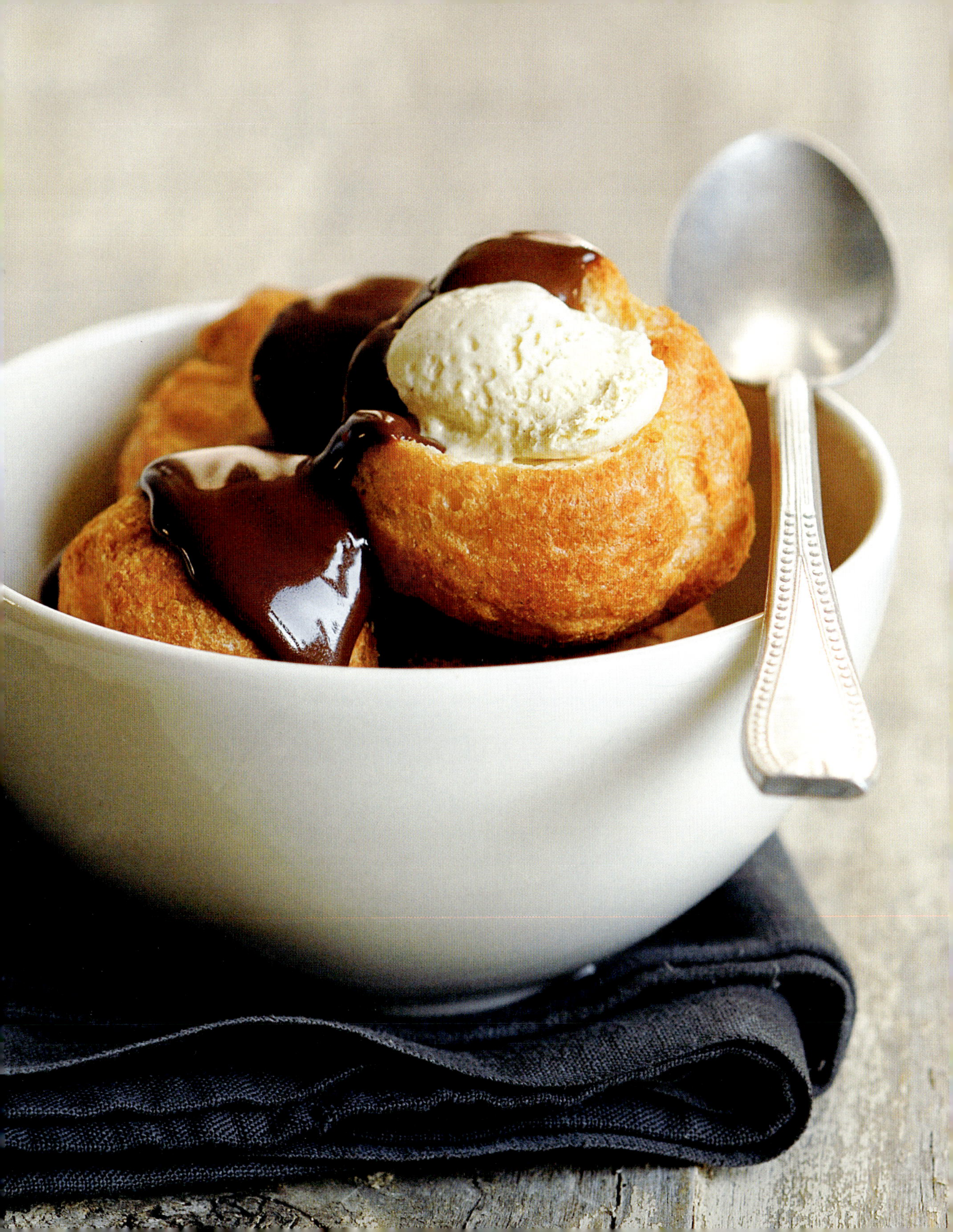

Chocolate-orange cookies

MAKES ABOUT 50 COOKIES
PREP TIME: 15 mins.
COOKING TIME: 10 to 15 mins. each batch

- 6 tbsp. butter
- 2/3 cup powdered sugar
- 1/4 organic orange
- 1 egg + 1 egg white
- 1-1/3 cups flour
- 1/2 teaspoon baking powder
- 3 oz. dark chocolate (70% cocoa solids)

Preheat the oven to 375° F.

Work the butter with a wooden or rubber spatula until soft and creamy. Mix in the sifted powdered sugar. Beat until light and frothy.

Grate the zest of the quarter orange. Mix the whole egg, the egg white and the orange zest into the mixture. Sift the flour with the baking powder and stir into the mixture.

Chop the chocolate with a serrated knife and melt in a saucepan placed in a double boiler. Pour the melted chocolate into the mixture and mix well. Spoon into a pastry bag fitted with a smooth tip.

Line a baking sheet with parchment paper. Pipe walnut-size dollops of mixture onto the paper. Bake for 10 to 15 minutes. Remove the cookies from the baking sheet and allow to cool on a wire rack.

never fails

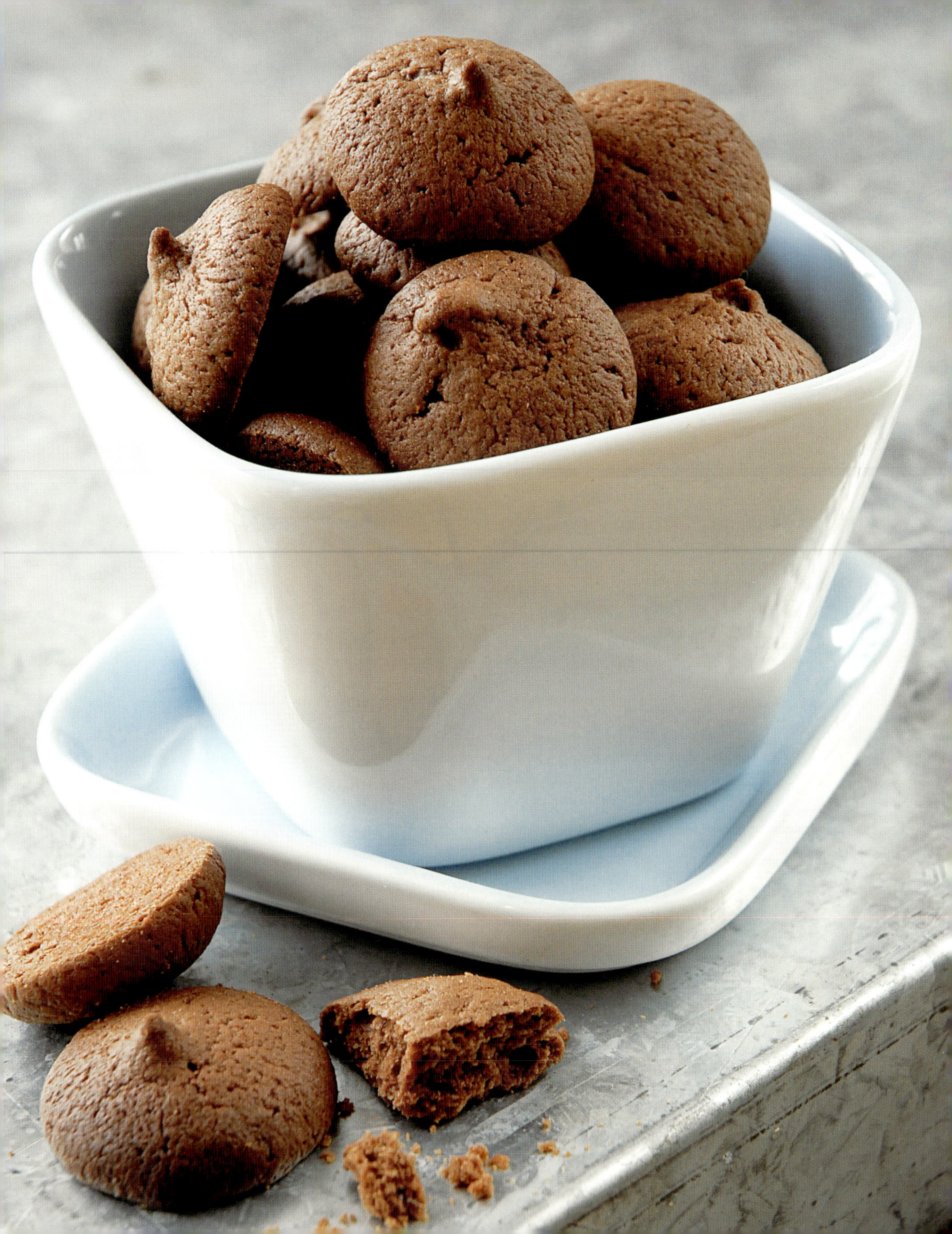

Old-fashioned hot chocolate

SERVES 4
PREP TIME: 10 mins.
COOKING TIME: 4 to 6 mins.

- 1/4 lb. dark chocolate (at least 67% cocoa solids)
- 2 cups mineral water
- 4 tbsp. sugar
- 3 tbsp. cocoa powder

Chop up the chocolate with a large knife and put it into a bowl.

Bring the water and sugar to a boil in a saucepan. Add the cocoa powder and whisk. Bring to a boil again, then remove from the heat.

Pour this mixture onto the chopped chocolate, a third at a time. Stir gently with a wooden spoon, starting in the center and working outwards in concentric circles.

Blend with a hand blender for 5 minutes.

Pour the hot chocolate into four large cups and serve right away.

quick & easy

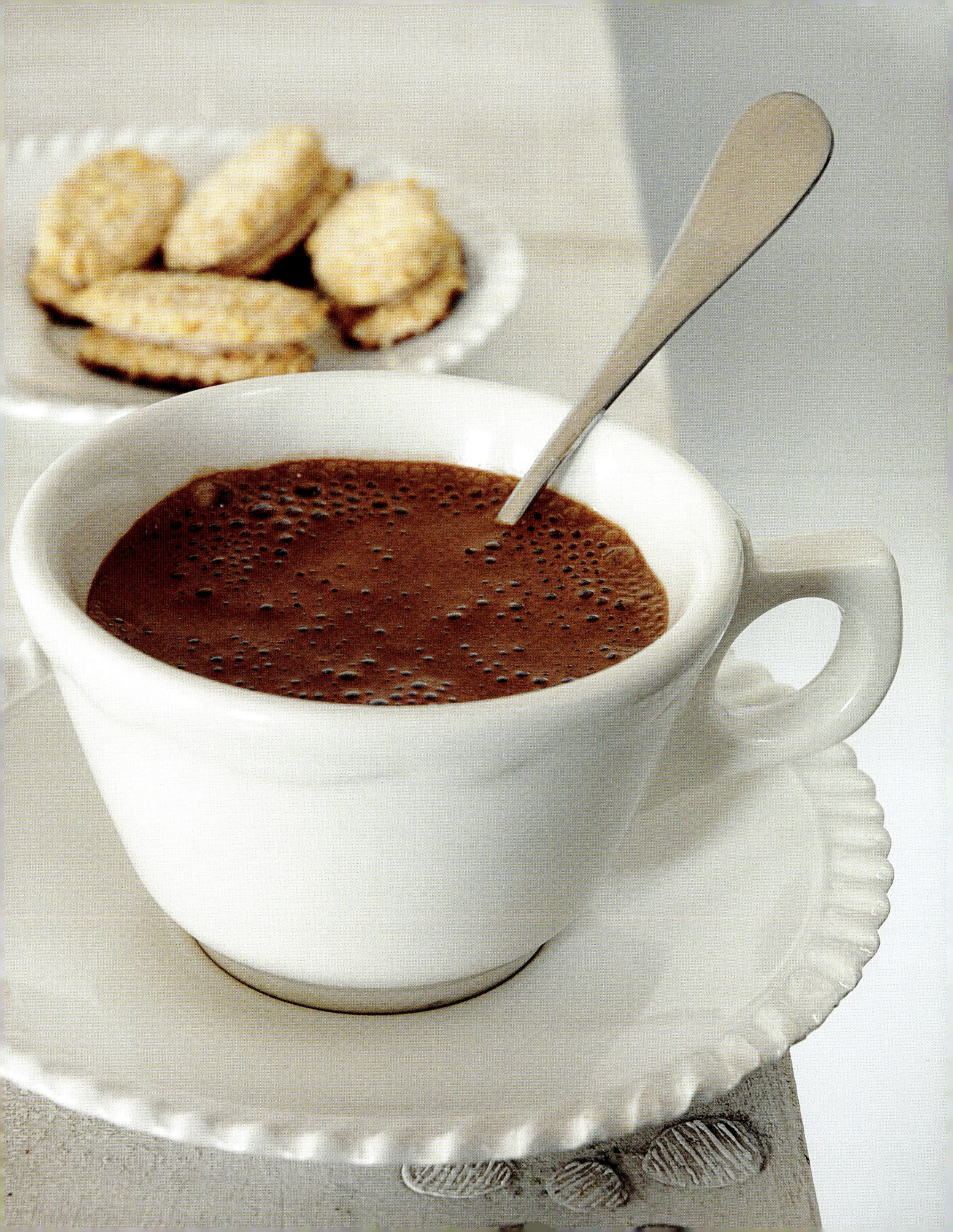

Florentines

**MAKES ABOUT
20 FLORENTINES
PREP TIME:** 10 mins.
COOKING TIME: 5 mins.
REFRIGERATION TIME: 2 hrs

- 1/4 lb. dark chocolate
- 20 toasted hazelnuts
- 20 unsalted pistachios
- 20 raisins
- A few pieces of candied orange peel

Break the chocolate into pieces and melt in a double boiler. Beat with a wooden or rubber spatula (it should remain liquid).

Spoon small rounds of chocolate onto a baking sheet lined with parchment paper. Pat with the back of the spoon.

When you've done five of these, place 1 hazelnut, 1 pistachio, 1 raisin and 1 piece of candied orange peel on each. Repeat with the rest of the chocolate and other ingredients until you've made 20. Allow to cool in a cool place (about 65° F) before removing the florentines with a spatula.

> To make a change

You can use almonds instead of pistachios, and milk chocolate instead of dark.

> Helpful tip

Your florentines will be all the more crisp and glossy if you use a thermometer: when the chocolate has melted, it should reach a temperature of about 120° F. Allow to cool to 84° F in a cold water bath, then heat again to 88° F before using.

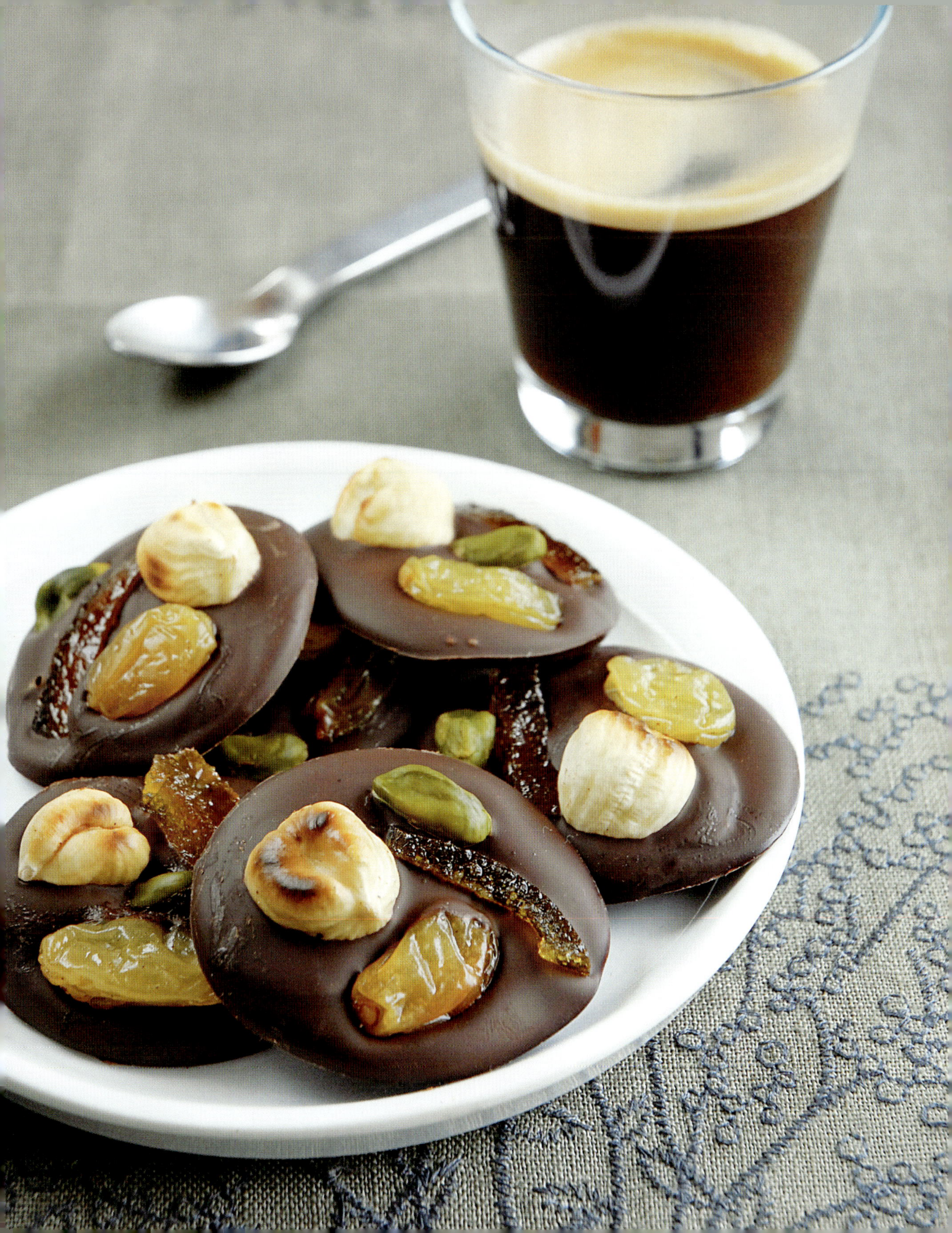

Chocolate cherries

MAKES 30 CHERRIES
PREP TIME: 15 mins.
SOAKING: 15 days

- 30 firm cherries
- 7 oz. cognac
- 9 oz. dark chocolate (70 % cocoa solids)

Choose only the very best cherries. Leave the stems on. Rinse them in fresh water, dry them carefully and put them in a tall container. Add the cognac, cover with plastic wrap and leave to soak in the refrigerator for 15 days.

Drain the cherries, spread them out on a thick pad of paper towels, and allow them to dry completely.

Cut the chocolate into small pieces or grate it. Place in a saucepan and melt over a very low heat or in a double boiler, stirring constantly.

Take the cherries one by one and, holding them by their stems, dip them quickly into the melted chocolate. Place them on a wire rack or a tray covered with parchment paper or plastic wrap and leave them to dry. Repeat the operation if you want thicker chocolate on your cherries.

Put the cherries in pleated paper candy cups and arrange them on a serving dish or store them in an airtight box (they will keep for several days).

> Find out more
In France, fruit prepared in this way is called "fruits déguisés" or "fruit in disguise." You can use bottled cherries in brandy instead of fresh ones, or if you prefer you can leave out the brandy altogether.

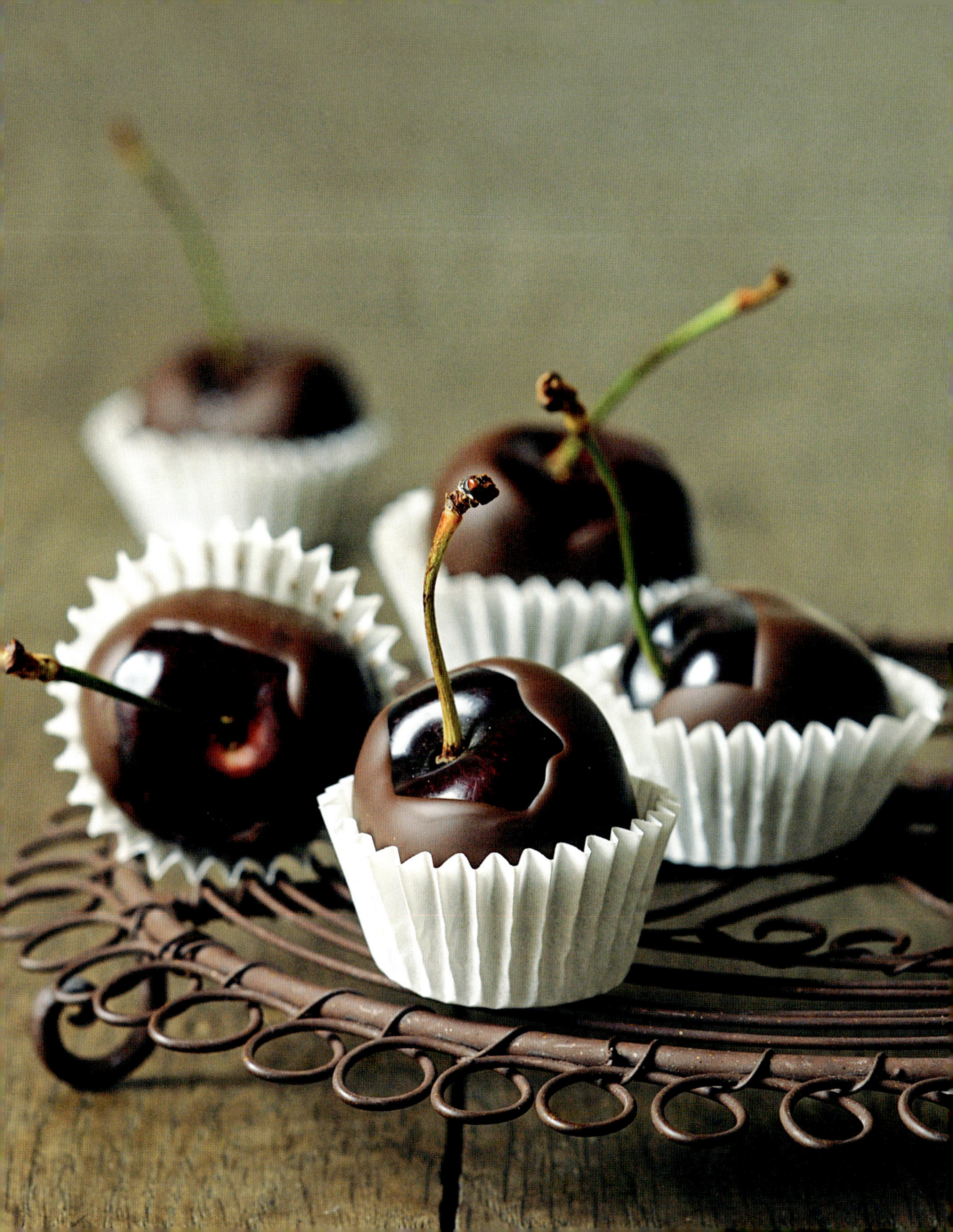

Chocolate caramels

MAKES 50 TO 60 CARAMELS
PREP TIME: 10 mins.
COOKING TIME: 10 to 12 mins.

- 2-1/4 cups sugar
- 3/4 cup crème fraîche or heavy cream
- 2 tbsp. honey
- 1/2 cup cocoa powder
- Peanut oil

Prepare the caramel: in a saucepan, mix the sugar, the crème fraîche or heavy cream, the honey and the cocoa. Heat, stirring constantly with a wooden spoon, until the caramel turns a deep amber color.

Lay the collar from a 10-inch springform cake pan on a piece of lightly oiled parchment paper. Pour in the caramel and allow to cool.

Remove the ring and cut the caramel into squares. Wrap in plastic wrap and place in an airtight container.

> To make a change
Make soft coffee caramels: follow the same procedure with 2-1/4 cups sugar, 3/4 cup fraîche or heavy cream, 2 tbsp. coffee extract and 12 drops of lemon juice.

never fails

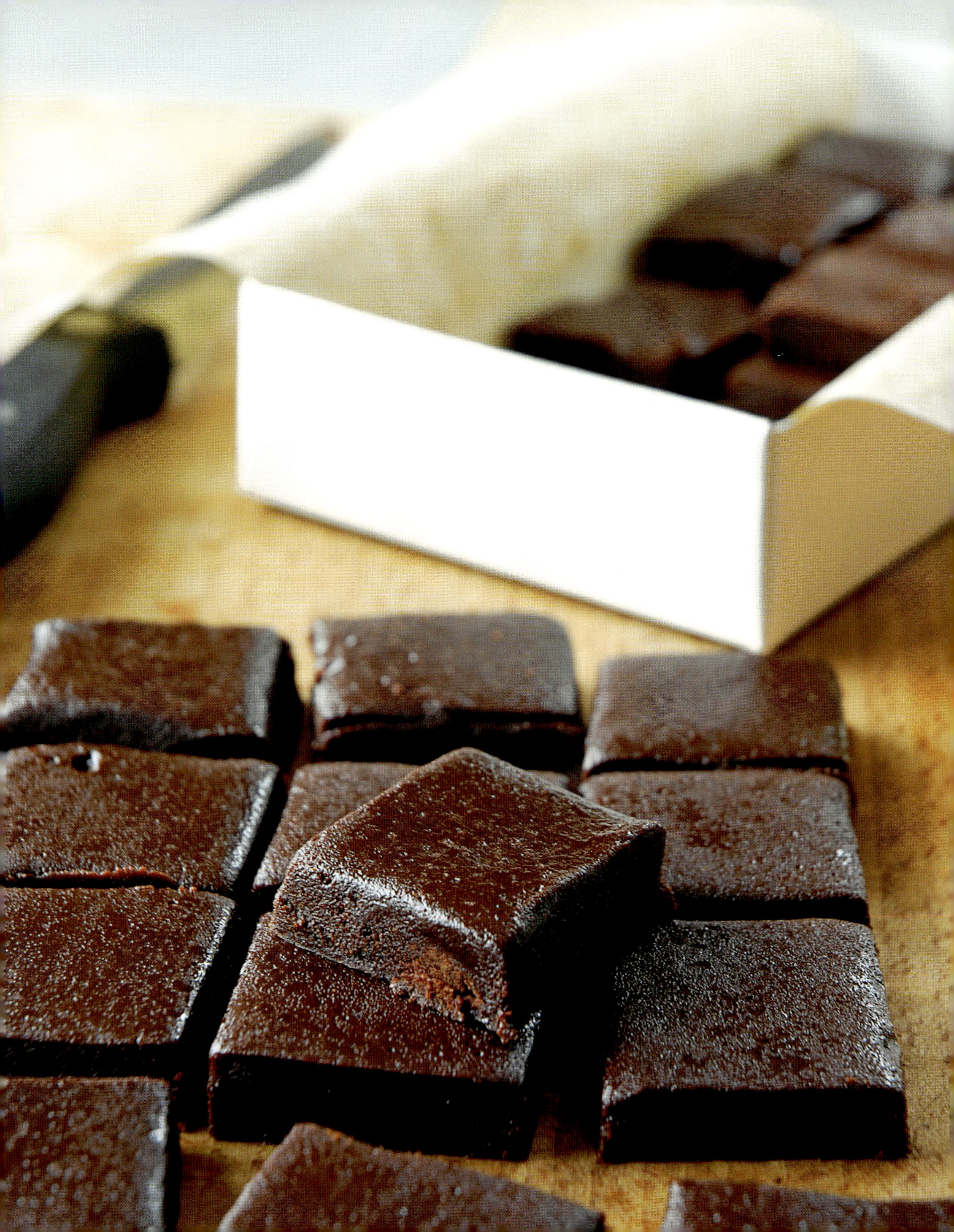

Chocolate truffles

MAKES ABOUT 20 TRUFFLES
PREP TIME: 30 mins.
REFRIGERATION TIME: 2 hrs
COOKING TIME: About 3 mins.

- 11 oz. dark chocolate
- 1 tbsp. milk
- 7 tbsp. butter
- 2 egg yolks
- 4 tbsp. crème fraîche or heavy cream
- 1 cup powdered sugar
- 1 tbsp. of rum or other alcohol (optional)
- 2 cups cocoa powder

Break the chocolate into pieces and heat in a double boiler with the milk, stirring until smooth.

Cut the butter into small pieces and gradually add them to the chocolate. Add the egg yolks one by one, then the cream and the powdered sugar. Add a dash of rum or cognac (optional). Whisk for 5 minutes.

Pour the mixture onto a baking sheet covered with parchment paper and place in the refrigerator for 2 hours.

Spread the cocoa powder over a baking sheet or large dish. Cut the chocolate mixture into small squares. Dip the palms of your hands in cocoa powder and roll the chocolate into a ball. Place the chocolate balls in the cocoa powder as you make them. Work as quickly as possible to avoid softening the truffles.

When the truffles are all made, remove from the cocoa powder and place in a serving dish. Keep in a cool place (but not in the refrigerator) until ready to serve.

> Helpful tip
You can also place your truffles in pleated paper cups.

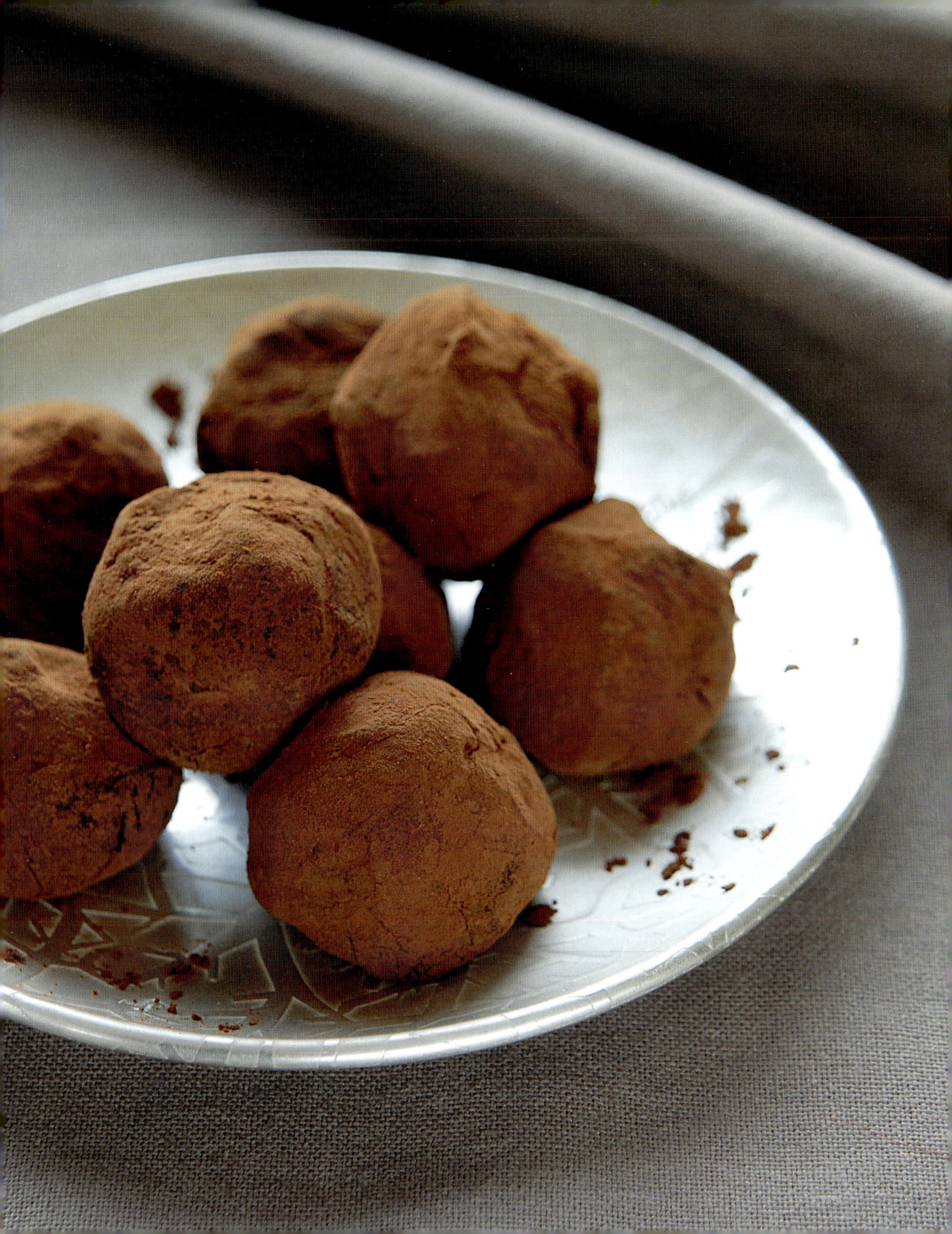

Chocolate fondue

SERVES 4 TO 6
PREP TIME: 20 mins.
COOKING TIME: 5 to 10 mins.

FOR THE FONDUE
- 3/4 lb. dark chocolate
- 2/3 cup crème fraîche or heavy cream
- 2 tbsp. rum (optional)

FOR DIPPING
- 3 pears
- 3 bananas
- The juice of 1/2 a lemon
- Strawberries
- 1 pineapple (or 3 slices of canned pineapple)
- Lady fingers
- 1 sponge cake

Prepare the fondue: grate the chocolate or break it into small pieces. Place in a saucepan. Add the crème fraiche and heat very gently for 5 to 10 minutes, stirring with a wooden spatula until you have a smooth cream. Add the rum if using and stir well.

Prepare the dipping ingredients: peel the pears and bananas, cut into large cubes, put them in a bowl and sprinkle with lemon juice to prevent them from discoloring. Quickly wash the strawberries, hull them and dry them with paper towels. If using fresh pineapple, peel it and remove the tough core. Cut into large cubes.

Share the fruit between several individual serving dishes.

Cut the lady fingers and sponge cake into bite-size pieces and put them in a dish.

Place your fondue heater in the center of the table and set it to its lowest setting (you can also use a small saucepan, heating it from time to time when the chocolate sauce starts to harden). Pour the very hot chocolate sauce into the fondue pot and keep it hot. Turn off the fondue heater from time to time to prevent the chocolate from coagulating.

Arrange the dishes of fruit and cake around the pot of sauce. Guests use their forks to dip ingredients into the chocolate sauce.

child's play

138 • OH CHOCOLATE!

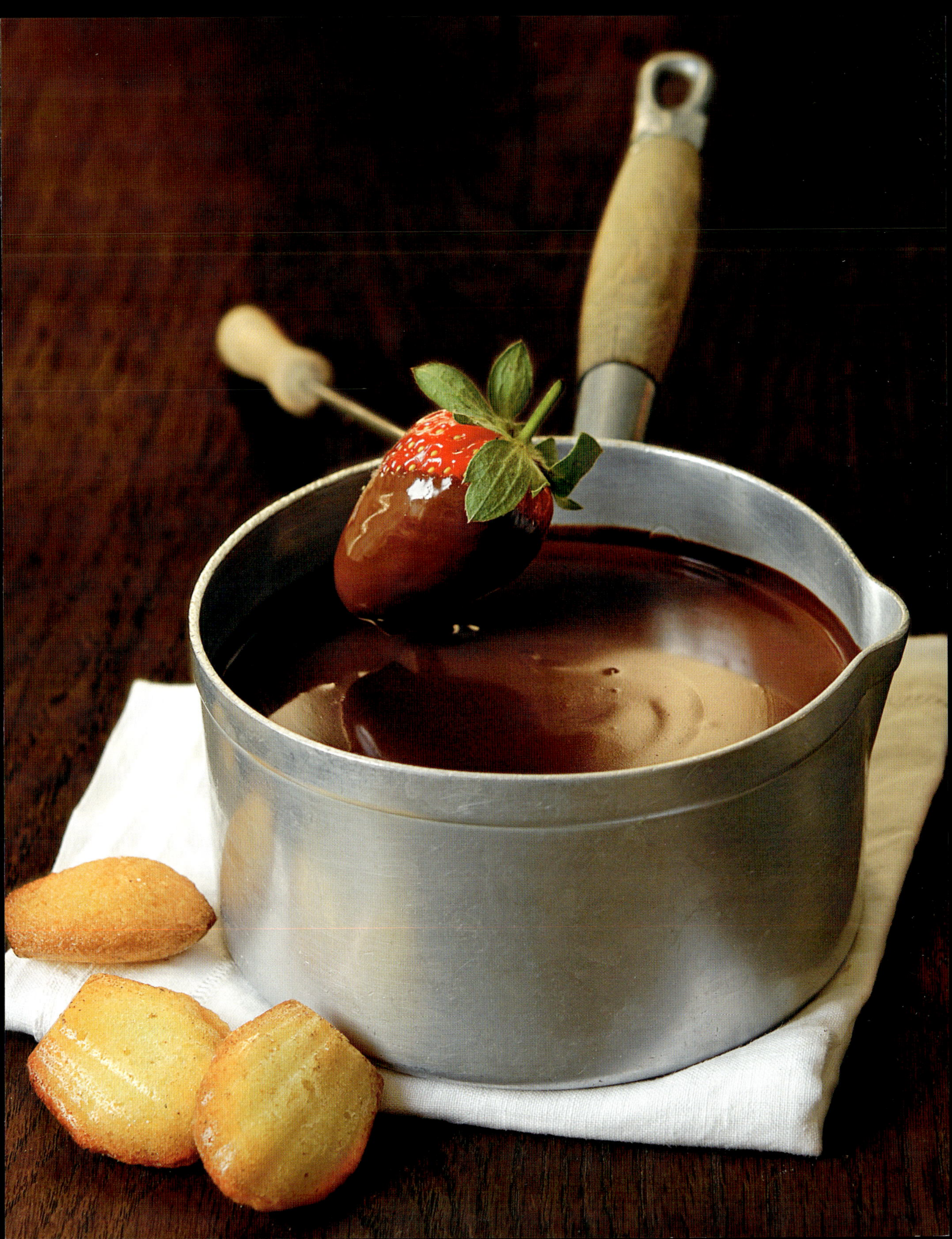

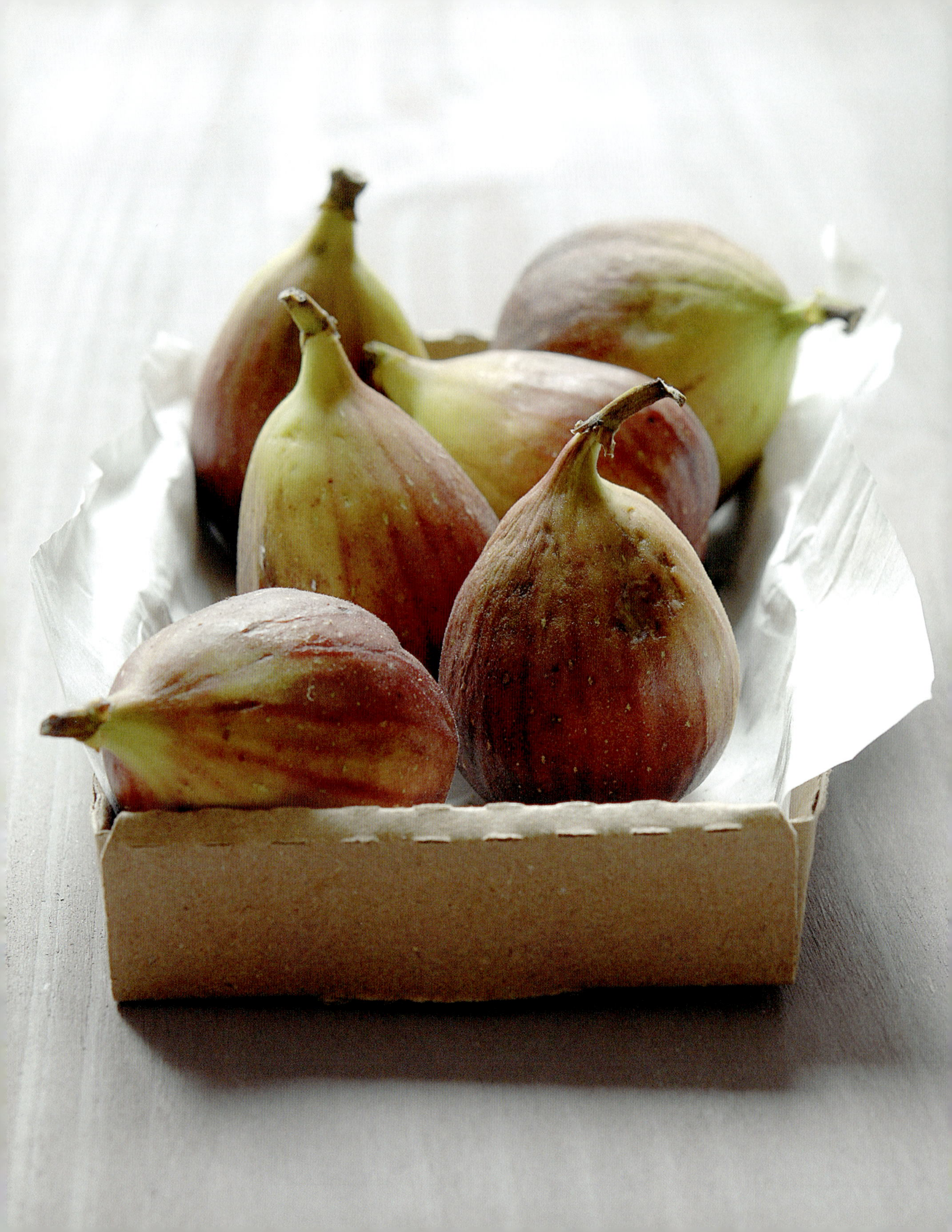

Fancy fruit

Strawberry tartlets 142
Rhubarb pie.. 144
Apple pie... 146
Tarte Tatin.. 146
Kiwi pie.. 148
Bourdaloue pie 150
Raspberry boats... 152
Lemon meringue pie................................. 154
Apricot and rosemary
   brioche pie 156
Fig tartlets.. 158
Mini mango
   and coconut pies................................... 160
Apple strudel 162
Pineapple upside down cake 164
Blueberry crumble 166

Apricot and almond gratin 168
Peach parcels
   with orange caramel 170
Apricot parcels with lavender 172
Banana phyllo parcels
   with orange sauce................................ 174
Strawberry charlotte 176
Lime mousse 178
Lemon curd.. 180
Panna cotta with coconut
   milk and berries..................................... 182
Banana-cinnamon mousse 184
Mirabelle plums with lemon 186
Baked spiced bananas............................. 188
Baked figs with tarragon 190
Broiled caramelized grapefruit 192

Strawberry tartlets

6 TARTLETS
PREP TIME: 30 mins.
RESTING TIME: 30 mins.
SOAKING TIME: 1 hr
COOKING TIME: 10 mins.

FOR THE SHORTBREAD
- 1 vanilla bean
- 4 tbsp. sugar
- 1 cup flour
- 3 tbsp. softened butter + some for the pans
- 1 egg

FOR THE FILLING
- 1 pint strawberries
- 4 tbsp. sugar
- 9 tbsp. butter

FOR DECORATION
- 6 fresh mint leaves

Prepare the shortbread: split the vanilla bean in two and scrape out the seeds. In a bowl, mix the vanilla seeds with the sugar. Sift the flour onto your work surface. Cut the butter into small pieces and add to the flour. Rub in with your fingertips until the mixture has the consistency of fine breadcrumbs. Make a well in the center and break the egg into it. Add the vanilla sugar and mix everything together with your fingertips. Don't overwork the mixture. Press the dough with the heel of your hand, then make it into a ball, wrap in plastic wrap and allow to rest for at least 30 minutes.

Quickly rinse the strawberries, hull them and cut them in two. Put half in a bowl with the sugar and let them soak for about 1 hour. Put the other half to drain on some paper towels.

Preheat the oven to 350° F.

With a cookie cutter or small bowl, cut out six disks of dough and use them to line six buttered tartlet pans. Prick each with a fork. Cut out six circles of parchment paper and place them on top of the dough. Add some dried beans to stop the dough from rising during baking. Bake for 10 minutes.

Prepare the filling: put the butter into a bowl and soften it by working it with a fork or a whisk. Drain the soaked strawberries, rub them through a sieve and add them to the butter. Mix to a smooth cream.

When the pastry shells are cool, carefully remove them and fill with strawberry cream. Put the fresh strawberries on top and decorate with mint. Serve cold.

142 • FANCY FRUIT

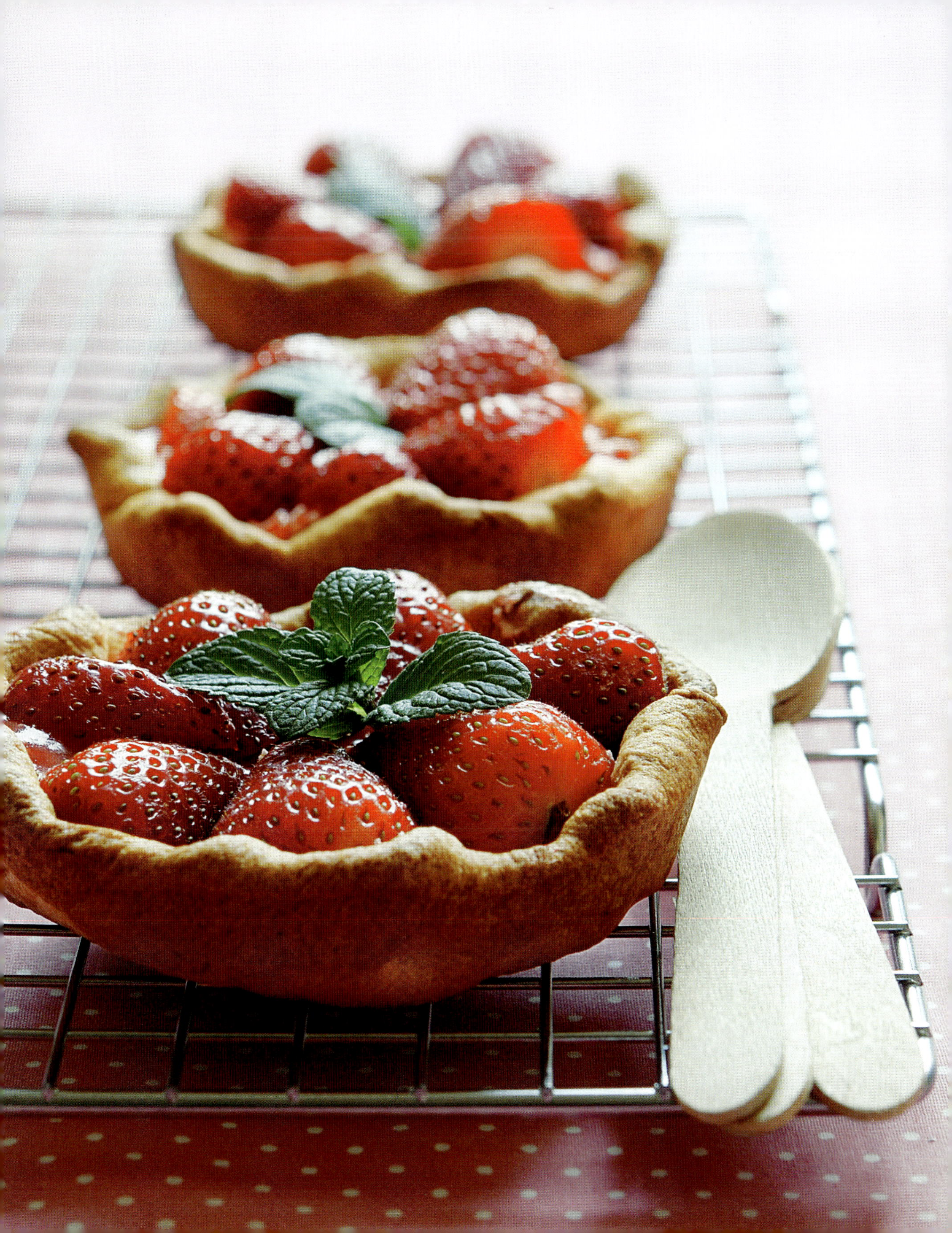

Rhubarb pie

SERVES 6 TO 8
PREP TIME: 30 mins.
SOAKING TIME: 8 hrs
RESTING TIME: 30 mins.
STRAINING TIME: 30 mins.
COOKING TIME: 30 mins.

- 5 tbsp. sugar

FOR THE RHUBARB
- 1-1/4 lbs. rhubarb
- 5 tbsp. sugar

FOR THE SHORTCRUST PASTRY
- 7 tbsp. softened butter
- 1-1/4 cups sifted flour
- A pinch of salt
- 2 tbsp. sugar

FOR THE CUSTARD
- 1 egg
- 6 tbsp. sugar
- 2-1/2 tbsp. milk
- 2-1/2 tbsp. crème fraîche or heavy cream
- 1/4 cup ground almonds
- 1/4 cup chilled butter

The day before, wash the rhubarb and cut into one-inch lengths. Place in a large bowl and sprinkle with sugar. Cover and allow to soak for at least 8 hours.

The following day, prepare the shortcrust pastry: cut the butter into very small pieces. Put the flour in a bowl and make a well in the center. Add the salt, the sugar, and then the butter. Quickly rub in the ingredients with your fingertips. Add some water to form a dough, and knead until supple (it should be neither too soft nor too sticky). Flour a work surface and place the dough on it. Flatten it with the heel of your hand but avoid kneading it at this stage. Make it into a ball, wrap in plastic wrap and leave to rest for at least 30 minutes.

Put the rhubarb in a large sieve and allow to strain for 30 minutes. Preheat the oven to 350° F.

Use the dough to line a non-stick 10-inch pie dish. Prick the dough all over with a fork. Cover with parchment paper and add a layer of baking beans. Bake for 15 minutes.

Prepare the custard: beat the egg and the sugar in a bowl, add the milk, the cream, the ground almonds and the butter. Mix well.

Remove the parchment paper and baking beans from the pie base. Arrange the rhubarb on the pie crust, pour over the custard and bake for about 15 minutes. Sprinkle liberally with sugar and serve cold or warm.

> Serving advice

This pie is delicious with strawberry coulis. You can also add a layer of Italian meringue (see p.417) and bake for 5 minutes until golden.

> To make a change

Instead of rhubarb you can use 1-1/2 lbs. blueberries or 1-1/4 lbs. mirabelle plums. Another variation is "old-fashioned" rhubarb pie: after baking for 15 minutes, cover the pie with crumble (9 tbsp. butter cut into small pieces rubbed in with 2/3 cup sugar, a pinch of salt, 1 cup flour and 1-1/4 cups ground almonds) and bake for another 20 minutes. Serve cold.

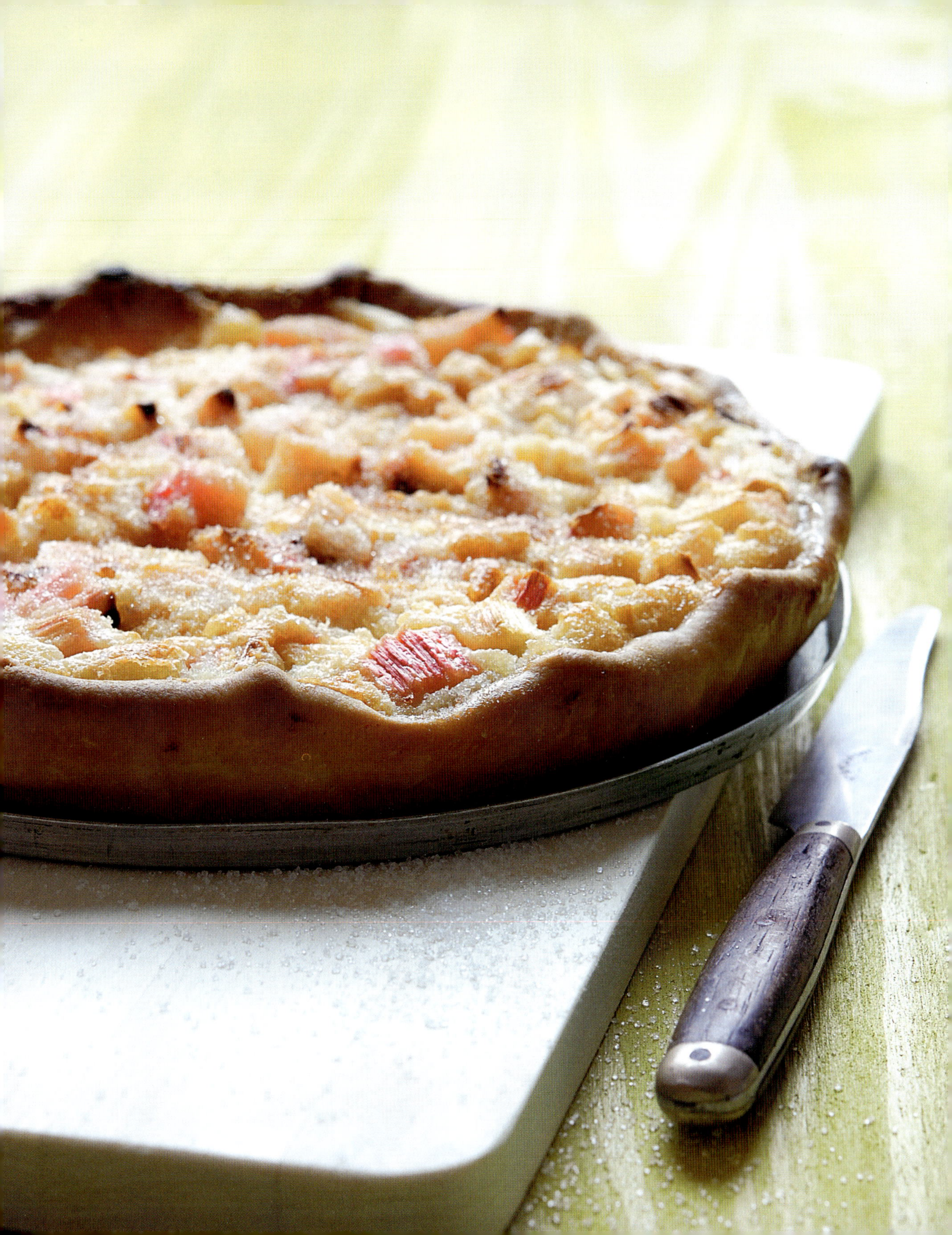

Apple pie

SERVES 6 TO 8
PREP TIME: 30 mins.
COOKING TIME: 50 mins.

- 1-3/4 lbs. apples
- The juice of one lemon
- 1 egg

FOR THE PIE CRUST
- 14 tbsp. softened butter
- 2-1/2 cups sifted flour
- A pinch of salt
- 4 tbsp. sugar

FOR THE SPICED SUGAR
- 1/3 cup flour
- 2-1/2 tbsp. brown sugar
- 1/2 tsp. of vanilla extract
- 1/2 teaspoon cinnamon
- A pinch of grated nutmeg

Prepare 1 lb. shortcrust pastry (see p.399); allow to rest for 30 minutes. Divide the dough into two pieces equivalent to two thirds and one third. Roll to a thickness of about 1/8 inch. Use the larger piece to line a 9-inch pie dish.

Prepare the spiced sugar: in a bowl, mix together the flour, brown sugar, vanilla, cinnamon and nutmeg. Place half of this mixture in the pie dish.

Preheat the oven to 400° F. Peel and slice the apples. Lay them in the dish in overlapping circles, adding more as you move inwards so that they form a dome in the center. Sprinkle with lemon juice, then cover with the remaining flour/brown sugar mixture.

Lay the smaller dough disk on top. Brush the edges with beaten egg and pinch them together to seal the pie. Make a chimney and glaze the top of the pie. Bake for 10 minutes. Remove from the oven, brush again with beaten egg and bake for 40 minutes longer.

Serve warm with cream, vanilla ice cream or blackberry coulis.

> To make a change
If you like apples, why not try our delicious recipe for English apple crumble.

Tarte Tatin (upside-down apple pie)

SERVES 6
PREP TIME: 40 mins.
RESTING TIME: 30 mins.
COOKING TIME: 30 mins.

FOR THE SHORTCRUST PASTRY
- 7 tbsp. butter
- 1-2/3 cups flour
- 1 generous pinch of salt
- 2 tbsp. sugar

FOR THE FILLING
- 1 lb. sweet, firm apples
- 1/3 cup butter
- 1-1/3 cups sugar
- 2/3 cup crème fraîche or heavy cream

Prepare the shortcrust pastry (see p.399) and allow to rest for 30 minutes.

Prepare the filling: peel the apples and cut into slices. Cut the butter into pieces. Butter a 9-inch metal pie dish and sprinkle liberally with 6 tbsp. sugar. Arrange the apples on top and sprinkle with the rest of the sugar. Distribute the butter evenly on top.

Preheat the oven to 350° F. Flatten the shortcrust pastry with your hand, then roll out to a thickness of about 1/8 inch. Cut out a disk that is 2 inches larger in diameter than the pie dish.

Lay the disk over the apples, carefully tucking the edges inside the dish. Caramelize the apples by placing the dish directly on high heat for three minutes. Place in the oven and bake for 30 minutes.

Remove from the oven, lay a plate over the pie dish and invert. Remove the dish and allow the pie to cool.

Serve with cream.

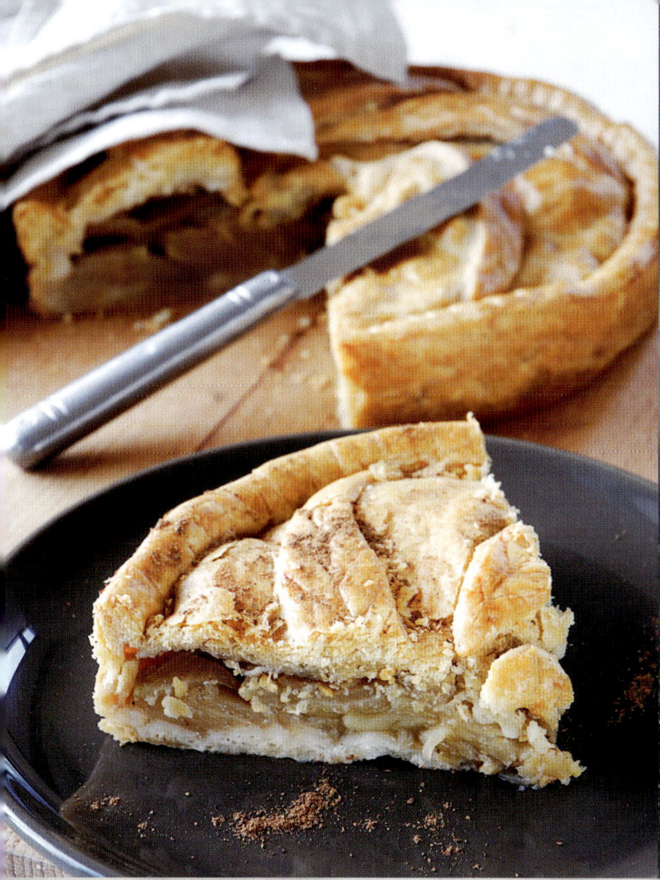
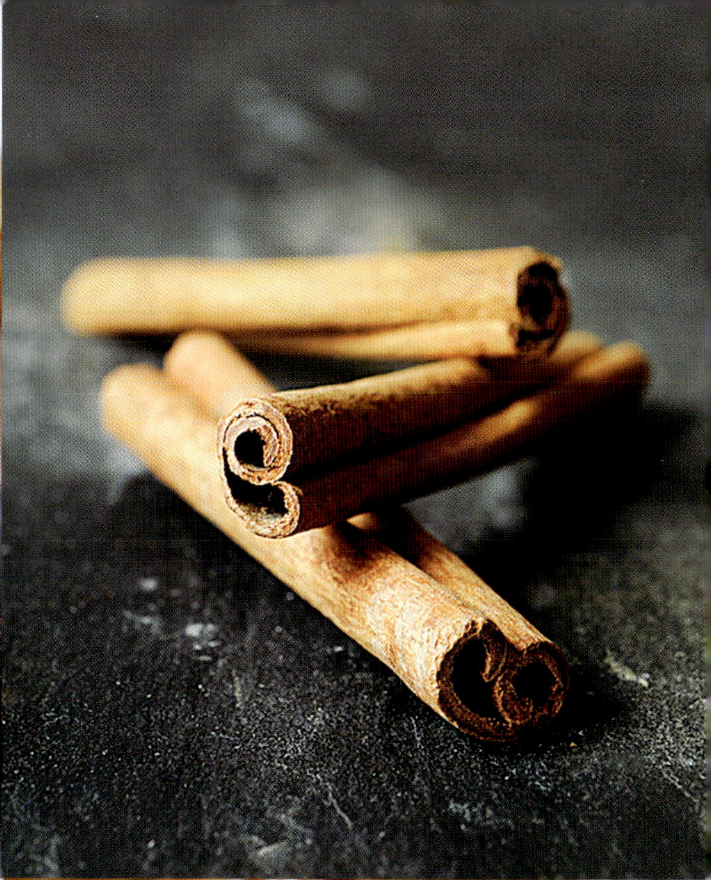
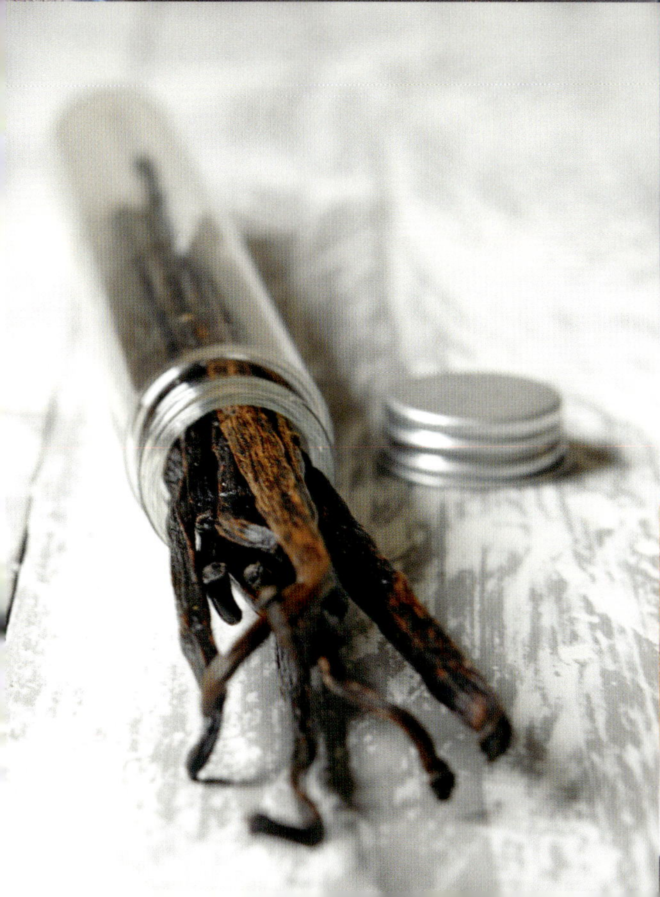
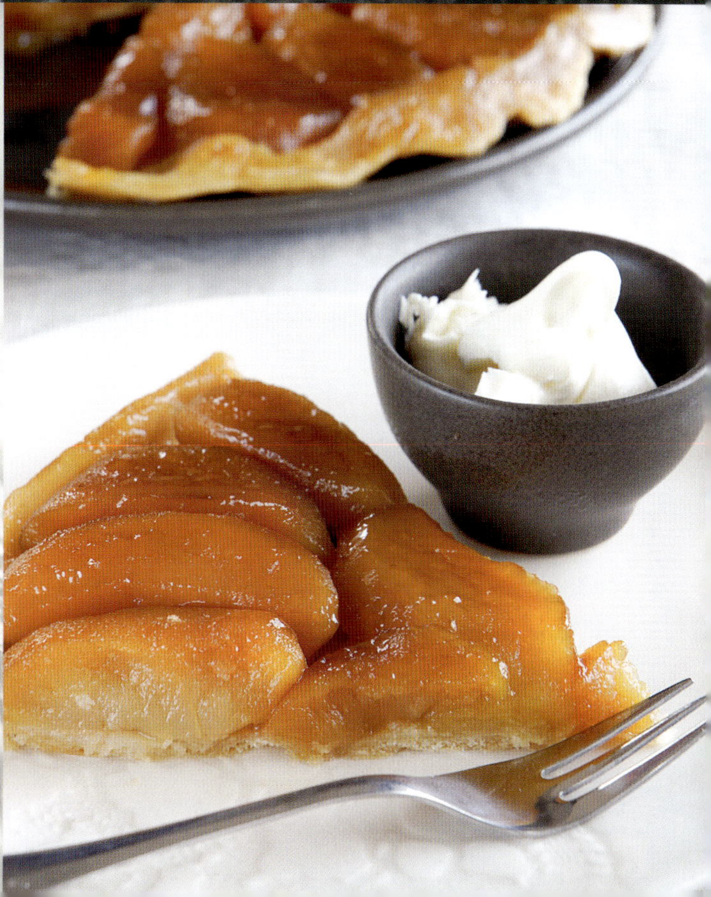

Kiwi pie

SERVES 4 TO 6
PREP TIME: 20 mins.
RESTING TIME: 30 mins.
COOKING TIME: 20 mins.

- 5 or 6 kiwis

FOR THE PIE CRUST
- 7 tbsp. softened butter
- 1-1/4 cups sifted flour
- A pinch of salt
- 2 tbsp. sugar
- 5 tbsp. cold water

FOR THE CUSTARD
- 2 egg yolks
- 6 tbsp. sugar
- 1 teaspoon flour
- 1 cup milk
- 1 tbsp. red currant jelly

Prepare the pie crust: cut the butter into very small pieces. Put the flour in a bowl and make a well in the center. Add the salt, the sugar and the butter. Quickly rub in the ingredients with your fingertips. Add some water to form a dough. Knead until supple (it should be neither too sticky, nor too soft). Dust your work surface with flour, lay the dough on it and flatten it with the heel of your hand (do not knead at this stage). Shape the dough into a ball, wrap in plastic wrap and allow to rest for at least 30 minutes.

Preheat the oven to 400° F.

Roll out the dough to a thickness of 1/8 inch and use it to line a buttered 10-inch pie dish. Prick with a fork, cover with parchment paper and fill with baking beans. Bake for 20 minutes.

Meanwhile, prepare the custard: in a saucepan, mix the egg yolks, the sugar, the flour and the milk. Cook over a gentle heat, stirring constantly until the mixture coats the back of the spoon. Remove from the heat and stir in the red currant jelly.

Remove the pie base from the oven and remove the beans and paper. Allow to cool and pour in the custard.

Peel the kiwis and slice them thinly. Arrange the slices on top of the custard, overlapping them slightly. Chill in the refrigerator until needed.

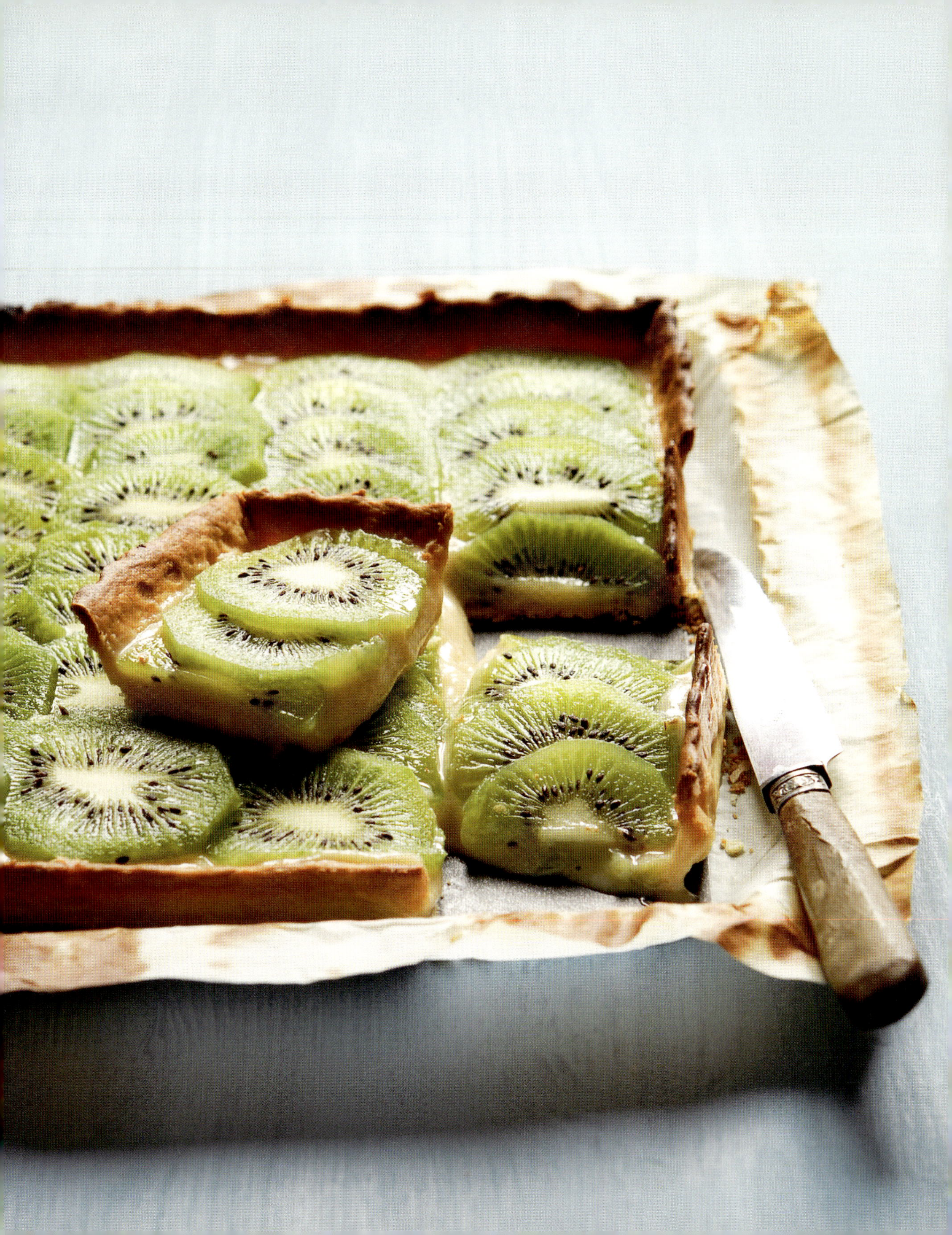

Bourdaloue pie

SERVES 4 TO 6
PREP TIME: 30 mins.
RESTING TIME: 30 mins.
COOKING TIME: 30 mins.

- 10 to 12 canned pear halves

FOR THE PIE CRUST
- 7 tbsp. softened butter
- 1-1/4 cups sifted flour
- A pinch of salt
- 2 tbsp. sugar
- 5 tbsp. cold water

FOR THE ALMOND CREAM
- 1/4 cup butter
- 1 small egg
- 5 tbsp. sugar
- 7/8 cup ground almonds

Prepare the pie crust: cut the butter into very small pieces. Put the flour in a bowl and make a well in the center. Add the salt, the sugar and the butter. Quickly rub in the ingredients with your fingertips. Add some water to form a dough. Knead until supple (it should be neither too sticky, nor too soft). Dust your work surface with flour, lay the dough on it and flatten it with the heel of your hand (do not knead at this stage). Shape the dough into a ball, wrap in plastic wrap and allow to rest for at least 30 minutes.

Cut the butter for the almond cream into pieces and allow to soften at room temperature.

Drain the pears and cut lengthwise into thin slices.

Preheat the oven to 375° F.

Prepare the almond cream: break the egg into a bowl, add the butter and sugar and beat by hand until you obtain a smooth cream. Beat in the ground almonds.

Roll out the dough and place in a 9-inch pie dish lined with parchment paper. Pour in the almond cream. Arrange the pear slices on top. Bake for 30 minutes. Allow to cool slightly before turning out. Serve cold.

never fails

FANCY FRUIT

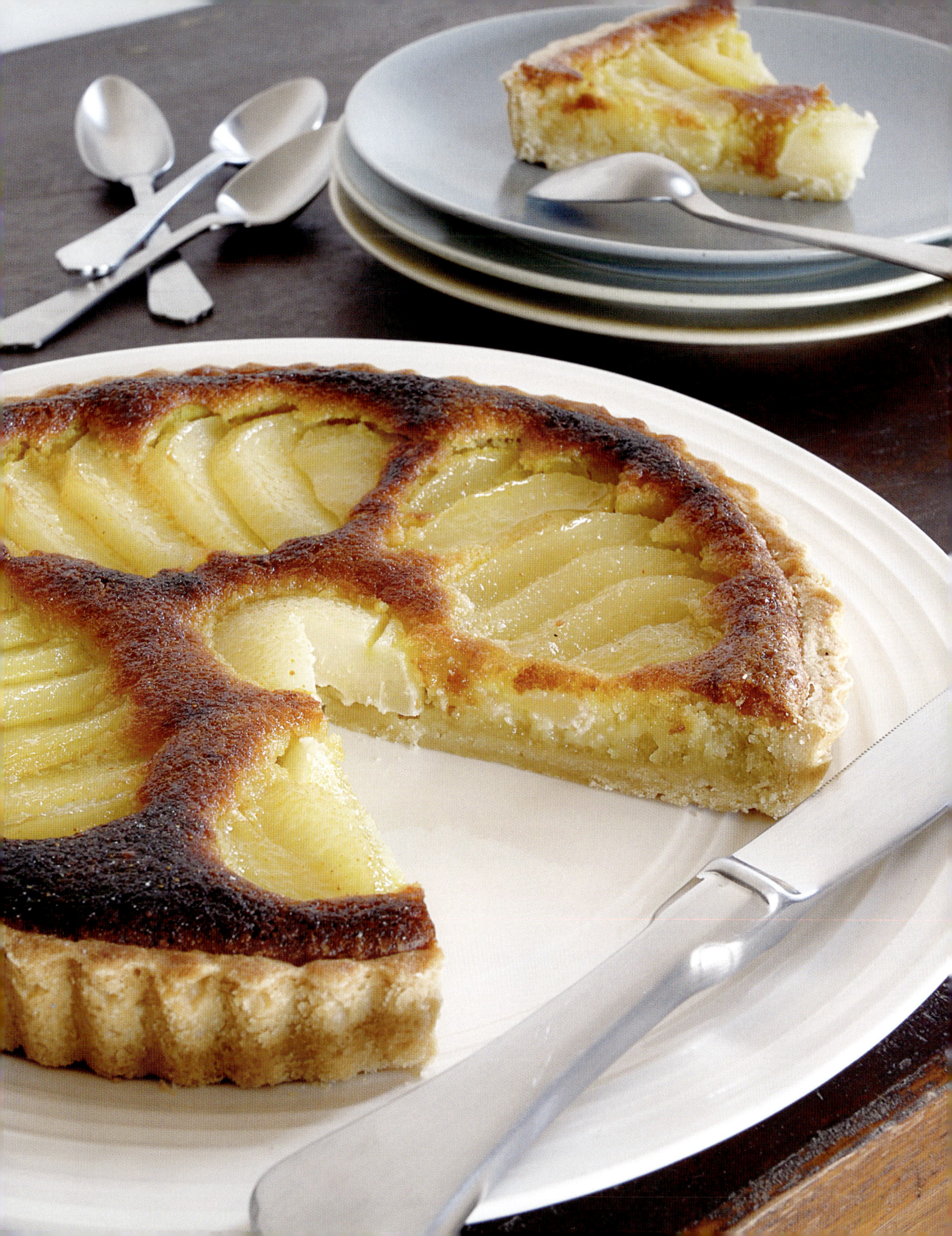

Raspberry boats

10 BOATS
PREP TIME: 15 mins.
RESTING TIME: 30 mins.
COOKING TIME: 15 mins.

- 1/2 lb. raspberries
- 5 tbsp. red currant (or raspberry) jelly

FOR THE PIE CRUST
- 7 tbsp. butter
 + some for the molds
- 1-1/5 cups sifted flour
- A pinch of salt
- 2 tbsp. sugar
- 5 tbsp. cold water

FOR THE PASTRY CREAM
- 3 egg yolks
- 3 tbsp. sugar
- 3 tbsp. flour
- 1 cup milk

Prepare the shortcrust pastry. Cut the butter into very small pieces. Put the flour into a bowl and make a well in the center. Add the salt, the sugar, and the pieces of butter. Quickly rub the ingredients together with your fingertips until they have the consistency of fine breadcrumbs. Add a few drops of water and knead the mixture into a soft dough. Add water if too firm; dust with flour if too sticky. Place the dough on a floured work surface and flatten it with the heel of your hand (avoid kneading it too much). Now make it into a ball, wrap it in plastic wrap and let it rest for at least 30 minutes.

Preheat the oven to 350° F.

Divide the dough into ten pieces and use it to line ten 4-inch boat molds, prick the dough with a fork and bake for 15 minutes.

Turn out the pastry boats and allow them to cool.

Prepare the pastry cream: put the egg yolks and sugar in a bowl and beat them together until the mixture turns pale yellow. Add the flour and mix it in quickly (don't overwork the mixture). While you're doing this, boil the milk. Pour the boiling milk into the mixture, stirring constantly with a wooden spoon until it's smooth and creamy. Pour into a heavy saucepan. Heat very gently and stir until the mixture thickens. As soon as the mixture begins to boil, remove from the heat and pour into a bowl.

Use a teaspoon to fill the pastry boats with pastry cream. Reserve any that is left over to use in other recipes.

Rinse the raspberries and pick through them. Arrange them on top of the custard in the boats.

In a small saucepan, warm the red currant (or raspberry) jelly and gently brush over the raspberries with a pastry brush. Serve chilled.

152 • FANCY FRUIT

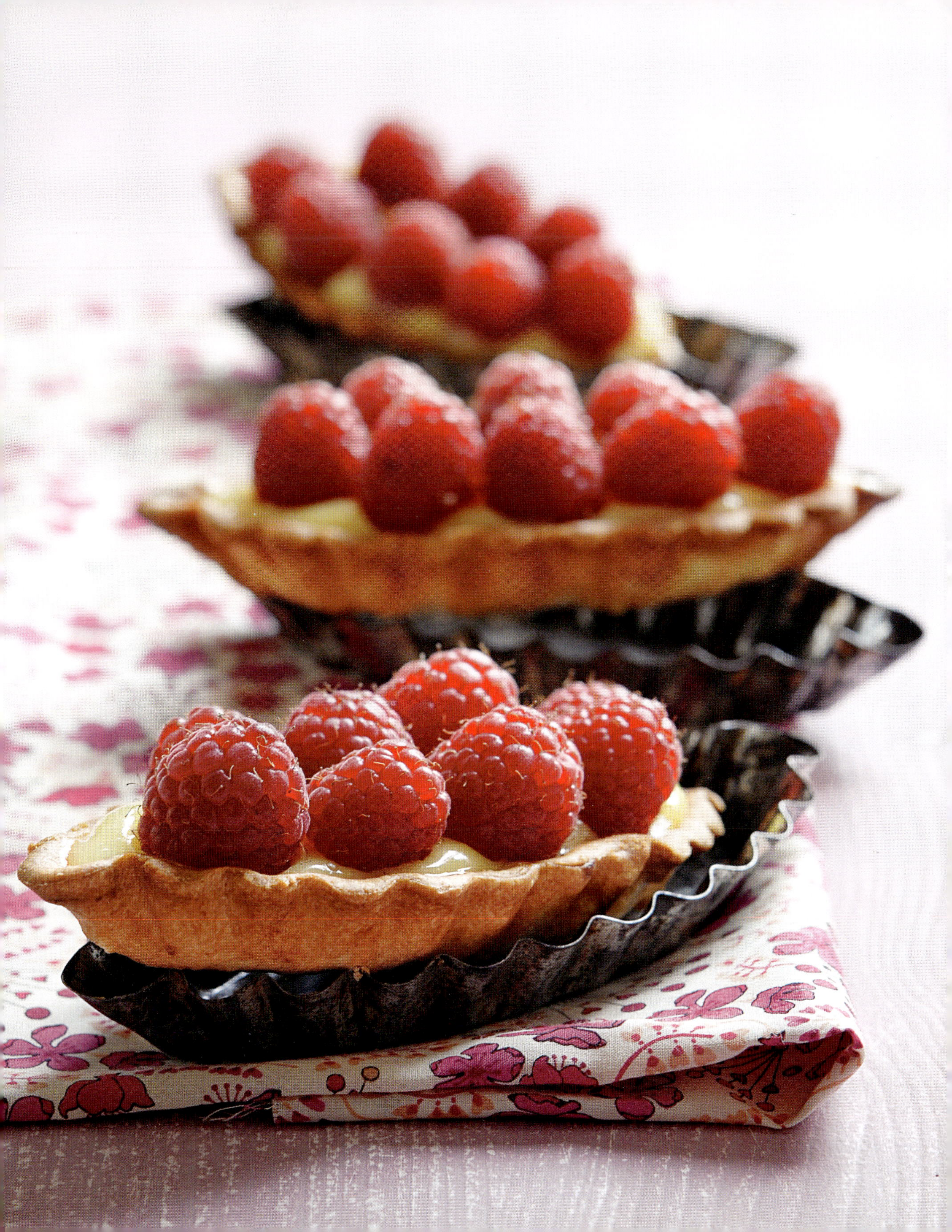

Lemon meringue pie

SERVES 6
PREP TIME: 35 mins.
RESTING TIME: 30 mins.
COOKING TIME: about 40 mins.

FOR THE PIE CRUST
- 1 vanilla bean
- 4 tbsp. sugar
- 1 cup flour
- 3-1/2 tbsp. softened butter
- 1 egg

FOR THE LEMON CREAM
- 3 lemons
- 3-1/2 tbsp. butter
- 1 tbsp. cornstarch
- 4 eggs
- 1 cup sugar

FOR THE MERINGUE
- 4 egg whites
- 3/4 cup powdered sugar

Prepare the pie crust: split the vanilla bean and scrape out the seeds. Mix the seeds with the sugar in a bowl. Sift the flour onto a work surface. Cut the butter into small pieces and rub into the flour until the mixture has the consistency of fine breadcrumbs. Make a well in the center and break the egg into it. Add the vanilla and sugar mixture. Mix the ingredients together with your fingertips, but don't knead. Flatten the dough with the heel of your hand, then make it into a ball and wrap in plastic wrap. Allow to rest for at least 30 minutes.

Roll out the dough and place in a 10-inch pie dish lined with parchment paper.

Prepare the lemon cream: rinse and finely zest the lemons, then squeeze the juice. Gently melt the butter in a small saucepan. Mix the cornstarch with 1 tbsp. water. Break the eggs into a bowl. Add the sugar and beat until the mixture turns pale. Beat in the cornstarch, the butter, the lemon juice and the zest.

Preheat the oven to 400° F. Pour the lemon cream into the pie base and bake for 35 to 40 minutes, until the edge of the crust is golden and the cream sets. Remove from the oven and allow to cool.

Prepare the meringue: beat the egg whites with a pinch of salt until they form stiff peaks, then carefully fold in the powdered sugar.

Turn on the broiler.

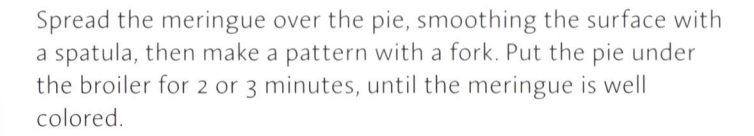

Spread the meringue over the pie, smoothing the surface with a spatula, then make a pattern with a fork. Put the pie under the broiler for 2 or 3 minutes, until the meringue is well colored.

Remove from the oven, turn out and place on a cooling rack. Serve cold.

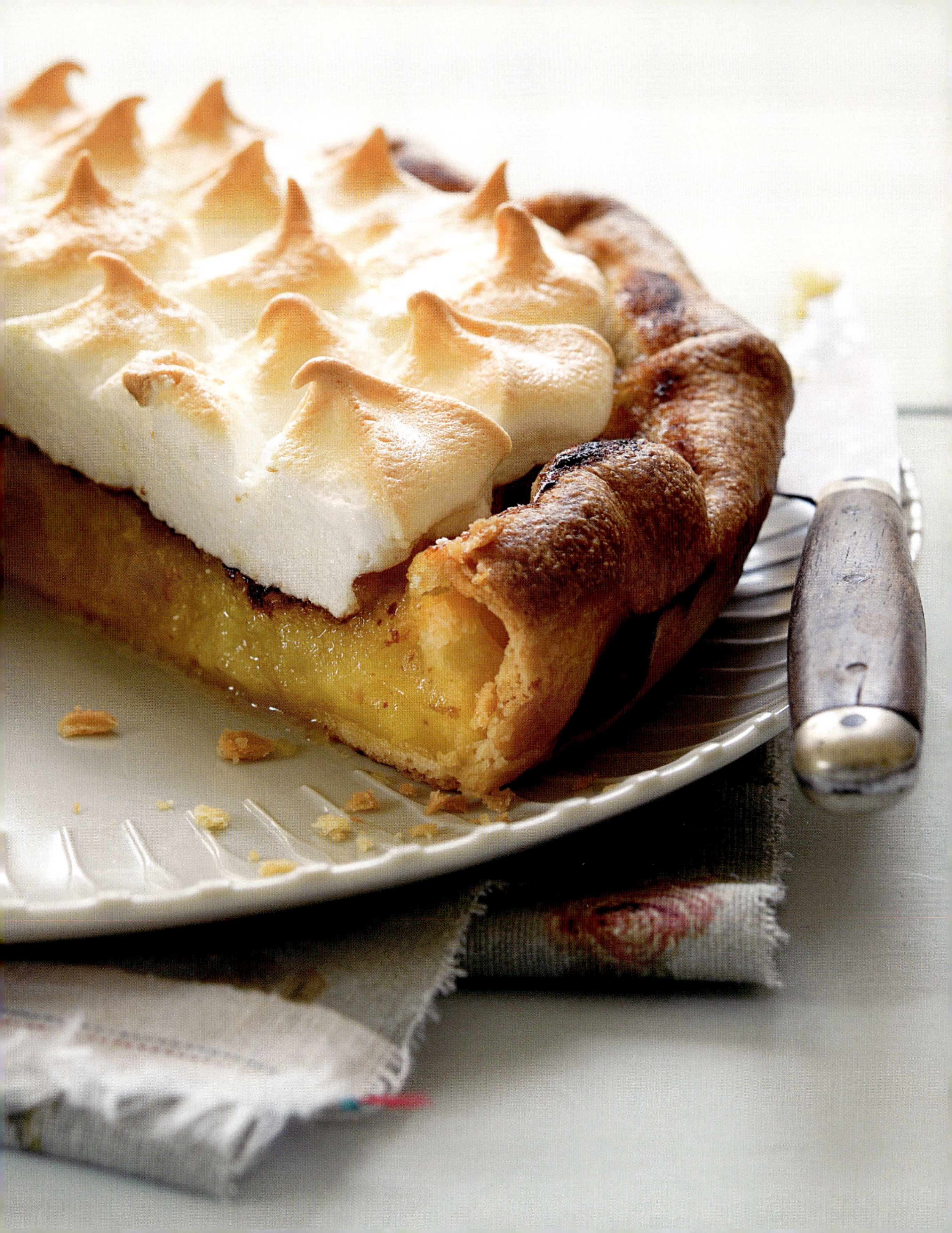

Apricot and rosemary brioche pie

SERVES 4 TO 6
PREP TIME: 20 mins.
RESTING TIME: 4 hrs
COOKING TIME: 25 mins.

- 2-1/4 lbs apricots

FOR THE BRIOCHE CRUST
- 1/4 tbsp. dried yeast
- 1 scant cup flour
- 1 heaping tbsp. sugar
- 1 small teaspoon salt
- 2 eggs
- 7 tbsp. butter

FOR THE FILLING
- 2 eggs
- 7 tbsp. softened butter
- 1/2 cup sugar
- 1-1/4 cups ground almonds
- 2 tbsp. chopped rosemary

Prepare the brioche crust: place the yeast in a bowl. Add the flour, the sugar and the salt and mix with a wooden spoon. Add the eggs one at a time, incorporating the first one before adding the second. Cut the butter into small pieces and gradually mix it in when the dough stops sticking to the bowl. Mix until the dough stops sticking to the bowl again. Cover with plastic wrap and leave for 3 hours in a warm place. It should double in volume. Press the dough with the heel of your hand until it shrinks to its initial volume (this allows the gas produced during fermentation to escape: a process called "knocking down"). Cover again and allow to rise once more for at least 1 hour. Knock down to its original volume a second time.

Preheat the oven to 350° F.

Roll out the dough to an 8-inch diameter circle and place it on a baking sheet covered with parchment paper.

Rinse the apricots, cut them in two and remove the pits.

Prepare the filling: beat the eggs in a bowl; beat in the softened butter, the sugar, the ground almonds and the rosemary. Mix well until smooth.

Spread this mixture over the dough and arrange the apricots on top, rounded side down. Bake for around 25 minutes. Serve warm.

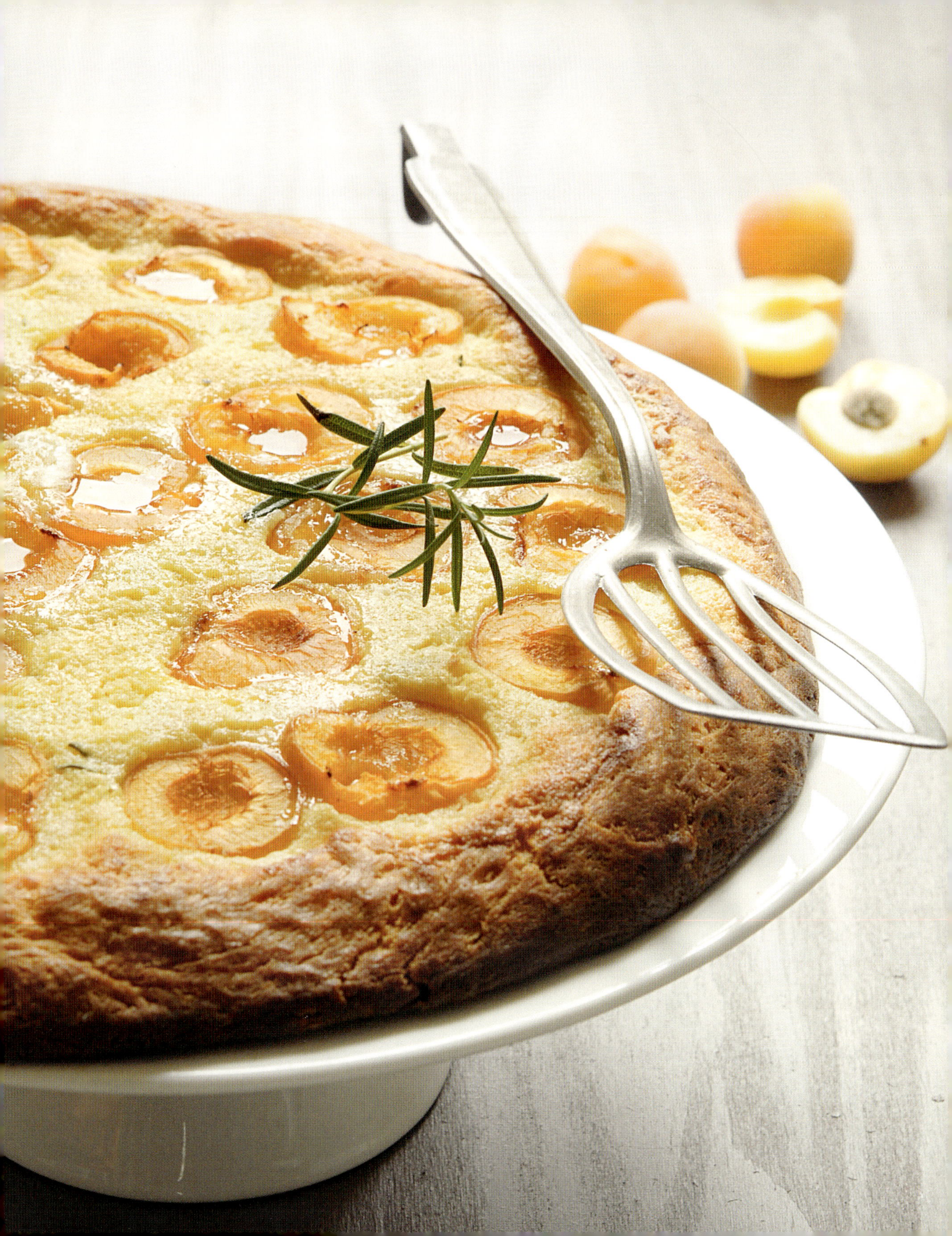

Fig tartlets

SERVES 4
PREP TIME: 15 mins.
COOKING TIME: 35 mins.

- 1/2 lb. pre-rolled puff pastry

FOR THE FILLING
- 1 tbsp. pine nuts
- 1 tbsp. almonds or hazelnuts
- 1 tbsp. unsalted pistachios
- 1 dozen fresh figs
- 3 tbsp. butter
- 2 or 3 tbsp. liquid honey
- 2 tbsp. balsamic vinegar

Preheat the oven to 350° F.

Cut out four 5-inch disks of puff pastry. Place them on a baking sheet, lay a sheet of parchment paper over them, then place another baking sheet on top. Bake for 10 minutes.

Prepare the filling: chop the nuts. Rinse and dry the figs.

Melt the butter in a skillet, add the halved figs and the honey and cook over a gentle heat for 3 minutes, turning the figs from time to time.

Remove the figs with a slotted spoon. Heat the cooking juice, add the vinegar, bring to a boil and remove from the heat.

Place the figs on the puff pastry disks, sprinkle with chopped nuts and spoon over 1 tbsp. of the cooking liquid. Bake for about 20 minutes. Serve hot.

never fails

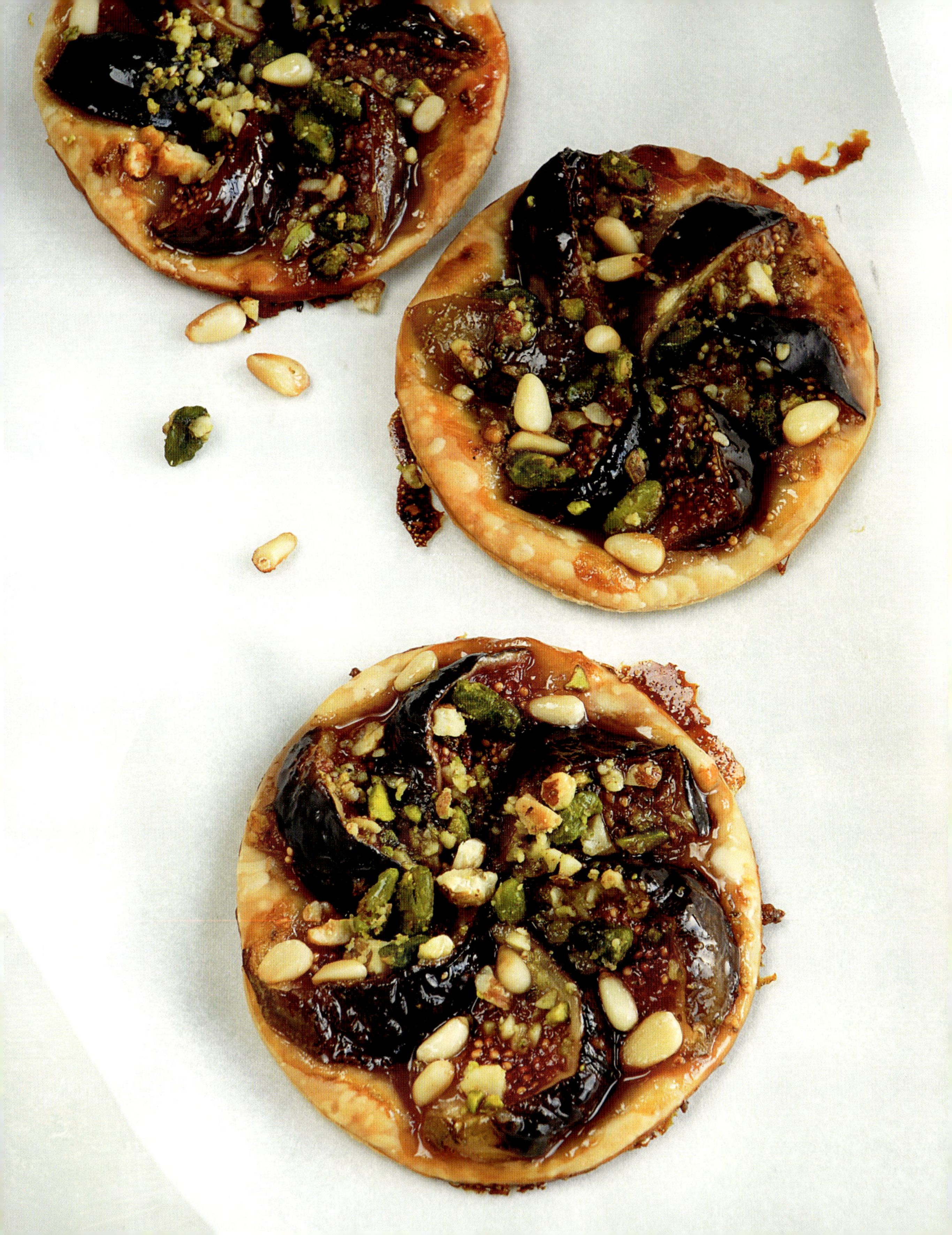

Mini mango and coconut pies

6 MINI-PIES
PREP TIME: 20 mins.
COOKING TIME: about 45 mins.

FOR THE SHORTCRUST PASTRY
- 14 tbsp. softened butter
- 2-1/2 cups sifted flour
- A pinch of salt
- 4 tbsp. sugar (optional)
- 5 tbsp. cold water

FOR THE FILLING
- 1/3 cup raisins
- 2 mangoes
- 3 tbsp. salted butter + some for the pans
- 1 teaspoon vanilla extract
- 4 tbsp. sugar
- 2 tbsp. grated coconut
- 1 egg

Prepare the shortcrust pastry: cut the butter into very small pieces. Put the flour in a bowl and make a well in the center. Add the salt, the sugar (if using) and the pieces of butter. Rub in the mixture with your fingertips. Add the water and mix to form a stiff dough, then work the dough until it is supple and smooth. Flour a work surface and flatten the dough on it with your hands (do not knead). Shape it into a ball, wrap in plastic wrap and allow to rest for at least 30 minutes.

Prepare the filling: soak the raisins in warm water; peel the mangoes, remove the pits and dice the flesh. Heat the butter over a low heat in a skillet and pour in the vanilla and sugar. When the mixture begins to caramelize, add the mango. Cook for about 10 minutes over a medium heat.

Preheat the oven to 350° F.

Cut the dough into twelve disks. Use them to line six 4-inch buttered patty pans. Sprinkle the pie bases with grated coconut, then fill with mango. Cover with another disk, seal the edges well and make a slit in the center to allow the steam to escape. Use a fork to make a pattern on the top of each mini-pie.

Brush the surface of the pies with beaten egg, and bake for about 35 minutes. Serve warm.

> To make a change
You can flavor these mini-pies with ginger: peel and chop a small piece of fresh ginger, and add to the mango and sugar mixture before caramelizing.

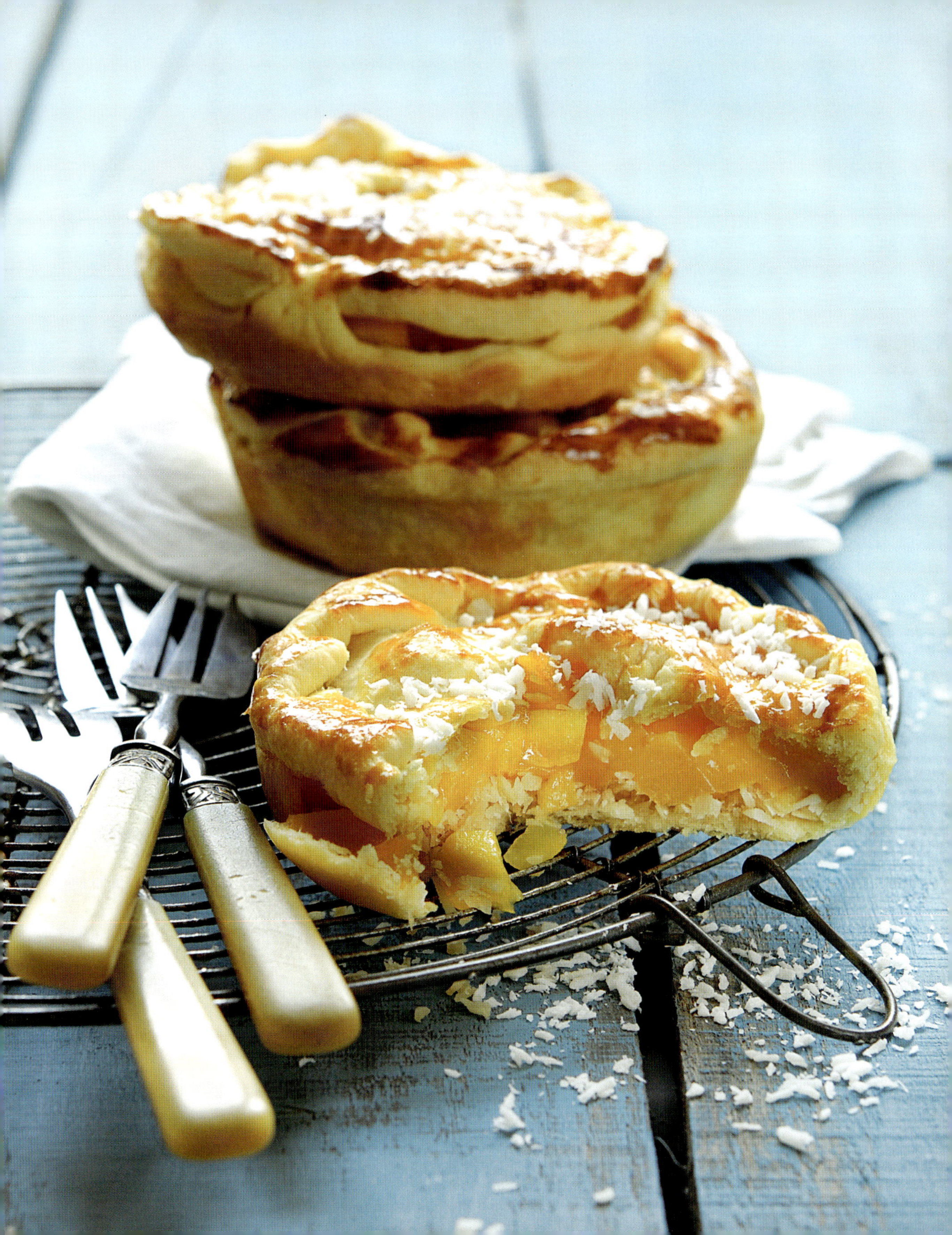

Apple strudel

SERVES 8 TO 10
PREP TIME: 50 mins.
RESTING TIME: 2 hrs
COOKING TIME: 35 mins.

FOR THE DOUGH
- 2-1/2 cups flour
- 1 teaspoon salt
- 1 egg yolk
- 1 cup warm water
- 2 or 3 tbsp. of cooking oil

FOR THE FILLING
- 1-1/2 lbs. apples
- 2/3 cup butter
  + some for the baking sheet
- 3/4 cup brown sugar
- 1 cup raisins
- 1/2 cup toasted and chopped walnuts
- 1 teaspoon cinnamon
- 2/3 cup fine breadcrumbs

Prepare the pastry: sift the flour into a bowl. Mix the salt and egg yolk into the warm water, pour into the center of the flour with the oil and bring together quickly to obtain a soft dough. Knead on a lightly floured surface until smooth and elastic. Cover and allow to rest for 2 hours.

Prepare the filling: peel, core and finely dice the apples; cook them gently in 7 tbsp. melted butter, then add the other ingredients and allow to cool.

Flatten the dough with a rolling pin, then lay it on a large floured cloth. Stretch the dough by placing your hands underneath it and pulling from the center outward: the dough should be so thin that you can see your hands through it. Trim the edges to form a large rectangle and and brush with half the remaining melted butter.

Spread the filling on the dough, stopping an inch or so from the edge. Roll up the strudel lengthwise, using the cloth to help you lift and roll the long edge of the rectangle.

Preheat the oven to 375° F. Butter a baking sheet.

Carefully lay the strudel on the baking sheet, folding the ends underneath it if it's too long. Brush with the rest of the melted butter and bake for about 35 minutes.

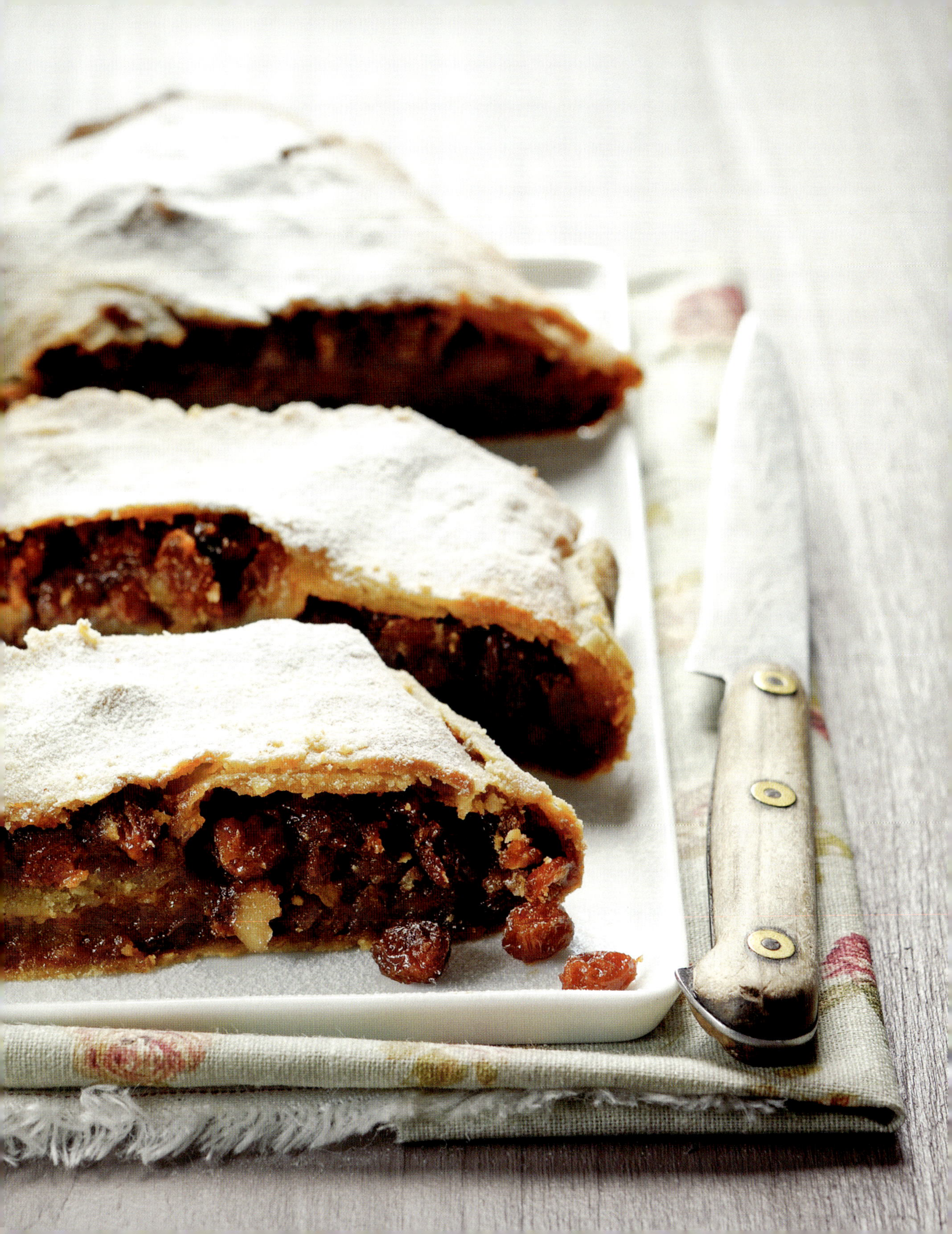

Pineapple upside-down cake

SERVES 8
PREP TIME: 30 mins.
COOKING TIME: 30 mins.

- 7 tbsp. butter
- 4 tbsp. brown sugar
- 4 slices canned pineapple
- A few canned cherries
- 6 tbsp. sugar
- 1 egg
- 1 cup sifted flour
- 4 tbsp. milk
- 1 teaspoon vanilla extract

Mix 3 tbsp. of softened butter with the brown sugar until creamy. Spread the mixture all over the inside of a 7-inch round cake pan.

Place the pineapple slices in the bottom of the pan and decorate with cherries.

Mix the rest of the butter with the sugar in a bowl. Add the egg and beat well. Mix in the flour and milk. Flavor with a few drops of vanilla extract.

Preheat the oven to 350° F.

Pour the cake mixture into the pan. Bake for about 30 minutes.

Allow the cake to cool. Turn out onto a serving dish and serve.

> Serving advice

You can serve this cake with crème anglaise or vanilla ice cream.

> Helpful tip

Slide a knife blade between the cake and the side of the pan to help turn it out.

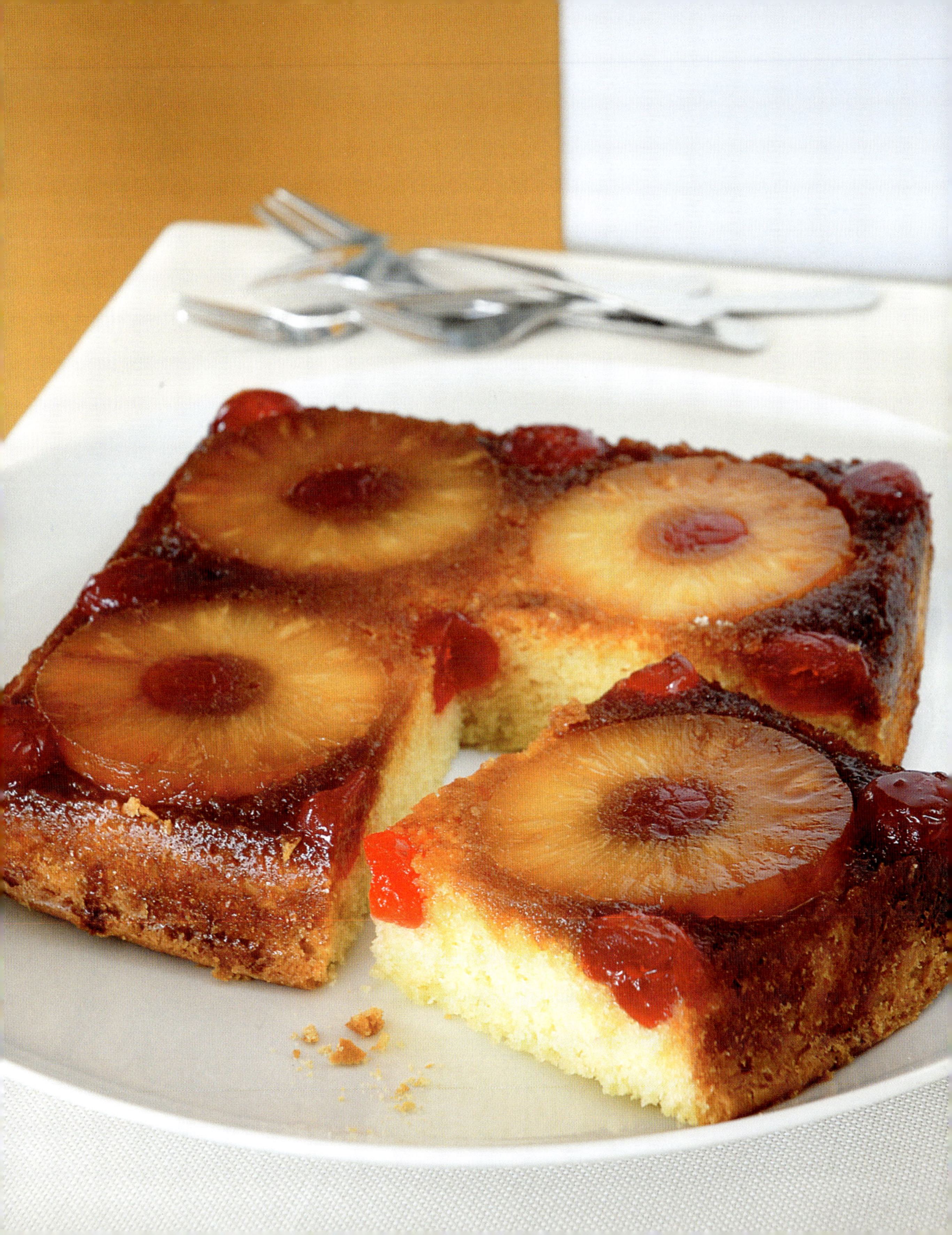

Blueberry crumble

SERVES 4
PREP TIME: 15 mins.
COOKING TIME: 30 mins.

FOR THE CRUMBLE TOPPING
- 1 cup flour
- 3 tbsp. brown sugar
- 4 tbsp. butter
- 6 drops vanilla extract

FOR THE FILLING
- 1 tbsp. honey
- 1-1/4 lb. fresh blueberries

Prepare the crumble topping: mix the flour and the brown sugar. Cut the butter into small pieces and add to the flour and sugar. Rub in with your fingertips until the mixture is the consistency of fine breadcrumbs. Add the vanilla extract and work the mixture again.

Preheat the oven to 350° F.

Prepare the filling: heat the honey in a small saucepan for 2 minutes and pour into a gratin dish. Add the blueberries and mix well. Cover the berries with the crumble topping and smooth the top with the back of a spoon.

Bake for 25 to 30 minutes, until golden. Serve warm or cold.

> To make a change
You can also make this crumble in small individual dishes.

> Serving advice
Serve blueberry crumble with a scoop of vanilla ice cream.

never fails

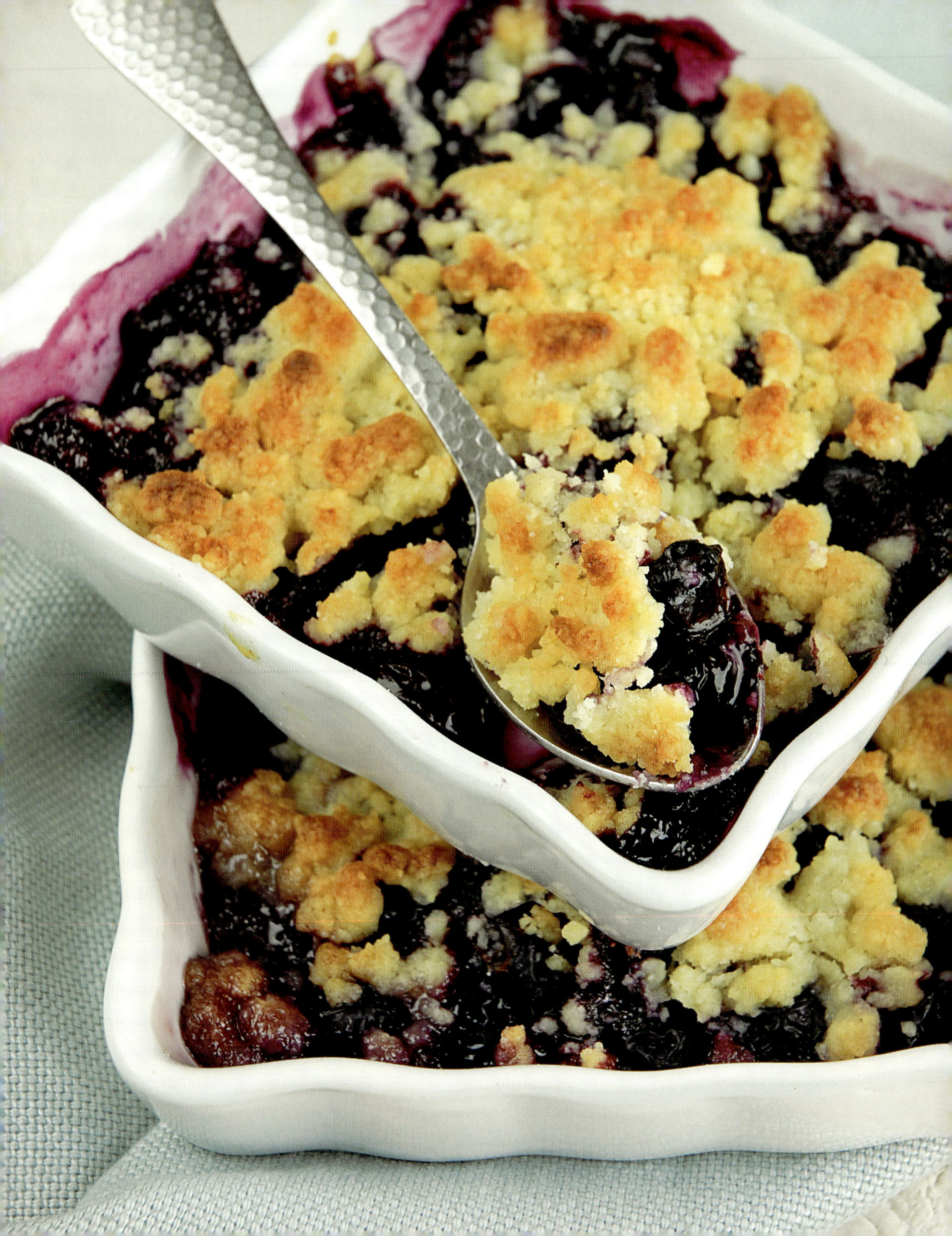

Apricot and almond gratin

SERVES 4
PREP TIME: 10 mins.
COOKING TIME: 20 mins.

- Butter for the gratin dish
- 16 large canned apricot halves
- 3 eggs
- 1 cup crème fraîche or heavy cream
- 6 tbsp. sugar
- 1 cup ground almonds
- 1/2 cup slivered almonds

Preheat the oven to 350° F.

Butter a gratin dish or four individual dishes. Drain the apricots and arrange them in the dish(es).

Break the eggs into a small bowl and beat them. Add the crème fraîche or heavy cream, then the sugar, then the ground almonds, beating constantly until smooth.

Pour this mixture over the apricots. Bake for 20 minutes. Remove from the oven and sprinkle with slivered almonds. Serve warm or cold.

> **To make a change**
If available, you can use ripe fresh apricots for this dish.

never fails

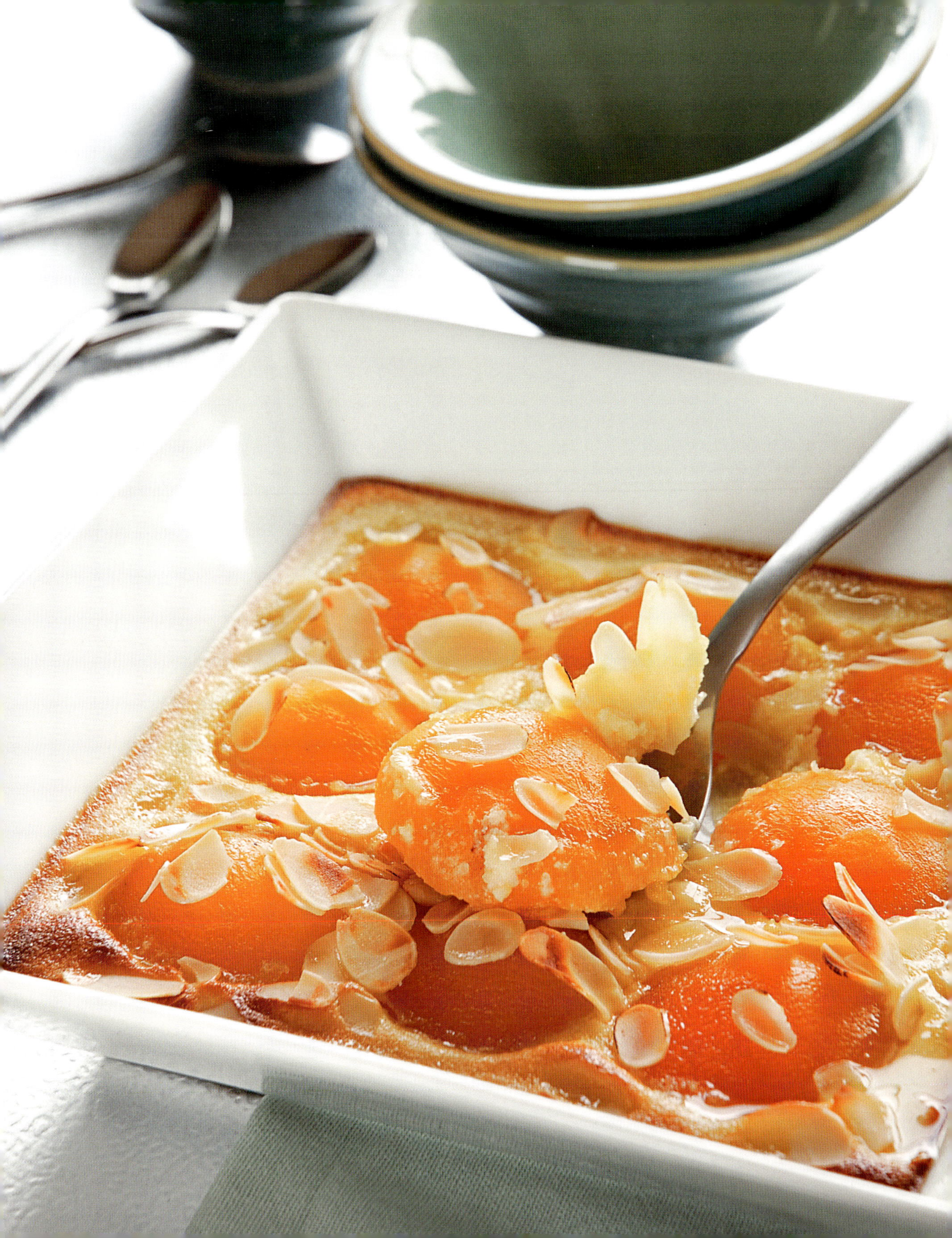

Peach parcels with orange caramel

SERVES 4
PREP TIME: 30 mins.
COOKING TIME: About 15 mins.

- 6 peaches (yellow variety)
- 7 tbsp. butter
- The finely grated zest of 1/2 an orange
- 4 tbsp. sugar
- 1-1/4 cups fresh orange juice
- The juice of one lemon
- 4 sheets phyllo pastry

Drop the peaches into boiling water for 30 seconds, strain and allow to cool slightly. Peel them, cut them in two and remove the pits. Cut 4 peaches into small cubes and the other 2 into quarters.

Melt half the butter over medium heat in a large skillet. When it starts foaming, add the orange zest, sprinkle with sugar and allow to caramelize slightly. Add the peaches and cook for 1 or 2 minutes, carefully turning them once to cover them with caramel. Carefully remove the peaches with a slotted spoon and put them to one side.

Increase the heat under the skillet, pour in the orange and lemon juice and reduce until you obtain a thick syrup.

Preheat the oven to 350° F.

Melt the rest of the butter and brush the phyllo sheets with it. Spoon the peach cubes into the center of each phyllo sheet. Gather up the edges of each phyllo sheet to form a round bag shape and secure the openings with toothpicks. Lay on a non-stick baking sheet and bake for 6 to 8 minutes until golden.

Warm four plates in the oven. Pour a pool of orange caramel into each, arrange a phyllo parcel on top and decorate with caramelized peach quarters.

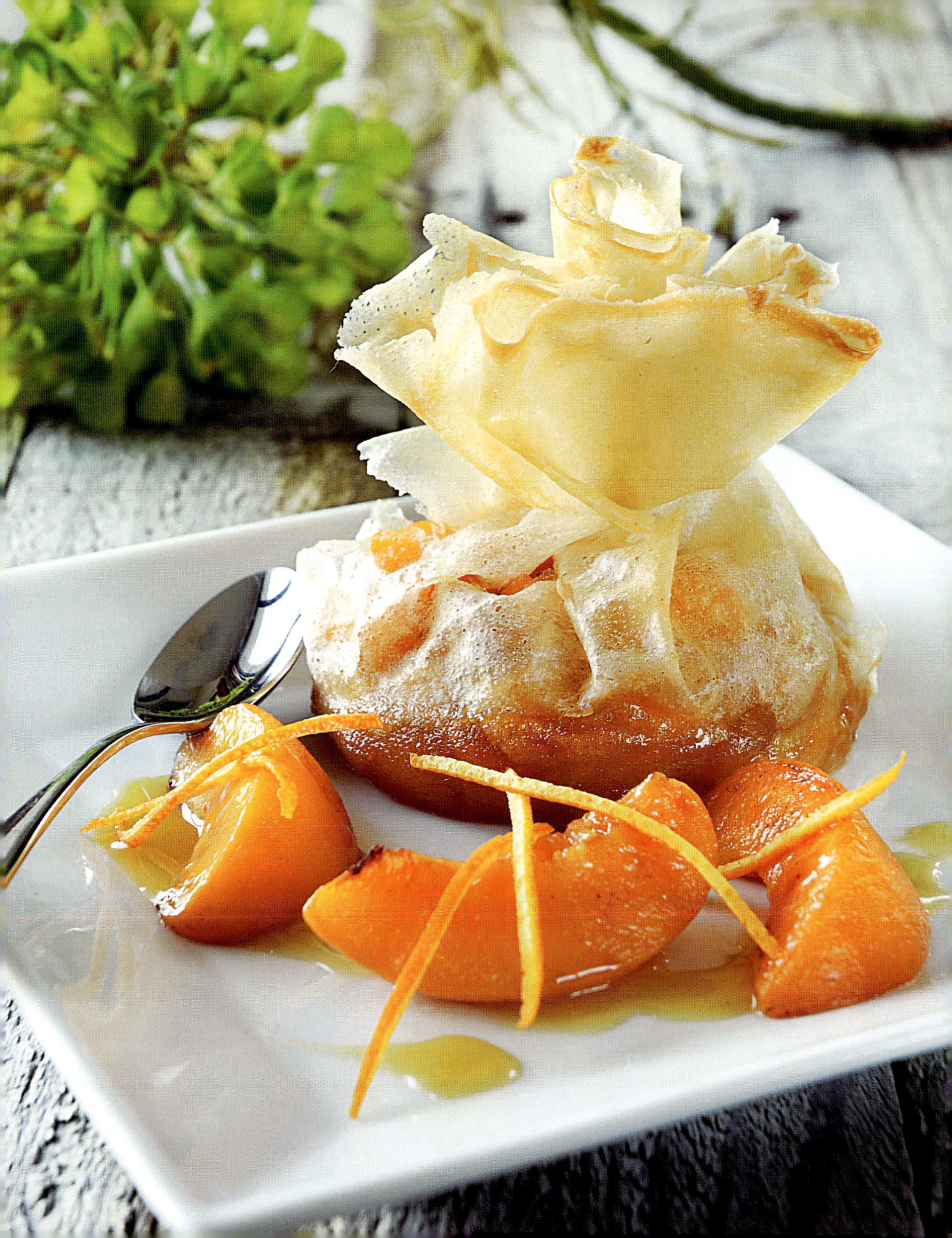

Apricot parcels with lavender

SERVES 4
PREP TIME: 15 mins.
COOKING TIME: 10 mins.

- 12 apricots
- 8 stems flowering lavender
- 4 tbsp. lavender honey

Rinse and dry the apricots. Cut them in two and remove the pits.

Preheat the oven to 350° F.

Rinse the lavender. Keep 4 stems aside for decoration and strip the flowers from the others.

Cut out four 15-inch squares of parchment paper. Place 6 apricot halves on each, round side down. Pour over the honey and sprinkle with lavender. Bring together the edges of the paper to make parcels, place on a baking sheet and bake for 10 minutes.

Serve warm, decorated with a stem of lavender, letting your guests open their parcels at the table.

never fails

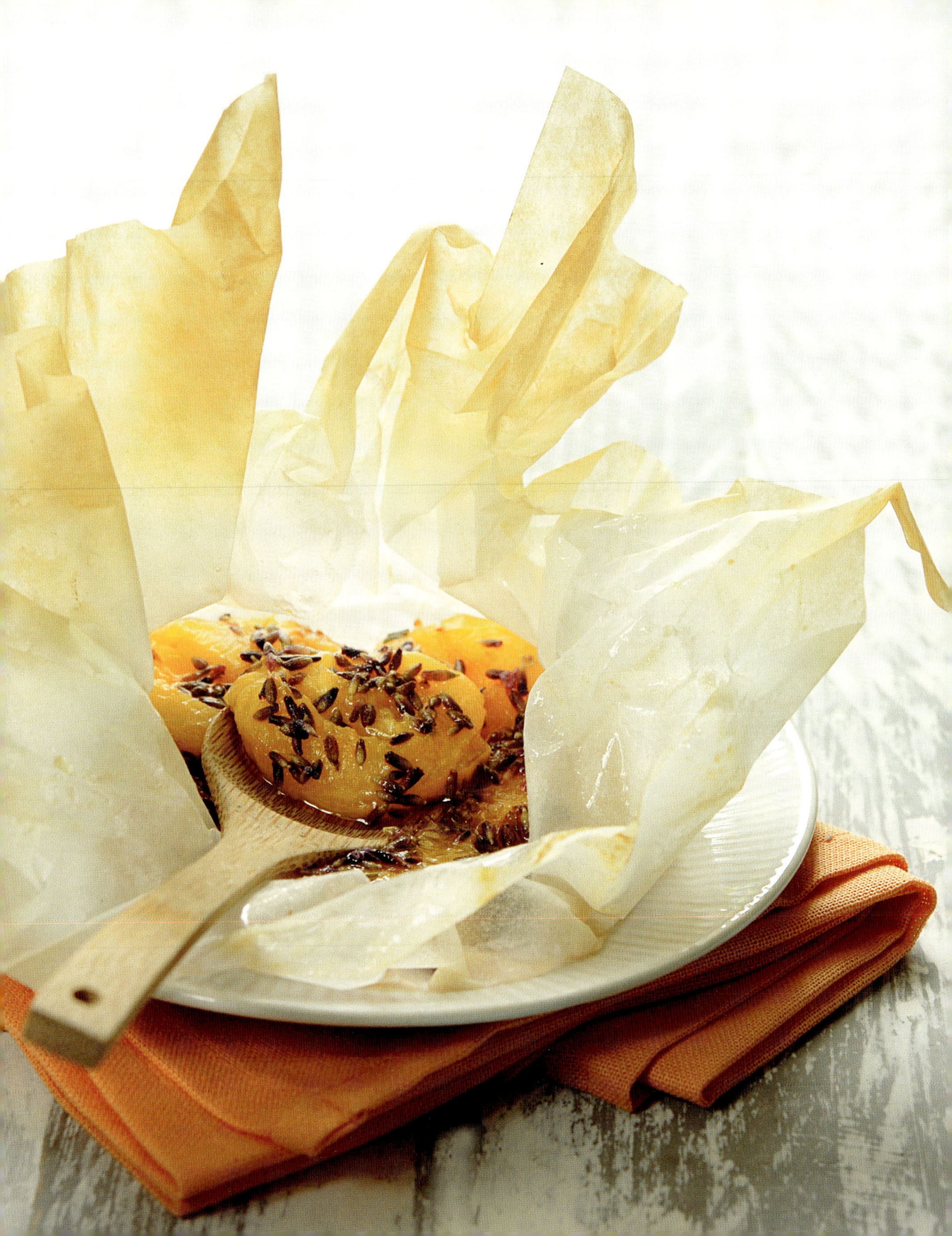

Banana phyllo parcels with orange sauce

SERVES 4
PREP TIME: 30 mins.
COOKING TIME: 10 mins.

- 7 tbsp. butter
  (+ a little for the baking sheet)
- 8 phyllo sheets
- 2/3 cup banana jam or chocolate spread
- 2 ripe bananas
- 1/2 lemon
- Sugar
- The juice of one orange
- 4 tbsp. rum

Preheat the oven to 400° F.

Melt 3 tbsp. butter. Brush a phyllo sheet with a little melted butter. Spread some banana jam (or chocolate spread) in the center of the phyllo sheet and place half a thinly sliced banana on top. Add a few drops of lemon juice and fold the phyllo sheet into a rectangular parcel.

Butter a second phyllo sheet and pleat it loosely around the first parcel. Dust with powdered sugar and place on a well buttered baking sheet. Do the same with the other 6 sheets.

Bake for 10 minutes.

While the parcels are baking, make the sauce. Heat the orange juice with the rum (do not boil). When the mixture is hot, add the remaining butter in small pieces and whisk until smooth. Spoon this sauce into 4 dishes and lay the phyllo parcels on top.

> Serving advice

Serve these banana parcels with a citrus fruit sorbet.

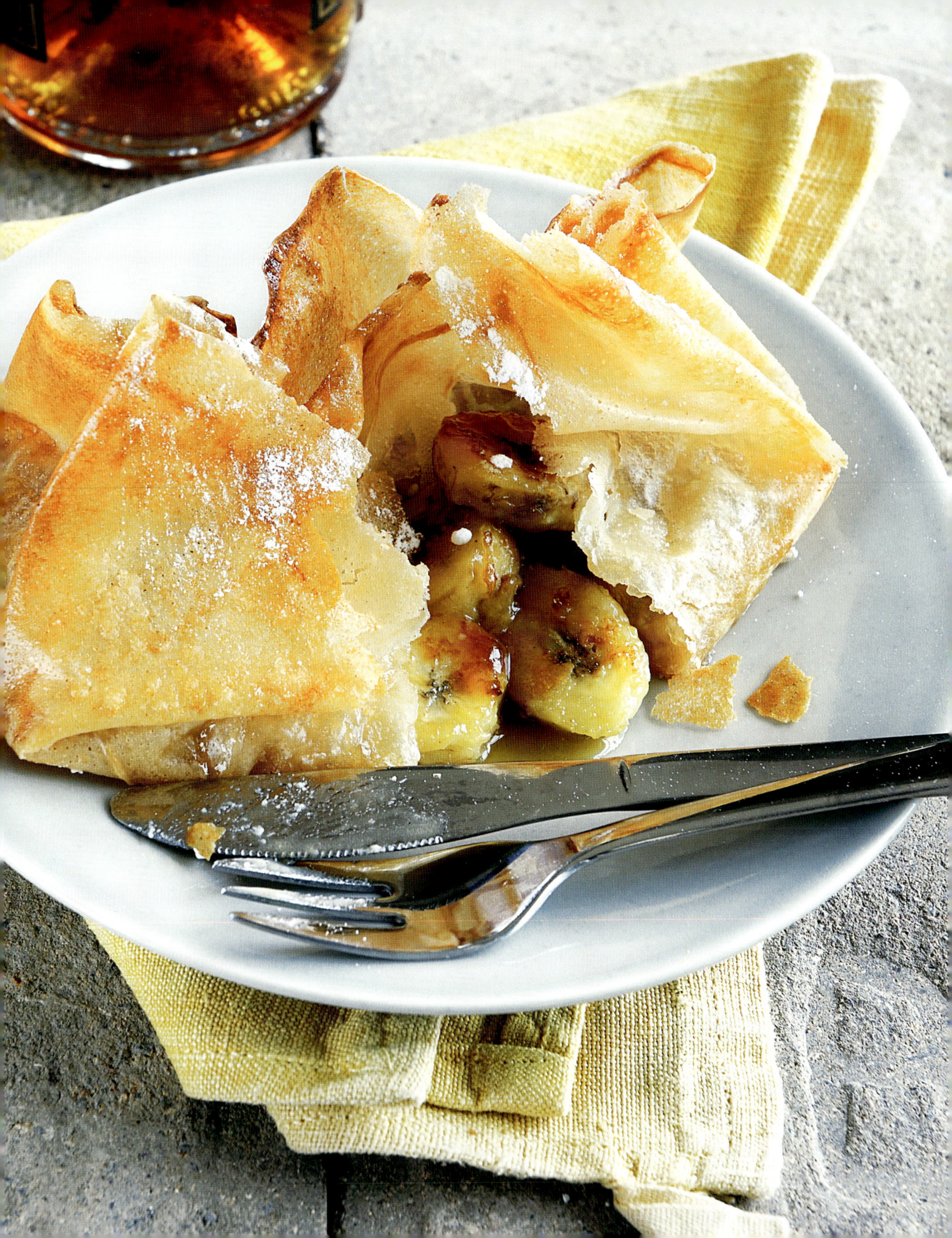

Strawberry charlotte

SERVES 6 TO 8
PREP TIME: 35 mins.
REFRIGERATION TIME: 4 hrs

- 2 pounds strawberries
- 1-1/2 packets gelatin
- 1/2 cup sugar
- 3-1/4 cups crème fraîche or heavy cream
- 9 oz. lady fingers

Quickly wash the strawberries, hull them and let them drain on some paper towels.

Dissolve the gelatin in a little cold water.

Keep aside a few strawberries (the prettiest ones) for decoration. Put the rest in the blender to make a purée, or run them through a food mill. Now rub the purée through a fine sieve to obtain a very smooth coulis.

Warm one quarter of the strawberry coulis with the sugar, then add the gelatin and stir. Now add the rest of the coulis and stir again. Add the crème fraîche or heavy cream and mix until completely blended with the strawberry mixture.

Dip the lady fingers quickly in water and use them to line a 6-1/4-inch charlotte mold, then pour in the strawberry mixture. Cover with a layer of lady fingers and place in the refrigerator for 4 hours.

To turn out the charlotte, quickly run the mold under the hot faucet and invert on a serving dish. Decorate with strawberries.

> **To make a change**
It's easy to make mini-charlottes using the same recipe! Just use individual molds instead of a single large one.

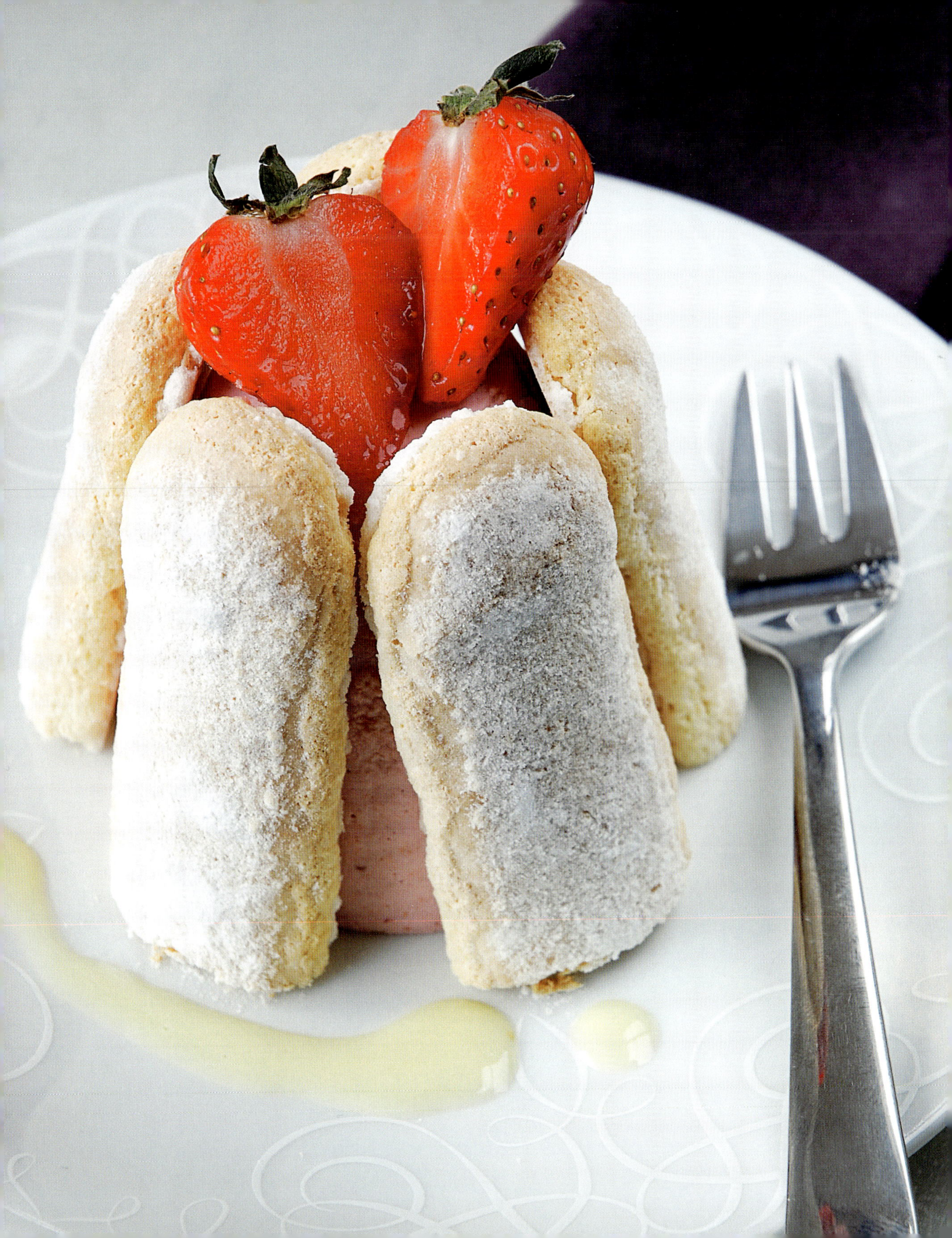

Lime mousse

SERVES 6
PREP TIME: 30 mins.
COOKING TIME: About 10 mins.
REFRIGERATION TIME: 4 hrs

- 4 limes
- 6 eggs
- 1/2 cup sugar
- 2 cups crème fraîche or heavy cream
- 3/4 cup powdered sugar
- A pinch of salt

Wash the limes in cold water and dry them. Grate the zest, cut the limes in two, squeeze out the juice and place in a saucepan.

Break the eggs and separate the yolks and the whites.

Put the sugar and lime zest in the saucepan and bring slowly to a boil. When it starts to boil, remove the saucepan from the heat and pour the mixture onto the egg yolks, whisking constantly. Put the mixture back into the saucepan and heat very gently, stirring constantly until the custard thickens. Remove from the heat and allow to cool.

Beat the chilled crème fraîche (or heavy cream) until it sticks to the wires of the whisk. Add the powdered sugar, mix well and fold carefully into the lime custard.

Beat the egg whites with a pinch of salt until they form stiff peaks. Fold them very carefully into the previous mixture.

Pour into a large bowl or individual bowls, and place in the refrigerator for 4 hours. Serve well chilled.

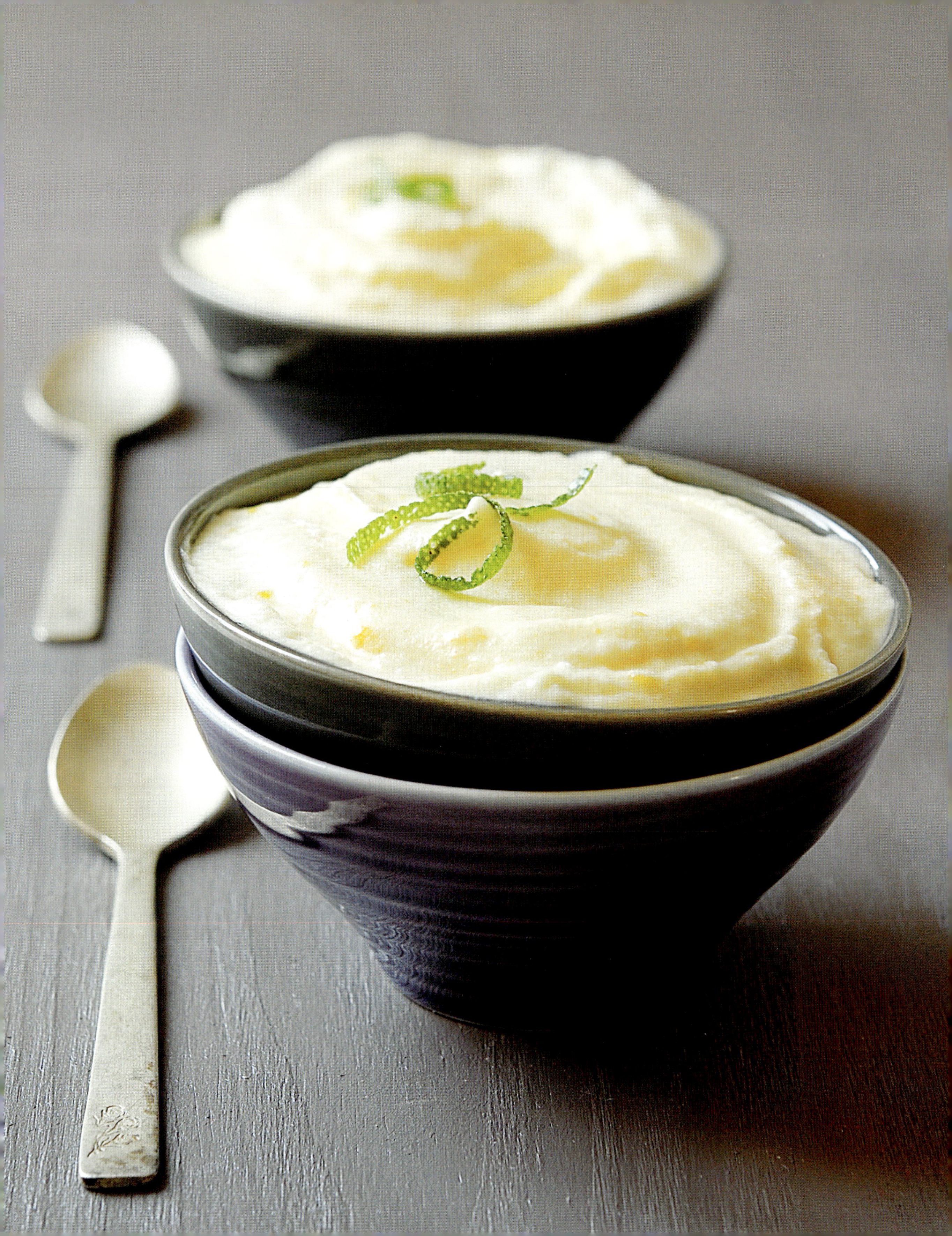

Lemon curd

MAKES ABOUT 3/4 POUND
PREP TIME: 15 mins.
COOKING TIME: 10 mins.

- 3-1/2 tbsp. softened butter
- 2 organic lemons
- 2 eggs
- 1/2 cup sugar
- 1 teaspoon cornstarch

Cut the butter into small pieces. Rinse and dry the lemons, zest them with a zester and squeeze the juice.

Put the zest in a saucepan and add the juice. Beat the eggs in a bowl. Beat in the sugar and butter. Stir the cornstarch into a tbsp. of this mixture and add to the saucepan.

Cook over a low heat, beating the mixture constantly until it thickens. When it is thick and creamy, sieve it through a fine sieve and pour into glass jars. Allow to cool and seal the jars.

> Helpful tip
Lemon curd can be used as a pie filling, or simply spread on bread or toast.

> To make a change
It can also be cooked in a double boiler. Lemon curd will keep for 2 weeks in the refrigerator.

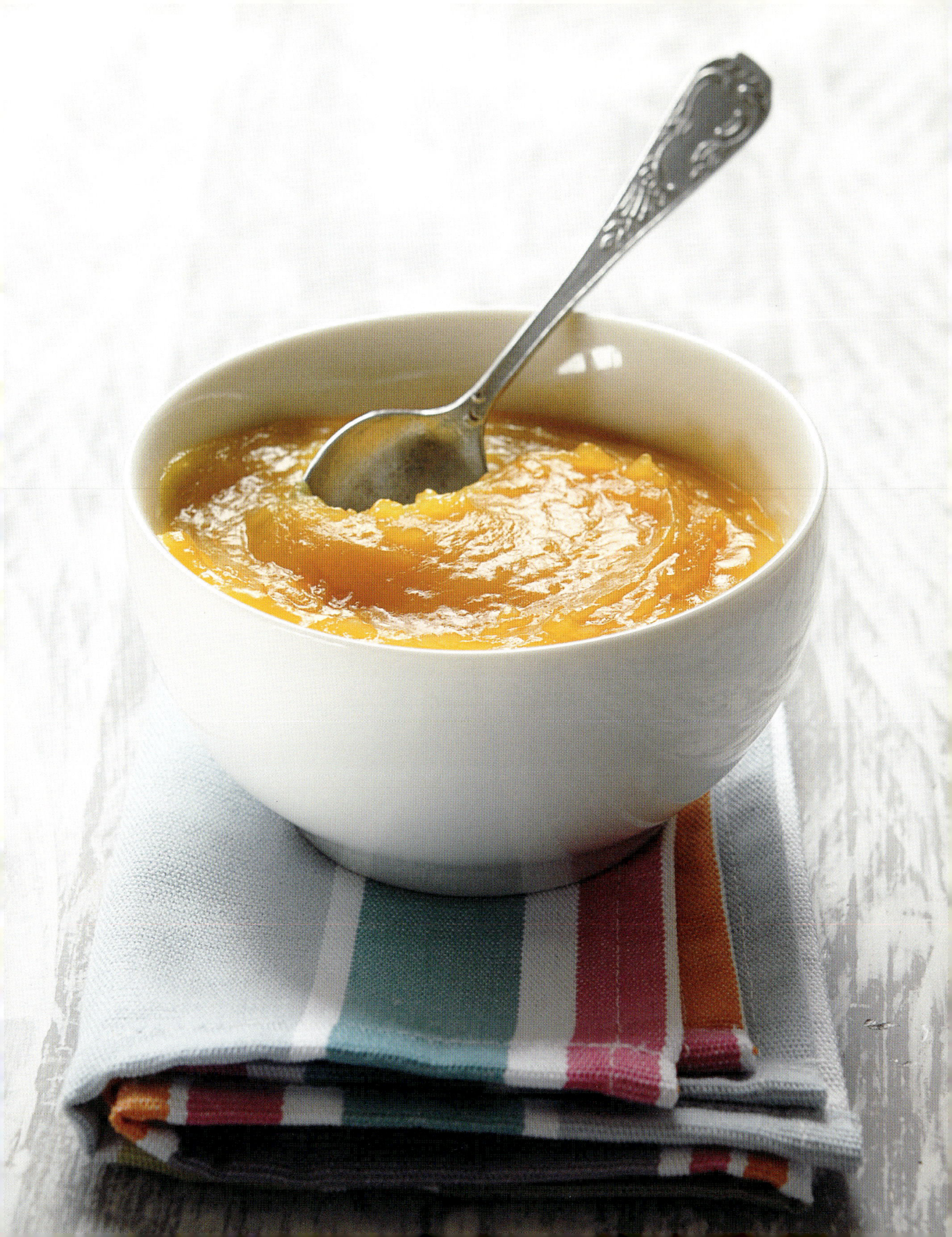

Panna cotta with coconut milk and berries

SERVES 4
PREP TIME: 30 mins.
COOKING TIME: 5 mins.
REFRIGERATION TIME: 4 hrs

- 1/2 packet gelatin
- 1 cup coconut milk
- 1 cup crème fraîche or heavy cream
- 1 vanilla bean
- 4 tbsp. sugar

FOR THE COULIS
- 1 lb. strawberries
- 1/2 lb. red currants
- 1 lb. raspberries
- 1/3 lb. wild strawberries
- 1 cup sugar
- 1 cup water

Dissolve the gelatin in a little cold water.

Put the coconut milk and cream in a saucepan. Split the vanilla bean, scrape out the seeds and add them to the milk and cream. Add the sugar, mix and bring to a boil. Remove the saucepan from the heat, cover and allow to infuse for a few minutes.

Add the gelatin to the saucepan and stir well. Divide the mixture between four glasses and place in the refrigerator for 4 hours.

Prepare the coulis: hull the strawberries and remove the stalks from the red currants. Puree the berries with a hand blender or in a food mill. Add the sugar and mix well with a wooden spoon. Add water until the coulis has the desired consistency.

Place a spoonful of coulis in each glass and serve the rest in a small pitcher. Serve immediately.

> Helpful tip
You can also turn out these panna cotta creams onto serving plates. Pour the coulis on top and decorate them with whole berries.

> Serving advice
Try this panna cotta with mango coulis, or served with slices of fresh mango.

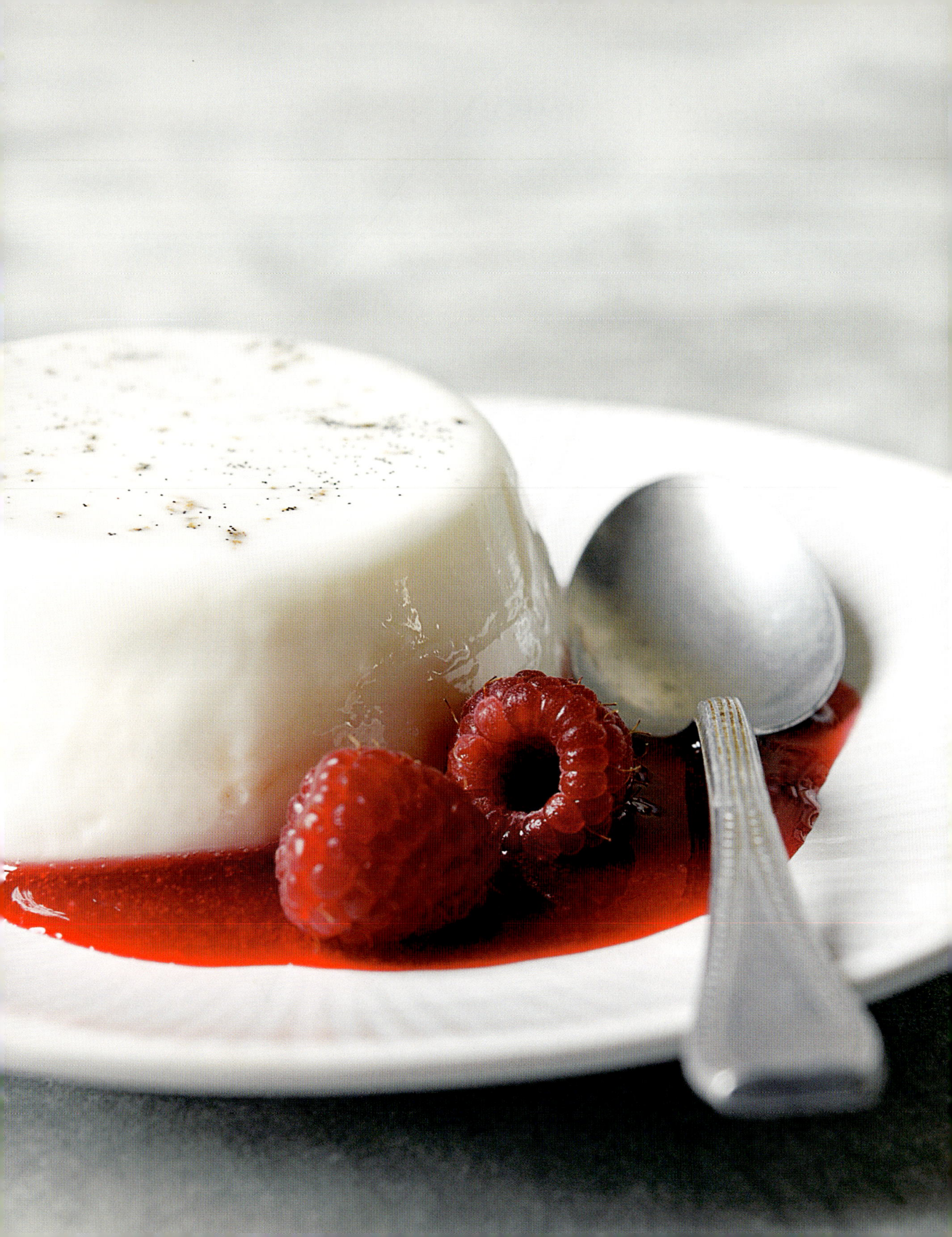

Banana-cinnamon mousse

SERVES 4
PREP TIME: 10 mins.
REFRIGERATION TIME: 1 hr

- 1 lime
- 4 large ripe bananas
- 4 tbsp. fromage frais or Greek yogurt
- 1 small teaspoon cinnamon
- 4 tbsp. sugar
- 3 egg whites
- A pinch of salt

Squeeze the juice from the lime. Peel and slice the bananas, place in a bowl and pour the lime juice over the top.

Add the fromage frais or Greek yogurt and reduce to a purée with a hand blender. Add the cinnamon and sugar and mix well.

Beat the egg whites with a pinch of salt in a large bowl until they form stiff peaks. fold them gently into the banana mixture. Pour the mousse into individual bowls and chill in the refrigerator for 1 hour.

Serve well chilled.

> Helpful tip

You can either serve this mousse on its own, with tropical fruit salad, or with a mixture of berry fruits.

> To make a change

Try banana and ginger mousse: replace the fromage frais or Greek yogurt with 3 or 4 tbsp. of coconut milk, and replace the cinnamon with the same quantity of ground ginger.

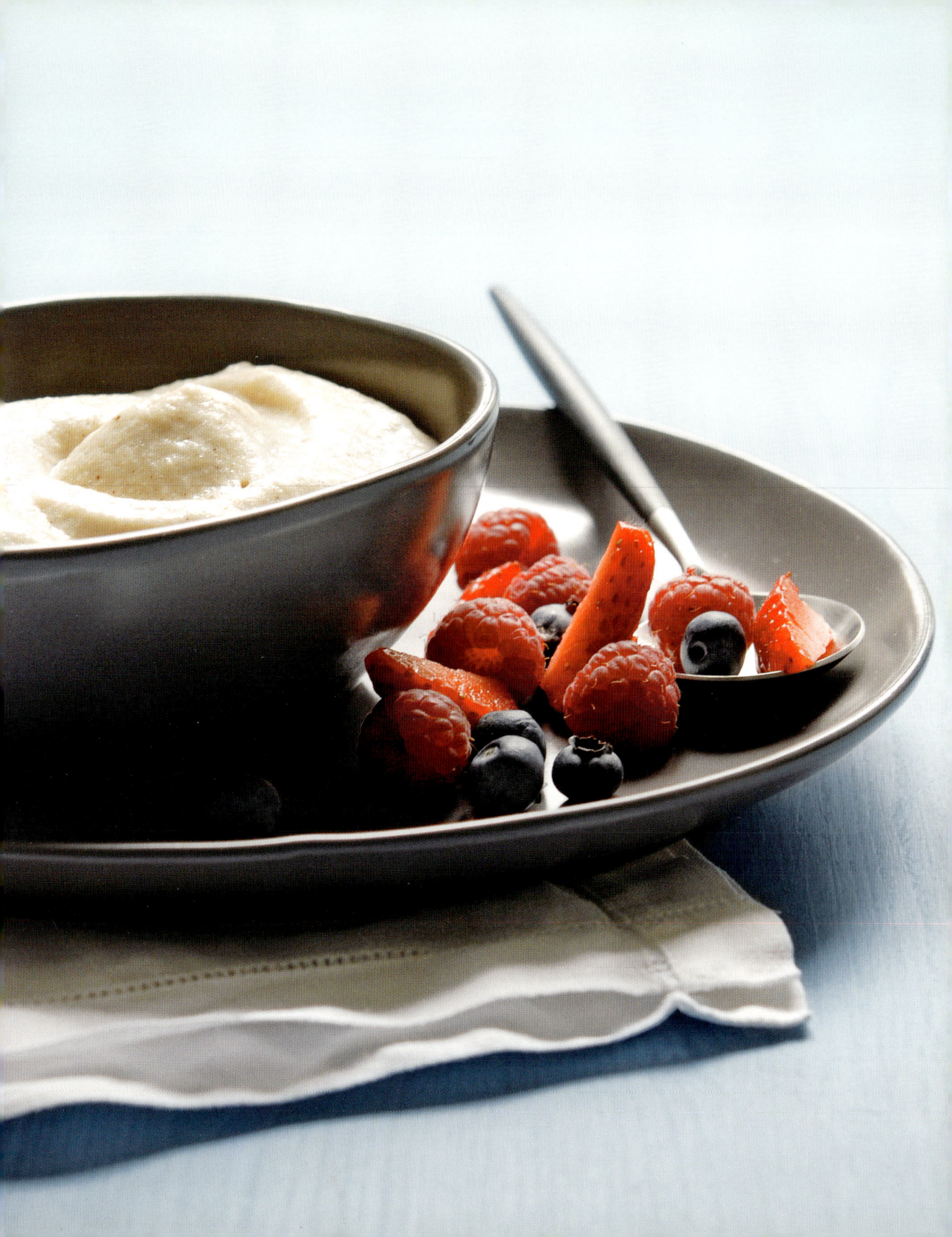

Mirabelle plums with lemon

SERVES 4
PREP TIME: 15 mins.
COOKING TIME: 15 to 20 mins.

- 1-3/4 lbs. mirabelle plums
- 6 tbsp. sugar
- 3 tbsp. water
- 6 tbsp. fresh lemon juice
- 1/2 vanilla bean

Rinse and dry the plums. Cut them in two and remove the pits.

Gently heat the sugar and water in a large non-stick skillet. Add the lemon juice and the split vanilla bean; stir until the sugar has completely dissolved.

Add the plums and bring to a boil slowly, then turn down the heat and cook for 10 to 15 minutes, spooning over the cooking juice from time to time.

Remove the plums with a slotted spoon, allowing as much liquid as possible to fall back into the pan. Place in a serving bowl or in individual bowls. Place the skillet on a high heat and reduce the cooking juice until it has thickened.

Scrape the vanilla seeds into this sauce and pour over the plums. Allow to cool slightly and place in the refrigerator until needed.

> Helpful tip
Mirabelle plums are small, yellow, firm-fleshed plums with a delicious flavor.

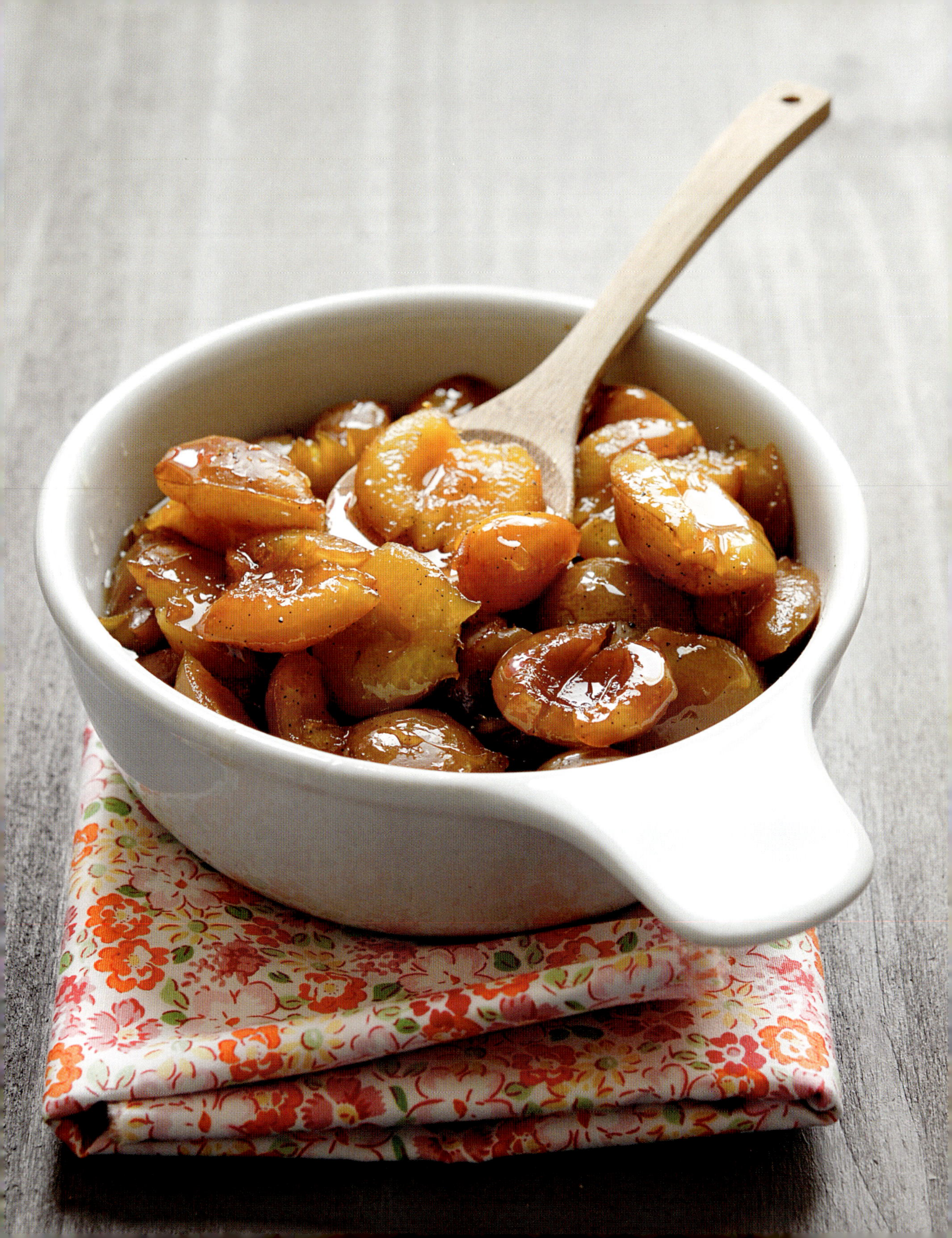

Baked spiced bananas

SERVES 6
PREP TIME: 10 mins.
COOKING TIME: 20 mins.

- 4 large ripe bananas
- 1/2 teaspoon cinnamon
- A pinch nutmeg
- 4 tbsp. sugar
- 7 tbsp. fresh lime juice
- 1/2 cup fresh orange juice
- 3 tbsp. dark rum (optional)

Preheat the oven to 400° F.

Peel bananas and cut into two lengthwise. Arrange them in a baking dish just big enough to hold them and dust with nutmeg and cinnamon.

Mix the sugar with the orange and lime juice until it dissolves. Pour this mixture over the bananas. Bake for 20 minutes, spooning the juices over the bananas at regular intervals. After 20 minutes there should be very little juice left in the dish.

If using rum, warm it in a saucepan, pour over the bananas, and ignite just before serving.

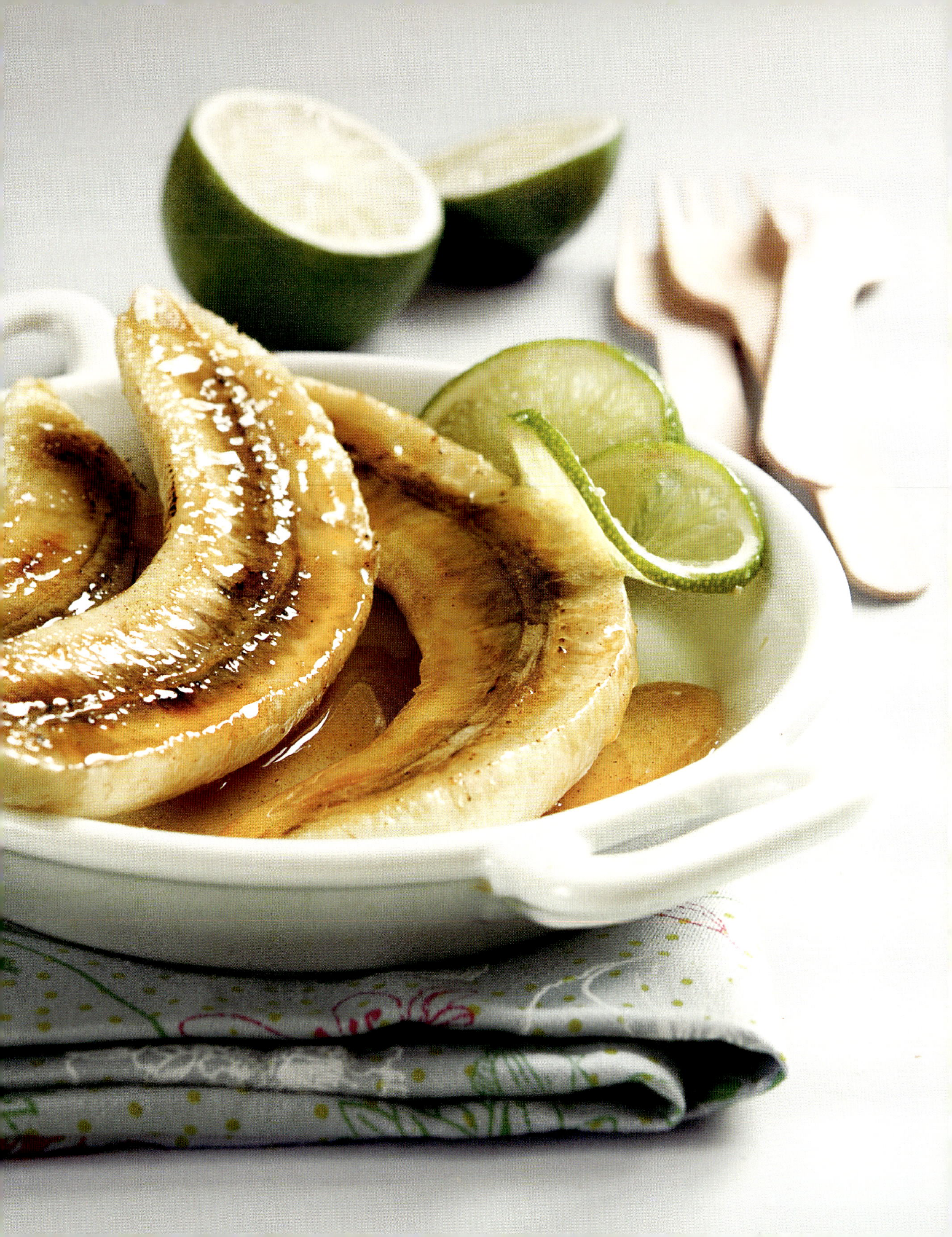

Baked figs with tarragon

SERVES 4
PREP TIME: 15 mins.
COOKING TIME: 20 mins.

- 12 fresh figs
- 4 sprigs fresh tarragon

FOR THE SYRUP
- The juice of 3 oranges
- 2 tbsp. honey

Preheat the oven to 350° F.

Wash the figs, dry them gently and cut them in half from top to bottom.

Prepare the syrup: mix the juice of 3 oranges and the honey in a small saucepan, bring to a boil and simmer for 5 minutes.

Lay the figs in a gratin dish with the flat side facing upward; pour the syrup over them and bake for 15 minutes. Take the dish out of the oven and allow to cool.

Wash and dry the tarragon. Strip off the leaves and discard the stalks. Chop the tarragon leaves finely and sprinkle over the figs just before serving.

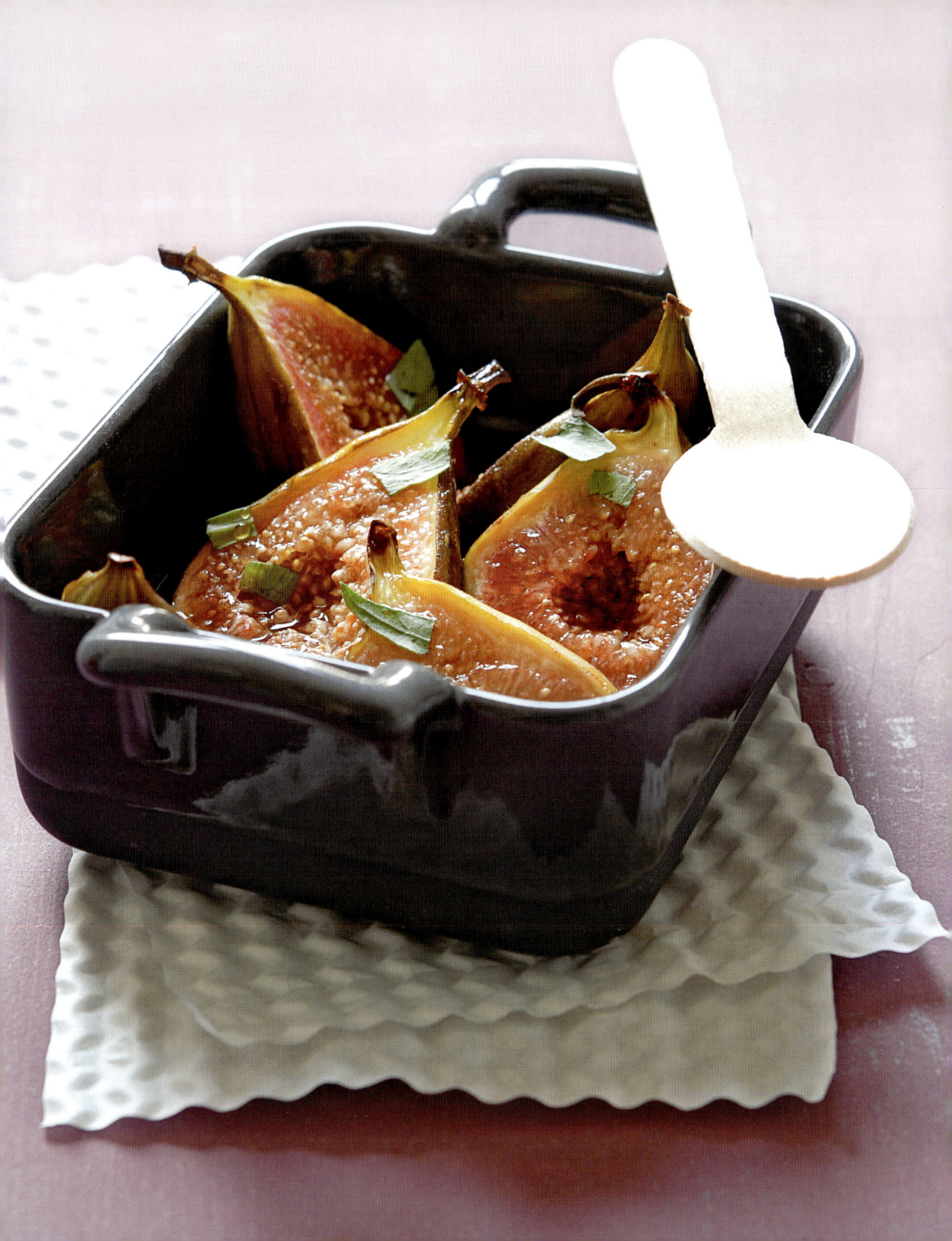

Broiled caramelized grapefruit

SERVES 4
PREP TIME: 10 mins.
COOKING TIME: 2 to 3 mins.

- 2 pink grapefruit
- 8 tbsp. sugar
- 2 tbsp. butter

quick & easy

Turn on your broiler.

Cut the grapefruit in half across their equators and use a grapefruit knife to loosen the flesh from the membrane.

Place the grapefruit halves in an ovenproof dish and sprinkle generously with sugar. Cut the butter into small pieces and scatter over the surface of the grapefruit.

Broil for 2 or 3 minutes, keeping a careful eye on the cooking process. When the sugar has caramelized, remove the fruit from the broiler and serve immediately.

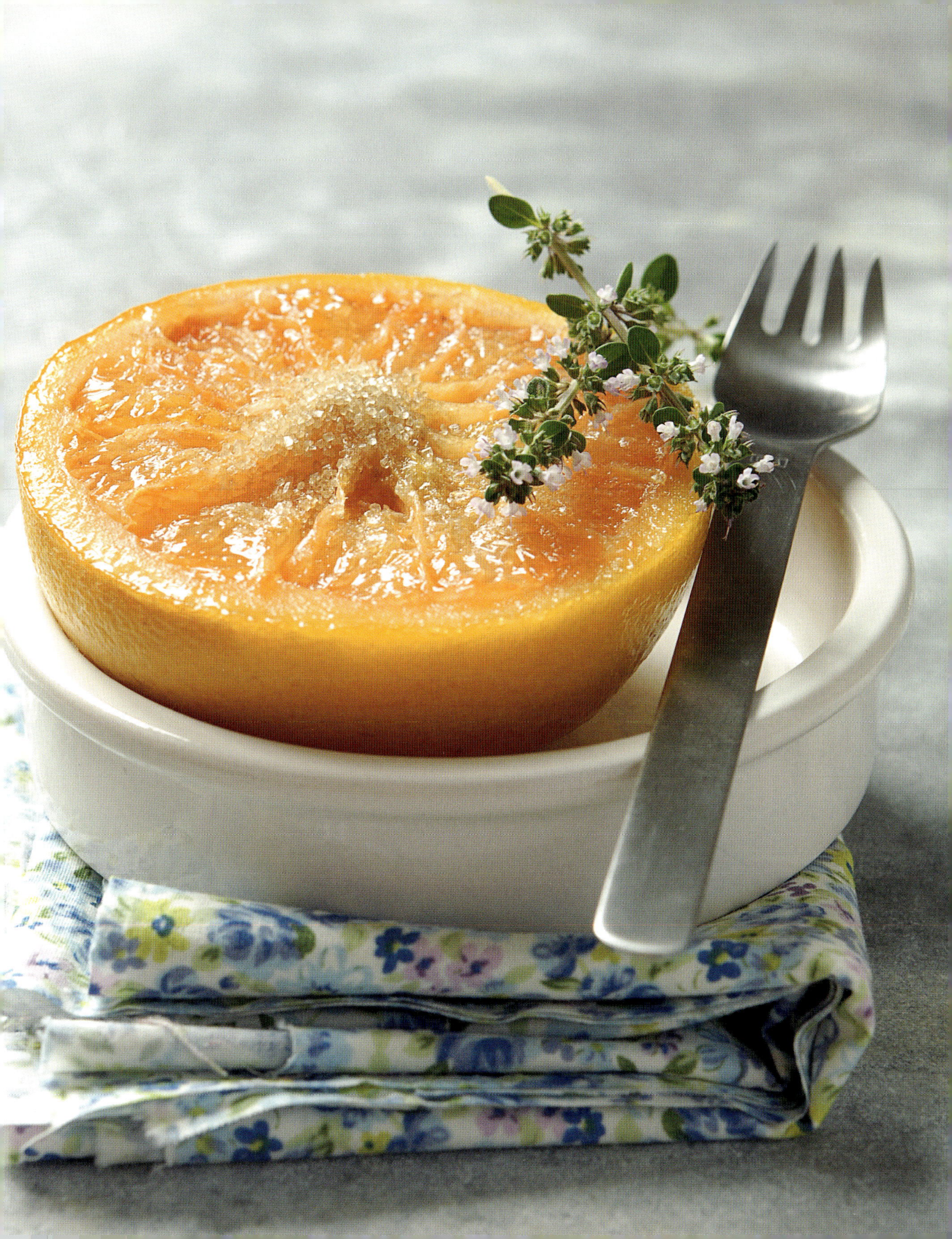

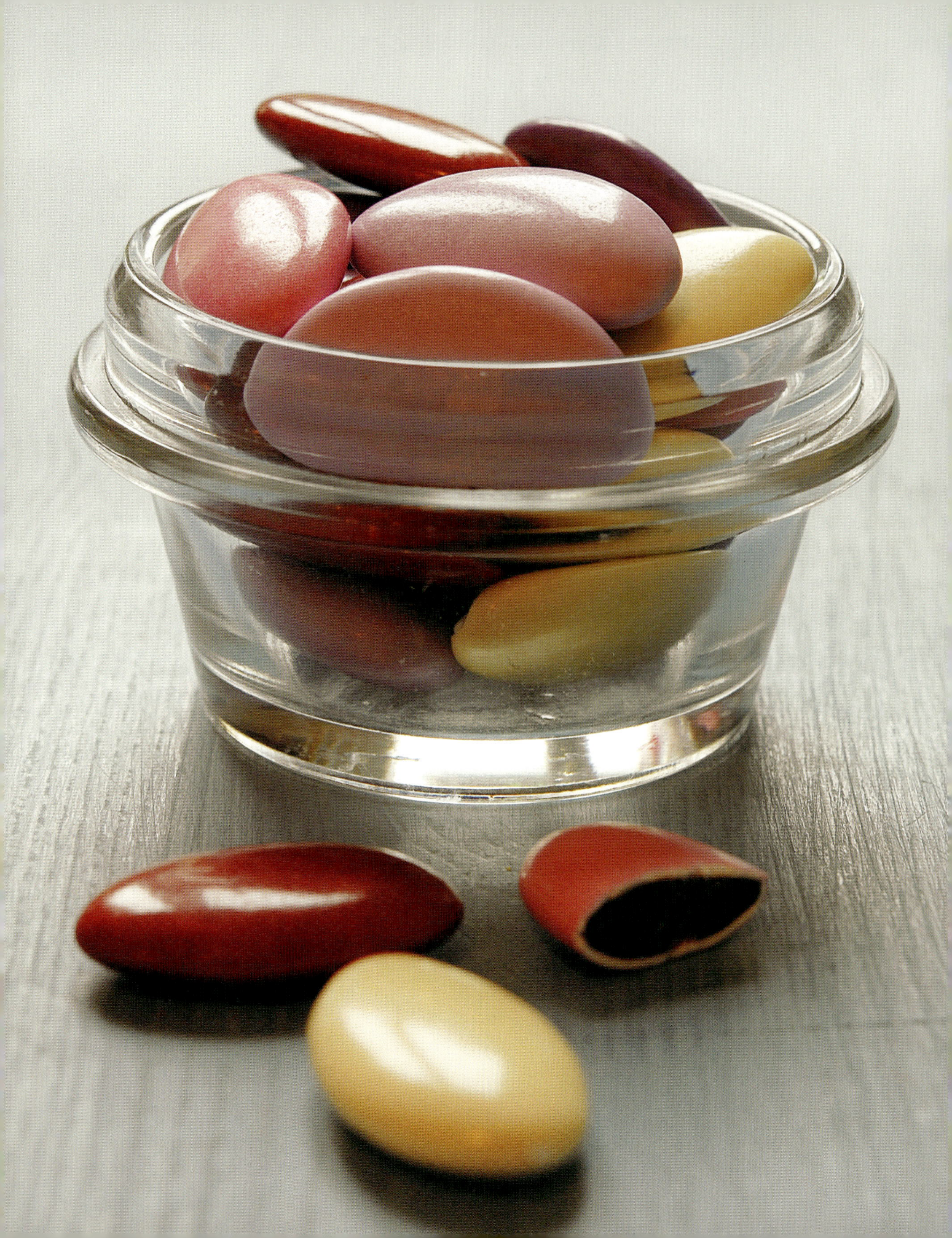

It's party time!

Croquembouche	196
Moka	198
Paris-Brest	200
Coffee cream puffs	202
Coffee dacquoise	204
Saint-Honoré	206
Raspberry (or apricot) roll	208
Walnut "délice"	210
Individual rum babas	212
Luxury coffee cake	214
Galette des Rois	216
Chestnut log	218
Spiced pineapple mille-feuilles	220
Black Forest gâteau	222
Berry fruit savarin with Chantilly whipped cream	224
Strawberry sponge cake	226
Raspberry pavlova	228
Raspberry soufflé	230
Trifle	232
Cooked vanilla cheesecake	234
Baked Alaska	236
Mont-Blanc	238
Grand Marnier® soufflé	240
Fig and mascarpone cups	242
Tiramisu	244
Candied orange peel	246

Croquembouche

chef style

SERVES 15
PREP TIME: 2-1/2 hrs (over two days)
COOKING TIME: 30 mins.

- 7 oz. Jordan almonds

FOR THE CHOUX PASTRY
- 1/2 cup water
- 2/3 cup whole milk
- 1 scant teaspoon salt
- 1 scant teaspoon sugar
- 9 tbsp. butter
- 1-1/4 cups flour
- 5 eggs

FOR THE SWEET PASTRY
- 3 tbsp. softened butter
- 1 egg
- 4 tbsp. powdered sugar
- 2 tbsp. ground almonds
- A pinch of salt
- 2/3 cup sifted flour

FOR THE PASTRY CREAM
- 8 egg yolks
- 3/4 cup sugar
- 7-1/2 tbsp. flour
- 3 cups milk
- 2 cups rum or kirsch

FOR THE CARAMEL
- 1-3/4 cups sugar cubes
- 1-1/2 teaspoons vinegar

The day before, prepare the choux pastry: pour the water and milk into a saucepan, Add the salt, the sugar and the butter. Bring to a boil, stirring constantly. Add the flour all at once. Stir with a wooden or rubber spatula until the dough is smooth. When it stops sticking to the sides of the pan, continue to work for 2 or 3 minutes, to dry it out a little. Place in a bowl. Break in the eggs one by one, stirring constantly. Lift your spatula from time to time: when the mixture forms a smooth ribbon, it's ready. Using a pastry bag, pipe 75 small spheres of the mixture onto a baking sheet covered with parchment paper and bake at 400° F for 10 minutes.

Prepare the sweet pastry: cut the butter into small pieces; add the beaten egg, the sugar, the ground almonds and the salt. Work the mixture until it turns pale yellow. Pour in the flour all at once and mix well. Take small quantities of the mixture between your fingers and rub in (it should break up like damp sand). Dust your work surface with flour and place the dough on it. Scatter the butter over it and knead to incorporate the butter. Form into a ball, wrap in plastic wrap and leave to rest in the refrigerator.

Prepare the pastry cream: beat together the egg yolks and sugar. Add the flour. Boil the milk and add to the mixture, stirring constantly.
Put into a saucepan and heat gently to thicken. Remove from the heat. Flavor the custard according to taste with rum or kirsch.

The following day, put the pastry cream in a pastry bag with a very fine tip, pierce the base of the choux pastry buns and fill with custard.

Preheat the oven to 350° F. Roll the sweet pastry to a thickness of 1/4 inch. Cut out a 9-inch disk, lay on a baking sheet covered in parchment paper and bake for 20 minutes. Prepare a pale caramel by heating the sugar cubes and 1 cup water together. Add the vinegar to stop the sugar from crystallizing. Dip the top of each bun into the caramel and put all the buns on a tray.

Put the sweet pastry disk on a serving dish. Oil the outside of a bowl about 7 inches in diameter and invert it on top of the disk. Dip the base of each choux pastry bun in the caramel and stick a circle of them around the base of the bowl with the caramel facing outwards. Remove the bowl and build a tall cone with the rest of the buns. Decorate with Jordan almonds stuck on with caramel. Serve within 45 minutes.

> Helpful tip
In France, this spectacular cone of custard-filled and caramel-covered choux pastry spheres is a familiar sight at weddings and baptisms.

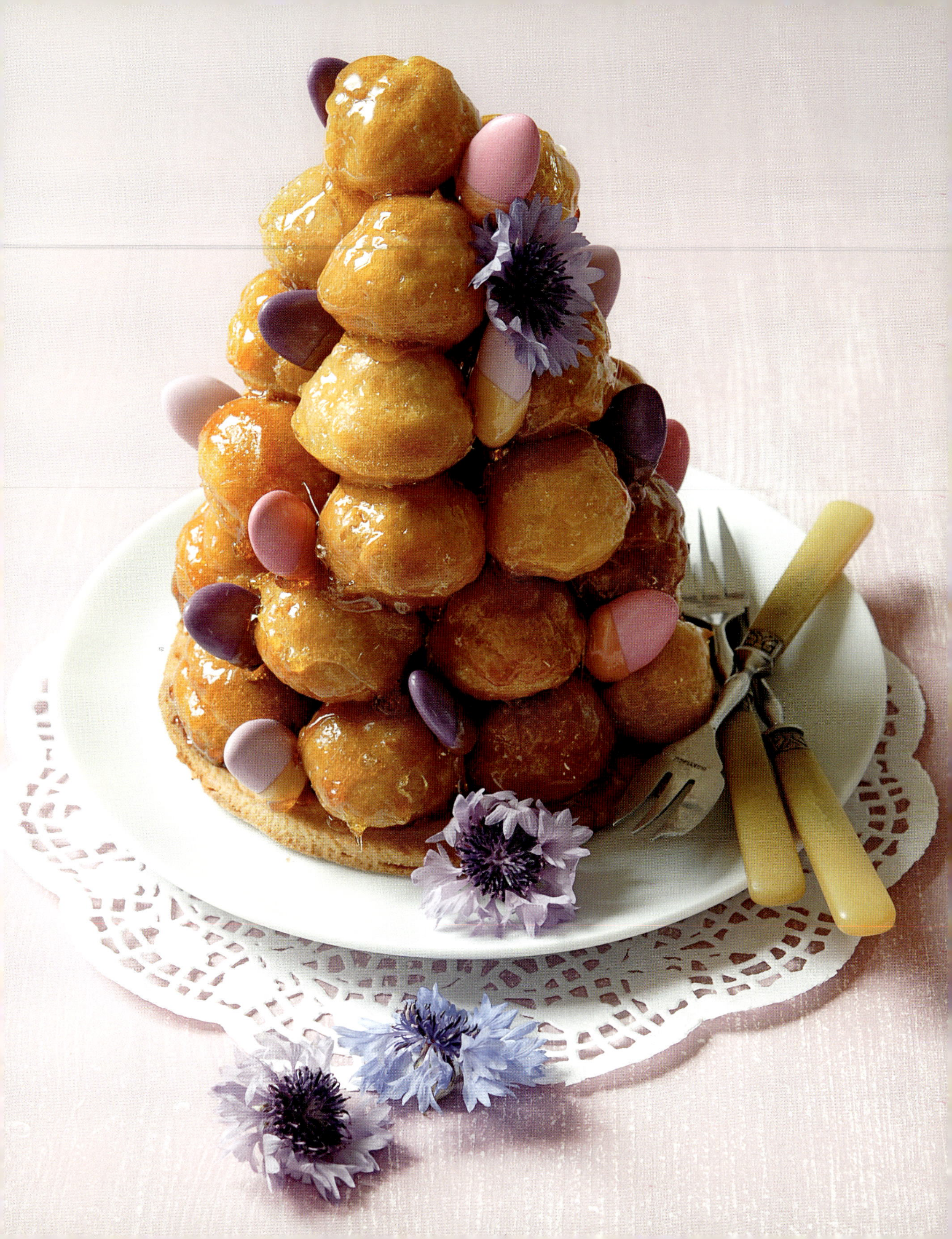

Moka

SERVES 6 TO 8
PREP TIME: 1 hr
COOKING TIME: 40 mins.
REFRIGERATION TIME: 3 hrs

FOR THE SPONGE CAKE MIXTURE
- 1/3 cup flour
- 2 tbsp. butter
- 2/3 cup powdered sugar
- 2/3 cup ground almonds
- 2/3 cup ground hazelnuts
- 4 whole eggs
- 4 egg whites
- 1-1/2 tbsp. sugar

FOR THE BUTTER CREAM
- 1-1/3 cups very soft butter
- 1/4 cup water
- 3/4 cup sugar
- 2 whole eggs
- 2 egg yolks
- 3 tbsp. instant coffee or 1 teaspoon coffee essence

FOR THE RUM SYRUP
- 2/3 cup sugar
- 6 tbsp. water
- 3 oz. rum

FOR DECORATION
- 3/4 cups blanched hazelnuts

Prepare the sponge cake: sift the flour; melt the butter. In a bowl, mix the powdered sugar, the ground almonds and the ground hazelnuts. Add 3 whole eggs, one by one. Beat very well (the mxture should double in volume). Add the last egg and beat again for 5 minutes. Pour in a little cooled melted butter, mix together, then pour in the rest of the butter. Beat the egg whites until they form stiff peaks, gradually adding the sugar. Fold them into the mixture, gradually adding the sifted flour.

Preheat the oven to 350° F. Butter an 8-inch round cake pan, pour in the mixture and bake for 35 minutes. Turn the cake out, allow to cool completely, then cover with a cloth and place in the refrigerator for an hour.

Prepare the butter cream: work the butter to a smooth cream with a wooden or rubber spatula; put the water and the sugar into a saucepan over a low heat and bring to a boil. Cook to the soft ball stage (240° F). Put the whole eggs and extra yolks into a bowl and beat them with an electric mixer. When the syrup is ready, pour it into the egg mixture in a thin stream, beating constantly, then add the butter little by little. Continue to beat until the mixture is cold, then add the coffee.

Prepare the rum syrup: boil the sugar and water together, allow to cool and add the rum.

For decoration, finely chop the hazelnuts and place in the oven for 5 minutes to toast them.

Cut the sponge cake horizontally into three disks. Divide the butter cream into five equal parts.

Using a pastry brush, moisten the first disk with rum syrup, then take a spatula and spread with butter cream. Scatter one quarter of the hazelnuts on the cream. Repeat the operation with the second disk, then the third.

Still using your spatula, spread the outside of the cake with butter cream and stud with whole hazelnuts. Put the rest of the cream into a pastry bag fitted with a fluted tip and pipe rosettes onto the cake.

Put the moka in the refrigerator for 2 hours and serve well chilled.

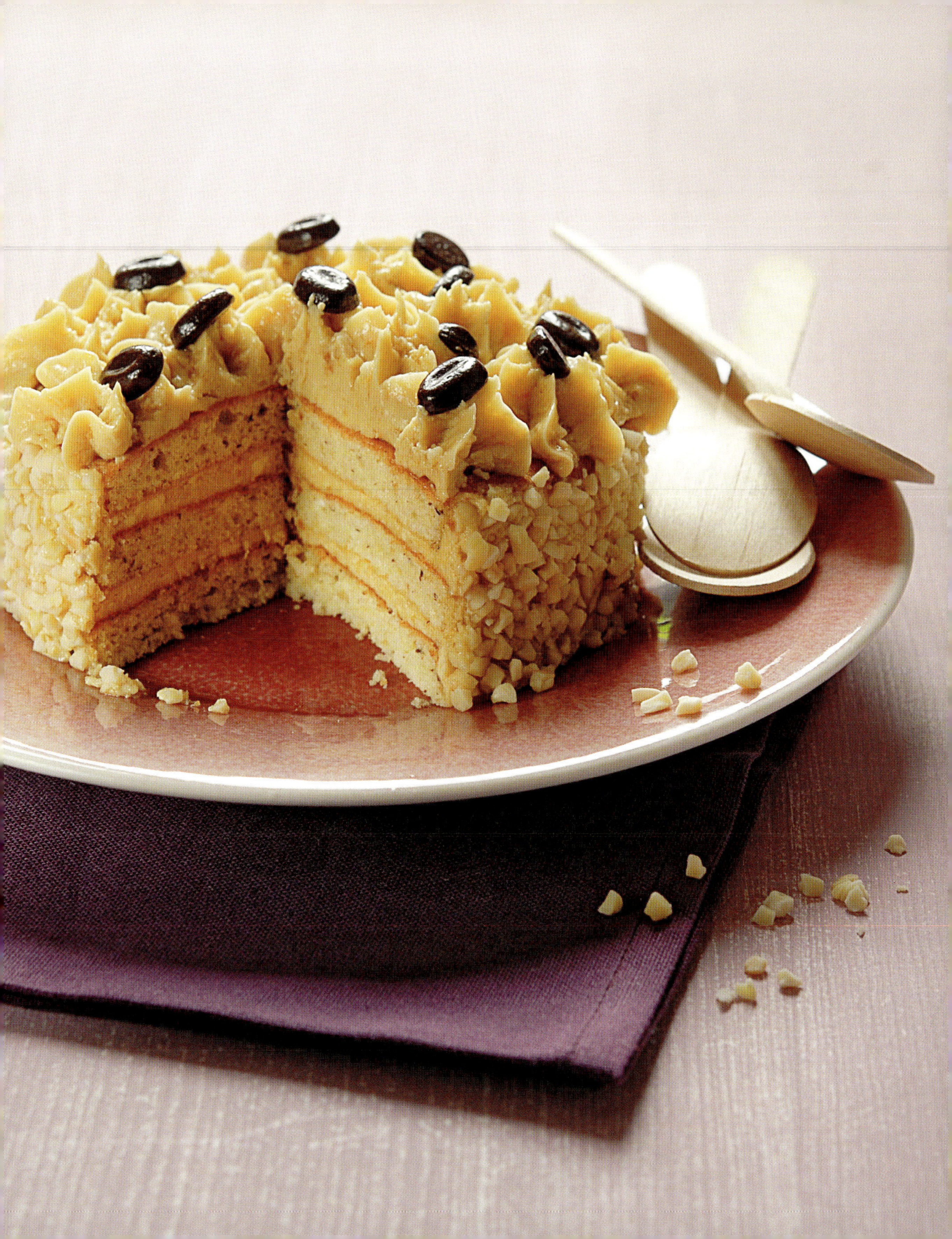

Paris-Brest

SERVES 6
PREP: 45 mins.
COOKING TIME: 30 to 45 mins.

- Powdered sugar

FOR THE PUFF PASTRY
- 1/3 cup sugar
- 4 tbsp. butter
  + some for the baking sheet
- 1 pinch of salt
- 1 heaping cup sifted flour
- 3 whole eggs
  + 1 egg yolk
- 1/2 cup of slivered almonds

FOR THE PRALINE CREAM
- 1 cup milk
- 9 tbsp. butter
- 1 whole egg
  + 1 egg yolk
- 1/2 cup sugar
- 3 tbsp. cornstarch
- 3/4 cup ground pralines

Prepare the puff pastry: warm 1 cup water in a saucepan. Add the sugar, butter and salt. Bring to a boil and remove from the stove. Add all the flour at once. Whip vigorously and put back on the stove. Cook while stirring continuously until the pastry can be completely separated from the saucepan. Remove from the heat again. Blend the 3 eggs in very quickly, one by one, until they are completely absorbed. Pour the mixture into a pastry bag.

Preheat oven to 350° F.

Lightly butter a baking sheet. Pipe a ring onto it roughly 8 inches in diameter.

Place the egg yolk in a bowl. Moisten the contents with a little water and mix thoroughly. Brush this mixture onto the ring with a pastry brush. Sprinkle the slivered almonds over it. Cover with aluminum foil to prevent it from browning too much. Place in the oven and bake for roughly 25 minutes. Take out of the oven and allow to cool.

Meanwhile, prepare the praline cream: boil the milk in a saucepan. Cut 4 level tbsp. butter into small pieces. Mix the whole egg and the egg yolk in a bowl. Add sugar and cornstarch and combine. Dilute with a little boiling water and pour the whole mixture into the saucepan while stirring vigorously. Leave on the stove until it comes to a boil, stirring constantly. Remove from the stove. Add pieces of butter and leave to cool.

Using a wooden spoon, combine the rest of the butter with the pralines until it becomes creamy. Pour this cream into the saucepan and mix until it is perfectly smooth.

Cut horizontally through the puff pastry ring to make two equal halves. Fill with the praline cream and place the almond-covered half on top. Sprinkle with powdered sugar and put into the refrigerator until ready to serve.

> For your information

This cake was created in 1891 by a baker whose shop was situated on the itinerary of the Paris-Brest bicycle race. He also imagined creating round éclairs to look like bicycle wheels.
Brest is a city at the western extremity of France.

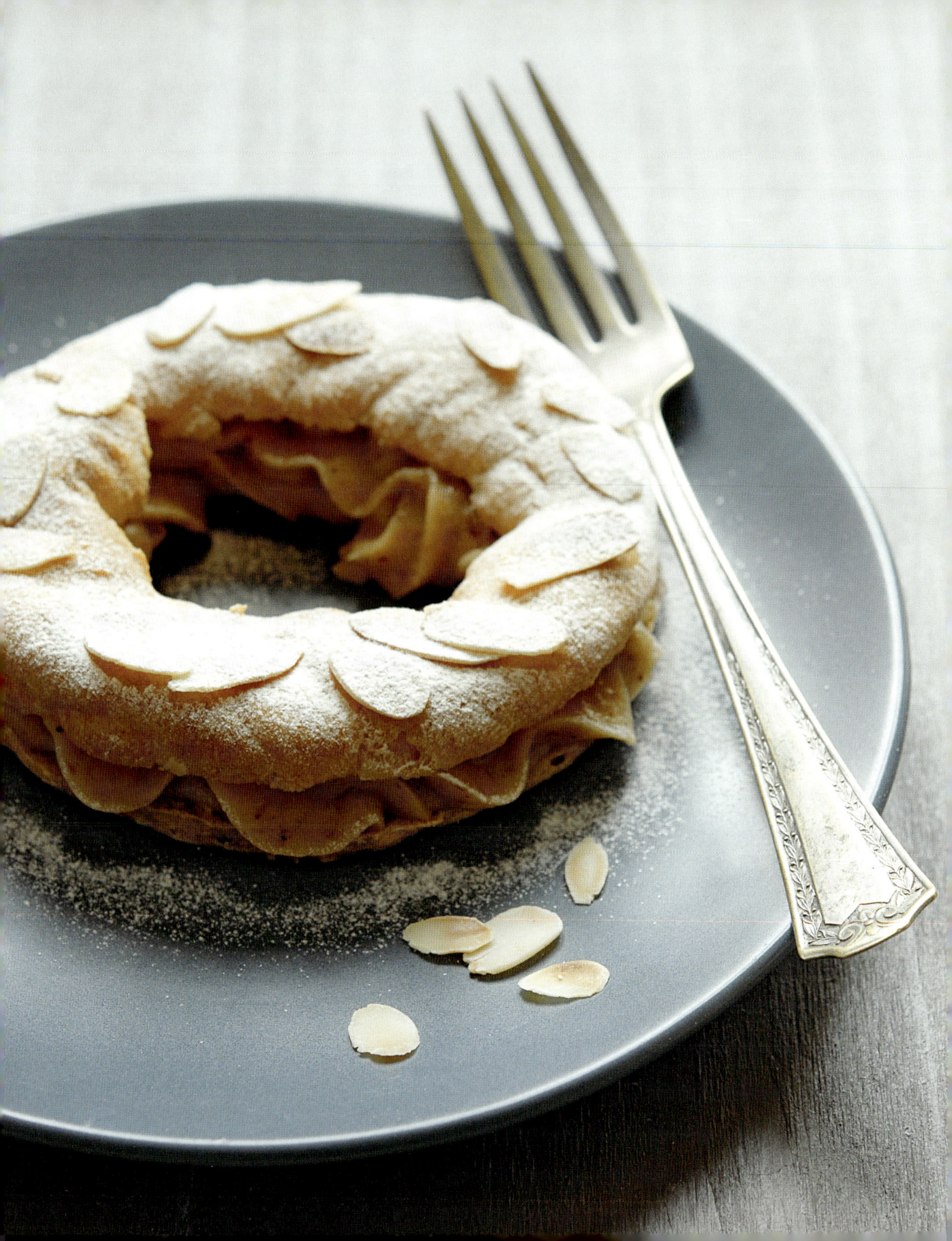

Coffee cream puffs

12 PASTRIES
PREP TIME: 40 mins.
COOKING TIME: 20 mins.

FOR THE CHOUX PASTRY
- 1/4 cup water
- 1/3 cup whole milk
- 1 scant teaspoon of salt
- 1 scant teaspoon of sugar
- 3 tbsp. butter
- 2/3 cup flour
- 2 eggs

FOR THE PASTRY CREAM
- 6 egg yolks
- 1/2 cup sugar
- 3/8 cup flour
- 2 cups milk
- 6 teaspoons soluble coffee extract

FOR THE FROSTING
- 6 oz. sugar cubes
- 2 tsp. glucose
- 4 tsp. coffee extract

Preheat the oven to 350° F.

Prepare the choux pastry: put the water and milk in a saucepan, add the salt, the sugar and the butter. Bring to a boil, stirring constantly. Add all the flour at once. Stir with a wooden or rubber spatula until the mixture is smooth. When it stops sticking to the sides of the pan, continue to stir for 2 or 3 minutes in order to dry it out slightly. Put the mixture in a bowl; add the eggs one by one, working the mixture constantly with the spatula. Lift the spatula out of the bowl from time to time: when the mixture forms a smooth ribbon, it's ready. Spoon into a pastry bag with a large fluted tip and pipe 12 circles of pastry onto a baking sheet covered with parchment paper. Bake for 20 minutes, leaving the oven door half open after the first 5 minutes.

Prepare the pastry cream: put the egg yolks and the sugar in a bowl and whisk vigorously. Stir in the flour. Boil the milk and pour it into the mixture, stirring constantly until it has a smooth, creamy consistency. Put the custard in a heavy saucepan over a low heat until it thickens, stirring constantly with a wooden spatula. Remove from the heat as soon as it starts to boil and add the coffee extract.

Prepare the fondant frosting: put 1 tbsp. water, the sugar and the glucose in a saucepan over a high heat. Heat until the syrup reaches 250° F. Pour onto a cold, oiled work surface; allow to cool. Work the frosting with a metal spatula, spreading it out and drawing it back in several times until it is perfectly smooth and white. Heat it in a double boiler and stir in the coffee extract.

Spoon the pastry cream into a pastry bag with a medium sized smooth tip and pipe the custard into the pastries, piercing their undersides with the tip. Dip the top half of each pastry in the coffee frosting and remove any excess frosting with your finger. Put the pastries on a wire rack to cool.

> **Helpful tip**
Fondant frosting requires a little care and attention. If it's too hot, it won't be glossy; if too cold, it'll be difficult to work with. The ideal working temperature is between 90 and 95° F.

> **Find out more**
Glucose syrup is a sticky substance made of various different sugars. It is also available in dehydrated form.

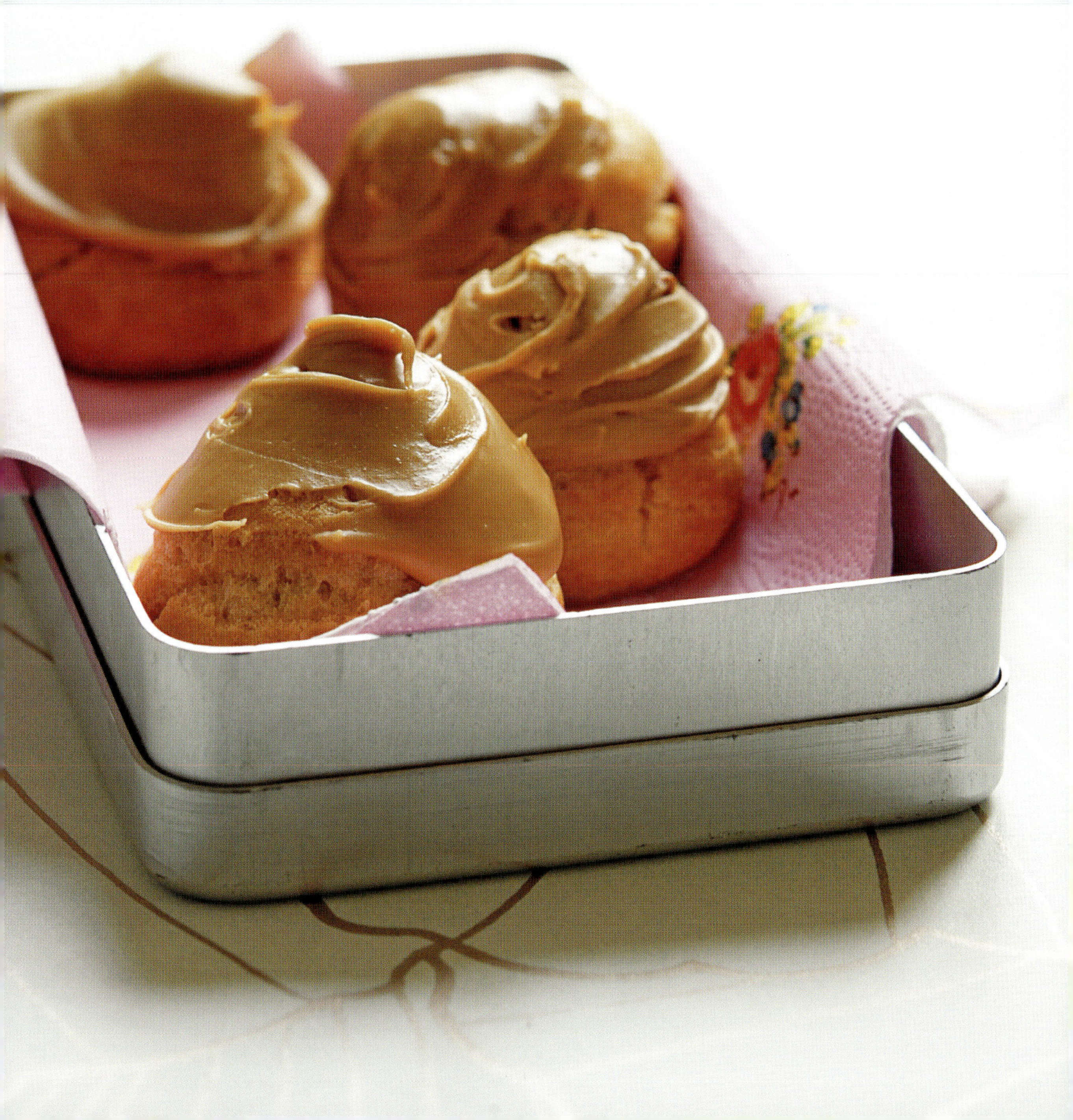

Coffee dacquoise

SERVES 6 TO 8
PREP TIME: 40 mins.
COOKING TIME: 35 mins.

FOR THE ALMOND CAKE
- 1-1/4 cups powdered sugar
- 1-1/2 cups ground almonds
- 5 egg whites
- 4 tbsp. sugar

FOR THE BUTTER CREAM
- 1 cup well softened butter
- 3 tbsp water
- 3/4 cup sugar
- 2 whole eggs
- 2 egg yolks
- 3 tbsp. instant coffee

TO DECORATE
- Lightly toasted slivered almonds
- Powdered sugar

Prepare the almond dacquoise: mix the powdered sugar and the ground almonds and sieve them onto a sheet of parchment paper. In a large bowl, beat the egg whites with an electric mixer. Beat in the sugar in three stages. Continue to beat the eggs until they form soft peaks. Carefully fold in the ground almonds and sugar (do not beat the mixture at this stage).

Preheat the oven to 350° F.

On one or two baking sheets covered with parchment paper, draw two circles 10 inches in diameter. Spoon the dacquoise into a pastry bag fitted with a number 9 tip and fill the circles, beginning at the center and spiraling outward. Bake for 35 minutes and allow to cool.

Prepare the butter cream: in a large bowl, work the butter with a wooden spatula until soft. Pour the water into a small saucepan. Add the sugar and bring to a boil over a gentle heat. Cook the syrup to soft-ball stage (250° F). Put the whole eggs and extra yolks into a bowl. Beat with an electric mixer until they turn pale yellow and frothy. When the syrup is ready, pour it onto the eggs in a thin stream, beating the mixture slowly. Continue beating until the mixture is cold. Add the coffee granules dissolved in a little water.

Put the butter cream into a pastry bag with a large smooth tip and pipe a thick layer onto the first disk. Lay the second disk on top and press down gently.

To decorate, sprinkle with toasted almonds and dust lightly with powdered sugar. Serve chilled.

> Helpful tip
When making dacquoise, many professional pastry chefs leave the egg whites in the refrigerator for 3 days before using them, as this helps the mixture keep its shape.

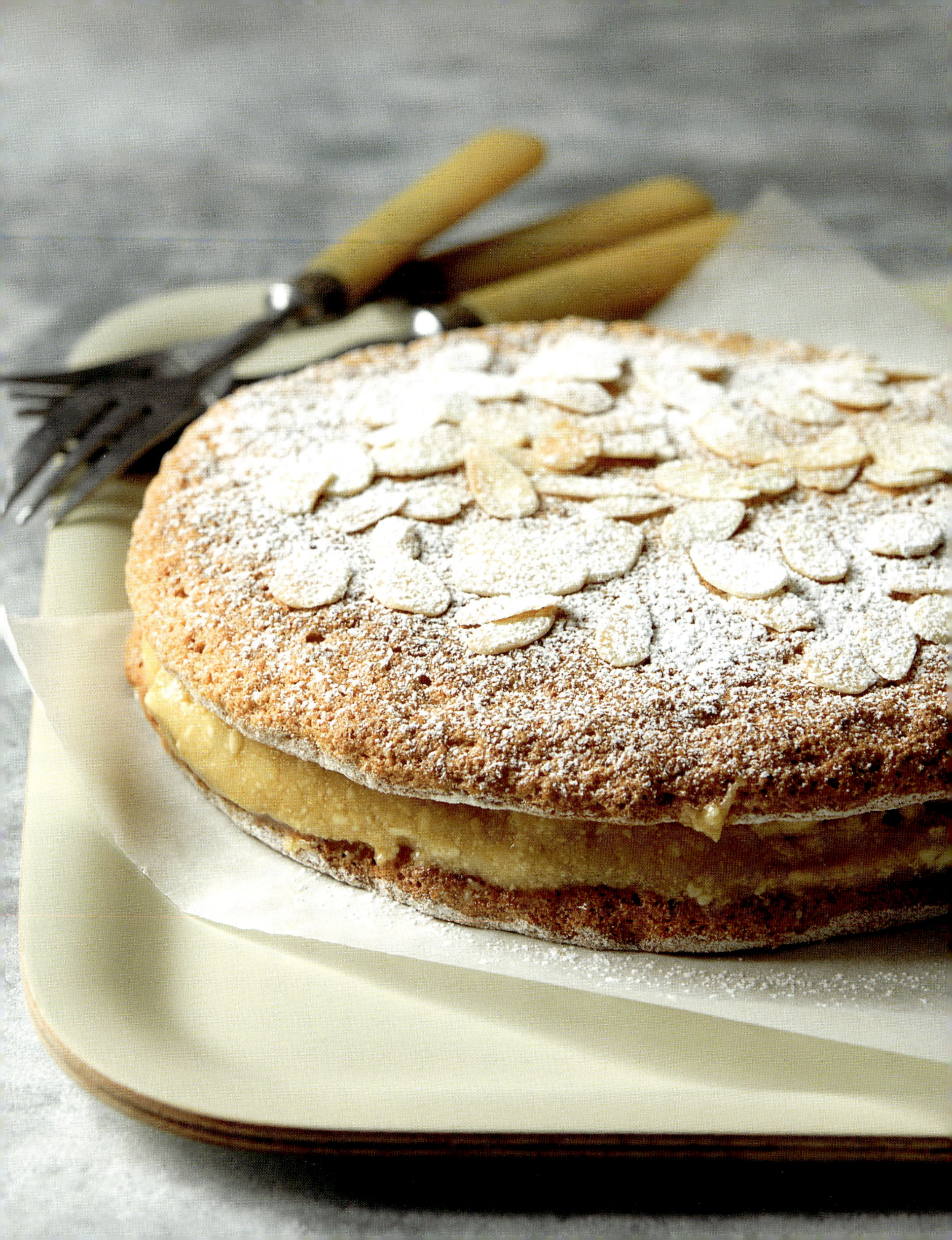

Saint-Honoré

SERVES 4
PREP TIME: 1 hr 15 mins.
COOKING TIME: 30 mins.

- 7 oz. store bought puff pastry

FOR THE CHOUX PASTRY
- 3 tbsp. water
- 3 tbsp. whole milk
- 3 tbsp. butter
- 1/2 tsp. salt
- 1/2 tsp. sugar
- 8 tbsp. flour
- 2 eggs

FOR THE PASTRY CREAM
- 1 cup milk
- 1/2 vanilla bean
- 3 egg yolks
- 1/3 cup sugar
- 6-1/2 tbsp cornstarch

FOR THE CARAMEL
- 1 cup sugar
- 4 tbsp. water

FOR THE CHANTILLY WHIPPED CREAM
- 1-1/4 cup heavy cream
- 2 tbsp. sugar

Prepare the choux pastry: pour the water and milk into a saucepan, add the salt, the sugar and the butter. Bring to a boil, stirring constantly. Add the flour all at once. Stir with a wooden or rubber spatula until the dough is smooth. When it stops sticking to the sides of the pan, continue to work for 2 or 3 minutes, to dry it out a little. Place in a bowl. Break in the eggs one by one, stirring constantly. Lift your spatula from time to time: when the mixture forms a smooth ribbon, it's ready.

Prepare the pastry cream: bring the milk to a boil with the split vanilla bean. Remove the bean. Beat the egg yolks with the sugar until they turn pale yellow; add the cornstarch. Pour in the boiling milk, stirring constantly, and pour the mixture back into the saucepan. Cook for 1 or 2 minutes, whisking constantly until the mixture thickens.

Roll out the puff pastry to form a 10-inch disk. Prick with a fork and place on a baking sheet lined with parchment paper.

Put the choux pastry into a pastry bag with a one-inch tip and pipe a circle of choux pastry on top of the puff pastry disk, half an inch from the edge. Now fill in the circle with a spiral of choux pastry.

Preheat the oven to 400° F. Put a smaller tip on your pastry bag and pipe 18 small spheres 1 inch in diameter on another baking sheet lined with parchment paper. Bake both sheets for about 30 minutes, keeping the oven door slightly open. Take the small spheres out of the oven 6 to 8 minutes before the main cake, as they will bake more quickly. Allow to cool.

Put the pastry cream into a pastry bag with a smooth medium tip and fill the spheres, piercing them with the tip. Do the same with the "crown," making several holes with the tip to fill it.

Prepare the caramel: gently heat the sugar with the water in a saucepan until it turns into a golden brown caramel. Dip the choux pastry spheres in the caramel and lay them caramel side down on a nonstick baking sheet. Allow to cool slightly, then take them off the sheet and dip the other side in the caramel. Stick the spheres all the way around the top of the "crown" as you go.

Make the Chantilly whipped cream: put the chilled cream in a bowl and beat with a whisk, gradually adding the sugar when the cream starts to thicken. Place in a pastry bag with a fluted tip and fill the center of the cake with a mound of cream. Serve immediately.

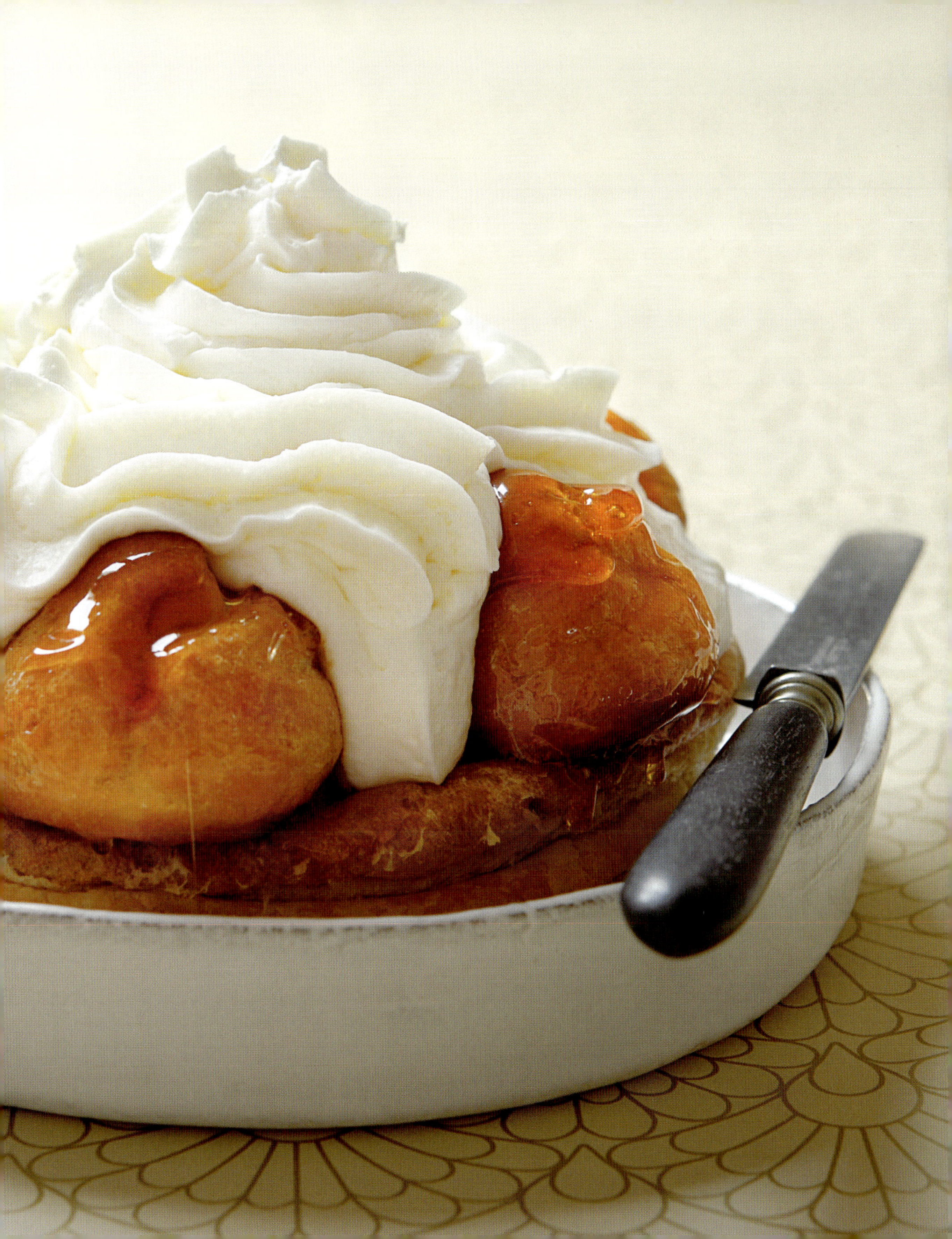

Raspberry (or apricot) roll

SERVES 4 TO 6
PREP TIME: 25 mins.
COOKING TIME: 10 mins.

- 6 tbsp. apricot or raspberry jam

FOR THE CAKE MIXTURE
- 6 eggs
- 3/4 cup sugar
- 2/3 cup sifted flour
- 1 tbsp. butter for the baking sheet

FOR THE SYRUP
- 1/2 cup sugar
- 1 teaspoon rum

FOR DECORATION
- 1-1/2 cups slivered almonds
- Apricot jam

Prepare the cake mixture: break the eggs and separate the yolks from the whites. Beat the 6 egg yolks with 3 of the egg whites and half the sugar until the mixture is frothy and pale yellow. Whisk the 3 remaining egg whites until they form stiff peaks and gradually beat in the rest of the sugar (you can use an electric mixer for this). Carefully fold in the egg yolk mixture. Add the sifted flour and mix in gently.

Preheat the oven to 350° F.

Melt the butter. Line a baking sheet with parchment paper and brush with melted butter. Pour in the mixture and spread it out to a thickness of half an inch using a metal spatula. Bake for 10 minutes: the top should turn a very light golden color.

Lightly toast the almonds in the oven at 350° F.

Prepare the syrup: mix the sugar with 6 tbsp. water, then add the rum.

Lay the cake on a clean dish towel and brush liberally with syrup. Spread thickly with apricot or raspberry jam.

Roll up the cake using the dish towel. Cut the two ends off at an angle. Spread a thin layer of jelly over the top of the roll and sprinkle with toasted almonds.

> Helpful tip
Why not make your own raspberry jam? (see p.392).

child's play

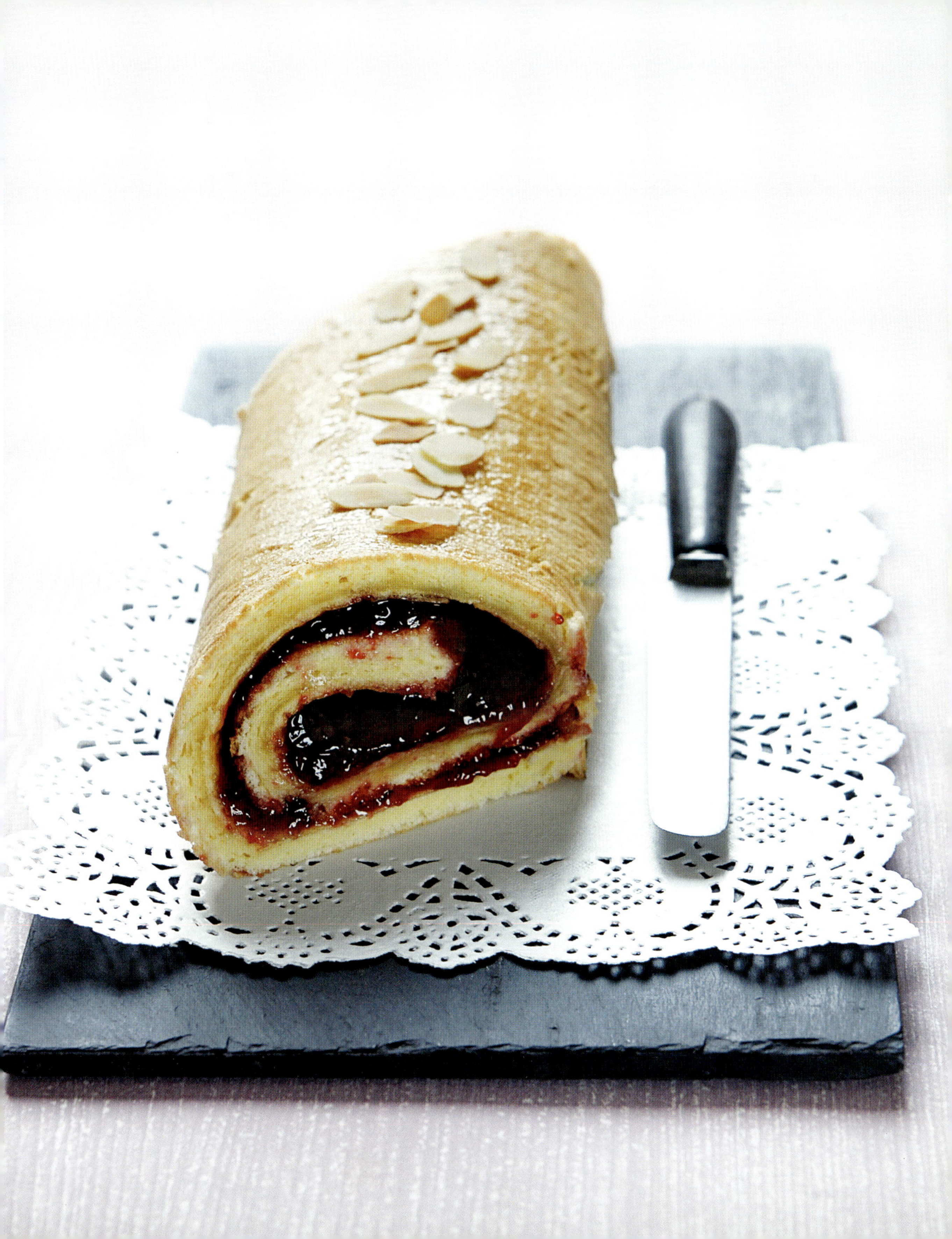

Walnut "délice"

SERVES 6
PREP TIME: 20 mins.
COOKING TIME: 50 mins.

- 2-1/2 cups shelled walnuts
- 6 eggs
- 3/4 cup sugar
- 1/2 cup cornstarch
- 2 tbsp. dark rum
- Butter for the pan

FOR THE FROSTING
- 1-1/4 cups powdered sugar
- 1 tbsp. water
- 2 tbsp. coffee extract

Keep 3 tbsp. walnuts for decoration and roughly chop the rest in a food processor. Break the eggs and separate the whites and yolks.

Put the egg yolks and sugar in a bowl and beat until the mixture turns a pale yellow. Add the cornstarch, the rum and the chopped nuts. Mix well with a wooden spoon.

Preheat the oven to 375° F. Generously butter an 8-inch round cake pan.

Beat the egg whites until they form very stiff peaks. Take two tbsp. of beaten egg white and fold into the nut mixture to lighten it. Now gently fold in the rest of the beaten egg whites.

Pour the mixture into the pan and place in the center of the oven. Bake for 50 minutes. Test by pushing the end of a knife into the cake: the blade should come out clean. Take the cake out of the oven and allow to rest for 10 minutes, then turn it out and allow to cool on a wire rack.

Prepare the frosting: mix the powdered sugar with the water, add the coffee extract and stir well to obtain a thick liquid paste. Spread on top of the cake with a soft spatula. Decorate with walnuts.

> To make a change
If you like walnuts you should try our recipe for walnut cookies (see p.258)!

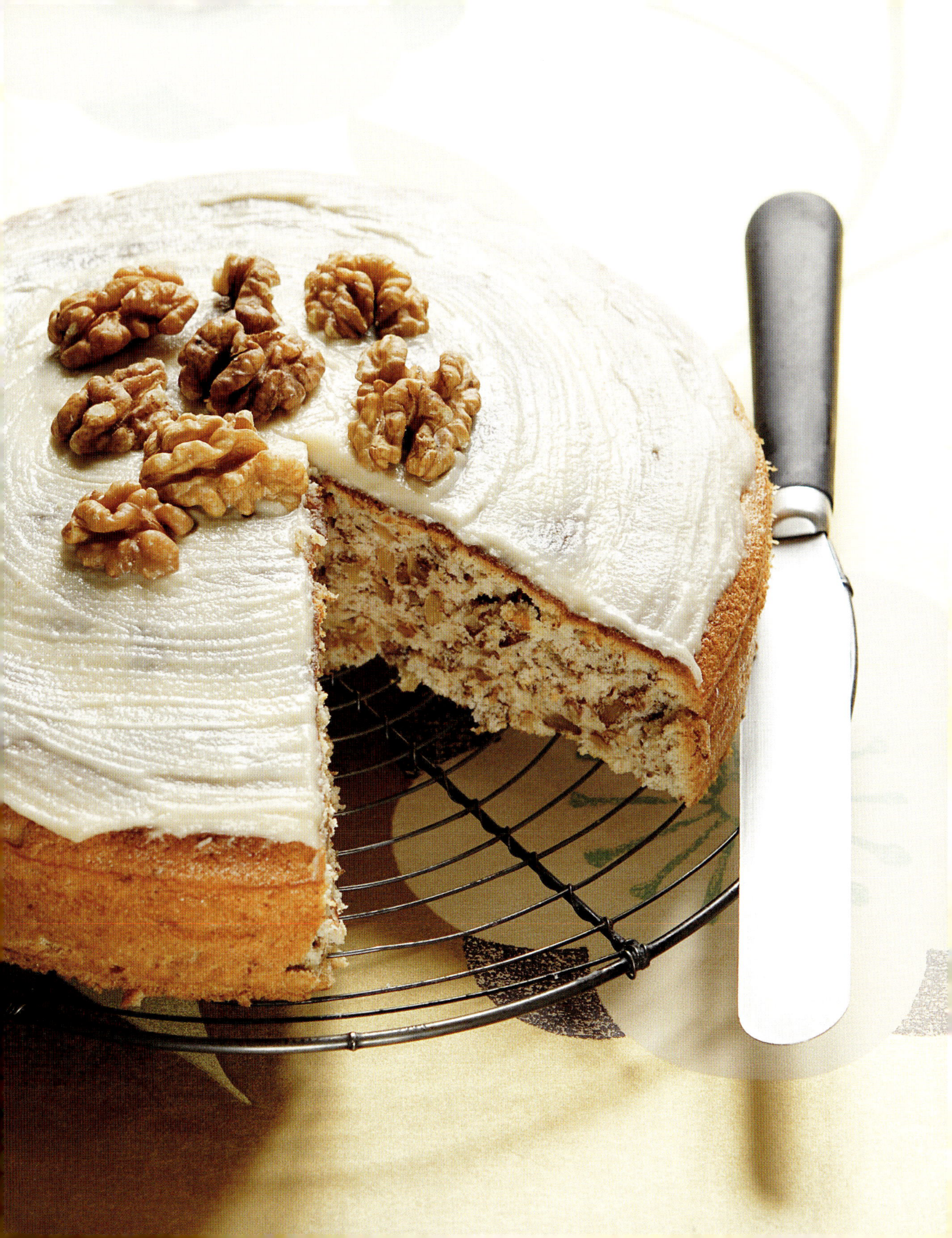

Individual rum babas

SERVES 6
PREP TIME: 45 mins.
RESTING TIME: 30 mins.
COOKING TIME: About 30 mins.

FOR THE YEAST MIXTURE
- 1/4 tbsp. dry yeast
- A little water

FOR THE BABA MIXTURE
- 3 tbsp. butter + a little for the molds
- 1 cup sifted flour
- A pinch of salt
- 2/3 cup sugar
- 2 eggs

FOR THE SYRUP
- 1 vanilla bean
- 2-1/4 cups sugar
- 5 oz. rum

Mix the dry yeast with 1 tbsp. warm water. Set aside.

Prepare the baba mixture: melt the butter and allow to cool slightly. In a bowl, mix together the flour, salt, sugar and 1 egg with a wooden spoon.

Add the yeast mixture, then add the second egg. Mix until the dough becomes smooth and supple. Add the melted butter and mix well.

Butter six 4-oz dariole molds. Fill them three-quarters full of mixture, cover them and allow them to rise for 30 minutes in a warm place.

Preheat the oven to 400° F. Bake the babas for 15 to 20 minutes.

While they're baking, prepare the syrup. Split the vanilla bean. In a heavy saucepan, dissolve the sugar in 2 cups of water over a low heat. Add the vanilla bean, bring to a boil for a few seconds and remove from the heat. Take the babas out of the oven and turn them out while they are still hot. When they are cold, plunge them into the warm syrup until no more bubbles appear. Drain them and put them on a large plate.

Mix the rum with the rest of the syrup. When the mixture is cold, pour over the babas. Chill until ready to serve.

> Helpful tip
Leave your yeast mixture to rest in a warm place and wait until it has doubled in volume before adding it to the rest of the mixture.

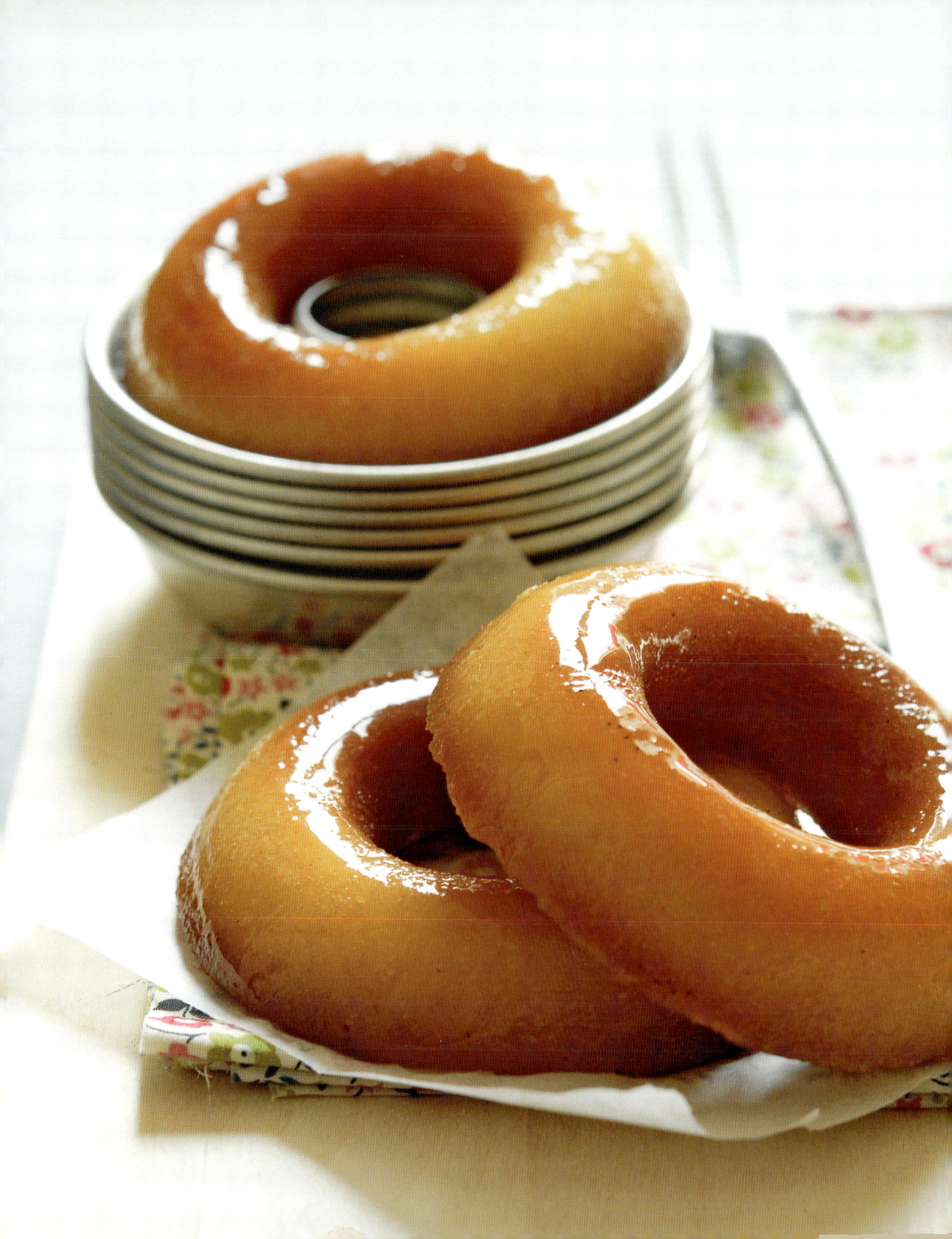

Luxury coffee cake

SERVES 6 TO 8
PREP TIME: 45 mins.
COOKING TIME: 45 mins.
REFRIGERATION TIME: 2 hrs

FOR THE CAKE MIXTURE
- 3/4 cup ground hazelnuts
- 1/3 cup ground unblanched almonds
- 1/2 cup ground blanched almonds
- 1-1/2 cups powdered sugar
- 1-1/2 tbsp. flour
- 6 egg whites
- 1 small pinch of salt
- Butter and flour for the pans

FOR THE COFFEE BUTTER CREAM
- 1 cup very soft butter
- 1/4 cup water
- 3/4 cup sugar
- 2 whole eggs
- 2 egg yolks
- 6 tbsp. instant coffee granules

FOR DECORATION
- 1-1/2 cups slivered almonds

Prepare the cake: mix the hazelnuts and ground almonds with the powdered sugar and flour. Beat the egg whites with a pinch of salt until they form stiff peaks. Fold them into the previous mixture.

Preheat the oven to 275° F.

Butter 2 (or 3) baking sheets, place 3 ten-inch plates on them, dust with flour and remove the plates: you now have three disk shapes. Spoon the cake mixture into a pastry bag with a no. 8 tip and cover the disks with the mixture, starting in the center and working outward in a spiral. Bake for about 45 minutes.

Allow the cake disks to cool on a wire rack. Toast the almonds to be used for decoration in the oven.

Prepare the coffee butter cream: work the butter with a wooden spatula until creamy. Place the water in a small saucepan, add the sugar and bring to a boil over a low heat. Cook this syrup to soft ball stage (240° F). Put the eggs and extra yolks in a bowl and beat with an electric mixer until pale yellow and frothy. When the syrup is ready, pour it onto the eggs in a thin stream, beating at low speed. Continue to beat until the mixture is cold. Add the coffee dissolved in a little water. Take out a quarter of the coffee cream and set aside. Divide the rest into three.

Using a frosting knife, cover the first disk with coffee cream. Place the next disk on top and spread with coffee cream. Do the same with the third disk. Use the remaining quarter of the coffee butter cream to frost the sides of the cake. Decorate with toasted almonds and place in the refrigerator for 2 hours.

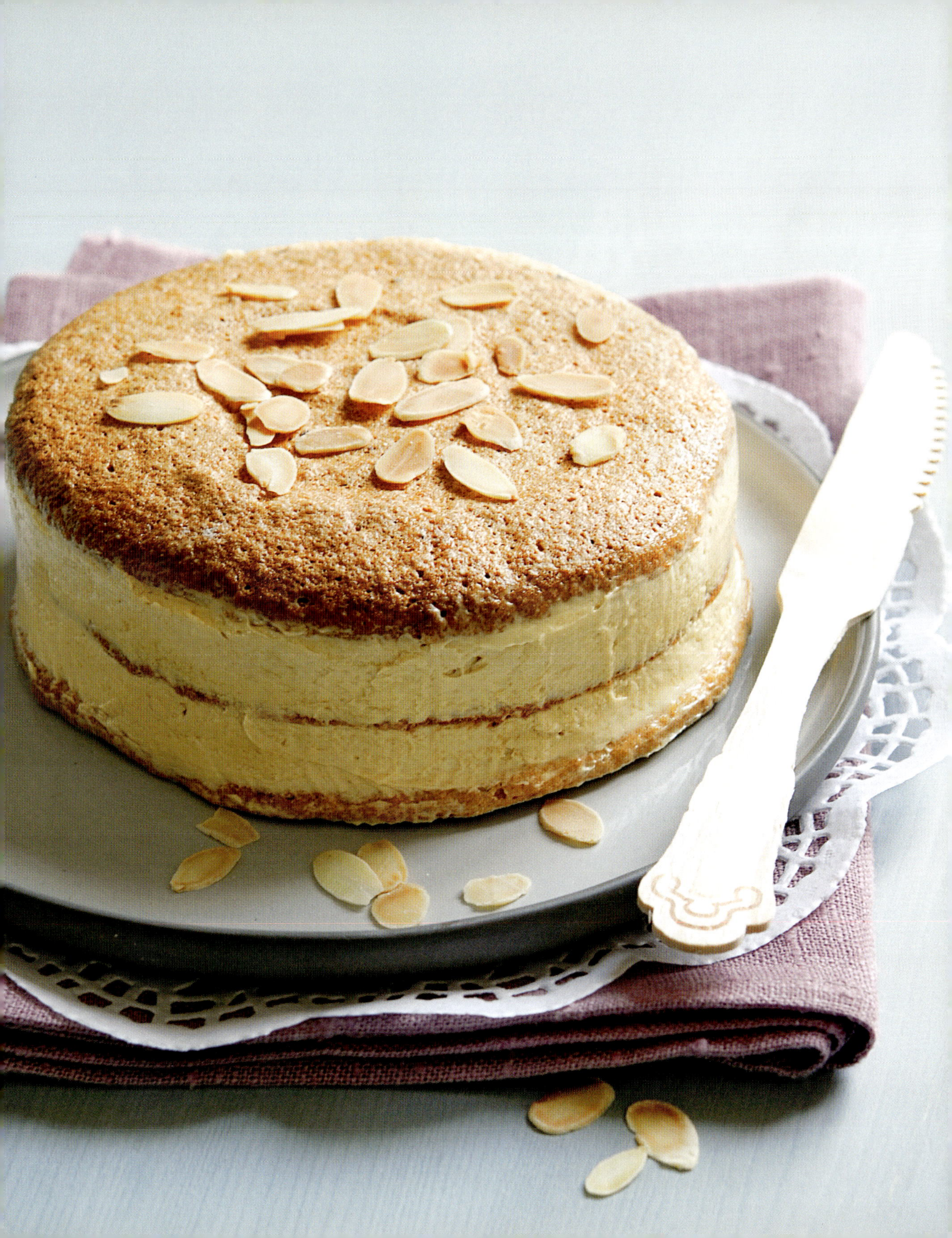

Galette des Rois
(Traditional French Twelfth Night cake)

SERVES 6
PREP TIME: 20 mins.
RESTING TIME: 30 mins.
COOKING TIME: 40 mins.

- 1 lb. store bought puff pastry
- 1 egg

FOR THE FRANGIPANE (ALMOND FILLING)
- 6 tbsp. butter
- 1 small egg
- 2/3 cup powdered sugar
- 3/4 cup ground almonds

child's play

Prepare the frangipane: cut the butter into small pieces. Break the egg into a bowl, add the butter and sugar. Beat to a smooth cream. Stir in the ground almonds.

Divide the puff pastry into two equal halves and roll out each half into a disk about 1/8 inch thick. Lay one of the disks on a large baking sheet covered in parchment paper.

Beat the egg and brush around the edge of the disk with a pastry brush. Spread the frangipane on the pastry, stopping just short of the edge.

Lay the other disk on top and pinch the edges together. Trace a criss-cross pattern on the top with a small knife. Place in the refrigerator for 30 minutes.

Preheat the oven to 475° F.

Brush the pastry with the rest of the beaten egg. Place in the oven, reduce the temperature to 400° F and bake for 40 minutes. Serve warm.

> Find out more

In France they put a small porcelain charm in the galette des Rois. The person who finds the charm is the "king" or "queen," and is given a cardboard crown to wear while the cake is eaten.

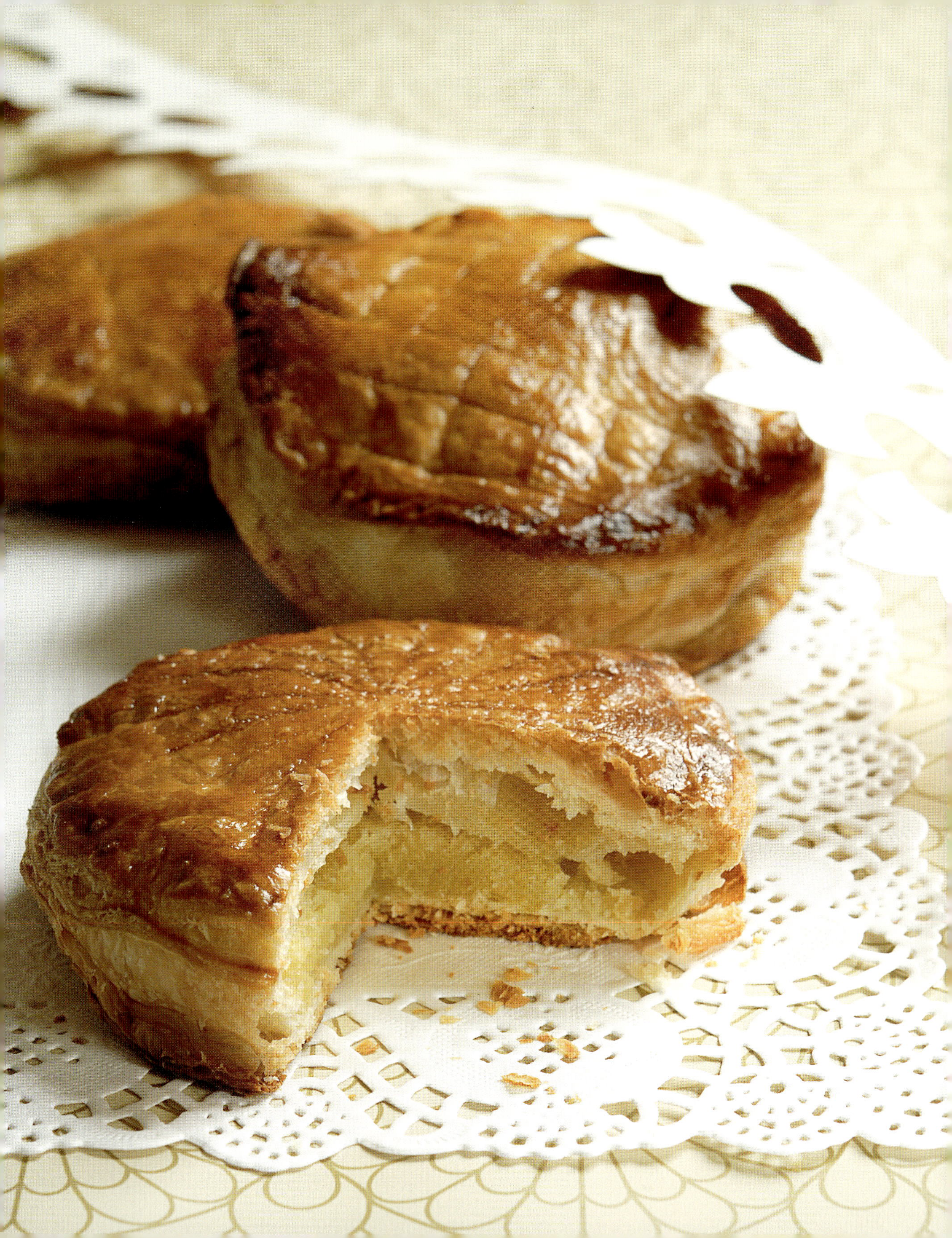

Chestnut log

SERVES 8
PREP TIME: 25 mins.
REFRIGERATION TIME: 24 hrs
- 1/4 lb. dark chocolate
- 9 tbsp. butter
- Just over 1 lb. chestnut purée
- 1 cup powdered sugar

Break the chocolate into pieces. Place in a small saucepan over very low heat. Add 2 tbsp. of water and allow to soften.

Put the butter in a bowl and soften with a spatula.

Put the chestnut purée in a bowl and mash it with a fork to remove any lumps. Add the butter and chocolate and half the powdered sugar. Stir until smooth.

Place a double thickness of aluminum foil on your work surface and spoon the mixture onto it. Make it into a thick cylinder shape and roll it up in the foil. Refrigerate for at least 24 hours.

When the cake is good and firm, peel off the foil and place it on a long serving platter. Cut off the ends at an angle. Run a fork along the top to make the "bark" and dust with powdered sugar. Refrigerate until needed.

> To make a change
You can flavor the mixture with a little rum if you wish. Use your imagination to decorate the log: holly leaves made of chocolate or marzipan, meringue mushrooms, festive figurines, etc.

> Helpful tip
If you're in a hurry, you can speed up the setting process by putting the log in the freezer for 2 hours.

never fails

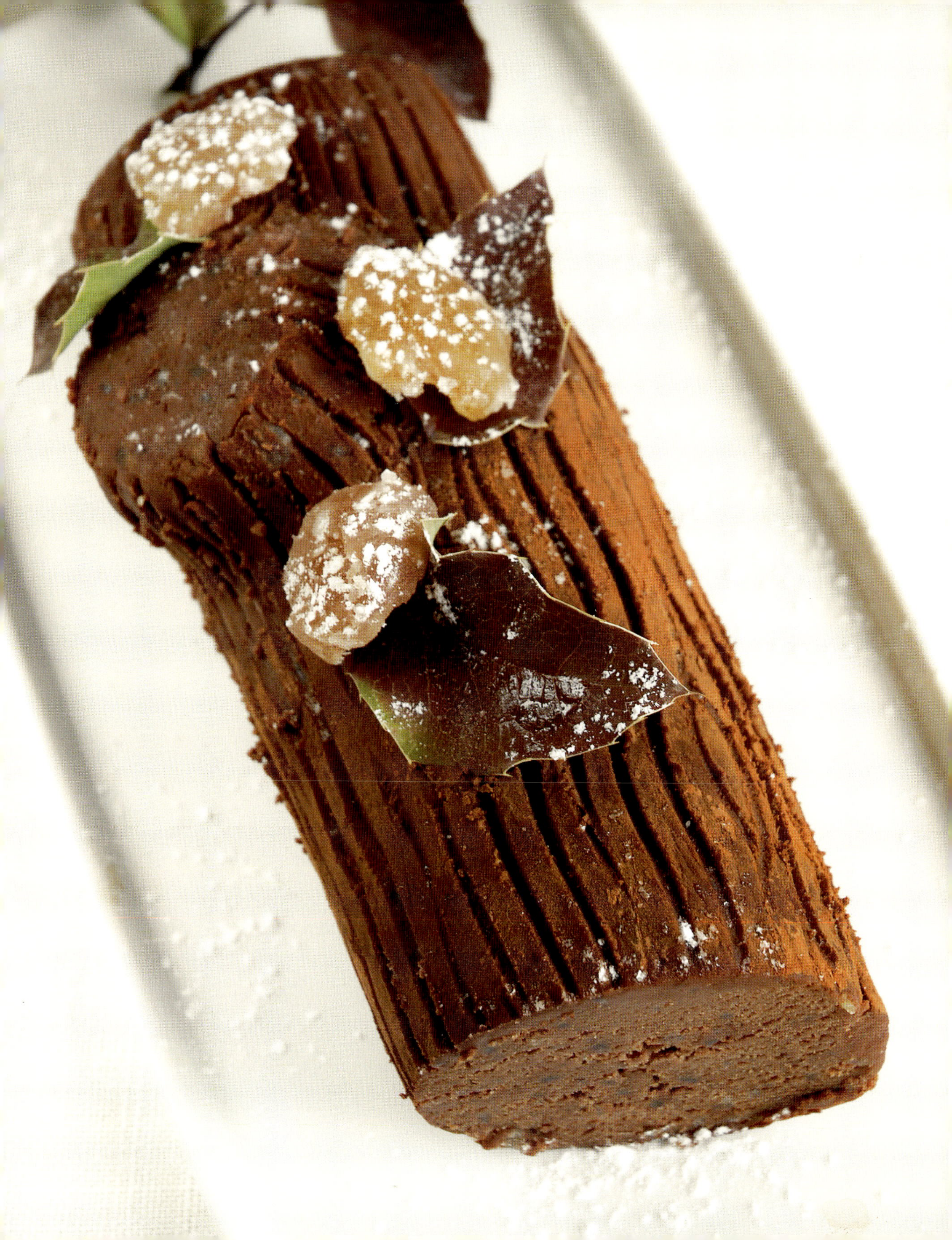

Spiced pineapple mille-feuilles

SERVES 6
PREP TIME: 25 mins.
COOKING TIME: 15 mins.

- 8 sheets phyllo pastry
- 4 tbsp. butter
- Powdered sugar
- 1 pineapple (about 1-1/2 pounds)
- 1 small piece of fresh ginger
- 4 green cardamom pods
- 4 tbsp. brown sugar
- 1 vanilla bean
- 1 tbsp. unsalted pistachios
- 1/2 cup berry coulis
- A few red currants

Preheat the oven to 350° F.

Place two sheets of phyllo pastry one on top of the other, brush with melted butter and dust with powdered sugar. Cut out six 6-inch disks and put them on a baking sheet lined with parchment paper.

Bake for 3 to 5 minutes until golden.

Do the same with the six remaining sheets of pastry.

Peel the pineapple and remove the "eyes" and tough core. Dice the flesh (you should end up with about a pound) and place it in a bowl.

Peel the ginger and grate it into a bowl. Open the cardamom pods, remove the seeds and roughly crush them. Place them in the bowl, along with the brown sugar. Split the vanilla bean and scrape the seeds into the bowl. Mix well.

Melt the rest of the butter in a skillet and add the pineapple; sprinkle with the spiced brown sugar and cook over medium heat for about 10 minutes, stirring frequently.

Roughly chop the pistachios and put them under the broiler for a minute until golden.

Make your mille-feuille: place a circle of pastry in each dish. Spread with pineapple and pistachios, top with a second pastry disk, and continue until you have used six disks for each one.

Pour a thin line of coulis around the mille-feuilles and decorate with powdered sugar, pistachios and a small bunch of red currants.

chef style

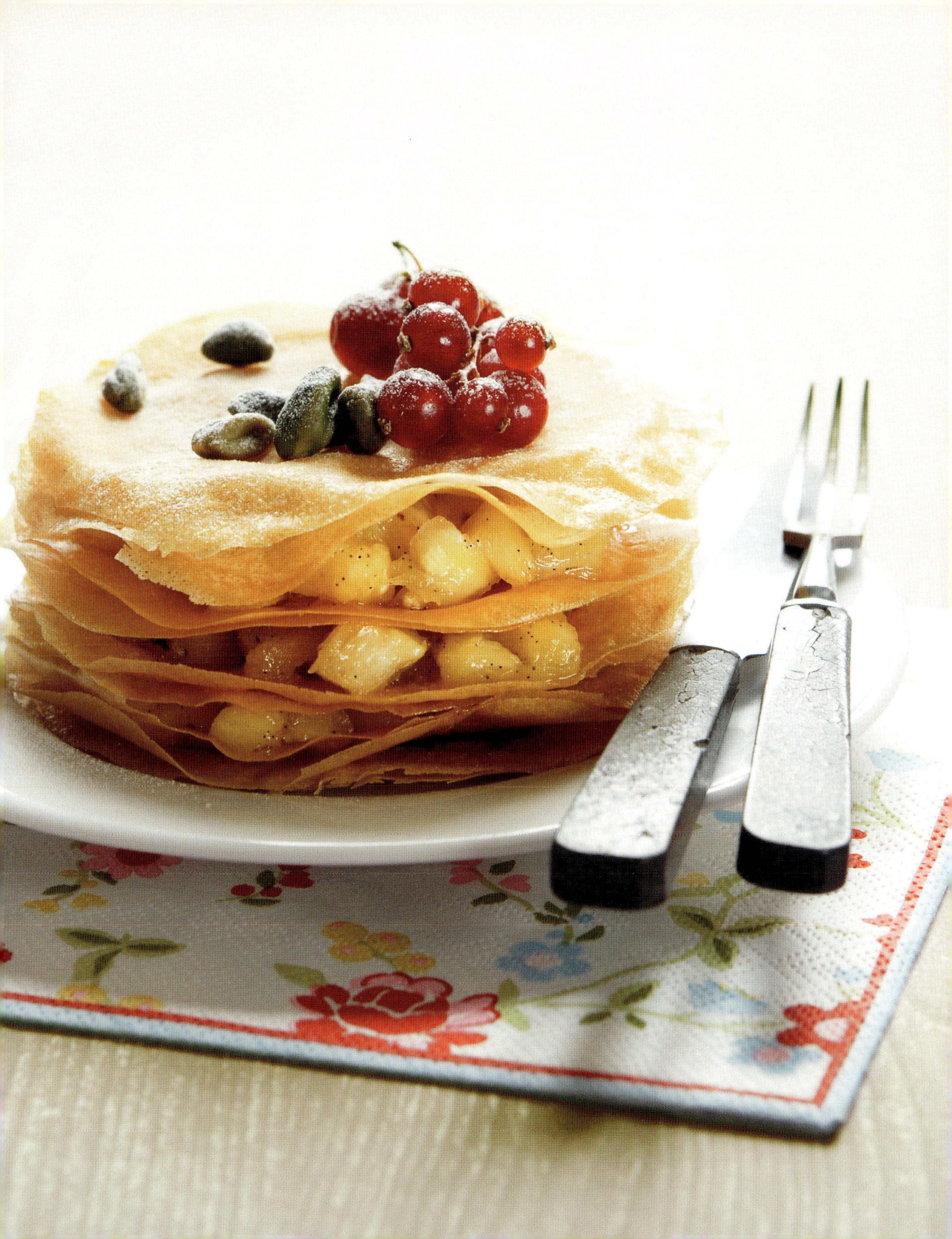

Black Forest gâteau

SERVES 8
SOAKING TIME: 2 hrs
PREP TIME: 45 mins.
COOKING TIME: 30 mins.
COOLING TIME: 2 hrs

FOR THE CHERRIES IN KIRSCH
- 1 lb canned cherries
- 7 tbsp. kirsch

FOR THE CAKE
- 6 eggs
- 7 tbsp. butter
  + more for the pan
- 1/2 cup sugar
- 3/4 cup ground almonds
- 1 cup cocoa powder
- 1-1/2 cups flour
- 2-1/2 tsp. baking powder
- 2 tsp. vanilla extract

FOR THE CHANTILLY WHIPPED CREAM
- 1 cup heavy cream
- 2 tsp. vanilla extract

FOR DECORATION
- Maraschino cherries
- Dark chocolate

Prepare the cherries in kirsch: soak the cherries in the kirsch for 2 hours.

Preheat the oven to 350° F.

Prepare the cake: break the eggs and separate the whites from the yolks; melt the butter gently in a saucepan. Put the egg yolks in a large bowl. Add the sugar, the melted butter, the almonds, the cocoa powder, the flour, the baking powder and the vanilla extract. Mix well until smooth. Beat the egg whites until they form stiff peaks. Fold them carefully into the mixture.

Butter an 8-inch round cake pan and pour in the mixture. Bake for about 30 minutes. Allow to cool for at least 1 hour.

Turn out the cake and cut horizontally into 3 disks. Put each disk onto a plate. Sprinkle with the cherry soaking juice and lay the cherries on 2 of the disks.

Prepare the Chantilly whipped cream: beat the cream until it thickens, gradually adding the vanilla extract. Stop beating when the cream has doubled in volume. Spread cream over the cherries on the two cake disks, then place the three disks on top of each other.

Decorate with Maraschino cherries and grated chocolate. Refrigerate for at least an hour before serving.

> Helpful tip

This cake is originally from the Black Forest in Bavaria, Germany. It can keep for 24 hours in the refrigerator.

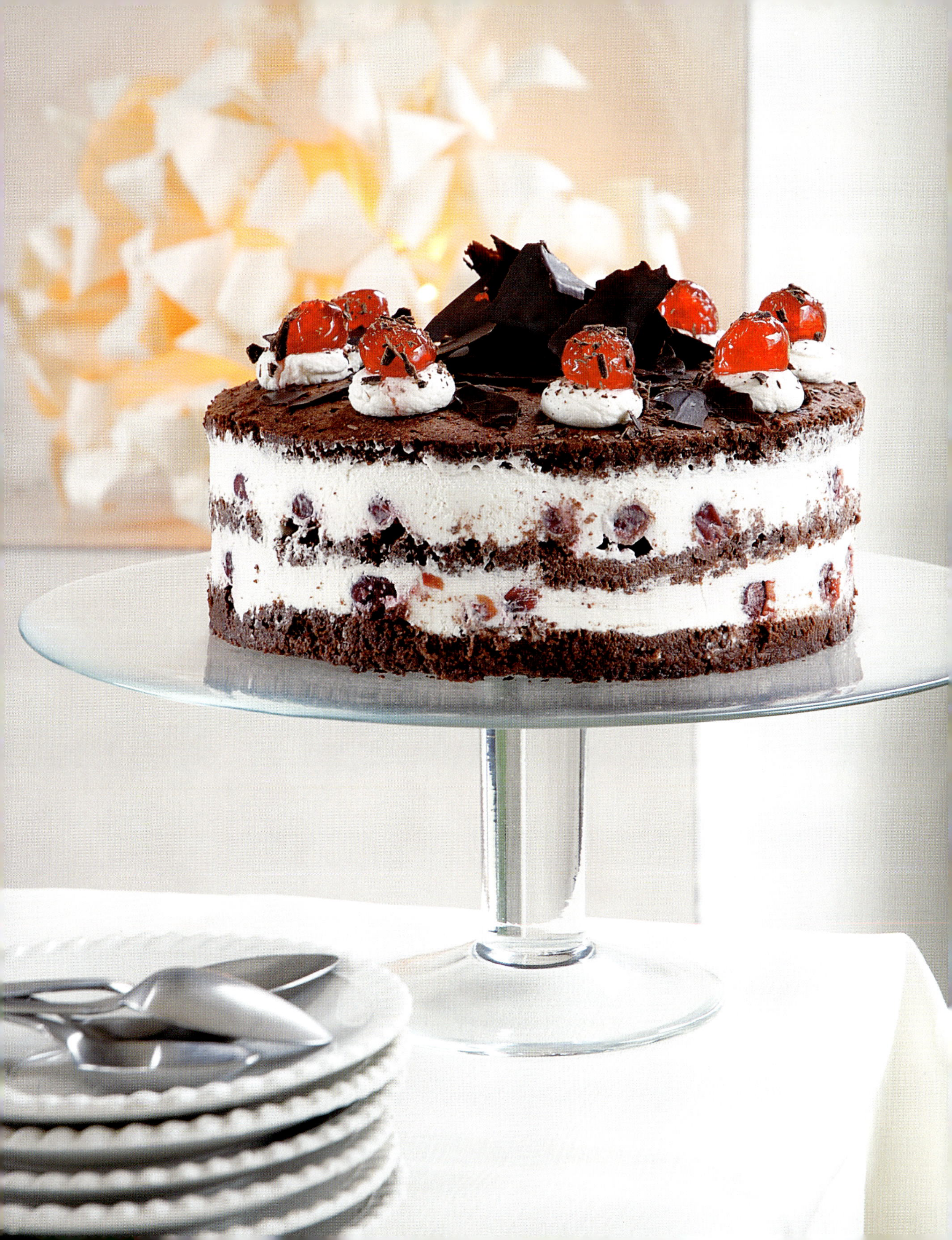

Berry fruit savarin with Chantilly whipped cream

SERVES 4 TO 6
PREP TIME: 25 mins.
RESTING TIME: 30 mins.
COOKING TIME: 20 to 25 mins.

FOR THE SAVARIN
- Zest of 1/4 lemon
- 4 tbsp. butter at room temperature
- 1 scant tbsp. dry yeast
- 1-1/4 cups flour
- 1/2 teaspoon vanilla extract
- 1 tbsp. honey
- 1 teaspoon salt
- 5 eggs

FOR THE SYRUP
- 1 vanilla bean
- 2-1/4 cups sugar
- 5 oz. rum

FOR THE CHANTILLY WHIPPED CREAM
- 1 cup crème fraîche or heavy cream
- 1 heaping tbsp. powdered sugar
- 1/2 tsp. vanilla extract

FOR THE FILLING
- 2-1/2 cups strawberries
- 3 tbsp. sugar
- The juice of half a lemon
- 1/2 lb raspberries
- 1/4 lb red currants
- 1/2 tsp. vanilla extract

Prepare the savarin: finely chop the lemon zest; cut the butter into small pieces. Put the yeast into a bowl. Add the flour, vanilla extract, honey, salt, lemon zest and one egg. Mix with a wooden spoon, then add the other eggs one by one. Work the mixture until it stops sticking to the sides of the bowl. Incorporate the butter and work until the mixture stops sticking to the bowl again. It should be elastic, smooth and shiny. Butter a 9-inch savarin mold, pour in the savarin mixture and allow to rest for 30 minutes in a warm place.

Preheat the oven to 400° F.

Bake for 20 to 25 minutes. Turn out the savarin and cool on a wire rack.

Prepare the syrup: split the vanilla pod and scrape out the seeds; dissolve the sugar in the water, add the vanilla seeds and heat until the mixture thickens into a syrup. Put the savarin into a dish and soak with warm syrup using a spoon. Allow to cool and sprinkle with rum.

Prepare the Chantilly whipped cream: whip the chilled crème fraîche or heavy cream for about 1 minute, then add the powdered sugar and the vanilla extract; continue to whip until it reaches the desired consistency (do not overwhip).

Prepare the fruit. Make a strawberry coulis: wash and hull the strawberries, blend them in a food processor and sieve the juice. Mix with the vanilla extract and the juice of half a lemon. Prepare the raspberries and red currants.

Put the cake on a serving dish. Carefully mix the raspberries and red currants with the Chantilly whipped cream and spoon into the center of the cake.

Serve the coulis in a small pitcher to accompany your savarin.

> Helpful tip

You can also make this cake in a food processor using a dough hook. Put the flour, yeast, salt, honey, lemon zest, vanilla and 3 eggs in the bowl. Turn on at medium speed until the dough stops sticking to the sides, add the other eggs, wait until the dough stops sticking again, then add the butter. Stop the machine when the dough is smooth, elastic and shiny.

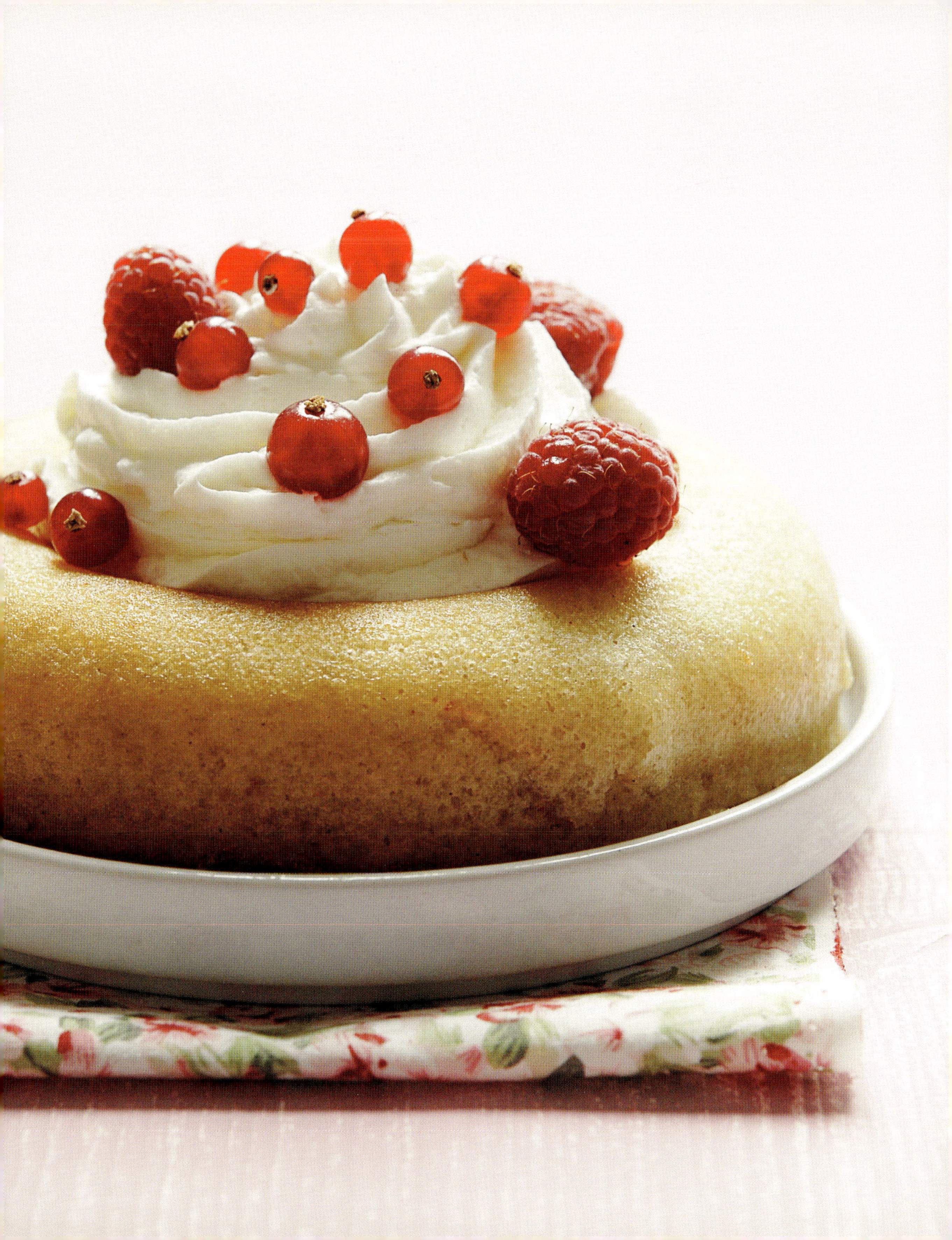

Strawberry sponge cake

SERVES 6
PREP TIME: 30 mins.
COOKING TIME: About 15 mins.

- 1 store bought sponge cake 9 inches in diameter
- 1 pound strawberries

FOR THE BUTTER CREAM
- 9 tbsp. very soft butter
- 2 tbsp. water
- 1/3 cup sugar
- 1 whole egg
- 1 egg yolk
- 1 tbsp. kirsch

FOR THE PASTRY CREAM
- 3 egg yolks
- 4 tbsp. sugar
- 3 tbsp. flour
- 1 cup milk

FOR THE KIRSCH SYRUP
- 2-1/2 tbsp. sugar
- 1 tbsp. kirsch

FOR DECORATION
- Powdered sugar
- Chantilly whipped cream

Prepare the butter cream: work the butter until creamy with a wooden spatula. Pour the water into a small saucepan, add the sugar and bring to a boil on a gentle heat. Cook the syrup to soft ball stage (240° F). Break the egg into a bowl and add the extra yolk. Beat with an electric mixer until the mixture turns pale and frothy. When the syrup is ready, pour it onto the eggs in a thin stream, beating slowly. Continue beating until the mixture is cold, then add the kirsch.

Prepare the pastry cream: beat together the egg yolks and sugar. Add the flour. Boil the milk and add to the mixture, stirring constantly. Pour the custard into a saucepan and allow to thicken over a gentle heat. Remove from the heat. Take out just over 1/8 cup of custard and put the rest aside to use in another recipe. Whip the butter cream and add the 1/8 cup of pastry cream.

Prepare the kirsch syrup: mix the sugar, 6 tbsp. water and the kirsch. Cut the sponge cake in two horizontally and brush each half with kirsch syrup.

Wash and hull the strawberries. Keep some aside for decoration.

Place one half of the sponge on a serving dish with the cut side facing upward. Spread thickly with custard using a spatula. Cover with tightly packed strawberries: they should be standing up with the fat end buried in the custard. Cover with another thick layer of custard, making sure it gets into the gaps but not covering the ring of strawberries standing around the edge.

Place the other half on top, cut face downward, and press down gently so that it all sticks together. Dust with powdered sugar, decorate with sliced strawberries and place in the refrigerator until needed. Serve with Chantilly whipped cream.

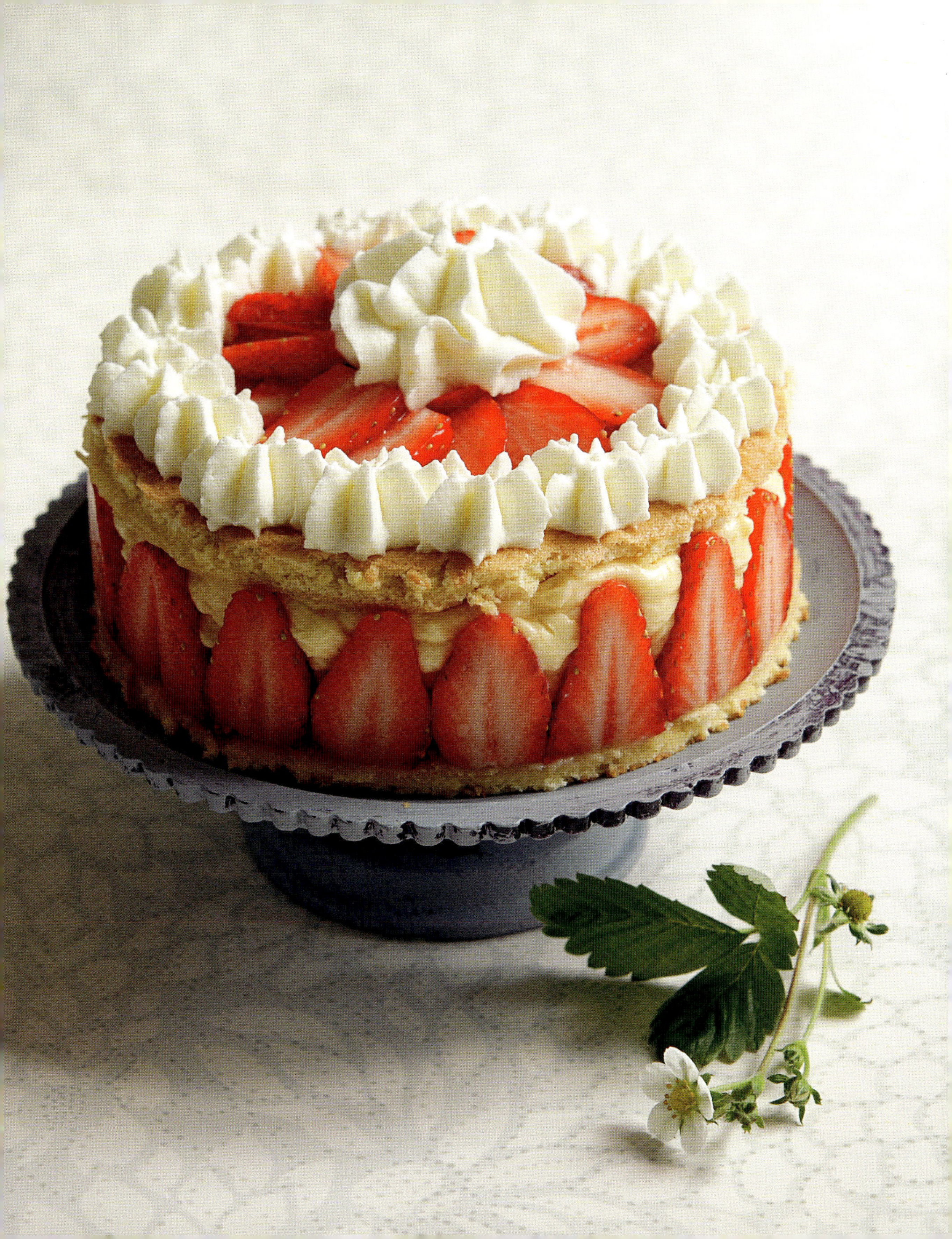

Raspberry pavlova

SERVES 4
PREP TIME: 20 mins.
COOKING TIME: 1 hr

- 1 lb raspberries

FOR THE MERINGUE
- 3 egg whites
- A pinch of salt
- 2/3 cup sugar
- 1 teaspoon cornstarch
- 1 teaspoon raspberry vinegar

Rinse the raspberries and put them in the refrigerator.

Preheat the oven to 300° F and line a baking sheet with parchment paper.

Prepare the meringue: beat the egg whites with a pinch of salt until they form very stiff peaks. When they stick to the whisk, add the sugar, the cornstarch and the vinegar and whisk again for 30 seconds.

Moisten the parchment paper and spread the egg whites onto it, forming a ten-inch disk. Use the back of a damp spoon to make a depression in the center. Bake for 1 hour.

Take the meringue out of the oven and allow to cool a little. Invert it, carefully peel off the parchment paper and allow to cool completely.

At the last minute, put the raspberries in the hollow of the meringue.

> Serving advice
Serve pavlova with raspberry coulis (see p.423).

> Helpful tip
Pavlova should be baked in a cool oven: it should be very pale gold in color, crisp on the outside, and soft inside.

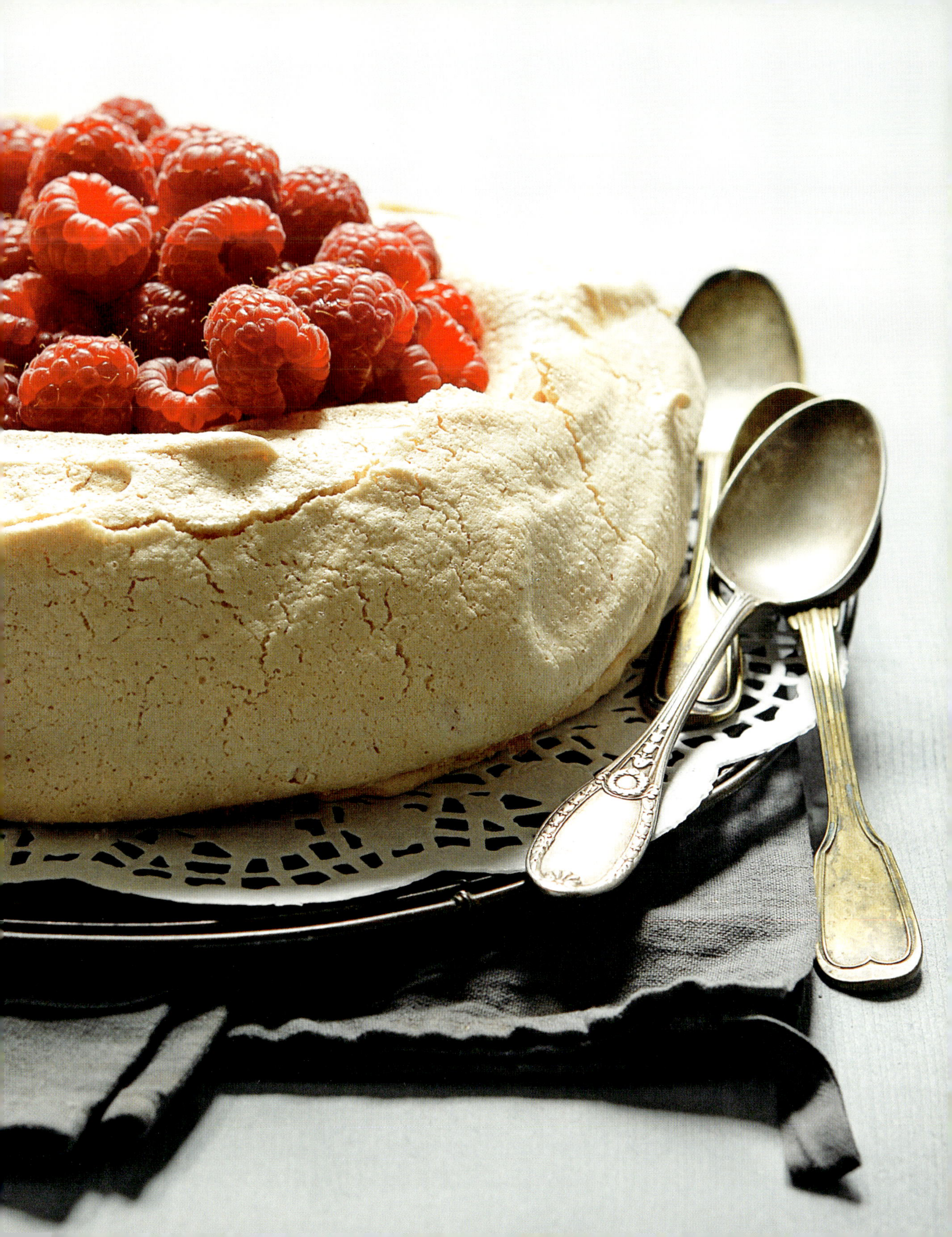

Raspberry soufflé

SERVES 6 TO 8
PREP TIME: 30 mins.
COOKING TIME: 25 mins.

- 1 pint raspberries
- 12 egg whites
- 2 pinches of salt
- Butter and sugar for the mold

FOR THE PASTRY CREAM
- 3 egg yolks
- 4 tbsp. sugar
- 3 tbsp. flour
- 1 cup whole milk

Prepare the pastry cream: put the egg yolks and sugar in a bowl and beat them together until the mixture turns pale yellow. Add the flour and mix it in quickly (don't overwork the mixture). While you're doing this, boil the milk. Pour the boiling milk into the mixture, stirring constantly with a wooden spoon until it's smooth and creamy. Pour into a heavy saucepan. Heat very gently and stir until the mixture thickens. As soon as the mixture begins to boil, remove from the heat and pour into a bowl.

Quickly rinse the raspberries and purée in a food processor. Add this purée to the pastry cream and mix well.

Beat the egg whites with the salt until they form very stiff peaks. Very gently fold in the raspberry pastry cream.

Preheat the oven to 400° F.

Butter a 7-inch soufflé dish and sprinkle with sugar. Pour in the mixture and bake for 5 minutes at 400° F, then 20 minutes at 350° F. Serve immediately.

> To make a change
For strawberry soufflé, simply replace the raspberries with strawberries and follow the same procedure.

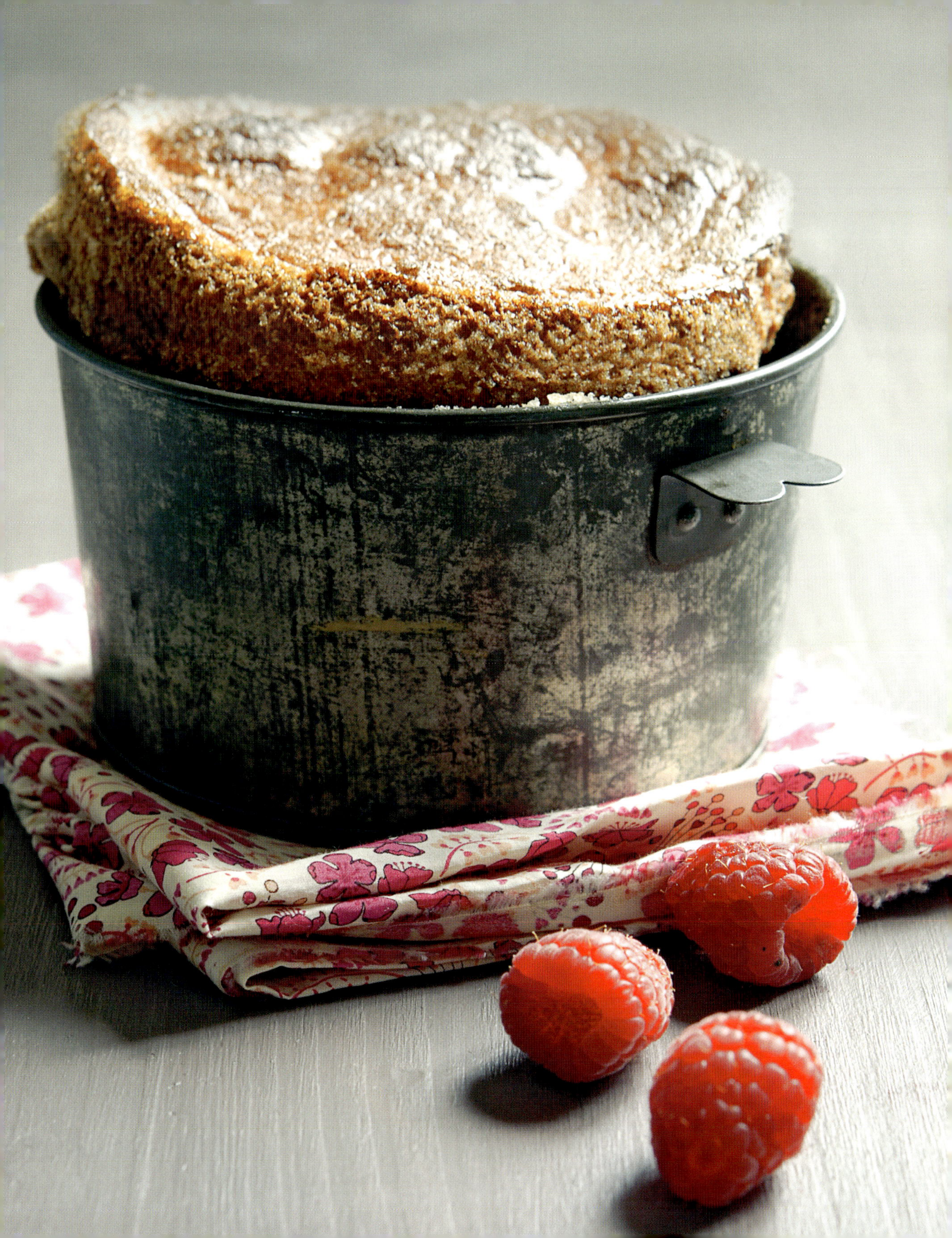

Trifle

SERVES 4
PREP TIME: 20 mins.
COOKING TIME: 15 mins.
REFRIGERATION TIME:
At least 1 hr

- 1/2 lb sponge cake
- Just over 1/2 cup sweet sherry or porto wine, as desired
- 3 to 4 cups mixed red berries (fresh or frozen) or other fruit, as desired
- 1 cup heavy cream
- 2 tbsp. Maraschino cherries

FOR THE CUSTARD
- 2 cups milk
- 4 egg yolks
- 6 tbsp. sugar

Cut the sponge cake into pieces about the size of brownies. Use these to line the bottom of a deep serving bowl and sprinkle with sherry.

Prepare the custard: bring the milk to a boil and remove from the heat. Beat the egg yolks and sugar until the mixture turns pale and frothy. Slowly whisk in the hot milk. Pour back into the saucepan and allow to thicken over a gentle heat for about 10 minutes, stirring with a wooden spoon. Allow to cool, stirring from time to time.

Spoon the fruit into the cake-lined bowl and add the crème anglaise. Chill in the refrigerator for at least 1 hour.

Just before serving, whip the cream. Cover the trifle with a thick layer of cream and decorate with Maraschino cherries.

> To make a change
There are endless variations on the trifle theme. You can replace the sponge cake with lady fingers or even macaroons, and use all kinds of different fruit.

> Helpful tip
You can also decorate your trifle with toasted slivered almonds or geometric patterns made of candied fruit.

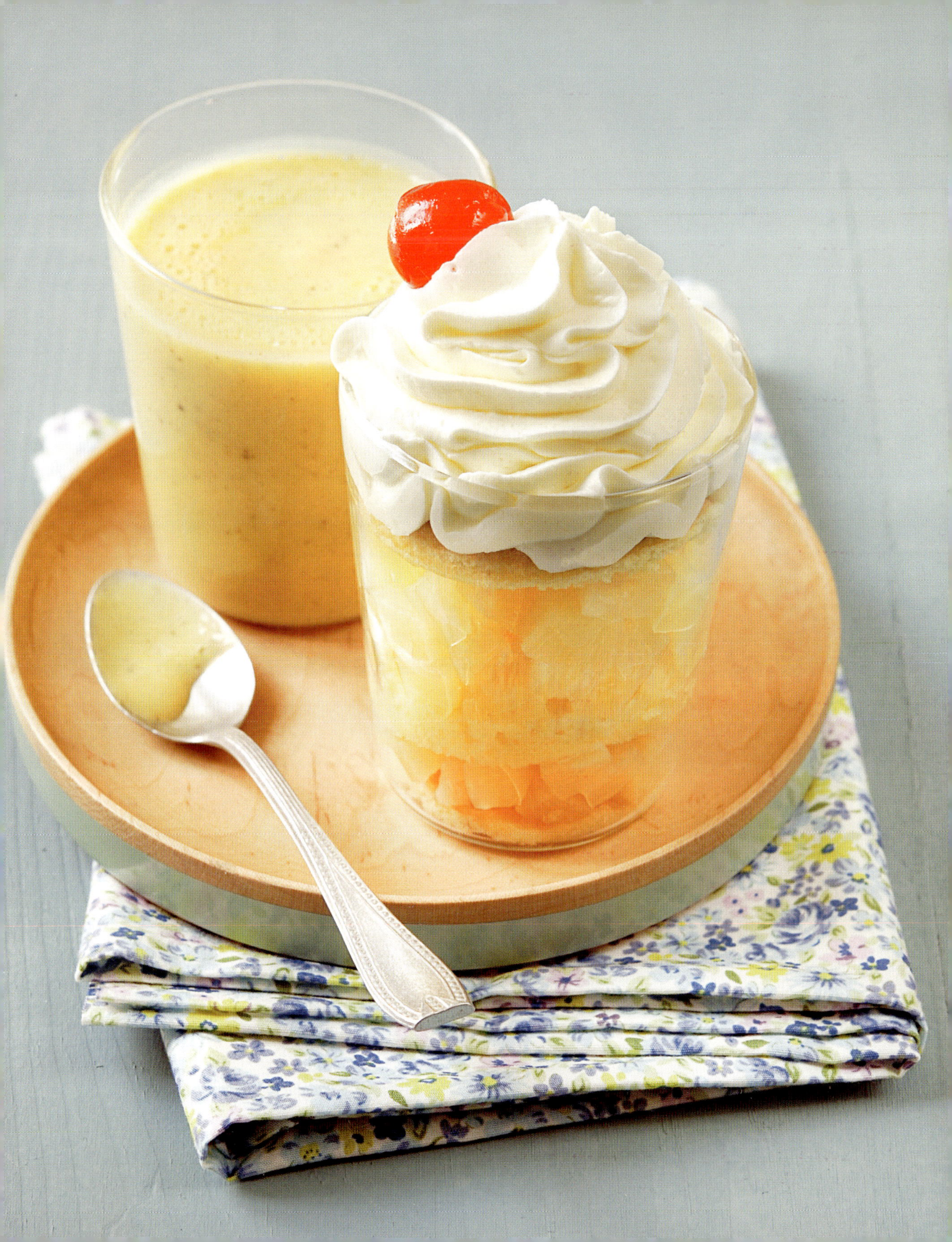

Cooked vanilla cheesecake

SERVES 6
PREP TIME: 20 mins.
COOKING TIME: About 45 mins.
REFRIGERATION TIME: At least 4 hrs

FOR THE BASE
- 9 tbsp. butter
- Just over 8 oz. butter shortbread

FOR THE FILLING
- 1 lb. cream cheese
- 3/4 cup crème fraîche or heavy cream
- 2/3 cup sugar
- 1 teaspoon vanilla extract
- 1 vanilla bean
- 3 eggs

Preheat the oven to 350° F.

Prepare the base: melt the butter over a gentle heat. Place the shortbread in a food processor with the butter and mix.

Use the shortbread mixture to line the bottom of a 9-inch springform cake pan. Pack the mixture down with the back of a spoon. Place in the refrigerator.

Prepare the filling: mix the cream cheese, the cream, the sugar and the vanilla extract in a bowl. Split the vanilla bean and scrape the seeds into the bowl. Beat the mixture until smooth and creamy.

Beat the eggs and add them to the bowl and mix well. Remove the base from the refrigerator and pour in the filling. Bake for about 40 minutes.

Allow to cool at room temperature, then chill in the refrigerator for at least 4 hours before serving.

> Serving advice
This cheesecake is delicious served with fruit coulis (see p.423).

never fails

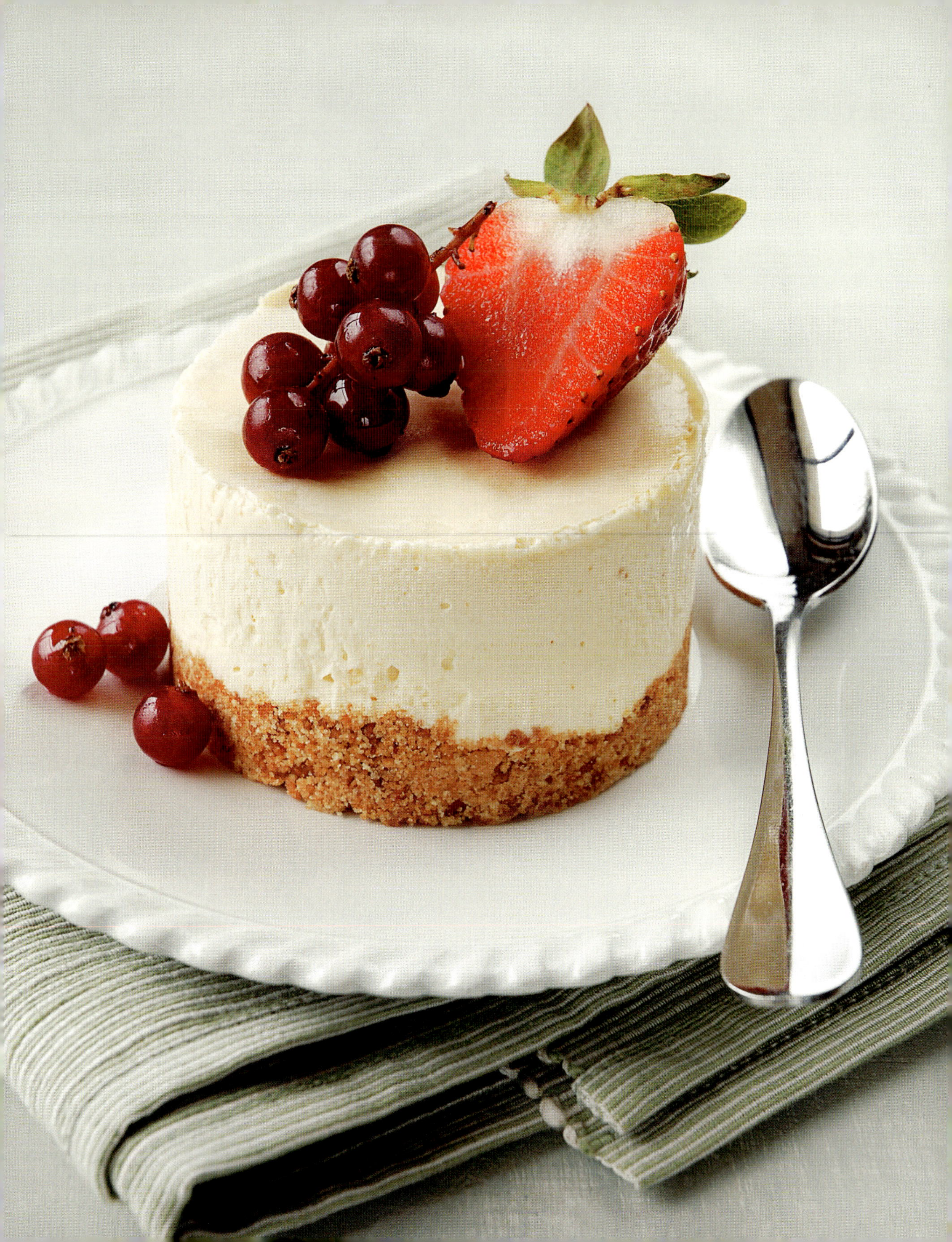

Baked Alaska

SERVES 6
PREP TIME: 1-1/2 hrs
COOKING TIME: 15 to 20 mins.

- 2 pints vanilla ice cream

FOR THE GENOISE SPONGE
- 1 heaping cup flour
- 3 tbsp. butter
- 4 eggs
- 3/4 cup sugar

FOR THE MERINGUE
- 3 egg whites
- 1 cup sugar
- 1 teaspoon natural vanilla extract

FOR THE SYRUP
- 1-1/3 cups sugar
- 1 cup water
- 7 oz. Grand Marnier®

TO DECORATE
- Powdered sugar

chef style

Preheat the oven to 400° F.

Prepare the genoise: sift the flour using a sieve placed over a bowl. Melt the butter over low heat in a small saucepan and allow to cool a little. Break the eggs into a heatproof bowl. Sprinkle in the sugar, stirring constantly. Put the bowl over a pan of simmering water (or use a double boiler) and whisk until the mixture thickens. Remove from the heat and beat with an electric mixer until cold. Put 2 tbsp. of this mixture in a small bowl and stir in the warm melted butter. Fold the sifted flour into the mixture in the other bowl with a wooden or rubber spatula. Add the mixture from the small bowl and stir gently.

Put the genoise mixture into a pastry bag with a smooth 1/2-inch tip. Pipe into an oval shape on a baking sheet lined with parchment paper and bake for 15 minutes. Check with the point of a knife (it should come out clean), remove from the oven and allow to cool.

Increase the oven temperature to 475° F.

Prepare the meringue: put the egg whites in a bowl and beat until they form soft peaks, gradually adding half the sugar. When the egg whites have doubled in volume, add the rest of the sugar and the vanilla. Continue to beat until the mixture is firm, smooth and glossy. Spoon the mixture into a large pastry bag fitted with a fluted 1/2-inch tip.

Prepare the syrup: put the sugar and water into a saucepan and bring to a boil. Allow to cool and add 6 tbsp. liqueur. Place the genoise on an ovenproof dish and brush with the syrup.

Spread the vanilla ice cream over the genoise. Cover the ice cream with half of the meringue and smooth it down with a spatula. Pipe the rest of the meringue on top in artistic patterns. Dust with powdered sugar and bake for 15 to 20 minutes until golden. Remove from the oven.

At the very last moment, heat the rest of the liqueur (6 tbsp.) in a small saucepan. Ignite and pour over the Baked Alaska in front of your guests. Serve immediately.

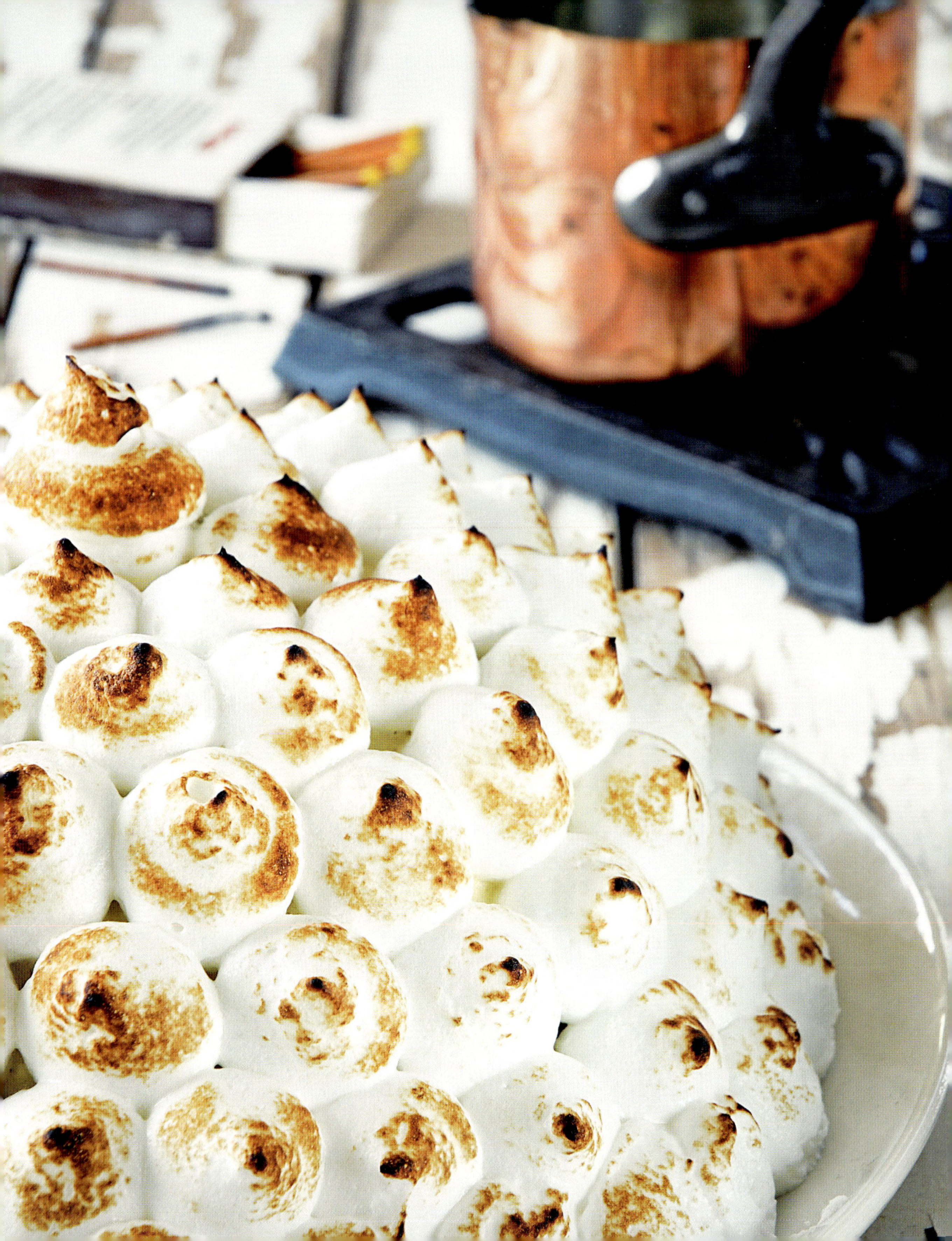

Mont-Blanc

SERVES 4
PREP TIME: 1 hr
COOKING TIME: 2 hrs 45 mins.

FOR THE FRENCH MERINGUE
- 2 egg whites
- 2/3 cup sugar
- 1/2 teaspoon natural vanilla extract

FOR THE CREAM
- 5 1/2 tbsp. butter
- 1 1/2 cups chestnut paste
- 2 cups chestnut cream
- 3 tbsp. rum

FOR THE WHIPPED CREAM
- 2 cups heavy cream
- 2-1/2 tbsp. powdered sugar
- 1 teaspoon vanilla extract

FOR THE DECORATION
- Tiny pieces of candied chestnuts

Preheat the oven to 250° F.

Prepare the French meringue: put the egg whites into a large bowl and beat until stiff peaks form, gradually adding half the sugar. When the mixture has doubled in volume, pour in half the remaining sugar and the vanilla. Keep beating until they are stiff, shiny and smooth. Add the rest of the sugar. Once it's been added, the mixture should be firm. Put the meringue into a pastry bag fitted with a 1/3-inch tip.

Cover the pastry tray with a sheet of parchment paper and make four meringue crowns 3 inches in diameter, each consisting of several small concentric circles, to make a base.

Place the tray in the oven for 45 minutes at 250° F, then for 2 hours at 225° F.

Prepare the cream: melt the butter in a double boiler or microwave oven until creamy. Add the chestnut paste and mix well. Once the mixture is smooth, add the chestnut cream followed by the rum and mix again.

Place this cream in a pastry bag with small holes at the end and cover the meringue base with piped chestnut cream strings.

Prepare the whipped cream: beat the chilled cream for about 1 minute, then add the powdered sugar and vanilla extract. Continue beating while checking the consistency of the cream. Put the whipped cream into a pastry bag with a fluted tip and make little rosettes on top of the chestnut cream.

Sprinkle little bits of chestnut on top of each rosette.

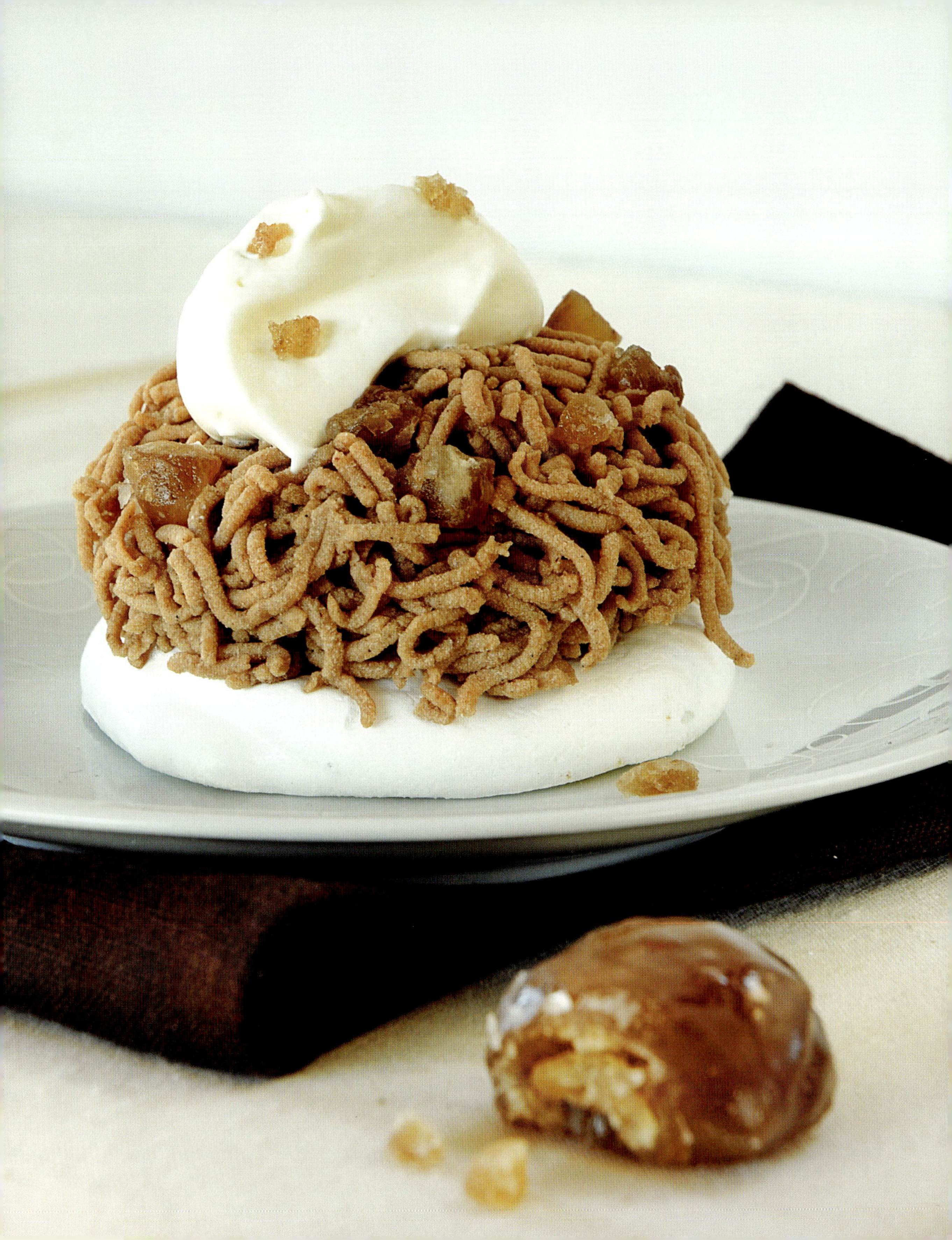

Grand Marnier® soufflé

SERVES 6
PREP TIME: 15 mins.
COOKING TIME: About 30 mins.

- 1 cup whole milk
- 1/3 cup sugar
- 5 tbsp. butter + some for the dish
- 1/2 cup flour
- 1 teaspoon vanilla extract
- 3 eggs
- 3 tbsp. Grand Marnier®

Heat the milk with 3 tbsp. sugar.

Melt the butter in a large saucepan. When it starts to foam, mix in the flour, add the vanilla extract, then add the boiling milk all at once. Bring to a boil, then lower the heat and cook, stirring, for 8 minutes to dry out the mixture.

Break the eggs and separate the yolks from the whites. Away from the stove, incorporate the egg yolks into the previous mixture and add the liqueur.

Preheat the oven to 400° F.

Beat the egg whites until they form stiff peaks and fold them into the mixture.

Butter a 7-inch soufflé dish and pour the mixture in. Bake for 20 minutes. Serve immediately.

> Helpful tip
You can also make soufflés in individual ramekins.

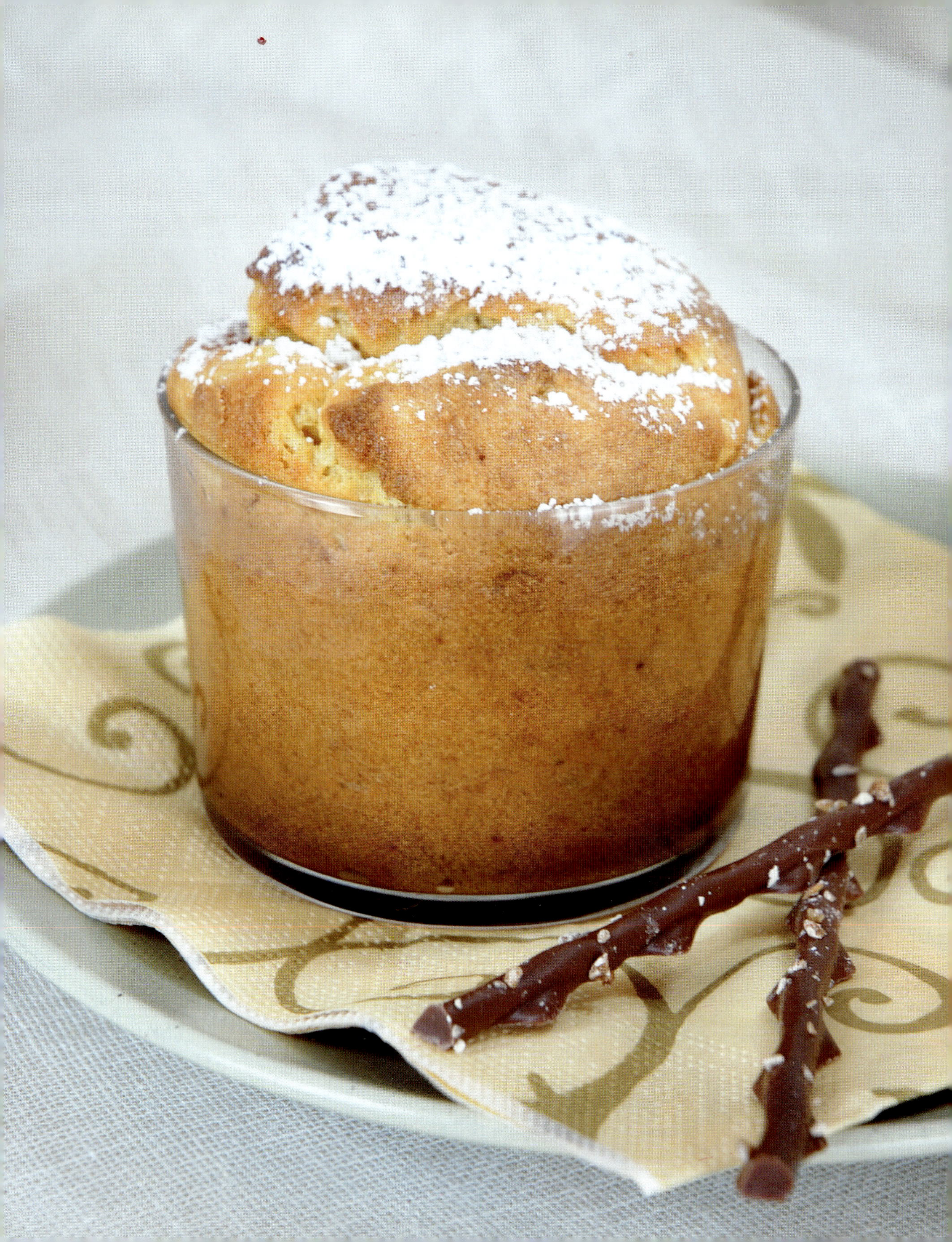

Fig and mascarpone cups

MAKES 8 CUPS
PREP TIME: 20 mins.
COOKING TIME: 10 mins.
REFRIGERATION TIME: 2 hrs

- 8 fresh figs
- 2 tbsp. butter
- 1 teaspoon vanilla extract
- 1 cup mascarpone
- 1-1/2 cups fromage frais or Greek yogurt
- 2-1/2 tbsp. demerara sugar
- 4 graham crackers

Rinse and dry the figs, remove the stalks and cut into quarters.

Melt the butter in a a skillet and add the vanilla extract. When the mixture is hot, add the figs and cook over a gentle heat for 10 minutes, turning them from time to time.

Put the mascarpone into a bowl and beat in the fromage frais or Greek yogurt and the demerara sugar.

Place the figs in small cups. Spoon the mascarpone mixture over the top and chill for 2 hours.

Just before serving, sprinkle with crushed graham crackers.

> **To make a change**
You can make this dessert with lightly cooked strawberries, stewed rhubarb, or caramelized pears.

> **Helpful tip**
Add quartered figs at the last minute.

never fails

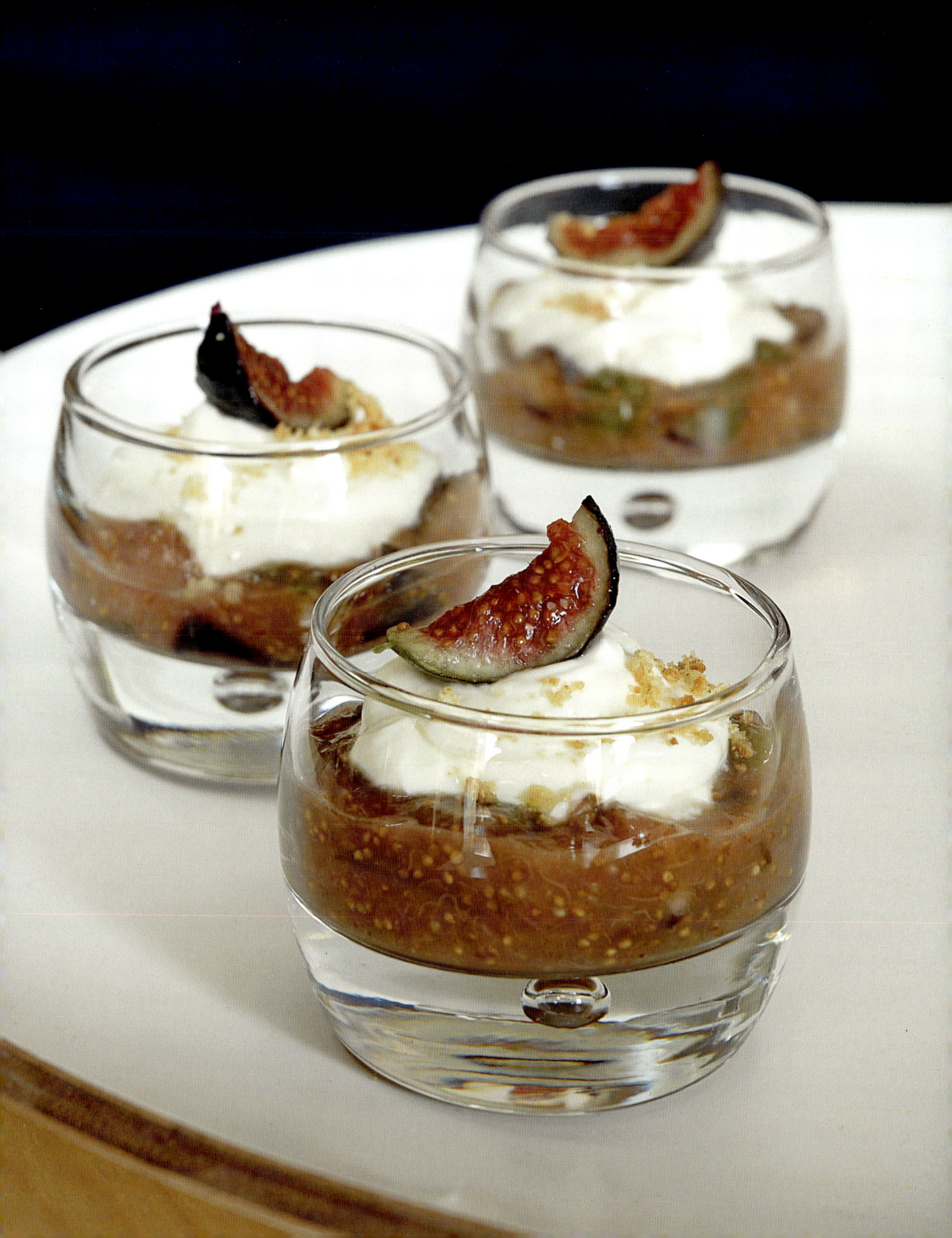

Tiramisu

SERVES 6
PREP TIME: 30 mins.
REFRIGERATION TIME: At least 2 hrs

- 3 eggs
- 1-1/3 cups sugar
- 1 cup mascarpone
- 7 tbsp. marsala
- A pinch of salt
- 12 lady fingers
- 2-1/2 cups very strong cold coffee
- A little cocoa powder

Break the eggs and separate the yolks from the whites. Beat the egg yolks with the sugar until the mixture turns pale. Add the mascarpone and the marsala.

Add a pinch of salt to the egg whites and whisk until they form soft peaks. Fold into the egg yolk mixture.

Dip the lady fingers in the cold coffee. Place a layer in the bottom of a rectangular mold about 4 inches deep. Pour in a layer of mixture and add a second layer of lady fingers. Add the rest of the mixture and dust with cocoa powder.

Place in the refrigerator for at least 2 hours before serving.

> Helpful tip
You can decorate your tiramisu with a sprig of fresh mint in the summer. The coffee must be really strong for this dessert to merit its name: "tiramisú" literally means "pick me up!"

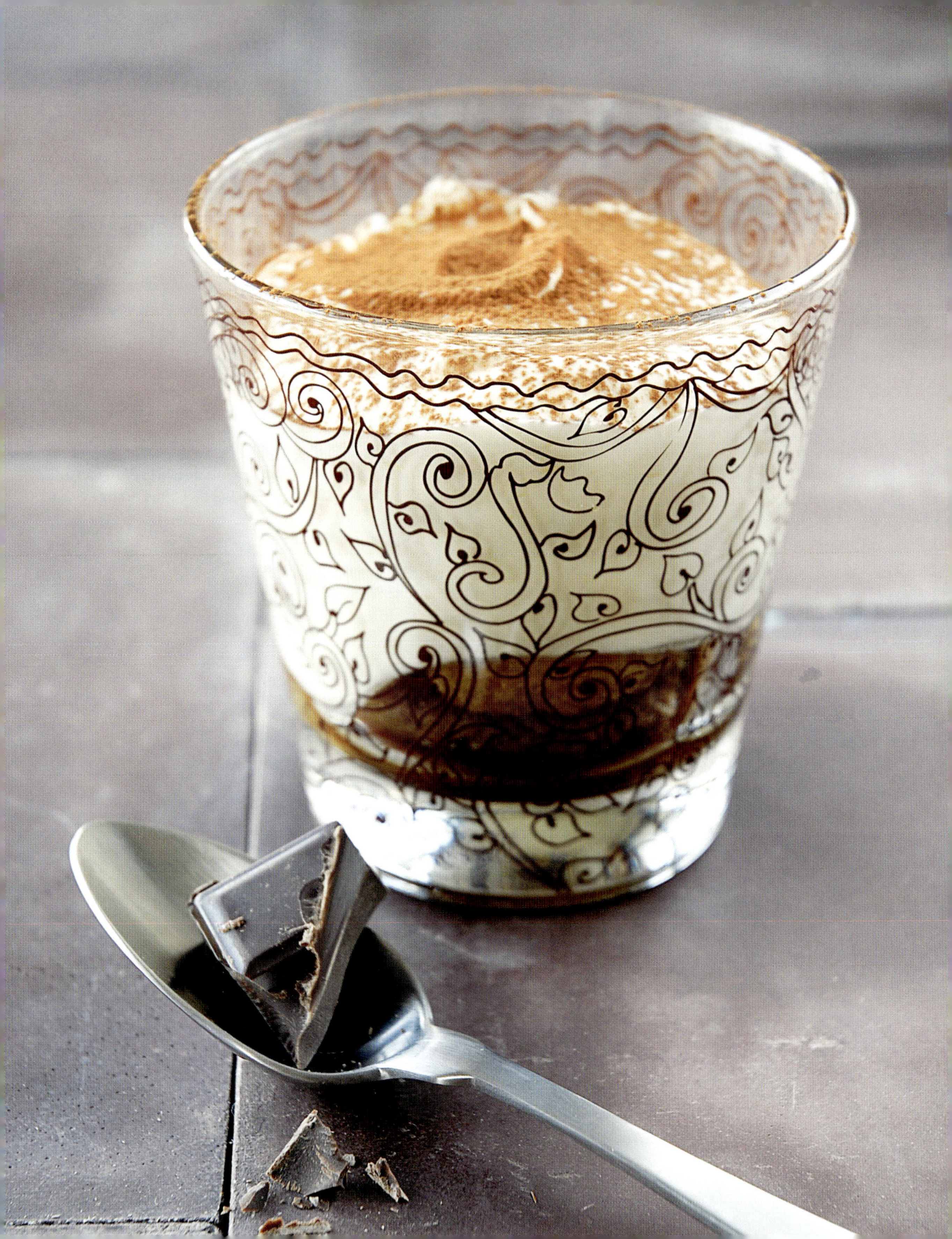

Candied orange peel

MAKES ABOUT 3/4 LB.
PREP TIME: 20 mins.
COOKING TIME: 1-1/2 hrs

- 6 thick-skinned organic oranges
- 2-1/2 cups sugar
- 6 tbsp. orange juice

Boil a saucepan of water. Cut off the top and bottom of each orange. Score the the skin in four places from top to bottom with a small knife to obtain four pieces of peel. Boil the peel for 1 minute, strain and rinse in cold water.

Put 2 pints of water in a large saucepan with the sugar and orange juice; bring to a boil. Add the orange peel, cover and simmer for 1-1/2 hours. Allow the peel to cool in the syrup.

Strain the orange peel in a sieve, then pat dry with paper towels. Allow to dry completely before placing in an airtight container. Store in a cool place.

> Serving advice

Candied orange peel can be used in a variety of cakes and desserts. You can also cut it into thin strips and roll them in sugar to make delicious orange candy.

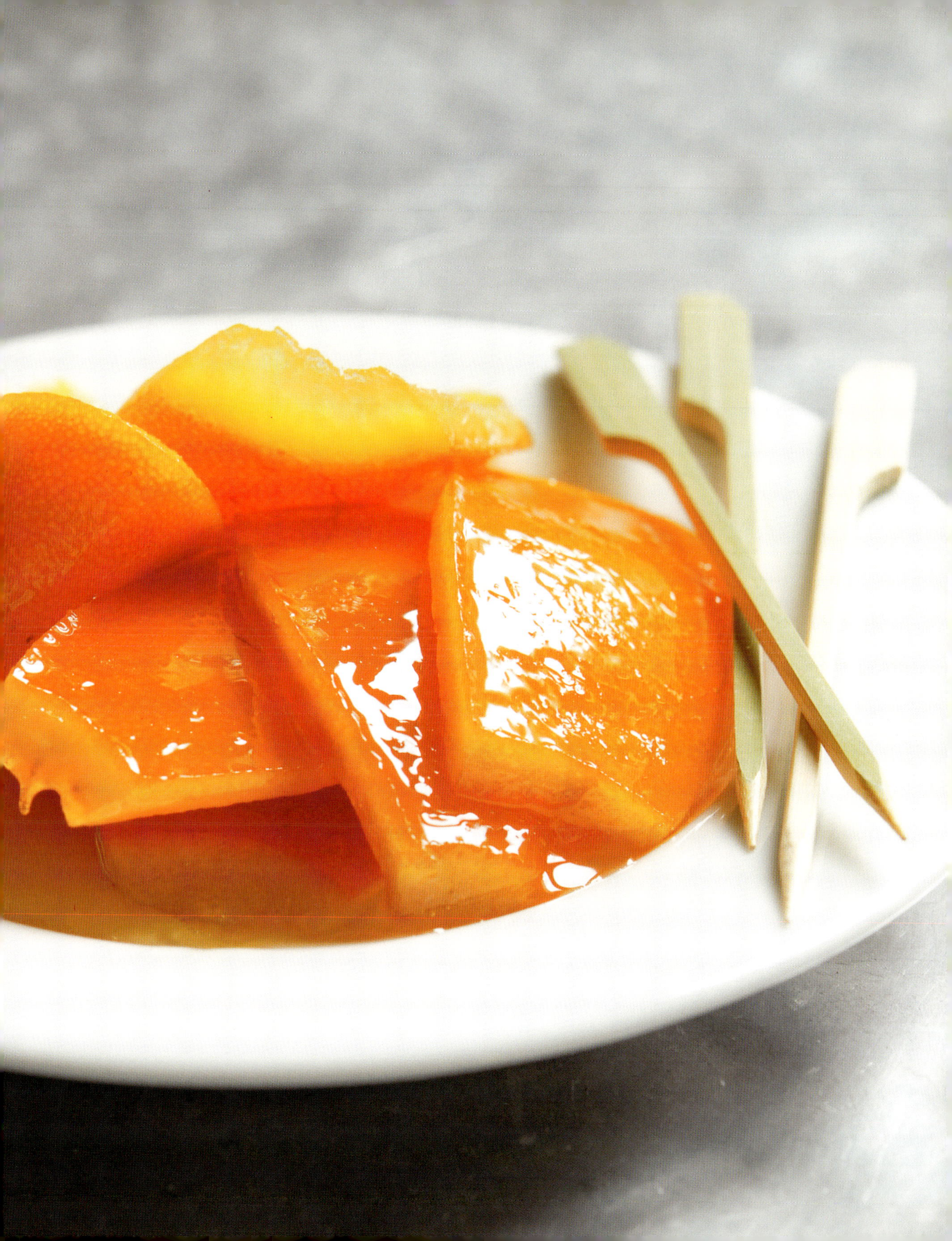

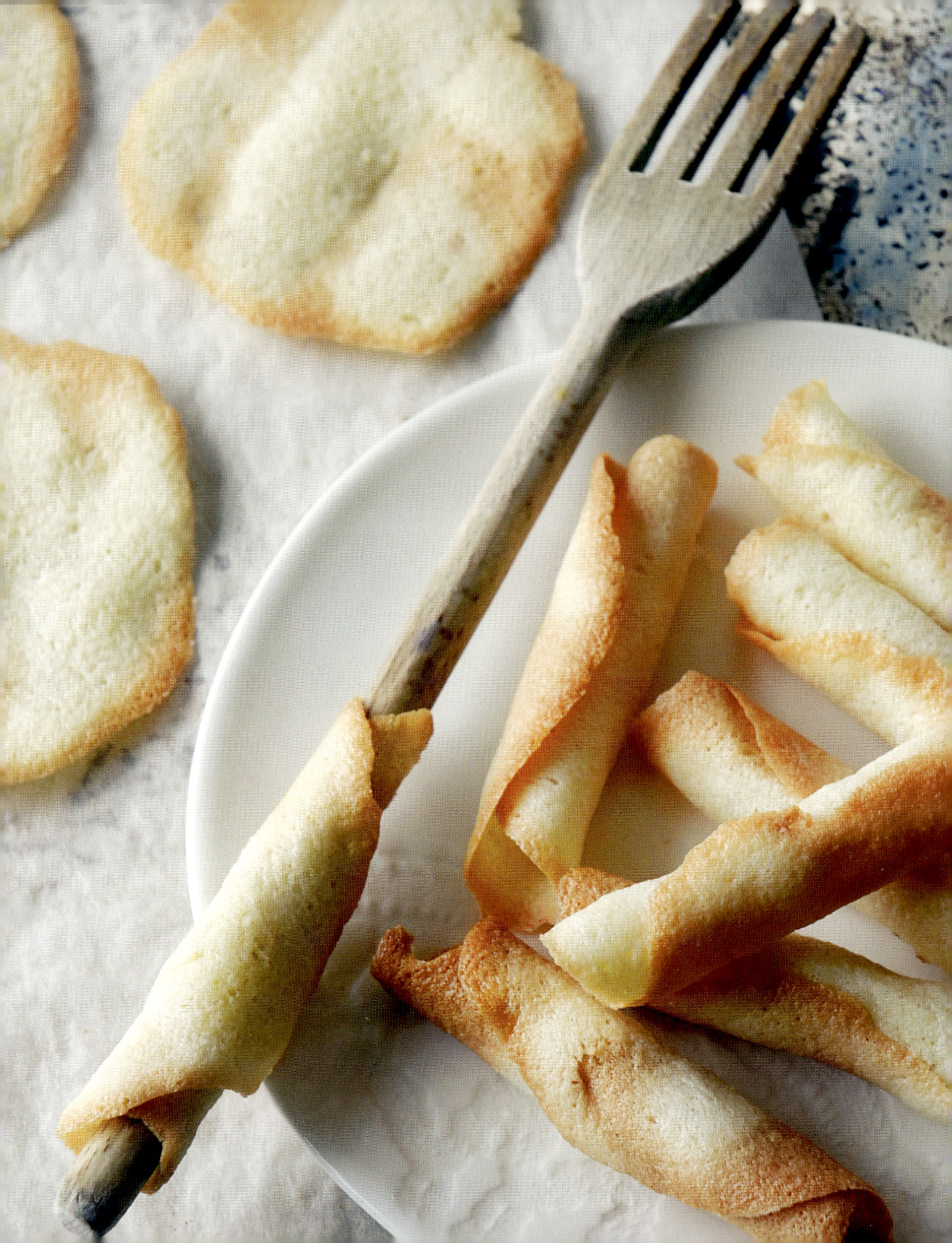

Munchy, crunchy cookies

Financiers de Sully 250
Madeleines 252
Coconut rock cakes 254
Cannelés 256
Walnut cookies 258
Visitandines 260
Almond slices 262
Macaroons 264
Langues-de-chat 266
Tuiles 268
Cigarettes russes 268
Galettes nantaises 270
Countess cookies 272

Palmiers 274
Coffee meringues 276
Rum-raisin cookies 278
Middle Eastern Easter pastries 280
Lemon cookies 282
Butter shortbread 284
Sablé-sur-Sarthe shortbread 286
Spiced "arlettes" 288
Pecan cookies 290
Cordoba cookies 292
Galettes bretonnes 294
Croquets de Bar-sur-Aube 294
Chocolate chip cookies 296

Financiers de Sully
(individual almond sponge cakes)

MAKES ABOUT 9 TO 12 FINANCIERS, DEPENDING ON MOLD SIZE
PREP TIME: 20 mins.
COOKING TIME: 10 mins.

- 14 tbsp. butter
- 1/2 cup flour
- 1 cup ground almonds
- 1-1/2 cups powdered sugar
- 1 teaspoon vanilla extract
- 6 egg whites
- 1/2 cup slivered almonds

Preheat the oven to 470° F.

Melt the butter over gentle heat and allow to cool. Mix together the sifted flour, the ground almonds, the powdered sugar and the vanilla extract in a bowl.

Beat the egg whites until slightly frothy, then beat them into the mixture. Add the melted butter.

Butter a 9-cup silicone cake pan with 3 x 1 x 1 1/4-inch cavities, or use twelve 1 3/4-inch round molds. Sprinkle slivered almonds into the bottom of the molds. Pour in the mixture, filling the molds three quarters full. Bake for 10 minutes. Turn out while still hot. Serve cold.

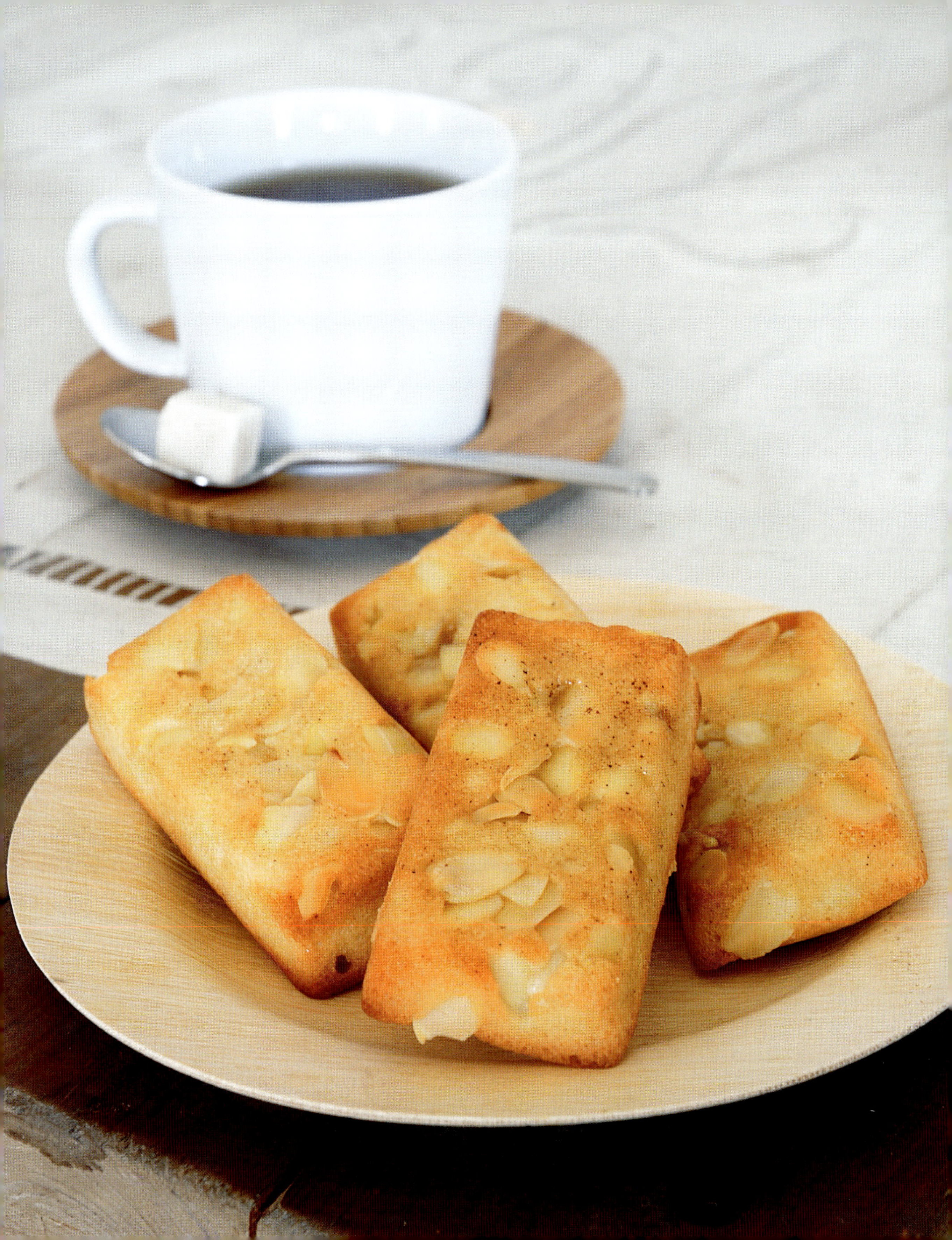

Madeleines

MAKES 12 MADELEINES
PREP TIME: 10 mins.
COOKING TIME: 15 mins.

- 1 scant cup flour
- 1 scant tsp. baking powder
- 7 tbsp. butter + some for the pan
- 1/4 organic lemon
- 2 eggs
- 2/3 cup sugar

Sift the flour and baking powder into a bowl. Melt the butter in a small saucepan and allow to cool.

Zest the quarter lemon and finely chop the zest.

Break the eggs into a bowl and add the sugar. Beat for 5 minutes until very frothy; add the flour and baking powder, then the butter and lemon zest, stirring constantly.

Preheat the oven to 425° F.

Lightly butter a madeleine pan and fill each compartment to two thirds full. Bake for 5 minutes at 425° F, then lower the temperature to 400° F and bake for 10 minutes longer.

Turn out the madeleines while still warm and allow them to cool.

child's play

MUNCHY, CRUNCHY COOKIES

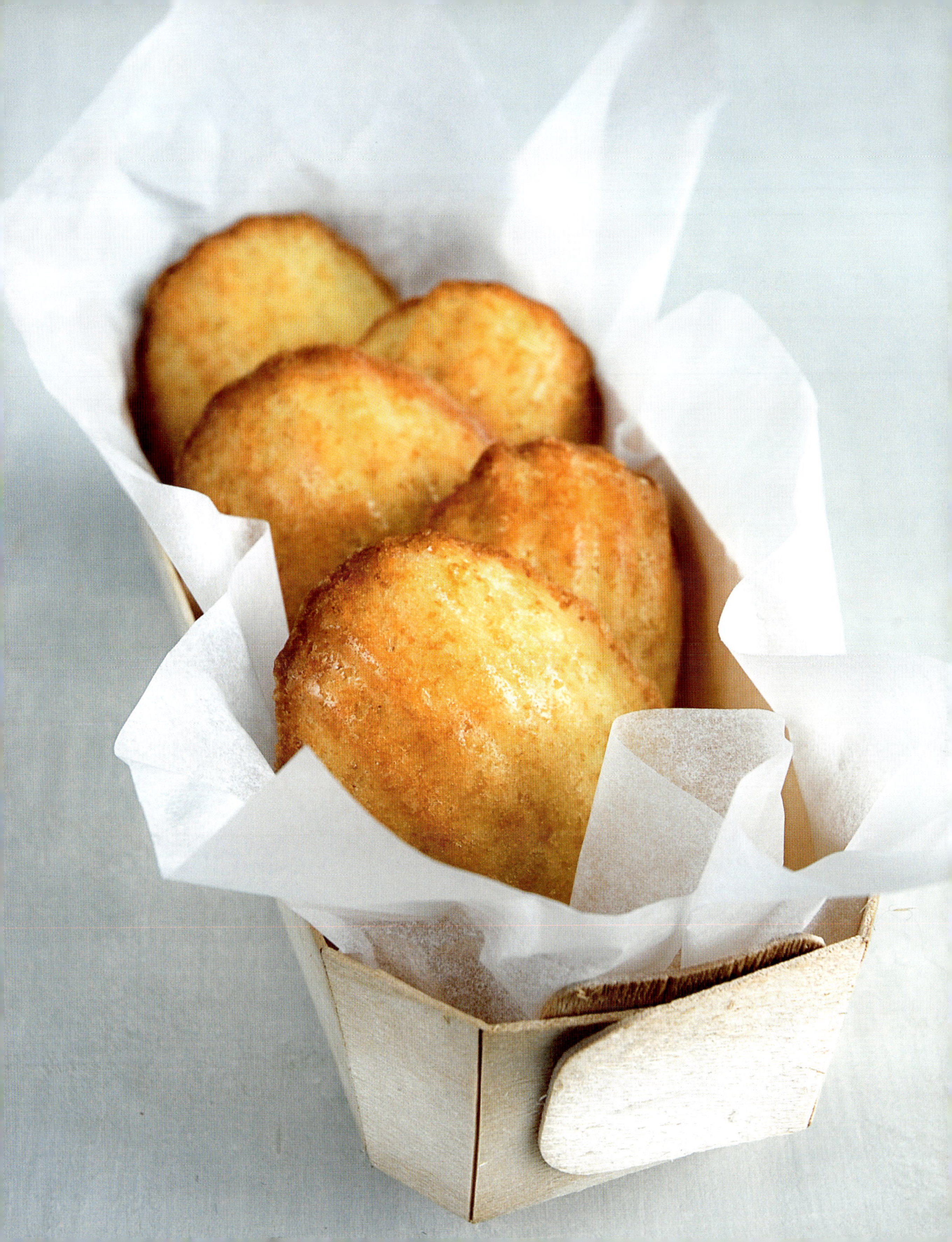

Coconut rock cakes

MAKES ABOUT 20 CAKES
PREP TIME: 20 mins.
COOKING TIME: 10 mins.

- 1-1/2 cups sugar
- A pinch of salt
- 5 egg whites
- 1/2 lb. grated coconut
- 1 teaspoon vanilla powder
- 2 tbsp. butter

Put a heatproof bowl over a saucepan of simmering water, or use a double boiler. Add the sugar, the salt and the egg whites.

Beat until the sugar has dissolved and the mixture is warm. Add the coconut and vanilla and stir. Remove from the heat.

Preheat the oven to 475° F. Line a baking sheet with parchment paper.

Place spoonfuls of mixture on the baking sheet, not too close together. Bake for about 10 minutes until golden.

Remove from the oven and allow to cool before taking them off the parchment paper.

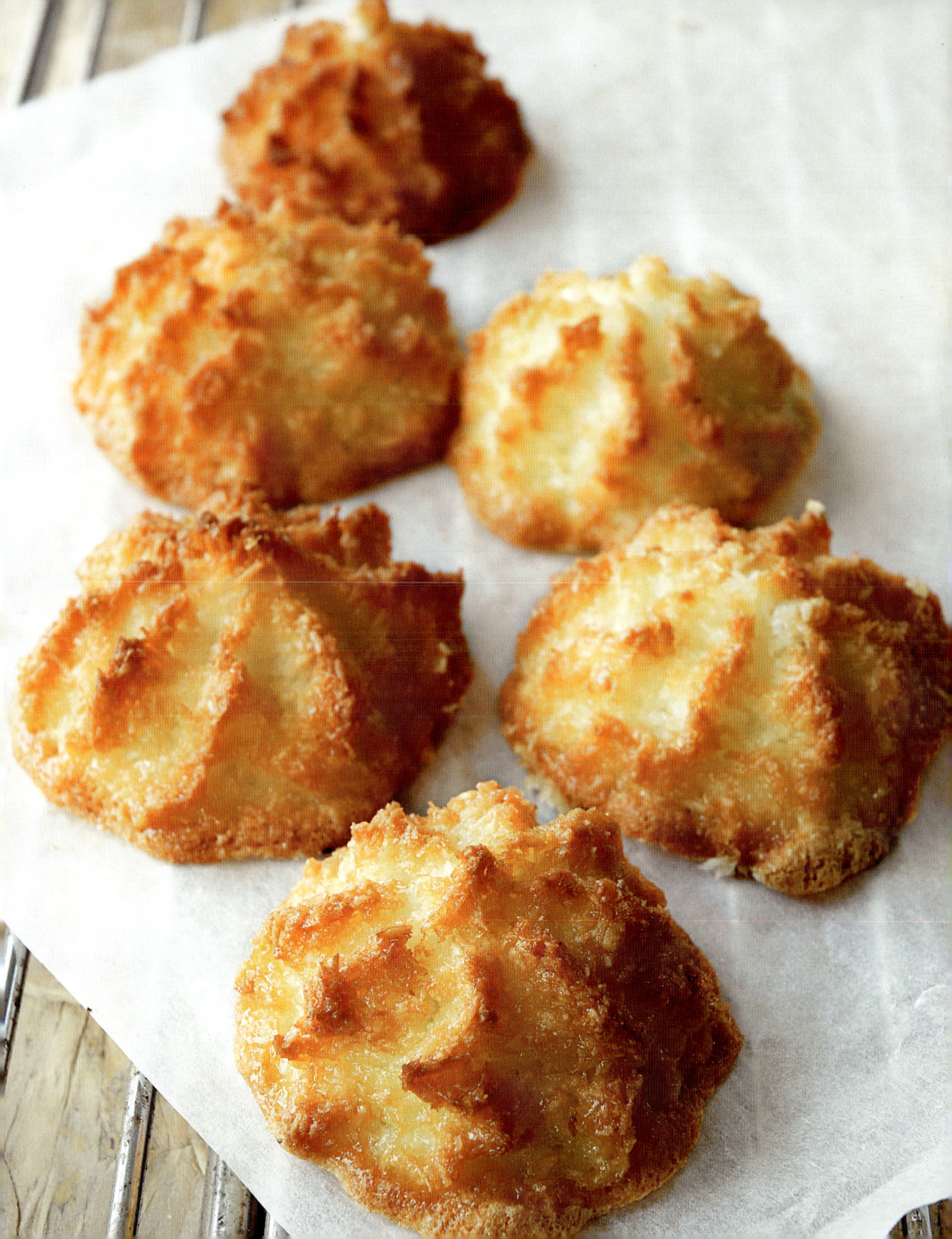

Cannelés

MAKES ABOUT 24 TO 36 CANNELÉS, DEPENDING ON MOLD SIZE
PREP TIME: 25 mins.
COOKING TIME: 45 mins.

- 1 vanilla bean
- 2 cups milk
- 3 tbsp. butter
- 2 eggs + 2 extra yolks
- 1-1/4 cups sugar
- 1 tbsp. orange flower water
- 1 cup flour

Split the vanilla bean and scrape out the seeds with a spoon or knife blade. Put the milk in a pan with the vanilla bean and seeds. Bring to a boil, turn off the heat, cover and allow to infuse for 15 minutes.

Preheat the oven to 400° F.

Melt the butter; beat the eggs and extra yolks with the sugar, until the mixture turns pale yellow. Add the melted butter and orange flower water. Mix in the flour and finally add the vanilla-flavored milk (discard the vanilla bean).

Generously butter two 18-cup mini cannelés trays with 1 1/4 x 1 1/4-inch cavities, or use twenty-four 1 3/4-inch dariole molds. Fill them three quarters full of the mixture. Bake for about 45 minutes.

Turn out the cannelés while they're still hot, but serve them cold.

> Find out more

These delicious cakes are a specialty of the region of Bordeaux. Their name comes from their fluted column shape. They are best eaten on the day you make them.

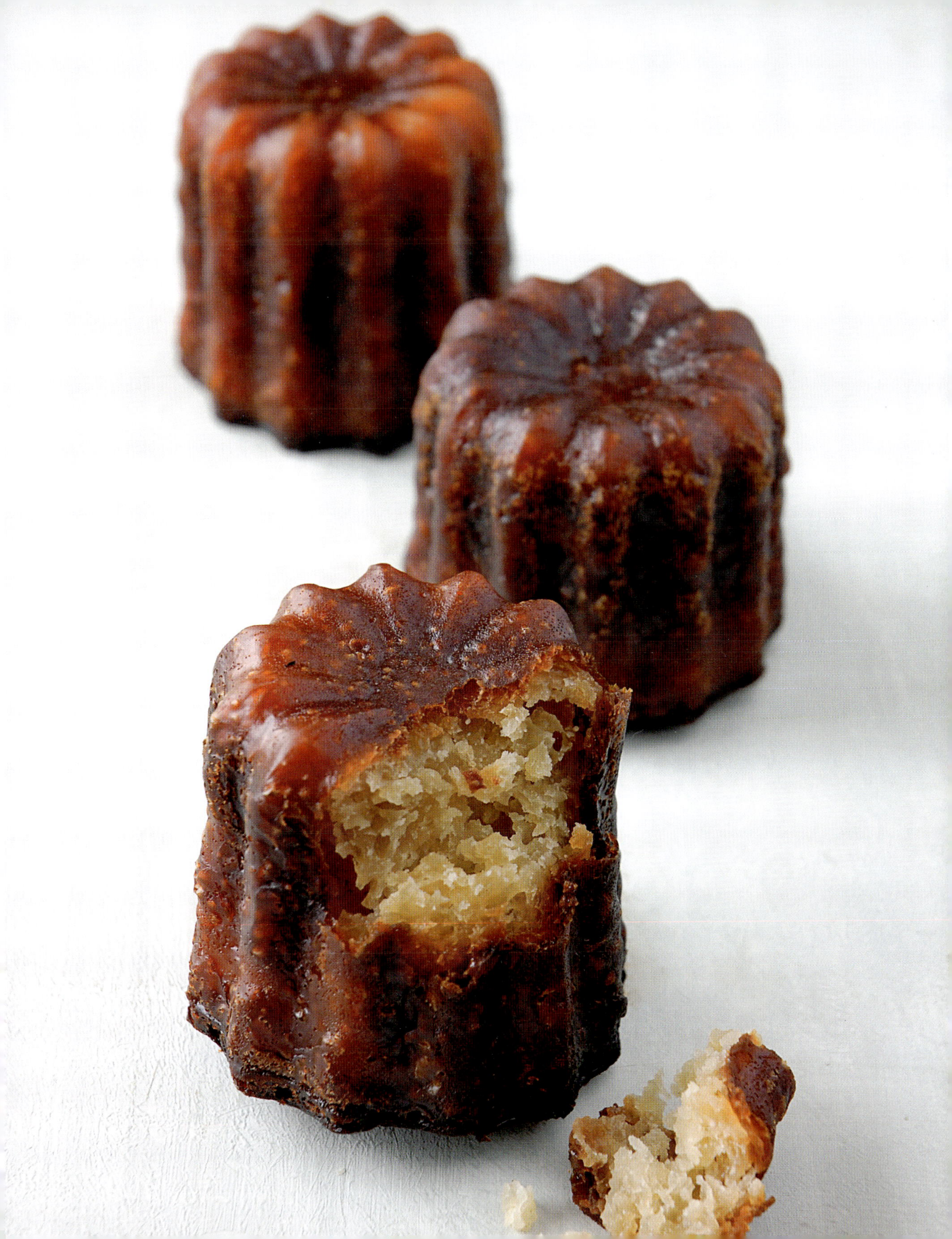

Walnut cookies

MAKES 30 TO 40 COOKIES
PREP TIME: 15 mins.
COOKING TIME: About 30 mins.

- 3 tbsp. shelled walnuts (or hazelnuts)
- 1/4 cup ground almonds
- 2 tbsp. cornstarch
- 4 tbsp. powdered sugar
- 4 egg whites
- A pinch of salt

Grind the nuts to a powder in an electric blender. Put them into a bowl with the ground almonds, the cornstarch and the powdered sugar; mix very well.

Beat the egg whites to very stiff peaks with a pinch of salt. Gently fold in the nut mixture.

Preheat the oven to 250° F. Line a baking sheet with parchment paper.

Spoon the mixture into a pastry bag with a round tip and pipe small circles of mixture onto the baking sheet, leaving plenty of space between them. Bake for 20 to 30 minutes: the cookies should be dry to the touch but still soft inside. Take them out of the oven and allow them to cool on a wire rack.

> To make a change

You can use hazelnuts instead of walnuts for this recipe.

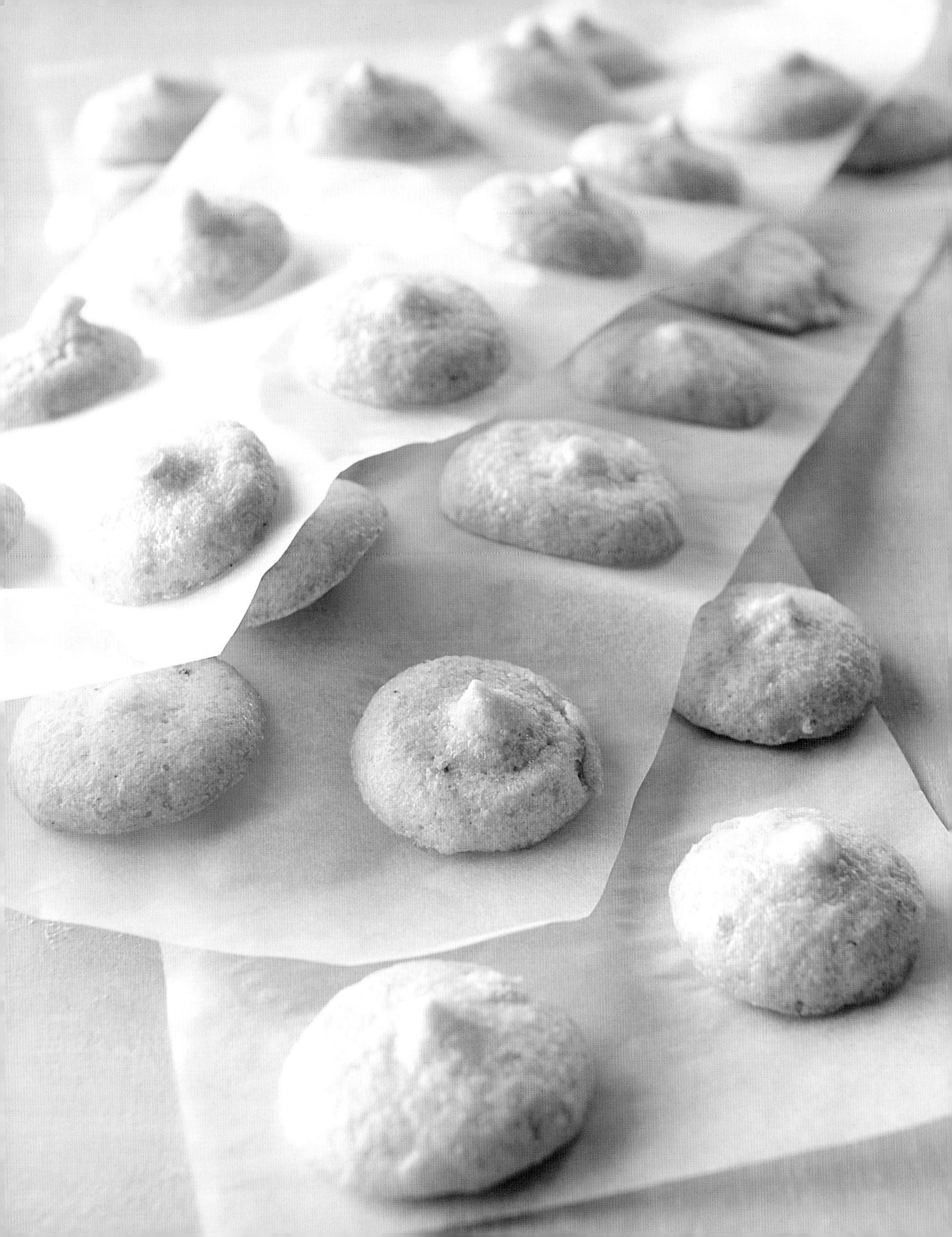

Visitandines

MAKES ABOUT 45 TO 48 VISITANDINES, DEPENDING ON MOLD SIZE
PREP TIME: 20 mins.
REFRIGERATION TIME: 1 hr
COOKING TIME: 8 to 10 mins. per batch

- 4 egg whites
- 1/3 cup flour
- 3/4 cup butter
- 2/3 cup sugar
- 1-1/4 cups ground almonds

Put 3 egg whites into one bowl and one egg white into another bowl. Place in the refrigerator for a good hour to chill.

Sift the flour. Melt the butter gently in a double boiler.

Whisk the single egg white until it forms stiff peaks and put back in the refrigerator.

Preheat the oven to 425° F.

Mix the sugar and the ground almonds. Add the flour, then beat in the 3 egg whites. Add the warm melted butter. Fold in the beaten egg white.

Butter three 15-cup silicone timbale molds with 1.3 x 1.5-inch cavities, or use two 24-cup mini muffin trays. Pipe the mixture into them using a pastry bag with a large, smooth tip.

Bake for 8 to 10 minutes; the cakes should be golden on the outside and soft in the middle. Allow to cool slightly and turn out.

> Helpful tip
Bake these cakes in batches according to the size of your oven and the number of molds you have. To turn them out, tap the molds on the table before inverting them.

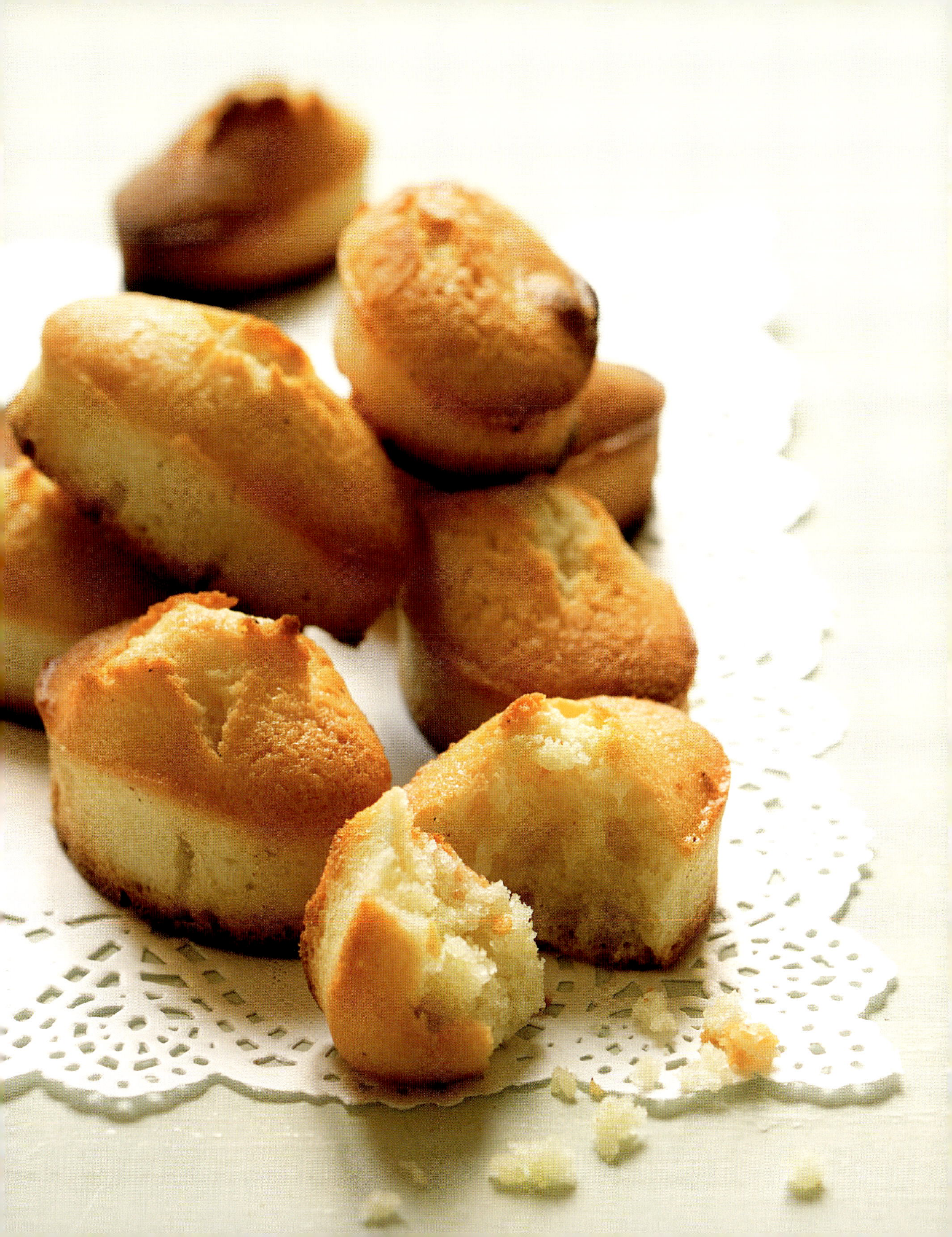

Almond slices

SERVES 6 TO 8
PREP TIME: 20 mins.
COOKING TIME: 50 mins.

- The zest of 1 organic orange
- 4 eggs
- A pinch of salt
- 1-1/4 cups sugar
- 2-1/3 cups ground almonds
- 1 cup orange juice
- 2 tbsp. butter
- 1/2 cup blanched almonds
- 2 tbsp. orange marmalade

Finely chop the orange zest.

Break the eggs and separate the yolks from the whites. Beat the egg whites with a pinch of salt until they form stiff peaks.

Preheat the oven to 400° F.

Whisk together the egg yolks and sugar in a bowl until the mixture turns pale yellow, then add the ground almonds, the orange zest and the orange juice. Mix well. Now gently fold in the beaten egg whites with a wooden spatula.

Cut out a piece of parchment paper to fit inside a shallow baking sheet. Butter the paper and use it to line the baking sheet.

Pour in the mixture and bake 30 minutes at 400° F; now lower the oven temperature to 350° F and bake for another 20 minutes.

Crush the blanched almonds. Allow the cake to cool, turn it out, brush the top with marmalade, cut into slices and scatter the crushed almonds over the top.

> Serving advice
These cakes are delicious served with chocolate mousse (see p.110) or chilled crème anglaise (see p.411).

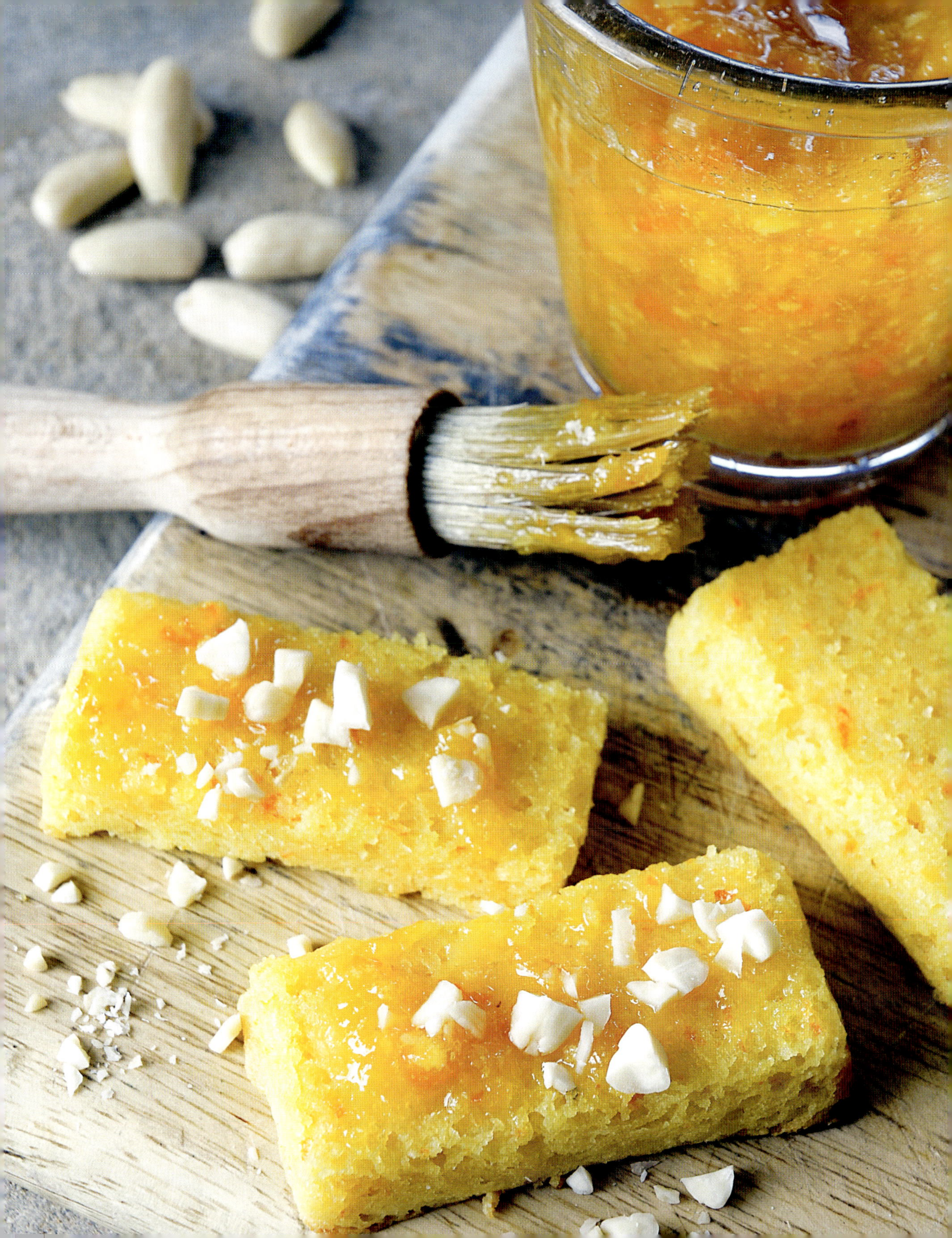

Macaroons

**MAKES 30 SMALL OR
15 LARGE MACAROONS
PREP TIME:** 10 mins.
COOKING TIME: 15 to 20 mins.

- 2 cups ground almonds
- 1 cup powdered sugar
- 1 teaspoon liquid honey
- 4 egg whites
- A pinch of salt

Mix the ground almonds with the powdered sugar and the honey in a bowl. Beat two egg whites with a fork until they turn white, then pour them into the bowl and stir with a wooden spoon until the mixture is very smooth.

Preheat the oven to 325° F and line two baking sheets with parchment paper.

Beat the 2 remaining egg whites with a pinch of salt until they form stiff peaks. Fold them carefully into the almond mixture.

Use a pastry bag with a smooth tip or a tablespoon to place small quantities of mixture on the baking sheet, leaving plenty of space between them. Flatten them slightly with the back of a damp spoon. Bake for 15 to 20 minutes, until golden.

Remove from the oven, take the macaroons off the paper with a spatula and place them on a rack to cool.

> Helpful tip
Macaroons will keep for a couple of days in an airtight container.

> Serving advice
You can serve macaroons with compote (stewed fruit).

> To make a change
Flavor your macaroons by adding one of the following to the powdered sugar: 3 tbsp. cocoa powder (chocolate macaroons); half a teaspoon of coffee extract (coffee macaroons); or half a teaspoon of vanilla extract (vanilla macaroons).

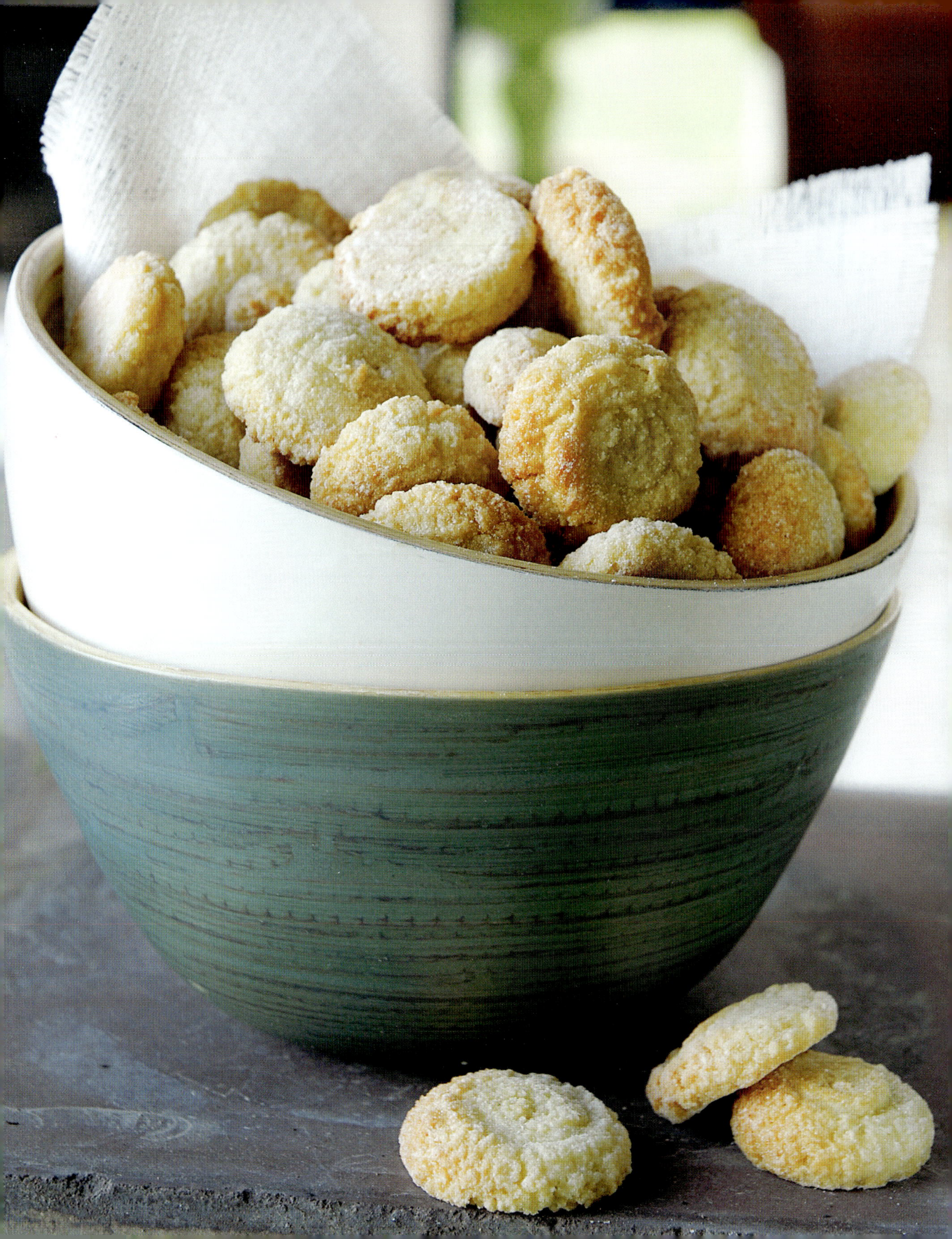

Langues-de-chat

MAKES 45 LANGUES-DE-CHAT
PREP TIME: About 20 mins.
COOKING TIME: About 5 mins.

- 9 tbsp. butter
- 1 teaspoon vanilla extract
- 6 to 8 tbsp. sugar
- 2 eggs
- 1 cup flour

Cut the butter into small pieces, place in a bowl and work with a wooden or rubber spatula until smooth. Add the vanilla extract and the sugar and mix well. Beat in the eggs one by one. Sift the flour, pour it onto the mixture and beat thoroughly.

Preheat the oven to 400° F. Line a baking sheet with parchment paper.

Spoon the mixture into a pastry bag fitted with a no. 6 tip and pipe 3-inch lengths of mixture, one inch apart. Bake for 4 to 5 minutes.

> Helpful tip
Not all these cookies (literally, "cat's tongues") will fit on one baking sheet, so bake them in batches. When they've cooled, place them in an airtight container.

> Serving advice
Serve with crème anglaise, chocolate mousse, fruit salad, stewed fruit, ice cream or sorbet.

never fails

266 • MUNCHY, CRUNCHY COOKIES

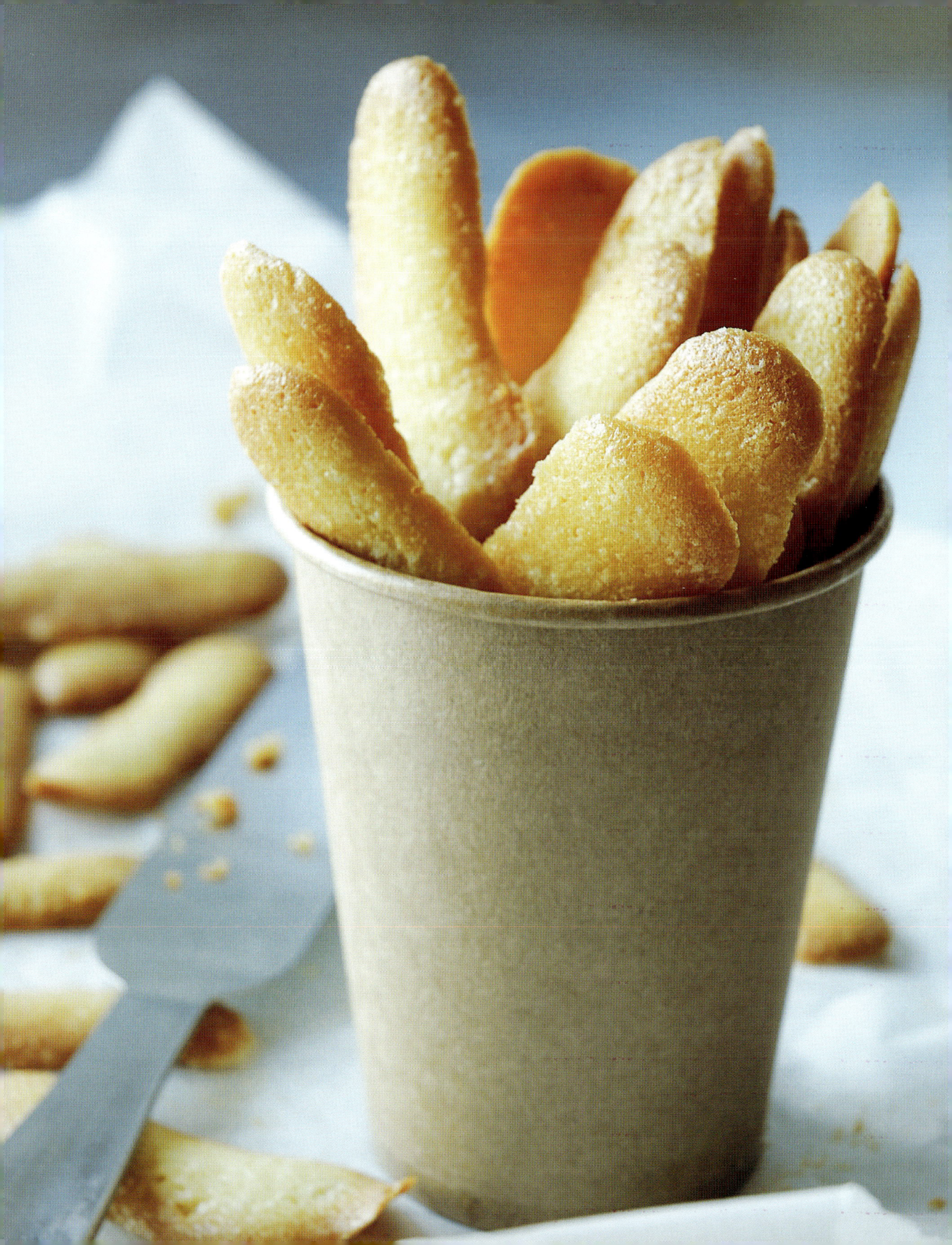

Tuiles

MAKES 25 TUILES
PREP TIME: 20 mins.
COOKING TIME: 4 mins. per batch

- 1/3 cup butter
- 2/3 cup flour
- 1/2 cup sugar
- 2 tsps. vanilla extract
- 2 eggs
- A pinch of salt
- 3/4 cup slivered almonds

Melt the butter, sift the flour. Preheat the oven to 400° F.

Place the sugar, the vanilla extract and the sifted flour in a bowl. Stir in the eggs one by one and add a small pinch of salt. Incorporate the melted butter and almonds. Stir gently to avoid breaking the almonds.

Line a baking sheet with parchment paper.

Spoon small quantities of mixture onto the baking sheet, leaving plenty of space between them. Flatten them with the back of a fork, dipping it in cold water each time. Bake for about 4 minutes.

Liberally oil a rolling pin. Unstick each tuile with a metal spatula and place it over the rolling pin to give it a curved shape. Allow to cool for a few seconds and place in an airtight container.

> Helpful tip
Bake these cookies in small batches to make it easier to organize the shaping process. Be careful as they are very fragile.

> Serving advice
Serve these classic French cookies with crème anglaise, chocolate mousse, fruit salad, stewed fruit, ice cream or sorbet.

Cigarettes russes

MAKES 25 TO 30 CIGARETTES RUSSES
PREP TIME: 30 mins.
COOKING TIME: 10 mins.

- 7 tbsp. butter
- 3/4 cup flour
- 3/4 cup sugar
- 1 teaspoon vanilla extract
- 4 egg whites

Preheat the oven to 350° F. Line a baking sheet with parchment paper.

Melt the butter in a double boiler. In a large bowl, mix the flour, the sugar, the vanilla extract, the egg whites and the melted butter.

Using a pastry bag or a spoon, spread this pastry in a very thin layer on the baking sheet and cut into thin four-inch diameter disks. Bake for 10 minutes: they should be a very pale golden color.

Remove the disks and roll them into cigarette shapes while still hot. Allow to cool and store in an airtight container.

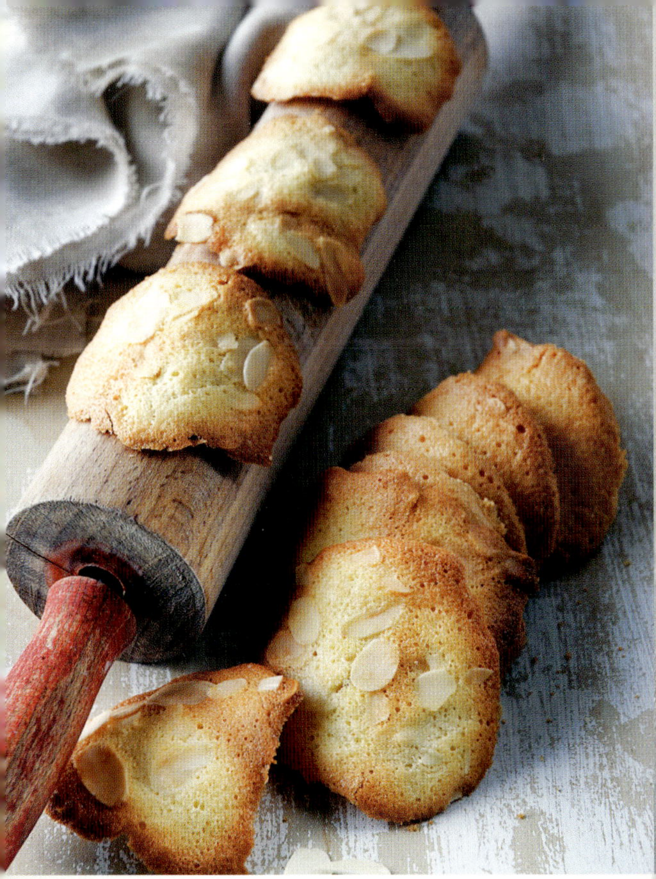
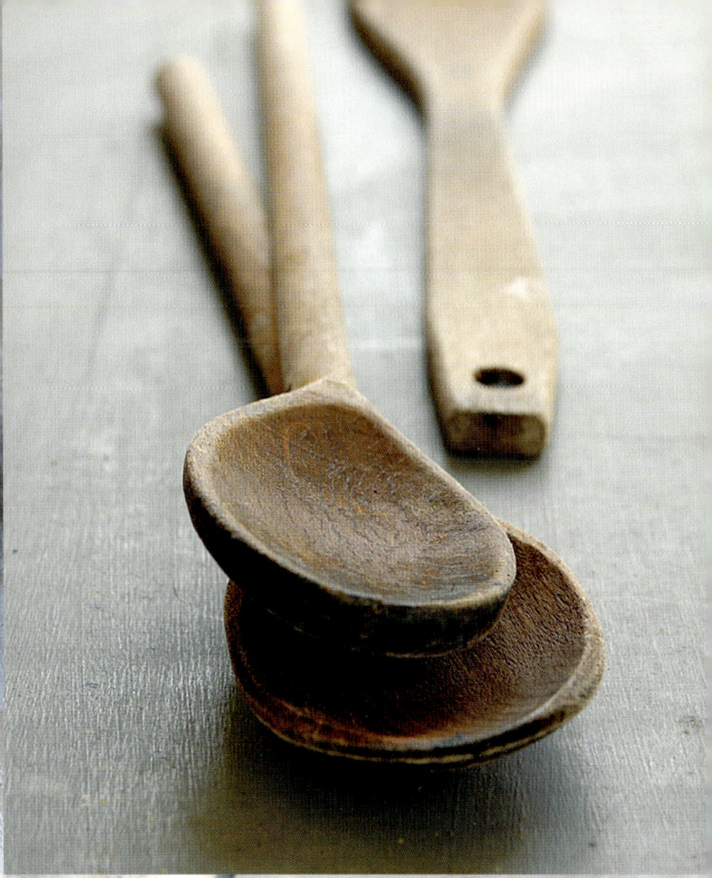
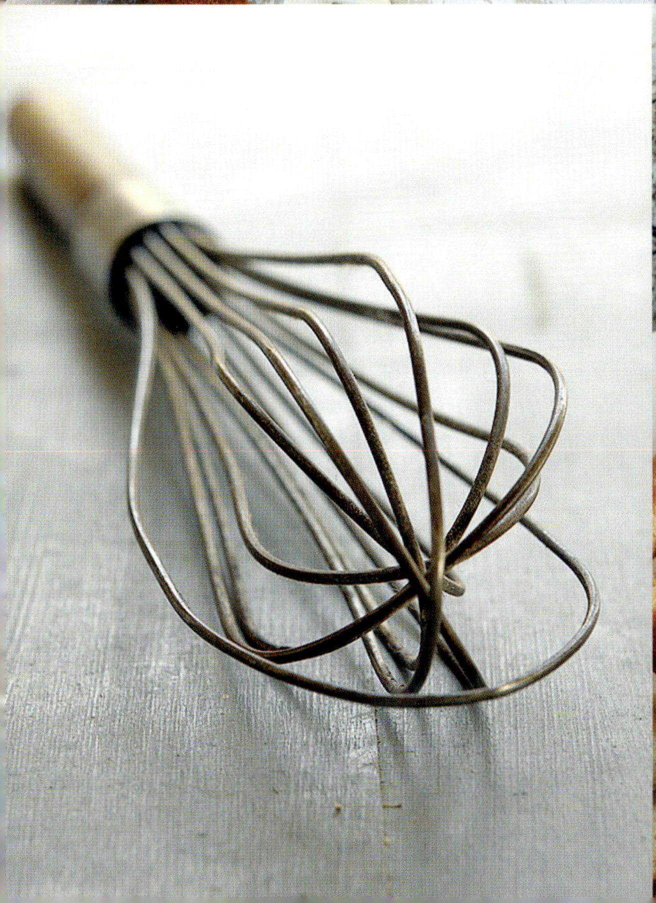
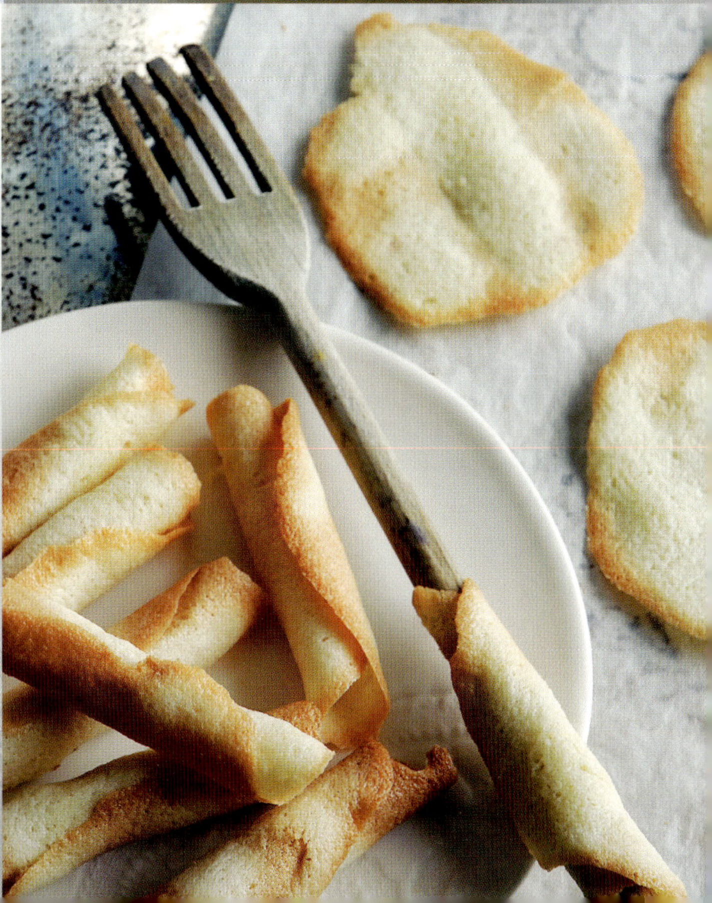

Galettes nantaises (Almond cookies)

MAKES ABOUT 25 COOKIES
PREP TIME: 15 mins.
COOKING TIME: 10 mins.

- 3 tbsp. butter
- 1/2 teaspoon salt
- 6 tbsp. sugar
- 2 eggs + 1 egg for glazing
- 1 cup flour
- 4-1/2 tbsp. ground almonds

Put the butter in a bowl and allow to soften at room temperature. Add the salt and work together with a spatula, then add the sugar. Beat in the 2 eggs one after the other. When the mixture is smooth, add the flour all at once and mix in very quickly (this helps make the cookie dough less brittle).

Preheat the oven to 350° F. Line a baking sheet with parchment paper.

Roll out the dough to a thickness of 1/8 inch on a lightly floured surface, then cut out round or rectangular cookies.

Lay them on the baking sheet and glaze with beaten egg. Draw a fork across the cookies to make a pattern of stripes and sprinkle with ground almonds. Bake for 10 minutes.

Allow to cool and place in an airtight container.

> Serving advice
Serve these cookies with crème anglaise, chocolate mousse, fruit salad, fruit compote, ice cream or sorbet.

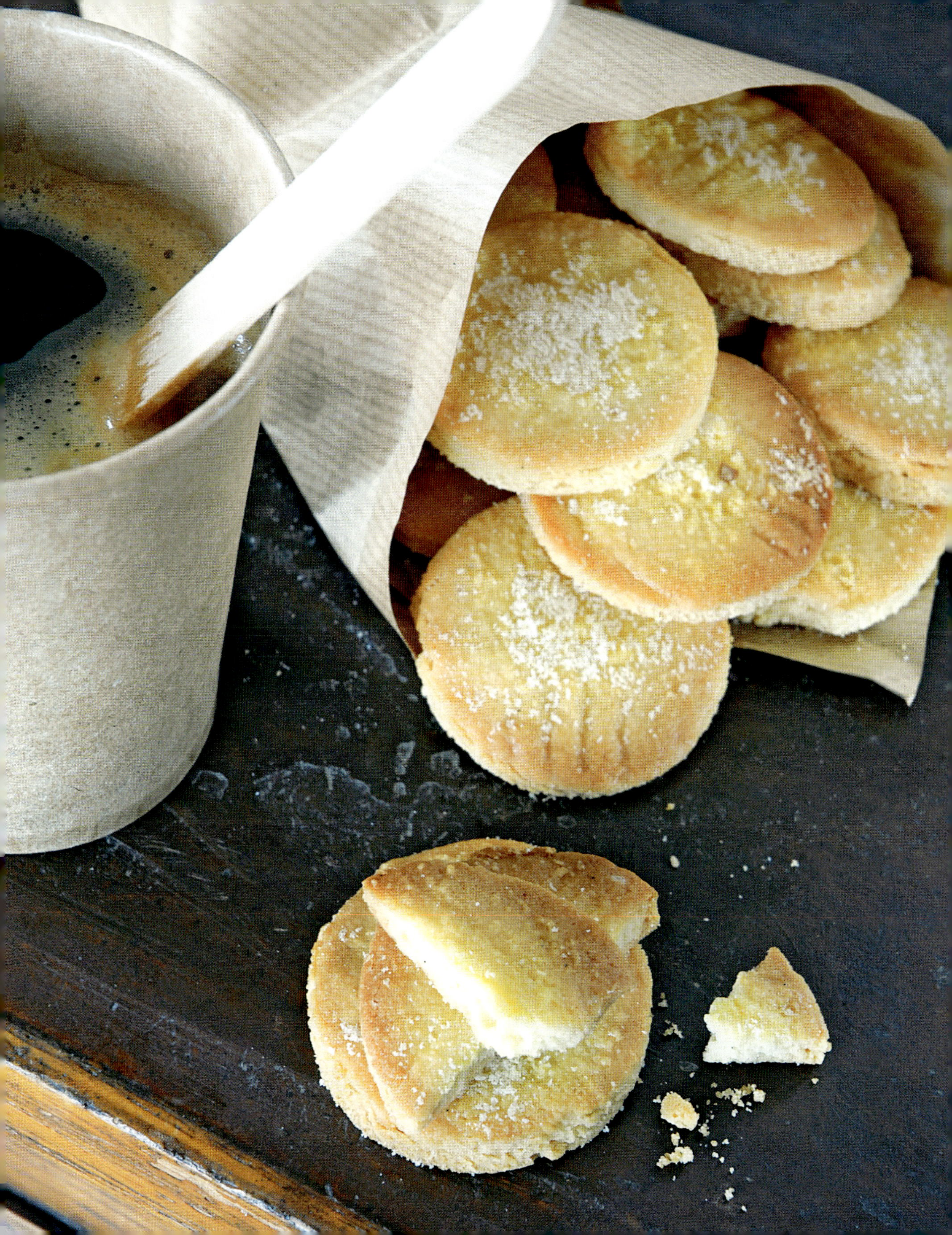

Countess cookies

MAKES 25 COOKIES
PREP TIME: 30 mins.
COOKING TIME: About 30 mins.

- 2 cups butter
- 4-1/2 cups flour
- 1/2 teaspoon salt
- 2 tbsp. sugar

never fails

Cut the butter into small pieces and allow to soften.

Sift the flour onto your work surface, add the salt and the butter. Knead into a smooth dough.

Preheat the oven to 300° F.

Roll the dough to a thickness of half an inch and cut into rounds with a cookie cutter. Arrange them on a parchment paper-lined baking sheet and sprinkle with sugar. Bake for about 30 minutes. These cookies should remain very pale in color. Store in an airtight container.

> Serving advice

These simple cookies go well with ice cream and fruit salad.

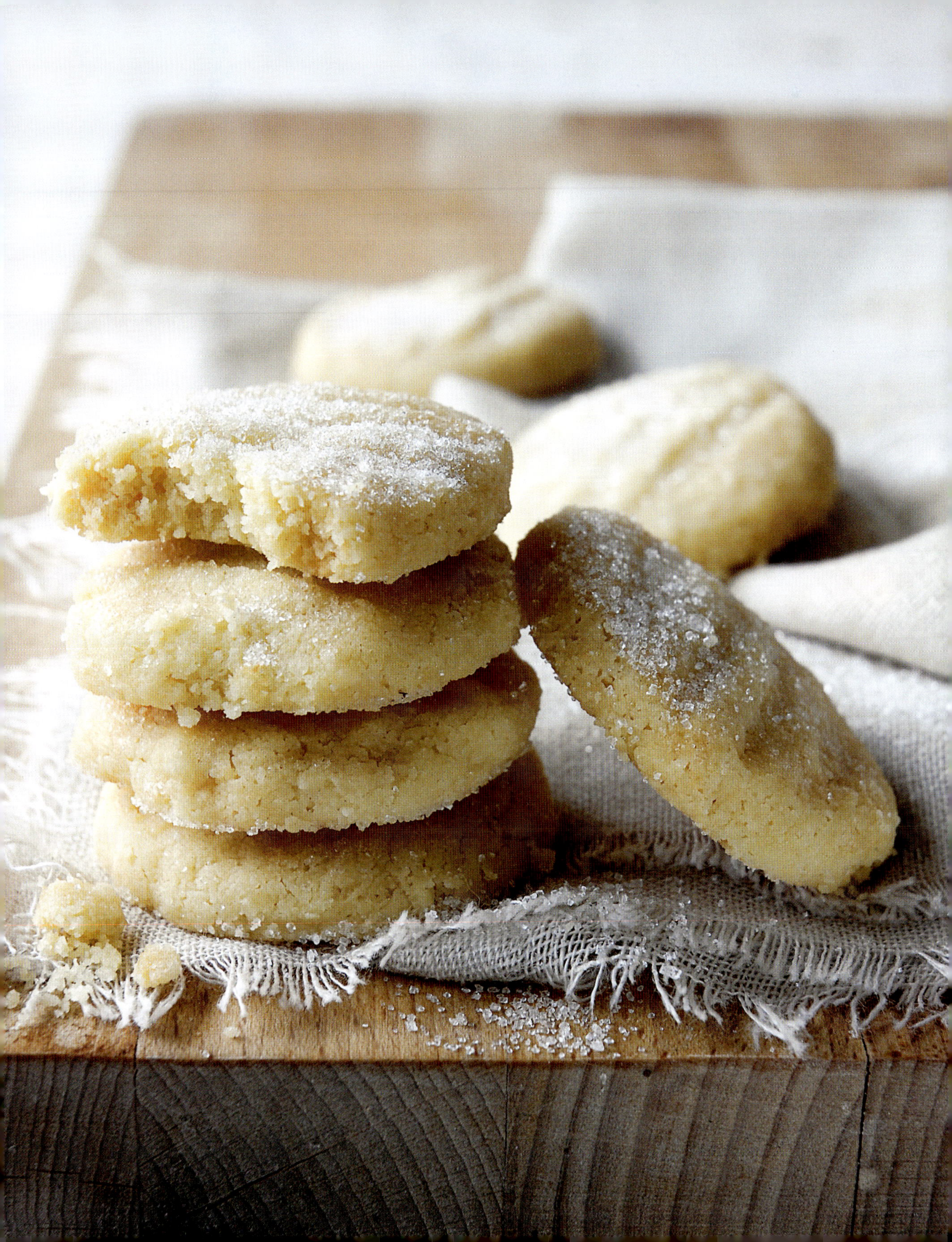

Palmiers

MAKES 20 PALMIERS
PREP TIME: 40 mins.
RESTING TIME: 1 hr
COOKING TIME: 10 mins.

- 1 lb. store bought puff pastry
- Powdered sugar

child's play

Roll out the puff pastry to form a rectangle three times as long as it is wide. Dust the surface with powdered sugar. Fold into three to make a rectangular envelope and allow to rest for 30 minutes in the refrigerator. Remove from the refrigerator, roll out again and repeat the operation.

Preheat the oven to 470° F.

Roll the pastry out to form a rectangle 1/2 an inch thick. Dust with powdered sugar. Fold each long edge into the center, then do the same again, so you end up with a kind of sausage with a heart-shaped cross-section.

Cut into 1/2-inch slices and place them on a baking sheet lined with parchment paper. Space them well apart, as the pastry will spread as it cooks.

Bake for 5 minutes, turn them over, and bake for another 5 minutes. They should be golden on both sides.

Allow to cool and store in an airtight container.

> Serving advice

You can serve palmiers on their own or as an accompaniment to ice cream or desserts such as chocolate mousse.

> Home made

If you want to prepare your own puff pastry, see p.402.

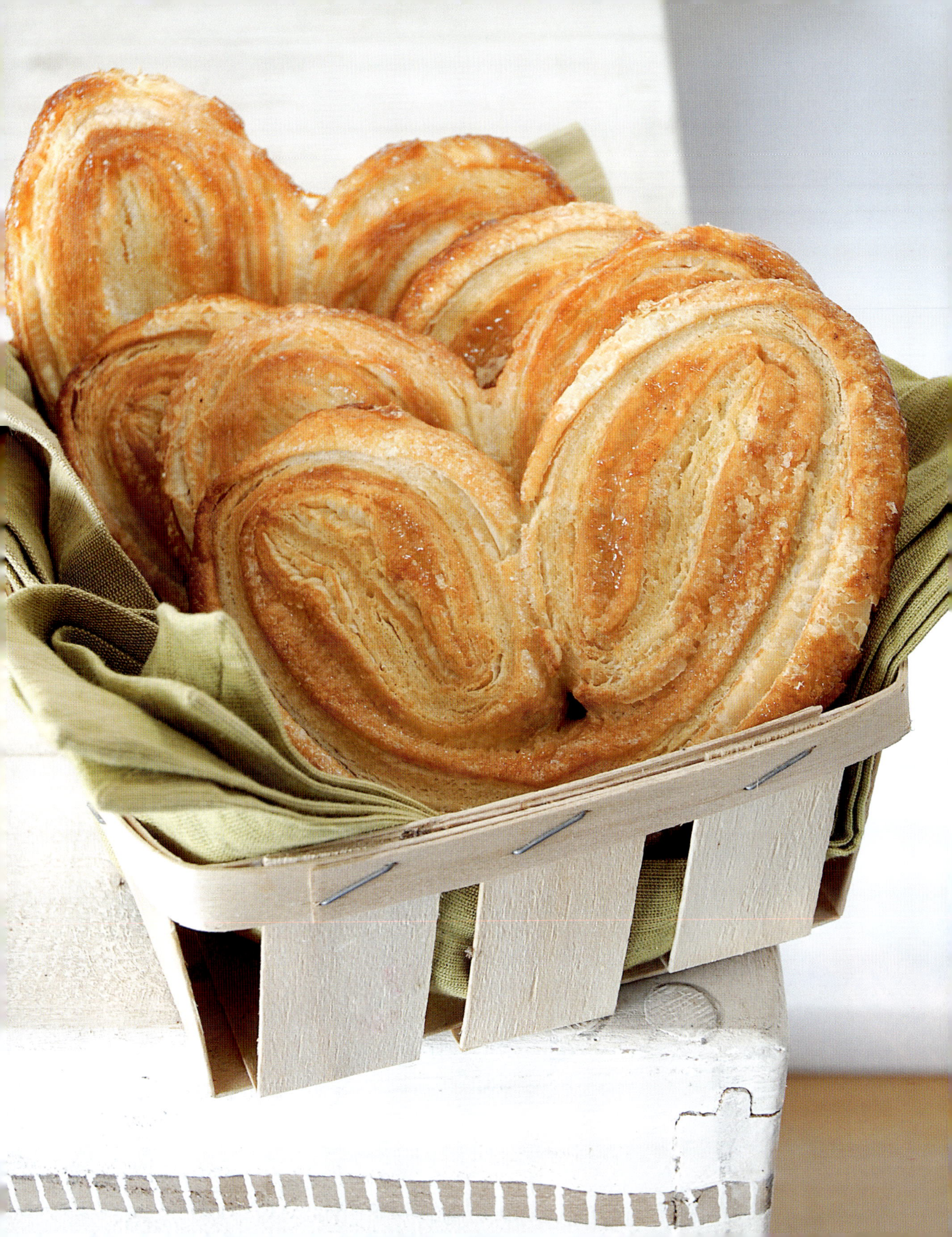

Coffee meringues

MAKES ABOUT 50 MERINGUES
PREP TIME: 15 mins.
COOKING TIME: 1 hr

- 3 egg whites
- A pinch of salt
- 5 tbsp. sugar
- 1 tsp. coffee extract
- 1 teaspoon cornstarch

Leave the egg whites for 1 hour at room temperature before using. Beat them with a pinch of salt until they form very stiff peaks. Gradually beat in the sugar, then the coffee extract and the cornstarch, and continue to beat for a few moments.

Preheat the oven to 225° F and line a baking sheet with parchment paper.

Spoon the mixture into a pastry bag with a wide, smooth tip and pipe spheres of meringue onto the parchment paper, making sure they don't touch each other. Bake for at least 1 hour, until the meringues are dry to the touch (they should not color).

Remove the meringues from the oven, allow to cool and carefully remove from the parchment paper.

> Serving advice
Serve these meringues on their own or with chocolate ice cream, for example.

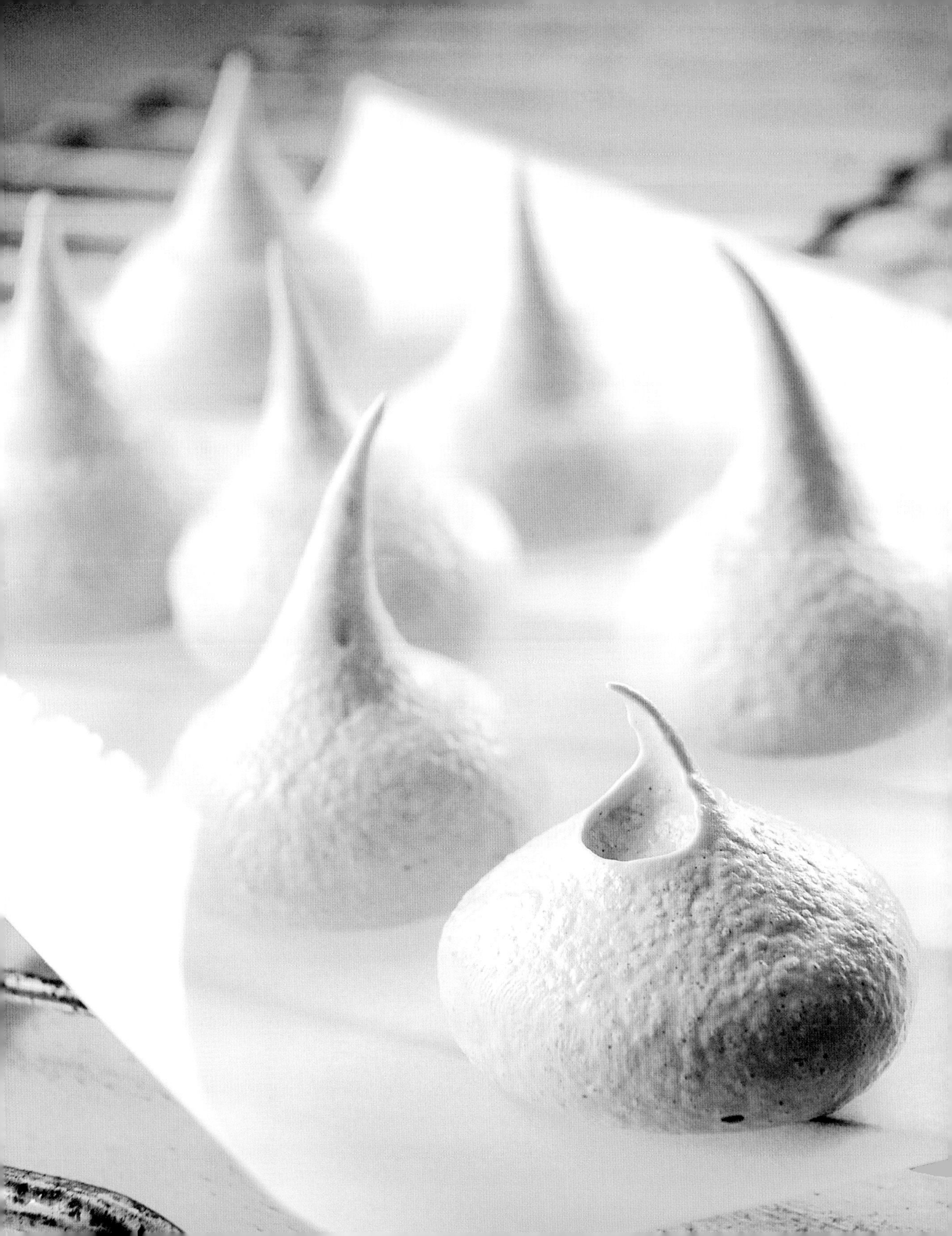

Rum-raisin cookies

MAKES 25 COOKIES
PREP TIME: 15 mins.
SOAKING TIME: 1 hr
COOKING TIME: 10 mins.

- 3/4 cup raisins
- 1/3 cup rum
- 9 tbsp. butter
- 2/3 cup sugar
- 2 eggs
- 1-1/4 cups flour
- A pinch of salt

Rinse the raisins and soak in the rum for about 1 hour.

Preheat the oven to 400° F.

Soften the butter in a bowl and beat together with the sugar, then add the eggs one by one and mix well. Add the flour, the raisins and rum, and a pinch of salt. Mix well after you add each ingredient.

Spoon small quantities of mixture onto a baking sheet lined with parchment paper, making sure they are spaced well apart, and bake for 10 minutes. Remove from the oven and allow to cool.

Keep in an airtight container.

never fails

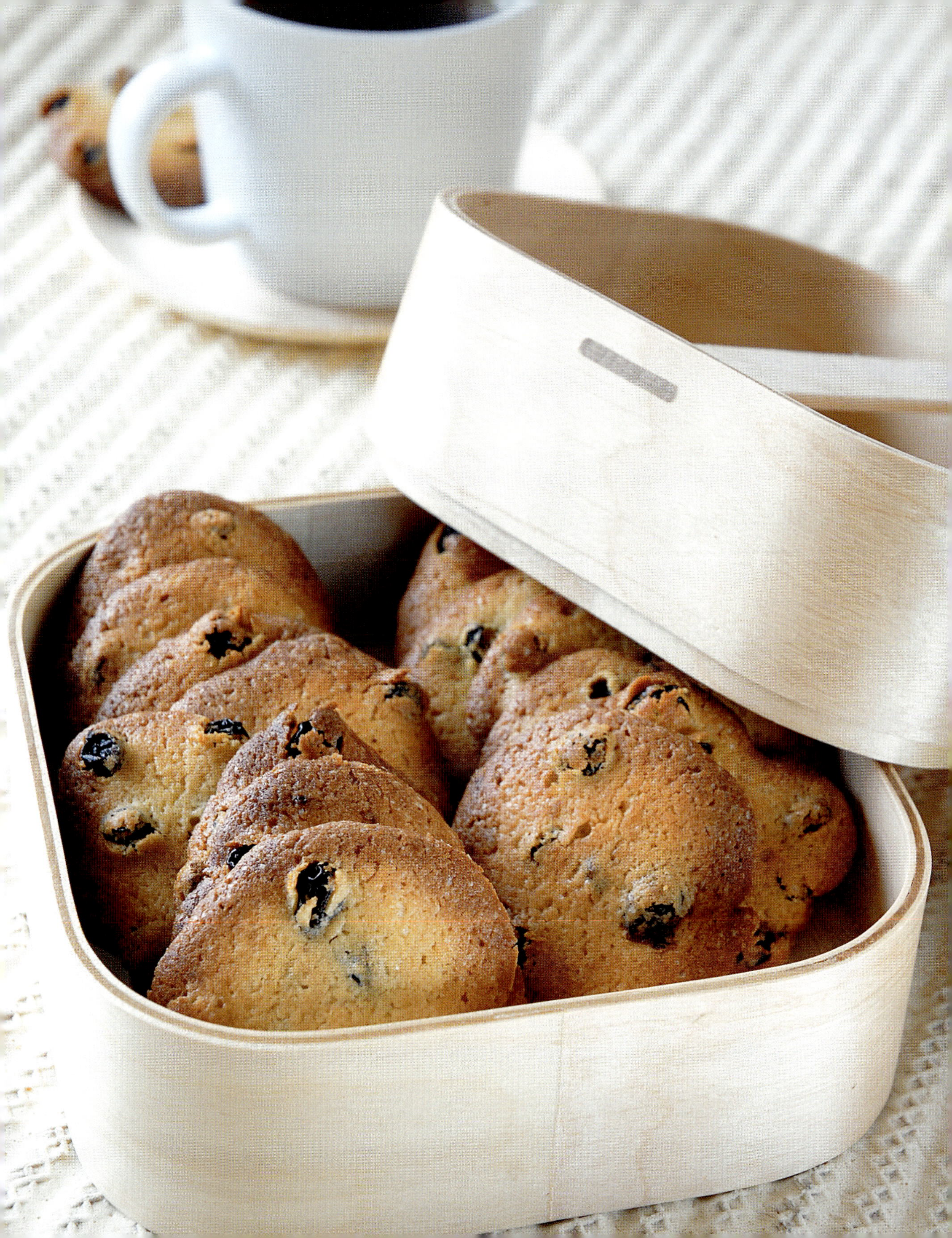

Middle Eastern Easter pastries

MAKES 20 COOKIES
PREP TIME: 45 mins.
RESTING TIME: 2 hrs
COOKING TIME: 35 mins.

FOR THE COOKIE DOUGH
- 1 cup butter
- 4 cups flour
- 3 tbsp. orange flower water
- 3 tbsp. rose water

FOR THE FILLING
- 1 cup shelled walnuts, blanched almonds or shelled pistachios
- 1 cup sugar
- 3 tbsp. orange flower water (or rose water)

Prepare the dough: melt the butter in a saucepan. Put the flour in a large bowl and pour in the melted butter. Add the orange flower water and rose water. Knead well until quite smooth (add a little water if the dough is too stiff). Allow to rest for 2 hours.

Prepare the filling: chop the walnuts, almonds or pistachios, then mix them with the orange flower water (or rose water).

Preheat the oven to 325° F.

Take a piece of dough the size of a small egg. Form into a hollow cone with your fingers. Fill with nut mixture and seal the open end. Continue with the rest of the dough.

Lay the pastries on a baking sheet lined with parchment paper and bake for 35 minutes. Remove from the oven and dust with powdered sugar.

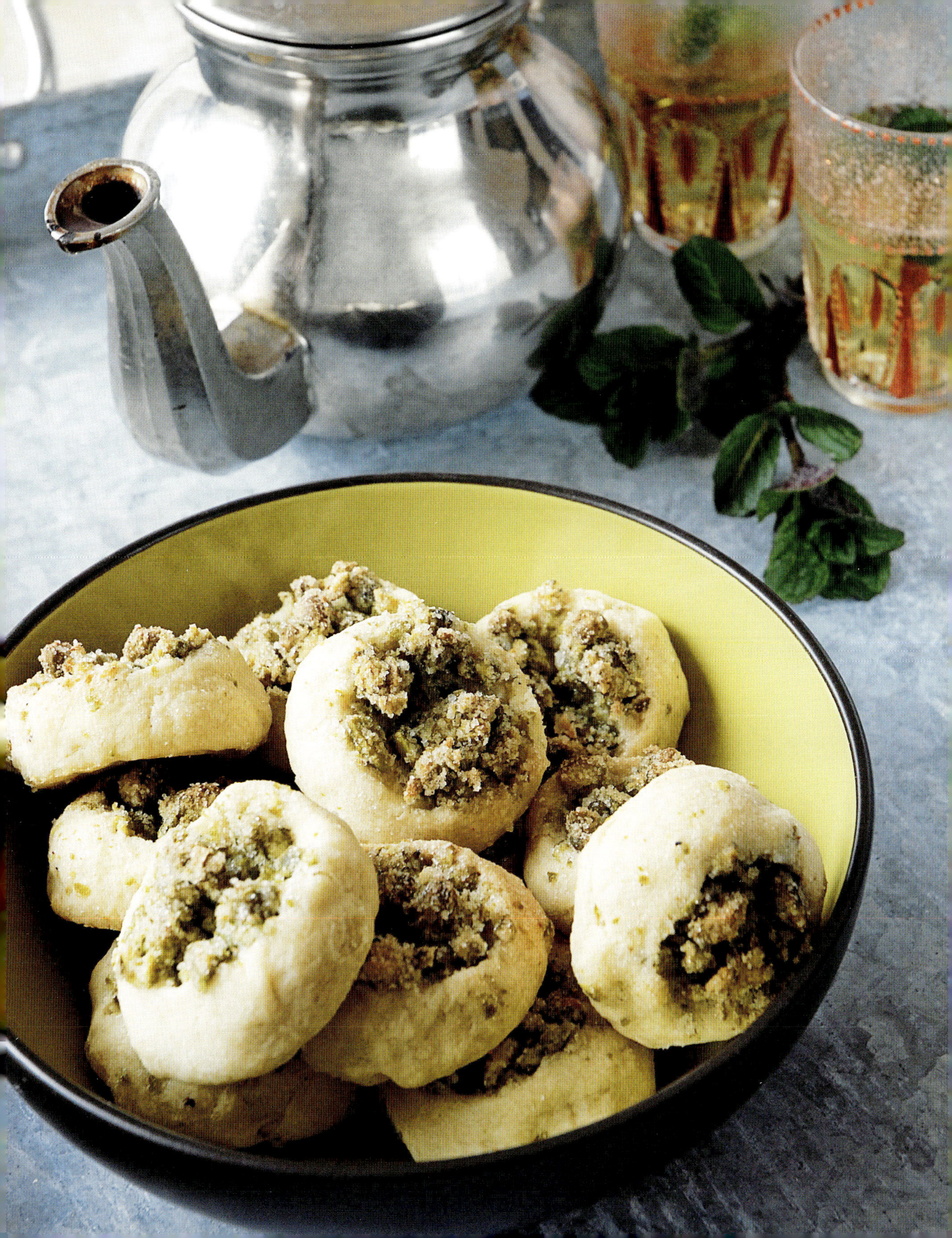

Lemon cookies

MAKES 40 COOKIES
PREP TIME: 25 mins.
COOKING TIME: 10 mins.

FOR THE LEMON CURD
- 2 tbsp. softened butter
- 1 lemon
- 1 egg
- 1/4 cup sugar
- 12 teaspoons cornstarch

FOR THE COOKIE DOUGH
- 1-1/3 cups flour
- 1 organic lemon
- 6 tbsp. butter
- 1-1/3 cups sugar
- 1 egg

Prepare the lemon curd: cut the softened butter into small pieces. Rinse and dry the lemon and grate the zest into a bowl. Now squeeze the juice from the lemon. Put the zest and juice into a saucepan. Beat the egg and whisk in the sugar and butter. Mix the cornstarch with a spoonful of this mixture. Add everything to the saucepan and cook over a very low heat, whisking constantly until the mixture thickens. When the mixture is thick and creamy, rub it through a fine sieve.

Preheat the oven to 350° F. Line a baking sheet with parchment paper.

Prepare the cookie dough: sift the flour. Grate the lemon zest. Work the butter to a soft consistency in a bowl, then add the sugar and continue to mix. When the mixture is white and smooth, beat in the egg and add the lemon zest. Gradually add the flour, stirring constantly. When the mixture becomes a stiff dough, knead it with your hands.

Roll out the dough to a thickness of 1/4 inch. Cut out shapes using a cookie cutter, arrange them on the baking sheet and bake for 10 minutes.

Remove the cookies from the baking sheet and place them on a wire rack to cool.

Spread half the cookies with lemon curd and lay the other half on top. Serve.

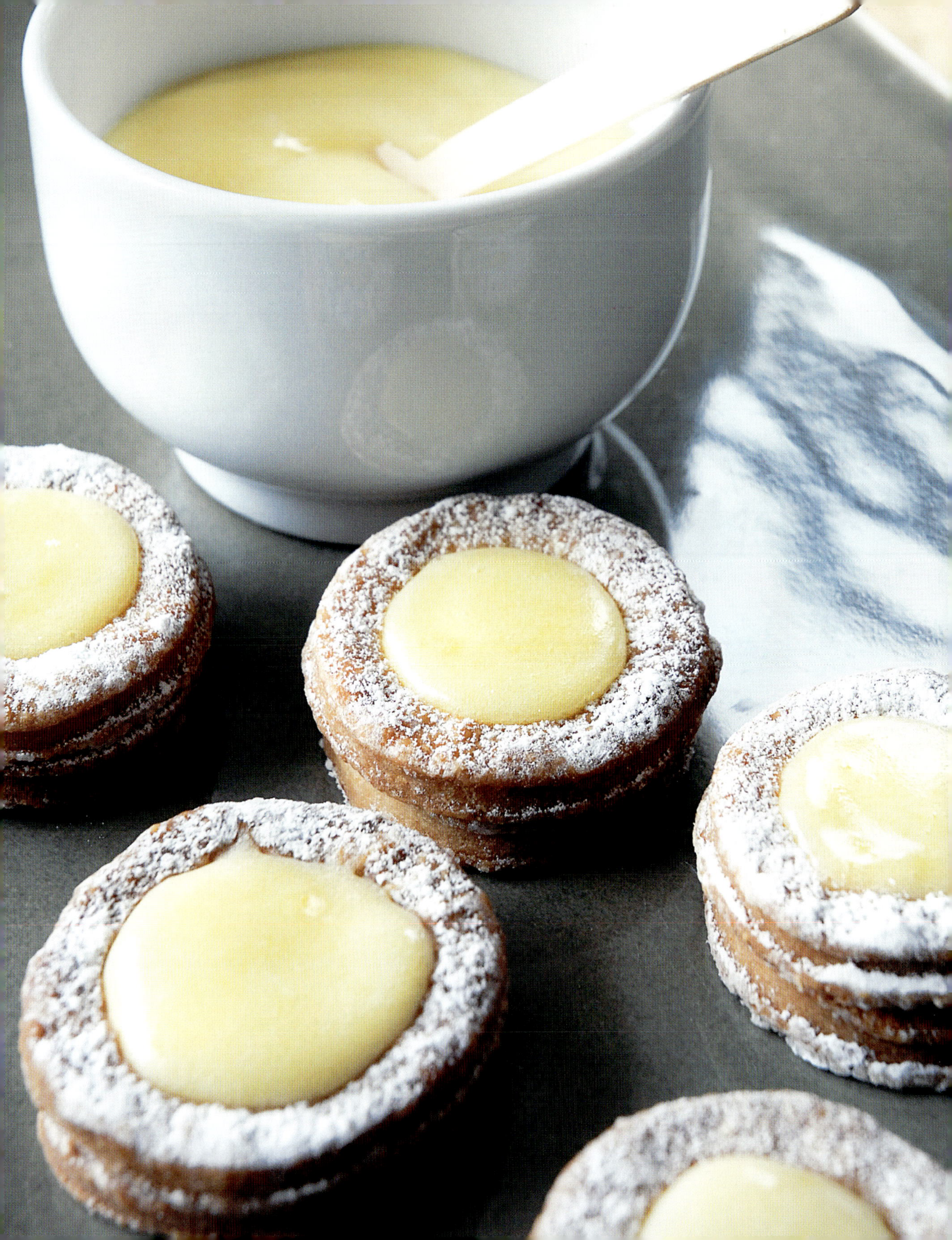

Butter shortbread (sablés)

MAKES 40 TO 50 COOKIES
PREP TIME: 15 mins.
COOKING TIME: 20 mins.

- 1/2 vanilla bean
- 14 tbsp. butter at room temperature
- 2/3 cup powdered sugar
- Small pinch of salt
- 1 egg white
- 1-3/4 cups flour

Split the vanilla bean in two and scrape out the seeds. Cut the butter into small pieces.

Put the butter into a bowl and work it quickly with a wooden or rubber spatula to soften it. Add the powdered sugar, the salt, the vanilla seeds, the egg white and finally the flour, combining each new ingredient before adding the next.

When everything is well incorporated, stop mixing so that the mixture keeps its "gritty" consistency.

Preheat the oven to 350° F. Line a baking sheet with parchment paper.

Put the dough in a pastry bag with a fluted tip. Pipe the dough onto the sheet in different shapes (strips, letters, etc). Bake for about 20 minutes.

> Serving advice

Serve these cookies with crème anglaise, chocolate mousse, fruit salad, stewed fruit, ice cream or sorbet.

child's play

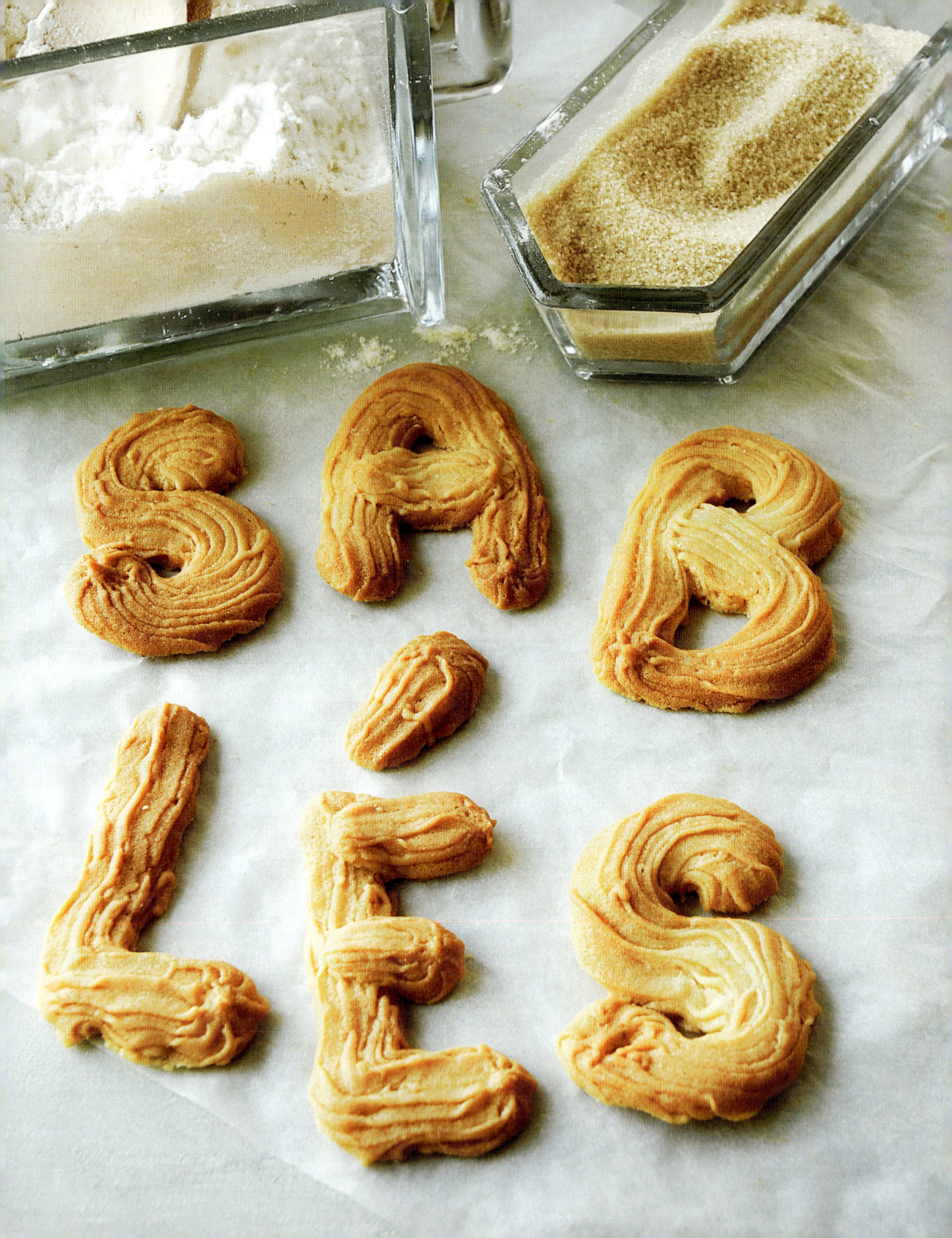
SABLÉS

Sablé-sur-Sarthe shortbread

MAKES 50 COOKIES
PREP TIME: 20 mins.
RESTING TIME: 30 mins.
COOKING TIME: 10 to 12 mins. each batch

- 14 tbsp. butter + some for the pan
- 1/2 cup sugar
- 4 egg yolks
- A pinch of salt
- 2-1/2 cups flour
- 1/2 cup of milk

never fails

Place the sugar, 3 egg yolks and a pinch of salt in a bowl and work them with a wooden or rubber spatula until creamy. Gradually stir in the flour, adding a little milk if necessary, until you have a slightly stiff but supple dough. Roll into a ball and allow to rest in a cool place for 30 minutes.

Preheat the oven to 425° F. Butter a baking sheet.

Roll out the dough to a thickness of 1/8 inch. Cut out shapes with a cookie cutter and lay them on the baking sheet.

Glaze with beaten egg yolk mixed with 3 tbsp. of milk.

Bake for 10 to 12 minutes, until just golden.

Remove from the oven and allow to cool on a rack. Keep in an airtight container.

> Helpful tip
Sablé-sur-Sarthe is the small town in western France where this recipe comes from. Serve these cookies with crème anglaise, chocolate mousse, fruit salad, stewed fruit, ice cream or sorbet.

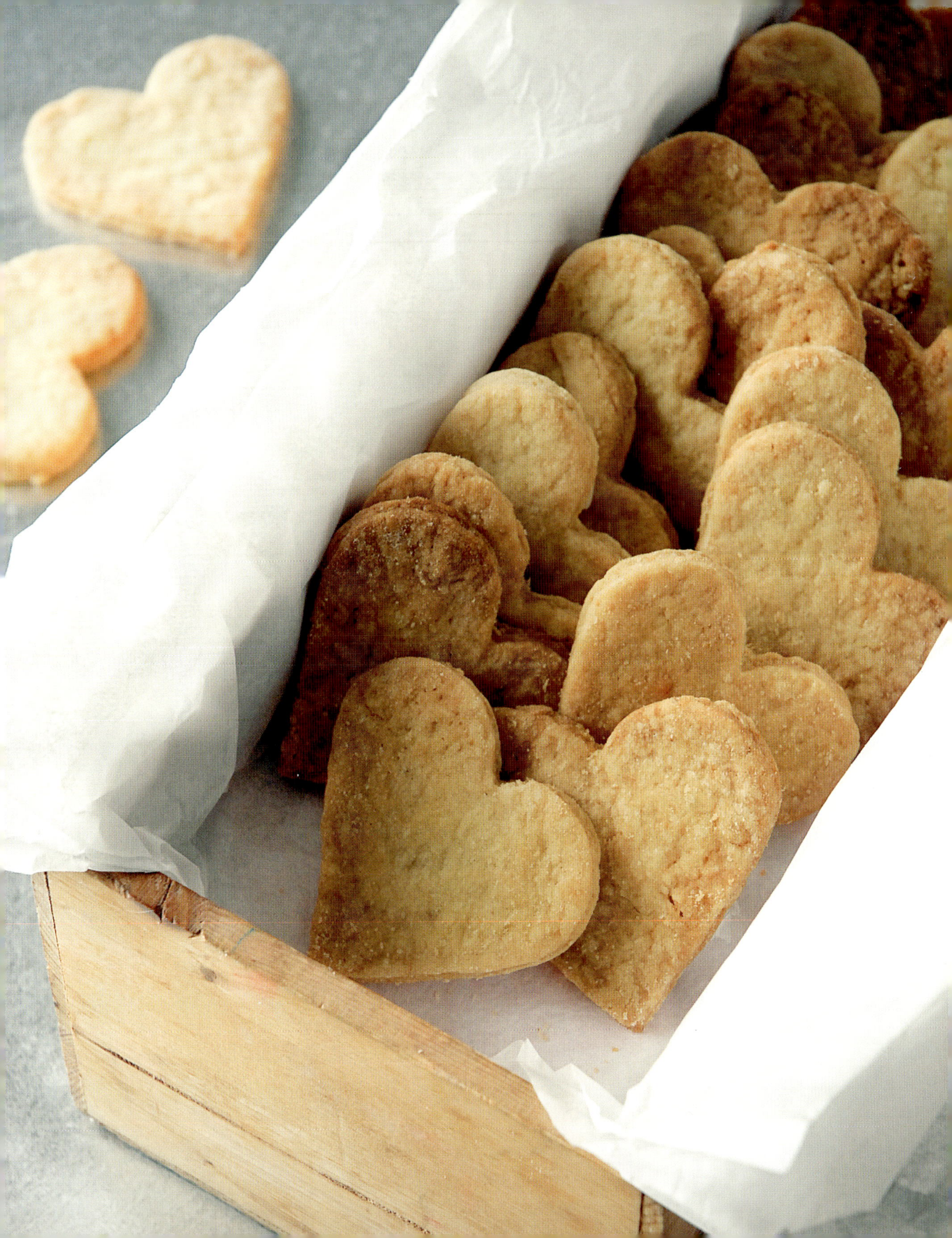

Spiced "arlettes"

MAKES 40 "ARLETTES"
PREP TIME: 30 mins.
RESTING TIME: 4 hrs
+ 10 mins.
COOKING TIME: 4 to 5 mins.

FOR THE SPICED SUGAR
- 1 tbsp. allspice
- 1 scant tbsp. vanilla extract
- 5 tbsp. sugar

FOR THE DOUGH
- 3 tbsp. butter
- 1 lb. chilled puff pastry

Prepare the spiced sugar: mix together the powdered sugar, the allspice and the vanilla extract.

Prepare the dough: melt the butter; roll out the puff pastry to a thickness of 1/16 inch and cut out a 20-inch square. Brush with melted butter. Roll up the dough into a cylinder shape and chill for about 4 hours, then place in the freezer for 10 minutes.

Preheat the oven to 450° F.

Cut the dough roll into slices 1/16 inch thick with a long, sharp knife.

Sprinkle your work surface with the spiced sugar. Lay the dough disks on the sugar two by two, cover them with sugar on both sides, then roll them out very thinly.

Put the cookies on a baking sheet lined with waxed paper and bake for 4 or 5 minutes.

> Helpful tip
These spiced cookies will keep in a tightly closed metal container for around two weeks in a dry place, or ten days in an airtight plastic container.

> To make a change
You can make these cookies into a delicious dessert by sandwiching them with chocolate mousse (see p.110) and serving with raspberry coulis (see p.423).

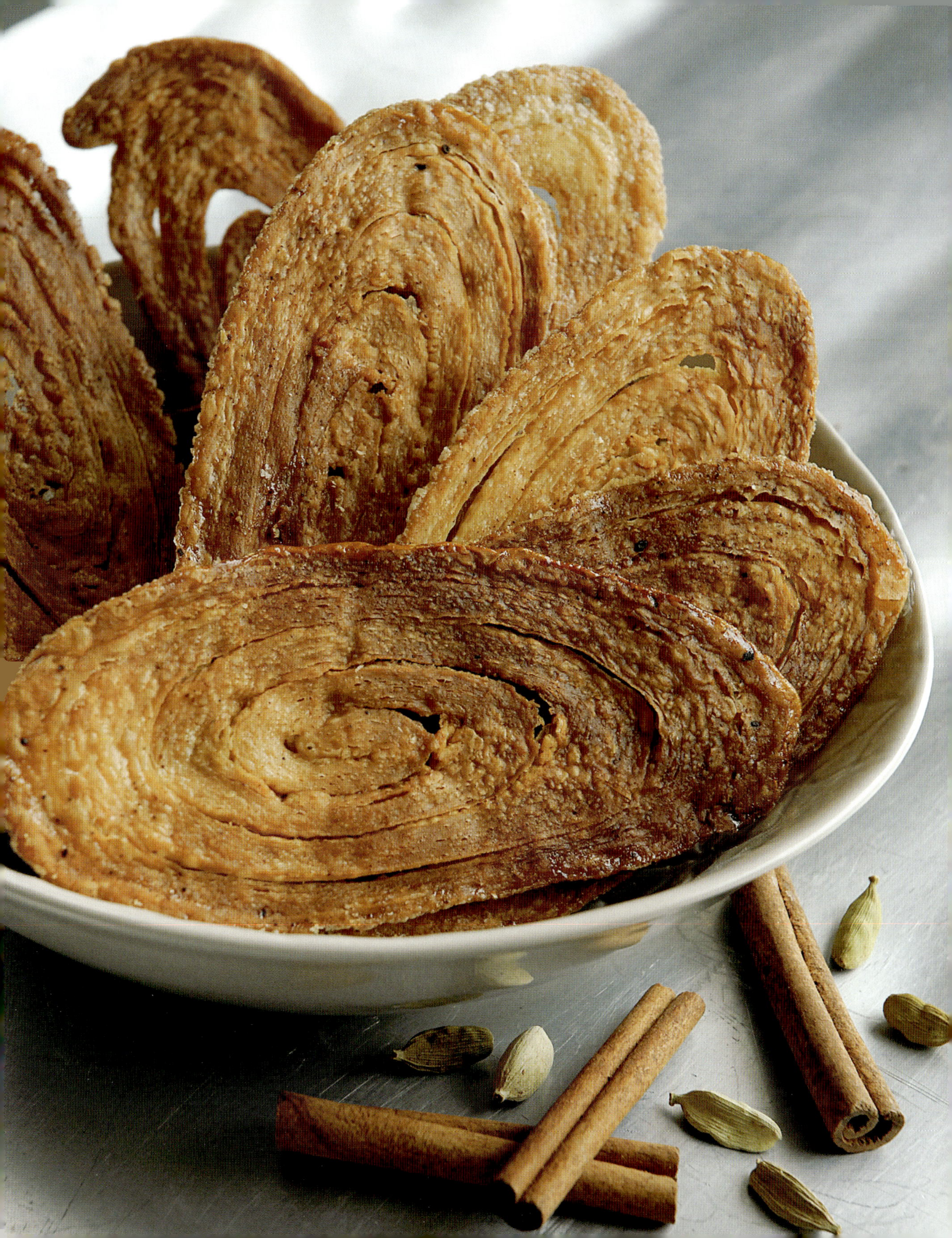

Pecan cookies

MAKES 25 COOKIES
PREP TIME: 30 mins
COOKING TIME: 15 mins.

- 2/3 cup butter
- 7 oz. pecans
- 4 eggs
- 1/2 cup sugar
- 3-1/4 cups flour

Allow the butter to soften at room temperature.

Wrap the pecans in a clean dish towel and crush them with a rolling pin, or use a food processor.

Break the eggs into a large bowl and beat them, then whisk in the sugar and the butter. Gradually add the flour, stirring constantly. Add the pecans and mix well.

Preheat the oven to 400° F. Line a baking sheet with parchment paper.

Place the dough on a work surface and roll into a sausage shape. Slice into 1/2-inch slices.

Place them on a baking sheet lined with parchment paper, leaving about 2 inches between them so they don't stick together. Bake for 15 minutes.

Allow to cool. Keep in an airtight container in a dry place.

> Serving advice

Serve these cookies with crème anglaise, chocolate mousse, fruit salad, stewed fruit, ice cream or sorbet.

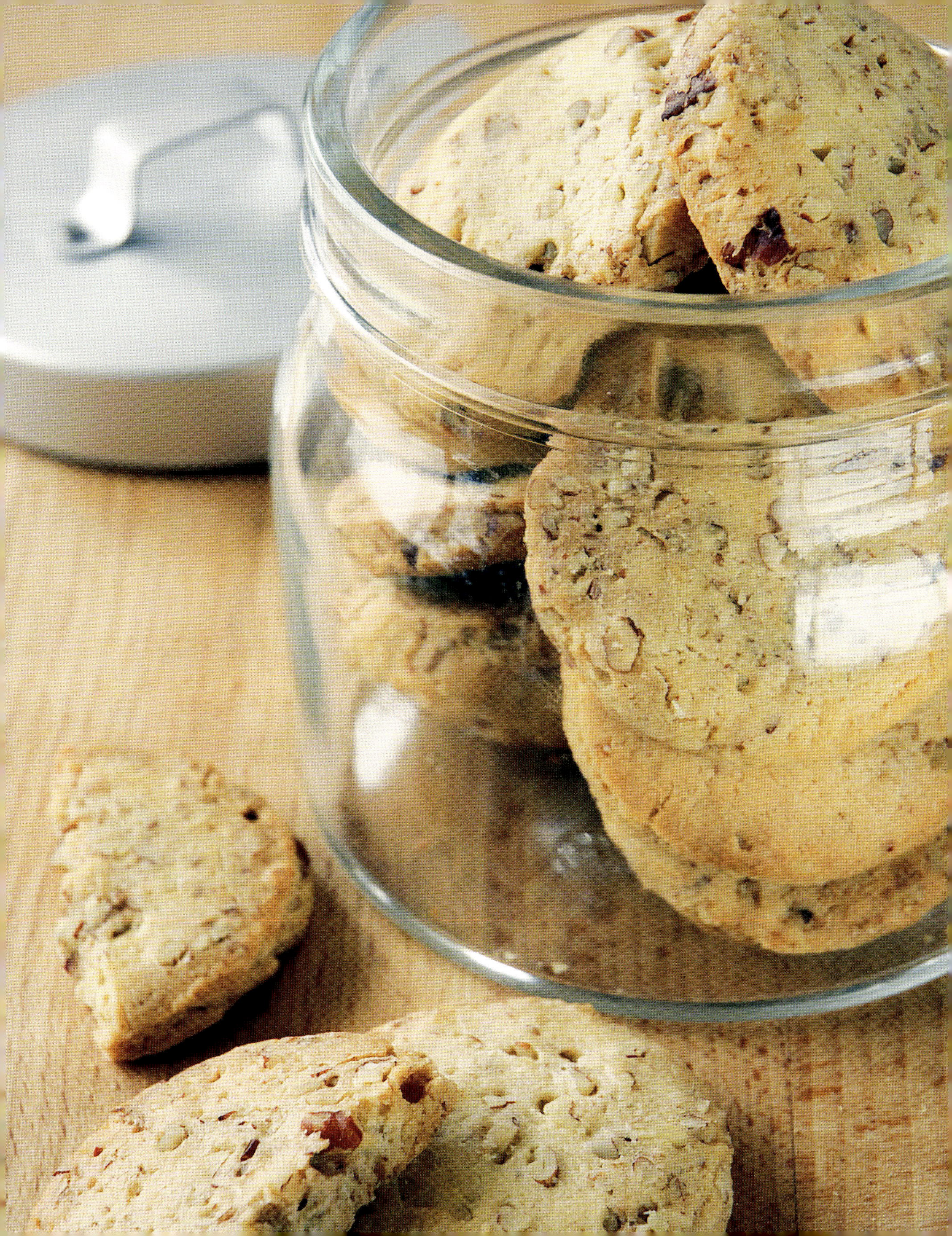

Cordoba cookies

MAKES 20 TO 25 COOKIES
PREP TIME: 15 mins.
RESTING TIME: 1 hr
COOKING TIME: 10 mins.

- 14 tbsp. butter
- 3-1/4 cups flour
- 1 tbsp. sugar
- 1 teaspoon vanilla extract
- 2 egg yolks
- 7 tbsp. whole milk
- Dulce de leche, guava jelly or papaya jelly

Cut the butter into small pieces. Sift the flour into a bowl and mix it with the sugar and vanilla extract. Gradually add the butter, then the egg yolks.

Add the milk and mix to a stiff dough (take care not to over-knead). Let the dough rest in the refrigerator for at least an hour.

Preheat the oven to 350° F.

Roll the dough out to a thickness of 1/8 inch. Cut out shapes with a cookie cutter. Arrange them on a baking sheet lined with parchment paper, leaving plenty of space between them. Bake for 10 minutes.

Remove the cookies with a spatula and put them on a rack to cool.

Sandwich the cookies with dulce de leche, guava jelly or papaya jelly and serve.

> Serving advice
Dulce de leche is really easy to make! Why not try to make your own? (see p.382).

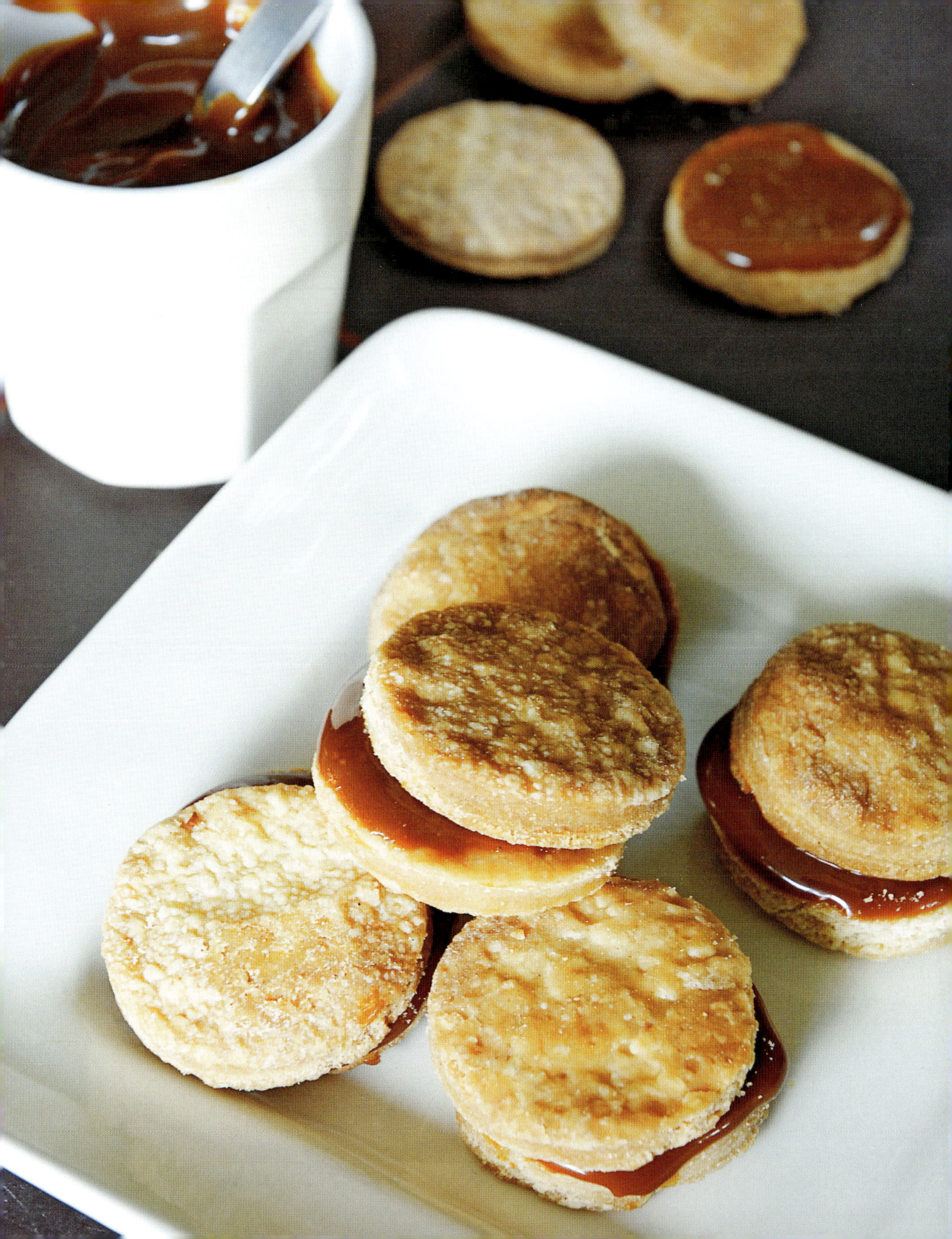

Galettes bretonnes
(Breton-style butter cookies)

MAKES 30 TO 35 COOKIES
PREP TIME: 10 mins.
REFRIGERATION TIME: 2 hrs
COOKING TIME: 10 mins.

- 9 tbsp. butter
- 2/3 cup sugar
- 2 pinches of salt
- 1 egg
- 1-3/4 cups flour
- 1-1/2 teaspoons baking powder

Soften the butter and mix with the sugar and salt. Add the egg and stir well with a wooden spoon for a few minutes. Add the flour and baking powder and knead until the dough is smooth.

Make the dough into a ball, wrap in plastic wrap and allow to rest for 1 hour in the refrigerator.

Cut the dough into four pieces. Make each into a sausage shape 2 inches in diameter, then cut into 1/2-inch disks. Lay the disks on a baking sheet lined with parchment paper and put back in the refrigerator for one hour.

Preheat the oven to 400° F. Bake for 10 minutes.

Allow to cool and keep the cookies in an airtight container.

> Serving advice
Serve these cookies with crème anglaise (see p.411), chocolate mousse (see p.110), fruit salad, fruit compote, ice cream or sorbet.

Croquets de Bar-sur-Aube
(Almond cookies)

MAKES 35 COOKIES
PREP TIME: 15 mins.
COOKING TIME: 10 mins.

- 2-1/4 cups sugar
- 1 tsp vanilla extract
- 1-1/2 cups ground almonds
- 4 egg whites
- 1 generous cup sifted flour

In a large bowl, mix the sugar, the vanilla extract and the ground almonds. Add the egg whites one by one. Gradually mix in the flour. Preheat the oven to 350° F. Lay the dough on a work surface and roll out to a thickness of half an inch.

Cut into narrow five-inch strips and place on a baking sheet covered in parchment paper. Bake for 10 minutes. Loosen the cookies with a metal spatula while they're still hot and allow to cool on the baking sheet. Place in an airtight container when cold.

> Helpful tip
These cookies are a specialty of Bar-sur-Aube, a village in the Champagne region of eastern France. They are often served with crème anglaise.

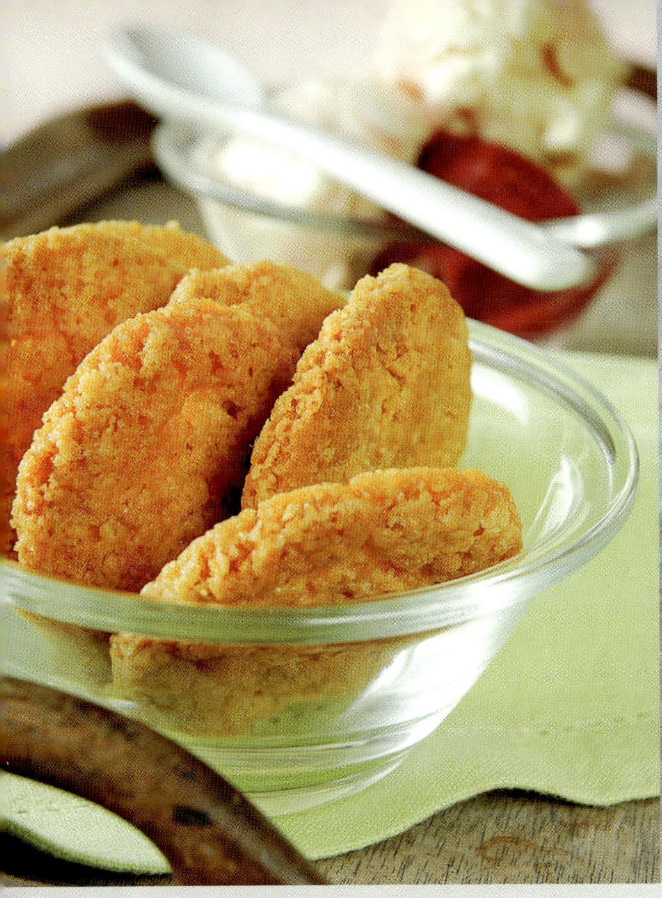
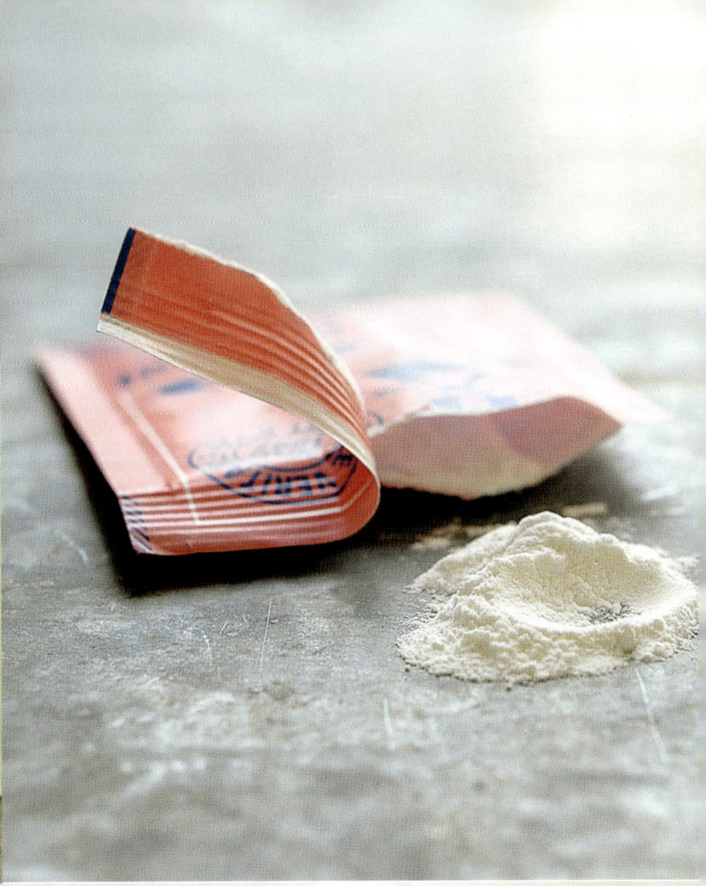
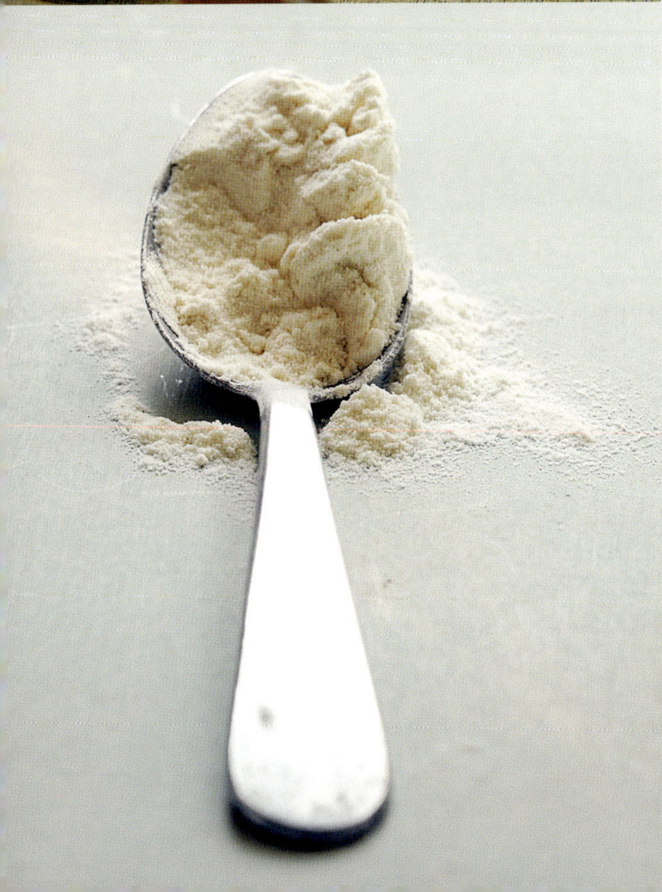
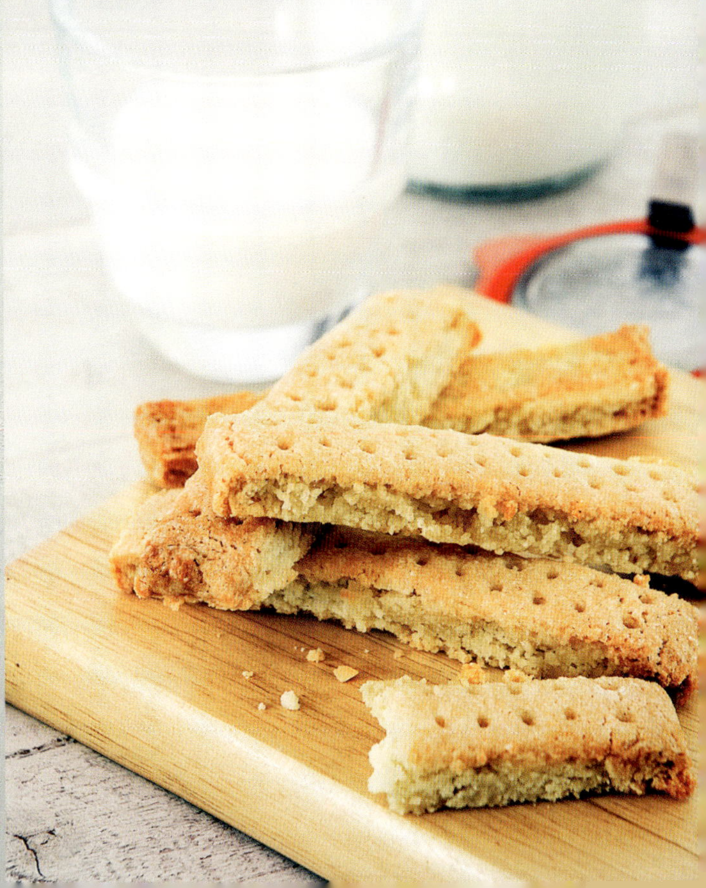

Chocolate chip cookies

MAKES 30 COOKIES
PREP TIME: 20 mins.
COOKING TIME: 8 to 10 mins. each batch

- 8 tbsp. softened butter
- 6 oz. dark chocolate chips
- 1/2 cup brown sugar
- 1/2 cup regular sugar
- 1 egg
- 1/2 teaspoon vanilla extract
- 1-3/4 cups flour
- 1/2 teaspoon baking powder
- A pinch of salt

Preheat the oven to 350° F.

Beat the softened butter with the two kinds of sugar in a bowl until the mixture turns pale yellow. Mix in the egg, then the vanilla extract.

Sift the flour with the baking powder and salt. Gradually add to the mixture, working it with a wooden spatula to avoid any lumps forming. Mix in the chocolate chips.

Place a sheet of parchment paper on a baking sheet. Spoon small quantities of dough onto the baking sheet with a tablespoon, dipping the spoon into a bowl of water each time. Flatten the dough with the back of the spoon to form disks about five inches in diameter.

Bake for 8 to 10 minutes.

Take the cookies out of the oven and put them on a wire rack. Serve warm or cold.

child's play

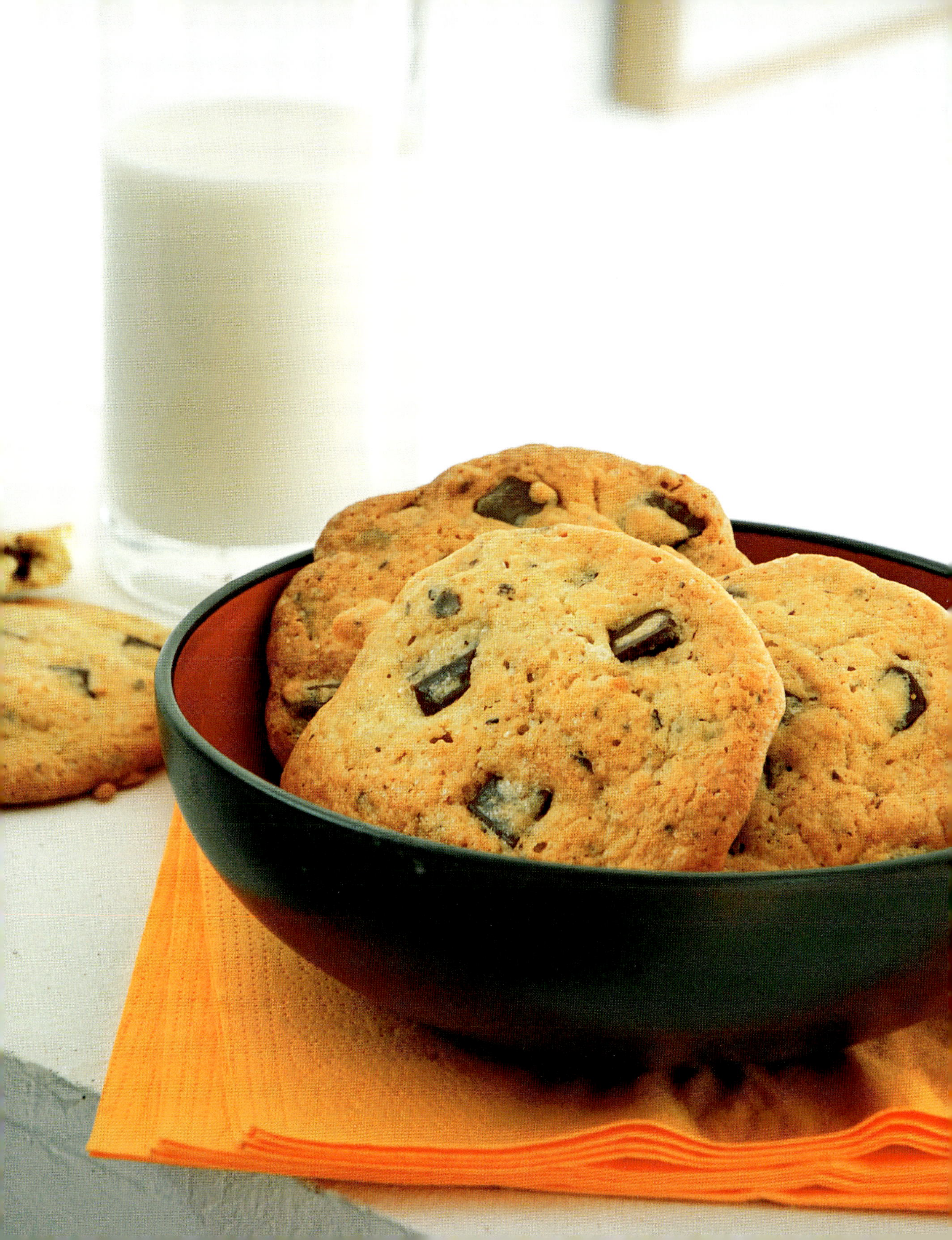

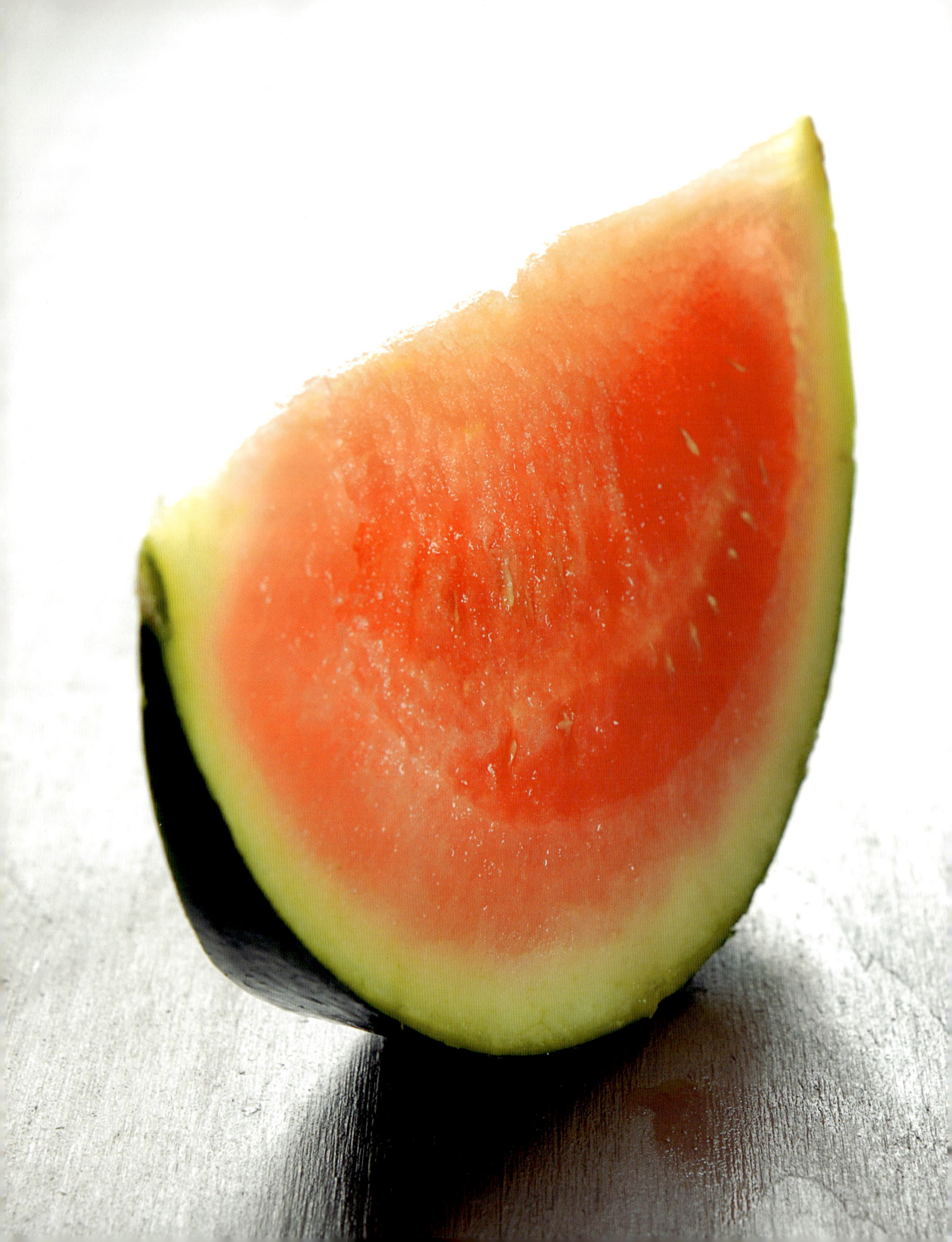

Summer sweets

Frozen black currant charlotte	300
Frozen pistachio parfait	302
Chestnut vacherin	304
Black currant and pear Bavarian cream	306
Cassata	308
Semifreddo	310
Frozen strawberry soufflé	312
Peach Melba	314
Pears Belle-Hélène	316
Mint ice cream	318
Lemon granita	320
Mango sorbet	322
Ginger and cardamom frozen yogurt	324
Strawberry tartare	326
Pineapple carpaccio with vanilla	328
Kiwi and citrus fruit salad	330
Berry soup	332
Watermelon and basil soup	334
Plum and ginger compote	336
Lychee and raspberry compote	338

Frozen black currant charlotte

SERVES 4 TO 6
PREP TIME: 40 mins.
FREEZING TIME: 2 hrs
COOKING TIME: About 25 mins.

FOR THE CAKE
- 1/4 cup black currant cordial (or crème de cassis)
- 24 lady fingers
- 2 cups black currant sorbet
- 1 cup fresh or frozen black currants

FOR THE CRÈME ANGLAISE
- 1/2 vanilla bean
- 2 cups milk
- 6 egg yolks
- 5 tbsp. sugar

Prepare the cake: dilute the black currant syrup with half a glass of water. Dip the lady fingers quickly into this liquid and use them to line a 7-inch charlotte mold.

Put a layer of black currant sorbet in the bottom of the mold and sprinkle with black currants. Add a layer of black currant flavored lady fingers. Continue alternating the ingredients until they have all been used up. Finish with a layer of lady fingers.

Put in the freezer for at least 2 hours.

Meanwhile, prepare the crème anglaise: split the vanilla bean lengthwise and put it in a saucepan with the milk, bring to a boil then turn off the heat and allow to infuse for 15 to 20 minutes. Put the egg yolks and sugar in a bowl. Whisk until the mixture turns pale yellow. Remove the vanilla and scrape out the seeds. Put the milk and seeds back on the heat and bring to a boil. Slowly pour onto the eggs and sugar, stirring constantly. Put the mixture back into the saucepan on a very low heat, stirring with a wooden spoon until it thickens. When it reaches the desired consistency, place the saucepan in a bowl of ice water (or pour the custard into a cold container) to stop the cooking process. Place in the refrigerator.

Turn out the charlotte just before serving. Serve the crème anglaise in a pitcher.

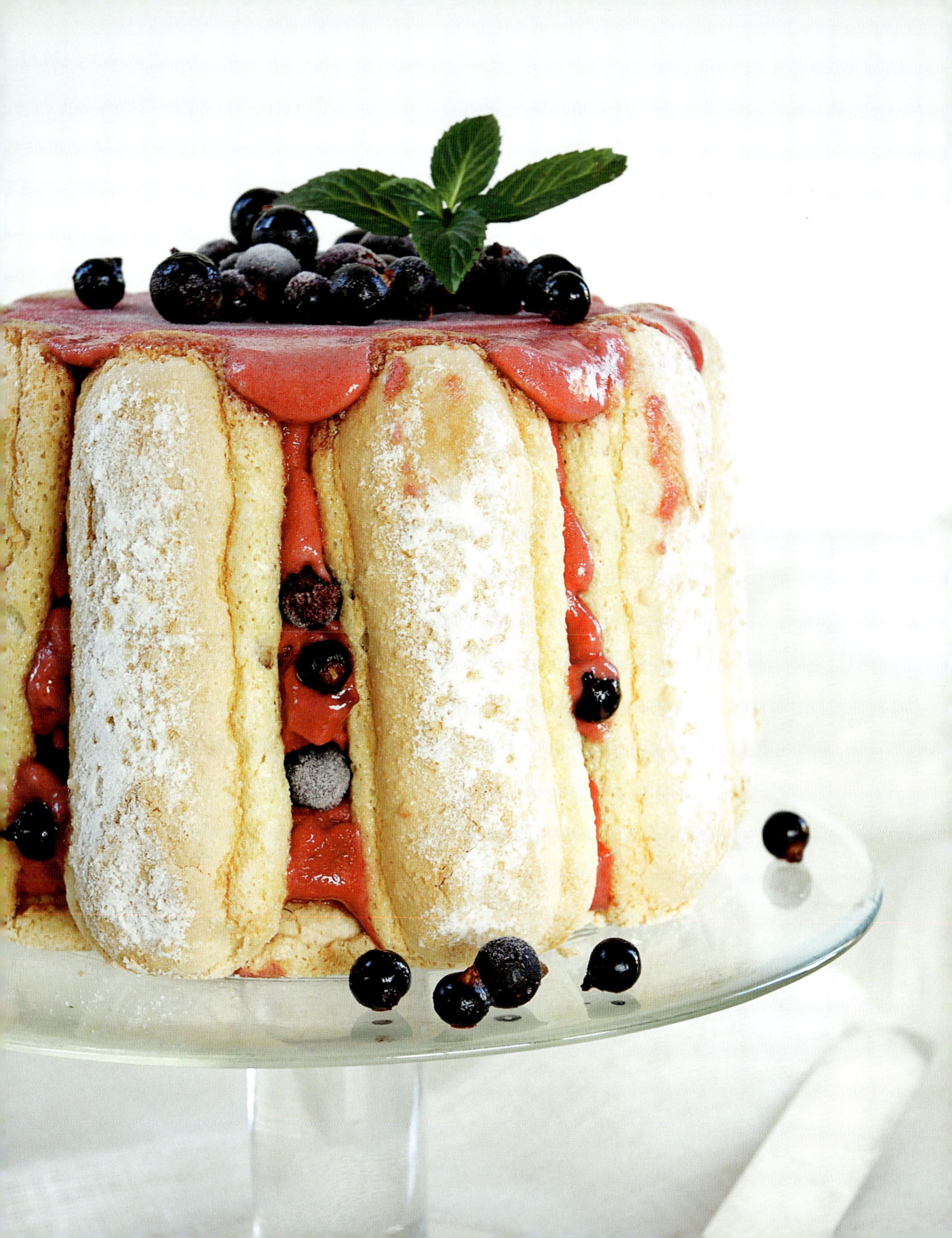

Frozen pistachio parfait

SERVES 6
PREP TIME: 30 mins.
COOKING TIME: 10 mins.
FREEZING TIME: 6 hrs

- 1/4 cup unsalted pistachios
- 1/3 cup water
- 1 cup sugar
- 8 egg yolks
- 1/2 cup pistachio butter

FOR THE WHIPPED CREAM
- 1-1/4 cup very cold crème fraîche or heavy cream

Lightly toast the pistachios and crush them.

Mix the water and the sugar and boil until soft ball stage (240° F on a sugar thermometer: a small amount dropped into cold water should form a soft ball).

Put the egg yolks into a bowl, add the pistachio butter and mix well. Gradually beat in the boiling syrup. Continue beating until cold.

Whip the cream.

Carefully stir the whipped cream into the pistachio mixture. Stir in the crushed pistachios.

Pour into a 7-inch charlotte mold and put in the freezer for 6 hours.

Run the mold quickly under hot water and turn the parfait onto a serving dish.

> Helpful tip
Don't overbeat the cream, otherwise it may turn to butter.

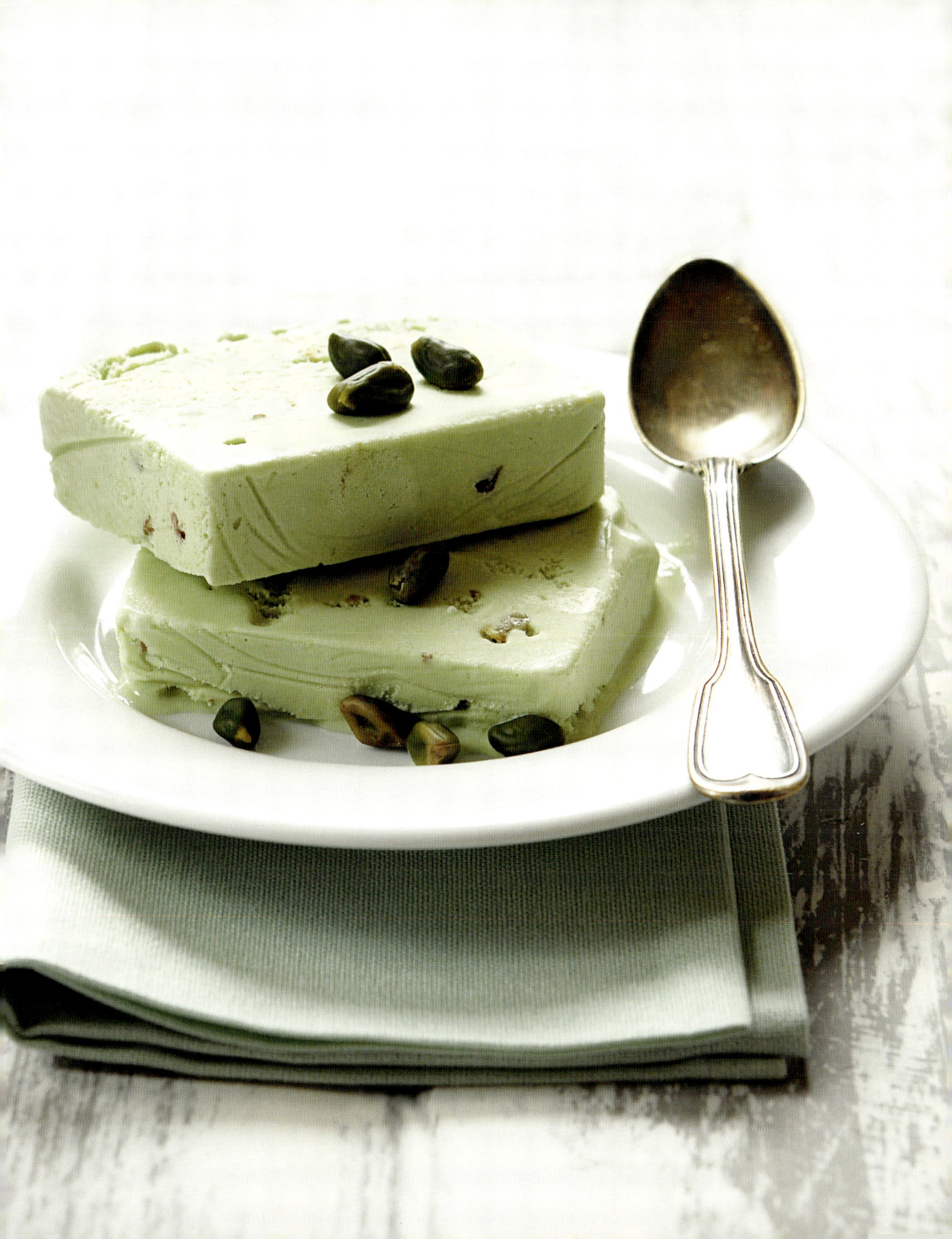

Chestnut vacherin

SERVES 6 TO 8
PREP TIME: 1 hr
(the previous day)
COOKING TIME: 1 hr 30 mins.
FREEZING TIME: 12 hrs

FOR THE CHESTNUT
ICE CREAM
- 2/3 cup whole fresh milk
- 2 cups crème fraiche
- 1 vanilla bean
- 7 egg yolks
- 3/4 cup granulated sugar
- 2/3 cup chestnut paste
- 2/3 cup chestnut puree

FOR THE DACQUOISE
- 1-1/2 cups ground almonds
- 1 heaping cup powdered sugar
- 8 egg whites
- 1-1/4 cups granulated sugar

FOR THE DECORATION
- Powdered sugar
- 4 beautiful candied chestnuts

The day before, prepare the chestnut ice cream: bring the milk and cream to a boil. Add the vanilla bean, split and scraped empty. Leave to infuse for 30 minutes, then strain. In a separate saucepan, beat the egg yolks and granulated sugar vigorously. Pour the flavored milk over the mixture and heat over a very low flame until it thickens (it must never be allowed to boil). Add the chestnut paste and puree. Leave to cool and put in the freezer.

Prepare the almond dacquoise: combine the ground almonds and granulated sugar, then strain in a sieve placed over a bowl. Beat the egg whites with a little sugar into stiff peaks. Then add all the rest of the sugar at once. Mix for 1 minute. Fold the sugar and almond mixture (as well as some almond flakes - optional) into the egg whites with a spatula. Place the dacquoise into a pastry bag with a 1/2-inch tip.

Preheat the oven to 325° F.

Pipe two disks of pastry 8 to 9 inches in diameter on a tray covered with a sheet of parchment paper, beginning in the center and spiraling outwards.

Place the tray into the oven for 30 minutes at 325° F, then lower the temperature to 275° F and bake for another hour. If your oven is too small, bake each disk separately.

Let the disks cool completely and remove them from the paper by placing them on a moist cloth spread on the work surface.

The next day, remove the chestnut ice cream from the freezer 1 hour before serving, so that it is soft enough. Using a spatula, spread a thick layer of ice cream over one disk. Then place the second disk on top.

Sprinkle powdered sugar on top and decorate with candied chestnuts.

chef style

304 • SUMMER SWEETS

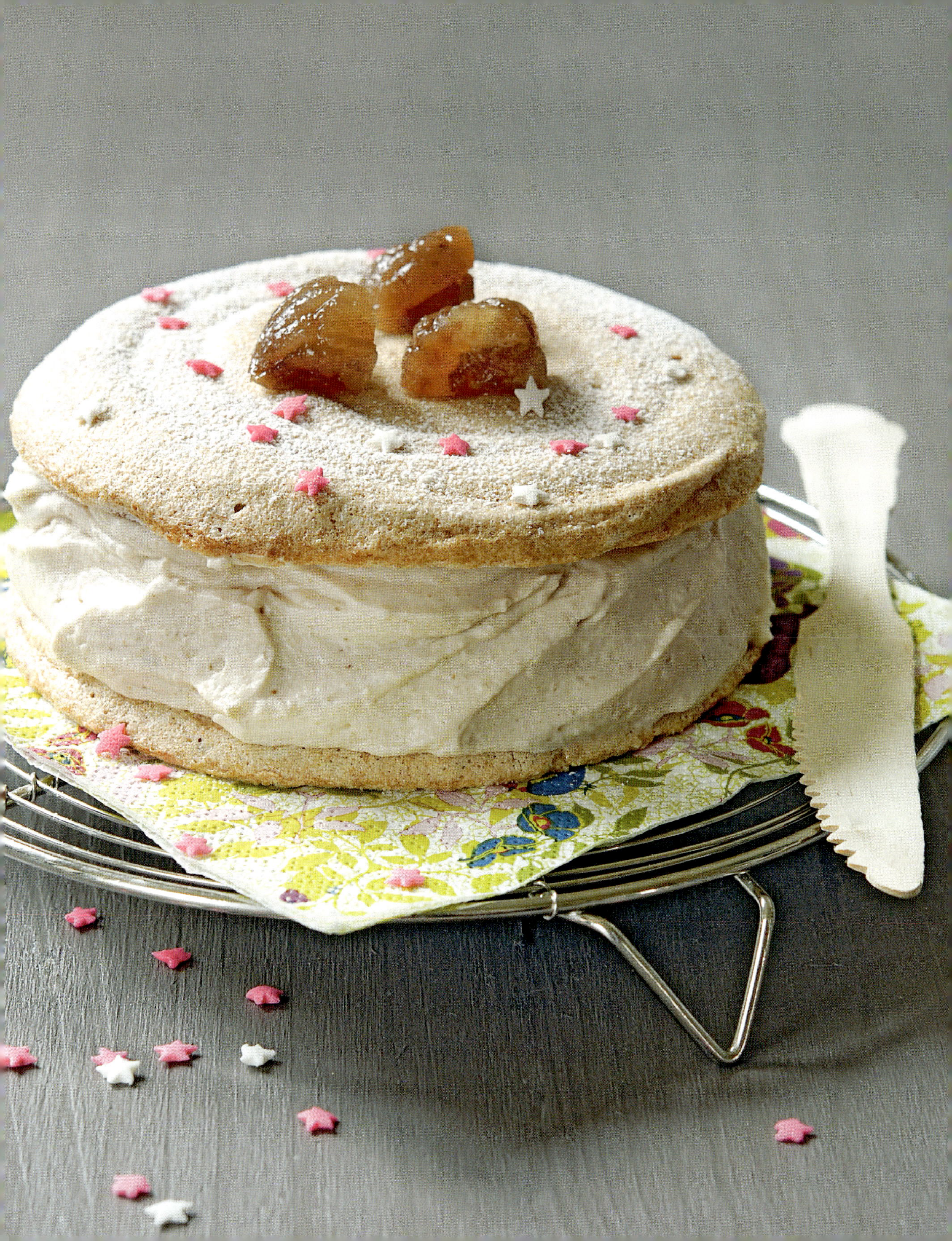

Black currant and pear Bavarian cream

SERVES 6
PREP TIME: 35 mins.
REFRIGERATION TIME: 2 hrs 15 mins.

- 1-1/2 packets gelatin
- 1 lb. black currants
- 2 pears
- The juice of one lemon
- 1-1/3 cups sugar
- 1/4 cup plus 2 tbsps. water
- 2-1/2 cups fromage frais or Greek yogurt

Dissolve the gelatin in cold water.

Rinse the black currants and remove stalks. Puree in a blender or food mill (fine mesh), then rub the puree through a sieve.

Peel the pears, cut them in two, remove core and pits. Cut into small dice and sprinkle with lemon juice.

Warm the sugar and water in a saucepan, stirring until completely dissolved. Bring to a boil and remove from the heat immediately. Stir in the gelatin. Add black currant coulis and mix well.

Line a rectangular 9 x 5-inch loaf mold with plastic wrap.

Whip the fromage frais or Greek yogurt until very smooth. Add to the black currant mixture. Pour half the mixture into the mold.

Place in freezer for 15 minutes to set. When the mixture is quite firm, scatter the pears over the surface, pour in the rest of the black currant mixture, and place in the refrigerator for 2 hours.

Turn out from the mold and peel off the plastic wrap. Slice into portions and serve.

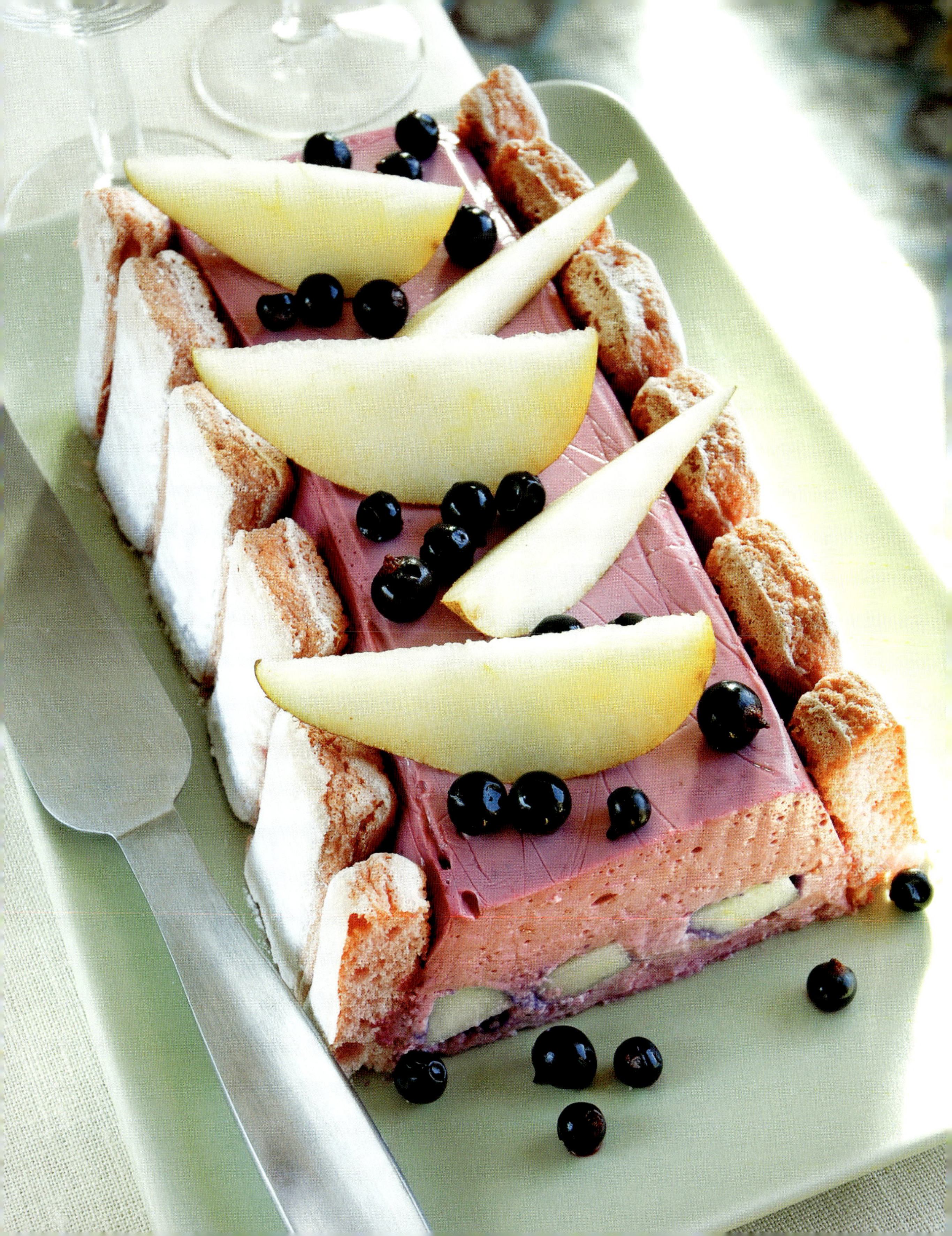

Cassata

SERVES 8
PREP TIME: 15 mins.
COOKING TIME: 15 mins.
FREEZING TIME: 4 hrs

- 2/3 cup slivered almonds
- 4 tbsp. mixed candied fruit, chopped into tiny cubes
- 1 small glass of kirsch
- 1-1/3 lb. vanilla ice cream

FOR THE BOMBE MIXTURE
- 1/3 cup water
- 6 tbsp. sugar
- 5 egg yolks
- 2 cups crème fraîche or heavy cream

Toast the almonds quickly in a skillet: they should be light golden brown in color.

Put the candied fruit and kirsch in a bowl to soak for a few minutes. Remove and strain.

Prepare the bombe mixture: make a syrup by boiling together the water and the sugar. Mix the syrup with the egg yolks in a saucepan. Place the saucepan over a pot of simmering water on medium heat, or use a double boiler, and beat with a whisk. Remove from the heat and continue beating until cold (it should now be frothy). Whip the crème fraîche or heavy cream and fold it into the mixture. Add the almonds and candied fruit.

Line a 7-inch charlotte mold with a thick layer of vanilla ice cream. Pour the bombe mixture into the center and put into the freezer for 4 hours.

To serve, hold the mold under a hot faucet for a few seconds and turn the cassata onto a serving dish.

> Helpful tip

To line the mold with ice cream, first put it in the freezer for 1 hour. Put some ice cream in the bottom of the mold with a wooden spoon or rubber spatula, pressing it down to get rid of any air bubbles. Now ease the ice cream up the sides of the mold by pressing it with the spatula. The layer of ice cream should be the same thickness all the way round. Flatten the top edge with your spatula for a smooth finish.

> To make a change

This classic dessert has many variations. You can use all kinds of candied fruit including cherries, angelica and melon. You can also decorate your cassata with hazelnuts, pistachios, strawberries, or raisins. What all authentic cassatas have in common is that they're made of two layers of ice cream, molded one inside the other.

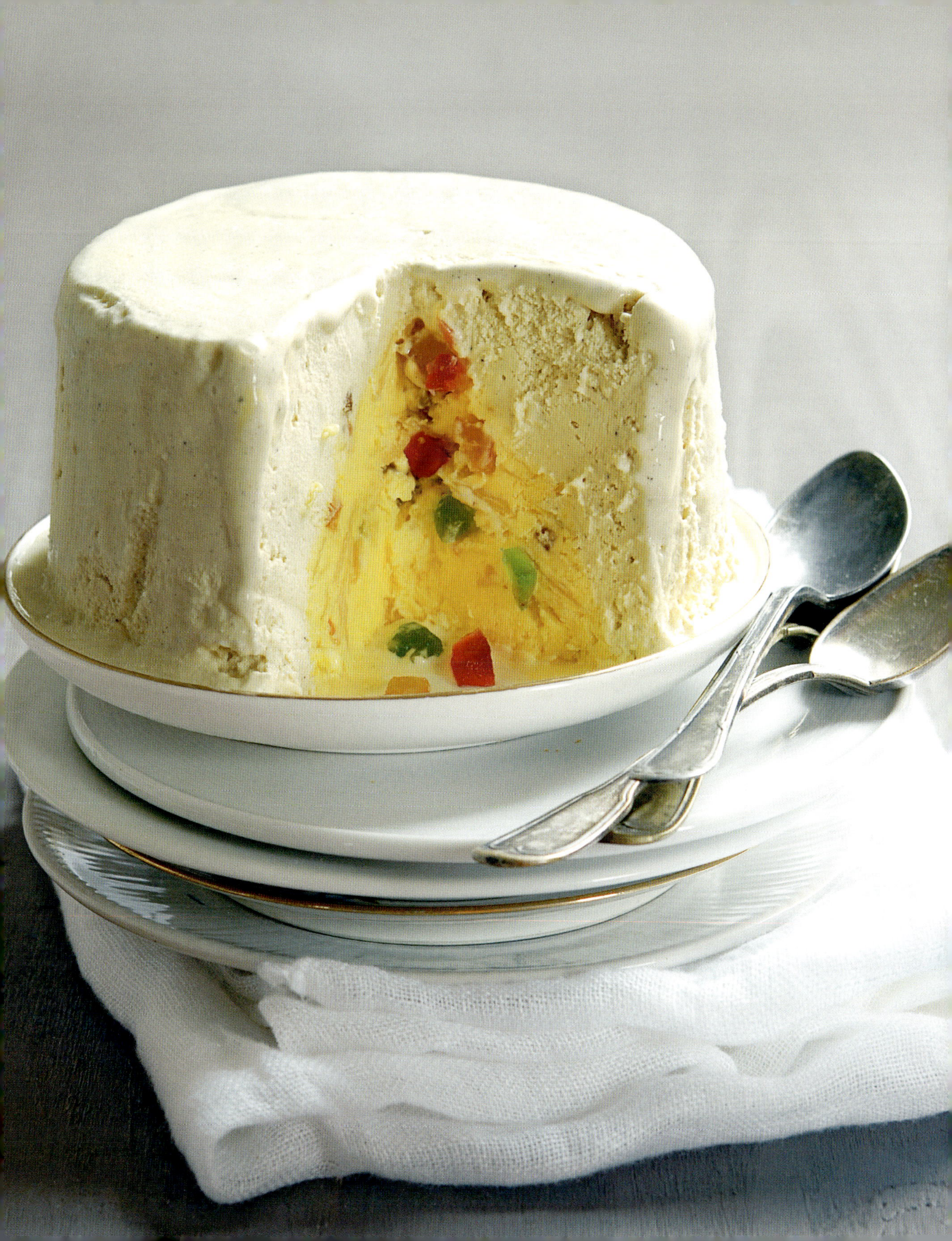

Semifreddo

SERVES 4 TO 6
PREP TIME: 45 mins.
COOKING TIME: 20 to 25 mins.
FREEZING TIME: 30 mins.

FOR THE "PAN DI SPAGNA"
- 1 cup flour
- 1 lemon
- 4 eggs
- A pinch of salt
- 2/3 cup sugar

FOR THE APPLES
- 4 sweet apples
- 1/3 cup sugar
- 1 lemon
- 1/2 cup white wine
- 3 tbsp. water
- Just less than 5 oz. amaretti

FOR THE SAUCE
- 1 cup crème fraîche or heavy cream
- 4 egg yolks
- 1/2 cup sugar

Prepare the "pan di Spagna": heat a large saucepan of water; sift the flour. Grate the lemon zest. Break the eggs into a bowl and mix with the salt and sugar. Preheat the oven to 350° F. put the bowl in the saucepan of simmering water and beat the eggs and the sugar until the mixture doubles in volume and thickens a little. Remove the bowl from the water and continue to whisk until the mixture is cold. Gradually add the sifted flour, folding it in with a wooden spoon, then add the lemon zest. Stir well to obtain a smooth batter. Butter a 7-inch round cake pan, pour in the mixture and bake for 20 to 25 minutes.

Prepare the apples: peel, core and cut into slices. Cook in a saucepan with the sugar, lemon zest, wine and water for 10 minutes on a gentle heat: the fruit should be tender and the liquid absorbed. Purée the apples with a fork. Crumble the amaretti.

Prepare the sauce: whip the cream. Beat the egg yolks and sugar in a saucepan until they turn pale yellow, then put in a double boiler; continue beating for a few seconds, then remove from the heat and continue beating until the mixture is cold. Carefully stir in the whipped cream.

Mix the cream with the apples and crushed amaretti.

Cut the pan di Spagna into three disks. Cut out a piece of parchment paper the same size. Place the first disk on the paper and, using a spatula, cover with apple cream. Place the second disk on top and repeat the operation, then lay the third disk on top.

Put the semifreddo in the freezer for 30 minutes, then keep in the refrigerator until needed.

> Helpful tip
Instead of the pan di Spagna, you can use a regular 9-inch diameter sponge cake.

chef style

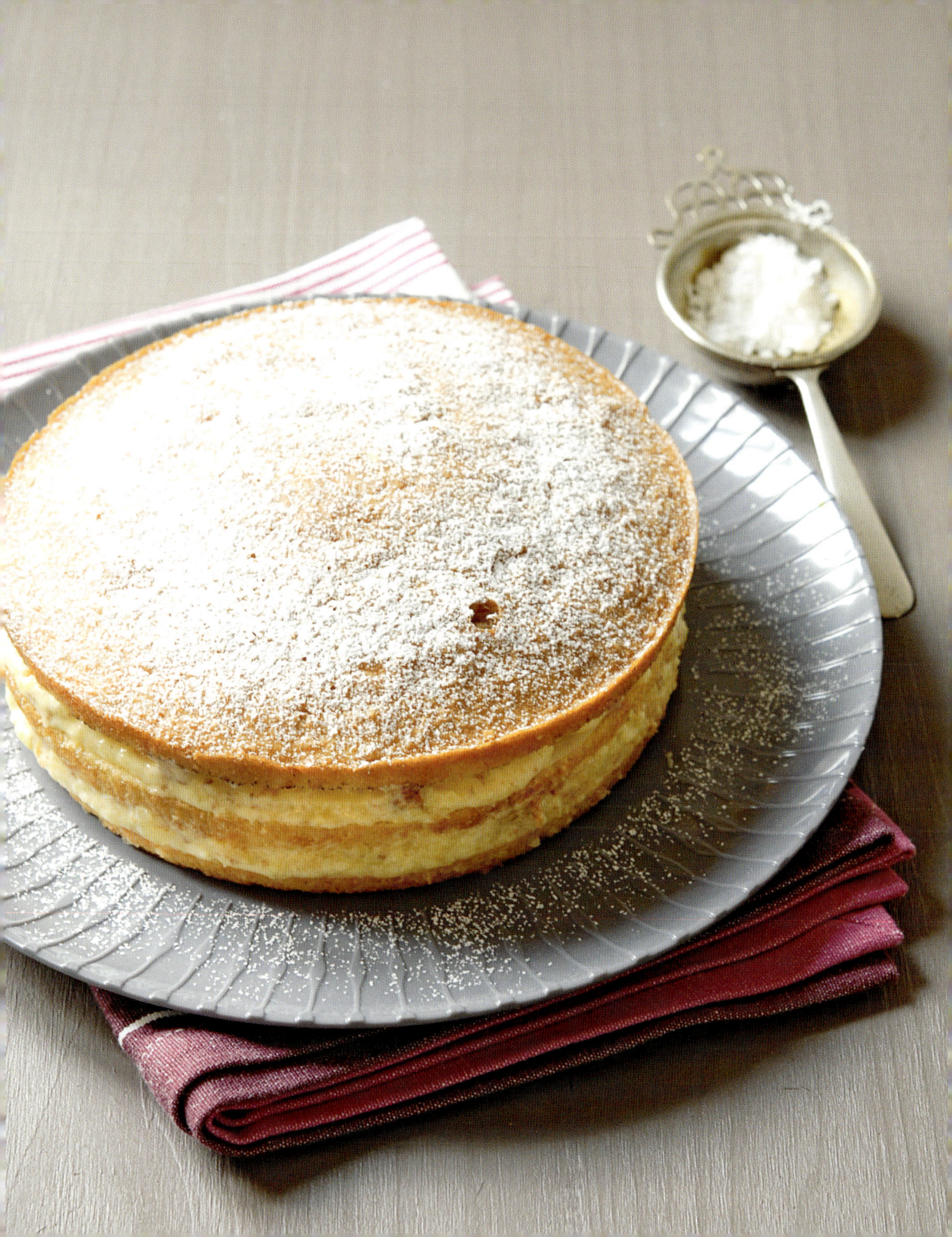

Frozen strawberry soufflé

SERVES 6
PREP TIME: 45 mins.
COOKING TIME: 20 mins.
FREEZING TIME: At least 12 hrs

- 8 egg yolks
- 1/2 lb. strawberry jam
- 2 cups crème fraîche or heavy cream
- 2 tbsp. butter for the dish
- 1 tbsp. cocoa powder

FOR THE SYRUP
- 3/4 cup sugar
- 1 cup water

Prepare the syrup: dissolve the sugar in the water and bring to a boil. Reduce by a third and allow to cool slightly.

Pour the warm syrup into a bowl standing in a pan of simmering water, or use a double boiler, over gentle heat. Whisk in the 8 egg yolks. Continue to whisk until it boils (about 10 minutes). Remove the bowl from the heat and beat until cold (about 10 more minutes).

Add the strawberry jam to this mixture, folding it in gently with a spatula.

Whip the chilled cream and fold it gently into the mixture.

Line a 7-inch soufflé dish with buttered parchment paper and pour in the mixture (the paper should be higher than the dish). Place in the freezer for at least 12 hours.

To serve, cut away the top of the parchment paper that extends above the soufflé dish and sprinkle the top of the soufflé with cocoa powder.

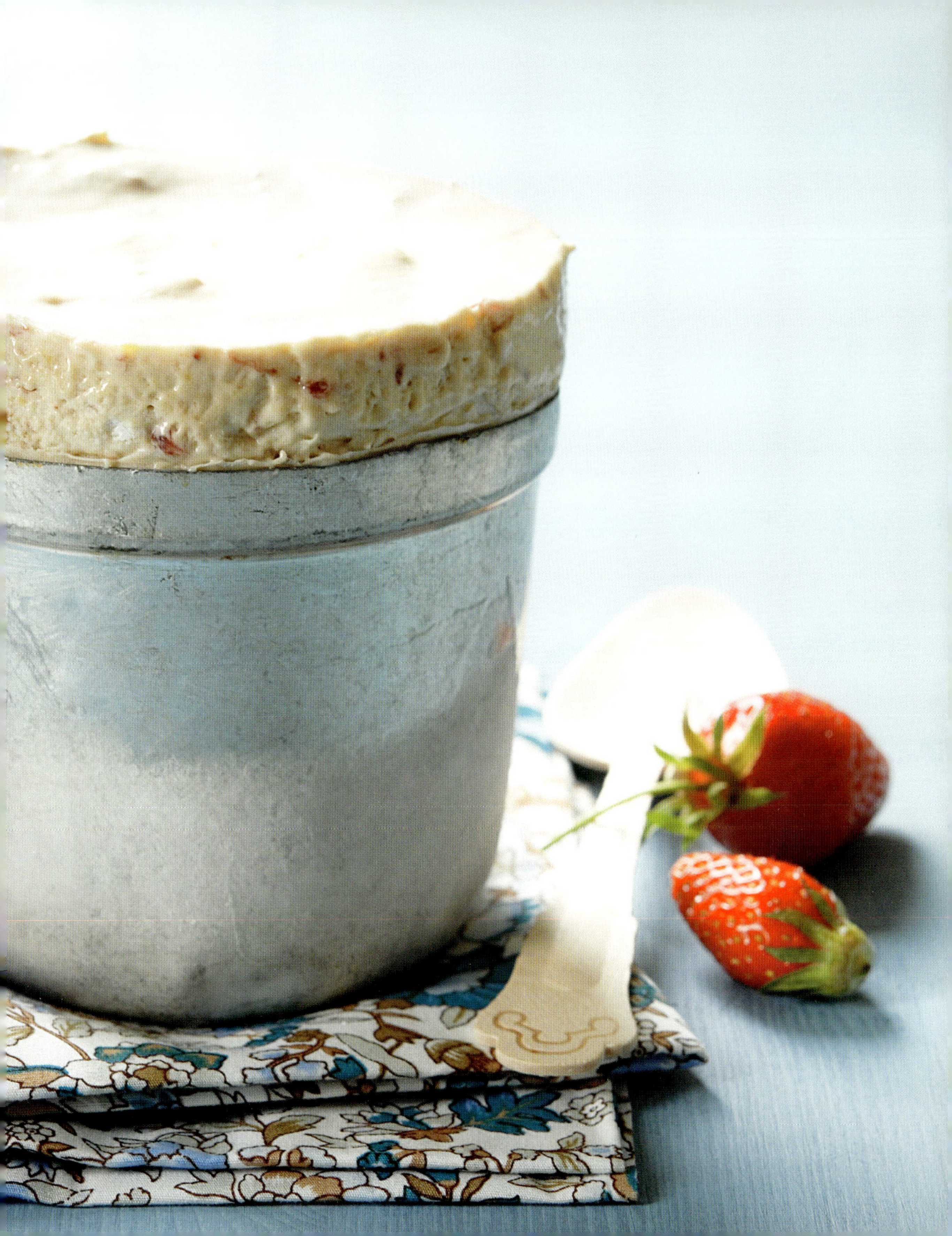

Peach Melba

SERVES 4
PREP TIME: 30 mins.
COOKING TIME: 12 to 13 mins.

- 1 lb. raspberries
- 4 peaches
- 2 cups vanilla ice cream

FOR THE SYRUP
- 2 pints water
- 2-1/2 cups sugar
- 1 vanilla bean

Prepare the raspberry purée: put the raspberries in a blender or run them through a food mill.

Prepare the peaches: plunge into boiling water for 30 seconds, then plunge into cold water and peel them.

Prepare the syrup: split the vanilla bean and scrape out the seeds. Put 2 pints water in a pan with the sugar and add the vanilla bean and seeds. Bring to a boil and add the peaches. Boil for 7 to 8 minutes.

Drain the peaches and allow them to cool completely. Cut them in two and remove the pits.

Put the ice cream in a large bowl or divide between individual bowls. Arrange the peach halves on top and pour the raspberry purée over the top.

> To make a change

Make pear melba in the same way by poaching pears in the vanilla syrup.

never fails

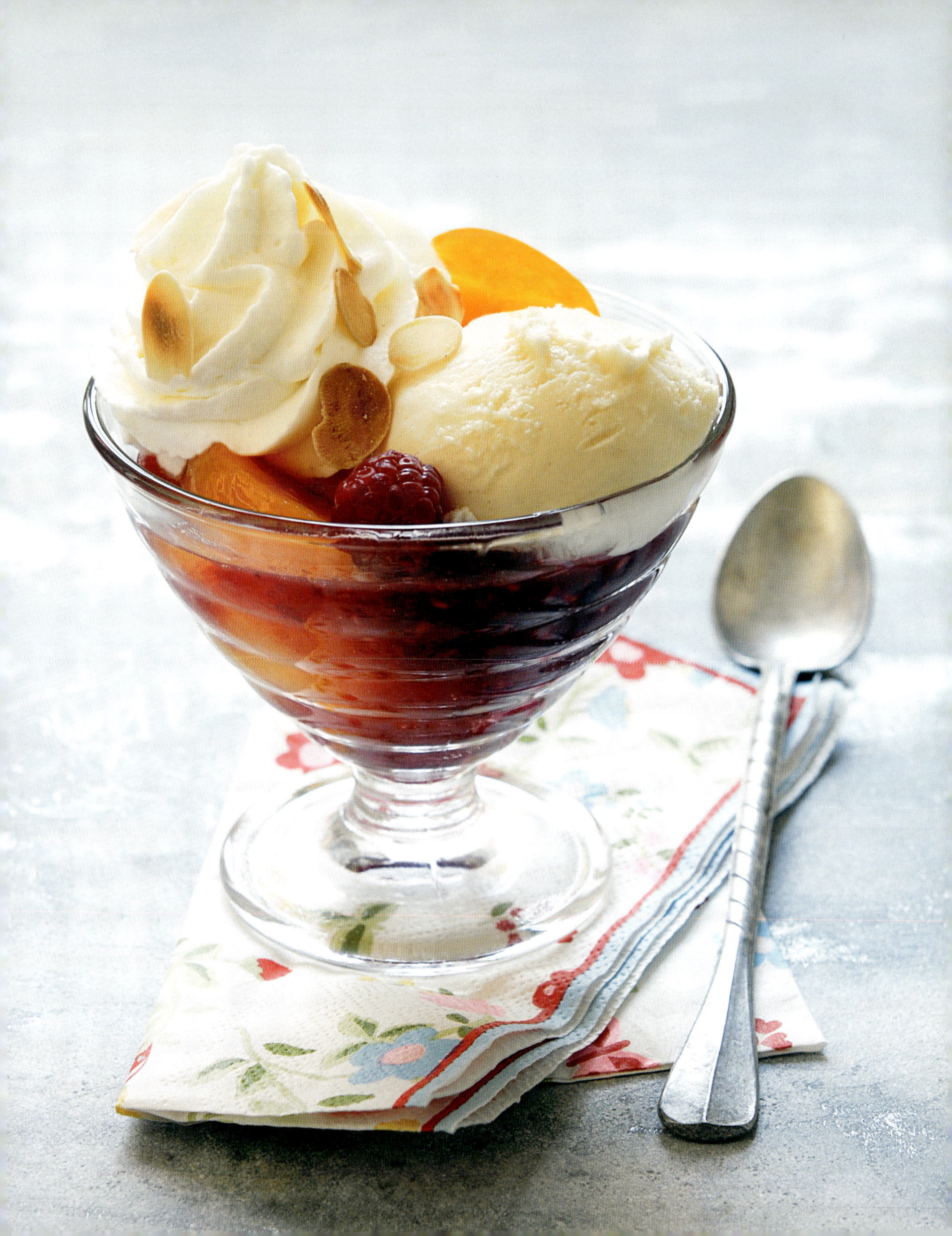

Pears Belle-Hélène

SERVES 6
PREP TIME: 45 mins.
COOKING TIME: 20 to 30 mins.

- 6 Williams pears
- 1/4 lb. dark chocolate
- 4 tbsp. crème fraîche or heavy cream
- 2 pints vanilla ice cream

FOR THE SYRUP
- 2-1/4 cups sugar
- 2 cups water

Prepare the syrup: boil the sugar and water together.

Prepare the pears: peel the pears but leave them whole and don't remove the stems. Poach in the syrup for 20 to 30 minutes. When they are tender, drain them and place them in the refrigerator.

Boil 1/4 cup water. Break the chocolate into pieces, chop it with a knife and put it in a saucepan. Pour in the boiling water and stir until the chocolate has melted. Stir in the cream.

Spoon some vanilla ice cream into each serving dish, place a pear on top and pour the hot chocolate sauce over the top.

> Find out more

Make 2 pints of vanilla ice cream yourself! Put 2/3 cup whole milk and 2 cups crème fraîche or heavy cream into a saucepan and bring to a boil. Add 1 split and scraped vanilla bean and allow to infuse for 30 minutes. Pour through a sieve. In another saucepan, beat 7 egg yolks with 3/4 cup sugar. Pour the flavored milk onto the eggs and heat over a low heat, stirring with a wooden spoon until the mixture thickens. Do not allow to reach boiling point. Allow to cool in the refrigerator, then place in the freezer.

never fails

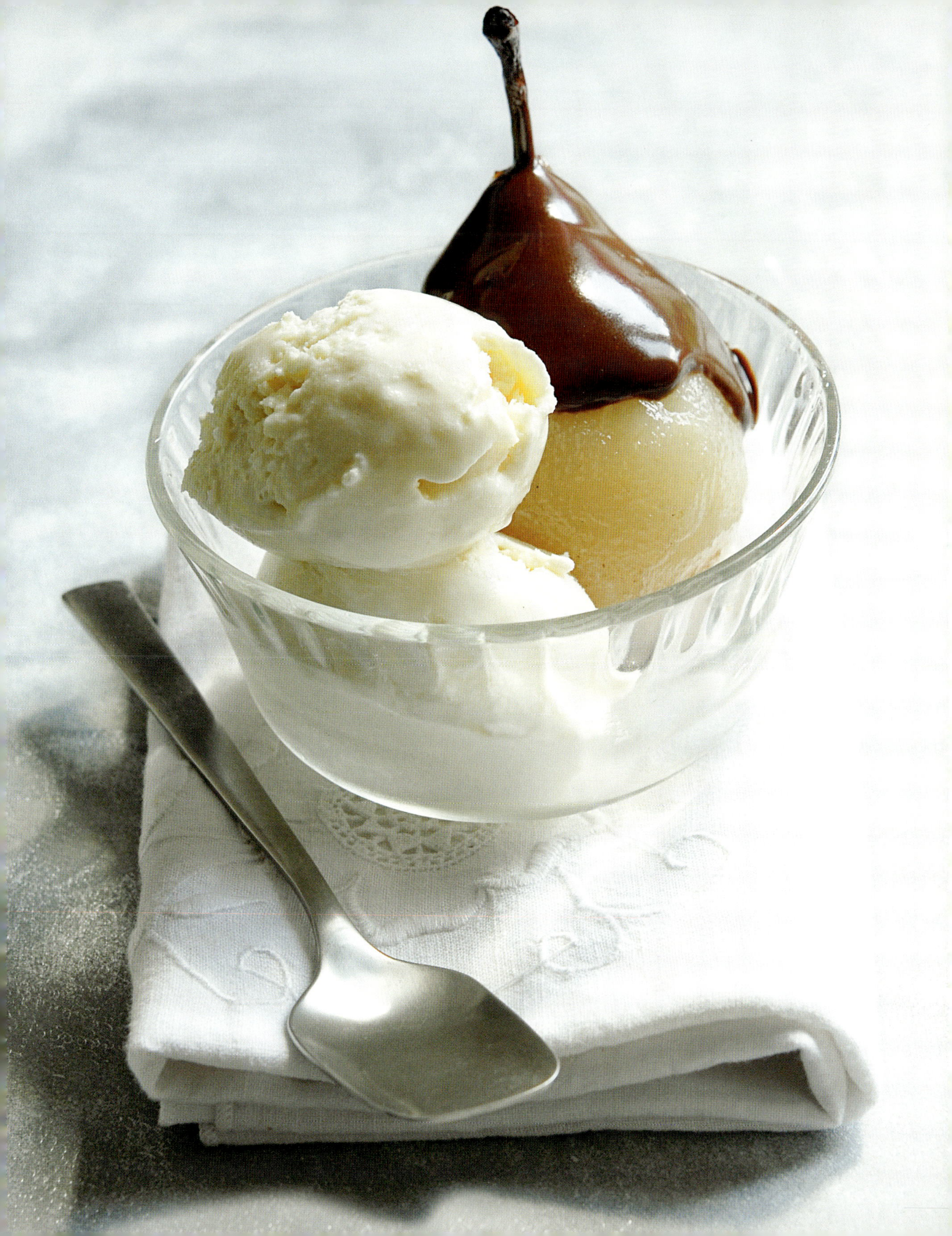

Mint ice cream

MAKES ABOUT 2 PINTS
PREP TIME: 30 mins.
COOKING TIME: 10 mins.
FREEZING TIME: 4 hrs

- 2/3 cup whole milk
- 2 cups crème fraîche or heavy cream
- 2-1/2 tbsp. chopped fresh mint
- 8 egg yolks
- 1 cup sugar
- 10 mint leaves

Bring the milk and crème fraîche or heavy cream to a boil in a saucepan.

Remove from the heat, add the chopped mint, cover and allow to infuse for 20 minutes. Strain the liquid through a fine sieve into a bowl.

In another saucepan, beat together the egg yolks and sugar. Add the flavored milk and cook over a very low heat (do not boil), stirring with a wooden spoon, until it thickens (180° F). Pour into a bowl.

Place the bowl in a large container full of ice, or in the refrigerator, to cool.

When completely cold, mix in the finely chopped mint leaves and freeze.

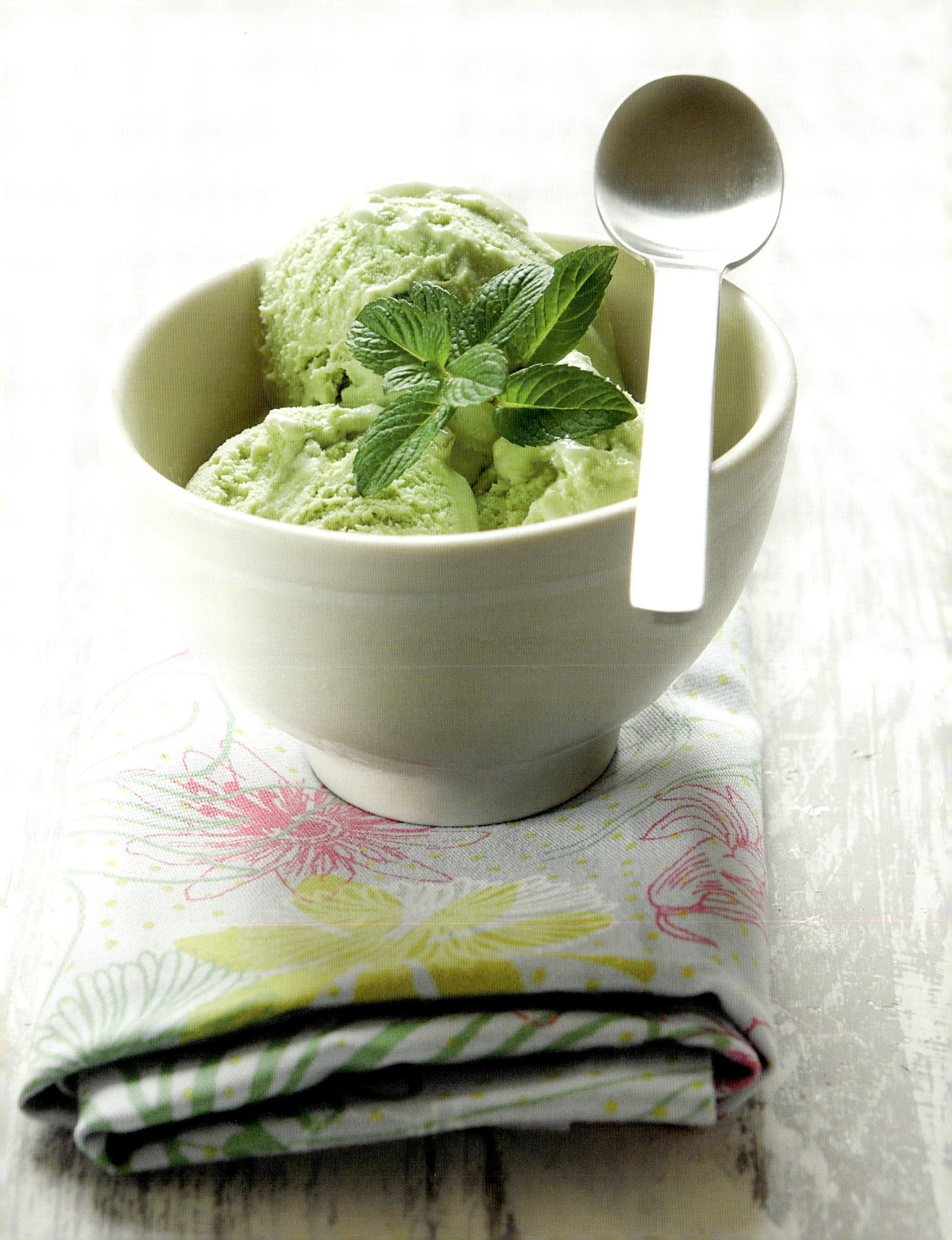

Lemon granita

MAKES 2 PINTS OF GRANITA
PREP TIME: 15 mins.
FREEZING TIME: About 2 hrs

- 2 lemons
- 3 cups water
- 1 cup sugar

Chop the zest of one lemon very finely. Squeeze both lemons and scrape out the flesh: you should end up with about 6 tbsp. juice.

Put the sugar and water in a bowl and stir until the sugar has dissolved. Add the lemon zest, juice and flesh. Mix well with a wooden spoon and put in the freezer.

After one and a half hours, take the granita out of the freezer and stir it well with a wooden or rubber spatula.

Put it back in the freezer until completely frozen.

> To make a change
You can use limes instead of lemons, and add a dash of vodka to the mixture.

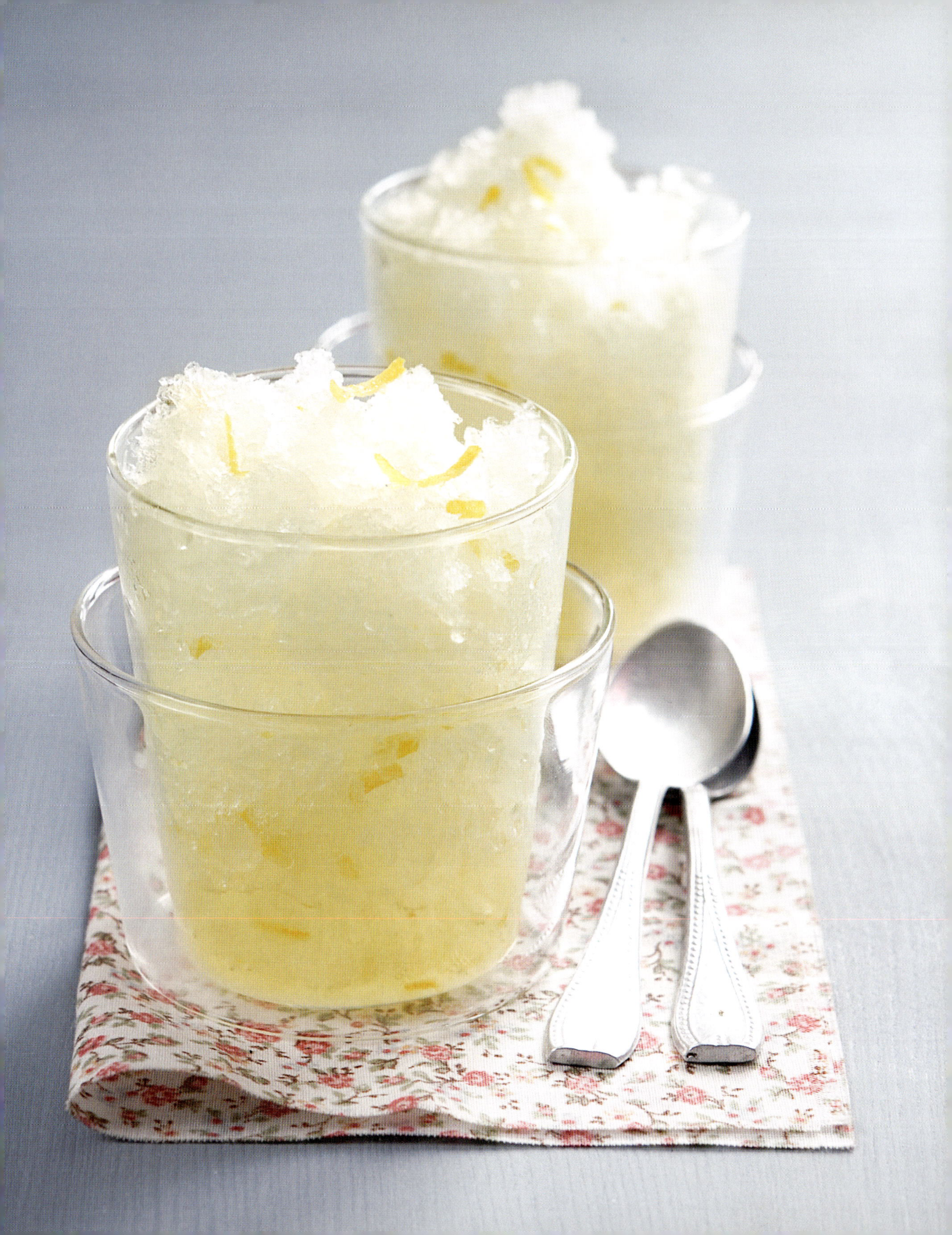

Mango sorbet

MAKES 2 PINTS OF SORBET
PREP TIME: 10 mins.

- 2-1/2 lbs ripe mangoes
- 1 lemon
- 1-1/3 cups sugar

Peel the mangoes, remove the pits and cut into pieces.

Purée in a food processor: you should end up with about 1 3/4 lbs. of purée. Squeeze the lemon.

Mix the purée with the sugar and 3 tbsp. lemon juice. Place in an ice cream maker.

> Helpful tip
Lime zest is also an excellent flavoring for this sorbet.

quick & easy

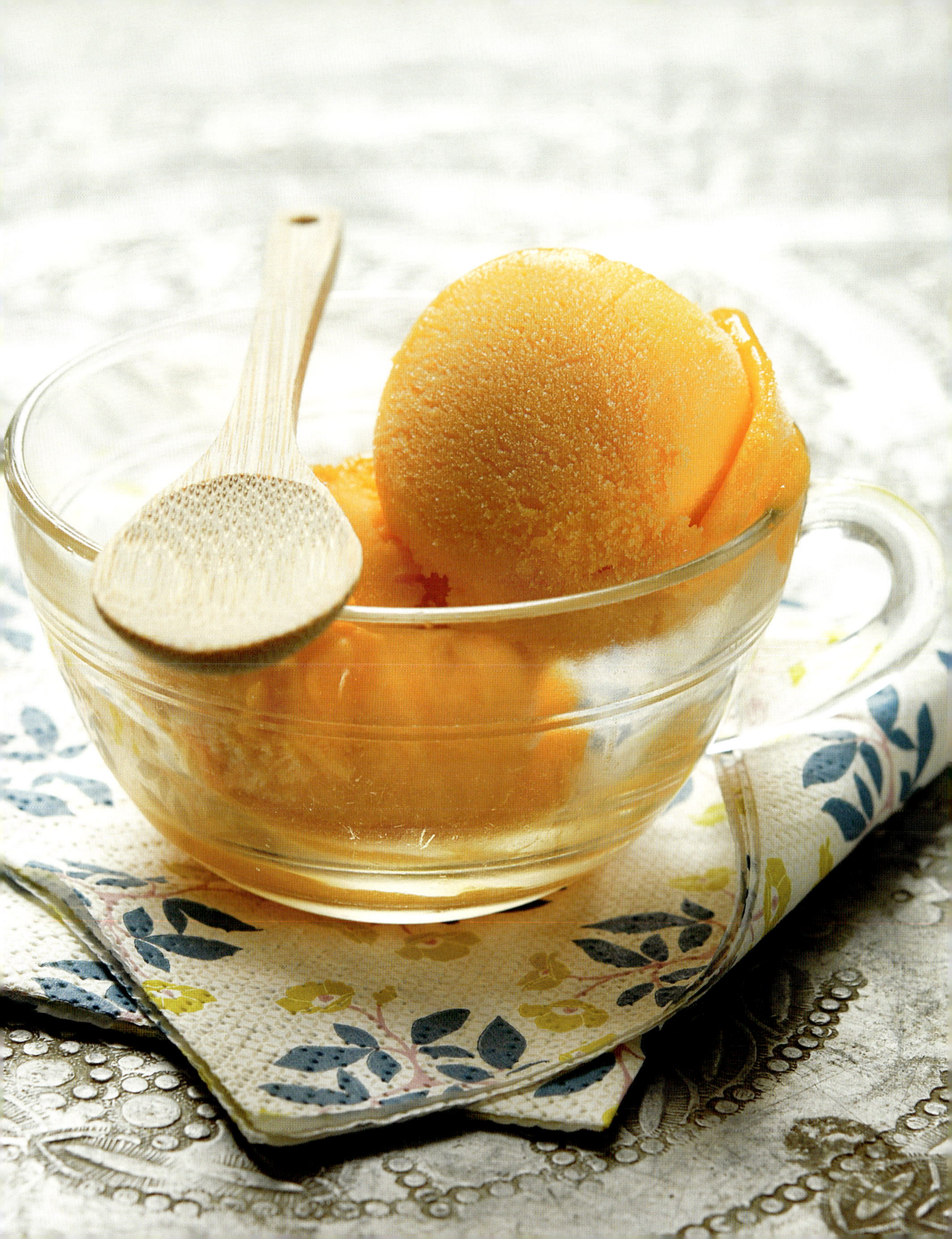

Ginger and cardamom frozen yogurt

SERVES 4
PREP TIME: 15 mins.
COOKING TIME: 1 to 2 mins.
FREEZING TIME: 30 to 45 mins.

- 1 oz. candied ginger
- 2 cups plain yogurt
- 2 tbsp. powdered cardamom

FOR THE SYRUP
- 6 tbsp. sugar
- 1/2 cup water
- The juice of 1/2 a lime

TO DECORATE
- A few cardamom seeds

Prepare the syrup: gently heat the sugar with the water and lime juice in a small saucepan, stirring until dissolved. Simmer for 1 to 2 minutes. Remove from the heat and allow to cool slightly.

Finely chop the ginger.

Put four glasses or individual serving dishes in the refrigerator to chill.

Pour the yogurt into a large bowl. Beat in the lemon syrup. Add the cardamom and ginger. Beat for a little longer and put the bowl in the freezer for 30 to 45 minutes.

When the yogurt begins to thicken (it should not be completely frozen), remove the bowl from the freezer and beat the mixture well. Spoon it into the glasses or dishes.

Sprinkle with cardamom seeds and serve.

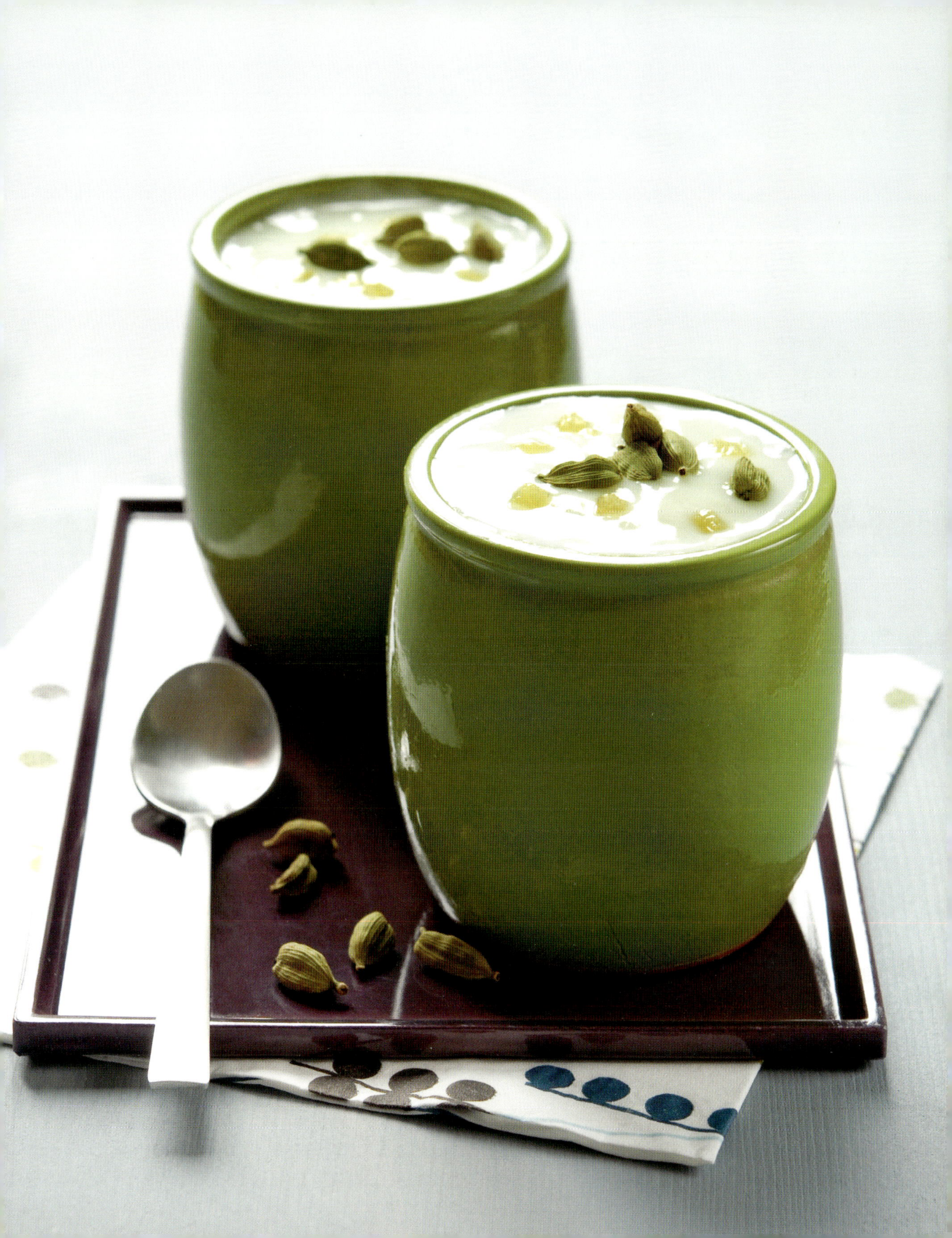

Strawberry tartare

SERVES 6
PREP TIME: 15 mins.
COOKING TIME: 6 to 8 mins.

- 1-3/4 lbs strawberries

FOR THE SYRUP
- 2 organic oranges
- 1 organic lemon
- 1 tbsp. dry white wine
- 1/2 cup water
- 2 tbsp. sugar
- 2 pieces star anise

Prepare the syrup: zest the oranges and the lemon and place the zests in boiling water for 30 seconds. Strain.

Place the white wine and 1/2 cup water in a small saucepan. Add the sugar and stir over a low heat until it dissolves. Add the zests and star anise, bring gently to a boil and simmer very gently for 6 to 8 minutes. Remove from the heat and allow to cool.

Prepare the strawberries: rinse quickly in a sieve, dry them, hull them and cut into small pieces. Place in a bowl with the syrup. Place in the refrigerator and serve well chilled.

never fails

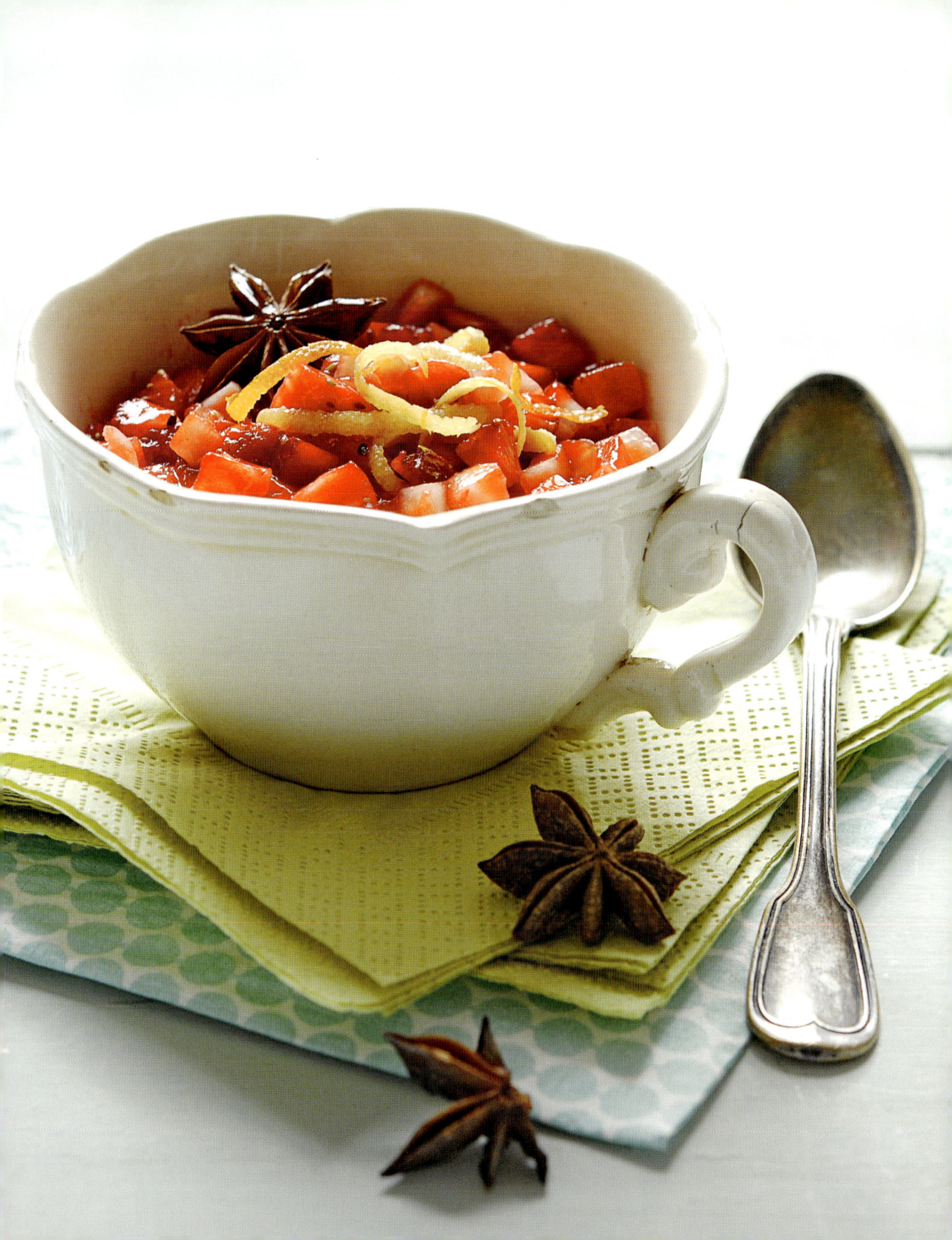

Pineapple carpaccio with vanilla

SERVES 4
PREP TIME: 20 mins.
REFRIGERATION TIME: 1 hr

- 1 large pineapple (about 2 pounds)
- 1 vanilla bean

FOR THE SYRUP
- 6 tbsp. water
- 4 sugar cubes

never fails

Prepare the pineapple: peel and remove the "eyes" with the pointed end of a peeler. Cut into very thin slices (there's no need to remove the core), and arrange them on a large platter so that they don't overlap.

Split the vanilla bean lengthwise and scrape the seeds out with a small knife. Sprinkle the seeds over the pineapple slices.

Prepare the syrup: put the water and the sugar into a small heavy saucepan and heat gently, shaking the handle of the pan to spread the heat evenly. When the sugar has dissolved, wait for bubbles to form on the surface of the syrup, allow to thicken slightly and remove from the heat.

Pour the syrup in a thin stream over the pineapple, cover with plastic wrap and place in the refrigerator for 1 hour. Serve chilled.

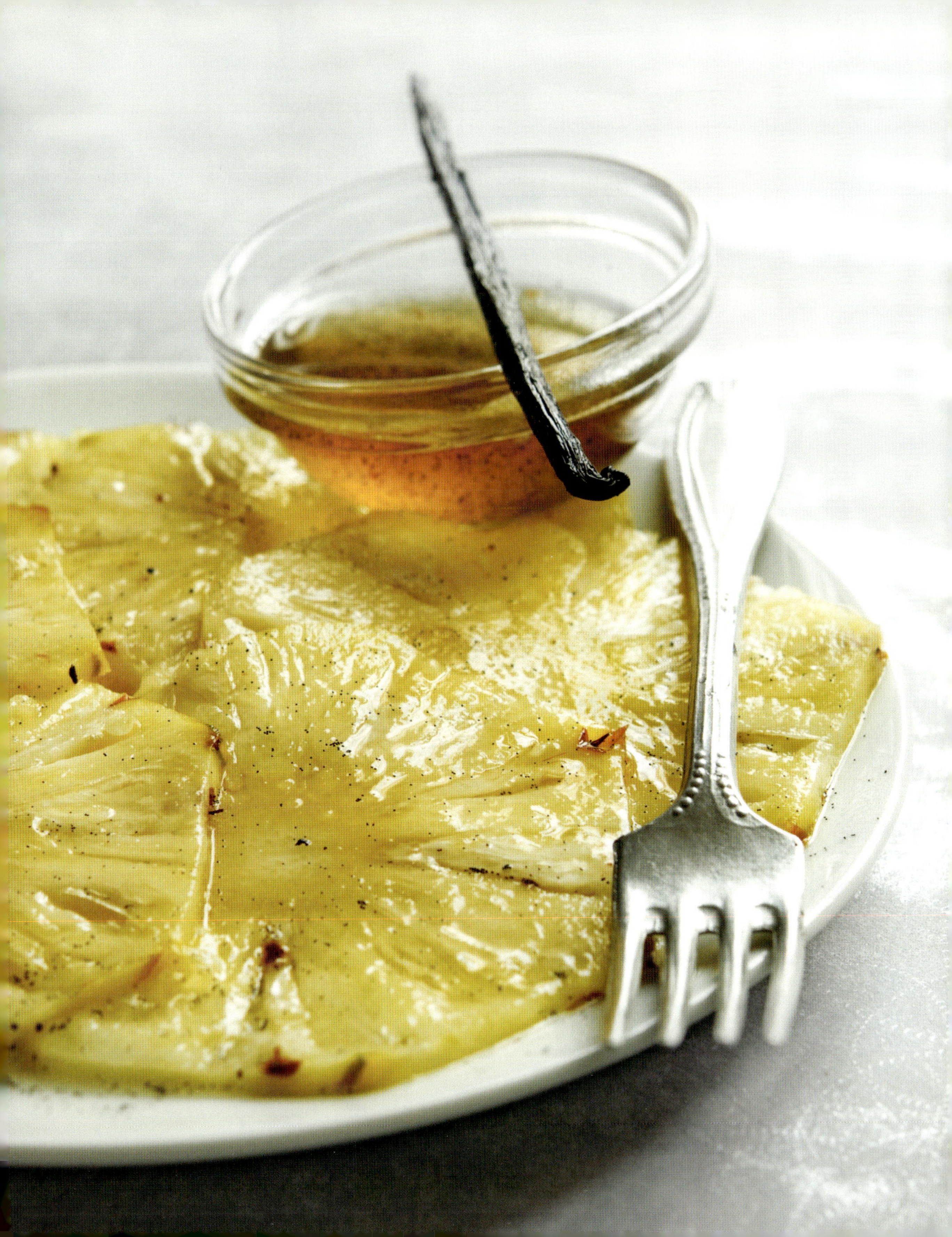

Kiwi and citrus fruit salad

SERVES 4
PREP TIME: 15 mins.
COOKING TIME: a few seconds

- 3 kiwis
- 1 orange
- 1 grapefruit
- 1 lemon
- 2 tbsp. liquid honey

TO DECORATE
- 1 tbsp. slivered almonds
- A few mint leaves

Peel the kiwis and cut into thin slices. Peel the orange and the grapefruit, cutting right through to the flesh so that you remove all the pith. Cut out the segments from between the membranes.

Cut the lemon in two and squeeze the juice into a bowl. Stir in the honey.

Place the fruit in a bowl, pour the honey and lemon over the top, and chill until needed.

Toast the almonds for a few seconds in a hot skillet. Sprinkle over the fruit salad and decorate with mint.

quick & easy

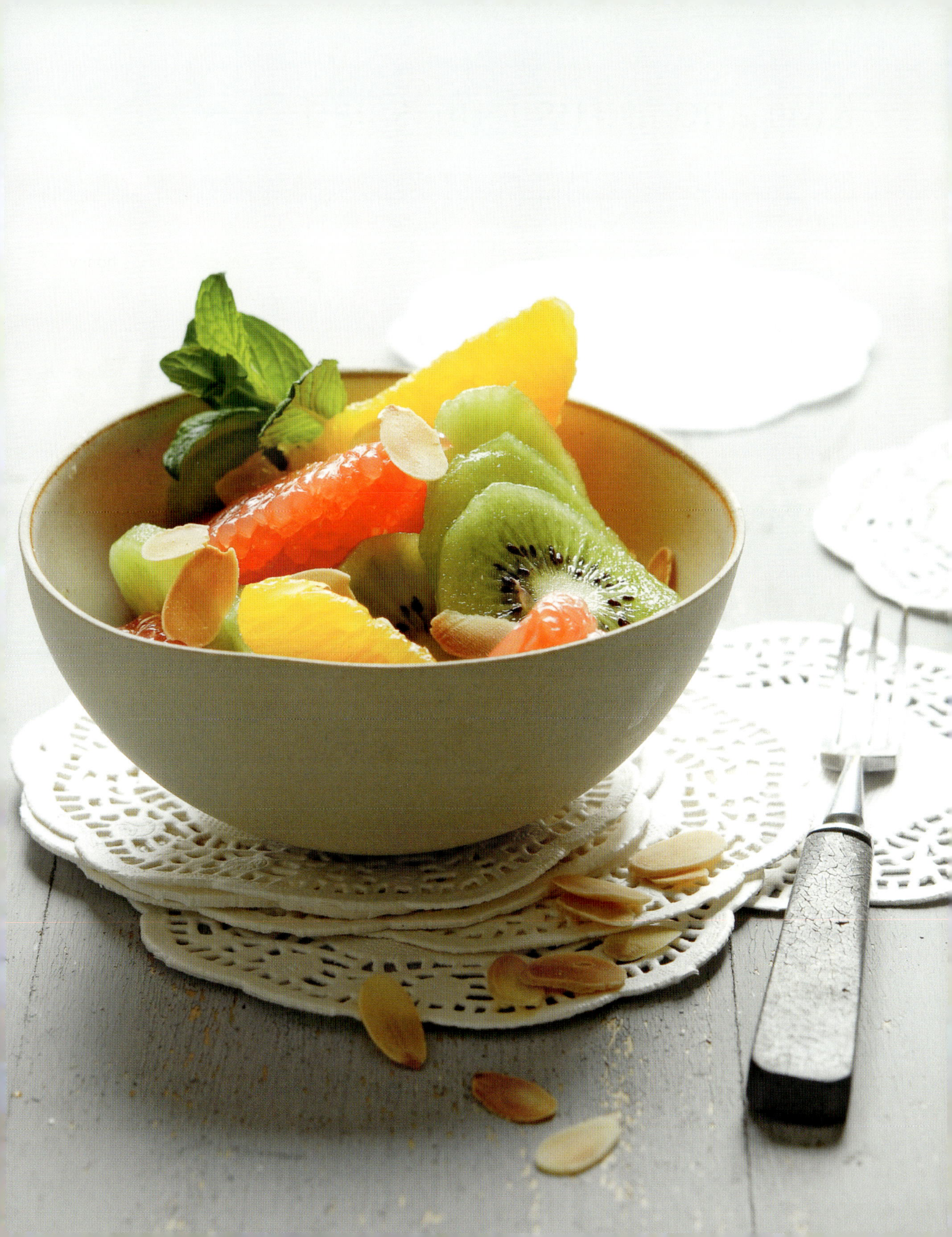

Berry soup

SERVES 6
PREP TIME: 20 mins.
COOKING TIME: 6 to 7 mins.

- 1 lb. red currants
- 2/3 cup black currants
- 1/2 lb. blackberries
- 1/2 lb. cherries
- 1/2 lb. raspberries
- 1 cup apple juice
- 1 cup grape juice
- 2/3 cup sugar
- 2 tbsp. cornstarch
- The zest of one lemon

never fails

Rinse the red currants, the black currants, the blackberries and the cherries (don't rinse the raspberries) and dry them on paper towels. Pick through the raspberries and blackberries and discard any damaged fruit. Remove the stems of the black currants and red currants with a fork. Pit the cherries.

Purée the blackcurrants and half the red currants in a food processor and put the purée in a saucepan. Add the apple juice, the grape juice and the sugar, and bring to a boil over gentle heat, stirring constantly until the sugar has dissolved.

Mix the cornstarch with half a cup of cold water and pour into the saucepan. Bring back to the boil, then carefully add the rest of the fruit and the lemon zest. Simmer very gently for 5 minutes, making sure the fruit doesn't get crushed.

Remove the saucepan from the heat, allow to cool slightly and pour into a large serving dish or individual bowls. Chill in the refrigerator until needed.

> Serving advice
Serve this dessert chilled, with vanilla ice cream or Chantilly whipped cream.

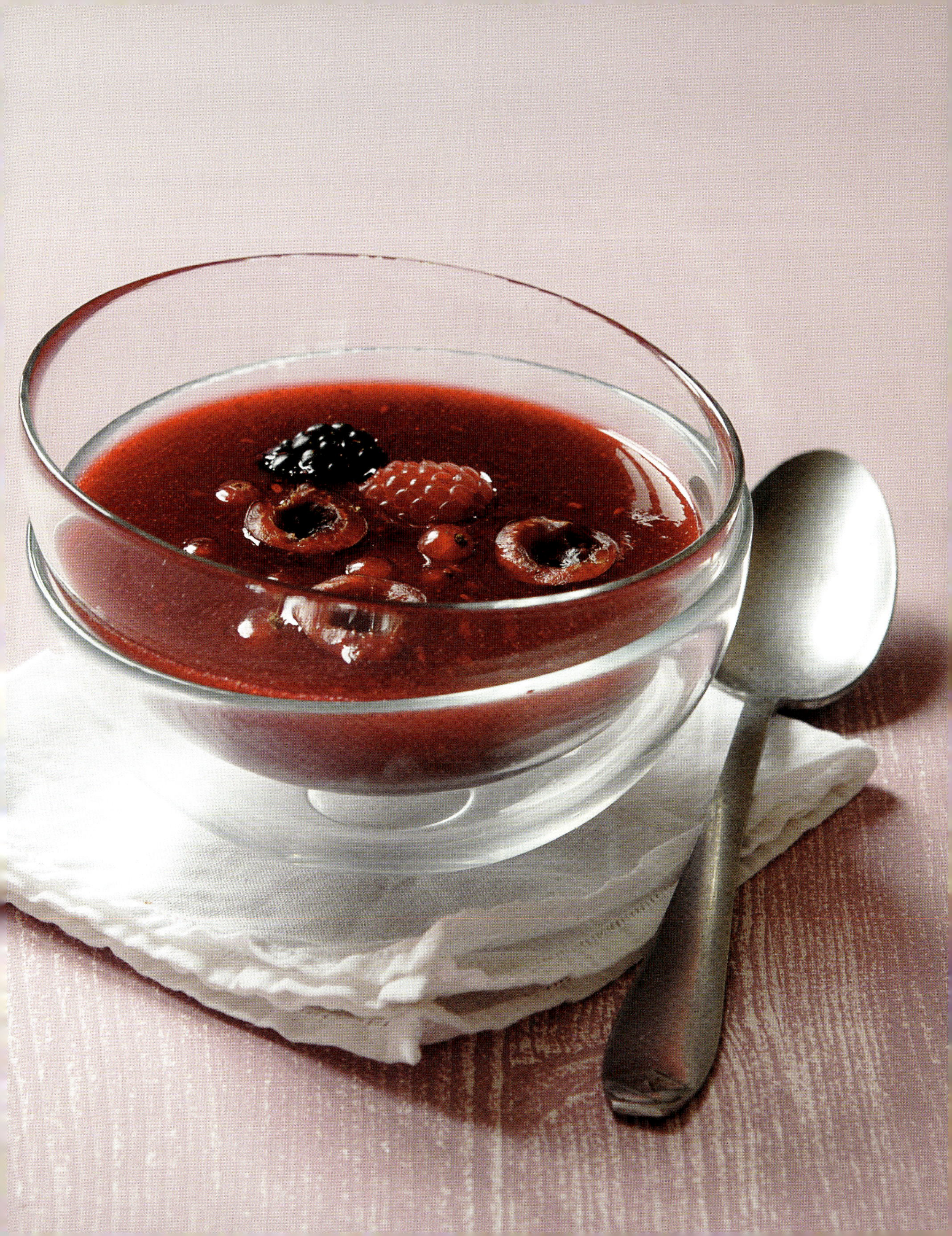

Watermelon and basil soup

SERVES 4
PREP TIME: 20 mins.
SOAKING TIME: 2 hrs

FOR THE WATERMELON COULIS
- 1 quarter watermelon (about 1-1/4 lb.)
- The juice of half a lemon

FOR THE BASIL SYRUP
- 2/3 cup water
- 3 tbsp. sugar
- 1 tbsp. finely chopped fresh basil

TO DECORATE
- 4 basil leaves

Prepare the watermelon coulis: remove the skin and seeds and cut the flesh into cubes. Keep one third of the flesh in the refrigerator and put the rest in a blender with the lemon juice. Blend until very smooth.

Prepare the basil syrup: put the water and sugar in a small saucepan, heat gently until the sugar dissolves, and bring to a boil. Immediately remove from the heat and add the chopped basil. Cover and allow to cool.

Mix the coulis and the syrup and allow to infuse in a cool place for 2 hours.

Just before serving, pour the mixture into four serving bowls and add the cubes of watermelon. Decorate with basil leaves and serve well chilled.

> Helpful tip

Watermelon is THE summer fruit: it's very refreshing and contains relatively little sugar! When buying a watermelon, make sure it feels heavy and doesn't sound hollow when you tap it.

never fails

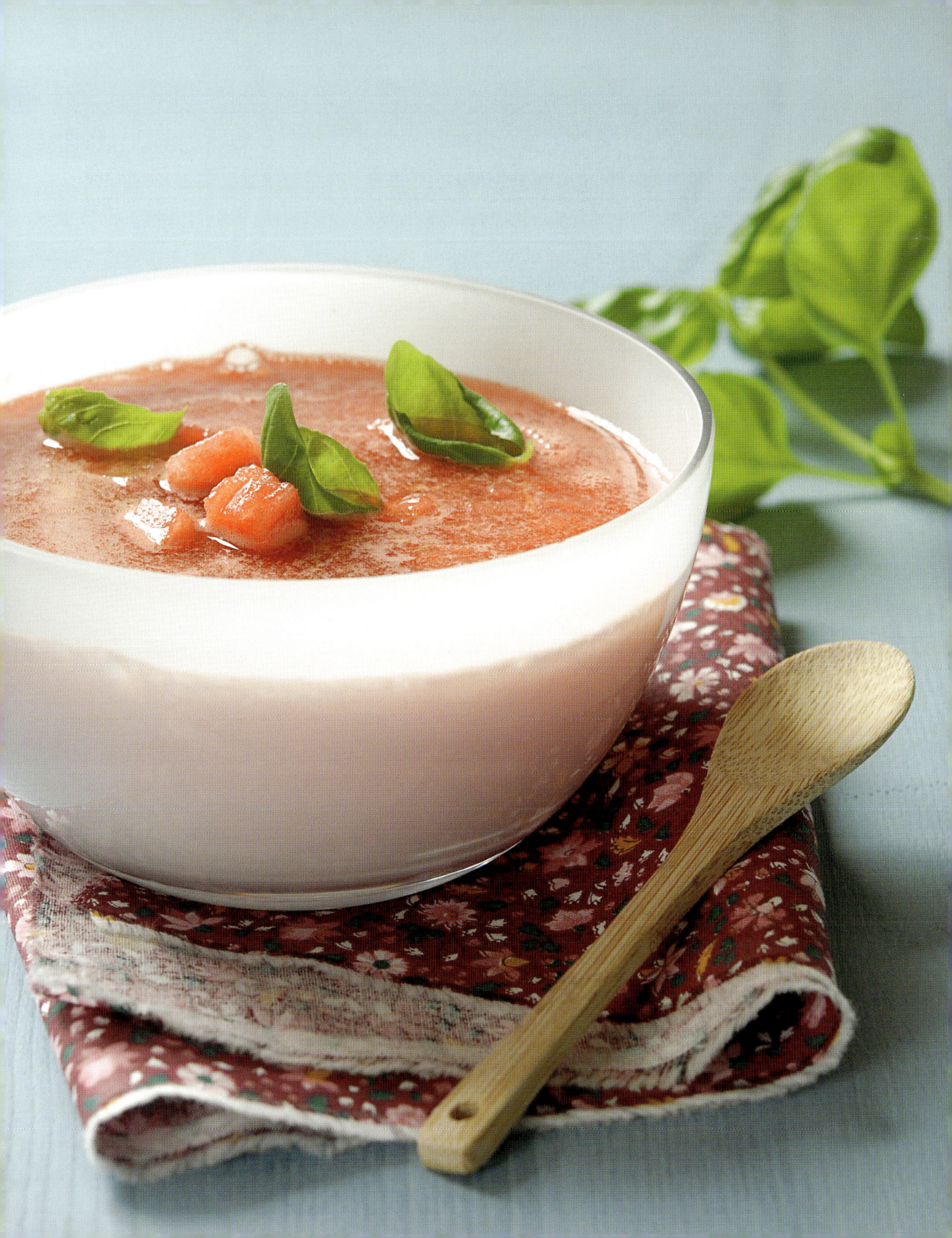

Plum and ginger compote

SERVES 6 TO 8
PREP TIME: 30 mins.
COOKING TIME: 1-1/2 hrs

- 2-1/2 pounds of ripe but firm plums
- 1 organic lemon
- A bit less than 4 oz. preserved lemon peel (optional)
- 3/4 cup sugar
- 1 oz. fresh ginger

Rinse and dry the plums, cut them in two and remove the pits. Put them in a pan and cook, stirring frequently, over medium heat for about 30 minutes, until they are soft. If you prefer a smooth compote, run them through a food mill.

Wash the lemon in cold water, dry it and zest it with a peeler. Finely chop the zest. Peel and finely chop the ginger.

Transfer the plums into a heavy pan and add the sugar, lemon zest, preserved peel (if using) and ginger. Cook over medium heat for one hour until the compote has reduced. Stir frequently as it will tend to stick to the pan.

Remove from the heat, pour into a serving bowl and allow to cool before refrigerating or freezing.

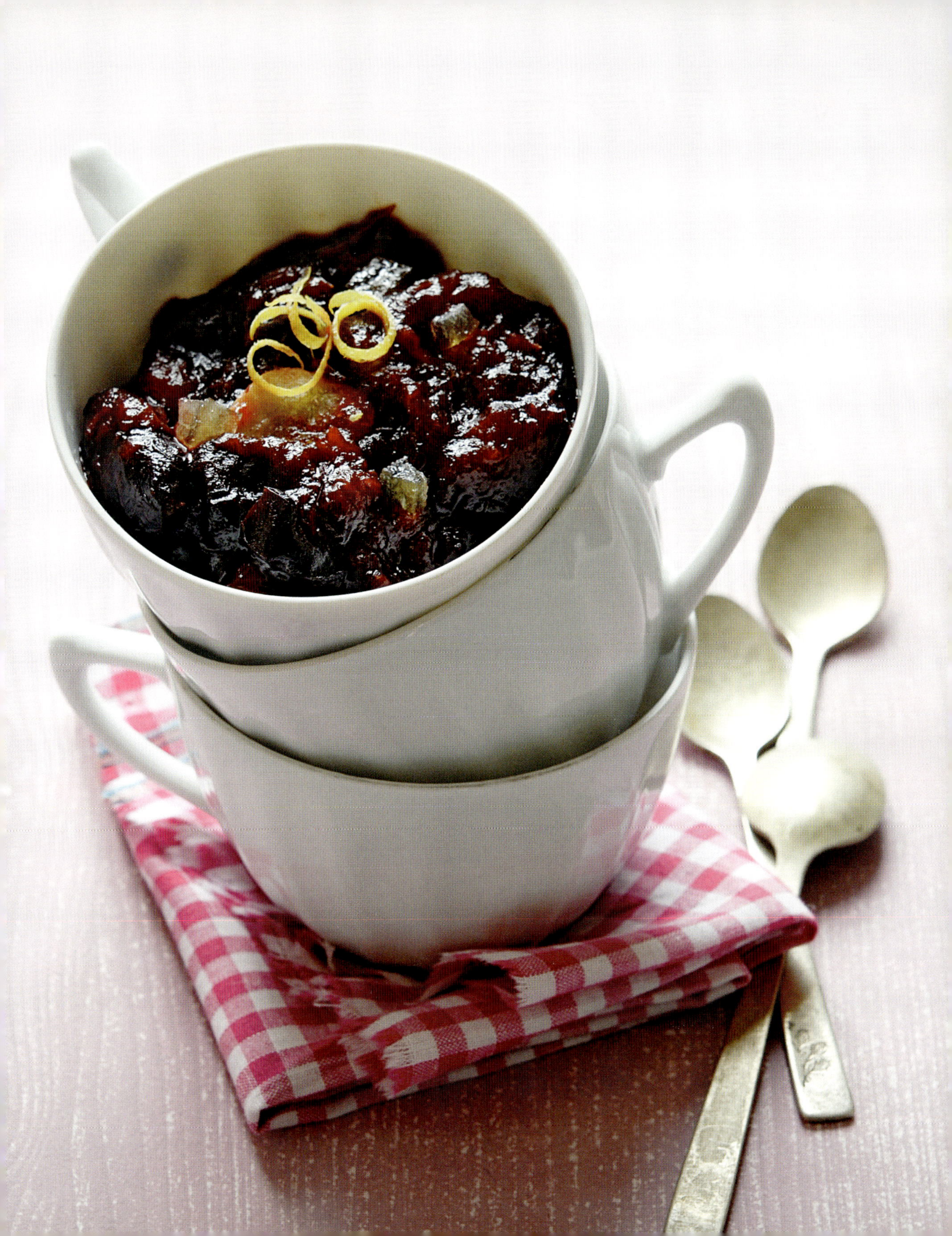

Lychee and raspberry compote

SERVES 4
PREP TIME: 20 mins.
COOKING TIME: About 3 mins.

- 1 lb. lychees
- The juice of half a lemon
- 1/2 lb. raspberries
- 1/2 cup granulated sugar

Peel and pit the lychees; sprinkle them with lemon juice. Process the raspberries and sugar in a blender to obtain a smooth coulis.

Pour the coulis into a saucepan. Bring to a boil, add the lychees and cook for about 3 minutes. Pour into a serving bowl and allow to cool. Chill in the refrigerator or freeze in plastic containers.

> Helpful tip

If fresh lychees are not available, use canned or frozen ones.

never fails

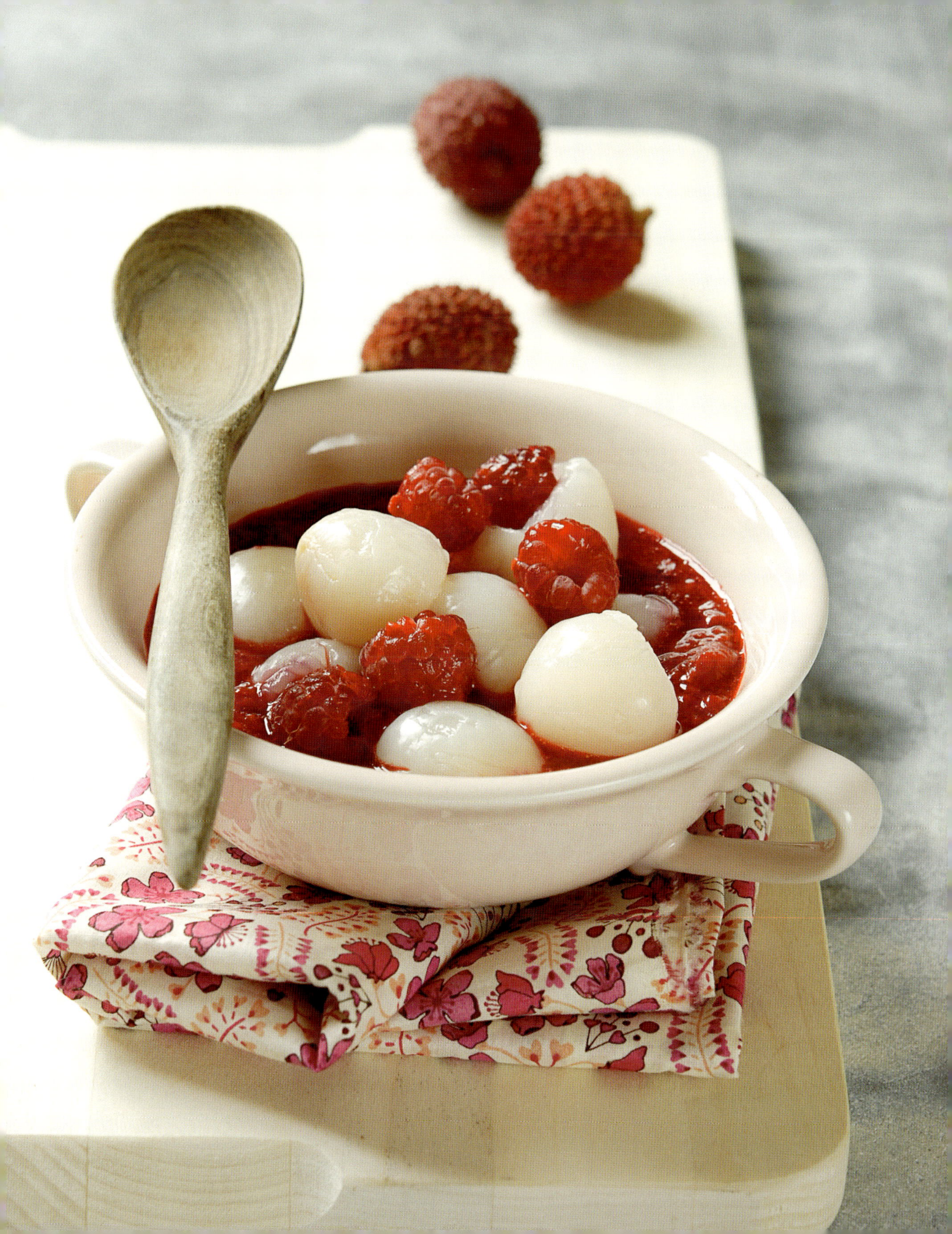

Rhubarb

Small snacks

Caramel and chocolate pie	342
Caramel and salt butter tartlets	344
Muffins	346
Currant buns	348
Cramique	350
Gâteau mollet	352
Pain d'épices	354
Praline brioche	356
French style fruit cake	358
Irish scones	360
Galettes Saint-Amour	362
French toast	364
Scotch pancakes	366
Crêpes Suzette	368
Waffles	370
Pets-de-nonne	372
Apple fritters	374
Churros	376
Bugnes	378
Salt butter caramel	380
Dulce de leche	382
Apricot-vanilla jam	384
Mandarin marmalade	384
Blueberry and caramel jam	386
Fig and honey jam	386
Cherry jam	388
Rhubarb and ginger jam	388
Rose petal jelly	390
Kiwi jam	392
"Quickie" raspberry jam	392
Quince jelly	394
Black currant jelly	394

Caramel and chocolate pie

SERVES 6
PREPARATION: 10 mins.
RESTING TIME: 30 mins.
COOKING TIME: 30 mins.
REFRIGERATION TIME: 2 to 3 hrs

FOR THE SWEET PASTRY
- 1/2 vanilla bean
- 5 tbsp. sugar
- 1 cup flour
- 1/4 cup softened butter
- 1 egg

FOR THE GANACHE
- 1 cup heavy cream
- 30 Carambar® candies
- 1/4 lb. milk chocolate

child's play

Prepare the pie crust: split the vanilla bean and scrape out the seeds; mix them with the sugar. Sift the flour directly onto a work surface, then cut the butter into small pieces and rub it into the flour with your fingertips until the mixture has the consistency of fine breadcrumbs. Make a well in the center and break the egg into it. Add the vanilla-flavored sugar. Mix with your fingertips, but don't knead. Flatten the dough with the heel of your hand until it is even-textured. Form into a ball, wrap in plastic wrap and allow to rest for at least 30 minutes.

Preheat the oven to 350° F.

Roll out the dough and place in a 10-inch pie dish lined with parchment paper. Bake for about 20 minutes.

Prepare the ganache: place the cream in a saucepan, add the Carambars® and place over low heat for about 10 minutes, until the candy has melted. Remove from the heat.

Break the chocolate into pieces, then add to the saucepan and mix with a wooden spoon until it has melted.

Pour this mixture into the pie base and leave in a cool place for 2 to 3 hours.

> Helpful tip
Carambars® are small sticks of caramel candy that are very popular in France. You can purchase them online.

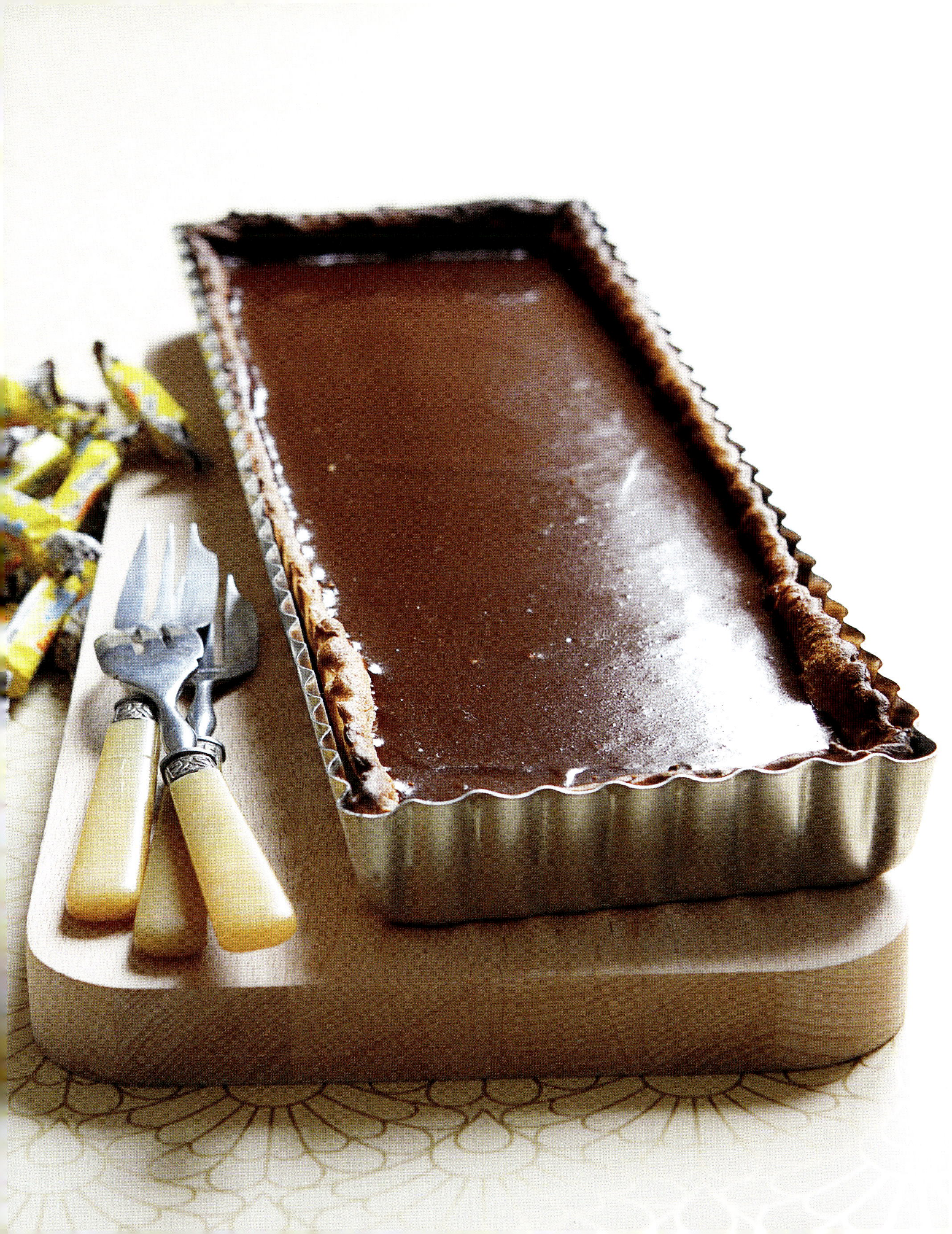

Caramel and salt butter tartlets

SERVES 6
PREP TIME: 20 mins.
RESTING TIME: 30 mins.
COOKING TIME: 25 to 30 mins.
REFRIGERATION TIME: 2 hrs

FOR THE PIE CRUST
- 1/2 vanilla bean
- 5 tbsp. sugar
- 1 cup flour
- 1/4 cup softened butter
- 1 egg

FOR THE CARAMEL
- 1/2 lb. sugar cubes
- 1-1/4 cup heavy cream
- 7 tbsp. softened butter cut into small pieces
- A pinch of sea salt flakes
- 2 eggs

Prepare the pie crust: split the vanilla bean and scrape out the seeds. Mix the seeds with the sugar. Sift the flour onto a work surface, then cut the butter into small pieces and rub into the flour until the mixture has the consistency of fine breadcrumbs. Make a well in the center. Break the egg into it and add the sugar flavored with vanilla. Combine the ingredients with your fingertips, but do not knead. Flatten the dough with the heel of your hand, then roll it into a ball and wrap in plastic wrap; allow to rest for at least 30 minutes.

Preheat the oven to 350° F.

Roll out the dough and use it to line six 4-inch buttered tartlet molds. Prick the dough, cover with parchment paper and baking beans and bake blind for 5 minutes. Remove the beans and paper and bake for another 5 minutes.

Prepare the caramel: put the sugar cubes in a saucepan, moisten them with water and allow to dissolve over gentle heat. Heat the cream in another saucepan. When the caramel takes on a dark golden color, add the boiling cream and stir well, taking great care to avoid splashing yourself. Incorporate the pieces of softened butter, then add the salt and the eggs.

Reduce the oven temperature to 300° F.

Fill the tartlets with caramel and bake for 15 to 20 minutes. Allow to cool and chill in the refrigerator for about 2 hours.

> Helpful tip
Don't overcook the caramel; this makes it taste bitter.

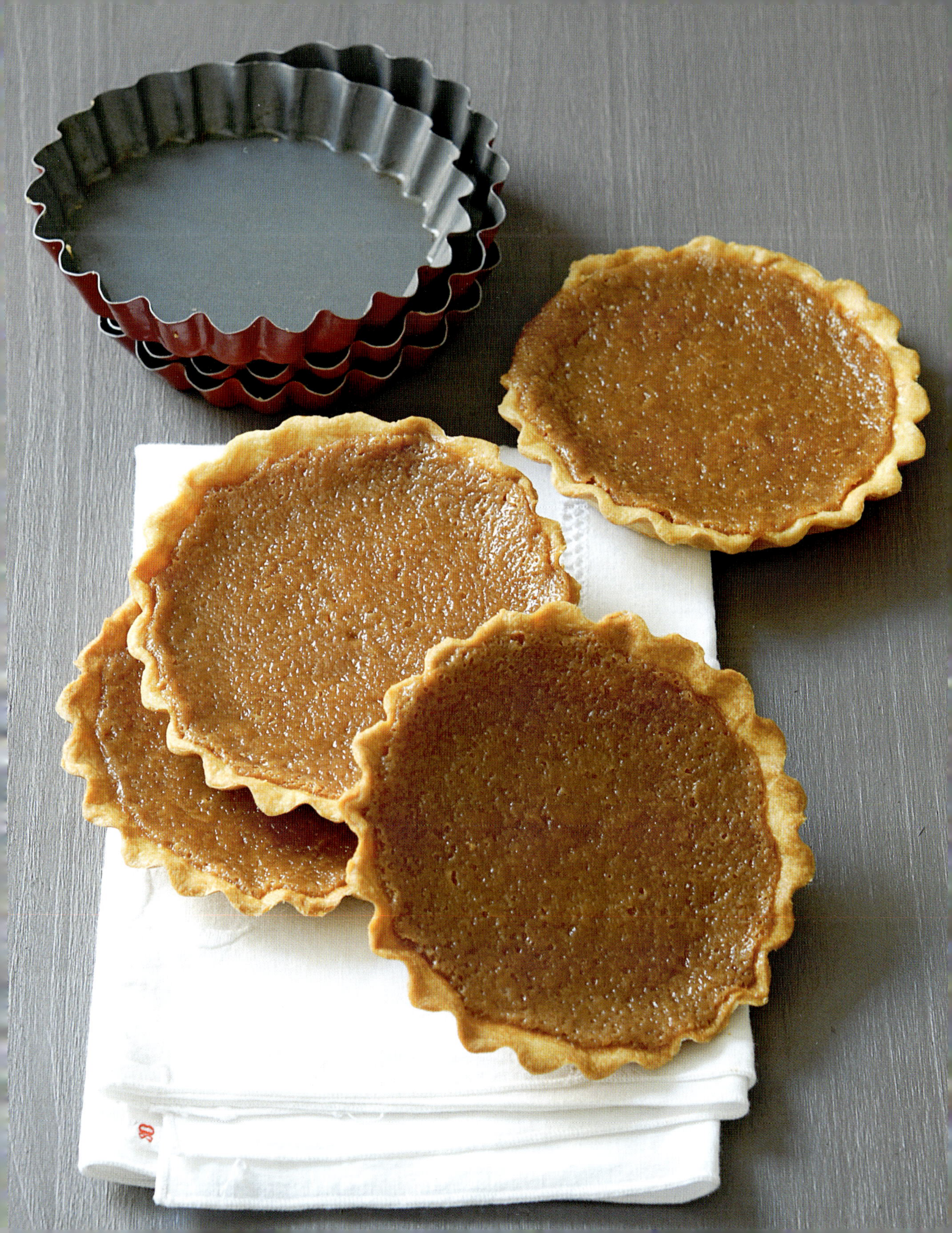

Muffins

MAKES 10 TO 12 MUFFINS
PREP TIME: 20 mins.
COOKING TIME: 25 mins.

- 2 cups flour
- 2-1/2 teaspoons baking powder
- 1/2 teaspoon baking soda
- A pinch of salt
- 1 cup milk
- 2 eggs
- 2/3 cup sugar
- 9 tbsp. melted butter + some for the pan
- 1 teaspoon vanilla extract

Put the flour into a bowl. Add the baking powder, the baking soda and the salt. Mix well. Warm the milk.

Preheat the oven to 350° F.

In another bowl, beat the eggs with the sugar until the mixture turns pale yellow, then incorporate the melted butter and the vanilla extract. Pour this mixture into the flour and mix together with a little warm milk (do not overbeat).

Pour the mixture into a buttered muffin pan and bake for 20 minutes until well risen and golden.

Turn out the muffins and leave to cool. Serve warm or cold.

> To make a change
To make a change from plain muffins, add blueberries, bananas or chocolate chips to the mixture.

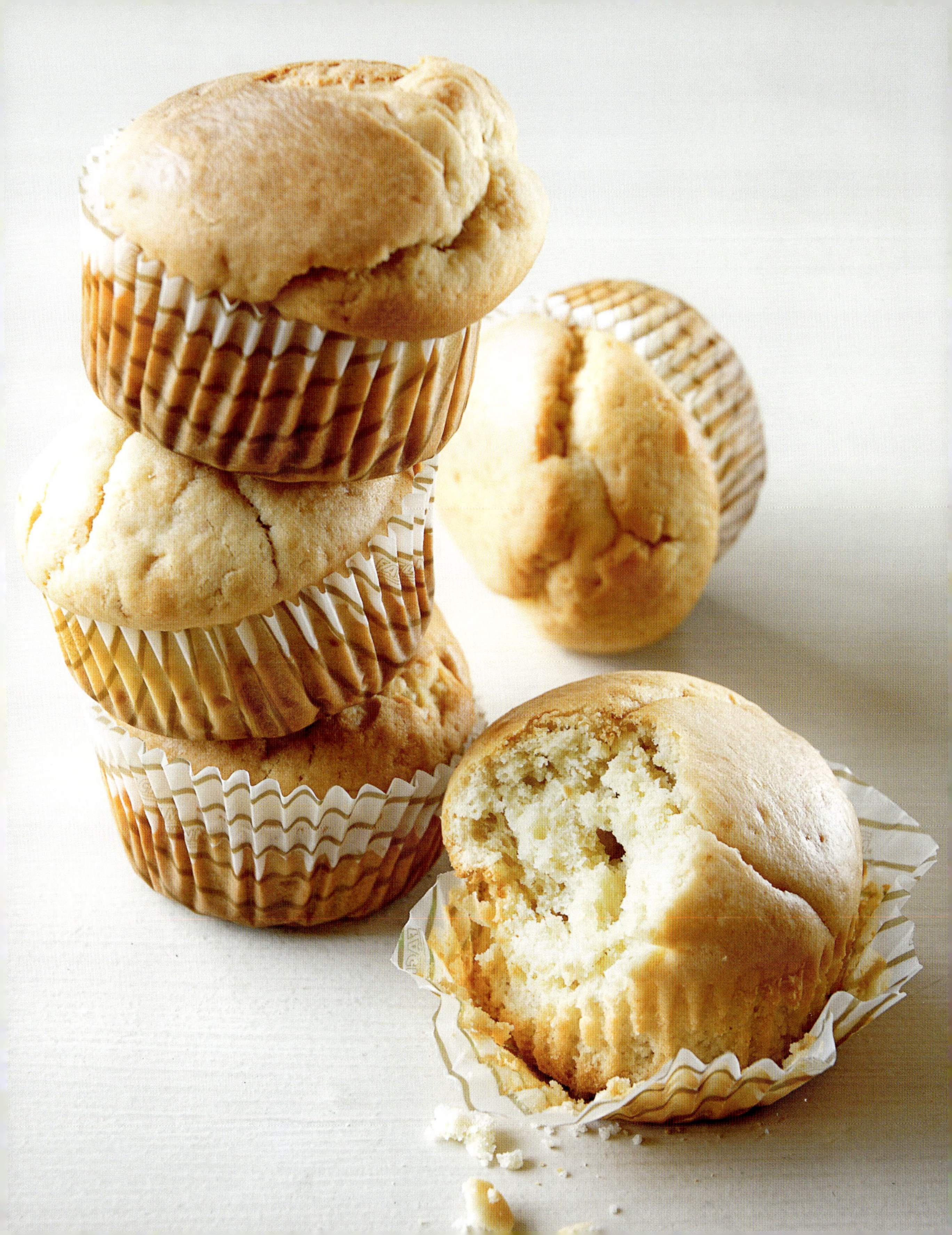

Currant buns

MAKES 15 TO 20 BUNS
PREP TIME: 15 mins.
RESTING TIME: 10 hrs
COOKING TIME: 20 mins.

- 2/3 tbsp. dry yeast
- 1-1/4 cups milk
  + 3 or 4 tbsp. to mix with the yeast
- 1 egg
- 2 pinches salt
- 1/2 lemon
- 7 tbsp. butter
- 5 tbsp. sugar
- 3/4 cup currants
- 2-3/4 cups flour

Mix the yeast with 3 or 4 tbsp. of warm milk in a bowl. Beat the egg with the salt. Grate the lemon and place the zest in a bowl with 1 cup milk, 1/3 cup softened butter, 5 tbsp. sugar and the currants. Mix well, then add the egg and yeast; incorporate the flour. Work into a supple dough and allow to rest for 5 hours (it will double in volume).

Divide the dough into little balls the size of tangerines. Butter a large metal or plastic container, place the dough balls inside it, brush them with the rest of the melted butter, close the container and allow to rest for another 5 hours. You can also lay them on a baking sheet and place them in a closet away from any drafts.

Preheat the oven to 400° F.

Place the buns on a baking sheet lined with parchment paper and bake for 20 minutes.

A few minutes before they are finished, mix the rest of the milk with 1 tbsp. sugar and brush over the buns.

> Find out more
Currant buns are a traditional favorite at tea time in the United Kingdom.

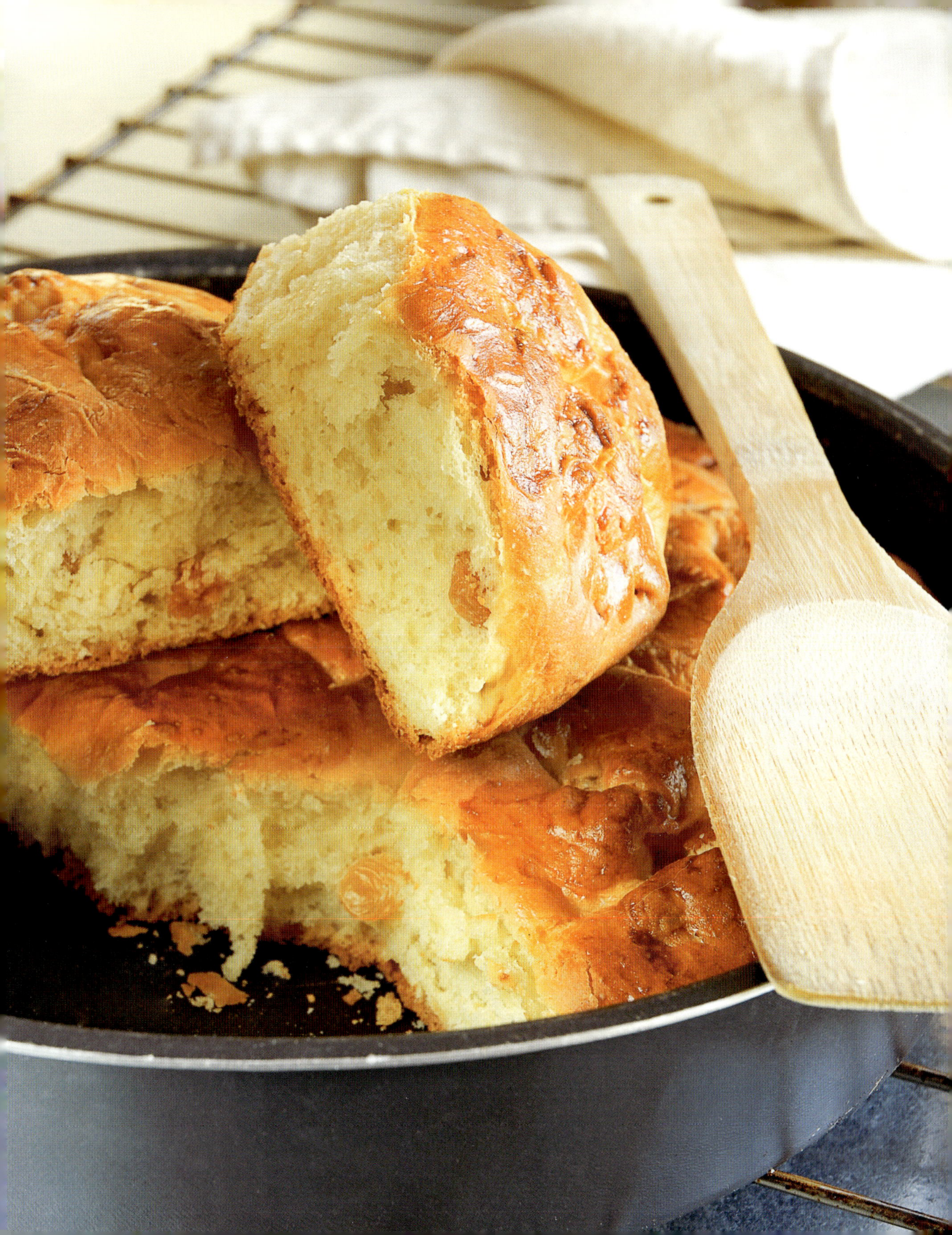

Cramique (Raisin loaf)

SERVES 6
PREP TIME: 25 mins.
RESTING TIME: 1 hr
COOKING TIME: 40 mins.

- 2 cups tea
- 2/3 cup raisins
- 7 tbsp. butter
- 3 eggs
- A pinch of salt
- 4 cups flour
- 1 tbsp. sugar

FOR THE YEAST MIXTURE
- 1 cup milk
- 1 tbsp. dry yeast
- Flour

Prepare the tea and put the raisins in it to soak.

Cut the butter into tiny pieces. Break 2 eggs and beat them with a pinch of salt.

Prepare the yeast mixture: warm the milk; sprinkle the yeast into a bowl, pour in a little warm milk and stir. Add the flour little by little, stirring with a wooden spoon until you have a soft dough.

Pour the flour onto your work surface and make a fountain. Add the yeast mixture. Add the beaten eggs and the rest of the warm milk.

Work the ingredients together with your hands and knead the dough until it becomes elastic. Add the butter. Continue kneading. Strain the raisins and add them to the dough. Knead some more to distribute the raisins evenly.

Preheat the oven to 400° F.

Make the dough into a sausage shape. Put it into a buttered 11-inch loaf mold. Beat the remaining egg and glaze the dough with a pastry brush. Allow to rise for 1 hour at room temperature.

Bake at 400° F for 10 minutes, then reduce the temperature to 350° F and bake for 30 minutes longer. Turn out the loaf and allow to cool.

> Serving advice
Serve cramique with fruit compote, chocolate cream or fruit-flavored ice cream.

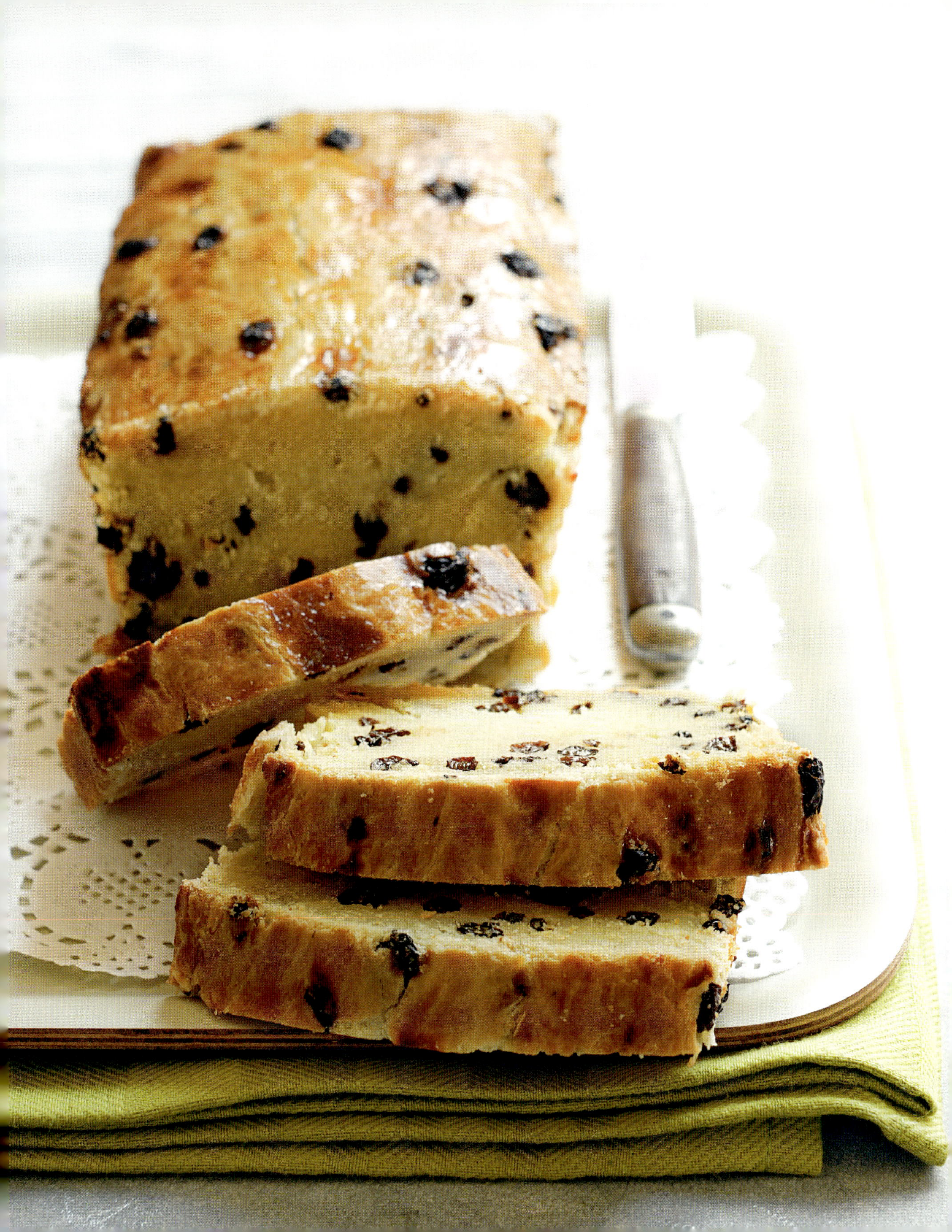

Gâteau mollet (Soft brioche)

SERVES 6
PREP TIME: 30 mins.
RESTING TIME: 1 hr
COOKING TIME: 30 mins.

- 1 scant tbsp. dry yeast
- 7 tbsp. warm milk
- 1-1/3 cups butter at room temperature + some for the pan
- 2-1/2 cups flour
- 4 eggs
- A pinch of salt
- 1-1/2 tbsp. sugar

Mix the yeast into the warm milk. Cut the butter into small pieces.

Sift the flour into a bowl and make a well in the center. Put the eggs, salt and sugar in the center and begin to mix. Add the butter and yeast and knead very well.

Generously butter a tall, 7-inch round brioche pan and put the dough into it. Allow to rise for 1 hour.

Preheat the oven to 350° F.

Bake for 30 minutes. Remove from the oven, allow to cool slightly and serve warm.

> Helpful tip
This soft brioche is a specialty of the Ardennes, in northern France. Serve with chocolate mousse or fruit compote.

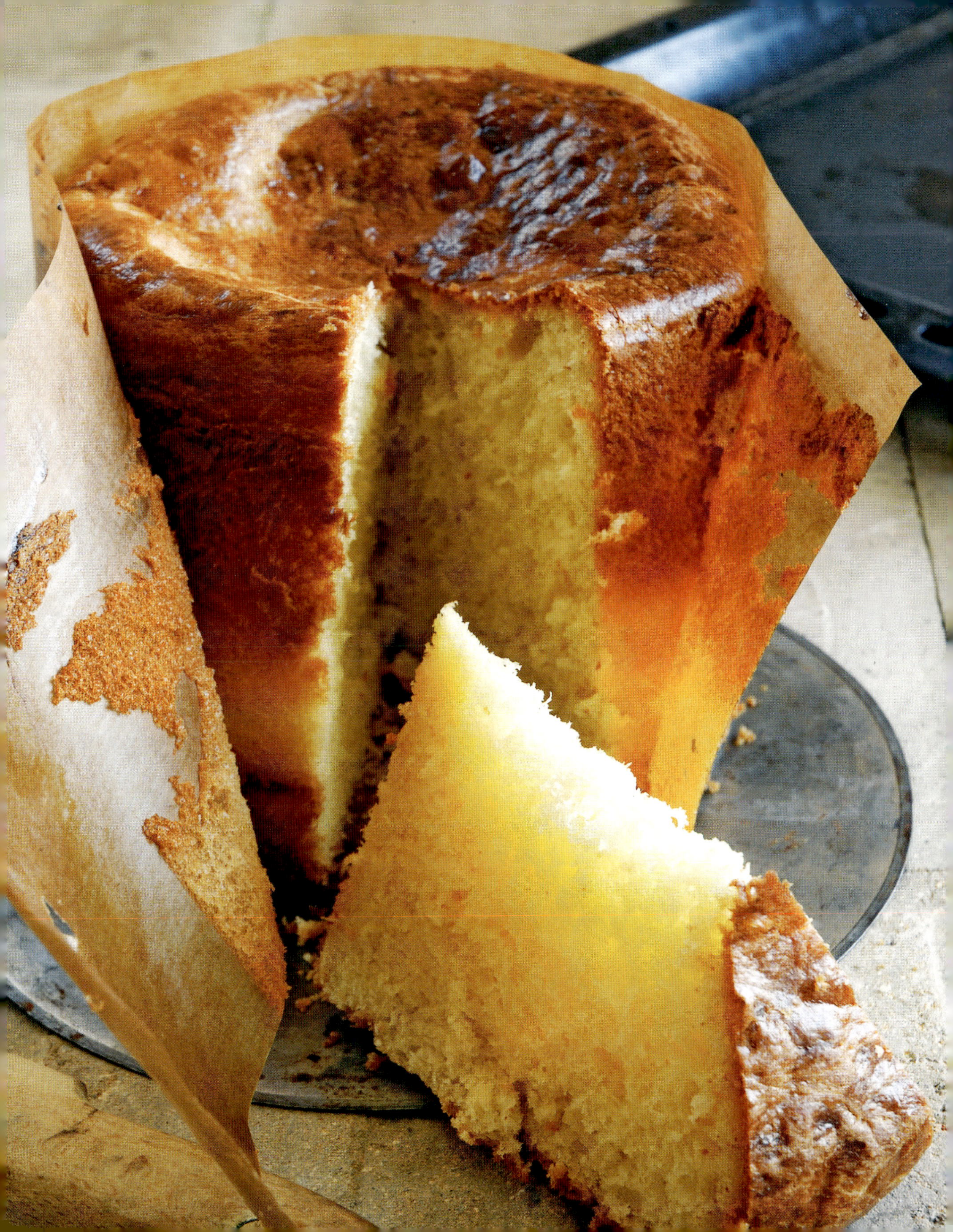

Pain d'épices (Spiced honey loaf)

SERVES 6
PREP TIME: 20 mins. (over 2 days)
COOKING TIME: 1 hr

- 6 tbsp. milk
- 1/2 cup strong-flavored honey
- 6 tbsp. sugar
- 2 egg yolks
- 1 teaspoon baking soda
- 2-1/2 cups flour
- 2 tbsp. lemon juice
- 1/2 cup chopped candied fruit
- 1 teaspoon cinnamon
- 2 tbsp. butter for the pan

Put the milk, honey and sugar into a small saucepan. Place over a low heat and stir.

Beat the egg yolks in a bowl and pour in half the milk and honey. Add the baking soda and the rest of the milk and honey. Mix well.

Preheat the oven to 350° F.

Sift the flour into a large bowl. Gradually add the previous mixture, alternating with 2 tbsp. of lemon juice, the candied fruit and the cinnamon. Beat this mixture for about 10 minutes.

Butter an 8- or 9-inch loaf pan and line it with parchment paper. Pour in the mixture and bake for 1 hour.

Turn out and allow to cool on a wire rack. Leave at least 24 hours before eating.

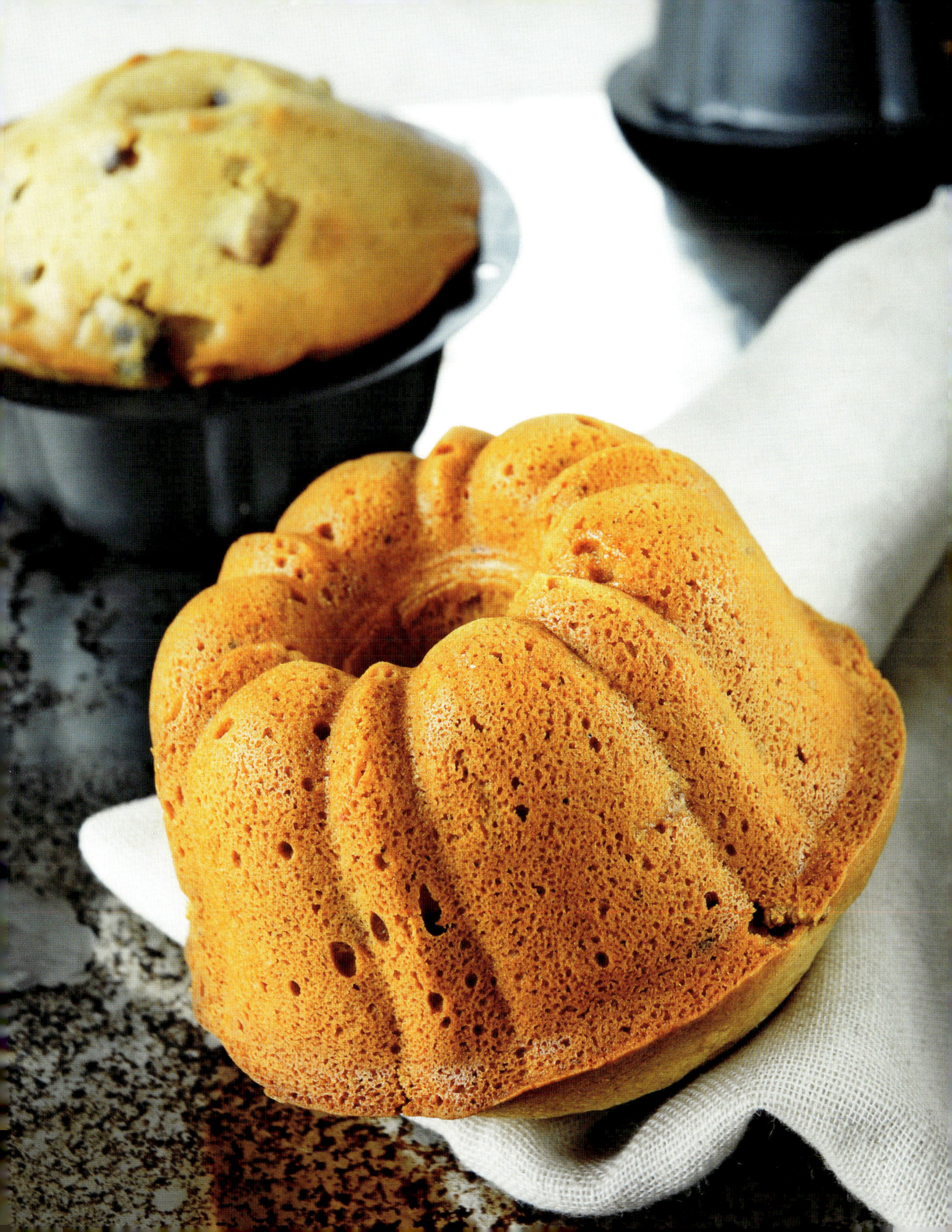

Praline brioche

SERVES 4 TO 6
PREP TIME
FOR THE PRALINES: 1 hr
COOKING TIME: 10 mins.
FOR THE BRIOCHE: 30 mins.
REST TIME FOR THE PASTRY: 4 hrs
COOKING TIME: 45 mins.

FOR THE PRALINES
- 1/2 cup shelled almonds
- 1-1/3 cups sugar
- 3/4 cup water
- 4 tbsp. powdered sugar
- 18 drops of red food coloring

FOR THE BRIOCHE DOUGH
- 1/4 tbsp. dry yeast
- 1-2/3 cups flour
- 1 1.2 tbsp. sugar
- 1 tsp. table salt
- 3 whole eggs
- 2/3 cup butter at room temperature

Prepare the pralines: in a saucepan with a thick base, boil the almonds along with 9 drops of coloring and half the sugar and water. Keep stirring with a wooden spoon until the sugar crystallizes around the almonds. Remove from the heat just as the sugar is about to caramelize (255° F on a candy thermometer).

Pour the contents onto a marble slab. Separate the almonds with a fork and dust them with half the powdered sugar, turning them over when necessary. Alternatively, you can also use slightly greased parchment paper to separate the almonds and then roll them separately in the powdered sugar. Place in a deep dish. Leave to cool.

Once the almonds are cold, boil the remaining 9 drops of coloring and the rest of the sugar and water without using the previous leftovers. Repeat the dusting operation with the almonds, watching the temperature as you do so. Again separate the almonds and dust with the powdered sugar. Leave to cool.

Prepare the brioche dough: break up the dry yeast into small pieces in a bowl. With a wooden spoon, stir in the flour, sugar and salt. Then add the eggs one at a time, blending them in carefully. Cut the butter into small pieces and mix into the dough. Work the dough well, until it comes away from the sides of the bowl.

Roughly crush 4 oz. of pralines and grind the remaining 1 oz. in the mixer or by placing them in a folded cloth and crushing them with a rolling pin. Add the 5 oz. crushed pralines to the brioche dough. Cover the dough with plastic wrap and leave it to rise for 3 hours in a warm place until it has doubled in volume.

Knead the dough quickly and roll it out over the remaining pralines so that they are spread over its entire surface. Place this ball on a baking sheet covered with parchment paper and leave to rise for 1 hour.

Preheat the oven to 450° F.

Place the sheet in the oven for 15 minutes, then lower the temperature to 350° F and leave to bake for another 30 minutes.

Turn the brioche out and serve while warm.

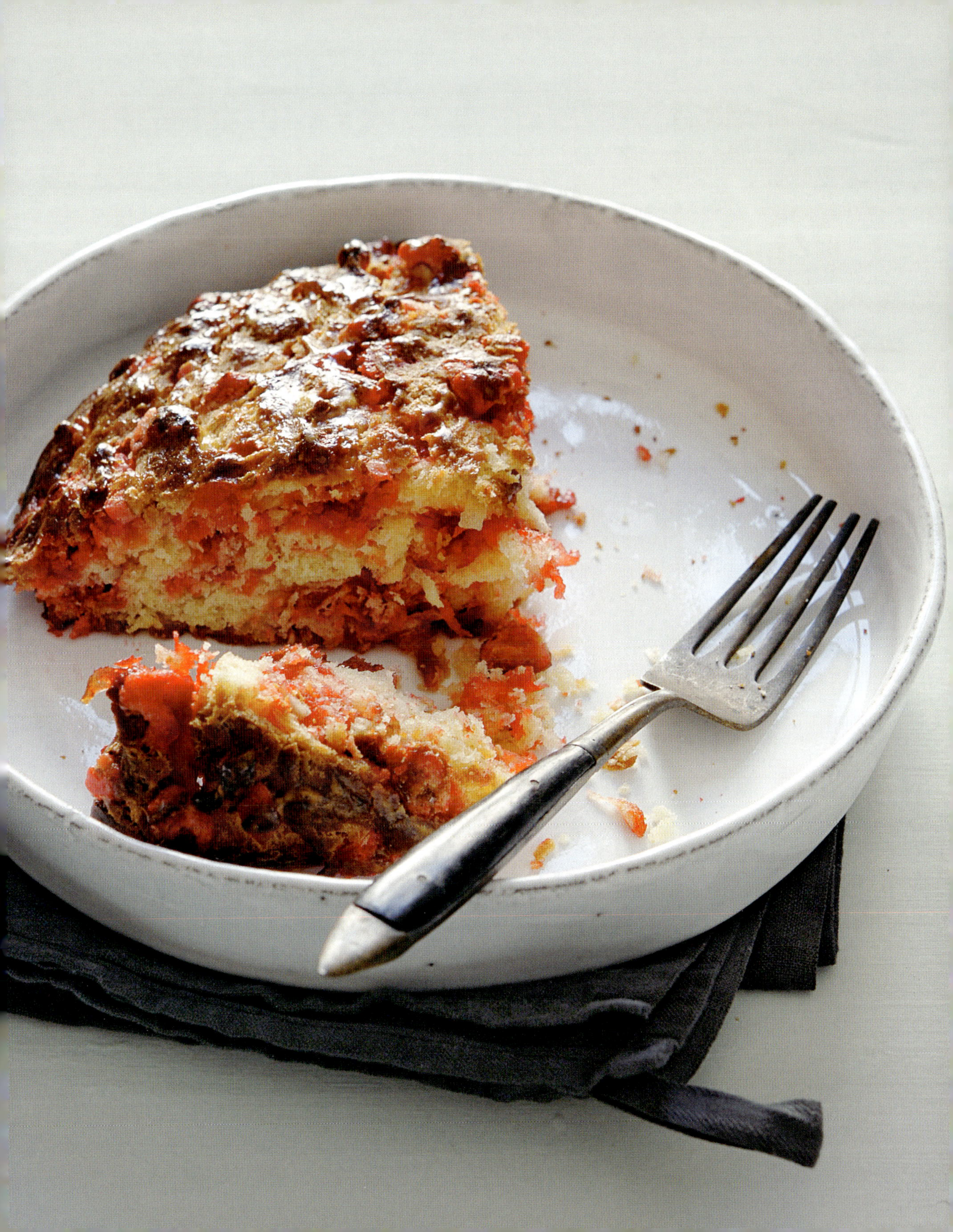

French-style fruit cake

SERVES 8
PREP TIME: 25 mins.
COOKING TIME: 45 mins.

- 2/3 cup raisins
- 1/2 cup candied fruit, cut into small cubes
- 2 oz. rum
- 3/4 cup butter + some for the cake pan
- 2/3 cup sugar
- A pinch of salt
- 3 eggs
- 2-1/2 cups flour
- 2-1/2 tsp. baking powder
- 1 tbsp. butter

never fails

Rinse the raisins. Soak them in the rum with the candied fruit.

Put the butter into a bowl and soften it with a spatula. Gradually add the sugar, then the salt. Mix until smooth. Add the eggs one by one. Finally, add 2 cups flour all at once. Drain the fruit and raisins and roll them in flour (this helps to prevent them from sinking to the bottom), then add them to the mixture with the rum. Add the baking powder and mix well.

Preheat the oven to 400° F.

Butter a piece of parchment paper and use it to line a 10-inch loaf pan. Pour in the mixture: the pan should be two thirds full.

Bake at 400° F for 10 minutes, then reduce the temperature to 300° F and bake for 35 minutes longer.

Remove the cake from the pan while it is still hot and stand it on a wire rack to cool.

> **For variety**
Make a honey and candied cherry cake: proceed in the same fashion but reduce the amount of sugar to 1/2 cup and add 2 tbsp. of liquid honey. Replace the raisins and candied fruit with 1/4 lb of candied cherries. Decorate the cake with strips of angelica.

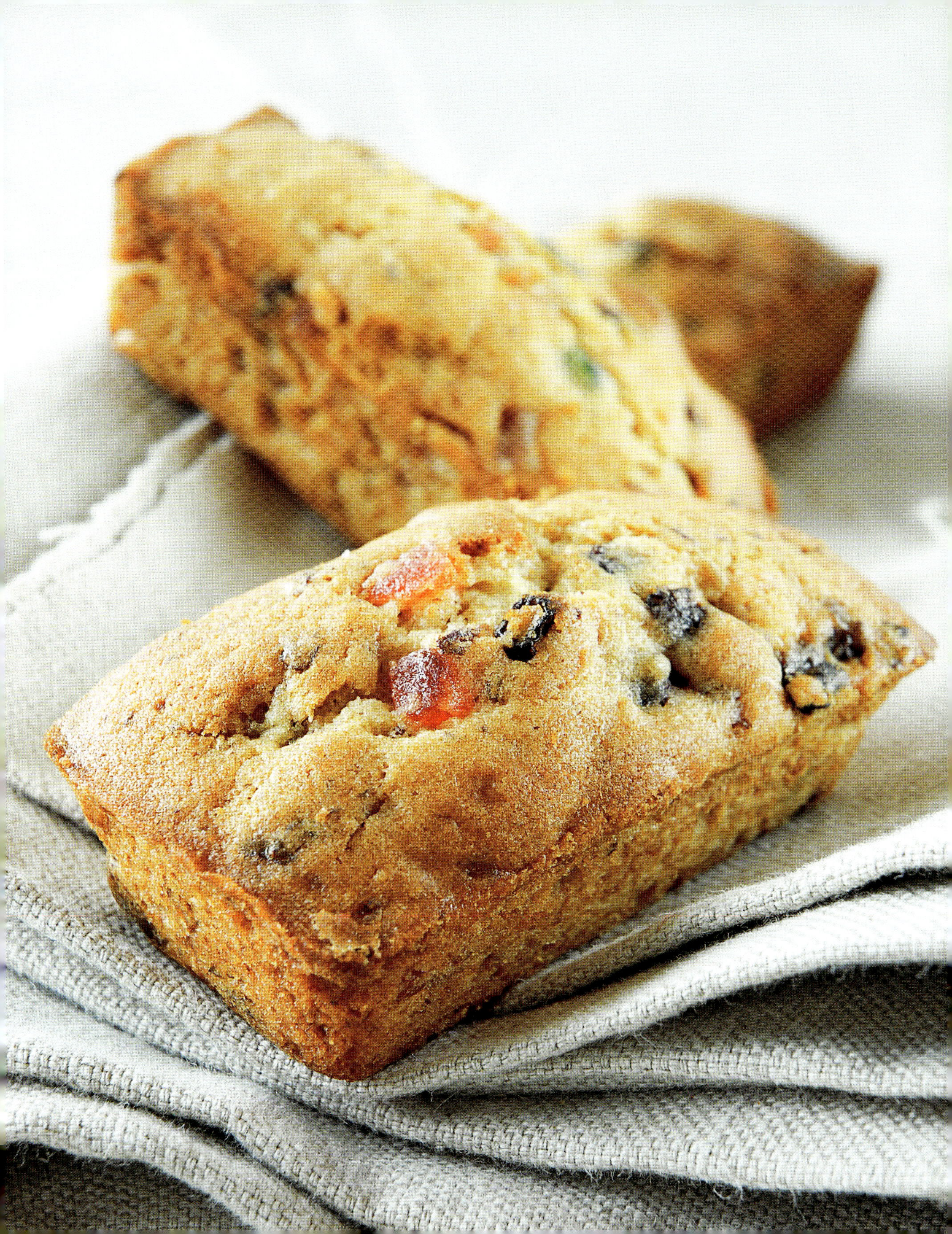

Irish scones

SERVES 6
PREP TIME: 25 mins.
COOKING TIME: 20 mins.

- 2 tbsp. butter + some for the baking sheet
- 2 cups flour
- 1 small pinch of salt
- A pinch of baking soda
- 1-1/2 tbsp. sugar
- 7 tbsp. sour milk

Cut the butter into small pieces. Put the flour and the salt into a bowl. Add the butter and rub in with your fingertips.

Mix the baking soda with the sugar and add this mixture to the bowl. Mix well. Add the milk and work into a stiff dough. Place on a floured work surface and knead until supple.

Preheat the oven to 425° F.

Roll out the pastry to a thickness of about an inch. Divide into eight, then trim each portion into a triangle.

Butter a baking sheet and place the triangles of dough on it.

Bake for 20 minutes until the scones are golden. Remove from the oven and place on a serving dish. Serve warm.

> Serving advice
Serve these scones with butter and jam in the afternoon or for breakfast.

> Helpful tip
To make sour milk, put 6 tbsp. whole pasteurized milk in a warm place for 48 hours.

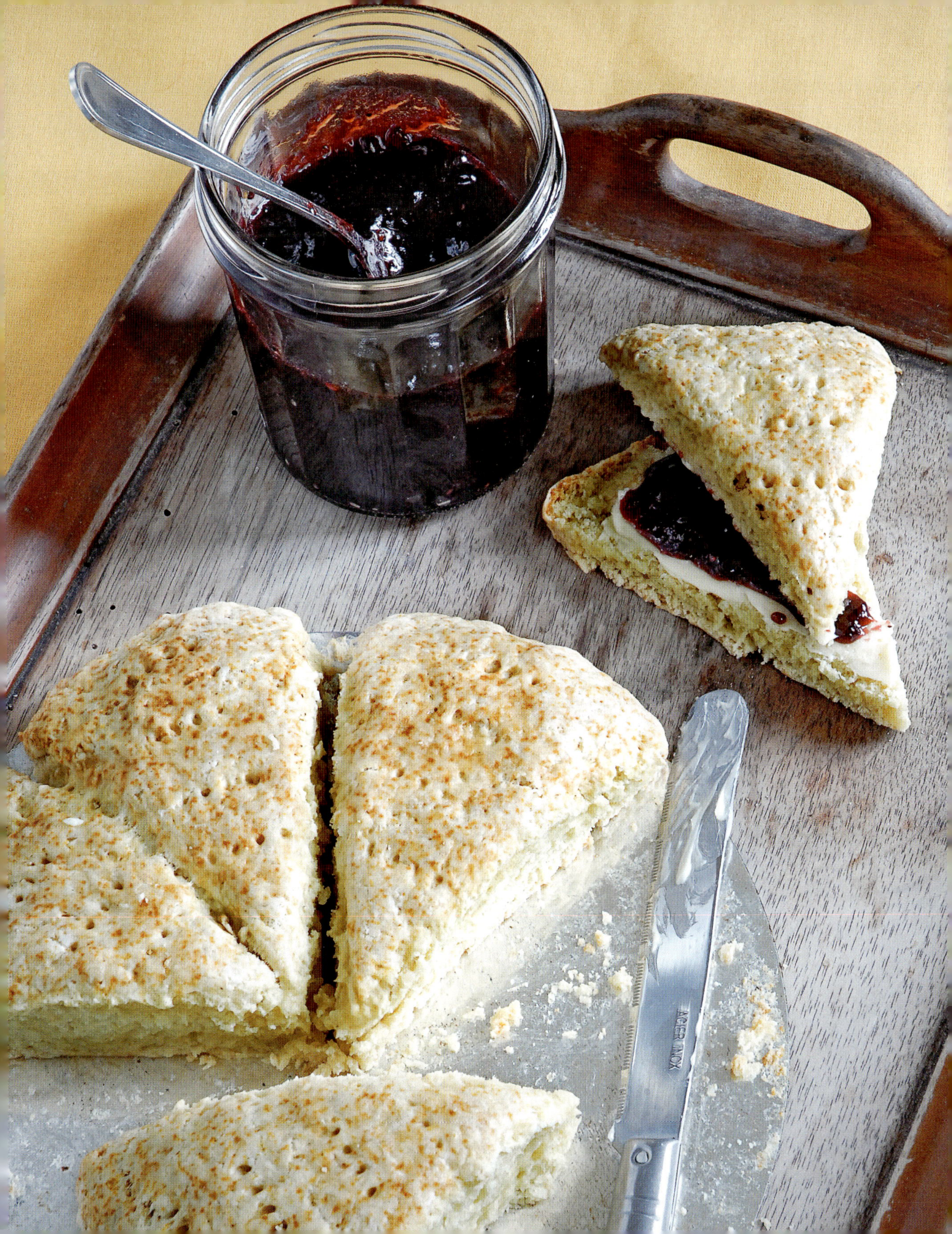

Galettes Saint-Amour
(Giant jam cookies)

MAKES 4 GALETTES
PREP TIME: 30 mins.
COOKING TIME: 35 mins.

- 7 tbsp. softened butter
- A pinch of salt
- 2 eggs
- 1-1/4 cups flour
- Just over 5 oz. red fruit jam
- 4 tbsp. crème fraîche or heavy cream

Preheat the oven to 400° F.

Cut the butter into small pieces and place in a bowl with the salt. Pour in two tbsp. of hot water, beating until the butter has melted.

Beat in 1 egg, then contine beating and gradually add the flour until the mixture is quite firm.

Form the mixture into a ball and divide into four smaller balls. Roll each ball out into a disk.

Butter a baking sheet and lay the 4 disks on it. Bake blind for 15 minutes.

Lower the temperature to 350° F.

Spread a thick layer of jam on each disk. Beat together the cream and the remaining egg and pour spoonfuls of this mixture onto the jam so that it forms spots. Bake again for 20 minutes. Serve warm.

> Helpful tip

To bake blind, prick the dough in several places with a fork; cut parchment paper to size and lay on top of the dough. Cover the surface with porcelain baking beans (or dried beans, peas or lentils) and bake. Remove beans and paper after baking.

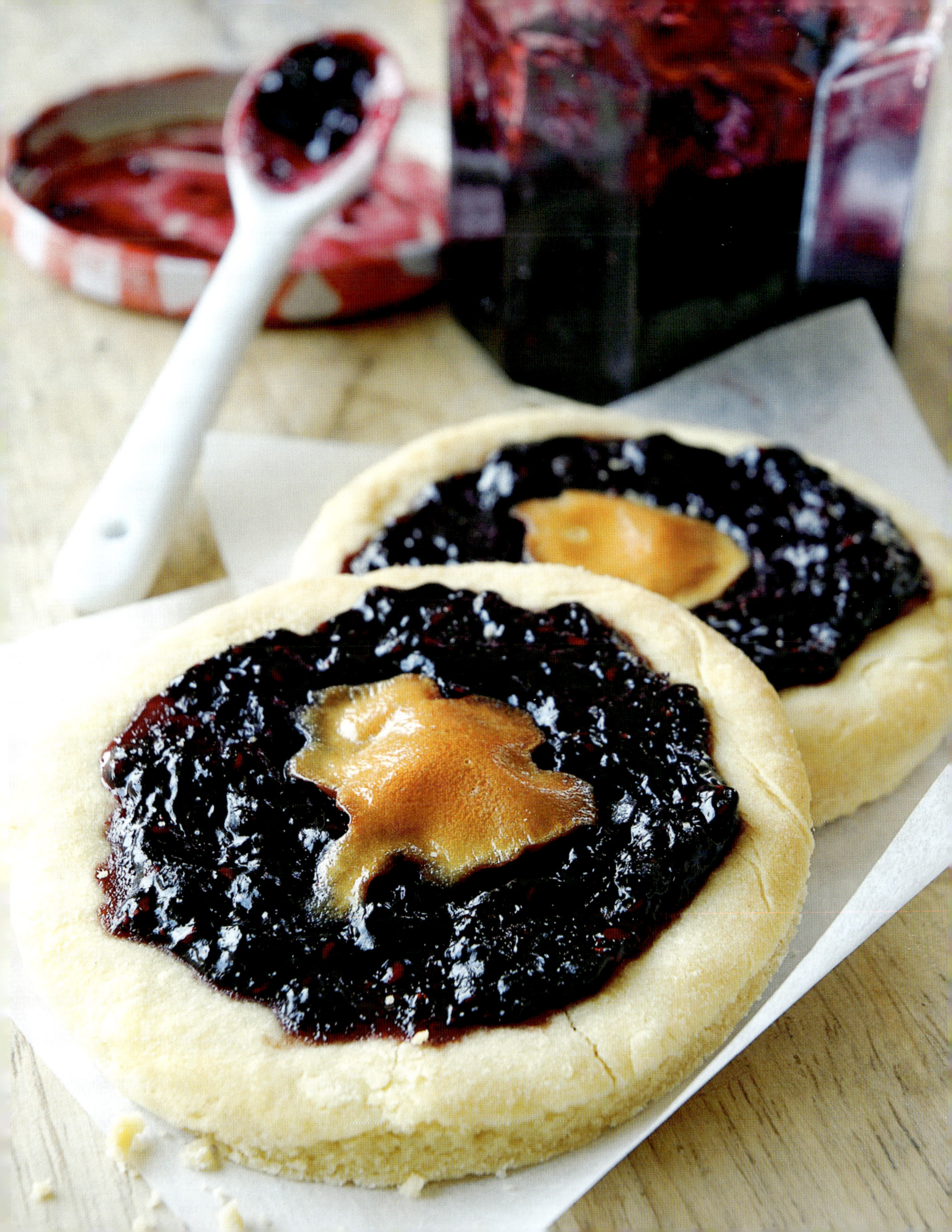

French toast

MAKES 12 SLICES OF BREAD
PREP TIME: 15 mins.
COOKING TIME: 15 mins.

- 1 cup milk
- 6 tbsp. sugar
- 1 teaspoon of vanilla extract
- 6 tbsp. brown sugar
- 5 medium eggs
- 12 slices fresh or stale bread
- 7 tbsp. butter

child's play

Heat the milk in a saucepan. Add the sugar and the vanilla extract. Mix until they dissolve and allow to cool.

Put the brown sugar in a flat dish. Beat the eggs in a bowl.

Dip the bread in the cooled milk then in the beaten eggs; when it has absorbed as much as it can, dip in the brown sugar so that both sides are coated.

Melt a large piece of butter in a large skillet and fry the bread (in batches) for 4 or 5 minutes until golden, turning once with a large spatula. The surface should be slightly caramelized.

Keep the French toast warm until needed. Add some more butter as you go, as the bread must not be allowed to stick to the pan.

> Helpful tip
You can eat French toast on its own or spread with jam.

> To make a change
In France, French toast is called "pain perdu" which means "lost bread." It used to be made with the crusts and bits of bread left on the table after a meal.

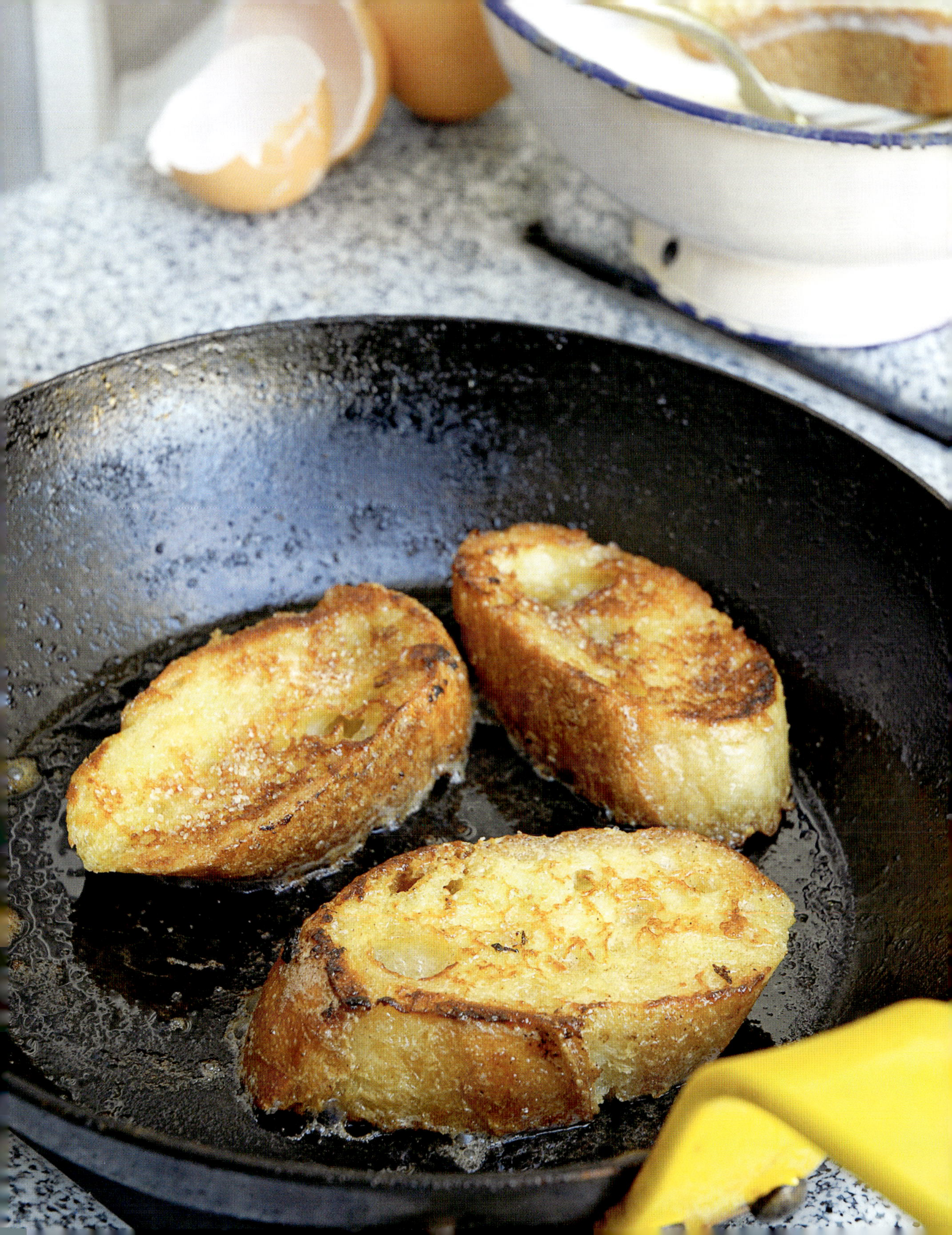

Scotch pancakes

MAKES 8 TO 12 PANCAKES
PREP TIME: 15 mins.
COOKING TIME: 4 to 5 mins. per batch

- 2 tbsp. butter
- 1 cup sifted flour
- 3 teaspoons baking powder
- 2-1/2 tbsp. sugar
- 1 egg
- 1 cup milk
- 1 tbsp. cooking oil

Melt the butter in a saucepan.

Place the flour, baking powder and sugar in a bowl and mix well. Break in the egg, add the milk and mix again. Stir in the melted butter.

Heat the oil in a large skillet and pour in small quantities of batter. Fry the pancakes for about 2 minutes, turning them so that they are golden all over.

Remove from the oil and drain on some paper towels.

Continue with the rest of the mixture.

> Serving advice
Serve these pancakes warm, with butter and jam. You can also serve them with caramel sauce for a delicious change!

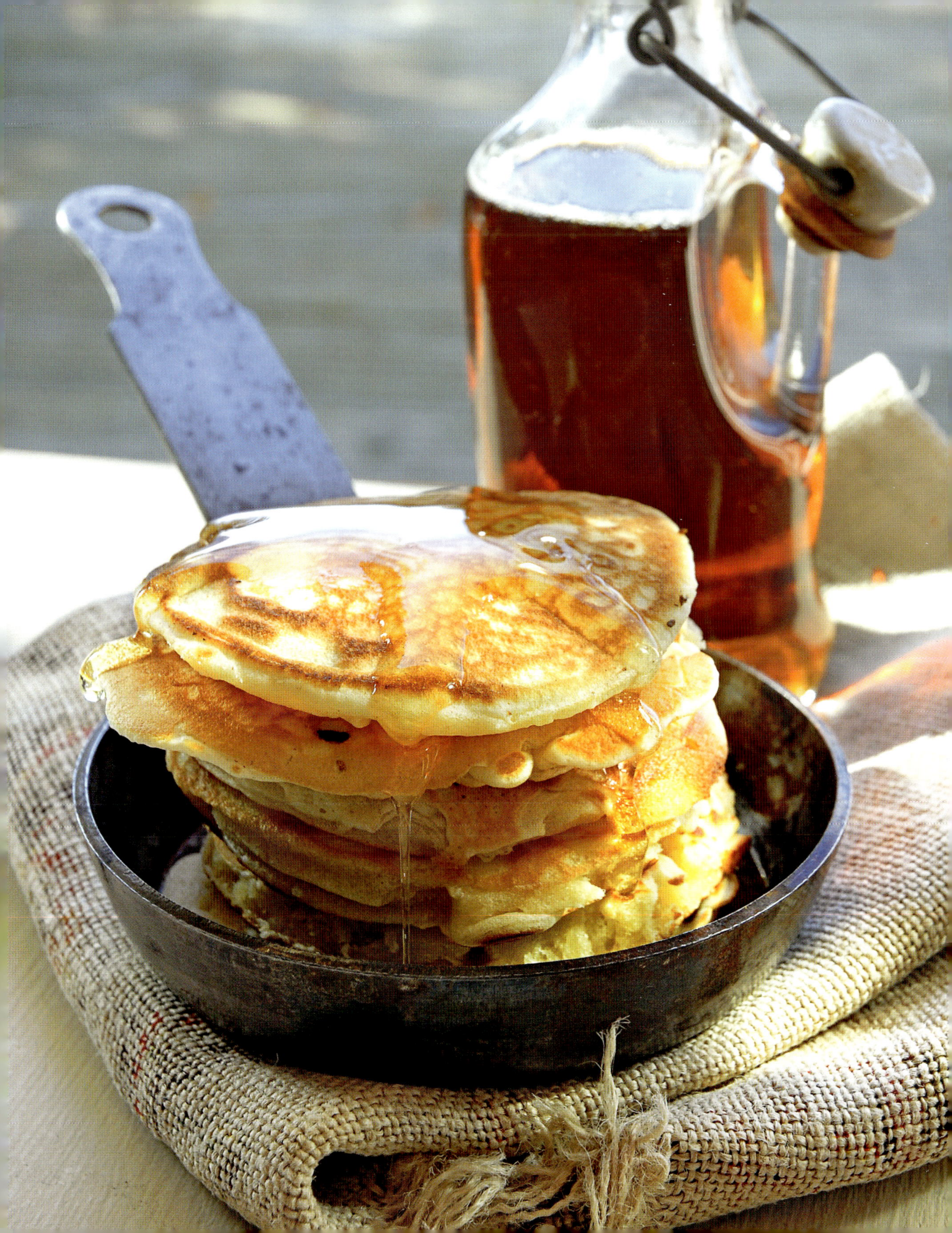

Crêpes Suzette

MAKES 6 CRÊPES
PREP TIME: 30 mins.
RESTING TIME FOR BATTER: 2 hrs
COOKING TIME: 30 mins.

- 2 mandarin oranges
- 3 tbsp. butter
- 1 tbsp. curaçao
- 4 tbsp. sugar
- 4 tbsp. Grand Marnier®

FOR THE BATTER
- 1 cup flour
- 1 cup milk
- 1 tbsp. butter
- 2 eggs
- 1 teaspoon salt
- 1 tbsp. curaçao
- 2 tbsp. corn oil

Grate the zest of one of the mandarin oranges and squeeze the juice from both.

Prepare the crêpe batter: put the flour into a bowl and make a well in the center. Pour in half the milk and mix with a wooden spoon, drawing the flour into the center little by little. Melt the butter over gentle heat in a small saucepan. Break the eggs into another bowl and beat them. Stir the eggs gradually into the flour, add the melted butter, the salt, half the mandarin juice, the curaçao and the oil. Continue to stir until the mixture is perfectly smooth. Gradually add the rest of the milk, stirring constantly to avoid any lumps forming. The batter should be of pouring consistency, but not too liquid. Cover and allow to rest for 2 hours.

Cut the butter into small pieces and put them in a large bowl. Add the rest of the mandarin juice, 1 tbsp. curaçao, the grated zest and the sugar. Work all these ingredients together until well blended.

Heat a lightly oiled nonstick skillet. Pour in a small ladleful of batter. Tilt the skillet in all directions to spread the batter in a thin, even layer. Put back on the heat. When the batter loses its shine, slide a spatula under the edge, loosen the crêpe and turn it over. Cook the other side for about 1 minute: the crêpe should be a pale golden color. Continue with the rest of the batter.

Spoon a little flavored butter onto each crêpe, fold in half, then in half again to form a triangle. Reheat gently in the skillet and place on a serving platter.

Warm the Grand Marnier® liqueur in a small saucepan, pour over the crêpes and flambé.

> **Helpful tip**
Getting crêpes just right depends on the consistency of the batter and how long you let it rest. To test consistency, dip a ladle into the batter, turn it over and drag your finger across the bottom: if the batter is not too fluid, your finger should leave a clear track. If the batter is too thick, you can thin it down with water or milk (up to 6 tbsp.) just before cooking.

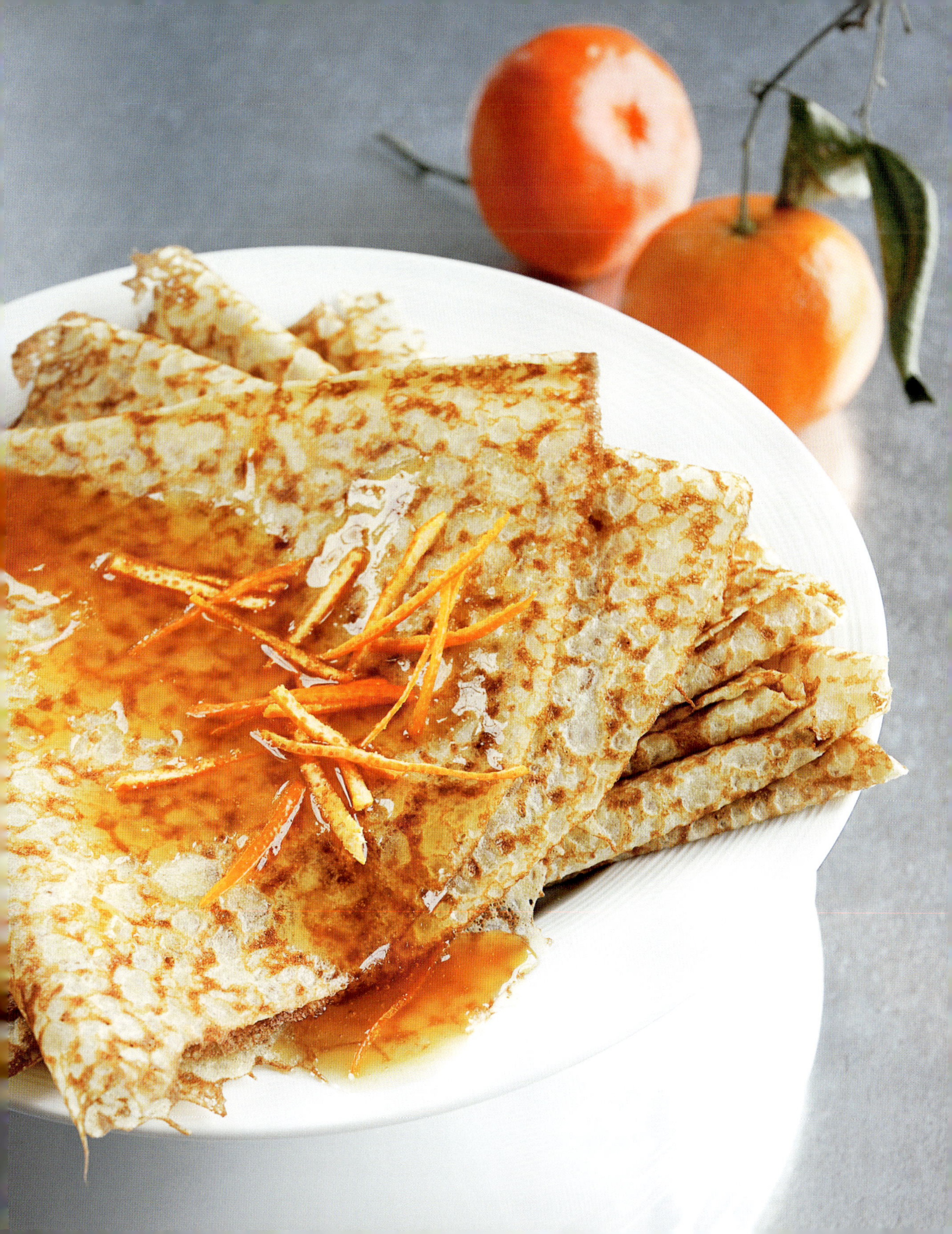

Waffles

MAKES 5 TO 10 WAFFLES
PREP TIME: 15 mins.
RESTING TIME: 1 hr
COOKING TIME: 10 mins.

- Oil for the waffle iron
- Powdered sugar

FOR THE BATTER
- 4 tbsp. crème fraîche or heavy cream
- 1 cup milk
- 1/2 tsp. salt
- 2/3 cup flour
- 2 tbsp. butter
- 3 eggs
- 1 tsp. orange flower water

Prepare the waffle batter: bring the cream and half the milk to boil in a saucepan. Allow to cool. In another saucepan, bring the rest of the milk and the salt to a boil. Add the flour and the butter. Allow to cook for 2 or 3 minutes, stirring with a wooden or rubber spatula as if making choux pastry. Place this mixture in a large bowl. Mix in the eggs one by one, then the boiled milk and cream, and finally the orange flower water. Mix well and allow to cool. Allow to rest for at least 1 hour.

Heat up your waffle iron. Carefully ladle in some mixture, taking care that it doesn't spill over the edge.

Close the waffle iron and cook for about 4 minutes. Open the waffle iron, turn out the waffle and sprinkle with powdered sugar.

> To make a change

Although waffles are delicious on their own, you can also serve them with jam or Chantilly whipped cream.

child's play

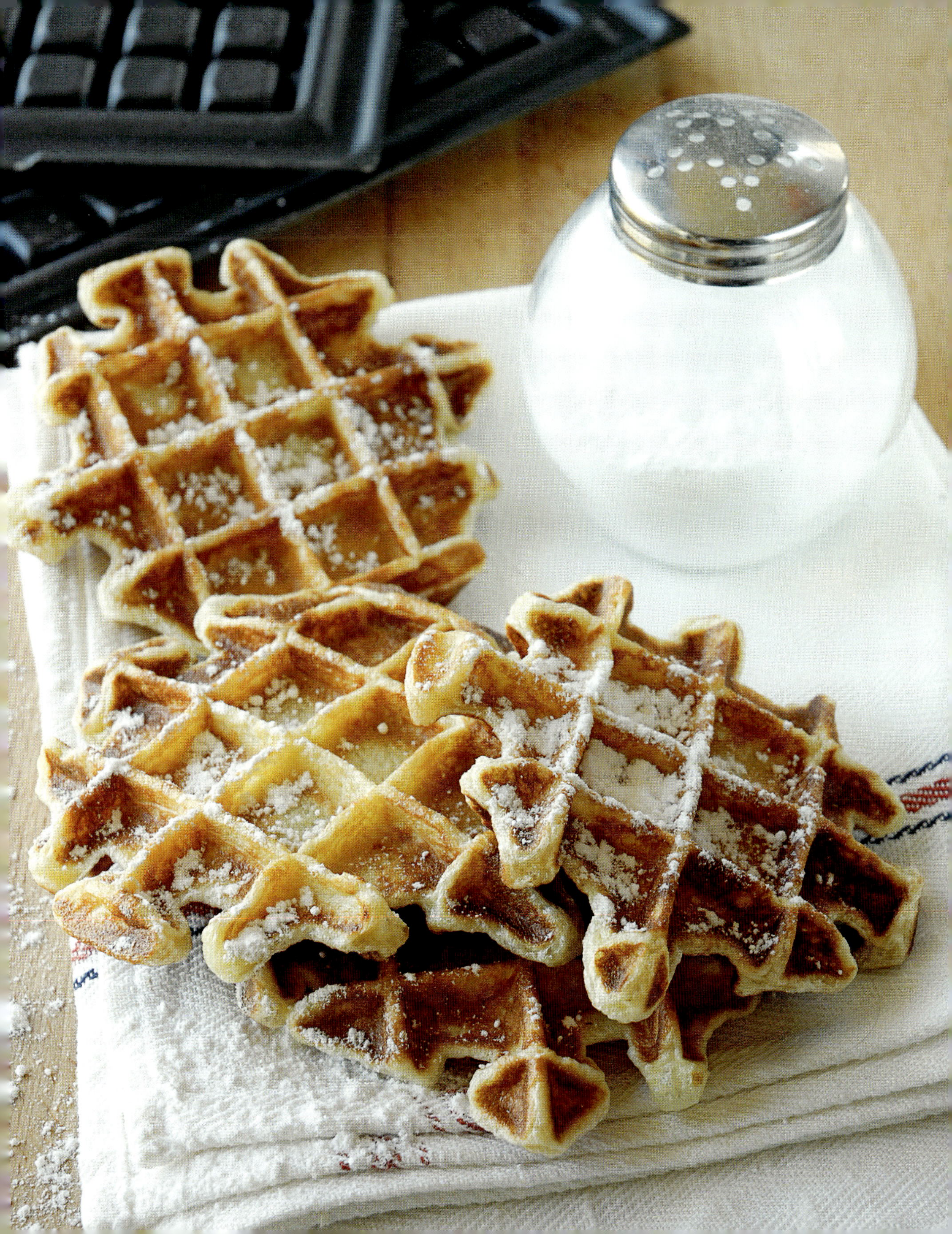

Pets-de-nonne (Choux pastry fritters)

MAKES 30 FRITTERS
PREP TIME: 30 mins.
COOKING TIME: 25 to 30 mins.

- Cooking oil for frying
- Powdered sugar

FOR THE CHOUX PASTRY
- 3 tbsp. water
- 3 tbsp. whole milk
- 1 small teaspoon salt
- 1 small teaspoon sugar
- 3 tbsp. butter
- 8 tbsp. flour
- 2 whole eggs

Prepare the choux pastry: pour the water and milk into a saucepan, add the salt, the sugar and the butter. Bring to a boil, stirring constantly. Add the flour all at once. Stir with a wooden or rubber spatula until the dough is smooth. When it stops sticking to the sides of the pan, continue to work for 2 or 3 minutes, to dry it out a little. Place in a bowl. Break in the eggs one by one, stirring constantly. Lift your spatula from time to time: when the mixture forms a smooth ribbon, it's ready.

Heat the oil to 350° F.

With a teaspoon, take a little choux pastry and drop it into the oil. Fry in batches of about ten, turning them with a spoon to ensure they are golden all over.

After 2 or 3 minutes, remove them with a slotted spoon and lay them on paper towels.

Continue until all the mixture is used up.

Place your pets-de-nonne on a serving dish and sprinkle with powdered sugar before serving.

> To make a change
You can make almond-flavored fritters by adding 1/2 cup slivered almonds to the choux pastry mixture. Serve warm with a fruit coulis.

> Find out more
"Pets-de-nonne" literally means "nuns' farts": they got their name because they are so light and airy!

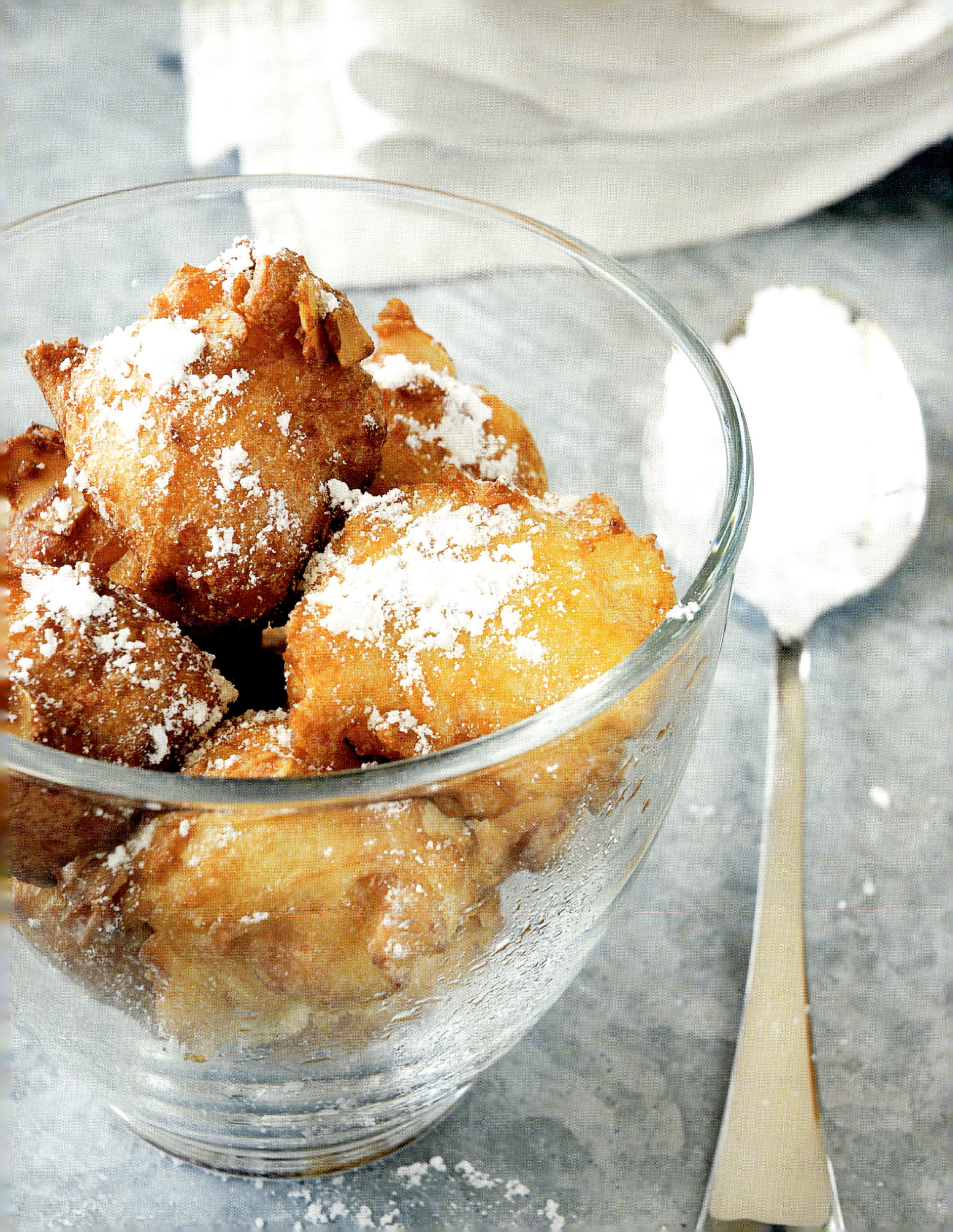

Apple fritters

MAKES 15 TO 20 FRITTERS
PREP TIME: 30 mins.
RESTING TIME: 1 hr
COOKING TIME: 20 mins.

- 4 apples
- oil for frying
- 3 tbsp. sugar

FOR THE BATTER
- 1 cup flour
- 1/2 teaspoon salt
- 1 egg
- 1 tbsp. peanut oil
- 2/3 cup beer

FOR THE CINNAMON SUGAR
- 3 tbsp. sugar
- 1 teaspoon cinnamon

Prepare the batter: pour the flour into a bowl and make a well in the center. Sprinkle the salt around the edge of the flour and break the egg into the center. Add the oil. Mix the egg and oil with a wooden spatula, drawing a little flour into the mixture. Continue to stir, then add the beer. Gradually incorporate the flour, stirring constantly, until the batter is perfectly smooth. Allow to rest for at least one hour.

Peel the apples and remove the cores with a corer. Cut into thick slices.

Heat the oil to 350° F.

Prepare the cinnamon sugar: mix half the sugar with the cinnamon in a bowl. Dip the apple slices into the cinnamon sugar, making sure it sticks.

Using a long fork, dip each apple slice into the batter and drop into the hot oil.

Use a slotted spoon to turn the fritters over and make sure they are cooked on both sides. Remove from the oil and place them on some paper towels to absorb the excess oil. Now put them on a serving platter and sprinkle with sugar. Serve immediately.

> To make a change
You can make these fritters with bananas or even cherries!

> Helpful tip
Never whisk your batter, as this tends to prevent it from adhering to the main ingredients. Always stir it with a wooden spatula.

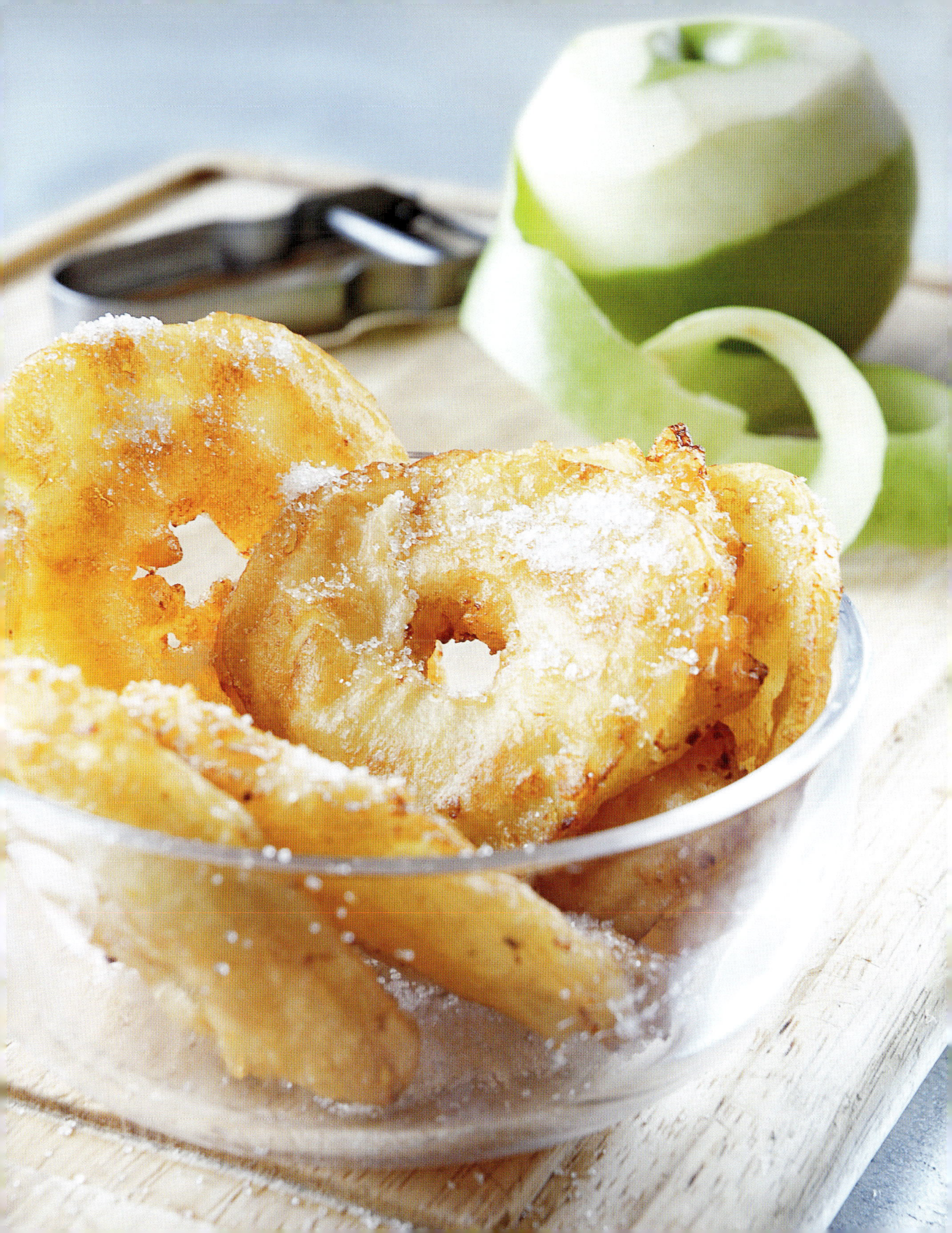

Churros

MAKES 45 CHURROS
PREP TIME: 10 mins.
RESTING TIME: 1 hr
COOKING TIME: 10 mins.

- 1 cup water
- 4 tbsp. butter
- A pinch of salt
- 5 tbsp. sugar
- 2 cups flour
- 2 eggs
- Grapeseed oil for frying

Bring the water to boil in a saucepan with the butter, the salt and 2 pinches of sugar.

Sift the flour into a bowl, make a well in the center and pour the boiling water into the center, stirring with a wooden spoon. You should quickly obtain a thick, smooth-textured dough.

Mix in the beaten eggs and allow the dough to rest for an hour in a cool place.

Heat the oil to 350° F.

Transfer the dough into a pastry bag with a fluted tip. Pipe 5-inch lengths of dough into the oil. Do this in batches so that the churros don't stick together.

Fry until light golden brown, turning them with a slotted spoon. Remove them and drain them on paper towels.

Sprinkle the churros with sugar and serve warm.

> Find out more

Churros are sold on street stands in Mexico and Spain. They're delicious for breakfast, served with sugar.

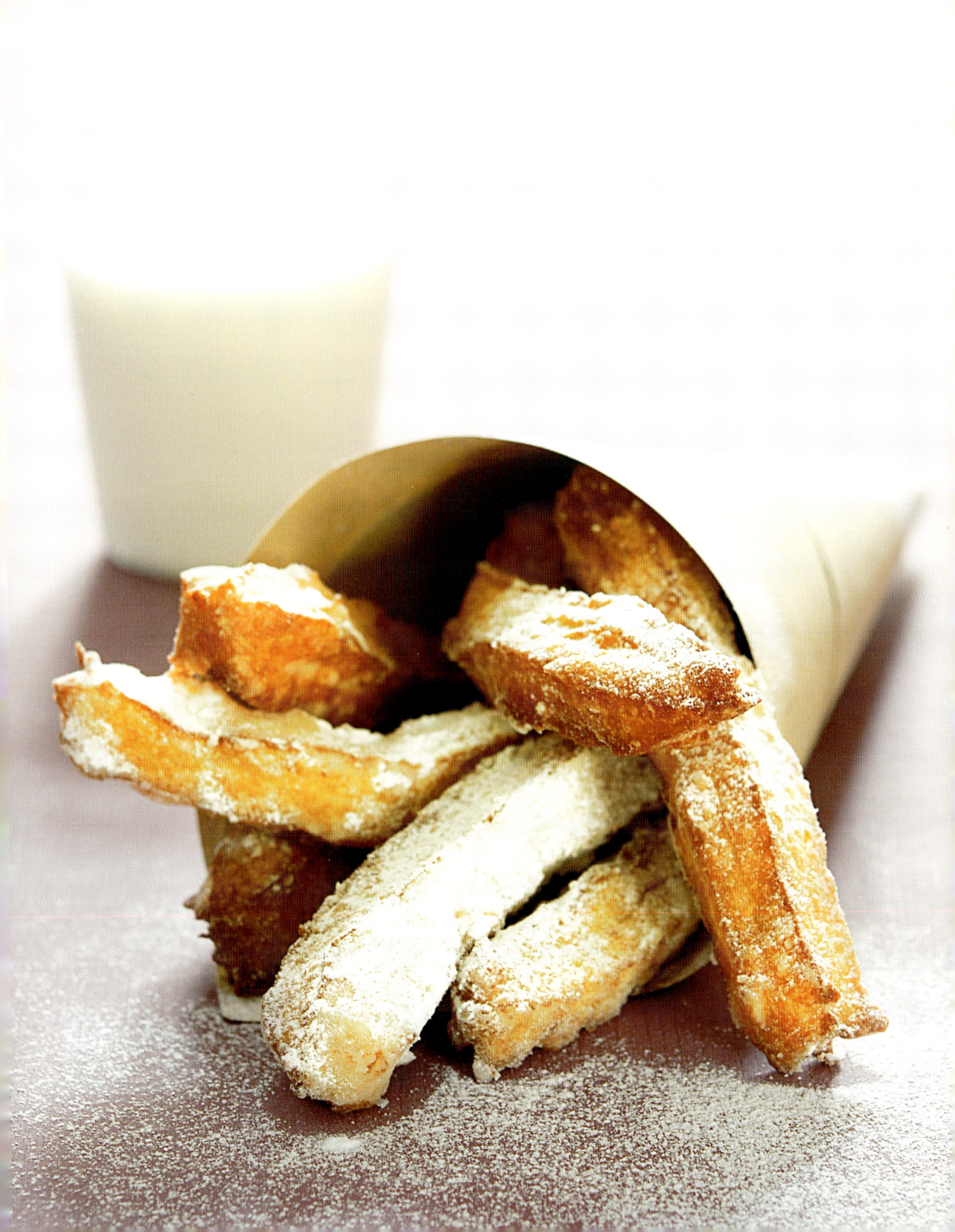

Bugnes (Traditional fritters from Lyon)

MAKES ABOUT 50 BUGNES
PREP TIME: 45 mins.
RESTING TIME: 12 hrs
COOKING TIME: 5 mins.

- 6 tbsp. butter
- 2-1/4 cups flour
- 2 eggs
- 3 tbsp. sugar
- 1 scant tsp. salt
- 2 tbsp. cooking oil
- the finely grated zest of half a lemon
- 3 tbsp. dark rum
- Oil for deep frying
- Powdered sugar

Allow the butter to soften at room temperature.

The day before, sift the flour into a pyramid-shaped mound on your work surface and break the eggs into the center. Add the sugar, salt, oil and softened butter, then mix by hand, gradually drawing the flour into the center. Knead very well until you have a smooth dough that no longer sticks to your fingers. Add the lemon zest and rum and knead again briefly. Put the dough in a bowl and leave to rest in a cool place.

The following day, roll out the dough on a lightly floured surface, as thinly as you can. Cut into 2 x 4-inch rectangles with a knife or a fluted pastry cutting wheel.

Heat the oil and drop in the rectangles one by one. Don't put too many in at one time: this means they'll puff up well. Turn them once to ensure they are golden on both sides.

Drain the bugnes on some paper towels and dust with powdered suger. Serve hot or warm.

> Find out more
Bugnes are traditionally eaten at holiday time in the Lyon region, especially for Mardi Gras.

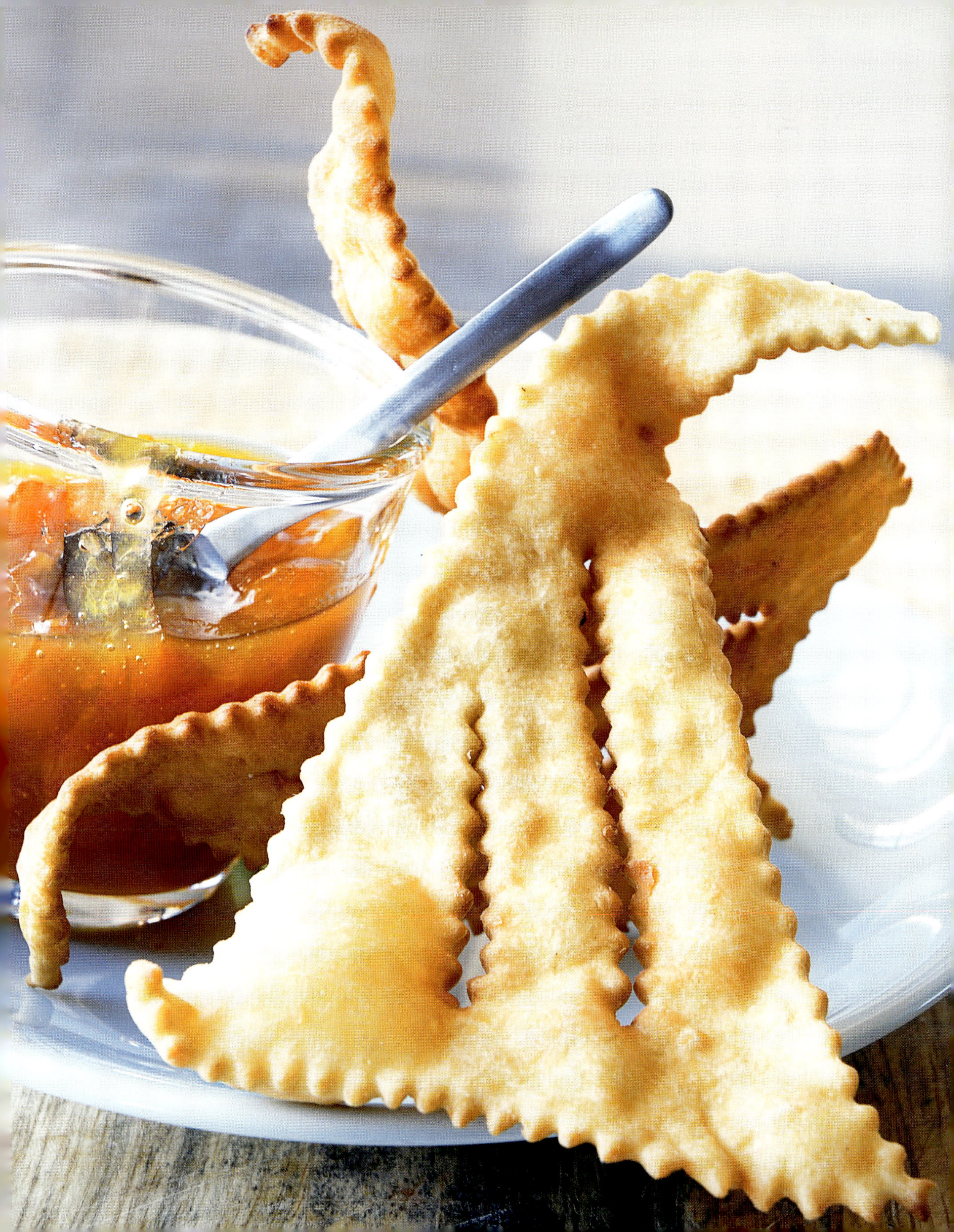

Salt butter caramel

MAKES ABOUT ONE POUND OF CARAMEL
PREP TIME: 5 mins.
COOKING TIME: 15 to 20 mins.

- 1-1/2 tbsp. chilled salted butter
- 1/2 lemon
- 1-1/3 cups sugar
- 7 tbsp. crème fraîche or heavy cream

Cut the butter into pieces and put them in a bowl in the refrigerator. Squeeze the half lemon and strain the juice.

Dissolve the sugar in the lemon juice in a heavy pan. Heat this mixture very gently. Don't add any water and above all, don't stir it! Using a pastry brush dipped in water, brush the sides of the pan to clean off any splashes.

In the meantime, gently heat the crème fraîche or heavy cream in a small heavy saucepan.

When the caramel is a light golden color, remove it from the heat. Pour in the hot cream in a thin stream, stirring constantly. Once the cream has been mixed in, add the butter and stir with a wooden spatula until very smooth.

> Helpful tip

This caramel stays soft if you keep it at room temperature. You can spread it on the crust before adding the fruit when making pies. It keeps for 3 days in the refrigerator, but be aware that it hardens when chilled.

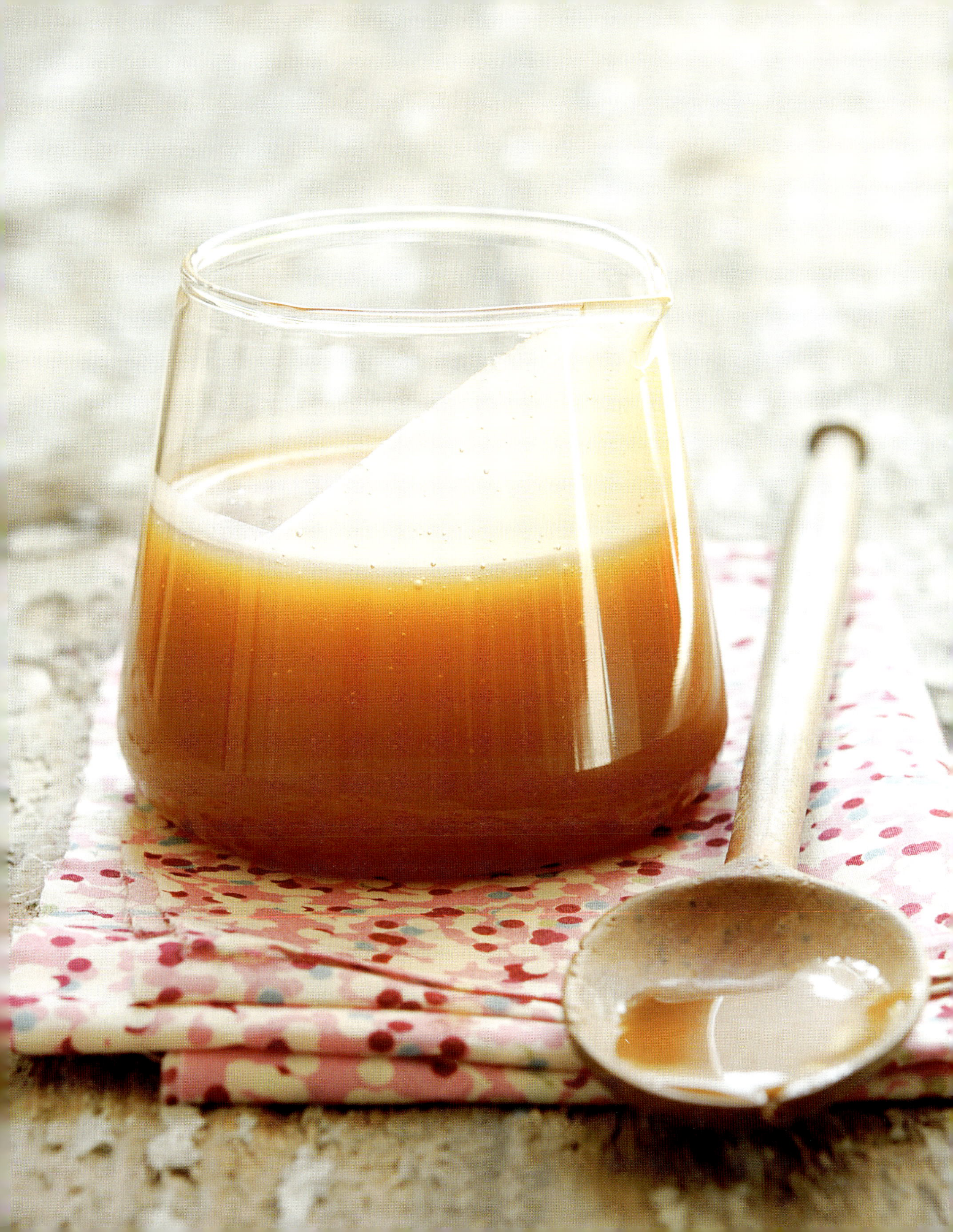

Dulce de leche

MAKES ABOUT 2-1/2 POUNDS
PREP TIME: 5 mins.
COOKING TIME: 4 to 5 hrs

- 4-1/4 cups whole milk
- 2-3/4 lbs granulated sugar
- 1 vanilla bean

Pour the milk and sugar into a saucepan. Place over gentle heat and stir until the sugar has completely dissolved. Place the saucepan over a pot of simmering water, or use a double boiler and cook for 4 to 5 hours, stirring frequently with a wooden spoon, until the mixture concentrates and thickens.

When the mixture has the consistency of thick honey and the color of golden caramel, remove it fom the heat. Stir, put into jars, seal while still hot and sterilize (see p.425).

> Helpful tip
If you don't want to sterilize the jars, keep it in the refrigerator and only prepare a small quantity at a time.

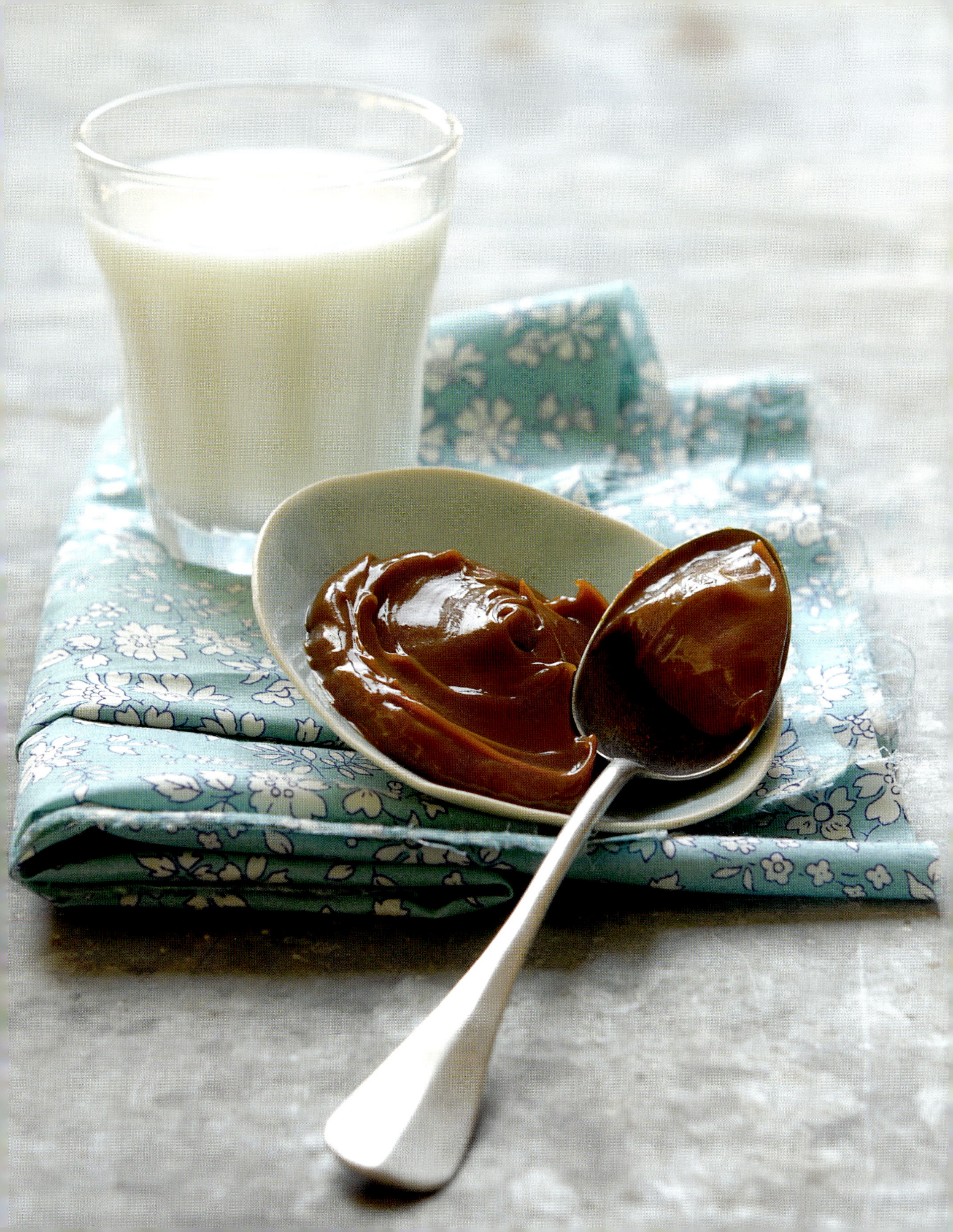

Apricot-vanilla jam

MAKES ABOUT 4 POUNDS
PREP TIME: 30 mins. (over 2 days)
SOAKING TIME: 12 hrs
COOKING TIME: About 20 mins.

- 2-1/2 pounds of firm, ripe apricots
- 4 cups granulated sugar
- 2 vanilla beans
- The juice of one small lemon

TO SEAL THE JARS
- 1 block of paraffin wax for sealing

The day before, rinse the apricots in cold water, dry them, cut them in two and remove the pits. Put the apricots into a bowl, alternating layers of fruit and sugar and distributing the split vanilla beans and lemon juice evenly throughout. Cover and allow to soak for at least 12 hours, until the sugar has completely dissolved.

The following day, transfer the mixture into a heavy pan and bring to a boil over medium heat. Skim the fruit, lower the heat and simmer gently for 20 minutes, stirring frequently with a wooden spoon. When the juice has reduced, check whether it is cooked by putting a drop of jam on a cold plate: it should not run, but set into a firm bead. Alternatively, use a sugar thermometer (220° F). Remove the pan from the heat and pour the jam into jars.

To seal the jars, melt the paraffin wax in a pan, remove from the heat and allow to cool slightly; pour onto the cold jam to a thickness of about 1/4 inch. Allow to harden.

> Find out more
Find out other ways of sealing jars in the step-by-step presentation on p.425.

Mandarin marmalade

MAKES 3 TO 3-1/2 POUNDS
PREP TIME: 40 mins.
COOKING TIME: About 20 mins.

- 2 lbs mandarin oranges with thin, close-fitting peel
- 4 cups granulated sugar
- The juice of one small lemon

TO SEAL THE JARS
- 1 block of paraffin wax

Wash the mandarin oranges, peel them and keep the peel to one side. Separate into segments and remove any pith. Remove the pits and place them in a muslin bag tied with string. Chop the peel, boil for 5 minutes in a pan of water, and strain. Put 1 cup water and the sugar into a heavy pan. Heat gently, stirring constantly, until the sugar has dissolved. Add the peel and the bag of pits and bring to a boil. Skim and cook on high heat to the thread stage (230° F). Add the mandarin oranges and lemon juice, bring to a boil again, skim once more and boil vigorously for 10 minutes until the fruit is translucent and stops rising to the surface. Check with a sugar thermometer (220° F) or plate (pour a drop of marmalade onto a cold plate: it should set into a firm bead). Remove from the heat. Take out the bag of pits. Pour into jars.

To seal the jars, melt the paraffin wax in a pan, remove from the heat and allow to cool slightly; pour onto the cold marmalade to a thickness of about 1/4 inch. Allow to harden.

> Find out more
Find out other ways of sealing jars in the step-by-step presentation on p.425.

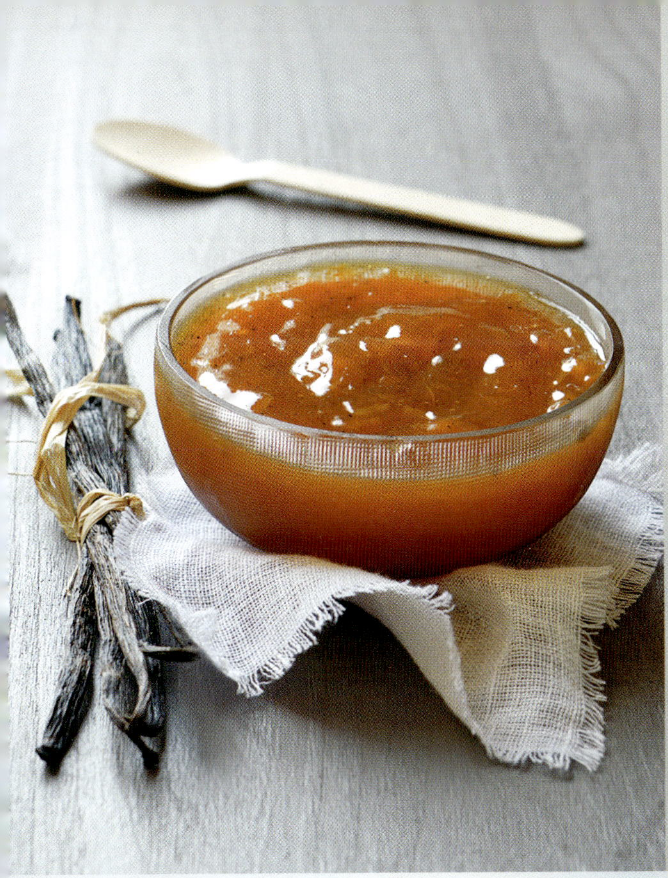
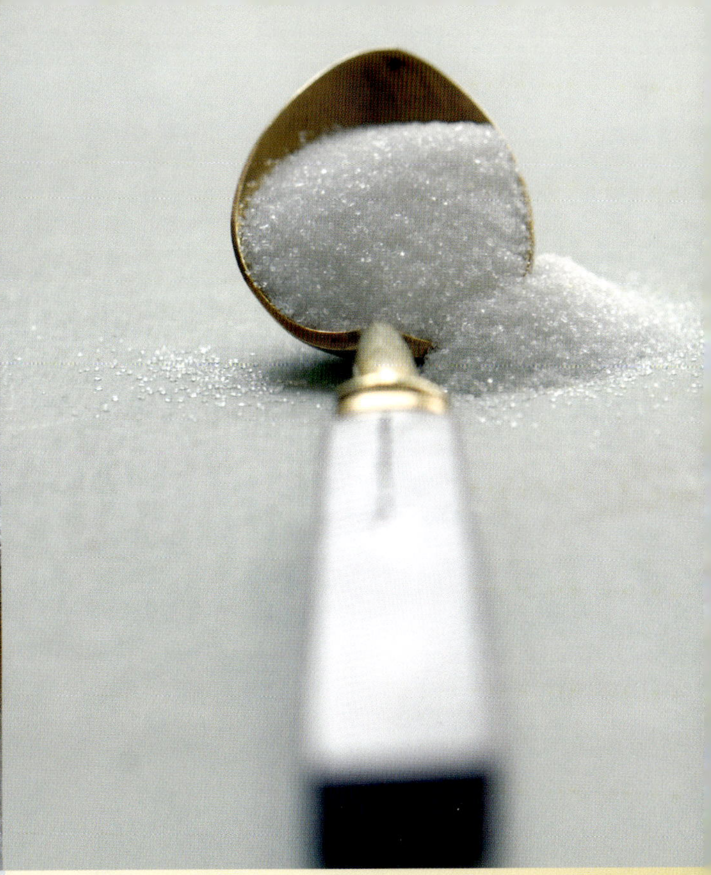
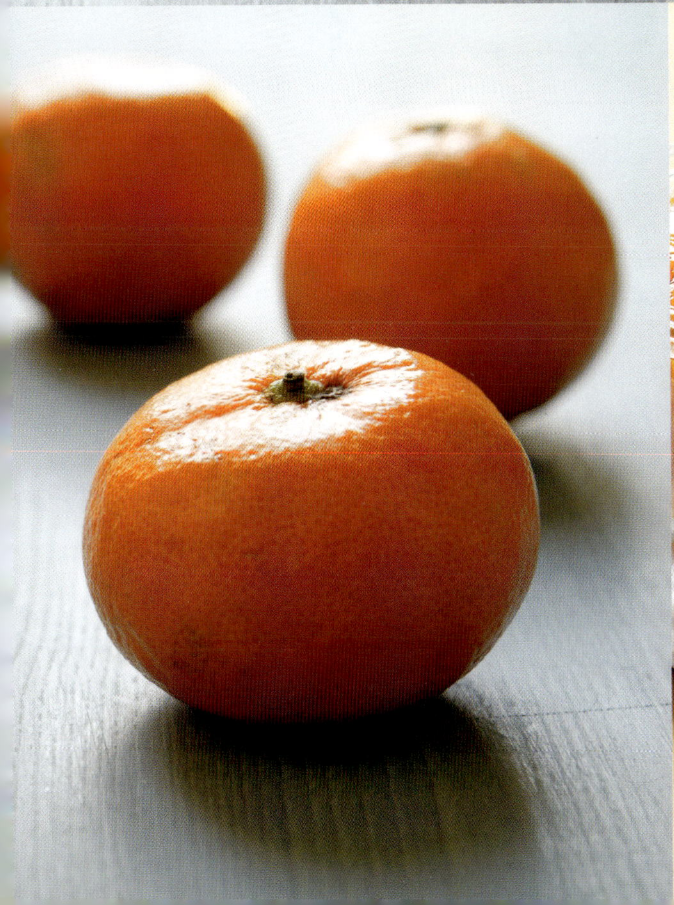
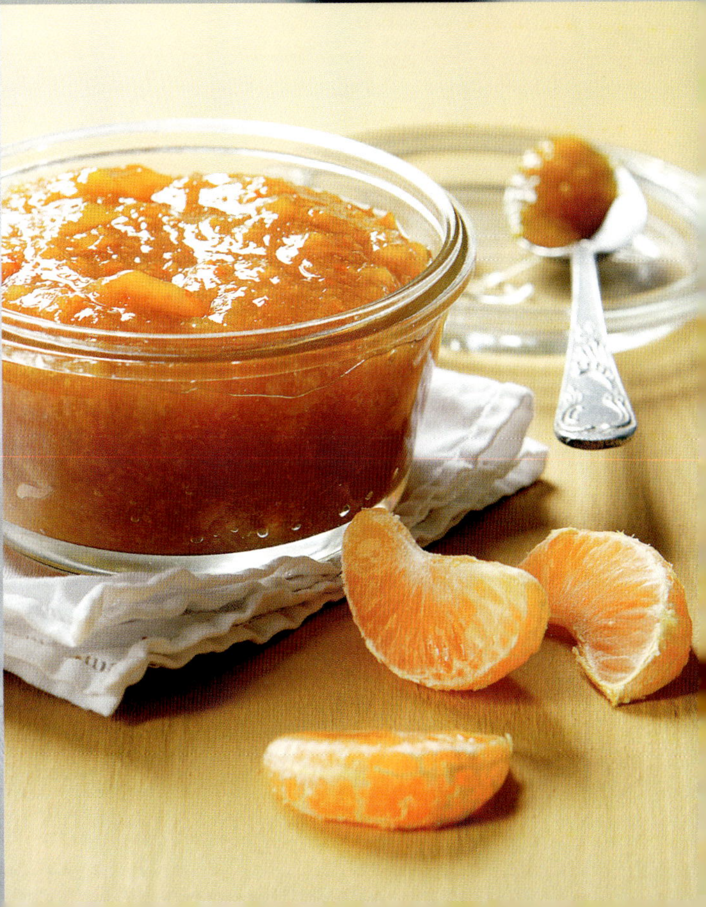

Blueberry and caramel jam

MAKES 3 TO 3-1/2 POUNDS
PREP TIME: 20 mins.
COOKING TIME: About 20 mins.
SOAKING TIME: 24 hrs

- 2-1/4 lbs. blueberries
- 3-1/4 lbs. sugar
- The juice of one small lemon

TO SEAL THE JARS
- 1 block of paraffin wax

The day before, pick through the blueberries, rinse them quickly and dry them. Put them in a heavy pan with 4 cups sugar, 1 cup water and the lemon juice. Bring gently to a boil, stirring constantly, and cook for 2 minutes. Transfer into a bowl, cover with plastic wrap or parchment paper, and leave to soak in a cold place for 24 hours.

The following day, prepare a caramel with 3 cups sugar and 1-1/4 cups water. Rub the blueberries through a sieve. Return them to the pan and cook for 15 minutes. Pour the caramel over the blueberries, mix well, and pour into jars.

To seal the jars, melt the paraffin wax in a pan, remove from the heat and allow to cool slightly; pour onto the cold jam to a thickness of about 1/4 inch. Allow to harden.

> **Find out more**
Find out other ways of sealing jars in the step-by-step presentation on p.425.

Fig and honey jam

MAKES 3 TO 3-1/2 POUNDS
PREP TIME: 15 mins.
SOAKING TIME: 12 hrs
COOKING TIME: About 10 mins.

- 2-1/4 pounds of small green figs
- A pinch of cinnamon
- 1/2 vanilla bean
- 2-1/2 cups granulated sugar
- The juice of one small lemon
- 3/4 cup honey

TO SEAL THE JARS
- 1 block of paraffin wax

The day before, rinse the figs and remove the stalks. Cut each one into six pieces and put in a bowl with the cinnamon, the split vanilla bean, the sugar and the lemon juice. Mix well, cover and allow to soak in a cool place for 12 hours.

The following day, transfer the fruit into a heavy pan. Add the honey and stir gently. Bring slowly to a boil, skim and allow to boil for about 10 minutes, until the mixture thickens and the figs remain below the surface of the syrup. Check that the jam is cooked with a sugar thermometer (220° F) or use the plate method (pour a drop onto a cold plate: it should not run but set into a firm bead), and remove from the heat. Pour into jars.

To seal the jars, melt the paraffin wax in a pan, remove from the heat and allow to cool slightly; pour onto the cold jam to a thickness of about 1/4 inch. Allow to harden.

> **Find out more**
Find out other ways of sealing jars in the step-by-step presentation on p.425.

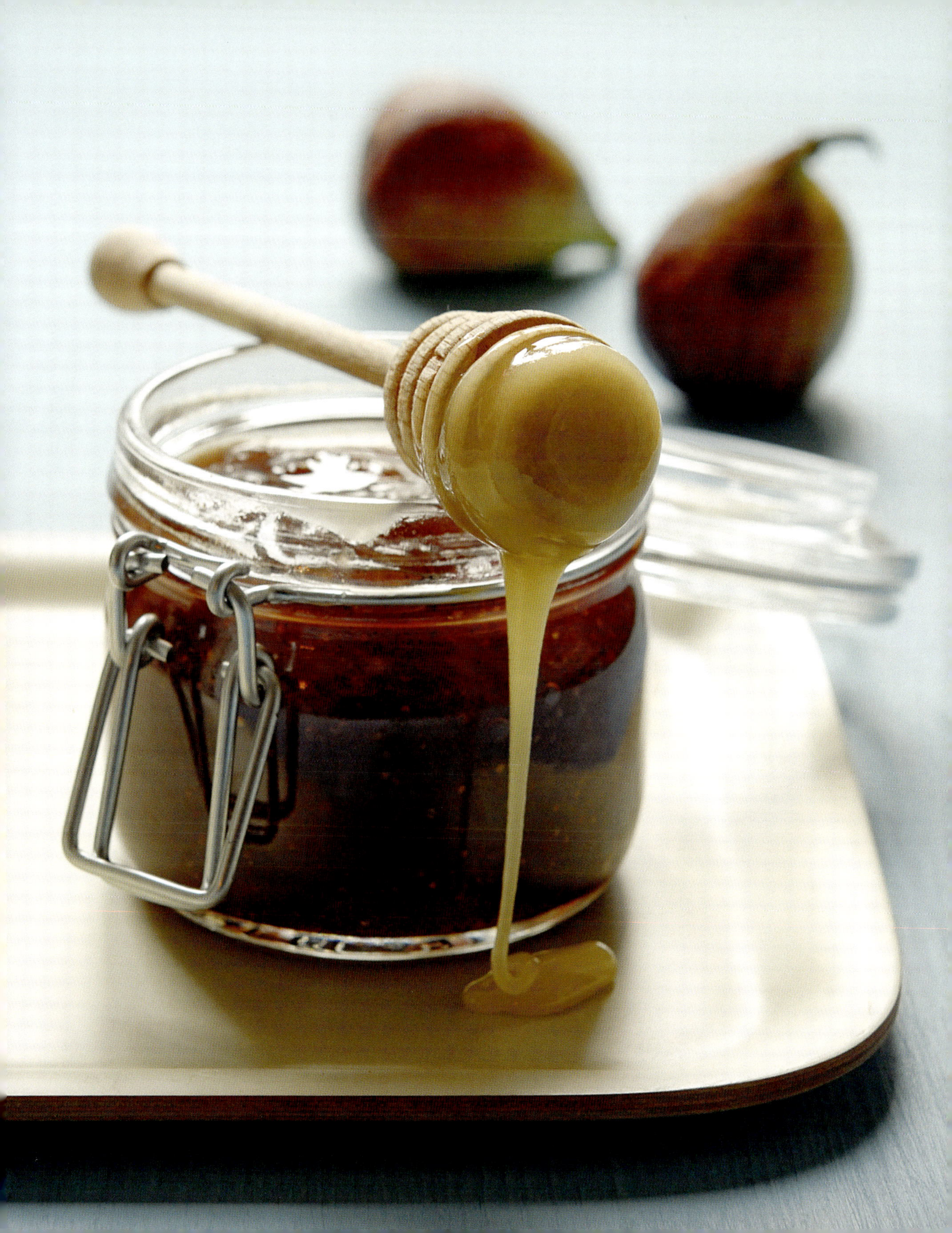

Cherry jam

MAKES 3 TO 3-1/2 POUNDS
PREP TIME: 20 mins.
COOKING TIME: About 15 mins.

- 2-1/2 lbs. cherries (2 lbs. pitted weight)
- 2-1/4 lbs. granulated sugar
- The juice of 1 small lemon
- 2/3 cup pectin-rich apple juice (or use regular apple juice and add one packet pectin powder)

TO SEAL THE JARS
- 1 block of paraffin wax

Rinse the cherries, dry them carefully, remove the stems and pit them. Pour the sugar, 1 cup of water and the lemon juice into a heavy pan and place over gentle heat, stirring until the sugar dissolves. Bring to a boil, skim and simmer until it reaches the thread stage (230° F on a sugar thermometer).

Add the cherries and apple juice, stir and bring to a boil again. Skim and boil vigorously for 10 minutes, until the fruit is translucent and stops floating to the surface. Check with a sugar thermometer (220° F) or plate (pour a drop of jam onto a cold plate: it should set into a firm bead). Remove from the heat.

Pour into jars: if using screwtops, screw onto the jar while it is still hot, then invert the jar until quite cold. If using wax, melt the paraffin wax in a pan, remove from the heat and allow to cool slightly; pour onto the cold jam to a thickness of about 1/4 inch. Allow to harden.

> **Find out more**
Find out other ways of sealing jars in the step-by-step presentation on p.425.

Rhubarb and ginger jam

MAKES 3 TO 3-1/2 POUNDS
PREP TIME: 30 mins.
COOKING TIME: 20 mins.

- 2-1/2 pounds rhubarb
- 1 oz. fresh root ginger
- 5 tbsp. candied ginger
- 2-1/4 lbs. granulated sugar
- The juice of one small lemon
- 7 oz. pectin-rich apple juice (or use regular apple juice and add one packet pectin powder)

TO SEAL THE JARS
- 1 block of paraffin wax

Wash and peel the rhubarb and cut into one-inch pieces. Peel the ginger root and finely chop the candied ginger.

Put the sugar, 1-1/4 cups water and the fresh ginger into a heavy pan and heat gently until the sugar dissolves. Bring to a boil, skim and cook to the thread stage (230° F on a sugar thermometer). Add the rhubarb, the crystallized ginger, the apple juice and the lemon juice. Bring back to a boil, skim and boil on a high heat for about 15 minutes, stirring until it sets.

Check with a sugar thermometer (220° F) or a plate (pour a drop of jam onto a cold plate: it should set firm). Remove from the heat. Take out the piece of fresh ginger. Pour into jars.

To seal the jars, melt the paraffin wax in a pan, remove from the heat and allow to cool slightly; pour onto the cold jam to a thickness of about 1/4 inch. Allow to harden.

> **Find out more**
Find out other ways of sealing jars in the step-by-step presentation on p.425.

Rhubarb

Rose petal jelly

MAKES 3 TO 3-1/2 POUNDS
PREP TIME: 30 mins.
(over 2 days)
SOAKING TIME: 12 hrs
COOKING TIME: About 15 mins.

- 1 lb. untreated rose petals
- 2-1/4 lbs. granulated sugar
- 3 tbsp. rose water
- 1-1/2 cups slivered almonds

TO SEAL THE JARS
- 1 block of paraffin

The day before, snip off the white base of each rose petal with scissors, put the petals in a bowl with 1-1/4 cup cold water, and leave to soak overnight until the water is colored (red roses give the best color).

The following day, strain the petals and pour the soaking juice into a heavy pan. Add the sugar. Bring to a boil, stirring constantly, skim the syrup and add the petals. Boil again for one minute.

Add the rose water and simmer for 5 minutes longer until the jelly thickens.

Remove the pan from the heat, add the almonds and allow to rest for 10 minutes. Bring to a boil once more, stir and pour into jars.

To seal the jars, melt the paraffin wax in a pan, remove from the heat and allow to cool slightly; pour onto the cold jelly to a thickness of about 1/4 inch. Allow to harden.

> Helpful tip

Sealing jars with paraffin is an old-fashioned but efficient way of sealing jars. Wash the paraffin wax disks carefully after use: you can use them again. Find out other ways of sealing jars in the step-by-step presentation on p.425.

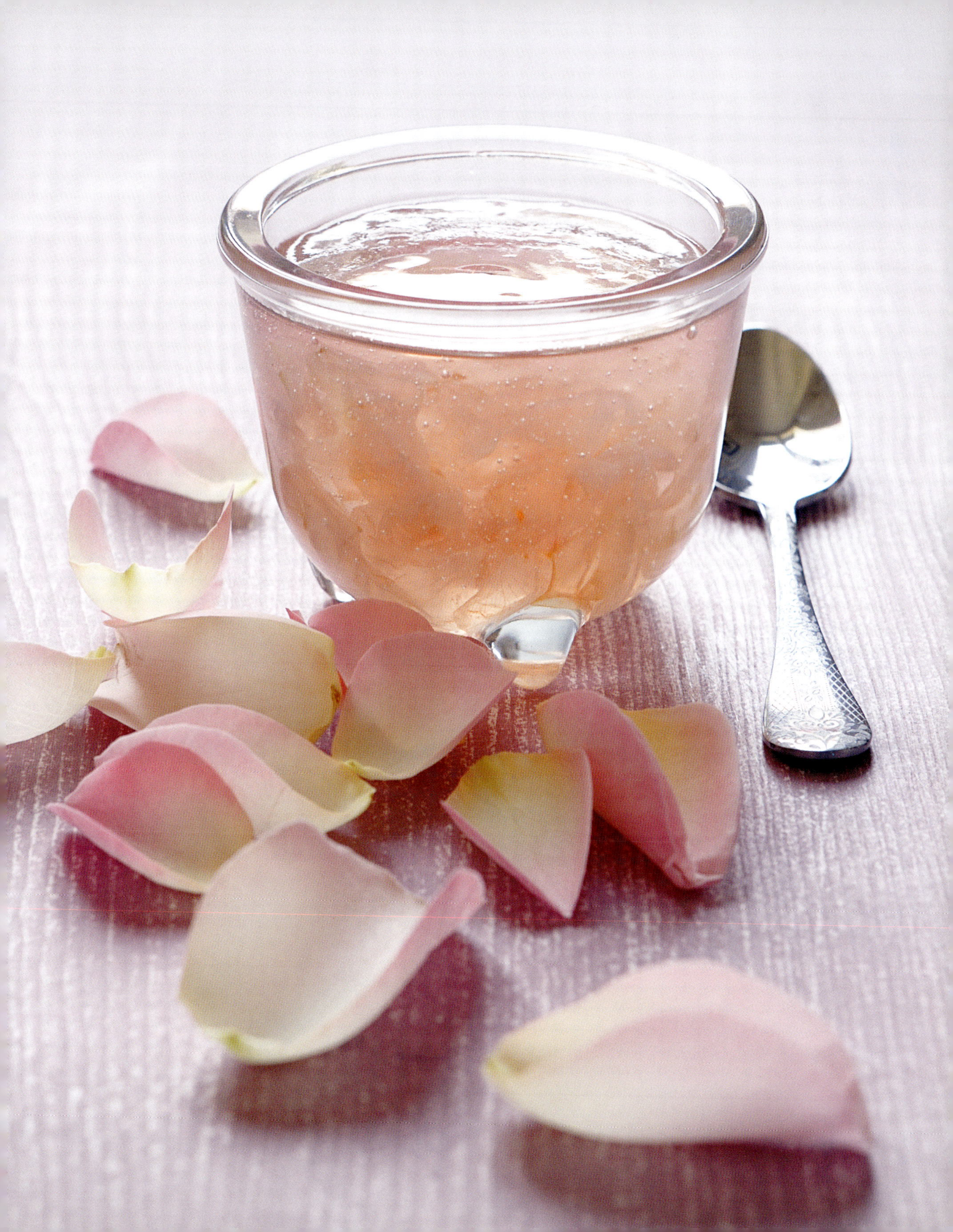

Kiwi jam

MAKES ABOUT 3-1/2 POUNDS
PREP TIME: 30 mins. (over 2 days)
SOAKING TIME: 12 hrs
COOKING TIME: About 15 mins.

- 2-1/2 pounds kiwis (peeled weight)
- 4-1/2 cups granulated sugar
- The juice of 4 limes
- 6 tbsp. pectin-rich apple juice (or use regular apple juice and add one packet pectin powder)

TO SEAL THE JARS
- 1 block of paraffin wax

The day before, peel the kiwis and cut into cubes. Mix with the sugar and lime juice, leave to soak in a bowl until the sugar has absorbed some of the liquid. Transfer the mixture into a heavy pan, bring to a boil and remove from the heat. Pour back into the bowl, cover with plastic wrap and leave to soak for 12 hours.

The following day, put the mixture back into the heavy pan. Add the apple juice and bring to a boil, skim and cook over high heat, stirring constantly, for about 10 minutes, until the fruit disintegrates and the mixture thickens.

Test with a thermometer (220° F) or plate (a drop of jam poured onto a cold plate should set into a firm bead), and remove from the heat.

Pour into jars and seal them: gently melt the paraffin, remove from the heat and allow to cool slightly. Pour onto the cold jam to a thickness of about 1/4 inch and allow to harden.

> Helpful tip
Find out other ways of sealing jars on p.425.

"Quickie" raspberry jam

MAKES ABOUT 3-1/2 POUNDS
PREP TIME: 10 mins.
COOKING TIME: About 5 mins.

- 2 lbs. raspberries
- 2 lbs. granulated sugar
- The juice of one small lemon

TO SEAL THE JARS
- 1 block of paraffin wax

Pick through the raspberries but don't wash them. Purée them quickly in a blender. Put the purée in a heavy pan with the lemon juice and bring to a boil. When it starts to boil, add the sugar. Bring to a boil again, stirring well. Skim the jam and cook for about 5 minutes.

Check with a thermometer (220° F) or a plate (a drop of jam poured onto a cold plate should set into a firm bead), and remove from the heat.

Pour into jars and seal them: gently melt the paraffin, remove from the heat and allow to cool slightly. Pour onto the cold jam to a thickness of about 1/4 inch and allow to harden.

> Helpful tip
Always fill the jars while the jam is hot and easy to pour. The jars must be very clean.

> Helpful tip
Find out other ways of sealing jars on p.425.

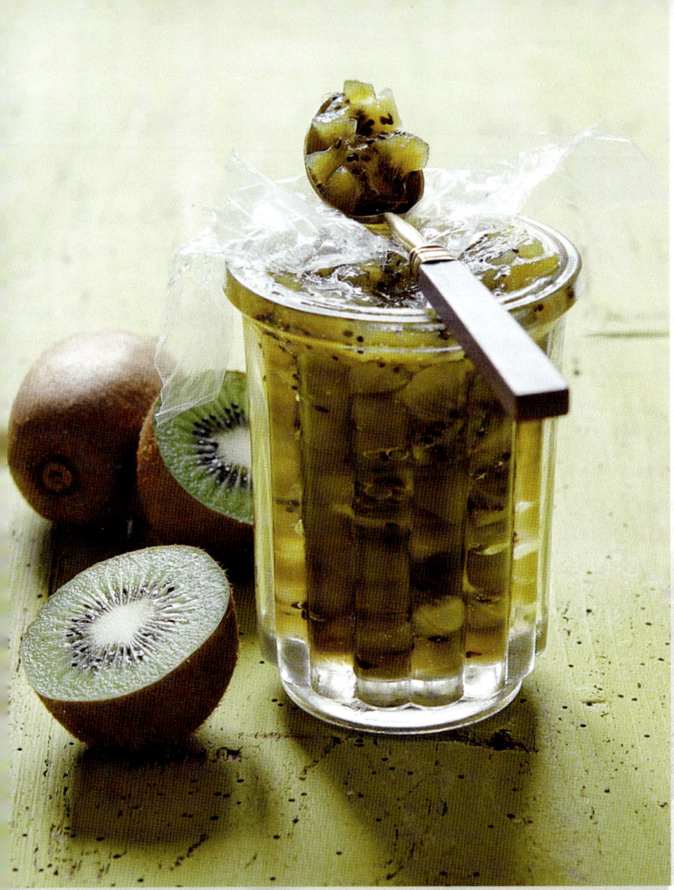
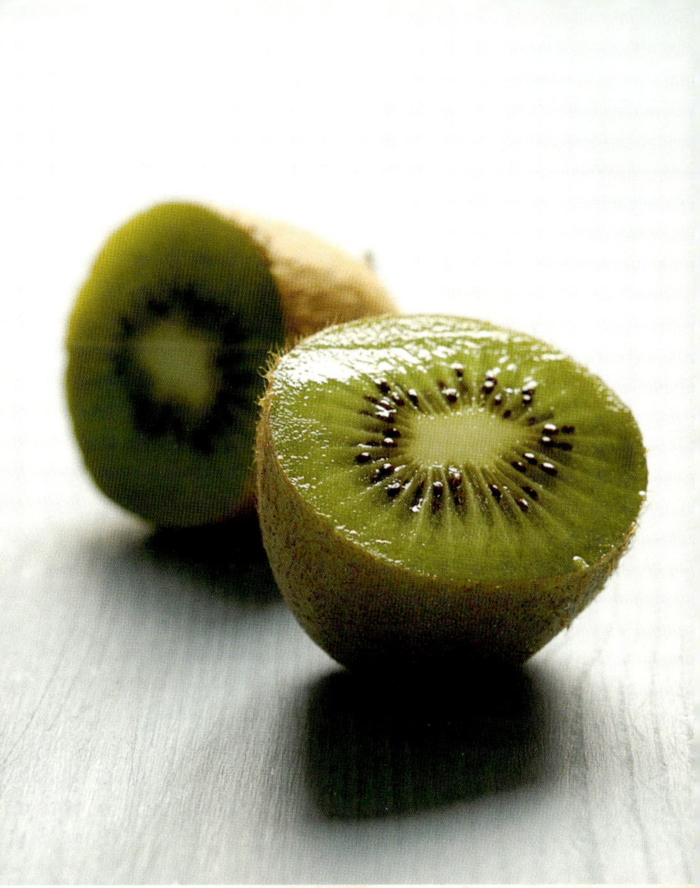
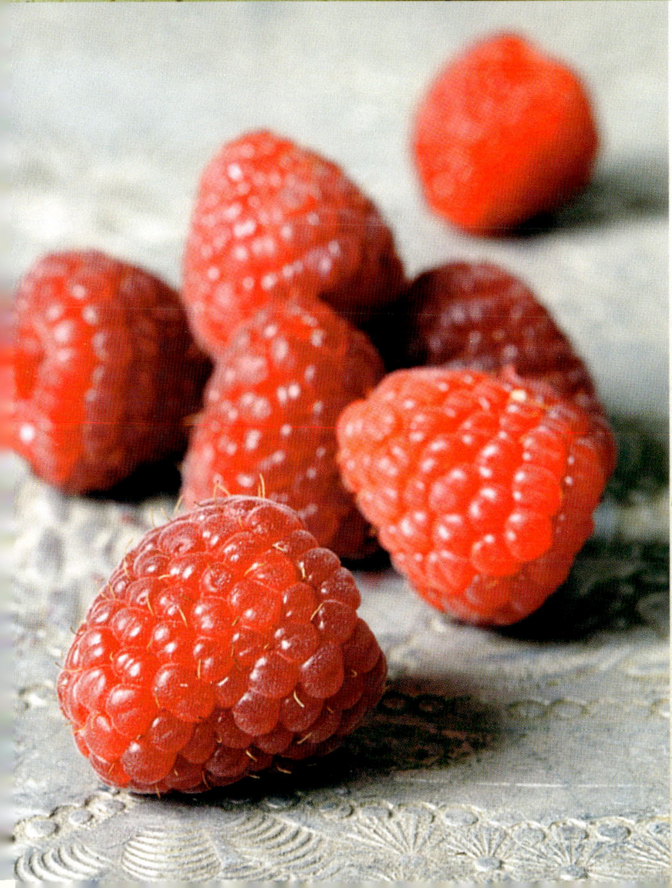
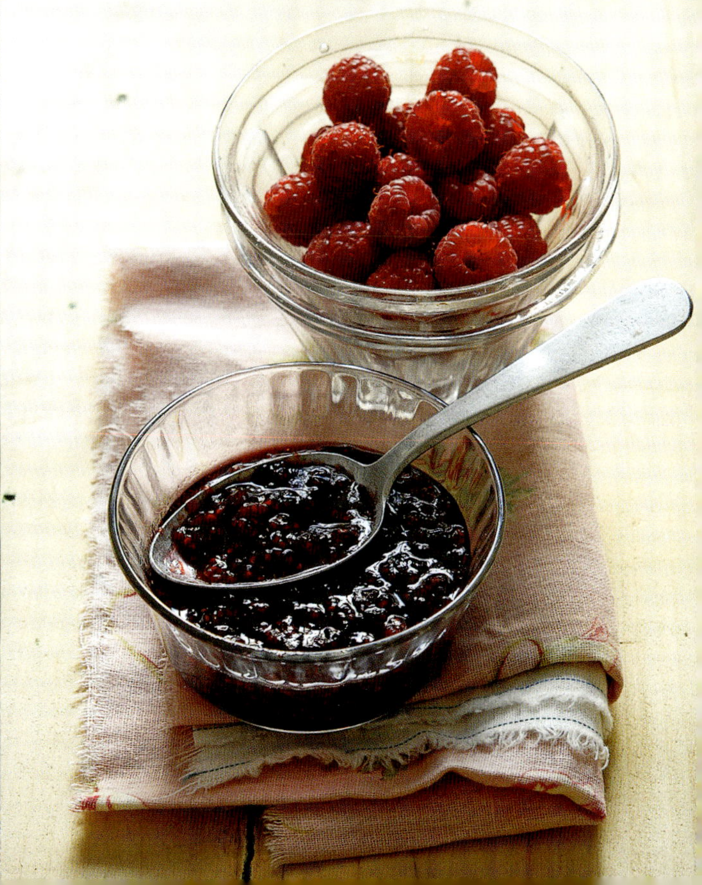

Quince jelly

Rub the fuzz off the quince with a cloth, then rinse them. Cut into pieces but do not remove the core or pits. Put the fruit into a pan with 4 pints water and cook over low heat for 30 to 40 minutes, until soft. Transfer to a large fine sieve and allow the juice to drip slowly into a bowl without exerting any pressure on the fruit.

Weigh the juice and set aside the same weight of sugar. Mix the quince juice, the sugar and the lemon juice in the heavy pan and heat gently, stirring constantly, until the sugar has dissolved. Bring to a boil, skim and boil quite fast for about 10 minutes, until the juice reaches jellying point. Check with a thermometer (220° F) or a plate (a drop of jelly should set into a firm bead on a cold plate). Remove from the heat.

Pour into jars and seal with plastic wrap: dampen squares of plastic wrap with water and stretch them over the jars with the damp side facing upward. Secure with an elastic band.

> Helpful tip
See the various different ways of sealing jam jars on p.425.

MAKES ABOUT 3-1/2 POUNDS OF JELLY
PREP TIME: 15 mins.
COOKING TIME: About 50 mins.
FILTERING TIME: 3 to 4 hrs

- 2-1/4 lbs quince
- The same weight of granulated sugar as fruit juice
- The juice of one small lemon

Black currant jelly

Rinse the black currants in cold water, remove the stems. Put them in a saucepan with 1 cup of water and bring to a boil. Cook over a high heat until the berries burst. Pour into a large fine sieve and allow the juice to drip slowly into a bowl for 2 to 3 hours. Weigh the juice and set aside the same weight of sugar.

Heat together the sugar, lemon juice and 1 cup water in a heavy pan, stirring until the sugar dissolves. Bring to a boil, skim and cook to the soft ball stage (240° F on the sugar thermometer). Add the black currant juice, stirring vigorously, skim again and cook over high heat for 5 minutes, until the juice reaches jellying point. Check with a thermometer (220° F) or a plate (a drop of jelly should set into a firm bead on a cold plate). Remove from the heat.

Pour into jars and seal with plastic wrap: dampen squares of plastic wrap with water and stretch them over the jars with the damp side facing upward. Secure with an elastic band.

> Helpful tip
See the various different ways of sealing jam jars on p.425.

MAKES ABOUT 3-1/2 POUNDS OF JELLY
PREP TIME: 20 mins.
FILTERING TIME: 2 to 3 hrs
COOKING TIME: About 10 mins.

- 3-1/3 lbs. black currants
- Same weight of granulated sugar as the juice obtained from the fruit
- The juice of one small lemon

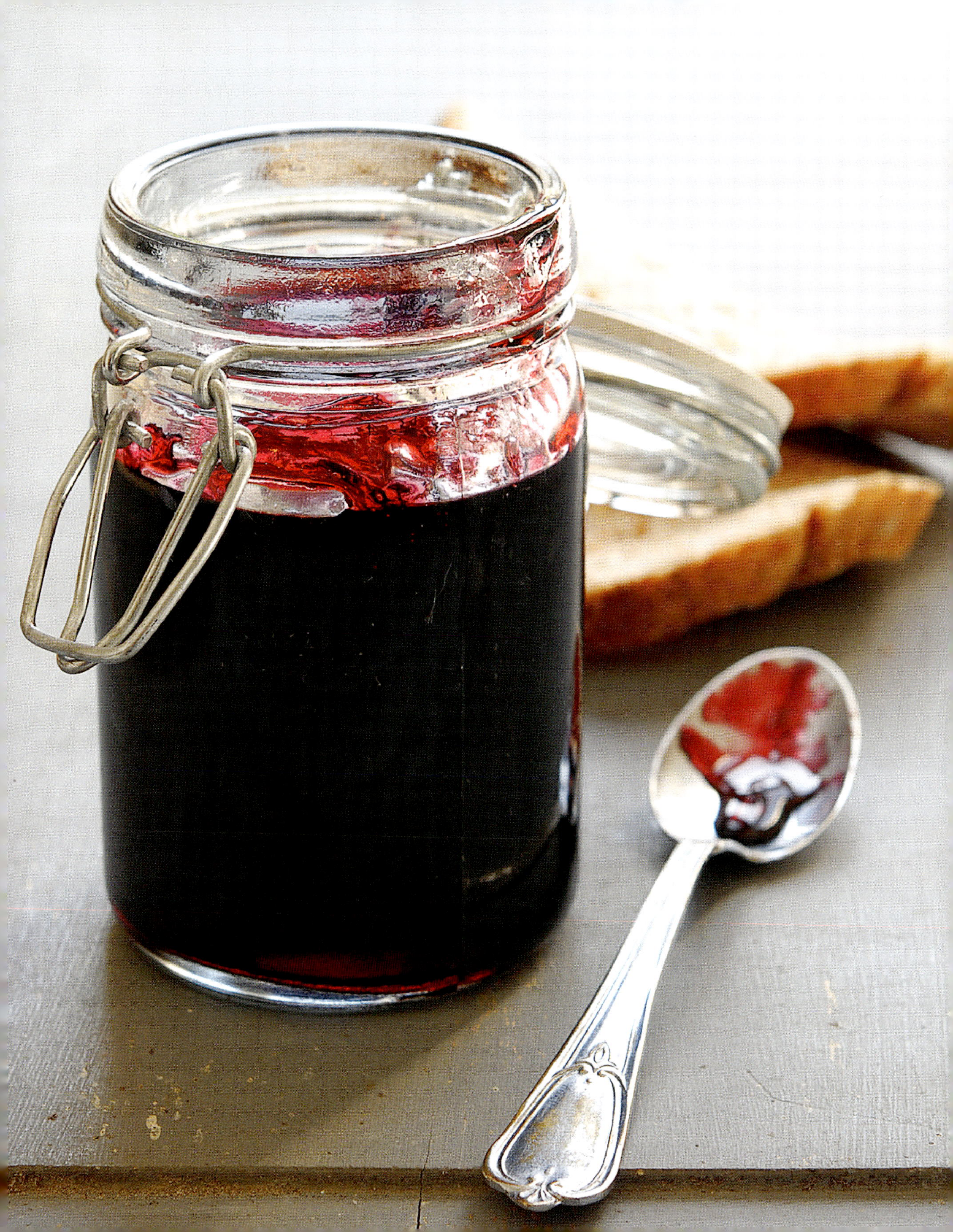

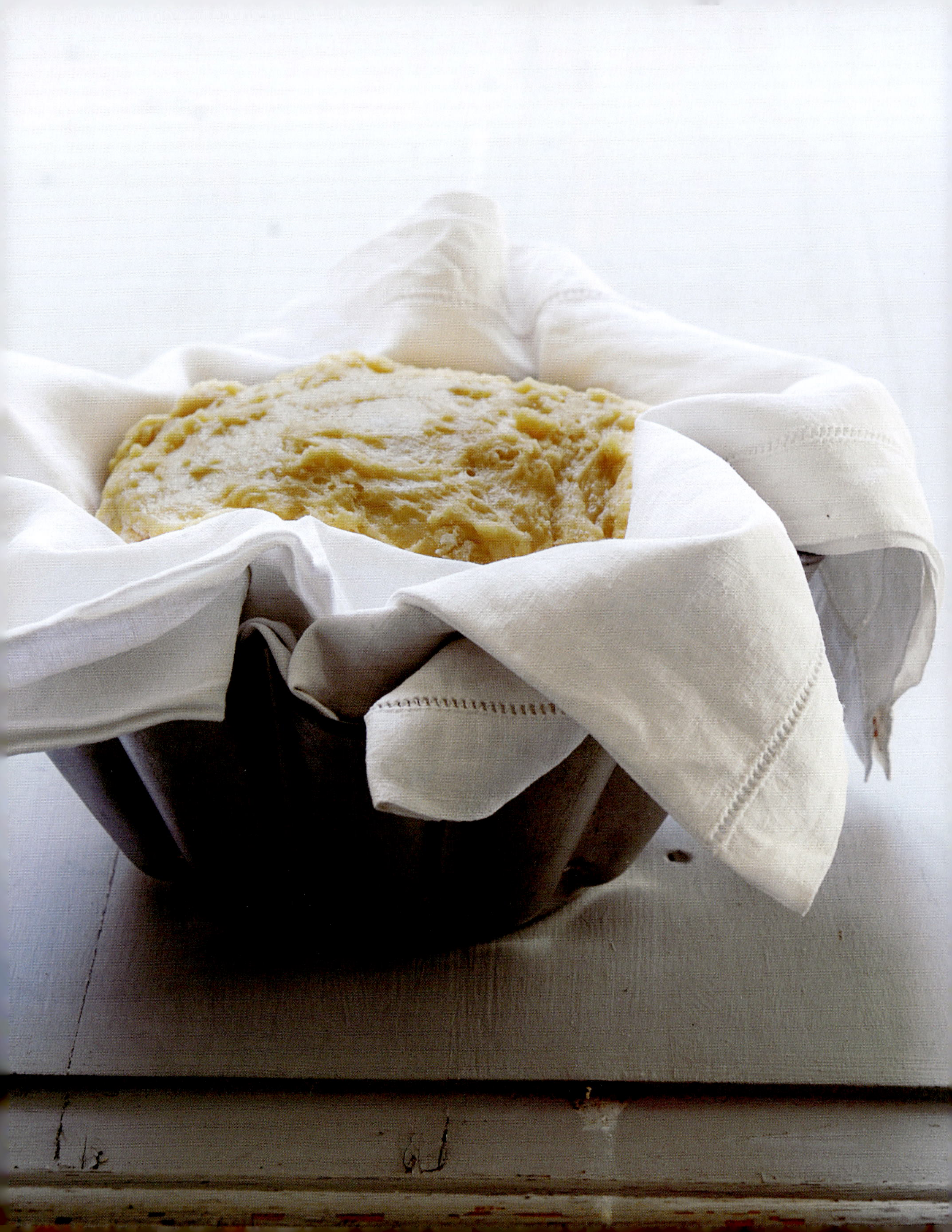

Pastry workshop

Lining tartlet molds	398
Blind baking	398
Shortcrust pastry	399
Pâte sablée	400
Sweet pastry	401
Puff pastry	402
Leavened dough	404
Choux pastry	405
Crêpe batter	406
Fritter batter	407
Génoise sponge cake	408
Almond dacquoise meringue	409
Pastry cream	410
Crème anglaise	411
Butter cream	412
Crème Chiboust	413
Pastillage	414
Chantilly whipped cream	415
French meringue	416
Italian meringue	417
Chocolate sauce	418
Chocolate frosting	419
Tempering chocolate	420
Chocolate curls and shavings	421
Caramel	422
Simple caramel decorations	423
Raspberry coulis	423
Jams and marmalades:	
one-stage cooking	424
two-stage cooking	424
Jam: cooking method	425
Sealing jam jars	425

Lining tartlet molds

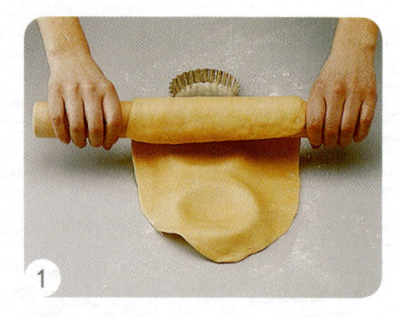

1 Butter your tartlet molds and arrange them in rows. Roll out the dough. Hang the dough over the rolling pin, then unroll it over the top of the molds.

2 Roll the rolling pin over the tops of the molds to trim off the excess dough.

3 Press the dough into the molds using a floured ball of dough. The process is the same for all kinds of mold.

Blind baking

1 Cut a circle of parchment paper to fit your baking pan.

2 Put the dough in the baking pan and pick it with a fork. Lay the parchment paper on top and pour in a layer of ceramic baking beans (or dried peas, beans or lentils). Bake according to the recipe.

3 Remove the beans and paper. Brush the crust with beaten egg and bake for 3 to 5 minutes.

Shortcrust pastry

Makes about half a pound of pastry

PREP TIME: 10 mins.
RESTING TIME: At least 30 mins.

- 7 tbsp. softened butter
- 1-1/4 cups sifted flour
- A pinch of salt
- 2 tbsp. sugar (optional)
- 5 tbsp. cold water

❶ Cut the butter into very small pieces. Put the flour in a bowl and make a well in the center. Add the salt, then the pieces of butter.

❷ Quickly rub in the ingredients with your fingertips. Add just enough water (1 tbsp. at a time) to make into a stiff dough, then quickly knead until supple and smooth. The dough should be neither too soft nor too sticky.

❸ Very lightly flour your work surface. Place the dough on it and flatten it with the heel of your hand (do not knead at this point).

❹ Form the dough into a ball and flatten it between your hands. Wrap in plastic wrap and leave to rest for at least 30 minutes in the refrigerator.

> **Find out more**
> Blind bake this pastry at 350° F for 10 to 15 minutes.

LAROUSSE ON PASTRY • 399

Pâte sablée (Rich, crumbly dessert pastry)

Makes about 1 pound
PREP TIME: 10 mins.
RESTING TIME: At least 30 mins.

- 2/3 cup sugar
- 2 cups flour
- 9 tbsp. softened butter
- 1 egg

❶ Sift the flour onto a work surface. Cut the butter into small pieces and rub into the flour with your fingertips until the mixture has the consistency of fine breadcrumbs and all the pieces of butter have disappeared.

❷ Make a well in the center and break the egg into it. Add the sugar and mix together with your fingertips (do not knead).

❸ Flatten the dough with the heel of your hand, pressing down and away from you, to give it an even texture.

❹ Make into a ball and flatten it between your hands. Wrap in plastic wrap and allow to rest for at least 30 minutes in the refrigerator.

> **To make a change**
> You can flavor this pastry according to how you are going to use it: add the zest of a lemon, a little rum, some almond or vanilla extract, or some cocoa powder to the flour.

Sweet pastry

Makes about 1/2 pound of pastry

PREP TIME: 10 mins.
RESTING TIME: At least 30 mins.

- 1 egg
- 1/3 cup powdered sugar
- 2 tbsp. ground almonds
- A pinch of salt
- 1/4 cup softened butter
- 1 scant cup sifted flour

❶ Break the egg into a bowl and beat it with a fork. Add the sugar, the ground almonds and the salt. Beat with a wooden spatula until the mixture turns pale yellow and frothy. Cut the butter into very small pieces.

❷ Pour in the sifted flour all at once and mix quickly with the spatula.

❸ Rub in the flour with your fingertips. The mixture should not stick together but form small grains the consistency of fine breadcrumbs.

❹ Place the mixture on a floured work surface. Dot with the butter and knead with your hands to incorporate the butter. Form the dough into a ball, wrap in plastic wrap and allow to rest for at least 30 minutes in the refrigerator.

> **To make a change**
> You can use ground hazelnuts instead of ground almonds if you wish.

Puff pastry

About a pound of pastry
PREP TIME: 30 mins.
RESTING TIME: 9 hrs

- 6 tbsp. cold water
- A pinch of salt
- 14 tbsp. softened butter
- 2 cups sifted flour

❶ First, prepare the basic pastry. Put the cold water in a glass, add the salt and allow to dissolve. Melt 2 tbsp. butter in a small saucepan. Put the sifted flour in a bowl and make a well in the center. Pour in the salted water, then the melted butter. Stir well, first with a wooden spatula, then with your hands to make a dough. Knead very briefly.

❷ Form this dough into a ball and flatten it between your hands. Wrap in plastic wrap and allow to rest for 2 hours in the refrigerator.

❸ Place the rest of the butter between two sheets of plastic wrap. Roll with a rolling pin to form a square of butter about 1/2 inch thick.

❹ Lightly flour your work surface and roll out the dough to a thickness of around one inch, making sure the center is thicker than the edges. Roll out to form a large square with right-angled corners. Place the square of butter on top.

❺ Fold the corners of the square over the butter to form a square envelope.

❻ Roll out this square into a rectangle three times longer than its width.

❼ Fold into three to form a square: this is the first "turn." Allow to rest for 2 hours in the refrigerator. Give the pastry a quarter turn, roll out into a rectangle once again, and fold into three to form a square: this is the second "turn." Allow to rest again for at least 1 hour in the refrigerator.

❽ Make a total of six "turns," allowing the pastry to rest for 2 hours in the refrigerator after each two "turns." Mark the surface of the pastry with a fingertip to remind you how many turns you've made.

> **Helpful tip**
> You can make croissants with puff pastry.

LAROUSSE ON PASTRY • 403

Leavened dough

About 1 pound of dough
PREP TIME: 20 mins.
RESTING TIME: 2 hrs 20 mins.

- 1-1/4 cups sifted flour
- A pinch of salt
- 1 tbsp. sugar
- 2 eggs
- 1 scant tbsp. dry yeast
- 1/2 cup milk
- 5 tbsp. melted butter

❶ Sift the flour into a bowl and make a well in the center. Add a pinch of salt and the sugar, then the eggs.

❷ Stir the yeast into the warmed milk (85 to 95° F). Pour this liquid into the well and mix with a wooden spoon. Add the melted butter and mix again.

❸ Cover the bowl with a cloth and allow to rest at room temperature in a draft-free place, for about 2 hours. In cool weather the dough will take longer to rise.

❹ When the dough has doubled in volume, flatten it with your hands until it reverts to its initial volume. This is called "knocking down" the dough. It should be supple and smooth-textured. Butter your baking pan to half its height only, place the dough inside it and allow to double in volume once more before baking.

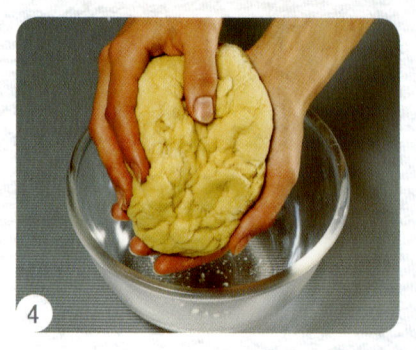

> **Find out more**
> This is the dough used for brioche, babas, savarins and kugelhopfs. You can add raisins or candied fruit to the mixture.

Choux pastry

1 lb. of pastry
PREP TIME: 15 mins.

- 1/3 cup water
- 7 tbsp. whole milk
- 1 small teaspoon salt
- 1 small teaspoon sugar
- 1/3 cup butter
- 1 scant cup flour
- 3 eggs

❶ Place the water and milk in a saucepan. Add the salt, the sugar and the butter. Bring to a boil, stirring with a wooden or rubber spatula.

❷ Add the flour all at once. Stir energetically with the spatula until the mixture is smooth. When it detaches itself from the bottom and sides of the saucepan, continue to mix for 2 to 3 minutes to dry it out a little.

❸ Place in a bowl; add the eggs one by one, making sure the first is well mixed in before adding the next. Continue to work the mixture, lifting the spatula from time to time. When the mixture forms a smooth ribbon, it is ready.

❹ Spoon the mixture into a pastry bag and pipe onto a baking sheet in the desired shape (sausage shapes for éclairs, for example).

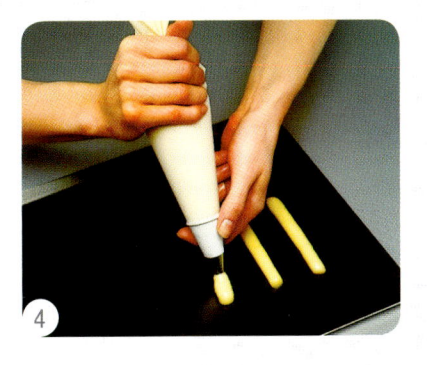

> **Find out more**
> Work the dough with a wooden spatula over a high heat until it stops sticking to the sides of the pan: this helps the water to evaporate before you add the eggs.

Crêpe batter

Makes enough for about 15 crêpes 10 inches in diameter
PREP TIME: 10 mins.
RESTING TIME: 2 hrs

- 2 cups flour
- 2 cups milk
- 2 tbsp. butter
- 3 eggs
- 1 teaspoon salt
- 2 tbsp. sugar (optional)

❶ Put the flour into a bowl and make a well in the center. Pour half the milk into the well and mix with a wooden spatula, gradually drawing the flour into the center.

❷ Melt the butter over gentle heat in a small saucepan. Break the eggs into another bowl and beat them. Gradually add them to the flour, stirring constantly, then add the melted butter, the salt and the sugar (if using). Continue to stir until the mixture is perfectly smooth.

❸ Gradually add the rest of the milk, stirring constantly so that no lumps form. The mixture should be of a smooth pouring consistency, but not too liquid. Cover and allow to rest at room temperature for 2 hours.

❹ Cook the crêpes over high heat in a flat skillet, turning once and allowing one minute for each side.

> **Helpful tip**
> It's best to use a nonstick pan: the butter in the mixture means it's not necessary to add any more.

Fritter batter

Makes 3/4 pound of batter (enough for 12 medium-sized fritters)

PREP TIME: 10 mins.
RESTING TIME: at least 1 hr

- 1 cup flour
- 1/2 teaspoon salt
- 1 egg
- 1 tbsp. peanut oil
- 2/3 cup beer

❶ Put the flour in a bowl and make a well in the center.

❷ Sprinkle the salt around the edge of the flour and break the egg into the center. Add the oil.

❸ Mix the egg and oil with a spatula, drawing in a little flour. Continue to stir (do not beat), and gradually add the beer.

❹ Continue to stir until all the flour has been incorporated and you have a perfectly smooth mixture. Allow to rest for at least 1 hour.

> **Find out more**
> Never beat fritter batter as this reduces its adhesive properties. Always use a wooden spatula.

LAROUSSE ON PASTRY • 407

Génoise sponge cake

Makes about one pound of génoise

PREP TIME: 30 mins.

- 1 heaping cup flour
- 4 eggs
- 3/4 cup sugar
- 3 tbsp. butter

❶ Sift the flour. Break the eggs into a heatproof bowl. Gradually mix in the sugar. Place the bowl over a pan of simmering water, or use a double boiler, and beat until the mixture thickens (130-140° F: you should be able to put your finger into the mixture without discomfort).

❷ Remove the bowl from the heat and beat the mixture with an electric mixer until cold.

❸ Melt the butter. Put 2 tbsp. of the previous mixture into a small bowl and stir in the warm melted butter.

❹ Gradually fold the flour into the main mixture using a wooden or rubber spatula, then add the contents of the smaller bowl, stirring very gently.

> **Find out more**
>
> Once cooked, this ultra-light sponge cake will keep in the freezer, wrapped in plastic wrap.

Almond dacquoise meringue

Makes about a pound of meringue

PREP TIME: 25 mins.

- 1-1/4 cups powdered sugar
- 1-1/2 cups ground almonds
- 5 egg whites
- 4 tbsp. sugar

❶ Mix the powdered sugar and the ground almonds and sift them together onto a sheet of parchment paper.

❷ Beat the egg whites in a bowl with an electric mixer. Beat in the sugar in three stages. Continue until you have a soft meringue.

❸ Carefully fold in the sugar and ground almonds.

❹ Spoon the mixture into a pastry bag with a number 9 or 10 smooth tip and pipe onto a baking sheet lined with parchment paper, forming two 10-inch diameter spirals, beginning at the center and working outward. .

> **Find out more**

When making meringue, professional pastry chefs often prefer to use egg whites that have been kept in the refrigerator for 3 days: this helps the mixture keep its shape.

Pastry cream

Makes about 4 cups
PREP TIME: 10 mins.
COOKING TIME: 10 mins.

- 6 egg yolks
- 1/2 cup sugar
- 1/3 cup flour
- 2 cups milk

❶ Put the egg yolks and the sugar into a bowl and whisk until they become pale yellow and frothy. Sprinkle with the flour and stir it in quickly. Meanwhile, boil the milk in a saucepan.

❷ Slowly pour the boiling milk into the mixture, stirring constantly with a wooden spoon to obtain a smooth cream.

❸ Pour the custard into a heavy saucepan. Heat very gently until it thickens, stirring with a wooden spoon. Remove from the heat just as it starts to boil.

❹ Pour into a bowl. Rub a piece of butter over the surface to stop a skin from forming, and leave to cool.

> **Find out more**
> Heating gently should be enough to thicken the custard. If it is still fluid when it starts to boil, continue boiling for 1 or 2 minutes, whisking constantly to stop it from sticking to the bottom of the saucepan.

Crème anglaise (Real custard)

Makes just over a pint
PREP TIME: 25 mins.
COOKING TIME: 10 to 15 mins.

- 1/2 vanilla bean
- 2 cups milk
- 6 egg yolks
- 5 tbsp. sugar

❶ Split the vanilla bean lengthwise. Put one half in a heavy saucepan with the milk. Bring to a boil, then turn off the heat and leave to infuse for 20 minutes.

❷ Put the egg yolks and the sugar in a bowl and whisk energetically until the mixture turns pale yellow and becomes frothy.

❸ Remove the vanilla bean from the milk and scrape the seeds into the pan. Return the milk to the heat, bring to a boil, and pour the boiling milk slowly into the eggs and sugar mixture, stirring all the time.

❹ Pour the mixture back into the saucepan and heat very gently, stirring constantly with a wooden spoon until it thickens. Check that the right consistency has been reached by drawing your finger across the back of the spoon. If the track left by your finger stays clear, the custard is ready. Now dip the saucepan into a bowl of ice water to stop the cooking process. Leave to cool.

> **Find out more**
>
> Crème anglaise will inevitably curdle if it boils. It's hard to rescue when this happens, but you can try removing it from the heat and whisking it, or processing it in a blender.

Butter cream

Makes about a pound of cream
PREP TIME: 20 mins.
COOKING TIME: 5 mins.

- 1 cup very soft butter
- 3 tbsp. water
- 3/4 cup sugar
- 2 whole eggs
- 2 egg yolks

❶ Work the butter into a smooth cream in a bowl with a wooden spatula.

❷ Pour the water into a small saucepan and add the sugar. Bring slowly to a boil, brushing the sides of the pan with a pastry brush dipped in water. Cook this syrup until it reaches the soft-ball stage (250° F on the sugar thermometer).

❸ Put the eggs and extra yolks into a bowl and beat them with an electric mixer until they are pale and frothy. Pour the syrup into the eggs in a thin stream, continuing to beat the mixture (set the mixer to slow). Keep beating until the mixture is cold.

❹ Add the butter, beating constantly. When the cream is quite smooth, put it in the refrigerator.

> **> Find out more**
> Butter cream is used as a filling for cakes, Yule logs, and petits-fours; It can also be used for decoration.

412 • PASTRY WORKSHOP

Crème Chiboust

Makes about a pound of cream for filling cakes

PREP TIME: 25 mins.
COOKING TIME: 5 mins.

- 1-1/4 cup whole milk
- 4 tbsp. sugar
- 2 tbsp. cornstarch
- 4 egg yolks
- 1 packet gelatin
- 5 egg whites

❶ Prepare some pastry cream: bring the milk to a boil with 1 tbsp. sugar and the cornstarch. In another bowl, beat together 1 tbsp. sugar and the egg yolks, add to the milk. Bring to a boil, whisking constantly, then remove from the heat.

❷ Dissolve the gelatin in a little water. Stir into the hot pastry cream. Remove from the heat.

❸ Beat the 5 egg whites to stiff peaks and gradually beat in 3 tbsp. sugar.

❹ Stir one quarter of the beaten egg whites into the pastry cream.

❺ Pour this mixture into the remaining beaten egg whites, gently mixing them together with the whisk.

> **Helpful tip**
>
> This cream must be used immediately after it is made. Cakes in which it is used must be eaten within 24 hours.

LAROUSSE ON PASTRY • 413

Pastillage (Sugar paste for cake decoration)

Makes about one pound
PREP TIME: 20 mins.

- 1/2 packet gelatin
- 6 tbsp. white vinegar
- 3-1/3 cups powdered sugar

❶ Dissolve the gelatin in cold water. Add the vinegar. Beat in the sugar: the mixture will be very stiff. Work the paste by flattening it repeatedly with the heel of your hand on a floured work surface, until it is smooth and even-textured.

❷ Roll out with a rolling pin in small quantities as it dries very fast.

❸ Cut out cardboard shapes and place them on top of the paste. Cut around them with the point of a knife.

❹ You can use small molds to shape the paste (circles, semicircles, stars, leaves, etc.).

> **Find out more**
>
> For colored pastillage, add food coloring when the mixture is finished.

Chantilly whipped cream

Makes about a pound of cream

PREP TIME: 10 mins.

- 2 cups liquid crème fraîche or heavy cream
- 4 tbsp. powdered sugar
- 1 tsp. vanilla extract

❶ Pour the cream into a bowl at least 1 hour before preparing the Chantilly whipped cream and place it in the coldest part of the refrigerator. Take it out at the last minute.

❷ Whip the cream gently with a hand whisk or electric mixer for 1 minute.

❸ Speed up the whisking as the cream increases in volume and becomes frothy. Add the powdered sugar and the vanilla extract and continue to whisk until the cream is the right consistency.

❹ Stop whipping the cream when it has doubled in volume and sticks to the wires of the whisk. Put the cream in the refrigerator until needed.

> **Find out more**
>
> For perfect Chantilly, the cream and the bowl must be very cold. Place the bowl in the freezer for about 10 minutes before pouring in the cream.

French meringue

About 1 pound of meringue

PREP TIME: 5 mins.

- 5 egg whites
- 1-2/3 cups sugar
- 1 teaspoon natural vanilla extract

❶ Put the egg whites in a bowl. Make sure there are no traces of egg yolk in them. Beat the egg whites with an electric whisk, gradually adding half the sugar.

❷ When they've doubled in volume, add the rest of the sugar and the vanilla. Continue to beat until they are very firm, smooth and glossy.

❸ Gradually stir in the rest of the sugar until it is thoroughly combined and the mixture is firm enough to adhere to the whisk

❹ Put the meringue in a pastry bag with a smooth tip and pipe onto a buttered and floured baking sheet in the required shape.

> **Find out more**
> Bake meringues at 225° F, leaving the oven door slightly open. Bake small meringues for 40 minutes and large meringue disks for 1-1/2 hours.

Italian meringue

Makes about a pound of meringue
PREP TIME: 20 mins.
COOKING TIME: 10 mins.

- 1/3 cup water
- 1-1/2 cups sugar
- 5 egg whites

❶ Bring the water and sugar to boil in a saucepan, brushing the sides with a damp pastry brush to clean off any splashes. Heat the mixture to hard ball stage (260-275° F on a sugar thermometer).

❷ Place the egg whites in a large bowl and beat to soft peaks with an electric mixer. Turn the mixer down to medium speed and pour in the syrup. Beat until the mixture has cooled slightly.

❸ Spoon the meringue into a pastry bag fitted with a smooth tip and pipe onto a cake in the required shape.

> **Helpful tip**
>
> Italian meringue can be used to make a mousse lighter and fluffier, as well as in ice cream sponges, butter creams, sorbets and ice cream soufflés, or even petits-fours.

LAROUSSE ON PASTRY

Chocolate sauce

Makes 2 cups of sauce
PREP TIME: 5 mins.
COOKING TIME: About 10 mins.

- 1/2 lb. bitter chocolate (at least 70 % cocoa solids)
- 2 tbsp. butter
- 1 cup whole milk
- 2 tbsp. crème fraîche or heavy cream
- 2-1/2 tbsp. sugar

❶ Break the chocolate into pieces and place in a bowl. Put the bowl in a saucepan of hot water. Gently melt the chocolate, stirring with a wooden spatula.

❷ Cut the butter into small pieces. Add to the warm chocolate and mix gently until smooth and creamy.

❸ Put the milk in a small saucepan and bring to a boil. Remove the saucepan from the heat and add the crème fraîche or heavy cream and the sugar. Whisk well and bring back to the boil.

❹ Pour the contents of the saucepan onto the chocolate mixture, whisking constantly until smooth. Pour into a bowl or pitcher. Serve hot poured over ice cream or profiteroles, or allow to cool and serve with cake.

> **Find out more**
> The chocolate used for this sauce should have a very high cocoa content and contain as little sugar as possible.

Chocolate frosting

Makes 1/2 lb. frosting
PREP TIME: 15 mins.
COOKING TIME: 10 mins.

- 3 oz. dark semi-sweet chocolate
- 1/3 cup crème fraîche or heavy cream
- 1 tbsp. softened butter
- 1/2 cup chocolate sauce (p.418)

❶ Chop or grate the chocolate and put into a bowl. Bring the crème fraîche or heavy cream to a boil in a saucepan. Remove from the heat and gradually add the chocolate.

❷ Using a wooden spatula, carefully mix the chocolate and cream together, starting at the center and moving outwards in concentric circles.

❸ When the temperature of the mixture falls below 140° F, cut the butter into small pieces and gently stir it in, along with the chocolate sauce you prepared earlier.

> **Find out more**
> This frosting sets easily but remains very lustrous.

Tempering chocolate

For 10 oz.
PREP TIME: 15 mins.
COOKING TIME: 5 or 6 mins.

- 10 oz. of couverture chocolate, either dark, milk or white

❶ Chop the chocolate. Place just 7 oz. of it into a bowl. Melt it over a saucepan of simmering water, being careful not to let the bowl touch the bottom of the saucepan. Stir gently with a wooden spoon, as the chocolate has to melt completely before you can measure its temperature: the chocolate has to be at 130° F (measure with an electronic probe).

❷ Immediately remove the chocolate from the heat. Sprinkle in the remaining 3 oz. of chocolate. Place this bowl into another bowl filled with water and 4 or 5 ice cubes. Stir the melted chocolate occasionally, to prevent its sides from hardening. Again take its temperature: it has to drop to 81° F. You can also simply leave the chocolate to cool without placing it in the bowl with iced water until its temperature falls to 81° F.

❸ As soon as the melted chocolate has reached this temperature, place the bowl over the saucepan of simmering water once more. Watch carefully as the temperature rises, as it must remain low. Stir gently with a wooden spoon. Take its temperature: it should be between 86° F and 91° F. The chocolate is now at the required temperature, ready for use.

> **Helpful tip**
> Only couverture chocolate, specially designed for use in pastry baking, can be tempered: it melts far more easily than other types of chocolate.

Chocolate curls and shavings

For 3 oz. chocolate
PREP TIME: 10 mins.
FREEZING TIME: 30 mins.

- 3 oz chocolate (dark, milk or white)

❶ Chop the chocolate with a serrated knife and leave to soften. Place a small square of marble in the freezer for 30 minutes. Place a clean dish towel on your work surface, and lay the marble on top. Put half the chocolate on the marble and very quickly spread the chocolate into a thin layer with a metal spatula.

❷ Using a triangular spatula, push the edge of the chocolate so that it forms curls. Don't touch them with your fingers, use a spatula to lift them off the marble and place them on a piece of parchment paper.

❸ Chill the tubes for 15 minutes in the refrigerator. For shavings, use the edge of the triangular spatula to break up the curls. Keep in the refrigerator until just before you need them.

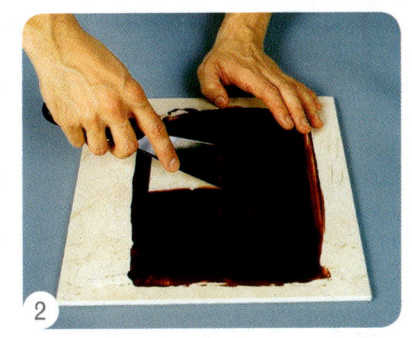

> **Find out more**
> Make sure you use top-quality cooking chocolate, otherwise it's likely to turn white when you work with it.

Caramel

Makes about 4 ounces of caramel
PREP TIME: 2 mins.
COOKING TIME: 8 to 12 mins.

- 2 tbsp. water
- 1/2 cup sugar
- lemon juice

❶ Put the cold water and the sugar in a heavy saucepan. Add the lemon juice (this will stop the caramel from going hard as it cools) and heat very gently, stirring with a wooden spatula, until the sugar has dissolved. Make sure no sugar gets onto the sides of the pan.

❷ When the syrup is clear, stop stirring and let it boil. As the water evaporates, the caramel will thicken and get darker.

❸ Remove from the heat when the caramel is the desired color. When it's a light gold color, it can be used for decorative purposes; when darker brown, it's used for both flavoring and decoration. If you want your caramel to stay liquid, add a little water before you stop cooking it (but beware of splashes!)

> **Find out more**
>
> To stop the cooking process once the caramel is the color you want, take the pan off the heat and dip it in a bowl of ice water.

Simple caramel decorations

❶ Prepare a dark golden caramel. Line a baking sheet with parchment paper. Dip a tablespoon into the hot caramel and let it fall onto the paper, "drawing" the shapes you require. When the caramel has set, remove from the paper.

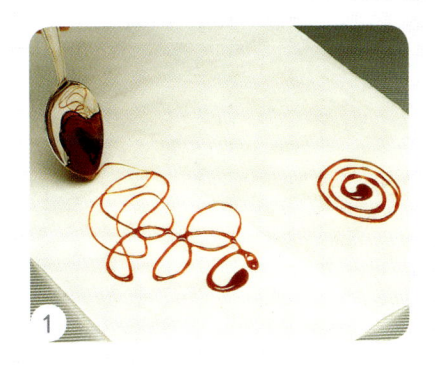

Raspberry coulis

For 2 cups of coulis
PREP TIME: 10 mins.

- 1 1/2 lbs raspberries
- 6 tbsp. sugar
- 3 tbsp. lemon juice
- 1/2 cup water

❶ Rinse and pick through the raspberries; discard any that are damaged. Put them into a large bowl with the sugar and lemon juice. Puree the raspberries with a hand blender, starting with small pulses and then continuously for 2 to 3 minutes, until you get a perfectly smooth liquid.

❷ Rub the purée through a sieve to remove the seeds. Press down on the fruit with a wooden or rubber spatula to collect as much juice as possible. Gradually add the water, stirring constantly, until the coulis reaches the desired consistency.

> **Find out more**
> The secret of a great coulis is to use perfect, fully ripened fruit.

Jams and marmalades: one-stage cooking

1 In a bowl, mix the prepared fruit with the lemon juice. Allow to soak for a few minutes, just enough to moisten the sugar.

2 Pour the mixture into a heavy pan, bring to a boil, stirring constantly, and boil until it reaches jellying point (the fruit should be translucent and stop rising to the surface).

3 Check with a sugar thermometer (220° F) or a plate (pour a drop of jelly onto a cold plate: it should set firm). Remove from the heat. Skim and pour into jars.

Jams and marmalades: two-stage cooking

1 Rinse and prepare the fruit. Place in a bowl, alternating layers of fruit and sugar sprinkled with lemon juice and leave to soak for several minutes, just enough to moisten the sugar.

2 Transfer to a heavy pan and bring to a boil, stirring gently. Remove from the heat as soon as it begins to boil.

3 Pour into a bowl, cover with plastic wrap laid directly onto the fruit, and leave to soak overnight. Press down on the fruit so that it is covered in liquid. The following day, put it back in the heavy pan, bring to a boil and cook until it reaches jellying point. Skim the fruit, and remove from the heat as soon as it reaches 220° F (use a sugar thermometer). Pour into jars.

Jams and marmalades: cooking method

1 Wash the fruit, remove pits if necessary and cut into small pieces. Roughly mix the fruit, the sugar and the lemon juice in a bowl, cover with plastic wrap or parchment paper and allow to soak overnight.

2 The following day, transfer the mixture into a heavy pan. Bring to a boil, stirring constantly with a wooden spoon.

3 The fruit will collapse into a purée. Mix briefly with a hand blender if you require a smoother consistency. Leave on the heat, stirring constantly until the thermometer reads 220° F. Skim the fruit, check consistency and pour into jars. For jam with neither skin nor pits, run the fruit through a food mill after maceration and before cooking.

Sealing jam jars

1 To seal hot jars with screwtop lids: fill the jars and screw the lids on while still hot. Invert until completely cold to create a vacuum. Use carefully sterilized jars and lids.

2 To seal cold jars with parchment paper: cut out circles of paper, brush one side with fruit brandy, lay the paper directly on the jam dry side up. Cover with plastic wrap and an elastic band.

3 To seal cold jars with paraffin wax: melt the paraffin wax over very gentle heat, then allow to cool slightly (it must remain transparent). Slowly pour a 1/4-inch layer onto the cold jam and allow to harden. Properly sealed, unopened jars can be stored for years.

LAROUSSE ON PASTRY • 425

Utensils for desserts, pastry and jams

Before beginning to make a dessert or jam, you need to make sure you have the right utensils.

The utensils, accessories and measuring instruments

When making pastry or jams, you need basic kitchenware as well as a number of specific utensils and appliances. For pastry making, you need to be able to measure ingredients most precisely. So a number of particular measuring instruments are essential.

The small basic utensils

- **MIXING BOWL.** It should be sufficiently wide and deep to allow you to whip ingredients, knead dough or let dough rest while rising.

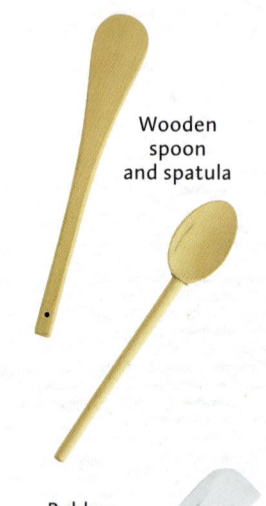

Wooden spoon and spatula

Rubber spatula

Whisk

Chinois

Metal mixing bowl

- **WOODEN SPOON AND SPATULA.** The former is used for stirring and mixing, the latter for turning out and scraping. Since wood does not conduct heat, it can be used without burning your hands. Spoons and spatulas which are used in making jam should be kept for this purpose only, because wood quickly absorbs the flavor of the ingredients involved.

- **RUBBER SPATULA.** This is used for smoothing, mixing or scraping dough.

- **BAKING SPATULA.** A flat, flexible blade used for glazing or frosting.

- **WHISK.** Available in a number of sizes, these are used for whipping cream or beating eggs.

- **CHINOIS.** A conical sieve used to strain out impurities from sauces, purees and syrups.

- **SIEVE.** Used to sift flour and remove lumps.

- **FOOD MILL.** With its set of blades, it is used in making marmalade, fruit purees and compotes to remove the skin and pits from fruit.

- **METAL MIXING BOWL.** This metal bowl comes in different sizes and is used particularly for beating egg whites and heating chocolate, eggs and sauces over simmering water.

- **PITTER.** This device resembles pliers and is used for removing the pits from cherries and plums, etc.

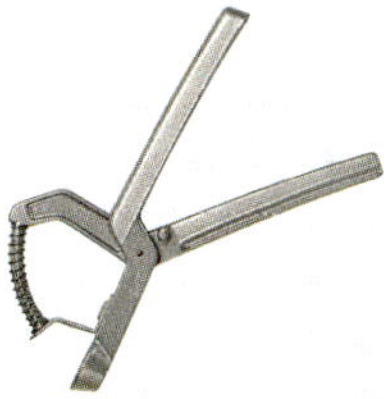

- **APPLE CORER.** This is a short cylinder with sharp edges used to remove apple cores while leaving the apple intact.

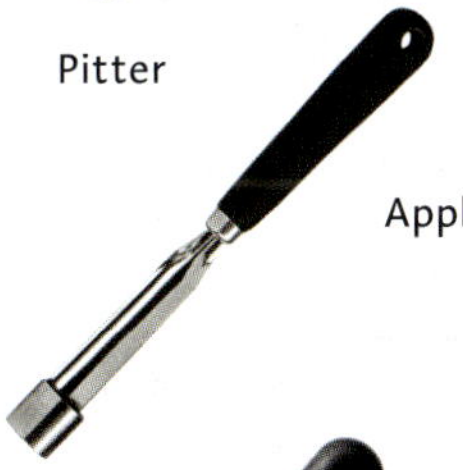

- **ZESTER.** A utensil with a blade for peeling fine strips of zest from a citrus fruit.

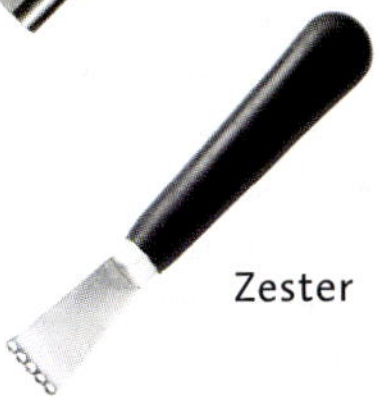

- **FLUTED PASTRY WHEEL.** Creates a fluted edge for pastry.

Articles used in pastry making

- **PASTRY CUTTER.** Made of stainless steel or plastic, it is available in a large array of shapes and sizes (human figures, animals, hearts, numbers etc.) which are used for cutting pastry into desired shapes (cutters with sharp edges are preferable, as they avoid crushing the pastry while cutting). For making cookies or decorating tarts.

- **PASTRY BAGS AND TIPS.** These are indispensable for filling choux, decorating cakes and piping certain kinds of dough onto the baking sheet. The tips are made either of plastic or stainless steel and come in a wide range of shapes and sizes to create a variety of decorations.

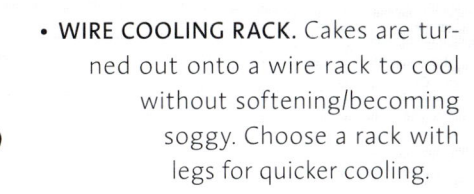

Pitter

Apple-corer

Zester

Fluted pastry wheel

Rolling pin

Pastry bag and tips

- **WIRE COOLING RACK.** Cakes are turned out onto a wire rack to cool without softening/becoming soggy. Choose a rack with legs for quicker cooling.

- **CERAMIC BAKING BEANS OR METAL PIE WEIGHTS.** Recommended for blind-baking a perfectly smooth pie crust. Flat dry beans or apricot kernels can be used as substitutes.

- **PASTRY CRIMPER.** This gives an attractive finish to pie edges.

- **FLAT PASTRY BRUSH.** Used for greasing molds, glazing pastry and sealing together the two halves of turnovers.

- **ROLLING PIN.** It is used for rolling out dough. Choose a wooden one (made of beechwood) with no handles at each end so that even pressure can be applied with both hands.

- **BAKING SHEET.** This goes into the oven for baking. Some sheets are covered with a nonstick coating to make cleaning easier.

LAROUSSE ON PASTRY • 427

Jam-making utensils

- **MASLIN PAN.** Usually made of copper lined with tin, the pan is wide and shallow, providing a large surface area so that water evaporates easily from fruit.

Its volume should be at least twice that of the fruit to be cooked. It should have a very thick base (about 1/4 to 1/2 inch) to allow heat to spread properly and prevent the jam from sticking to the bottom. The pan should never be used for soaking fruit.

To clean the pan, rinse then rub with a moist cloth dipped in a mixture of coarse salt and vinegar (1 tbsp. of each).

- **MASLIN PAN LID.** For some recipes which need the fruit mixture to be covered while cooking.

- **JUICE EXTRACTOR.** It consists of three sections which fit together and is used for collecting the juice of fruit for making jelly. The lower section is filled with water and the fruit is placed in the upper section. When the water boils, its steam bursts the fruit open and the juice runs down into the central section which is fitted with a faucette.

- **CHEESECLOTH OR MUSLIN.** This is used for making a pouch filled with fruit pits and kernels which is hung by a string from the handle of the pan to help certain jellies or jams set more efficiently.

Maslin pan

Jam funnel

Slotted spoon

Jam jars

- **SIEVE AND CHEESECLOTH.** For straining the juice from fruit. One can also use muslin placed in a narrow chinois or a nylon jelly bag.

- **SQUARES OF PLASTIC WRAP.** Like parchment paper, these are used to cover lidless jam jars.

- **JAM FUNNEL.** Its wide opening makes filling jam jars easy.

- **PARAFFIN WAX.** This is used to cover jellies and jams after they have cooled. It comes in blocks and pastilles which are melted in a double boiler. The wax is highly flammable and all contact with the flame must be avoided.

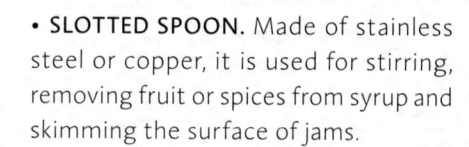

- **SLOTTED SPOON.** Made of stainless steel or copper, it is used for stirring, removing fruit or spices from syrup and skimming the surface of jams.

- **LABELS.** For marking the date when the jam was made, the kind of jam and other details.

- **JAM JARS.** These come in different shapes, but the traditional ones, with flat sides and wide openings, are the most practical to use.

Some have a simple threaded neck for flat, metal tops with integrated rubber seals. Those with a plain neck are covered with a piece of plastic wrap, parchment paper or paraffin wax. The most common sizes are 8 oz., 12 oz. and 16 oz.

Various kinds of baking paper

• **PARCHMENT PAPER.** This is treated to withstand heat (up to 450° F) and can be placed in microwave ovens. It is used for lining cake molds (to avoid greasing them) or to cover a baking sheet before placing the pastry on it to prevent it from sticking to the sheet. It is also used for covering lidless jam jars.

• **ALUMINUM FOIL.** Used for wrapping food during cooking (the shiny side should be on the inside, in contact with the food). Keeps food hot, as well.

• **PLASTIC WRAP.** Extremely thin, it keeps in the flavor of food stored in the refrigerator and prevents uncooked dough from drying out. It is also used to cover lidless jam jars. Thicker wrap is available for use in microwave ovens.

• **RE-USABLE BAKING PARCHMENT PAPER.** This nonstick paper withstands a temperature of 500° F. It is spread onto a baking sheet in the same way as other parchment paper, but can be used over and over again. It is very flexible, can be cut to fit any mold, does not require greasing and can be cleaned quickly and easily with a moist sponge.

• **DIPPING PAPER.** This "paper," made of transparent polyethylene, is used (especially by professionals) for shaping and hardening chocolate. The pieces obtained (decorations or florentines, for example) can be easily removed and have a glossy surface.

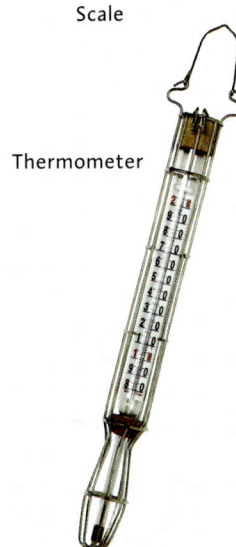

Scale

Thermometer

Timer

Electric mixer beaters

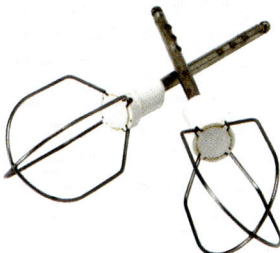

Measuring instruments

• **KITCHEN SCALES.** These have a bowl and tray, with a maximum capacity between 4 to 10 lbs. Automatic scales have a dial with a needle to show the weight. They are graduated in both gram and ounce increments. Electronic scales with a digital display are more precise.

• **THERMOMETER.** In pastry making, several very different kinds of thermometers are used. A cooking thermometer (glass tube, red liquid) is graduated from 0 to 250° F and is used for checking the temperature of creams which need to be heated, for example. A sugar or candy thermometer is graduated from 175° F to 400° F; it is used for checking the stage of cooking when making jam.

• **MEASURING CUP.** Measures the volume of ingredients, typically with markings for 1/8 cup, 1/4 cup, 2/3 cup, 3/4 cup and 1 cup. It can be made of plastic, glass or stainless steel, and is more practical if equipped with a handle and a pouring spout. However, it is sometimes easier to use an everyday object (mustard glass, soup spoon, teaspoon etc.).

• **SYRUP DENSITY METER.** This is used to measure the amount of sugar in syrups, as in making confectionery. It consists of a float with a graduated stem which sinks into the liquid to a degree determined by its density - the lower the density, the deeper the stem will sink into the liquid.

• **TIMER.** This allows you to measure the cooking time, rest time, etc., of food you are preparing.

LAROUSSE ON PASTRY • 429

Electrical equipment

- **ELECTRIC MIXER.** It has a variety of interchangeable beaters which replace the manual whisk, allowing you to beat egg whites into stiff peaks or make whipped cream very easily. Some models also have a set of dough hooks for kneading.

- **BLENDER.** The simplest kind can be placed inside the saucepan, while the more sophisticated models have a deep, glass bowl with sharp blades set into the base for crushing and blending food. The latter type is recommended for making stewed fruit, coulis, marmalades etc.

- **STAND MIXER.** It usually consists of a stand to which a bowl is fixed. In addition to the three indispensable accessories which come with it (a whisk for blending, a dough hook for kneading and a beater for mixing), there are optional accessories, such as a mincer, slicer or strainer. There are huge differences in price according to the brand and performance of the machines.

- **ICE CREAM MAKERS.** These are used for making ice cream and sorbets by mixing the ingredients while chilling them at the same time to a temperature far below 32° F. Electric ice cream makers have a motor-driven paddle and a removable bowl which absorbs cold and must be placed in the freezer for at least 12 hours before the ice cream is ready. Automatic ice cream machines are very expensive, smaller versions of those used by professionals. They can make ice cream in only thirty minutes.

Blender

Brioche mold

Loaf pan

Charlotte mold

- **JUICE EXTRACTOR.** Used for extracting the juice from fruit for jellies without using filters and sieves.

- **MICROWAVE OVEN.** Not recommended for pastry making, because, although dough can be baked in it, it will neither rise nor become golden-brown. It is nevertheless very useful for a number of purposes: quickly defrosting goods, warming milk without it sticking or overflowing; softening butter which has been kept in the refrigerator and melting butter and chocolate without a double boiler (if one does this in several successive stages of a few seconds each). Warning: for warming up or cooking food in this kind of oven, always use "transparent" containers, which let the waves in without deflecting or absorbing them. Nothing metallic should ever be placed in a microwave oven.

Molds and Pans

These are available in a large range of shapes, materials and qualities. Cake molds, fireproof dishes, chocolate or ice cream molds and single- or multi-cavity molds can be found for all purposes.

The most common molds and pans

- **BRIOCHE MOLD.** These are made of metal, sometimes covered in a nonstick coating. The sides can be fluted and sloping; they can be round or rectangular in shape. They are used for making brioches and certain desserts.

430 • UTENSILS FOR DESSERTS, PASTRY AND JAMS

- **LOAF PAN.** Rectangular in shape, they can have straight or slightly sloping sides. They come in a variety of sizes. It is preferable to use one with a nonstick coating.

- **CHARLOTTE MOLD.** Made in one piece, they are bucket-shaped with handles (for easy turning out), and can be made of metal or, sometimes, of plastic, with ridges to hold the lady fingers which line them. They are also used for making flans and puddings.

- **CAKE PAN.** These are made of metal and can be either ridged or smooth, and round, rectangular or square. They are used for baking Génoise or other sponge cakes, as well as tartes tatins and other tarts.

- **SAVARIN MOLD.** Often made of metal, they have a characteristic hole in the center, for making crown-shaped cakes.

- **SOUFFLÉ DISH.** These round pans are usually made of white, fired porcelain with straight, high, fluted sides. They can also be made of glass and are available in a variety of sizes.

- **SILICONE MOLD.** These solid, flexible, nonstick molds make for quick baking, as well as easy removal and cleaning (particularly in a dishwasher). No greasing is necessary. This new generation of molds comes in all the traditional shapes (for tarts, cakes, etc.). Their weak point is that, if too flexible, they can be difficult to use when filling with liquid mixtures (the mold should be placed on the oven rack or tray before lining or decorating). These molds must be used with care and never placed on a hot plate or in an oven heated to more than 475° F, for example.

- **PIE PAN.** These have smooth or fluted sides and come in a large array of different materials (metal, glass, porcelain or silicone). To avoid greasing and make turning out easier, the pie dish can be lined with parchment paper, but nothing beats a nonstick coating, such Teflon (on aluminum) or Exopan (on steel). Their diameters can vary from 6 to 12 inches. Round pans with removable bottoms are recommended for baking fruit tarts, as they make removal easier. Pans with deep, flared sides are best for one- and two-crust pies.

Round cake pan

Savarin mold

Pie dish

Silicone molds

Madeleine molds

Mini molds

- **DARIOLE MOLD.** A small round mold for rice puddings or rum babas (individual portions).

- **MULTI-CAVITY MOLD.** These can be either rigid and nonstick coated, or flexible silicone molds with cavities in the shape of tartlets, boats, little cakes or madeleines; they can hold up to 24 articles.

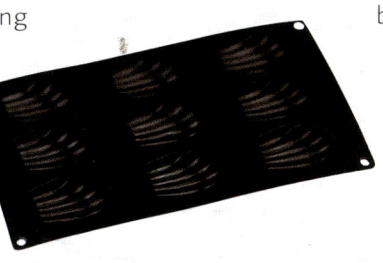

- **TARTLET MOLDS AND BOAT MOLD.** The former are round, the latter oval. They come in different sizes and are generally made of tin-plate or stainless steel (with removable bottoms for tart molds with a diameter over 4 inches).

- **PETIT FOUR MOLD.** These are miniature molds made of metal or silicone in a variety of shapes. They are also used in making confectionery.

- **RAMEKIN.** These are a kind of small soufflé dish for making caramel custard or crème caramel. Generally made of fired porcelain, they can be used in the oven or the fridge and then used to serve the dish.

Special-purpose molds

- **ICE CREAM MOLDS.** Metal molds are the most suitable. They have lids for hermetic sealing to prevent crystals from forming. Their smooth sides make removal easier. The bottom often has a design in relief on it. There are also small popsicle molds.

- **SPRINGFORM PANS.** These are round, metal pans with high sides. By unlatching the side buckle, the circle widens and releases the bottom, making it easier to remove certain items, such as cheesecakes, flans and pies.

Tartlet molds and boat molds

Ramekins

Springform pan

Ring and frames

- **KUGELHOPF MOLDS.** These are crown-shaped molds with diagonal ridges. Traditionally, they are made of glazed ceramic. However, it is better to choose molds with nonstick coating for easier removal.

- **TARTE TATIN MOLDS.** These are very thick molds, designed to be placed directly on the heat to make the caramel. It is preferable to choose a mold with nonstick coating.

- **CROQUEMBOUCHE CONES.** Used for tiered cakes, they make it easier to stack choux.

- **LOG CAKE PAN.** Mold for making a Yule log.

- **WAFFLE IRON.** These molds consist of two hinged metal plates, generally of cast iron, for making waffles and wafers. There are two kinds, one for placing on a stove hot-plate or burner, the other electric.

- **RINGS AND FRAMES.** These are bottomless, stainless steel molds which are placed on a baking sheet covered in re-usable parchment liner, bakery release paper, a pastry mat or regular parchment paper. This avoids the trouble of turning out the items. They come in single rings, tart rings (with two rolled edges) and cake rings (with higher edges). They are available in various diameters. Though previously used only by professionals, these rings are now sold in large retail outlets.

Pastry glossary

B

Beat: to work an element or a mixture vigorously to alter its consistency, appearance or color. To beat egg whites into stiff peaks, beat them with a whisk in a bowl.

Blanch: to remove the skin of fruit or nuts that have previously been placed in a sieve and plunged into boiling water for a few seconds. The skin is gently removed with the tip of a knife without damaging the pulp itself.

Blind-bake: to pre-bake a pastry base without its filling. This is done when the filling needs to be cooked for only a short time, is already cooked, or doesn't need any cooking (delicate fruit, for example). Blind baking is also necessary when the filling is moist or slightly liquid and could make the crust soggy; in this case, beaten egg is brushed on to the crust, which is left in the oven for another 3 to 5 minutes.

Butter: to add butter to a mixture or brush melted or softened butter onto a mold, ring or pastry sheet to prevent the mixture from sticking to the bottom and sides during baking.

C

Candy: to immerse fruit filled with almond paste, or soft sweets in a cold sugar syrup so that they are covered in a layer of fine sugar crystals.

Caramelize: to make sugar into caramel by heating it gently. To coat a mold with caramel. To flavor a rice pudding with caramel. To caramelize also means to color the top of a pastry or mixture sprinkled with sugar under a grill.

Chop: to reduce a food (fruit, almonds, nuts, pistachios, herbs, citrus zest, etc.) to small fragments of a particular size but, if possible, of equal thickness (for example, strips, slices, or cubes), using a knife or mincer.

Clarify: to make a syrup or jelly clearer by filtering or decanting. Clarifying butter consists of melting it in a double boiler, without stirring, to remove the whey which forms a whitish deposit.

Coat: to pour a coulis or cream, etc. over a dish so that it is covered as completely and evenly as possible. To cover a food in a layer of a mixture, e.g., to coat confectionery, petits-fours etc. with chocolate, fondant or cooked sugar.

Combine: to mix two or more ingredients of varying color, taste or texture.

Cool: to place a cake, cream dessert, fruit salad, etc. in the refrigerator to be served cold.

Core: to remove the inside of an apple with a corer.

Cream: to cream butter means to stir softened butter until it has a creamy consistency.

Crush: to reduce substances (almonds, nuts) to powder or paste.

Crust: a piece of pastry which is rolled out with a rolling pin on a lightly floured work surface to give it the desired shape and thickness.

D

Decant: to pour a cloudy liquid into another container after letting it stand until the floating impurities have settled to the bottom. To remove from a mixture the flavor-adding elements which are not to be served.

Density: the relation between the mass per unit of volume of a substance and that of the same volume of water at 39.2° F. The concentration of sugar (particularly in making jams, candy and confectionery) is now measured in density and no longer in degrees Baumé. A syrup density float with a graduated stem is used. This will sink into the liquid to a degree determined by its density.

Double boiler: also called a bain-marie, this is a utensil for either keeping a mixture warm, melting ingredients (chocolate, gelatin, butter) without burning them, or cooking items very gently, by means of the heat from boiling water. The receptacle with the mixture is placed inside another, larger receptacle containing boiling water.

Drain: to remove excess liquid from a mixture (or an ingredient) by placing it in a colander, sieve, chinois or on a rack.

Dry out: to remove excess water from a mixture by warming over low heat. This is used particularly during the first time a choux pastry is cooked: work the mixture of water, butter, flour, salt and sugar over high heat with a wooden spatula until it detaches from the sides of the saucepan, to allow excess water to evaporate before adding the eggs.

F

Fill: to cover the inside of a dessert with cream, fondant, etc.

Flambé: to pour alcohol (or liqueur) over a hot dessert and ignite it.

Flavor: to incorporate a flavored ingredient (liqueur, coffee, chocolate, rose water, etc.) into a mixture.

Flour: to cover a food in flour or spread flour onto a mold or a work surface. One can also flour a marble slab or a pastry sheet before rolling out or kneading dough.

Flute: to make parallel V-shaped furrows on fruit (lemon, orange) with a fluting knife. "Fluted" pie crusts are cut with a special pastry wheel. A "fluted" tip is one with a serrated edge.

Frappé: to chill a cream, liqueur, mixture or fruit very quickly.

Frost: to cover hot or cold dishes in a thin layer of fruit or chocolate glaze to make them shiny and appetizing. To cover the top of a cake with a layer of fondant, powdered sugar, syrup, etc.

Fry: to cook an ingredient, or finish cooking it, by immersing it in very hot fat. It is often covered in flour, fritter batter, crêpe batter, choux pastry, etc., which gives it a lovely golden crust.

G

Glaze: to give a sheen to a dish by coating the top with a substance, such as beaten eggs, sometimes thinned with a little water or milk, or butter for hot dishes. This is usually brushed on to the top. Glazing makes pastry crusts shiny and golden after baking. For cold dishes, jelly is used. For some desserts and pastries, the gloss is obtained by using fruit jelly or frosting.

Grease: to spread a greasy substance over a pastry sheet or on the inside of a ring or mold so that a mixture will not stick during baking and can be turned out more easily.

I

Incorporate: to add an ingredient to a mixture and mix in well (flour and butter, for example).

Infuse: to pour boiling liquid over a fragrant substance and let it stand until it absorbs its flavors. Vanilla can be infused in milk, or cinnamon in red wine.

K

Knead: to work a substance until it is smooth or soft. To mix flour with other ingredients using your hands or a food processor (with a dough kneader) to obtain a smooth dough.

Knock down: or to punch down dough is to stop a dough which has risen from fermenting momentarily by folding it over several times. This is done twice while preparing the dough and helps it develop better.

L

Line: to cover the bottom and sides of a mold with rolled-out dough, making sure it fits perfectly, either by cutting out the dough first with a pastry cutter, or by placing the dough into the mold with some hanging over the sides and running a rolling pin over the edges of the mold to trim off the excess dough. One can also cover the sides and/or bottom of a mold either with a thick layer of a mixture to prevent the food from sticking to the mold and enable it to be turned out easily, or with a number of ingredients which are an integral part of the dish (for example, a mold is lined with ice cream to make an ice cream bombe). Alternatively, molds can be lined with parchment paper to enable the food to be removed more easily.

M

Macerate: to soak fresh, candied or dried fruit in liquid (alcohol, liqueur, syrup, wine, tea) for a certain time so that it absorbs the liquid's flavor.

Melt: to liquify an ingredient like chocolate or solid fats, etc. by heating. To avoid burning, a double boiler is often used.

Mold: to place a liquid or dough into a mold which will give it its shape as the consistency of the substance changes through being cooked, refrigerated or frozen.

O

Oil: to cover a baking tray or the sides of a mold with a thin layer of oil to prevent food from sticking.

P

Press: to remove the juice, cooking water or excess liquid from an ingredient. To press citrus fruit, a citrus squeezer is used.

Pipe: to place choux pastry on a baking tray using a pastry bag with a tip.

Pit: to remove the stones from fruit with a pitter, which resembles a pair of pliers.

Poach: to simmer fruit in a certain quantity of liquid (water, syrup).

Prick: to make small regular holes with a fork on the surface of a rolled-out dough so that it will not swell during baking.

R

Reduce: to diminish the volume of a liquid or a sauce through evaporation by keeping it at boiling point. This increases its flavor by concentrating the juice, and makes it much smoother or thicker.

Reserve: to put aside mixtures or ingredients in a cool or warm place while awaiting further use. To prevent them from spoiling, they are often wrapped in parchment paper, aluminum foil or plastic wrap, or even in a cloth.

Ribbon: A hot or cold mixture of egg yolks and sugar, sufficiently smooth to flow from a spatula or whisk without breaking up (for example: a sponge mixture flows like a ribbon).

Rise: said of a dough, cream or cake which increases in volume through fermentation, cooking or baking.

Roll out: to spread and flatten dough with a rolling pin.

Roast: to place slivered almonds, nuts, pistachios etc. on a baking tray in a hot oven and move them about often to give them a light, even color.

S

Score: to make a slit with a sharp knife. Fruit is scored to make it easier to peel or cut. The top of a pastry crust is scored with a knife tip or fork after glazing to add a decorative touch before baking. For example, a galette des rois (French Twelfth Night cake) is traditionally scored with lozenges.

Set: to give greater consistency or firmness to a dough or mixture by leaving it in a refrigerator or freezer for a certain time.

Shape: to give a particular form or shape to a dough or mixture.

Sift: to pass flour, yeast or sugar through a sieve to remove lumps. One can also sift certain more or less liquid mixtures.

Simmer: said of a liquid when it bubbles just before reaching the boiling point.

Skim: to remove the foam which forms on the surface of a liquid or mixture while cooking (boiling syrup, cooking jam). This is done with a slotted or ordinary spoon, or a small ladle.

Sliver: to cut lengthwise into thin strips, for example, almonds etc.

Soak: to moisten cakes using syrup, alcohol or liqueur to soften and give them flavor (babas, sponges, etc.).

Strain: to pass thin cream, syrup, jelly or coulis which need to be very smooth through a sieve or chinois.

Striate: to make striations or lines using a fork, comb or brush on the top of a cake.

T

Thicken: to give a thicker consistency to a liquid or cream; for example, by adding cornstarch, egg yolks or crème fraiche.

Topping: This is usually a liquid jelly made of marmalade (apricot, strawberry, raspberry, for example), which has been strained and to which a gelling agent has been added. It gives a glossy finish to fruit tarts, babas, savarin cakes and other desserts.

Turn out: to remove an item from a mold.

W

Whip: to beat egg whites, heavy cream or a sweet mixture with an electric beater or hand whisk so that it absorbs a certain quantity of air, which increases the volume and gives it a particular consistency and color.

Whisk: to beat a mixture energetically using an electric beater or hand whisk to give it a smooth consistency: for example, to whisk eggs into stiff peaks, or cream until it becomes light and compact, etc. > See also **Beat.**

Work: to combine the elements of a paste or liquid mixture more or less energetically to incorporate the various ingredients, either to make it smooth or to give it body or a creamy texture. Depending on the kind of mixture, this may be done on or away from the heat, or on ice, with a wooden spatula, an electric beater or hand whisk, a mixer beater, a blender or even by hand.

Y

Yeast mixture: a paste obtained by combining flour, dry yeast and water, which is left to double in volume before being added to dough.

Z

Zest: to remove the colored and fragrant outer skin from citrus fruit using a peeler or a zester.

Index of recipes by ingredient & category

The entries in SMALL CAPS **refer to the "Pastry workshop"**

A

Almond
Almond cookies 294
ALMOND DACQUOISE MERINGUE 409
Almond slices 262
Apricot and almond cake 24
Apricot and almond gratin 168
Baked apples 52
Blancmange 72
Bourdaloue pie 150
Breton-style butter cookies 294
Croquets de Bar-sur-Aube 294
Financiers de Sully 250
Galette des Rois 216
Galettes bretonnes 294
Gâteau nantais 24
Individual almond sponge cakes 250
Macaroons 264
Middle-Eastern Easter pastries 280
Paris-Brest 200
Traditional French Twelfth Night cake 216
Tuiles 268
Visitandines 260

Apple
Apple crumble 48
Apple fritters 374
Apple pie 146
Apple strudel 162
Baked apples 52
Caramelized apple cake 30
Normandy apple cake 30
Semifreddo 310
Tarte Tatin 146
Upside-down apple pie 146

Apricot
Apricot and almond cake 24
Apricot and almond gratin 168
Apricot and rosemary brioche pie 156
Apricot parcels with lavender 172
Apricot-vanilla jam 384
Raspberry (or apricot) roll 208

B

Banana
Baked spiced bananas 188
Banana chocolate pie 104
Banana-cinnamon mousse 184
Banana phyllo parcels with orange sauce 174

Bavarian cream
Black currant and pear Bavarian cream 306
Chocolate and vanilla Bavarian cream 98

Beverages
Old-fashioned hot chocolate 128

Black currant
Berry soup 332
Black currant and pear Bavarian cream 306
Black currant jelly 394
Frozen black currant charlotte 300

Blueberry
Blueberry and caramel jam 386
Blueberry crumble 166

Brioches
Cramique 350
Gâteau mollet 352
Kugelhopf 26
LEAVENED DOUGH 404
Praline brioche 356
Raisin loaf 350
Soft brioche 352

Butter cream
BUTTER CREAM 412
Coffee dacquoise 204
Custard-filled brioche 40
Luxury coffee cake 214
Moka 198
Strawberry sponge cake 226
Tropézienne 40

Brownies
Pecan brownies 84

C

Cakes
Apple strudel 162
Apricot and almond cake 24
Berry fruit savarin with Chantilly whipped cream 224
Caramelized apple cake 30
Carrot cake 18
Chocolate cake from Nancy 80
Chocolate "délice" 82
Chocolate fondant cake 78
Croquembouche 196
Double-choc muffins 92
Financiers de Sully 250
French-style fruit cake 358
French-style pound cake 8
Gâteau basque 14
Hazelnut cake 12
Kouign-amann 28
Lemon cake 32
Madeleines 252
Marble cake 16
Montpensier 22
Muffins 346
Normandy apple cake 30
Paris-Brest 200
Pineapple upside-down cake 164
Queen of Sheba 86
Raspberry (or apricot) roll 208
Rice pudding with caramel 54
Rich chocolate cake 90
Saint-Honoré 206
Semifreddo 310
Semolina pudding with sultanas 60
Spiced chocolate slab cake 94
Walnut "délice" 210
Yogurt cake 10

Candied fruits
Candied orange peel 246
Cassata 308
French-style fruit cake 358

Candy and Chocolates
Chocolate caramels 134
Chocolate cherries 132
Chocolate truffles 136
Florentines 130

Caramel
Blueberry and caramel jam 386
CARAMEL 422
Caramel and chocolate pie 342
Caramel and salt butter tartlets 344
Chocolate caramels 134
Chocolate-caramel pizza 106
Crème caramel 66
Floating island 70
Peach parcels with orange caramel 170
Rice pudding with caramel 54
Salt butter caramel 380
SIMPLE CARAMEL DECORATIONS 423

Carrot
Carrot cake 18

Chantilly
› see **Cream**

Charlottes
Chocolate charlotte 76
Frozen black currant charlotte 300
Pear charlotte 34
Strawberry charlotte 176

Cheese
Cooked vanilla cheesecake 234
Fiadone 42
Fig and mascarpone cups 242
Mascarpone pie 44
No-bake cheesecake 46
Tiramisu 244

Cherry
Berry soup 332
Black Forest gâteau 222
Cherry clafoutis 50
Cherry jam 388
Chocolate cherries 132

Chestnut
Chestnut and chocolate verrines 120
Chestnut log 218
Chestnut vacherin 304
Mont-blanc 238

Chocolate
Banana chocolate pie 104
Black Forest gâteau 222
Caramel and chocolate pie 342
Chestnut and chocolate verrines 120
Chestnut log 218
Chocolat liégeois 122
Chocolate and pear "mi-cuits" 88
Chocolate and vanilla Bavarian cream 98
Chocolate cake from Nancy 80
Chocolate-caramel pizza 106
Chocolate caramels 134
Chocolate charlotte 76
Chocolate cherries 132
Chocolate chips cookies 296
CHOCOLATE CURLS AND SHAVINGS 421
Chocolate "délice" 82
Chocolate éclairs 108
Chocolate fondant cake 78
Chocolate fondue 138
Chocolate frosting 419
Chocolate marquise 114
Chocolate mousse 110
Chocolate-orange cookies 126
Chocolate pie 100
CHOCOLATE SAUCE 418
Chocolate soufflé 96
Chocolate truffles 136
Dark chocolate crème brûlée 116
Double-choc muffins 92
Florentines 130
Old-fashioned chocolate creams 118
Old-fashioned hot chocolate 128
Pears Belle-Hélène 316
Pecan brownies 84
Profiteroles with ice-cream and chocolate 124
Queen of Sheba 86
Rich chocolate cake 90
Spiced chocolate slab cake 94
TEMPERING CHOCOLATE 420
Two-chocolate mousse 112
White chocolate mousse 112
White chocolate tartlets 102

˃ see also **Cocoa**

Choux
CHOU PASTRY 405
Choux pastry fritters 372
Coffee cream puffs 202
Croquembouche 196
Pets-de-nonne 372
Saint-Honoré 206

Cinnamon
Banana-cinnamon mousse 184

Cocoa
Chocolat liégeois 122
Marble cake 16
Old-fashioned hot chocolate 128

Coconut
Coconut rock cakes 254
Mini mango and coconut pies 160

Coconut milk
Panna cotta with coconut milk and berries 182

Coffee
Coffee cream puffs 202
Coffee dacquoise 204
Luxury coffee cake 214
Moka 198
Tiramisu 244

Compotes
Lychee and raspberry compote 338
Plum and ginger compote 336

Cookies
Almond cookies 270, 294
Breton-style butter cookies 294
Butter shortbread 284
Chocolate chips cookies 296
Chocolate-orange cookies 126
Cigarettes russes 268

Coconut rock cakes 254
Coffee meringues 276
Cordoba cookies 292
Countess cookies 272
Croquets de Bar-sur-Aube 294
Galettes bretonnes 294
Galettes nantaises 270
Galettes Saint-Amour 362
Giant jam cookies 362
Langues-de-chat 266
Lemon cookies 282
Macaroons 264
Middle-Eastern Easter pastries 280
Palmiers 274
Pecan cookies 290
Rum-raisin cookies 278
Sablé-sur-Sarthe shortbread 286
Spiced "arlettes" 288
Tuiles 268
Walnut cookies 258

Coulis
RASPBERRY COULIS 423

Creams
BUTTER CREAM 412
CHANTILLY WHIPPED CREAM 415
CRÈME ANGLAISE 411
Crème brûlée 62
Crème caramel 66
CRÈME CHIBOUST 413
Dark chocolate crème brûlée 116
Egg custard 64
Little pots of cream 64
Old-fashioned chocolate creams 118
Paris-Brest 200
PASTRY CREAM 410
Pear charlotte 34
REAL CUSTARD 411
Trifle 232

Crème anglaise
CRÈME ANGLAISE 411
Pear charlotte 34
Trifle 232

Crêpes
CRÊPE BATTER 406
Crêpes Suzette 368
Scotch pancakes 366

Crumbles
Apple crumble 48
Blueberry crumble 166

D

Dacquoises
ALMOND DACQUOISE MERINGUE 409
Coffee dacquoise 204

Doughs and Batters
ALMOND DACQUOISE MERINGUE 409
Berry fruit savarin with Chantilly whipped cream 224
Chestnut vacherin 304
CHOU PASTRY 405
CRÊPE BATTER 406
FRITTER BATTER 407
GÉNOISE SPONGE CAKE 408
Individual rum babas 212
LEAVENED DOUGH 404
PÂTE SABLÉE 400
PUFF PASTRY 402
Raspberry (or apricot) roll 208
SHORTCRUST PASTRY 399
SWEET PASTRY 401
Waffles 370

F

Fig
Baked figs with tarragon 190
Fig and honey jam 386
Fig and mascarpone cups 242
Fig tartlets 158

Flans
Parisian flan 38

Fritters
Apple fritters 374
Bugnes 378
Choux pastry fritters 372
Churros 376
FRITTER BATTER 407
Pets-de-nonne 372
Traditional fritters from Lyon 378

Frosting
Chocolate éclairs 108
CHOCOLATE FROSTING 419
Lemon cake 32

Fruit salads
Kiwi and citrus fruit salad 330
Strawberry tartare 326

Fruit soups
Berry soup 332
Watermelon and basil soup 334

G

Gâteaux
Black Forest gateau 222
Luxury coffee cake 214
Moka 198
Semifreddo 310
> see also **Sponge cakes, Cakes**

Ginger
Ginger and cardamom frozen yogurt 324
Plum and ginger compote 336
Rhubarb and ginger jam 388

Granita
Lemon granita 320

Grapefruit
Broiled caramelized grapefruit 192

H

Hazelnut
Florentines 130
Hazelnut cake 12

Honey
Fig and honey jam 386
Pain d"épices 354
Spiced honey loaf 354

I

Ice creams
Baked Alaska 236
Cassata 308
Chestnut vacherin 304
Mint ice cream 318
Peach Melba 314
Pears Belle-Hélène 316
Profiteroles with ice-cream and chocolate 124

J

Jam
COOKING METHODS 424-425
Apricot-vanilla jam 384
Blueberry and caramel jam 386
Cherry jam 388
Dulce de leche 382
Fig and honey jam 386
Galettes Saint-Amour 362
Giant jam cookies 362
Kiwi jam 392
"Quickie" raspberry jam 392
Raspberry (or apricot) roll 208
Rubarb and ginger jam 388

Jelly
COOKING METHODS 424-425
Black currant jelly 394
Quince jelly 394
Rose petal jelly 390

K

Kiwi
Kiwi and citrus fruit salad 330
Kiwi jam 392
Kiwi pie 148

L

Lavender
Apricot parcels with lavender 172

Lemon
Fiadone 42
Lemon cake 32
Lemon cookies 282
Lemon curd 180
Lemon granita 320
Lemon meringue pie 154
Lime mousse 178
Mirabelle plums with lemon 186
Lemon curd 180
Lemon cookies 282

Lychee
Lychee and raspberry compote 338

M

Mandarin
Crêpes Suzette 368
Mandarin marmalade 384

Mango
Mango sorbet 322
Mini mango and coconut pies 160

Marmalade
COOKING METHODS 424-425
Mandarin marmalade 384

Marron
> see Chestnut

Mascarpone
Fig and mascarpone cups 242
Mascarpone pie 44
Tiramisu 244

Meringues
Almond dacquoise meringue 409
Baked Alaska 236
Chestnut and chocolate verrines 120
Coffee meringues 276
FRENCH MERINGUE 416
ITALIAN MERINGUE 417
Lemon meringue pie 154
Mont-blanc 238
Raspberry pavlova 228

Mint
Mint ice cream 318

Mirabelle
Mirabelle plums with lemon 186

Mousses
Banana-cinnamon mousse 184
Chocolate mousse 110
Lime mousse 178
Two-chocolate mousse 112
White chocolate mousse 112

Muffins
Double-choc muffins 92
Muffins 346

O

Orange
Almond slices 262
Banana phyllo parcels with orange sauce 174
Candied orange peel 246
Chocolate-orange cookies 126
Peach parcels with orange caramel 170

P

Pan di Spagna
Semifreddo 310

Parcels
Apricot parcels with lavender 172

Parfait
Frozen pistachio parfait 302

Pastry cream 410
Chocolate éclairs 108
Coffee cream puffs 202
Croquembouche 196
Custard-filled brioche 40
Gâteau basque 14
Prune diplomate 36
Raspberry boats 152
Raspberry soufflé 230
Saint-Honoré 206
Strawberry sponge cake 226
Tropézienne 40

Peach
Peach Melba 314
Peach parcels with orange caramel 170

Pear
Black currant and pear Bavarian cream 306
Bourdaloue pie 150
Chocolate and pear "mi-cuits" 88
Pear charlotte 34
Pears Belle-Hélène 316

Pecan
Pecan brownies 84
Pecan cookies 290

Phyllos
Banana phyllo parcels with orange sauce 174
Peach parcels with orange caramel 170
Spiced pineapple mille-feuilles 220

Pies
Apple pie 146
Apricot and rosemary brioche pie 156
Banana chocolate pie 104
Bourdaloue pie 150
Caramel and chocolate pie 342
Chocolate pie 100
Galette des Rois 216
Kiwi pie 148
Lemon meringue pie 154
Mascarpone pie 44
Mini mango and coconut pies 160
Rhubarb pie 144
Tarte Tatin 146
Traditional French Twelfth Night cake 216
Upside-down apple pie 146

Pineapple
Pineapple carpaccio with vanilla 328
Pineapple upside-down cake 164
Spiced pineapple mille-feuilles 220
Trifle 232

Pistachio
Florentines 130
Frozen pistachio parfait 302
Middle-Eastern Easter pastries 280
Old-fashioned chocolate creams 118

Plum
Plum and ginger compote 336

Praline
Praline Brioche 356

Prune
Far Breton 38
Prune diplomate 36

Puddings
Rice pudding with caramel 54
Rice pudding with citrus peel 56
Semolina pudding with sultanas 60
Traditional rice pudding 58

Q
Quince
Quince jelly 394

R
Raisins
> see **Sultanas**

Raspberry
Berry fruit savarin with Chantilly whipped cream 224
Berry soup 332
Lychee and raspberry compote 338
"Quickie" raspberry jam 392
Raspberry boats 152
Raspberry coulis 423
Raspberry (or apricot) roll 208
Raspberry pavlova 228
Raspberry soufflé 230

Real custard
> see **Creams, Crème anglaise**

Rhubarb
Rhubarb and ginger jam 388
Rhubarb pie 144

Rice
Rice pudding with caramel 54
Rice pudding with citrus peel 56
Traditional rice pudding 58

S
Sablés
> see **Shortbreads**

Semolina
Semolina pudding with sultanas 60

Shortbreads
Butter shortbread 284
Sablé-sur-Sarthe shortbread 286

Small cakes
Almond slices 262
Cannelés 256
Chocolate and pear "mi-cuits" 88
Chocolate éclairs 108
Coffee cream puffs 202
Individual rum babas 212
Middle-Eastern Easter pastries 280
Profiteroles with ice-cream and chocolate 124

> see also **Cookies**

Sorbets
Mango sorbet 322

Soufflés
Chocolate soufflé 96
Frozen strawberry soufflé 312
Grand Marnier® soufflé 240
Raspberry soufflé 230

Sponge cakes
Génoise sponge cake 408
Individual almond sponge cakes 250
Raspberry (or apricot) roll 208
Real French sponge cake 20
Strawberry sponge cake 226
Trifle 232

Strawberry
Frozen strawberry soufflé 312
Strawberry charlotte 176
Strawberry sponge cake 226
Strawberry tartare 326
Strawberry tartlets 142

Sultanas
Cramique 350
French-style fruit cake 358
Kugelhopf 26
Raisin loaf 350
Rum-raisin cookies 278
Semolina pudding with sultanas 60

T

Tartlets
Caramel and salt butter tartlets 344
Fig tartlets 158
Raspberry boats 152
Strawberry tartlets 142
White chocolate tartlets 102

V

Vanilla
Apricot-vanilla jam 384
Chocolate and vanilla Bavarian cream 98
Cooked vanilla cheesecake 234
Pineapple carpaccio with vanilla 328

W

Waffles 370

Walnut
Middle-Eastern Easter pastries 280
Walnut cookies 258
Walnut "délice" 210

Watermelon
Watermelon an basil soup 334

Y

Yogurt
Ginger and cardamom frozen yogurt 324
Yogurt cake 10

Index of recipes from A to Z

The entries in SMALL CAPS refer to the "Pastry workshop"

A

ALMOND DACQUOISE MERINGUE 409
Almond slices 262
Apple crumble 48
Apple fritters 374
Apple pie 146
Apple strudel 162
Apricot and almond gratin 168
Apricot and rosemary brioche pie 156
Apricot parcels with lavender 172
Apricot-vanilla jam 384

B

Baked Alaska 236
Baked apples 52
Baked figs with tarragon 190
Baked spiced bananas 188
Banana chocolate pie 104
Banana-cinnamon mousse 184
Banana phyllo parcels with orange sauce 174
Berry fruit savarin with Chantilly whipped cream 224
Berry soup 332
Black currant and pear Bavarian cream 306
Black currant jelly 394
Black Forest gâteau 222
Blancmange 72
Blueberry and caramel jam 386
Blueberry crumble 166
Bourdaloue pie 150
Broiled caramelized grapefruit 192
Bugnes 378
BUTTER CREAM 412
Butter shortbread 284

C

Candied orange peel 246
Cannelés 256
CARAMEL 422
Caramel and chocolate pie 342
Caramel and salt butter tartlets 344
Caramelized apple cake 30
Carrot cake 18
Cassata 308
CHANTILLY WHIPPED CREAM 415
Cherry clafoutis 50
Cherry jam 388
Chestnut and chocolate verrines 120
Chestnut log 218
Chestnut vacherin 304
Chocolat liégeois 122
Chocolate and pear "mi-cuits" 88
Chocolate and vanilla Bavarian cream 98
Chocolate cake from Nancy 80
Chocolate-caramel pizza 106
Chocolate caramels 134
Chocolate charlotte 76
Chocolate cherries 132
Chocolate chip cookies 296
CHOCOLATE CURLS AND SHAVINGS 421
Chocolate "délice" 82
Chocolate éclairs 108
Chocolate fondant cake 78
Chocolate fondue 138
CHOCOLATE FROSTING 419
Chocolate marquise 114
Chocolate mousse 110
Chocolate-orange cookies 126
Chocolate pie 100
CHOCOLATE SAUCE 418
Chocolate soufflé 96
Chocolate truffles 136
CHOUX PASTRY 405
Churros 376
Cigarettes russes 268
Coconut rock cakes 254
Coffee cream puffs 202
Coffee dacquoise 204
Coffee meringues 276
Cooked vanilla cheesecake 234
Cordoba cookies 292

Countess cookies 272
Cramique 350
CRÈME ANGLAISE 411
Crème brûlée 62
Crème caramel 66
CRÈME CHIBOUST 413
CRÊPE BATTER 406
Crêpes Suzette 368
Croquembouche 196
Croquets de Bar-sur-Aube 294
Currant buns 348

D

Dark chocolate crème brûlée 116
Double-choc muffins 92
Dulce de leche 382

E-F

Egg custard 64
Far breton 38
Fiadone 42
Fig and honey jam 386
Fig and mascarpone cups 242
Fig tartlets 158
Financiers de Sully 250
Floating island 70
Florentines 130
FRENCH MERINGUE 416
French-style fruit cake 358
French-style pound cake 8
French toast 364
FRITTER BATTER 407
Frozen black currant charlotte 300
Frozen pistachio parfait 302
Frozen strawberry soufflé 312

G

Galette des Rois 216
Galettes bretonnes 294
Galettes nantaises 270
Galettes Saint-Amour 362
Gâteau basque 14
Gâteau mollet 352
Gâteau nantais 24
GÉNOISE SPONGE CAKE 408
Ginger and cardamom frozen yogurt 324
Grand Marnier® soufflé 240

H-I

Hazelnut cake 12
Individual rum babas 212
Irish scones 360
ITALIAN MERINGUE 417

J-K

JAMS AND MARMALADES 424-425
Kiwi and citrus fruit salad 330
Kiwi jam 392
Kiwi pie 148
Kouign-amann 28
Kugelhopf 26

L

Langues-de-chat 266
LEAVENED DOUGH 404
Lemon cake 32
Lemon cookies 282
Lemon curd 180
Lemon granita 320
Lemon meringue pie 154
Lime mousse 178
Little pots of cream 64
Luxury coffee cake 214
Lychee and raspberry compote 338

M

Macaroons 264
Madeleines 252
Mandarin marmalade 384
Mango sorbet 322
Marble cake 16
Mascarpone pie 44
Middle Eastern Easter pastries 280
Mini mango and coconut pies 160
Mint ice cream 318
Mirabelle plums with lemon 186
Moka 198
Mont-Blanc 238
Montpensier 22
Muffins 346

N-O

No-bake cheesecake 46
Normandy apple cake 30
Old-fashioned chocolate creams 118
Old-fashioned hot chocolate 128

P

Pain d"épices 354
Palmiers 274
Panna cotta with coconut milk and berries 182
Paris-Brest 200
Parisian flan 38
PASTILLAGE 414
PASTRY CREAM 410
PÂTE SABLÉE 400
Peach Melba 314
Peach parcels with orange caramel 170
Pear charlotte 34
Pears Belle-Hélène 316
Pecan brownies 84
Pecan cookies 290
Pets-de-nonne 372
Pineapple carpaccio with vanilla 328
Pineapple upside down cake 164
Plum and ginger compote 336
Praline brioche 356
Profiteroles with ice cream and chocolate 124
Prune diplomate 36
PUFF PASTRY 402

Q

Queen of Sheba 86
"Quickie" raspberry jam 392
Quince jelly 394

R

Raspberry boats 152
RASPBERRY COULIS 423
Raspberry (or apricot) roll 208
Raspberry pavlova 228
Raspberry soufflé 230
Real French sponge cake 20
Rhubarb and ginger jam 388
Rhubarb pie 144
Rice pudding with caramel 54
Rice pudding with citrus peel 56
Rich chocolate cake 90
Rose petal jelly 390
Rum-raisin cookies 278

S

Sabayon 68
Sablé-sur-Sarthe shortbread 286
Saint-Honoré 206
Salt butter caramel 380
Scotch pancakes 366
Semifreddo 310
Semolina pudding with sultanas 60
SHORTCRUST PASTRY 399
SIMPLE CARAMEL DECORATIONS 423
Spiced "arlettes" 288
Spiced chocolate slab cake 94
Spiced pineapple mille-feuilles 220
Strawberry charlotte 176
Strawberry sponge cake 226
Strawberry tartare 326
Strawberry tartlets 142
SWEET PASTRY 401

T

Tarte Tatin 146
TEMPERING CHOCOLATE 420
Tiramisu 244
Traditional rice pudding 58
Trifle 232
Tropézienne 40
Tuiles 268
Two-chocolate mousse 112

V-W

Visitandines 260
Waffles 370
Walnut cookies 258
Walnut "délice" 210
Watermelon and basil soup 334
White chocolate mousse 112
White chocolate tartlets 102

Y

Yogurt cake 10

Photos Credits

Photos of recipes

Olivier Ploton © coll. Larousse (design Bérengère Abraham): pages 6, 7 (m.; r.), 9, 15, 24, 27, 29, 33, 35, 37, 41, 45, 47, 49, 53, 55, 57, 61, 67, 75, 77, 89, 91, 95, 99, 103, 105, 107, 109, 111, 113 (t. l.), 117, 121, 123, 125, 133, 135, 139, 141, 143, 145, 149, 153, 155, 157, 161, 163, 173, 179, 181, 183, 185, 187, 189, 191, 193, 195 (g.; c.), 197, 199, 201, 203, 205, 207, 208, 209, 211, 212, 213, 215, 217, 221, 225, 227, 229, 231, 233, 247, 249 (l.), 261, 292, 299, 303, 305, 309, 311, 313, 315, 317, 319, 321, 323, 325, 327, 329, 331, 333, 335, 337, 339, 340, 341 (m.), 343, 345, 351, 357, 377, 381, 383, 385, 386, 387, 389, 391, 392, 393, 394.

Olivier Ploton © coll. Larousse (design Noëmie André): pages 7 (l.), 11, 13, 17, 19, 21, 23, 25, 31, 39, 43, 51, 59, 63, 65, 68, 69, 71, 73, 79, 81, 83, 85, 87, 93, 97, 101, 113 (b. r.), 115, 119, 127, 129, 131, 137, 147, 151, 159, 165, 167, 169, 171, 175, 177, 194 (r.), 219, 223, 235, 237, 239, 241, 243, 245, 248, 249 (m.; r.), 251, 253, 255, 257, 259, 263, 265, 267, 269, 271, 273, 275, 277, 279, 281, 283, 285, 287, 289, 291, 293, 295, 297, 301, 307, 341 (r., l.), 347, 349, 353, 355, 359, 361, 363, 365, 367, 369, 371, 373, 375, 379.

Other photos

Olivier Ploton © coll. Larousse (design Bérengère Abraham): pages 4, 8, 10, 12, 16, 18, 20, 22, 28, 31, 32, 34, 36, 39, 40, 44, 46, 50, 52, 54, 56, 58, 60, 62, 65, 70, 72, 76, 78, 80, 82, 84, 86, 100, 102, 104, 113, 116, 118, 122, 128, 132, 140, 142, 147, 148, 150, 154, 156, 160, 162, 164, 166, 172, 174, 178, 182, 188, 190, 192, 194, 204, 210, 214, 222, 226, 242, 244, 246, 250, 254, 256, 258, 260, 262, 264, 269, 270, 272, 276, 278, 280, 286, 295, 298, 302, 310, 314, 316, 318, 320, 322, 324, 326, 328, 330, 332, 334, 336, 338, 344, 348, 350, 354, 356, 366, 370, 372, 374, 382, 385, 389, 390, 392. Éric Fénot © coll. Larousse (design Delphine Brunet): pages 48, 130, 168, 282, 304, 346. Massimo Pessina © coll. Larousse (design Rosalba de Magistris): pages 74, 92, 136. Christian Adam © coll. Larousse (design Noëmie André): pages 88, 90, 94, 120, 252. Pierre-Louis Viel © coll. Larousse (design Valéry Drouet): pages 96, 138

Photos of the step-by-step pastry workshop

Olivier Ploton © coll. Larousse: pages 398-412, 415-417, 422, 423 (t.), 424-425. Studiaphot © coll. Larousse: pages 413- 414, 419. G et S photographie © coll. Larousse (design Isabelle Dreyfus): pages 418, 423 (b.). Nicolas Bertherat © coll. Larousse (design Sabine Paris): pages 420-421

Photos of the cover

Olivier Ploton © coll. Larousse except the small one, in the middle, under the title, Éric Fénot © coll. Larousse

Photoengraving: Nord Compo, Villeneuve d'Ascq.